JURISPRUDENCE:
from the Greeks
to post-modernism

Cavendish
Publishing
Limited

JURISPRUDENCE:
from the Greeks
to post-modernism

Wayne Morrison, LLB, LLM, PhD,
Barrister and Solicitor (New Zealand)
Lecturer in Law
Queen Mary & Westfield College

Cavendish
Publishing
Limited

First published in Great Britain 1997 by Cavendish Publishing Limited, The Glass
House, Wharton Street, London WC1X 9PX
Telephone: 0171-278 8000   Facsimile: 0171-278 8080

Morrision, Wayne
Textbook on Jurisprudence
I Title
344.1

ISBN 1 85941 134 7

Printed and bound in Great Britain

For Juliana Georgiadis

PREFACE

This text reflects my experience of teaching at the Faculty of Law, Queen Mary and Westfield College (QMW), and on the External Programme of the University of London, both in England and Malaysia. It began its life one Easter in Athens where I was ploughing my way through the complete lectures of John Austin (given between 1828–32 in London). After largely having relied for my previous opinion upon secondary sources – in particular the writings of HL Hart in the *Concept of Law* (1961) – encountering Austin's actual words was both a shock and a source of bewilderment. How could Hart have been so limited in his reading? What is the status of the past in contemporary discussions in jurisprudence? How were students meant to relate to contemporary issues and debates if they were presented with caricatures of previous positions instead of a rich intellectual heritage? Why did so many texts expect students to take on face value simplistic assertions as to what previous writers have said?

I therefore decided to attempt a text which would both serve as an introduction to the study of jurisprudence and also contextualise the efforts of the various writers normally studied in jurisprudence courses. Three years on, my sense of dissatisfaction and acute frustration has not evaporated. In part, my own text has become the focus of frustration, as I came to realise the impossibility of creating a book which can adequately span both projects. This book is, of course, a compromise. On the one hand it is an attempt to provide an introductory text which can serve to orientate the reader who wishes to learn something of the nature of jurisprudence and which strives to be faithful to the chronology and interactionism of scholarly writing. In this respect part of its aim is exegesis; to put forward an account of various writers projects and material within some contextuality. On the other hand, the book is also a particular narrative of the development of the material; a narrative developed in terms of the pre-modern, modernity and the onset of post-modernity.

The resulting text is a personal creation and makes no claims to universal coverage. Each reader will possibly have his or her own view on which particular writers they feel ought to have been included, or, alternatively, feel that I have underemphasised, or, conversely, overemphasised, aspects of their work. My only defence is to agree: the task is endless and this text is a pragmatic offering.

In terms of the production of this text my greatest debt is to Terence Kelly who not only offered tireless encouragement, but painstakingly read early drafts of the majority of chapters and proved invaluable in transforming disjointed incoherence into relative coherence. Roger Cotterrell and Peter Fitzpatrick both read later versions of several chapters and offered perceptive comments. Rupert Chandler proof read the majority of the finished versions. I am also thankful to Stephen Guest for his support, and for providing me with an unpublished guide to Kelsen several years ago. A small grant from the External System Research Fund, administered by the Institute of Advanced Legal Studies, London, and another from the Faculty of Law, QMW, provided temporary research assistance. Cavendish have continued to prove to be a joy to be involved with and my thanks go out to Kate Nicol, Jo Reddy and Sonny Leong. Responsibility for any mistakes, however, remains with me.

This book has been worked on in London, Athens and Kuala Lumpur. Each location has left its own imprint. The narrative stems from the revision several years ago of the QMW jurisprudence course and the response of successive years of students who have found jurisprudence at first daunting and then stimulating. In these times where the British Conservative government appears determined to refuse appropriate resources for a first class university system, more burdens than ever fall upon academic staff and secretaries. It is a source of wonder that the atmosphere of the QMW Law Faculty has remained favourable and friendly. I have benefited from the dedicated professionalism of all the staff, and the organisational and secretarial skills of Sophia Oliver and Julie Herd in particular. From various students in Kuala Lumpur I owe the hope that the necessarily complex material of jurisprudence can be rendered both understandable and relevant, when appropriate energy and enthusiasm is applied. On a more personal level, Elespeth and Stuart MacKenzie (not to forget James) provided hospitality in KL, Johti Ram supported the writing up of an early version of my lectures (published as *Elements of Jurisprudence)* and engaged in several stimulating and enjoyable sessions at the Bull's Head tavern, and Annup Sidhu constantly urged on the project. But it has been the calmness, wisdom and understanding that I have found in Athens that ensured the project reached fruition.

In conclusion I return to my original complaint aimed at the work of Hart. Although he acknowledged that he drew upon the writings of others, Hart declared his text would not be a presentation of their views. He hoped 'that this arrangement may discourage the belief that a book on legal theory is primarily a book from which one learns what other books contain. So long as this belief is held by those who write, little progress will be made in the subject; and so long as it is held by those who read, the educational value of the subject must remain very small' (*Concept of Law*, 1961: Preface). This is a viewpoint with merit, but it also encourages a new ignorance. It is of course easy to write a text-book which claims that it will not be merely a book repeating the claims of others, particularly if that discourages the reader from reading those 'others' to check what they actually said. And one ought not to forget that the writing of those 'others', were in turn the result of doings, or projects of activity. This present text is an opposing sort of project. That 'we' have pasts which are multi-layered and complex, that 'we' are the result of histories so diverse that no one school or set of projects can encompass them, is simply 'our' 'reality'. It is the fate of humanity for our essence to remain a mystery to ourselves, but that should not mean we ought not to engage in processes of articulation, memory and discussion. This text is not a text-book which lays out the truth of jurisprudence – no such text is possible. But if it encourages the reader to look at many of the writers of our past with a fresh interest, if it encourages the raising of questions and the further pursuance of issues, it will have succeeded in its limited aims.

Wayne Morrison
December 1996

CONTENTS

Contents

CHAPTER 1

THE PROBLEM OF JURISPRUDENCE, OR TELLING THE TRUTH OF LAW:
an entry into recurring questions?

Why do philosophers ask the meaning of quite ordinary words? … Have they forgotten it? (L Wittgenstein, quoted in Redpath, 1990: 82)

Law, says the judge as he looks down his nose,
Speaking clearly and most severely,
Law is as I've told you before,
Law is as you know I suppose,
Law is but let me explain it once more,
Law is The Law.
(WH Auden, *Collected Poems*, 1976: 208)

Do we in our own time have an answer to the question of what we really mean by the word 'being'? Not at all. So it is fitting that we should raise anew *the question of the meaning of Being*. But are we nowadays even perplexed at our inability to understand the expression 'Being'? Not at all. So first of all we must reawaken an understanding for the meaning of this question. (Heidegger, *Being and Time* [1929] 1962: 1)

THE SCOPE OF JURISPRUDENCE, OR WHAT IS INVOLVED IN ASKING 'WHAT IS LAW?'[1]

The linguistic philosopher Ludwig Wittgenstein (1889–1931) believed we enquire into the meaning of words so that we can better orientate ourselves in the practical tasks of life. He also contended that the study of our language usage soon showed us how complicated social life was. Uncertainty is often the result when we look for meaningful answers to questions which on the surface appear simple. So it is with jurisprudence. At its simplest jurisprudence may be defined as the corpus of answers to the question 'what is law?' This is a deceptively easy definition – surely a response can be quickly agreed? If the subject has such a simple core task, however, why is it that the question has been posed from at least the time of the classical Greeks, some 2,500 years ago, and no settled answer to the question 'what is law?' has been arrived at?

---

1   There cannot be an uncontroversial beginning to a book on jurisprudence written in the mid 1990s. There are simply too many perspectives and so many different ways of posing the questions that no one opening can be assumed to be the normal or natural way of beginning. Indeed, a basic distinction can be posed between seeing the object of analysis as an entity - as law seems traditionally to be seen - or as an activity. In the second example to see 'law' as the object of analysis may be unduly reductionist. Some other terminology such as 'legalism', which more easily conveys the idea of a variable field of social practice and ideologies may be preferable.

In broader terms jurisprudence may be defined as the wisdom of law, or the understanding of the nature and context of the 'legal enterprise'.[2] This definition of the task changes the focus to one where we are not just asking 'what is this enterprise?' and 'how does one answer the question, what is law?', but we are also trying to gain an understanding of the sorts of things involved when asking these questions. The first point to notice may appear deceptively obvious: there are many perceptions of the basic subject matter. Is law a discrete entity, or is it a process, or a set of processes, or is it perhaps a complex social phenomenon? Is legality a mode of thinking? Or is it the ability to predict the outcome of court cases? Is law an argumentative attitude? It has been called all of these things and more. Thus our broader conception of jurisprudence must not remain within the confines of one or other idea of law, but rather ask how it is that so much diversity is possible?

THE NEED FOR REFLEXIVITY?

In other words we seek awareness not only of the sorts of issues which are raised by the various answers to the question 'what is law?', or 'what is the nature of the legal enterprise?', but endeavour to understand the conditions and stimuli which actually cause these questions to be asked and which drive our need for meaning. This sort of self-questioning is often called *reflexivity*; reflexivity is the process whereby the action of questioning is turned back upon the questioner, or the conventions of the tradition in which the questioning takes place, in an effort to become more self-conscious.

But reflexivity is problematic. It invites an endless process of questioning. Once this is apparent, it is obvious that no total or final account of these processes can be authoritatively offered – there could always be another twist to the tale, another item to be considered. All accounts emphasise certain features and neglect others.

Is there any way in which clear guidelines can be laid down as to what material is properly called jurisprudence, and which approaches are relevant to it and which irrelevant? Until quite recently Western jurisprudence was dominated by a particular philosophy of law – specifically *legal positivism* – with contrasting approaches from the traditions of *legal realism* or *natural law*. Now, however, the range of material included in jurisprudence courses, or which is clearly of interest, has expanded dramatically; moreover the field has become so contentious, so divided, that it appears jurisprudence has no settled framework, or agreement, as to its nature or area of study. What does this indicate? Is this a mark of progress within the jurisprudential project, or an indication of failure in key areas? How can we know?

To peruse jurisprudence is to strive for self-consciousness, for a degree of transparency as to law's nature and the social projects of using law. Guided by our

---

2   I take the etymology of jurisprudence from '*juris*', law, or the right, and '*prudence*', wisdom. Thus I read it as searching for the wisdom of law, or the prudential understanding of law. In using the terminology of the 'legal enterprise' I follow Beyleveld and Brownsword (1986), themselves building upon Fuller's *dictum* of law as 'the enterprise of subjecting human conduct to the governance of rules' (Fuller, 1969: 96).

concern for reflexivity we understand that to judge the quality of our awareness we need to consider the presuppositions of analysis; not only to understand the different methodologies utilised in the search for knowledge about law, but also to ponder the different reasons why it is important to seek answers to the question of what law is. We face also the problem of contextuality: can we ask the question 'what is law?' (and propose a definition or model which can then be further discussed) independently of particular social and historical circumstances, or is the question always asked within some or other context, and the answer to it dependent upon that context? Therefore in discussing the various answers and attempting to gain wisdom about law do we need to be sympathetic to the contextuality of the very enterprise of jurisprudence? And do methodologies improve, or simply provide different perspectives? It seems we are invited to wander endlessly in an intellectual labyrinth. Soon, however, we are forced to return to the basic question. Is law a single phenomenon – or is there a range of different phenomena which are loosely grouped together under the label 'law'? And what, reflexively, are we to make of the projects which ask these very questions? What is the appropriate methodology for ensuring that our enterprise of approaching jurisprudence is self-conscious?

The second and third extracts with which this chapter opens represent opposing attitudes towards social phenomena. In the second, the poet Auden presents, through the figure of the legal professional, a view of law which holds that the law just 'is', and thereby can be related to in a relatively straightforward, self-evidential way. The law is autonomous, it can be viewed as self-sustaining and, irrespective of how it came about – we may, for example, be aware of its historical creation through power politics – once in existence it has some kind of essential form to which we can relate. In modern times Anglo-American jurisprudence has largely tried to develop a science of law which relies upon the assumption that law has some identifiable common feature and form and that this can be clearly identified as a matter of fact; the law either exists in a particular area, or there is no law covering the area. This view is usually referred to as *legal positivism*. It asserts that the question 'what is the law' *should* be viewed as a question which can be answered by some relatively simple definition providing a truthful answer (such as, law is the command of the state, or, law is a body of rules), which then enables us to construct some process for recognising valid law.[3] Having made the question of defining law a relatively simple matter, legal positivist approaches are then generally concerned to describe the mechanism for recognising law. A further and important issue becomes the separate, though related, issue of analysing the content of law (ie the various doctrines and sets of legal relationships). The question of what the law ought to be is an additional

---

3   The words *should* or *ought* are used deliberately. There is a 'moral' argument for legal positivism and ease of identification is not only an epistemological side effect but a desired effect. The opening of HLA Hart's modern classic *The Concept of Law* involves a discussion of the vast efforts that have been taken to define what is law. Hart implies not only that this effort would be better spent clarifying our understanding of the various categories of law, but that by keeping our identification process of law simple we preserve our everyday critical moral ideas for deciding whether particular laws are morally good or bad. Several commentators refer to this as the positivist 'critical citizenship thesis', or the desirability of keeping the issue of identifying the existence of law separate from the issue of judging the moral worth of law.

issue?[4] Before considering the final quotation heading this chapter, it is as well to establish a clearer idea of the nature of legal positivism, given that it has been the dominant tradition in the jurisprudence of modernity.

LEGAL POSITIVISM AS THE DOMINANT TRADITION IN THE JURISPRUDENCE OF MODERNITY

Legal positivism is a label for a set of related approaches to law which have dominated western jurisprudence in the last 150 years. Using such labels is always a matter of including a number of varying projects and answers to the question 'what is law', but, in general, legal positivism has asserted two essential defining elements: (i) law is a human creation, it is 'posited' by humans in some way, for example through the express volition of political rulers – the sovereign – via a process of legislation; (ii) law can be studied and properly understood by adopting the methodology developed by the so-called 'natural' or 'physical' sciences during the 18th and 19th centuries known as the positivist approach; this approach sought to strip all subjective considerations from the scientist in the interests of objectivity. When appropriate data had been collected – usually the concepts that legalism worked with – a purely analytical methodology appeared ideal to break down the objects into manageable form and the legal scientist must be careful to prevent his values from intruding upon the investigation.

In recent years legal positivism has lost its previous dominance within jurisprudence, partly because its projects of conceptual analysis occurred at the expense of asking questions concerning the entirety of the legal enterprise and they lacked social awareness as to law's social effectivity. Its critics, moreover, have claimed that instead of being a value-free approach to law, it is itself a particular value-laden approach, reflecting a certain body of assumptions, which in turn lead us on to thinking of law in a particular way.[5] The contrasting projects of different writers take on a different complexion when we locate them as historical constructions, rather than treating them as if they were all concerned with dealing with some common pure essential form, some trans-historical entity. Sociologically inclined commentators, for example Cotterrell (1989), have stressed that many of the so-called contradictory features in jurisprudence and socio-legal studies may be explained by the simple – but usually ignored – fact that different writers have been engaged in different projects, and hence employed disparate

---

4   Two famous early exponents of legal positivism, Jeremy Bentham (discussed in Chapter 8 of this text) and John Austin (discussed in Chapter 9), both distinguished *expositional jurisprudence* from *censorial jurisprudence*, or the *science of law* from the *science of legislation*.

5   A prominent modern criticism was that of Judith Shklar (1964:3) in *Legalism*: 'The deliberate isolation of the legal system - the treatment of law as a neutral social entity - is itself a refined political ideology, the expression of a preference ... Here a legal system can be treated as something "there", an entity to be analysed only by looking at it in purely formal terms, even if it does not have the static timelessness really required for such an enterprise ... Formalism creates this "thereness" because its promoters think that a legal system ought to be "there" in order to function properly. To be "there" it must be self-regulating, immune from the unpredictable pressures of politicians and moralists, and manned by a judiciary that at least tries to maintain justice's celebrated blindness. That is why it is seen as a series of impersonal rules which fit together neatly.'

methodologies with distinct considerations in mind. Law is not some stable or essentially trans-historical phenomenon, but differently constituted empirical phenomena in varying socio-historical locations. It is not only that asking different questions leads to dissimilar answers, but a variety of perspectives may be a consequence of inherent diversity and variation in the basic material of investigation. Thus variation in the answers proposed to the asking 'what is law?' may be not so much proof that some writers are right and some wrong, but evidence of the wealth of questions and perspectives on offer when looking at the issue of law and legality across the richness of history.

How did those writers who saw themselves as legal positivists define the tradition? In the late 1950s HLA Hart (widely regarded as the foremost legal positivist of modern times) offered a summary of several possible tenets of legal positivism:

(1) the contention that laws are commands of human beings;

(2) the contention that there is no necessary connection between law and morals, or law as it is and ought to be;

(3) the contention that the analysis (or study of the meaning) of legal concepts is (a) worth pursuing and (b) to be distinguished from historical enquiries into the causes or origins of laws, from sociological enquiries into the relation of law and other social phenomena, and from the criticism or appraisal of law whether in terms of morals, social aims, 'functions', or otherwise;

(4) the contention that a legal system is a 'closed logical system' in which correct legal decisions can be deduced by logical means from predetermined legal rules without reference to social aims, policies, moral standards; and

(5) the contention that moral judgments cannot be established, or defended, as statements of fact can, by rational argument, evidence, or proof ('non-cognitivism' in ethics) (Hart, 1957–58: 601–602).

A core element of legal positivism is the understanding that modern law – positive law – is something posited by humans for human purposes. Thereby modern law can be viewed as an important tool. It is variously presented as an instrument of governmental power, or simply as an instrument for facilitating a basic social interaction and laying out the conditions for individuals to enter into contracts, make wills, transfer property, rely upon public institutions, and so forth. Moreover a fundamental tenet of legal positivism is that while the laws of any one society may reflect moral and political choices, there is no necessary or conceptual link between law and morality. Law does not need to be moral to be recognised as valid law.[6] As John Austin, widely regarded as the founder of the academic tradition of legal positivism, stated in lectures published in the early 1830s: 'the existence of law is one thing; its merit or demerit is another'. This 'separation thesis' is crucial in another element of positivism; law should be identified by using a relatively

---

6   This point is often misunderstood. Scholars who hold legal positivist approaches recognise that empirically law is the product of social, political and moral processes, but argue that the idea or concept of law can be analysed independently of morality. Law can be immoral or moral; unjust or just; repressive or socially progressive.

simple (usually empiricist) methodology. The existence of the law was a factual question answerable by observation, rather than some complex process of moral interpretation and evaluation.[7] To determine the legality of some enactment, for example, it was only necessary to follow through some *de facto* source test. This highlights an important feature of legal positivism: it was a jurisprudence deeply concerned with reinforcing the use of law as an instrument of the modern state. As we shall see, in the work of Thomas Hobbes (discussed in Chapter 4 of this text), who laid out a foundation upon which Austin was to build the modern approach of legal positivism, the core of intellectual questioning turns its back upon any other-worldly transcendental being – God – as the ultimate author of the pure or just ideal of law. Instead concern is transferred to the authority of the state. From Hobbes onwards sovereignty has been a key concept (for example in Bentham and Austin),[8] however as modern western societies developed into social structures administered by bureaucracy, 'officials' replaced the sovereign as the central figure(s) of authority (for example in the work of HLA Hart, 1961, see Chapter 13 of this text, and Ronald Dworkin 1978, 1986, Chapter 15 of this text). But in linking law to its institutional and instrumental role as the servant of the state, legal positivism was always in danger of becoming a methodology without a soul. For how could there be an essence to law if law lost its pre-modern connection with a transcendental signifier, becoming instead solely a mutable human instrument? Would this not mean that there are as many kinds of (non-)law as there are forms of human/social arrangements? Legal pluralism has always been the 'other' of state law.[9]

ALTHOUGH LEGAL POSITIVISM HAS DOMINATED MODERN PERSPECTIVES THERE IS CURRENTLY A POST-POSITIVIST PLURALITY OF PERSPECTIVES: THIS IS THE PROBLEM OF ASKING THE LAW QUESTION IN POST-MODERNITY

Positivism appeared to offer a relatively simple methodology for identifying law. By contrast, in the third of the opening quotations to this chapter, Heidegger opens up the idea that any social phenomenon is capable of various and multi-faceted

---

7   As Joseph Raz (1979: 37) put it: 'In its most general terms the positivist social thesis is that what is law and what is not is a matter of social fact (that is, the variety of social theses supported by positivists are various refinements and elaborations of this crude formulation).'

8   Another important intellectual influence was the French jurist Bodin, see Skinner (1978, vol 2: 284–301); Franklin (1963).

9   In fact, the classical legal positivist - John Austin (1832, 1873) - realised this. His position was conscious of legal pluralism and his theory was specifically one of what he called 'positive law', or law as a technique of political domination. Austin recognised an array of non-state processes which operated to reinforce state law, but others have not been so subtle. In text-book after text-book, Austin's theory is presented as if it were a theory of law, all law. Having made such a claim, later commentators can easily undercut the image of Austin which they present as overly simplistic.

interpretations.[10] *The question of true being – what is the nature of X? – cannot be reduced to one perspective other than by an act of intellectual domination by that perspective or methodology of enquiry over others.* Substitute the word 'law' for 'being' and the second of the opening quotations then reads:

> Do we in our own time have an answer to the question of what we really mean by the word 'law'? Not at all. So it is fitting that we should raise anew *the question of the meaning of 'law'*. But are we nowadays even perplexed at our inability to understand the expression 'law'? Not at all. So first of all we must reawaken an understanding for the meaning of this question.

It is this paradox – that we have no settled meaning for the word law, and yet, for most of the time, we go about our daily lives without the need for such a settled meaning – which served as the inspiration for HLA Hart's *Concept of Law* (1961). The absence of such a settled meaning helps to 'leave everything as it is' (to paraphrase the linguistic philosopher Wittgenstein, upon whom Hart relied for a philosophical methodology) and makes it possible to accept the official or bureaucratic definition of law as the 'truth' of law to be relied upon for all practical purposes. But any question about social phenomena – here law – is also a question about social reality and our ability to know it.

Legal realism

From at least the time that OW Holmes (1897) stated that to 'tell it as it really is', or to find the 'truth' of law, we must look at 'law in action', as opposed to the doctrinal analysis of 'law in books', a tradition of *legal realism* has existed which seeks to locate law as an integral piece of an inescapably complex social world. In this tradition telling the 'truth of law' is a part of telling the 'truth of social reality'. But if scholars hoped that by adopting legal realism they would find a set of answers about the real nature of law, in fact seeking to position law in society has served to complicate, rather than simplify, competing accounts to the self-referential claims of legal positivism.

The addition of sociological perspectives

For some time sociology has been chipping away at the confidence of legal academics to speak the 'truth' of jurisprudence. The mature Karl Marx (discussed in Chapter 10 of this text) viewed the jurisprudence of the lawyer as ideology, or superficial rhetoric. While social theorists in the Marxist tradition tried to denigrate jurisprudence as ideology of the capitalist system, less critical scholars, such as Roscoe Pound (1943), attempted to go beyond jurisprudence in search of the 'social interests' of law, and

---

10 The German philosopher Martin Heidegger was driven by the need to reawaken our sense of wonder at the very fact of our existence. That we are, rather than are not, we take for granted. We must accept the fact of our being in order to live; yet, reflexivity, or exposing our being to scrutiny, is the essence of the fully human life and ascertaining its meaning the central question of cultural existence. Heidegger argues that if we live without asking the meaning of our life, are we not simply following the pattern of the instinctive creatures which surround us? In other words, is it not the central task of human intellect to wonder at our very being, perpetually questioning its nature; to peer beyond the ordinary and the familiar, in search of the ultimate?

scholars who have been influenced by the writings of the German social theorist Max Weber (who drew links between the modernisation of legality and the rationalisation of modern society, discussed in Chapter 11 of this text) have differentiated the kinds of knowledges that the different disciplines can provide and have tended to describe jurisprudence as the discourse of, and for, legal professionals which enabled the 'profession' to explain itself to itself and to its public. Writers influenced by the Weberian tradition, for example Cotterrell (1989), distinguish 'normative legal theory' (or jurisprudence as traditionally viewed – ie the philosophy of law – which is depicted as bound to the interests of the legal profession), from 'empirical legal theory' (or more sociologically based accounts). In later work (1995) Cotterrell implies that any claim that traditional jurisprudence may make to contain the truth of law is inconsequential in the face of competing sociological claims.

The appeal of sociological accounts lies in the image of critical distance from the material analysed

The advantage of sociological accounts over the perspectives of those 'keyed into' the legal process lies in distance. Through sociology one may both interpret and relate the ideas and subjective perceptions of the legal actors within accounts of the larger context. Reflexively, however, all sociological theses are the narratives of humans trying to 'tell it as it truly is' while locked inescapably into an hermeneutical circle of fellow human beings interpreting the practices and institutions created by other human beings. Where to stand? Where can a secure grounding be found from which legitimately to 'tell it as it truly is'? It may be that there is no secure ground to be found in sociology that will correct and (re)position traditional jurisprudence in such a way that we can produce a faithful rendition of the story of law; providing not only an answer to the question 'what is law', but also to other questions concerning the conditions under which we ask that question and apply the answer(s).

How are we to relate to the diversity of theory? Or, conversely, what are we to make of the urge for a master-theory of law?

An immediate and pressing issue for the contemporary student of law is how to relate to the diversity of theoretical perspectives on law. Jurisprudence is orientated towards clarification, towards making us wiser regarding law and legality, but diversity threatens to create incoherence and bewilderment. Or is this the wrong way to approach the issue? Should we approach the study of law from another direction, encouraging diversity in opinions and perspectives? In which case the question might be, 'what are we to make of the urge for one master-theory of law?'

Throughout history, those who have written on law have generally been inclined to produce one master-account of law, to offer one authoritative story of law's truth. One theorist went so far as to call his theory *The Pure Theory of Law* (Kelsen, 1934, 1970, discussed in Chapter 12 of this text). Why has this tendency to search for unity, coherence and consistency been so dominant, even in theorists who considered themselves to be specifically modern scientists? Some scholars (for example, Unger,

1976, 1987) have suggested the answer lay in fear. Fear of the social responsibility which results if we really face up to the fact that law is our creation, and modern society is an artefact. For Unger (and others) we delude ourselves if we think we have become modern; in reality we have never been truly modern and are afraid of becoming modern; instead we look for substitutes for God so that we may be absolved of the responsibility for making and caring for social bonds and relationships. Thus it may be that the search for some master-discipline – which either displays law's self-sufficiency or, conversely, destroys the image of the (relative) autonomy of legality in the name of proclaiming the truth of its social position – is the search for a replacement for the transcendent figure modernity dispatched when it turned religion from a relationship with 'God' into a mere social and cultural practice. Modernity has thrown up many candidates both to replace God and to pronounce the different ways of reading God's will. Modernity has sought to replace God's will by knowledge of the natural world (as John Austin explicitly stated, utilitarianism was to provide an index of God's commands). A current and very fashionable attempt is the law and economics movement (cf Richard Posner, *The Economic Analysis of Law*, 4th edn, 1992). But each candidate has rivals. The extent of this plurality has intensified within the context of social changes many refer to as the onset of post-modernity.

CONFRONTING POST-MODERNITY: FROM DWORKIN TO BLADE RUNNER

Legal positivist approaches asserted law was a crucial instrument for governing modern societies. Other accounts have claimed that law is more than an instrument. It expresses truths about the type of society we have and the kinds of public commitments we make. Which interpretation is correct; or, do both capture some aspect of legality? In both accounts, telling the truth of law implicitly involves answering the question 'who are we?' and 'what is the nature of the times we find ourselves in?' But these are vast and perhaps open-ended questions which we can understand as the constant travelling companions of mankind's historical journey. They are questions which have needed to be, and have been, asked throughout history. While they are not often explicit in texts called jurisprudence, they are always implicit.

All texts embody hopes and dreams, fears and analysis; the texts of our contemporary situation carry a long history. Consider two texts from the 1980s. The first is from the introduction to a leading work of jurisprudence written by Ronald Dworkin (1986) – a professor of jurisprudence who holds simultaneously academic appointments in jurisprudence at New York University in the United States and Oxford, England. Dworkin is the subject of Chapter 15 of this text; our purpose here is to gain a feel of his rhetoric.

> We live in and by the law. It makes us what we are: citizens and employees and doctors and spouses and people who own things. It is sword, shield, and menace: we insist on our wage, or refuse to pay our rent, or are forced to forfeit penalties, or are closed up in jail, all in the name of what our abstract and ethereal sovereign, the law, has decreed. And we argue about what it has decreed, even when the books that are supposed to record its command and directions are silent; we act then as if law had muttered its doom, too low

to be heard distinctly. We are subjects of law's empire, liegemen to its methods and ideals, bound in spirit while we debate what we must therefore do.

> What sense does this make? How can the law command when the law books are silent or unclear or ambiguous? [The] answer [is] ... legal reasoning is an exercise in constructive interpretation, that our law consists in the best justification of our legal practices as a whole, that it consists in the narrative story that makes of these practices the best they can be. The distinctive structure and constraints of legal arguments emerge on this view, only when we identify and distinguish the diverse and often competitive dimensions of political value, the different strands woven together in the complex judgment that one interpretation makes law's story better on the whole, all things considered, than any other can. (Ronald Dworkin [*Law's Empire*], 1986: vii)

For Dworkin 'we' are the products of the law and our terrain is *Law's Empire*. We are the products of an historical journey in which the construction of a structure of law – a towering edifice of rights and principles – underpinning our social interactions is a crowning achievement. Our contemporary lives, our identities, are mapped out, sustained and energised by legality. To breathe life into the empire we must make the best sense of our story and combine the sometimes disparate strands into a comforting and uplifting whole. In this process we will both inform and secure our social identity. We will offer a justification for the coercion which lies behind our institutions and also demand that such coercion be morally legitimated. Through a philosophical and interpretative jurisprudence we can answer questions of identity, assuage our need for identification with our key social institutions, and further the progressive development of our socio-political legal history. We can then know what to do in this post-modern world.[11]

The second text is Ridley Scott's 1982 film, *Blade Runner*, often called the acme of post-modern movies (for discussions see Bruno, 1987; Harvey, 1990: 308–14; Vattimo, 1992: 83 ff). *Blade Runner* is set in an imaginary Los Angeles in 2019. A group of 'replicants', bio-engineered near-people who normally reside out of the city, have returned to confront their makers, the high-tech Tyrell Corporation. The replicants object to the shortness of their pre-programmed four-year life span – the ultimate in consumerism – and want extension to full human status. The Tyrell Corporation can only respond negatively: 'There is no way. You are doomed to live your programmed life as a simulated human being and your feelings are all false!' Deckard – the 'blade runner' – is assigned to track down the replicants and eliminate (or 'retire') them.

The replicants are not robots, but skin jobs, simulacra who live a fast and furious existence. How are we to determine whether those whom Deckard suspects are

---

11 Dworkin is the subject of Chapter 15 in particular; suffice here to say that the opening quotations are not self-explanatory. The quotation needs interpretation: how are we to understand it? It says many things and assumes many things. Who (is) are (this) 'we'? What is law? Or should the question be, what are laws? Or what is particular to [the essence within the various appearances of] law(s)? That fact that all statements require interpretation is an obvious point, but one which needs constant restatement since it is often overlooked. In literary theory Stanley Fish stresses that the meaning of words is always a question of context and our understanding, even at the most commonsensical level, is a matter of interpretation. As Fish puts it: 'A sentence is never not in context. We are never not in a situation ... A sentence that seems to need no interpretation is already the product of one' (1980: 284. In a chapter of his *Is There a Text in This Class?* entitled 'Normal Circumstances, Literal Language, Direct Speech Acts, the Ordinary, the Everyday, the Obvious, What Goes Without Saying, and Other Special Cases').

replicants or not? One, Rachel, produces a photograph of her 'mother', which enables her to achieve a sense of a real past, a life story, as though human. This inspires Deckard to form an emotional attachment with her and, after dispatching the other replicants, he escapes – at least in the original, commercially released, version – with her to nature; the film ends with them on a journey to a land of forests and mountains. By chance she is special, she was programmed for indefinite life; the scenery of mountains and forests appears to offer the potential for a mode of life enabling them to realise a 'real' human existence.

Blade Runner is set in a terrain of urban decay where once-grand buildings lie damaged, positioned in crowded cosmopolitan streets with endless shopping malls, where incredible high-rise buildings – dwellings for the rich – tower over the street level where Asians ride bicycles and tend stalls. Uncollected garbage is piled high and it constantly drizzles. In the late 1980s and 1990s Los Angeles has become the motif of the post-modern city, the place in which the future is displayed; but if the terrain of *Blade Runner* is indeed Los Angeles it has now become a giant, polluted, overcrowded, Asian-dominated, mega-city. Every street corner is a dangerous arena filled with punk-oriental-heavy-metal-Krishna-lowlifes. While many of the signs are recognisable to the viewer, some – such as the sign which shows a Japanese woman popping pills while a loudspeaker proclaims the pleasures of 'off world vacations' – are not. What has happened? Does this imagery portend the results of a nuclear holocaust? Or does it seek to warn of a more unfocused form of self-destruction? A testament to a modern society which simply fell apart because of the multiplicity of its own internal pressures? What of human values? Paradoxically, the replicants seem to embody more 'human virtue' than the humans. Undoubtedly 'progress', in the sense of things improving for the social body, is no longer credible; what then can offer salvation? In *Blade Runner* we are living amidst signs which date from a time when they would be recognised as having relevance. Roman and Greek columns, Chinese dragons and Egyptian pyramids merge with giant neon ads for Coca-Cola, Atari, Jim Beam, Trident, Michelob and PanAm. Although well-lit transporters hover above the streets and there are momentary scenes of plush corporate suites, the totality is a disorienting collage.

Blade Runner is perhaps the most easily recognised early example of a set of films which announce the strangeness of the post-modern sense of reality. The future is depicted as frightening – it cannot be trusted and neither can man trust himself. The replicants of *Blade Runner* epitomise the ideas of robots, cyborgs, androids, and the growth in biological engineering, which stand in for, and become the simulacra for humans. How is a real human existence possible within the hallucinatory surrounds of electronic billboards broadcasting sex and non-feeling, where narcissistic clones fake orgasms, and 'virtual' reality machines provide (non-)experiences more 'real', more exhilarating than anything real 'reality' can provide. In this portrayal individuals, love, families, jobs, religion, have all disappeared – only the glorious fruits of reproduction technologies rule. Is it possible to keep any hope in utopia?

Vattimo (1992) suggests a lesser kind of utopia is present in *Blade Runner*, a feeling of relief that the disaster modernity seemed destined for has occurred, and we can now get on with living without the relentless urge to be(come) modern that drove us into catastrophe. But this utopia is a retreat from modernity; with the world of 'progress' in ruins, the ending of *Blade Runner* indulges in an ironic-nostalgic retreat to a more 'natural' existence. It is a message that central elements of our modern period have been founded upon misunderstandings and miscalculations. If the enlightenment announced that the goal of human life was happiness in freedom, it was mistaken in believing that abstract scientific analysis could provide us with the truth of the human condition or that technology could build cities worth living in; instead we need to recreate the communities now long lost. The message we hear from existentialist writers, such as Albert Camus (1956), and moral philosophers, such as John Finnis (1980) or Alasdair MacIntyre (1981, 1988), or communitarians, such as Sandel (1982), Taylor (1985, 1990), is that truly human existence is only possible on the basis of living in natural groups. We need to reinterpret past stories and find the true 'natural law' we ought to be living by.

IS IT POSSIBLE TO BELIEVE IN A JURISPRUDENCE WHICH COULD TELL A TRUE STORY OF LAW'S EMPIRE IN POST-MODERNITY? OR IS POST-MODERNITY A LOSS OF FAITH IN COHERENT NARRATIVES, PROGRESS AND THE POSSIBILITY OF JUSTICE?

In recent years jurisprudential scholars have looked from the task of analysis and tried to connect their work to broader stories of social development. Some – such as radical feminists – have challenged the stories of social progress liberalism has implicitly relied upon. Liberalism also has its defenders. The normative jurisprudence of Ronald Dworkin attempts to revitalise liberal legality in the face of the post-modern challenge. To many writers he is a romantic, a 'noble dreamer' who weaves a web of coherence and principled consistency when the reality underlying post-modern legality is incoherence, inconsistency and political battle. What part could be possibly found for Dworkin in *Blade Runner*? Or, in that celebration of contemporary glamour, *LA Law*? In contrast to Dworkin, it appears an easy task to identify a broad set of opponents who are either loosely grouped under the banner of the Critical Legal Studies Movement, or are influenced by similar concerns to those which motivated that movement. Characterised by scepticism and suspicion towards liberalism, there appears, at first sight, no way of reconciling their respective projects with that of Dworkin or those who espouse legal positivism. In fact there seems little way of presenting a narrative of jurisprudence which can contain both sets of positions in such a way that any dialogue between them is possible.[12]

---

12 Strangely, many of the proponents appear not to want dialogue. Dworkin is clear that he cannot have a conversation with those he calls 'external sceptics' (ie commentators who step outside of the confines of internal perspectives to legality and refuse to search first for a favourable and constructive interpretation of the tradition of liberal legality); while other writers claim one can only converse after everybody has admitted the ideological nature of their discourse and deconstructed all texts that they will refer to.

THE PROBLEM OF OFFERING COHERENT NARRATIVES IN THE PLURALIST AND DIVERSE CONDITIONS OF LATE-MODERNITY OR POST-MODERNITY

Modernity – the period of social history since the enlightenment in the 18th century – is founded partly on the belief that it will be possible to attain full self-consciousness concerning social reality. Mankind will analyse the world, gain secure knowledge(s) and use these to build a just society. Post-modernity can be defined as the realisation that such a belief is radically flawed. The more knowledges we gain, the harder it becomes to tell a master story, to present a rationally coherent picture of social reality and the core institutions. Telling the truth of social reality has become problematic. We have defined this as the post-modern problem. Of course, identifying the nature of reality and of our own selves is no new issue: it has been a core project since mankind first started recording its intellectual reflections. We need to construct big stories which both define the nature of our institutions and confer our social identities. As Rosen put it: 'A freedom which cannot give an account of itself is indistinguishable from slavery' (1969: 157).

Why has it apparently become so difficult to give coherent narratives of social progress and the meaning of our institutions in our time? Clearly, what is different is our context and our history. We have so many investigations that we should have some certainty, yet each new discovery undercuts confidence in past certainties. We recognise that: (i) the development of scientific knowledge plays a crucial role in the development of modern society; (ii) the development of new forms of knowledge and new technologies of communication and representation do not make modernity more transparent, but rather offer more and more frequently conflicting perspectives, images, communication networks, and technological capabilities; (iii) such an explosion of imagery and knowledge complicates all forms of social identity creating existential doubts which make coherent action difficult, fears of meaninglessness arise and demands for techniques of certainty intensify; (iv) facing up to this apparent chaos is the post-modern dilemma.

THE PARTICULAR PROBLEMATIC OF ANALYSING LAW IN THE CONDITIONS OF POST-MODERNITY

We live in uncertain times; many commentators feel that the promises of modernity to construct societies of social justice where people would be happy have proved false. The two great opposing political and social narratives of modernity face difficulties: although still providing many of the critical concepts by which we try to understand the social structure of our times, Marxism stands discredited as a political doctrine, while liberalism seems to many to be an empty shell incapable of providing a source of social meaning.

The fate of contemporary law reflects this story of social development. We are surrounded by law. Some have called this the *juridification of social spheres* (Teubner, 1987). Others have alluded to a proliferation of legal and quasi-legal forms of regulation and wondered if any sense can be made of the myriad of effects. In this narrative law has lost its identity, it has surrendered to new Gods: it is seen as a servant of economics, of policy, of utility, while we demand that it should be a moral phenomenon. Never before, it seems, have so many tasks been asked of law; never before has so little authority been invested in it. Is this a cause for concern? Do we need to have an institutional imagination for law which offers us optimistic and uplifting messages, or can we be content to think of law as an instrument of whatever political or ideological power currently dominates the social order?[13] For writers like Dworkin, arguments in jurisprudence are debates over part of our social identity. How we think of law becomes a reflection of how we think of the purposes and contents of our institutions and our societies' public commitments to moral and political decision-making. For both Dworkin and members of the Critical Legal Studies Movement legal positivism weakened our jurisprudential imagination and it is necessary to adopt new forms of interpretation to understand the role of law in constituting our present situation. In what sort of mood should this process be conducted? For Dworkin it is essential to keep our optimism; thus he claims it is possible to read in legality and in legal documents – the US Constitution is the great example – stories of the moral and political principles of our societies (Dworkin (1996) offers lessons on 'The Moral Reading of the [US] Constitution'). Others demand that we face up to our disenchanted world and avoid making the mistake of overestimating the capabilities of law. While other voices argue that we should be wary of all attempts to construct coherent narratives *per se;* we should, rather, deconstruct all narratives refusing to tell any large-scale story of law at all; paradoxically such a refusal is to engage in story telling.[14] We cannot escape from the need to interpret and reinterpret the nature of our social history and the mechanisms by which we orient ourselves in this world. That is the task of jurisprudence; to offer us means by which we can understand and relate to the complex phenomenon of law. Perhaps there is no limit to the stories we can tell? And accepting that our stories cannot be reduced to one master-story may seem like failure to some who need the comfort of an answer to life's questions. Conversely, however, accepting that we are destined to offer interpretations and reinterpretations also implies that being human has to do with continual change, with events and projects, with dialogue and interpretation. And with the need to construct structures of orientation; hence the law.

---

13 Some writers have demanded that this is the correct reading and only if we become radically realist in our appreciation of law can we retain our moral and political integrity. The writer often regarded as the most extreme legal positivist, Hans Kelsen, required that we not only strip our methods of interpreting law of any moral or ideological impurity but also recognise that – in itself – law was nothing but a vehicle for coercion (Kelsen, 1934, 1970).

14 These sides do not appear to be speaking to each other. How do we resolve this? One temptation is to recast this dilemma as a matter of language. This has been tried before. That the 'flight into *logoi* (ways of saying things)' - the constant dialogue of language with language - may obscure the reality of being has never been in doubt. One reading of Plato's distrust of the Sophists has been that he is aware how much the pragmatic things of language, namely, names, concepts, ideas, may all assert themselves instead of the thing they were meant to bring to 'light'. While language offers us the opportunity to bring things out, to analyse things, to see them in a better light, we may lose ourselves in the clarification of the words - thus language obscures as well as helps to illuminate. The Sophists seized upon this potentiality of language to confuse and obfuscate, and were concerned with manipulation and emotional effects, rather than with truth. (See our discussion of the cave myth in Chapter 2.)

ORIGINS:
Classical Greece and the idea of Natural Law

PART ONE
LAW AND THE EXISTENTIAL QUESTION

I am content to think of law as a social institution to satisfy social wants – the claims and demands and expectations involved in the existence of civilised society – by giving effect to as much as we may with the least sacrifice, so far as such wants may be satisfied or such claims given effect by an ordering of human conduct through politically organised society. For present purposes I am content to see in legal history the record of a continually wider recognising and satisfying of human wants or claims or desires through social control; a more embracing and more effective securing of social interests; a continually more complete and effective elimination of waste and precluding of friction in human enjoyment of the goods of existence – in short, a continually more efficacious social engineering (Roscoe Pound, *Introduction to the Philosophy of Law*, 1954: 47).

A single summer grant me, great powers, and
   A single autumn for full ripened song
      That, sated with the sweetness of my
         Playing, my heart may more willingly die.
The soul that, living, did not attain its divine
   Right cannot repose in the nether world.
      Holy, my poetry, is accomplished ...
Be welcome then, stillness of the shadows' world!
   I shall be satisfied though my lyre will not
      Accompany me down there. Once I
         Lived like the gods, and more is not needed.
(The German poet Hölderlin, extract from the poem 'Nur einen Sommer', translated by W Kaufmann in his essay 'Existentialism and Death', 1965: 59).

ASKING THE BASIC QUESTIONS, OR BECOMING AWARE OF THE EXISTENTIAL FOUNDATIONS OF LAW

Roscoe Pound (1870–1964) is often called the founder of American sociological jurisprudence. Looking for the social phenomenon at the basis of legal philosophy, Pound (1954) defined law as the social institution that enabled human wants to be satisfied. A substantial part of his academic work (1921, 1943) consisted in the cataloguing of various claims, demands and desires, and classifying them as individual, public or social. Pound took the legal framework as an essential structure of a modern liberal society, and did not offer any qualitative evaluation of human desires, wants or demands. Instead he offers a narrative history of legal development in which modern law increasingly came to recognise individual 'rights' (particularly from the 18th century), and grant recognition to a wider diversity of human wants, claims, demands and social interests. Law is a technique of social engineering, and recent history shows the legal project as relatively successful; the mere fact of greater wants, demands, claims and desires indicates social progress.

By contrast, the German poet Hölderlin presents a radically different set of concerns wherein the aim of life is not simply to enjoy the goods of existence, rather existence needs *expressive meaning*. For Hölderlin, to simply live out our lives is not enough: humanity transcends animal life by its demand for meaning and its search for criteria of qualitative conceptions of living. We must live in such a way that we are prepared for death – we must seek to live, at least for some time, like the gods.

Every human society is, in the last resort, persons banded together in the face of death. This is the core understanding of liberal political philosophy, jurisprudence, and the sociology of religion.[1] Death is the fundamental evidence of mankind's ontological inadequacy; the irremovable limit to human existence. In the myths of the pre-modern, and the philosophical myths of the modern – for example, in variations of the social contract narrative – men and women join together in loneliness before death to sustain life and form society. In the tradition of liberal jurisprudence, founded by Thomas Hobbes (1651) and developed in recent decades by HLA Hart (1961), the basic aim of legality is survival. While the liberal finds it difficult to say what society is for, he is certain of what it is not: society is not a suicide club (Hart, 1961: 188) But what are the limits to this 'society'? And what is the meaning to be given to the 'social'?

THE PHYSICAL AND EXISTENTIAL ASPECTS OF SOCIAL EXISTENCE

Social existence comprises at least two differing aspects: the *physical* and the *existential*. To combat physical or biological death humans need to find shelter from the elements, eat, drink, engage in procreative activity, and so forth. But biological survival is not the entirety of existence: humans also face the issue of existential survival and existential death. Sex is necessary for biological survival but love is not. To love is to exist in a different frame than merely to survive, and to love may mean that death is of lesser importance. As Gabriel Marcel (1964: 241) once wrote: 'As long as death plays no further role than that of providing man with an incentive to evade it, man behaves as a mere living being, not as an existing being'. That *human existence transcends the merely biological* is the paradox of sociality; it provides the ground for the twin extremes of terror and love that denote the truly human.

Physical security and existential security are two demands which invoke two sets of enemies. One set revolves around the pole of hunger, disease, killings, violence to the body, and lack of material resources. The other revolves around a less obvious pole involving fears of the unknown, desires for knowledge and esteem, the desire to create,

---

1   The sentence is adapted from Peter Berger (1967: 52) and reads in its context: 'Every human society is in the last resort, men banded together in the face of death. The power of religion depends, in the last resort, upon the credibility of the banners it puts in the hands of men as they stand before death, or more accurately, as they walk, inevitably, toward it.'

to find beauty, and to be an individual. Law, utility, contract, economics – symbols of existential distance and calculation – provide the relational tools of the late-modern. By contrast, love not law, encounter not utility, contact not contract, denote concern for a different existential relation. How are they to be reconciled? Where is the beginning?

In the beginning there was nothing; no words, no vision, only the void. Call this what you wish – 'black holes' is the currently fashionable idea – but we now know that there was no God to lay out the foundation, to name the entities of the cosmos and prepare the script of our destiny. We now know that our societies are social-historical constructions; they, and we, could have become something different than they are today. We are a *contingency*. How can we face this? Is this realisation of social construction specifically a modern consciousness – as we tend to think – or did certain people always realise that humanity alone interpreted and laid out the meaning of the cosmos? And what does this realisation imply? Do we need to have a grasp of the totality of existence to answer questions of the meaning of social life; or is human history a constant movement of pragmatic enterprises and arguments within overall mystery?

INTELLECTUAL THOUGHT BEGINS IN MYTH AND THE MYSTERY OF THE HOLY

We cannot know the totality of existence. While fashionable intellectuals announce this as the post-modern message, in pre-modern times this essential mystery went by the name of the *holy*. And the holy defies all attempts to partition it up into neat divisions for our consumption. In Hindu piety, for example, the holy is sometimes represented as gods but in doing so a (dialectical) unity of creator and destroyer is present. Consider Krishna, the most beloved of the Hindu gods. In the *Bhagavad-Gita* he is presented as 'world destroying time', but he also tells Arjuna, 'I am the origin of all; from Me all [the whole creation] proceeds'. And he combines and contains those apparently incongruent features: 'I am the origin and the dissolution ... I am immortality and also death: I am being as well as non-being ... I am death, the all devouring and [am] the origin of things that are yet to be' (for these and following quotes see Kinsley, 1975, aptly entitled *The Sword and the Flute: Kali and Krishna, Dark Visions of the Terrible and the Sublime in Hindu Mythology*).

In the development of Hinduism the divine invokes both attractiveness and repulsiveness. The young Krishna epitomises the former, while the goddess Kali embodies the latter. The *Gita* is the central text, but beyond it those who identify with Krishna esteem the image of the child – the object of love and the physical relations of coddling and cuddling – who in time grows into a youth whose sexual cavorting, in particular with the equally young and beautiful cowherdess Radha, can only be described as a 'carnival of joy'. Krishna brings to the world freedom and spontaneity, beauty and grace, fragrance and harmony, wildness and play, warmth and intimacy; approachable, irresistible, hypnotising, intoxicating, bewitching, he is spellbinding. Ecstatic love provides his route to the ultimate.

Coercion and consensus – the power to destroy and the power to enable, to create – lie intertwined. The flute is the symbol of the intoxicating beauty of the eternally youthful Krishna, while the sword is the symbol of Kali, who represents all the horrifying aspects of destructive forces. Descriptions portray her as bloodthirsty, ruthless, and fierce.

> Of terrible face and fearful aspect is Kali the awful. Four-armed, garlanded with skulls, with dishevelled hair, she holds a freshly cut human head and a bloodied scimitar in her left hands ... Her neck adorned with a garland of severed human heads dripping blood, her earrings two dangling severed heads, her girdle a string of severed human hands, she is dark and naked. Terrible, fang-like teeth, full, prominent breasts, a smile on her lips glistening with blood, she is Kali whose laugh is terrifying ... she lives in the cremation ground, surrounded by screaming jackals. She stands on Shiva, who lies corpse-like beneath her ... In her left hand she holds a cup filled with wine and meat, and in her right hand she holds a freshly cut human head. She smiles and eats rotten meat.

These readings are not the work of two sects or cults and mythologies; instead, while the images of Krishna and Kali denote different phenomena, the identity of each depends upon the existence of the other. And each embodies aspects of the other. Krishna cavorts with the cowherdesses but also makes Arjuna's hair stand on end, and is both the life-giving origin of all and the destroyer of all. The same is true of Kali, to whom the faithful cry out: 'Thou art the Beginning of all, Creatrix, Protectress, and Destructress that Thou art'.[2]

In time philosophy grew out of mythology. The aim of philosophy has always been to maintain the delicate balance between humanity and the cosmos. It interprets our intellectual creations, our rational models, in such a way to strip them of their mystery and turn them into entities we can relate to. For example, in ancient Greek mythology one of the functions of Zeus (the King of the Gods) was that of the patriarchal guardian of the city and its laws. Zeus was capable of terrible retribution to those (such as Prometheus) who used cunning to defeat reason, and preferred arbitrary will to justice. But Zeus was also capable of many changes of mood, particularly when influenced by the sexual attraction and wiles of women. The first consort of Zeus, Metis, was a source of discord and Zeus devoured her, but his second, Themis, became the God of communal order and 'collective conscience' or social sanction. Mythology becomes philosophy through our increased range of interpretations. Thus the union of the belligerent Zeus and the pacific Themis may represent both the need to distinguish and balance the active and aggressive enforcement of commands (laws), with the ideal of social stability and quiescence, as well as illustrating that domestic safety requires at least the ability to have recourse to the sword. Although we can give this a gender-aware reading, in which the respective realms of the public and the sword are the domain of

---

2   In the writings of the 19th-century Hindu saint, Sri Ramakrishna (1974: 11 and 17), a passionate devotee of Kali, the Divine Mother, the being of the goddess is to contain at the same time a unity of opposites. In the temple her image stands in basalt, spectacularly bedecked in gold and jewels, upon the prostrate body of Shiva in white marble: 'She has four arms. The lower left hand holds a severed human head and the upper grips a bloodstained sabre. One right hand offers boons to her children; the other allays their fear. The majesty of Her posture can hardly be described. It combines the terror of destruction with the assurance of motherly tenderness. For she is the Cosmic Power, the totality of the universe, a glorious harmony of the pairs of opposites. She deals out death, as She creates and preserves. In an early vision of Ramakrishna, Kali emerged from the Ganges, came to the land, and presently gave birth to a child, which she began to nurse tenderly. A moment later she assumed a terrible aspect, seized the child between her grim jaws, and crushed it. As she swallowed the child, she re-entered the waters of the Ganges.'

the male, while that of domestic peace is the female, another reading is of the necessity for the power of the sword to be joined to the wisdom of its social effects. As Zeus, without the influence of Themis, can be a terrible and uncivilised tyrant, so can law, blind to its social effectivity and consequences, be an uncivilised weapon. Several of the children of Zeus and Themis became the guarantors of the laws and social stability: most notably Dike, Eunomia, and Eirene. Dike came to personify the ideal of justice which raised men above the animal world. Over time dike would become the standard term for a law case. As a Goddess, Dike made judges strive to deliberate with logical straightness and not make arbitrary decisions; her sister Eunomia stood for the social and legal harmony attendant upon such reasoned behaviours, and Eirene embodied peace. Together they constituted the social idea of *homonoia*, or the ideal of a harmonious city community; the later philosophy of Plato and Aristotle takes up the task of understanding that idea.[3]

THE EXISTENTIAL PROBLEM REFLECTED IN GREEK LITERATURE AND PHILOSOPHY: THE EXAMPLE OF *ANTIGONE*

From our vantage point it appears that in the Homeric world 'the basic values of society were given, predetermined, and so were a man's place in the society and the privileges and duties that flowed from his status' (MI Finley, 1954: 134). But this is a modern judgment, made with the benefit of 2,000 years of historical writings – it did not look so to the participants. Any discussion of concepts concerning morality or justice takes place within a mode of life which provides not only the resources but also the context for writing and speculation. To the Greeks we owe the origins of our western philosophical and social theoretical traditions. One aim of this tradition has been to transcend uncritical acceptance of the conventional life – to identify the conditions for a rationally meaningful existence. But how were the tools for understanding and criticising the context for ancient Greek life established? Greek literature and, in time, its developing philosophy, seem to reflect fundamental divisions in the human spirit: divisions between acceptance of the *status quo* and rejection of it, between desire for order and desire to transgress, between immanence and transcendence; between defence of conventional standards and scepticism towards those standards, between accepting one's fate/role in life and desiring something else or *other*.

Consider the famous and tragic example of *Antigone*, the third of the Theban plays by Sophocles written in the 5th century BC (text used is the Penguin Classics, 1947).

---

3   Philosophy comes out of mythology, but perhaps, never fully escapes from a mythological foundation. Western philosophy's birth with Plato and Aristotle contains the grace of the gods. In *Protagoras* Plato gave a foundational natural explanation of society in that while primitive men could feed themselves they came together to seek protection from wild animals. However, social life was virtually impossible since man was without civil skill (*politike techne*), or the capacity to live in community with others. The city life men entered into was dangerous because of their own ill-behaviour, but Zeus bestowed upon man the faculties for mutual respect and a sense of justice that civic life requires. The philosophy of Plato then takes on the task of finding rational and concrete methods for constituting the ideal city-state. For an argument that highlights the role of mythology in contemporary jurisprudence see Fitzpatrick, (1992) *The Mythology of Modern Law*.

Antigone was one of the daughters of Oedipus, that tragic figure of male power who had been cursed by the Gods for mistakenly killing his father (the King of Thebes) and subsequently marrying his mother and assuming the throne of Thebes.[4] After the death of Oedipus, civil war broke out and a battle was waged in front of the seventh gate of Thebes – his two sons led opposing factions and at the height of the battle fought and killed each other. Oedipus' brother, Creon, uncle of Antigone, was now undisputed master of the city. Creon resolved to make an example of the brother who had fought against him, Polynices, by refusing the right of honourable burial. The penalty of death was promulgated against any who should defy this order, and the order was accepted as the lawful command of the ruler throughout the city. The play begins with Antigone confronting her sister Ismene.

Antigone is distraught, while her brother Eteocles 'has been buried in full honour of the state, Polynices has been left unburied, unwept, a feast of flesh for keen eyed Carrion birds'. Antigone asks Ismene if she had heard of the order which she perceives as personally addressed to them:

> It is against you and me he has made this order. Yes, against me. And soon he will be here himself to make it plain to those who have not heard it, and to enforce it.

This is no idle threat; the punishment for disobedience is death. For Antigone the dilemma is acute and a challenge to her royal blood: 'Now is the time to show whether or not you are worthy of your high blood ... is he not my brother, and yours, whether you like it or not? I shall never desert him – never!' But Ismene responds: 'How could you dare – when Creon has expressly forbidden it?'

Antigone feels bound by a normative obligation which transcends her position as a subject of Creon. Ismene, however, recalling the horrors of the events their family has suffered, appeals to Antigone to be realistic:

> ... now only we two left; and what will be the end of us, if we transgress the law and defy our king? Oh think, Antigone; we are women; it is not for us to fight against men;[5] our rulers are stronger than we and we must obey in this, or in worse than this. May the dead forgive me, I can do no other but as I am commanded; to do more is madness.

With a touch of bitterness, Antigone releases her sister from the obligation to help her, but argues she cannot shrug off the burden:

> If I die for it what happiness!
> Convicted of reverence – I shall be content to lie beside a brother whom I love ...
> Live if you will; live, and defy the holiest laws of heaven.

Antigone juxtaposes two sets of obligations and laws. She feels bound by the laws of Heaven to bury her brother while she is bound by the laws of Thebes not to bury him.

---

4 Antigone is destined to a tragic life from the circumstances of her birth. In *Oedipus Rex* Oedipus realises the awful plight of the identity of his children by Jocasta (his natural mother). Antigone is both his sister and his daughter; the unwritten rules of kinship and the attribution of identity had been breached.

5 This is frequently translated as 'we were born women, showing that we were not meant to fight with men'; in the Greek Ismene uses the verb *phyo*, indicating that it is by nature (*physis*) rather than social convention that women do not attempt to rival men.

Her sister's response demonstrates she also recognises the conflict: 'I do not defy them; but I cannot act against the state, I am not strong enough'. For Antigone this is merely an excuse;[6] she leaves to bury her brother resigned to her punishment. Her death will be 'honourable'; to live in the knowledge of her failure to act would be to deny meaning to her life and make it a non-existence.[7] The scene of the play shifts to the Assembly of Thebes where Creon is addressing his counsellors. After Creon explains the necessity for his command the counsellors announce their concurrence:

> ... you have given the judgment for the friend and the enemy. As for those that are dead,
> so for those who remain, your will is law.

Antigone gives symbolic burial to her brother. When the burial is discovered by the guards and reported to Creon he immediately suspects it to be the work of a man. In time, however, the sentries apprehend Antigone and bring her before him. Rather understandably, given the fact that he is now her official guardian and she is engaged to his son, Creon presents Antigone with the opportunity to deny she had knowledge of the command or, alternatively, that she had misunderstood its meaning. Antigone, however, does not take the opportunity:

> I knew it, naturally. It was plain enough.
> CREON: And yet you dared to contravene it?
> ANTIGONE: Yes, that order did not come from God. Justice that dwells with the gods below, knows no such law. I did not think your edicts strong enough to overrule the unwritten unalterable laws of God and heaven, you being only a man. They are not of yesterday or today, but everlasting, though where they came from, none of us can tell. Guilty of their transgression before God I cannot be, for any man on earth. I knew that I should have to die, of course, with or without your order. If it be soon, so much the better. Living in daily torment as I do, who would not be glad to die?

When the punishment of death is about to be carried out, and its burden lies heavily on Creon, he offers a justification for its absolute necessity.

> He who the state appoints must be obeyed to the smallest matter, be it right – or wrong. And he that rules his household, without a doubt, will make the wisest king, or, for that matter, the staunchest subject. He will be the man you can depend on in the storm of war ... There is no deadlier peril than disobedience: states are devoured by it, homes laid in ruins, armies defeated, victory turned to rout. While simple obedience saves the lives of hundreds of honest folks. Therefore, I hold to the law, and will never betray it.

---

6   Several scholars have depicted Antigone as a masculinised woman. Antigone shared the exile of her father, while Ismene stayed in Thebes. Ismene has therein been indoctrinated into the beliefs of patriarchal society - men are born to rule, woman to obey - while Antigone has known greater self-sufficiency. In later scenes of the play Antigone often refers to herself with a pronoun in the masculine gender, and Creon - in deciding to punish her - states 'I am not a man, she is the man if she shall have this success without penalty.' In the later stages Antigone even refers to herself as the sole survivor of the house of Oedipus - thus casting her sister in the role of the living dead. In choosing physical survival Ismene has lost her existential status, her life has no meaning in the eyes of her sister.

7   To writers who can loosely be described as existential - for example Marcel, Jaspers, Nietzsche, Heidegger - individual human life comes with the burden that the individual is called upon to give it meaning. The idea of death serves as the ultimate testing ground. *Life is the challenge of living and testing the meaning of living while conscious of human mortality.* While mere existence is a matter of biological and social functions, existentialism points to a subjective, self-determining aspect of life - the task of using life wisely, lovingly, and honestly.

Creon further adds a patriarchal note:

> Least of all for a woman. Better be beaten, if need be, by a man, than let a woman get the better of us.[8]

There are many tensions apparent in the words of the play, such as those between love and power, between family and state, between what we might call the public and the private, but the overriding tension is between the obligation to the legitimate commands of Creon – established as the rightful laws of Thebes – and the obligation to the laws of Heaven. Sophocles offers no way out. Antigone is doomed to die, as indeed is Creon's son in despair at her fate.[9]

INTERPRETATIONS OF THE LEGAL TENSIONS IN *ANTIGONE*

While the main dilemma focuses around the conflict between Antigone and Creon, the play offers a multitude of layers and possible readings including the conflict between love and duty,[10] between men and women, between nature and culture, and between different conceptions of law and their 'fit' with the natural order. These 'legal' tensions are variously represented as:

(i)   the demands of natural law verses legal positivism. The 19th-century German philosopher Hegel (see this text, Chapter 7), in his *Phenomenology of Spirit,* read the play as exposing the latent tensions of Greek society. Greek culture operated on the belief of total unity, based on a communal, 'natural' way of life. Antigone refused, however, to follow Ismene's obedience to the natural law which subordinated women to men and which reinforced the human law of Creon's commands, following instead the divine law which dictates that a member of the family must be buried by its relatives and its spirit will know no rest unless it is. Each is compelled to obey one law and disobey another. Creon's ruling, moreover, made sense on its own terms. It was opposed, however, by divine law, carrying a contrary but strict authority, which insisted that Polynices be buried and that a member of the family assume special responsibility for this task. Hegel presents both demands as non-negotiable. Antigone is not able to operate as an autonomous individual choosing to

---

8   Creon consistently displays patriarchal prejudices. He fails to understand his son Haemon's love for Antigone, refers to his own wife as a 'field to plow' (line 569; a sentiment which reflected the belief that it was the male seed which produced children, and saw the female as merely providing a fertile soil for the seed) In *The Second Sex,* Simone de Beauvoir argues the phallus/plow – woman/furrow symbolism is a common tactic reinforcing patriarchal authority and the subjection of woman. Creon is clearly afraid of being bettered by a woman and warns his son against such an event (lines, 484, 525, 740, 746, 756).

9   Ultimately Antigone reverts to the female role: she first laments that she will die a virgin, unwed and childless, and then commits suicide after being entombed alive in a cave under Creon's orders. Suicide is regarded as a feminine mode of death - however Haemon, Creon's son, also commits suicide as does Eurydice, Creon's wife.

10   After they have heard the fate of Creon's son, Haemon, the chorus announces the destructive force of love: 'Love, invincible love, who keeps vigil on the soft cheek of a young girl, you roam over the sea and among homes in wild places, no one can escape you, neither man nor god, and the one who has you is possessed by madness. You bend the minds of the just to wrong, so here you have stirred up this quarrel of son and father. The love kindling light in the eyes of the fair bride conquers.'

do one thing rather than another; rather, she is the bearer of a divine injunction which is absolute. The tension is between the communal demand to follow the laws of the community as strict injunctions, accepting their immemorial status as the ground of their truth, and the supra-communal demand to obey the law to bury her brother and acknowledge the sacred character of the familial bond. Creon is charged with the responsibility of shaping the laws of the community, and he is equally bound, both as male and ruler, to obey the principle that an enemy of the state must not receive the honour of a burial, and to punish the woman who disobeys his edict. The community does not have the intellectual resources to resolve this internal conflict.[11]

(ii) an example of the command theory of law;

(iii) an early and undeveloped site of civil disobedience; an action impossible to conceptualise successfully since the social order did not provide the intellectual resources to sustain a concept of civil disobedience. The concept of civil disobedience, which came into existence in the enlightenment, allows an individual a 'right' to oppose part of the legal order in the name of the true spirit of the legal order. The right did not exist for the classical Greek, rather we have opposing sets of 'duties', specifically:[12]

(iv) the duty to one's family versus one's duty to the state, two conflicting and irreconcilable forms of duty which also represent the bonds of civil society in opposition to the ties of the political state;[13]

---

11 Hegel (*Phenomenology of Spirit*, AV Miller, trans 1977: para 466): 'Since it sees right only on one side and wrong on the other, that consciousness which belongs to the divine law sees in the other side only the violence of human caprice, while that which holds to human law sees in the other only the self-will and disobedience of the individual who insists on being his own authority. For the commands of government have a universal, public meaning open to the light of day; the will of the other law, however, is looked upon in the darkness of the nether regions, and in its outer existence manifests as the will of an isolated individual which, as contradicting the first, is a wanton outrage.'

12 Again, following Hegel's reading, the tragedy highlights the inner contradiction in the life of a community which does not have the intellectual resources that the concepts of individuality and subjectivity provide. Law of its nature implies that the subject has the ability to disobey. It is always a relationship of one entity to another. The individual or the corporate personality versus the state. The law requires that it be obeyed, but the reality of social life creates circumstances where obedience also begets disobedience. Without a developed notion of individuality – without the legal space created by a concept of civil disobedience – the focus of Greek culture upon functionality within a totality left no space for the individual-totality relationship to be mediated without contradiction. The play thus brought out actual and potential conflicts in the traditions of the land; and revealed the lack of unity in a world which demanded that unity exist. Antigone displayed the contradiction in Greek spirit, and the Sophists, on Hegel's reading, revealed both its need for the principle of subjectivity and its inability to assimilate it. Greek life simply could not continue once a philosophy of individuality became more common.

13 Continuing Hegel's reading, it is impossible for either Creon or Antigone to escape guilt. The structure presents multiple duties: each obeyed one set of laws at the expense of another. Guilt in Greek life does not reside so much in the evil intention of the agent, for agency is, by later standards, undeveloped or at least underdeveloped – the structural imagery of fate carries all before it. Guilt inheres in actions against the law of the social order even if they did not intend that result and could not have acted differently. It is a tragic position in which both Antigone and Creon, in disobeying one law and obeying another, assume guilt, although neither could have acted other than they did.

(v) the irrationality of women's arbitrary subjectivity versus the cold reason of the male state expressed through the abstract duty to formal law;[14]

(vi) the demands of a practical reason which faces up to an immediate dilemma versus the demands of a theoretical rationality (Creon's utilitarianism) which looks to a category of the state's interests;

(vii) the early beginnings of individual rationality – subjectivity – against the view of justice as following the objective rules of the social body.

Writing in the early 1990s, Douzinas and Warrington (1994), suggest another, perhaps 'post-modern', reading. In their eyes Antigone's dilemma is the subject of so much analysis partly because the existential quandary occurred at the beginning of our traditions of writing and needs to be captured in writing for us to understand it. The desire(s) of Antigone to face (a personal) justice – Antigone's *Dike* – is a precursor to modern ethics, a state of primordial being before the ordering methodologies of rational thought and writing have established their demarcations. Antigone's *Dike* is a very personal existential crisis – there were no rules which could resolve the issue successfully. Later systems of intellectual thought define existential dilemmas as unorderlessness and turn the rawness of existence into things that can be analysed – in other words, transform existential dilemmas into conceptual discussions – so that 'ought' structures of moral systems arise and demarcate themselves from the 'is' of 'natural being'. As a result we hand over moral dilemmas to specialised technocrats and live out our lives within a bureaucratically administered social space.[15]

Antigone speaks to the tragic and contradictory aspects of human existence; perhaps there is no solution, no master reading. *Antigone* has constantly demanded philosophical

---

14 Again epitomised by Hegel's reading of *Antigone*. In his *Philosophy of Right*, published in 1821, Hegel is concerned with the types of rationality in the world and he views world history as a matter of the development and clash of modes of rationality. For Hegel man seeks knowledge of universal conditions through conceptual thought and willing objectivity. Women are concerned with the substantive matters identified through concrete individuality and feeling. Men look to the external world and thus:

'Man has his actual substantive life in the state, in learning, and so forth, as well as in labour and struggle with the external world ... woman has her substantive destiny in the family, and to be imbued with family piety is her ethical frame of mind.

For this reason, family piety is expounded in Sophocles' *Antigone* ... as principally the law of woman, and as the law of a substantiality at once subjective and on the plane of feeling, the law of the inward life, a life which has not yet attained its full actualisation; as the law of the ancient gods, "the gods of the underworld"; as "an everlasting law, and no man knows at what time it was first put forth". This law is there displayed as a law opposed to public law, to the law of the land. This is the supreme opposition in ethics and therefore in tragedy; and it is individualised in the same play in the opposing natures of man and woman.' (TM Knox, trans, 1952: para 166)

15 Douzinas and Warrington work their analysis for a specific purpose: to advance a thesis that modern legality and ethics have lost any real connection with moral being and become mere technique. Their project in reading Antigone is to invoke a time and a place where justice was a more pressing figure, less de-humanised, more 'real' in that it was a set of demands at the level of the 'other's' (here Polynices') real presence ('the beloved head and face of my brother'), rather than of some abstract formal argument, or being bound by a moral idea. In their argument, the intellectual categories and demarcations which modernity has constructed have lowered our appreciation of the reality of human ties and interactions. Douzinas' and Warrington's post-modern demand is to reinstate the 'face' of the 'other' as a real phenomenon in our moral discussions.

interpretation and serves as a beginning to jurisprudence since the task of philosophy is to provide rational guidance for practical life, to enable us to relate to our institutions, and to interpret and criticise our practices. When institutions do not have a settled intellectual tradition of debate – of justification and critique – their forms and functions remain deeply ambiguous and liable to abuse (if we can even identify abuse from use).[16] It is a task of literature to (re)present life; it is one task of jurisprudence to interpret and provide critiques of the ethos of legality in life. Perhaps we can take a message: jurisprudence 'ought' to remember its basis is life, and not become obsessed by analysing an 'idea' thought up out of the conditions of life. One idea that labelled a prominent tradition is that of Natural Law, given birth to by the Greeks.

---

16 For Leo Strauss (1953: 101) the analysis of law cannot escape from ambiguity:

'Law reveals itself as something self-contradictory. On the one hand, it claims to be something essentially good or noble: it is the law that saves the cities and everything else. On the other hand, the law presents itself as the common opinion or decision of the city, ie of the multitude of citizens. As such, it is by no means essentially good or noble. It may very well be the work of folly and baseness. There is certainly no reason to assume that the makers of laws are as a rule wiser than "you and I"; why, then, should 'you and I' submit to their decision? The mere fact that the same laws which were solemnly enacted by the city are repealed by the same city with equal solemnity would seem to show the doubtful character of the wisdom that went into their making.' The question, then, is whether the claim of the law to be something good or noble can be simply dismissed as altogether unfounded or whether it contains an element of truth.

'The law claims that it saves the cities and everything else. It claims to secure the common good. But the common good is exactly what we mean by 'the just'. Laws are just to the extent to which they are conducive to the common good.'

We can accept Strauss's highlighting of the issue, without needing to commit ourselves to Strauss's particular definition of the just.

PART TWO
THE CONTEXT FOR THE NATURAL LAW OF
THE CLASSICAL GREEKS

THE EXISTENTIAL LOCATION OF THE BEGINNING OF CLASSICAL GREEK PHILOSOPHY: THE NATURAL DEPENDENCY OF EARLY MANKIND

If you control the way children play, and the same children always play the same games under the same rules and in the same conditions, and get pleasure from the same toys, you'll find that the conventions of adult life too are left in peace without alteration ... Change, we shall find, except in something evil, is extremely dangerous. (Plato, *The Laws*, Penguin edn, 1970: 797.)

It is difficult to obtain a right education in virtue from youth up without being brought under right laws; for to live temperately and hardily is not pleasant to most men, especially when young; hence the nature and exercises of the young should be regulated by law...
We shall need laws to regulate the discipline of adults as well, and in fact the whole life of the people generally; for the many are more amenable to compulsion and punishment than to reason and moral ideas. Hence some persons hold that, while it is proper for the lawgiver to encourage and exhort men to virtue on moral grounds, in the expectation that those who have the virtuous moral upbringing will respond, yet he is bound to impose chastisement and penalties on the disobedient and ill-conditioned, and to banish the incorrigible out of the state altogether (Aristotle, *Nicomachean Ethics* 10. 9. 8–9) .

The writings of the two Greek thinkers hailed as the founders of western philosophy – Plato and Aristotle – display differing approaches to the task of stabilising social order and creating mechanisms for structuring social existence. While they adopted contrasting methodologies, however, both sought the security of a 'truth' which resided in nature. While the world may seem full of variation, chaos, diversity and disorder, both asserted that a natural order lay behind or inherent within it, and this order, once its basic principles were known, could found man's social order.

While 'pure truth' is independent of particular social relations, all human knowledge is pragmatic, perspectival and methodological. The story of the development of classical Greek social thought is beyond this text, but, in summary, it arose with the development of a multitude of city-states and was spurred on by the need to handle new issues created by the advancement of knowledge and trade. Its change from 'primitive' mythology to (what we now give the status of) revered 'classical flowering of man's reason' spanned eight centuries at least. While modern anthropology has tried to escape from eurocentric views of an irrational primitive society which later become a modern rational society, we remain with ideas of 'primitive' societies as dependent upon the forces of the natural world to an extent which is hard to understand today. In these early societies the level of social power and technology was such as to make the paramount issue that of the connection with, and relationship to, the forces of nature.

Certainly there was a time (and perhaps we are at risk to assert that it is not still with us) when nature imposed itself so imperatively on humanity as almost totally to control humanity. So-called primitive mankind shared in the life of nature, was initiated via rituals and ceremonies into its routine, in order to participate in the structure of that life – and thereby keep within nature's grace. The natural – conceived as the numinous and the sacred – imposed respect, and became the source of norms for their behaviour. Life involved norms and practices, rituals and ceremonies, regarding agriculture, fishing, hunting, mating, giving birth, the transition from childhood to adulthood, coping with illness, death and burial. The same natural imperatives that were believed to operate throughout nature – the climate, the terrain (mountains, rivers, the sea, the desert, the forest), the sun and the moon – bound mankind. But whereas primitive humanity may have felt either powerless before nature, or one minor power amongst many, they felt embedded in nature; by contrast modern man understands nature as a site for man's activities – an arena where man may impose his will via technology.[17] For the *modern* person, natural law can no longer be felt to be just there, since nature is no longer just there.[18] The modern understands that a view of natural law as man acting in obedience to the dictates of nature downplays the aspect of man's collective and individual will; the modern wants to assert his/her 'rights', and sees the world as a space to play and construct, to develop individual life projects. Conversely, classical natural law did not imply natural rights, rather it implied natural functions, ends and duties. It constructed a web of relations which positioned and gave the self meaning, outside of which was existential death.

---

17 For Antony Giddens (1990) pre-modern cultures faced a different combination of trust and risk than modern cultures. The general context of the pre-modern was of the overriding importance of localised trust. The mechanisms which provided trust were:

(i) kinship relations as an organising device for stabilising social ties across time-space;

(ii) the local community as a place providing a familiar milieu;

(iii) religious cosmologies as modes of belief and ritual practice providing a providential interpretation of human life and nature;

(iv) tradition as a means of connecting present and future, the culture being past-orientated in time;

While the environment of risk consisted of:

(i) threats and dangers emanating from nature, such as the prevalence of infectious diseases, climatic unreliability, floods, or other natural disasters;

(ii) the threat of human violence from marauding armies, local warlords, brigands or robbers;

(iii) risk of a fall from religious grace or of malicious magical influence.

18 By contrast the modern person lives a life disembedded from nature and re-embedded in abstract social systems. By the disembedding of social systems, Giddens refers to the lifting out of social relations from local contexts of interaction and their restructuring across indefinite spans of time-space.

Abstract systems depend upon symbolic tokens (media of interchange which can be passed around without regard to the specific characteristics of individuals or groups that handle them at any particular juncture) for example, money, and the establishment of expert systems. Systems of technical accomplishment or professional expertise organise large areas of the material and social environment in which we live today. The lawyer and the system of legal knowledge, the car designer and factory production. Everyday life requires 'faith' in the fact that the numerous things we interact with - cookers, washing machines, cars, public transport, buildings, road traffic systems, bank accounts, credit cards, insurance, etc - work as they are 'supposed to do'. This is a faith occasioned by participation in the practices of everyday life and reinforced by recourse to law. (Behind much of the activities and the conditions of operation of the entities are regulatory agencies over and above professional bodies whose function is to supervise and protect the consumers of expert systems, bodies which licence machines, keep a watch over the standards of aircraft manufacturers etc).

THE CONTEXT FOR CLASSICAL GREEK PHILOSOPHY WAS THE DEVELOPMENT OF THE CITY-STATE

As Mycenaean power crumbled under the pressure of the Dorian tribes who invaded mainland Greece in the 12th century BC, a whole type of kingship and form of social life, centred on the palace, was destroyed forever. While the religion and mythology of classical Greece (the 4th century BC) was rooted in the Mycenaean past, the social and cultural structure was dramatically different. The person of the divine king vanished from the Greek social and cultural universe. As this centre disappeared, the resulting psychological change prepared the way for the development of those twin innovations which are the foundation of the legacy of classical Greece: the institution of the city-state, and the development of abstract, rational, or conceptual thought (for an account see Vernant, 1982).

The city-state was both the creation of man's power to organise, and the place of imperfections. A living reality, it invited betterment. It required rational analysis in the hope of problem solving and improvement:

> The origin and ordering of the world for the first time took the form of an explicitly posed problem to which an answer must be supplied without mystery, an answer gauged to human intelligence, capable of being aired and publicly debated before the mass of citizens like any question of everyday life (Vernant, 1982: 107).

The government of the city was bound up with a new idea of space. Vernant argues the institutions of the *polis* were designed and embodied in what may be called a political space. The first urban planners – for example Hippodamus of Miletus – were political theorists, and the organisation of urban space was but one aspect of a more general effort to order and rationalise the human world.[19]

In this organisational process the Greeks tended to describe the world in terms of polar opposites, which for them differed in kind; for example:

rational|irrational	culture|nature	moving|at rest	deep|shallow
dry|wet	fast|slow	strong|weak	dark|bright
big|little	far|near	heavy|light	many|few
hot|cold	male|female	earth|sky	

Law knew its own polar opposition: legal\|illegal. As the Greeks understood it, things have particular sets of qualities which make things that are, say, *hot*, a different kind of

---

19 Vernant (1982: 126–7) points out the new social space was organised around a geographical centre which thus became the most valued. The welfare of the *polis* rested on those who were known as *hoi mesoi*, since, being equidistant from the extremes, they constituted a fixed point on which the city was balanced. Individuals and groups occupied symmetrical positions in relation to this centre. The *agora*, which represented this spatial arrangement on the ground, formed the centre of a common public space. All those who entered it were by that fact defined as equals, *isoi*. By their presence in that public space they entered into relations of perfect reciprocity with one another. Note also the restricted space that women moved in within classical Athens. Garner (1987: 84–5) points out that even though it is possible to list times and places where it was acceptable, and even expected, that women would make public appearances, there is much evidence that they were generally confined to the inner quarters of the house, and that the wealthier the house, the more the servants did away with the need for the mistress to go outside. Women did not even accompany their husbands to dinner parties in other houses, or appear for dinner in their own home in the presence of their husband's guests.

thing from those that are *cold*. The Greeks appeared to believe that these were qualities that could exist on their own. The hot could exist independently from the cold, the legal from the illegal, the male from the female.

This process of making clear-cut distinctions enabled Plato to identify the structure of the mathematical and geometric as the foundation for secure knowledge;[20] to 'be' was to exist in such a form as to be countable and easily visualised.[21] This structure to knowledge both linked, and yet separated into their respective domains, heaven and earth, epitomising both the orderliness of justice and providing the means of keeping self-advantage at bay (see the words of Socrates addressed to Callicles in *Gorgias*, 508a).

THE PRACTICAL NATURE OF GREEK PHILOSOPHY: PLATO'S WRITINGS FOUNDED ON THE DESIRE TO FIND A PLACE FROM WHICH TO CRITICISE THE CONVENTIONS OF THE SOCIAL ORDER[22]

The talk about the universal idea of (the) good always takes as its point of departure the *human* question: what is (the) good for us?[23] To have done otherwise would have seemed inauthentic. Even in the most clear-cut 'idealist' of Plato's writings, the *Republic*

20　In *The Open Society and Its Enemies: Vol I Plato*, Popper (1945: 31) argues that Plato exemplifies this 'methodological essentialism'. The task of pure knowledge or science is to discover and describe the true nature of things, that is their hidden reality which resides elsewhere than in the appearances our senses reveal to us.

21　By contrast if everything is interlinked how can we be sure that something is actually hot and not cold? Legal and not illegal? Bad and not good? The contrary view, that instead of pairs of polar opposites we have a continuous scale of degrees of the one and same quality (for example, that darkness is a zero intensity of light, and rest is a zero degree of motion), requires a wholly new form of mathematical calculation, and one which is difficult to visualise. An example is the difficulty of Japanese leaders to plead in the war trials of the Second World War either guilty or not guilty. Their argument was that they were both, since the structure of their social order, and their ideas of duty and responsibility, meant that elements of guilt and innocence were completely intertwined and impossible to separate.

22　Plato (c427-347 BC) is recognised along with his 'teacher' Socrates and his own pupil Aristotle as one of the vital definers of the western tradition in philosophy and social thought. He came from a family that had played a prominent part in Athenian politics and it would have been natural for him to follow the tradition. He was shocked by its corrupt nature, however, and sickened by the execution in 399 BC of his teacher and friend, Socrates. In Plato's youth the democratic movement consisted of men of humble origins who had the power to sway the popular assembly through rhetoric; once in power the policies tended to be populist, what would please the people, rather than a rational analysis of what the situation required. In 386 he founded the Academy, a school for statesmen. This reflected Plato's belief that nothing could be done with the contemporary political situation, and the best hope lay in training a future generation in the rational pursuit of true knowledge and the necessity of applying this to the practical realm of politics. His ideal was rule by philosopher-king. His opponents were the Sophists, who had a school of their own which taught the qualities required for success in everyday life; the key being rhetoric, or the art of self-expression and persuasion. Plato felt that a training in rhetoric alone was dangerous since it gave a person the power to express his/her desires and persuade others, without guidance in its proper use or providing any guards against abuse. *The Republic* (written c 375 BC; references to Penguin revised edition 1974, trans D Lee) his best-known treatise, was a set of dialogues on the ideal state; *The Laws* (another written in dialogue style; a description of a Utopian state to be founded in Crete in the 4th century BC) was written towards the end of his life (text used Penguin edn, 1970, trans Trevor Saunders).

23　See Socrates' self-portrayal in the *Phaedo* and the discussion in the *Philebus* as to the extent to which the passion of our drives and our consciousness can be balanced into an harmonious whole in our lives.

– which laid out a template for the creation of the 'ideal' state, where the legal regime leads to the good life – the foundation is an understanding of the nature of the practical and the practical life. The *Republic* opens with a discussion of whether the good is pleasure (*Hédoné*), as the mass of the population (*hoi polloi*) appear to believe, or reason (phron'esis). Does it consist in the satisfaction of one's immediate drives, or insight into the good? At stake is the arrangement of a practical rationality which will legitimate legal power. The tensions of communal life are to be balanced by the directional power that (transcendental) knowledge of the just, the good and the right, offers. Our belief that the concepts of the just, of the right, of the good, refer ultimately to phenomena which lie somewhere beyond the messiness of the practical life, is essential to enable the intellect to direct the operations of the practical life. But how are we to know the reality of the just, the good, the right? Can we trust the opinions which surround us? Can we reach the true through discussion or argument? No, argues Plato; our circumstances deceive us: we need to transcend our opinions and conventions and see, or grasp, pure reality.[24] Plato is certain of his epistemological methodology. In the *simile of the sun* (*Republic*) Plato combines his thesis of the world of pure essences (the 'ideas'), as contrasted to the world of appearances, with the thesis of our divided selves, wherein the temporal is downgraded compared to a soul which knows essences. It would appear that genuine knowledge comes about when the soul ceases wandering within the narrow sphere of material bodies, detaches itself from sense perceptions, and liberates a kind of intelligence which looks to the unchanging aspect of things (*eidos*). Genuine knowledge, then, requires an intelligence that is not tied to sense perceptions. It also requires an intelligible world that can be distinguished from the material world. The 'eye of the soul' and 'ideas' will be the preconditions of knowledge. The soul must free itself from the body and its changeable senses, and put its intellectual faculties to work. It must turn its gaze toward objects full of light, and, bathed in the light that emanates from those objects, see essential truth, beauty and permanence.

To reach the truth, to ascertain what is truly natural and good for humanity, we need to surpass the empirical situation we find ourselves in. Of course our deliberation and choice is located within a communal sense of what it is fitting to do. We are authentically ethical by virtue of participating in the language, customs, and practices located in institutions, which define what 'we' are. As each human child grows and comes out of the site of natural dependency into personhood, he/she finds – in the language, customs and institutions of the place – a pre-given set of social things which he/she must learn, and internalise or appropriate, so that he/she can make his/her own

---

24 Plato is usually read as the pupil of Socrates. Socrates was not content with accepting conventional explanations, but kept asking for the meaning of expressions and upset the confidence of the debater in his opinions. While this argumentative process was in pursuit of truth or the essential nature of things, Socrates does not appear to believe that the process can give an absolute answer. Thus Socrates appeals to the modern liberal, such as Karl Popper, who holds that while truth is the object of scientific and philosophical enquiry we will never reach absolute truth. Plato, by contrast, seems to believe that humans cannot understand the subtlety of this position and must, absolutely must, believe that some things are simply true. Not true in the sense of the very best that we can argue for as the result of our methodologies and our investigations, or by agreement, but simply true; absolutely, trans-historically, true.

space; the 'I' and the 'We' are co-dependent. The successful adult has made these resources his/her own and has lived in and through them. The danger, as Plato makes clear in his *simile of the cave*, lies in a suffocation within convention (*Republic*, 514a–521c).[25]

PLATO'S MYTH OF EMANCIPATION THROUGH TRUTH: THE SIMILE OF THE CAVE

Plato illustrates the need to enlighten mankind by offering a story in which a group of people have been living in a large cave, where from childhood they have been so positioned that they cannot see the light, but live according to shapes and shadows which they take to be 'real'. They have created a social existence based on illusions and practices which bear no relation to 'true' reality; however, they believe these illusions and are content.

Plato asks what would happen if one of these prisoners were forced to be free, namely if he were forcibly taken out of the cave and released into the sunlight. While at first he would be virtually blinded, and he would be unable to see any of the things that he was now told were real, gradually he would come to see the real objects themselves. In the light of the sun the prisoner would come to realise the falseness of the life of the cave.

If he went back to his former seat in the cave, he would at first have great difficulty, and not compete effectively with the other prisoners in their conventional practices. Their conclusion would be that it was not worth trying to go up out of the cave. Indeed, Plato concludes they would kill the person who was trying to set them free. It would be extremely difficult to 'correct' the practices of the cave. Left to their own habitual devices there is no escape for an individual from the life of the cave as great effort and strength of resolve are required.

Obviously, one theme of this story is Plato's desire to defend philosophy from the claim that it made men unfit for the rough and tumble of everyday political life.

---

25 The point of the narrative is practical; as Plato puts it, who should ideally take on the role of guardians of the state if not those who know most about the principles of good government and have an interest in a way of life that does not cause them to abuse their power position? The contrasting reality of Athenian politics can be gauged from Plato's letters. In the seventh letter, after discussing his reaction to the injustice of the trial and death of Socrates, he talks of his interest in politics and disgust at the reality which led to his formulation of the *Republic*.

'... the more closely I studied the politicians and the laws and customs of the day, and the older I grew, the more difficult it seemed to me to govern rightly. Nothing could be done without trustworthy friends and supporters; and these were not easy to come by in an age which had abandoned its traditional moral code but found it impossibly difficult to create a new one. At the same time law and morality were deteriorating at an alarming rate, with the result that though I had been full of eagerness for a political career, the sight of all this chaos made me giddy, and though I never stopped thinking how things might be improved and the constitution reformed, I postponed action, waiting for a favourable opportunity. Finally, I came to the conclusion that all existing states were badly governed, and that their constitutions were incapable of reform without drastic treatment and a great deal of good luck. I was forced, in fact, to the belief that the only hope of finding justice for society or for the individual lay in true philosophy, and that mankind would have no respite from trouble, until either real philosophers gain political power or politicians become, by some miracle, true philosophers.' (Quoted in the translator's introduction to the *Republic*, Penguin edn 1970: 16.)

Epistemologically, Plato is arguing that one can only be rational in the practical life by knowledge of the 'other' realm – the realm of pure truth – and that real knowledge is only of use if one returns and applies it to the practical life. Those with the real knowledge must be prepared to fight hard for its acceptance and ensure their societies are governed according to the precepts of that knowledge.

This is a myth of enlightenment. Mankind lives the life of the cave and we can only create the correct structures for social existence through the pursuit and attainment of pure truth. We need a new education, an enlightenment, which converts our ways of life. Truth exists, and we can know it if we shift our focus from the world of appearances to the world of ideas (the realm of 'true reality'). How is this enlightenment to be achieved? And what if people do not wish to be enlightened? Instead of looking in the wrong direction, our gaze must be turned 'the way it ought to be'. Since even the 'noblest natures' do not always want to look in the right direction, the rulers must 'bring compulsion to bear' upon them to ascend upward from darkness to light. Similarly, when those who have been liberated from the cave achieve the highest knowledge, they should not be allowed to remain in the higher world of contemplation, but must be made to come back down into the cave and take part in the life and labours of the prisoners. This narrative of two worlds – the dark world of the cave and bright world of light – is Plato's way of rejecting the scepticism and relativism of the Sophists, who argued that no perfect knowledge of the way society ought to be ordered was possible. Against them, Plato is arguing that not only is real knowledge possible, but it is also infallible. Real knowledge is infallible because it is based upon what is truly real. The dramatic contrast between the shadows and reflections of life in the cave and the actual objects, was for Plato the decisive clue to the different degrees to which human beings could be enlightened. Plato saw the counterparts of shadows in all of human life and discourse. Disagreements between men concerning the meaning of justice, for example, were the result of each one looking at a different aspect of the reality of justice. One person might take justice to mean whatever the rulers actually commanded the people to do, on the assumption that justice has to do with rules of behaviour laid down by the ruler. Just as a shadow bears some relation to the object of which it is the shadow, so this conception of justice has some measure of truth to it. Different rulers, however, command different modes of behaviour, and there could be no single coherent concept of justice if men's knowledge of justice were solely derived from the wide variety of examples of it.

The Sophists were sceptical about the possibility of true knowledge; impressed by both the variety and constant change in things, they argued that since knowledge comes from individual experience, our knowledge reflects this variance and is, therefore, relative to each person. Plato agreed that the result of basing knowledge upon our senses is variation, but claimed that real knowledge is of the essence, of the idea. It is not a question of what is believed, but of what is truly right. In the story of the cave, pursuing real knowledge can correct the distorted lifestyle of those engrossed in the practical life. Plato is often accused of dangerous elitism in claiming that individuals who know the good are superior to those who remain caught in existing moral or political conventions.

But this is to miss the very real human concern and sacrifice of those who have obtained a sense of the just, of the good, and so forth. Guided by their experience of the real essence of the just, the good, they can move beyond the conventional 'just and good' and enter into the fray with vigour. However, they will have to battle with others who accept the actual operation of the conventions of the society as the only measure of the good and the just; they will have to battle with the shadows and images of the dikaion, that is, with human things (*tá ton anthropon*), and that which is of human concern (*tá anthropeia*). He who has the knowledge of the right and just, or the good, may not win. For in the struggle he who knows the way of the cave, the bribes, the lies, the use of the shadows, the 'incomplete information to the people', the vicious cross-examination of the witness, is only too well fitted for the contest. But who is the realist? And must the man who aspires to do more than merely play the games of fear or survival need to believe in something 'other' than the common life in order to transcend its pettiness?[26]

Real knowledge is not simply a set of knowledges of essences, of the real forms of things lurking within their varying appearances, but adds up to *sophia* (wisdom).[27] Specialised knowledge is required, but it must be distributed and applied (see Book IV of the *Republic*); the city is to be well advised by it.

---

26 The question must be faced, however, what is the actual basis of this knowledge of the true and of the good? In Plato's case his discourse, particularly in his autobiographical writings (namely the *Epistles*), appears as a mystical or religious experience, wherein the light suddenly breaks through to the consciousness of the self: 'As a result of continued application to the subject itself and communion therewith, it is brought to birth in the soul on a sudden, as light that is kindled by a leaping spark, and thereafter nourishes itself' (*Epistle* VII, 341). But what does this mean? Does this mean that for Plato the totality of reality - the realm of the pure ideas, where pure truth and good reside - is actually a mystery? That it is only by some spiritual or mystical experience that we can be sure that we have come across the 'true' truth? If so, then the secret of justice can never be reached by rational processes - all that the 'law and justice of jurisprudence' can amount to is human, or debased and fallible accounts of law and justice. Did Plato actually realise that pure justice will always remain a mystery?

27 Take a rule-bound model of a legal system. The theory of the *techné* is to learn the methodology of applying general rules, but the gap between theory and practice may be only too obvious. The living practice of the institution, the day-to-day arrangement of courts, magistrates, lawyers, witnesses, plaintiffs and defendants, may demand a methodology which comes from the realm of general experience having to do with the relationship of ends and means in practical or pseudo-political action. The knowledge of rules, *per se*, contains nothing to ensure that they are applied correctly. In *Metaphysics* Aristotle argues that the practitioner, for instance the healer, can be more successful than the specialist (in that case the scientifically trained doctor). And while Plato stresses the importance of practical experience in his programme of education, he goes further, realising that all rules must be interpreted in order to be applied. But here, as in all activities, practice is a form of living theory, and creating theory is a form of practice. One can undertake a theoretical examination of interpretation, but to engage in interpretation is to enter into a practice.

PART THREE
PLATO'S JURISPRUDENCE

THE PLATONIC CONCEPTION OF JUSTICE AS EVIDENCED IN THE REPUBLIC

The ideal state has two key attributes: (i) it is founded upon justice; (ii) all the citizens within it are happy. To achieve this Plato seeks to create a small scale city-state modelled upon the rather tribalist and closed societies of pre-classical Crete and Sparta. Plato's naturalism is not a scientific analysis of the reality of contemporary Athens – which he appeared to find distasteful – but an intellectual nostalgia for the supposed purity of a mythical golden age where all things belonged to their 'natural station'. To avoid his image of the ideal society being seen as a return to the past, Plato presents a narrative of the development of city life. While the first city came about purely as the result of material self interest, it soon began to pursue the idea of the *common good*. What is the common good? How is it to be known? Plato appears confident that some can understand what the common good truly entails, and is quite ready to advocate compulsion and manipulation in realising these goals. Justice then means something like 'what is necessary for the functioning of the common good'. Democracy has the appeal of freedom of thought, but this also is the reason for its self-destruction. Democracy espouses 'liberty' whereby 'every individual is free to do as he likes' (*Republic*, 375). Although many today find pluralism, diversity and variety attractive, Plato stressed its disintegrating effects. Authority is stripped of its foundations, the young do not look up to their elders, 'and the minds of the citizens become so sensitive that the least vestige of restraint is resented as intolerable' (384). He warns that dissension grows on the lack of social cohesion, and class struggle will develop. We need a comprehensive social vision that assures us that the social structure is just. This runs counter to the liberal image of freedom but, Plato asks, what price freedom in a society which displays its inequalities? Such a society will inevitably give rise to a struggle between the opposing sections – the rich and the poor – over the material resources of society. And what of the moral condition of the society in which experimentation and diversity are seen as values? Plato gives a warning in his description of a permissive society in Book VIII. Lee (1974: 30) suggests that 'disunity, incompetence and violence, which he had seen at Athens and at Syracuse, were the main dangers against which Plato thought society must be protected'.

What is the role of law? Law ensures collective action. Referring again to the narrative of the cave, Plato has a main character in the dialogue argue that:

> our job as lawgivers is to compel the best minds to attain what we have called the highest form of knowledge, and to ascend to the vision of the good ... and when they have achieved this and see well enough, prevent them ... [from] remaining in the upper world, and refusing to return again to the prisoners in the cave below and share their honours and rewards ...
>
> The object of our legislation is not the special welfare of any particular class in our society, but of the society as a whole; and it uses persuasion or compulsion to unite all

34

citizens and make them share together the benefits which each individually can confer on the community; and its purpose in fostering this attitude is not to leave everyone to please himself, but to make each man a link in the unity of the whole (*Republic*, 519e-520).

The 20th century liberal philosopher Karl Popper is scathing in his analysis of this 'natural law', seeing it as the attempt to recreate a 'natural', ie tribal and collectivist, mode of social life' (1945, vol I: 80). The law pervades the thought patterns of all, sustaining a social existence in which the collective overwhelms individuality.

The sense of law constituting the ideal republic is vastly different from the liberal idea which has come to stress tolerance and plurality. First we must understand that even Plato's use of the concept we translate as 'republic' meant something different to its modern usage. In his time the Greek word indicated rather an interlinking of 'constitution', 'state', and 'society'. Law was not viewed as something autonomous from the social; the ideas of modern constitutional law, infused by the ideology of the rule of law and the separation of powers (Barnett, 1995; Loveland, 1996), find little resonance. In part this was a reflection of the smaller scale which the Greek city-state operated within – courts, for example, were not usually staffed by legal professionals but were more a popular institution – and it was also a reflection of the belief that virtue and law were co-penetrative. Good law led to virtue and virtue gave good law. Ethics, politics, education, law and philosophy, made up a practical, indivisible whole.

THE ROLE OF EDUCATION INTO THE 'TRUTH'

The primary force sustaining the republic is the character and education of the ruling classes or a specialised set of 'guardians'. All individuals are to undergo training of the intelligence to control the passions, and this training is mirrored in a system of education or widespread nurturing and instruction of the young to accord with the character of the ruler. Education, however, is not seen as a transfer of knowledge into the soul, like putting sight into blind eyes; it is more like turning the eye to the light (*Republic*, 518b-c). The educator is to provide the conditions in which the right kind of mind can develop its capacities. The system is authoritarian in that it is the only education offered; no alternative system is presented, nor are alternative values represented as desirable. For the average citizen there is no encouragement to question social beliefs; free educational enquiry is the preserve of the elite who have come through a long secondary education. The education system imposes on the young a single set of values in such a way that they will not be seriously sceptical about them in later life. It is not simply that Plato appears to hold that there is moral truth to be known, and we can be confident that we can come to know it, but he has little wish to educate people to be autonomous. Plato can see no point in subjectivism; rather, it is crucial to establish authority. Since it is only the elite that have the resources of education, time and support to engage in sustained intellectual questioning, it follows that the mass of the people cannot hope to achieve anything by such enquiry, and to encourage them in widespread questioning of the social conventions underpinning order would be dangerous. What value could there be in a person struggling and engaging in a personal process of speculation and not coming to the right answer, or only partially arriving at the answer? Those who know the answer ought to simply give it to that other person.

For the modern liberal, Plato has not only a misplaced confidence in absolute truth actually being found, but displays a naive trust in the ability of the elites to perceive it and act with integrity so that they use their power according to the dictates of such knowledge. Contemporary philosophers of knowledge and science are much less sanguine about claims to 'truth'; Plato simply trusts the elites too much in the exercise of power. Furthermore, as Aristotle was to point out, Plato appears unable to distinguish between unity and uniformity. Given his division of people into various social roles, the unity of the society comes from the performance of the roles with uniform sameness. Moreover, Plato has little time for those who cannot perform their role with the appropriate success. It is clear from his discussion that he regards it as impossible for someone with a chronic, debilitating illness to have a life that is worth living (*Republic*, 407a–407b), and that he cannot concede that someone can find sources of value in their life other than the approved ones. Consider the oft-discussed example of the carpenter who develops a chronic disease. Plato states there is no point in supporting what is left of his life with the help of medicine, it is better for him to die and be rid of his troubles, since his life is of no benefit to him if he cannot perform his job (*Republic*, 406d–407a). If a person cannot fulfil the social role that structures his life, his life is not worth living. The view of the person is irrelevant, it is mere subjectivity at odds with the objective reality.

In the ideal Republic each person belongs to one of three social orders or social classes legitimated by the system of education and upbringing. The ultimate bedrock is an acceptance of the underlying truth of the natural position and role of persons. Those who have successfully completed their education as 'guardians' will become rulers (*phylakes*) or warriors (called auxiliaries, *epikouroi*). Plato further stressed the imperative to maintain unity at all times, a need which causes him to suggest the requirement for a foundational myth; a magnificent narrative which would carry conviction for the whole community and provide legitimation for the division of classes and the various institutions (414–415d).[28] First the rulers and the soldiers are persuaded that the upbringing and education given them was something that happened in a dream, in reality they were fashioned in the depths of the earth, and their mother, earth herself, brought them up, when they were complete, into the light of day. They should, therefore, think of the land in which they live as their mother and protect her if attacked, while their fellow-citizens must be regarded as brothers born of the same earth. Then the Guardians should tell the rest of the citizens another 'noble falsehood', to the effect that while all citizens (members of this community) are siblings, born of the same mother, the earth, they are different in composition, some having gold in their nature,

---

28 Plato is recognising that the system needs a source of *legitimacy* which is greater, and other, than itself. Traditionally, the commentators stress, legitimacy must always come from some other source than the act of seizing itself. All systems require a process whereby their *power is seen as authority* by those who are subjected to it: that is, as somehow 'natural'. Legitimation, the process whereby we refer to a posited source of value that renders power as authority, is a complex circular event. The source of authority must always be posited, brought into being, and yet it is always posited as prior, as coming before the very process. The legitimating urge refers back to some event, a founding, a state of original being - no matter how remote - which fixes the truth of the present state of being.

some silver, others iron or bronze.[29] Moreover, it is important that the metals, which differentiate the classes, neither be mixed nor confused. So while a parent who recognises that its child has gold in its composition should ensure it is promoted to the class of potential Guardians and its education intensified, the parents of the child with iron or bronze in its make-up must harden their hearts and degrade it to the ranks of industrial or agricultural workers.

THE UNDERLYING STRESS UPON UNITY OF SOCIAL PURPOSE

Three points underlie Plato's ideal republic: (i) the unity of the state is paramount; (ii) this is not maintained primarily by laws and rules but by the Guardians' character and the general education system that produces the Guardians and others; and (iii) the Guardians do not hesitate to command and use the resources at their disposal, including those both discursive and hegemonic, in pursuit of the interests of the state. Unity is vital. There are certain pragmatic factors at work: to be unified, the state must not be too big or too small, and further, it must not contain extremes of wealth; since a real city is a unity and not a divided phenomenon (422e). A city requires unity of purpose – this is the real *constitutive mechanism*.[30]

Plato is undoubtedly an elitist as well as a centralist; power is to be held by a systematically produced and educated body of experts. The system will produce citizens of good character who in turn produce children better than themselves, and so forth. Law has a limited role and should not hinder the rulers: 'good men need no orders ... they will find out easily enough what legislation is in general necessary' (425e). The education of the Guardians, rather than a legal constitution or code of statutes, provides structural strength to the republic, and the Guardians are not constrained by a constitution or laws in their relationship to the other classes which are the objects of their rule. To modern sensibilities the social order is wrapped in a total ideology of rank reflecting a supposed natural order; ultimately even the rulers come to believe the myth

29 The great theorist of legitimacy, Max Weber (discussed in Chapter 11 of this text; for his major work see *Economy and Society*, 1978), stressed that, when the fortunate classes or individuals wish to justify their position, the appeal to tradition is the usual method. Weber refers to the common myth of 'blood superiority' as similar to the line of succession a king would use to justify his own reign. Tradition is one of the three dominant modes of legitimation along with the 'charismatic' and 'legal-rational' modes. But tradition is the widest, since even the 'modern' mode of legal-rational authority requires long standing common values, and in the modern legal system - the ideal form of legal-rational domination - the imagery of custom, precedent and veneration for decisions of the past is central.

30 Thus, actual existing entities, which are referred to as cities, may not be true states for Plato, since they do not have the sense of purpose and unity that a real city (state) should have. The Guardians are empowered to employ measures to ensure unity and remove sources of conflict and instability. Property is to be held in common, and nuclear families destroyed, replaced by state nurseries and regulated breeding programmes. Both measures are designed to make the city more of a unity. Conflicts of interest are not regulated by a legal framework, they are simply done away with. Thus a pluralist society would be seen as a failure by Plato, in that its members regard themselves as belonging to a number of smaller groupings, many of which have conflicting aims.

of their origin and superior composition. Thus, the security of this 'ideal state' is, in reality, founded upon the readiness of the population to believe a myth.[31]

THE MORE PRAGMATIC APPROACH OF *THE LAWS*

If we were to get a dictator who is young, restrained, quick to learn, with a retentive memory, courageous and elevated … and 'lucky' too, in this point: he should be the contemporary of a distinguished lawgiver, and be fortunate enough to come into contact with him. If that condition is fulfilled, God will have done nearly all that he usually does when he wants to treat a state with particular favour (Plato, distillation of dialogue in *The Laws*, 710).

Plato's *Republic* is often presented as all one needs to know of Plato, since it represents his purest statements; sometimes commentators argue it is actually an extreme programme designed to shock the reader into thinking about how the contemporary social order could be changed (Plato, it is claimed, knew full well it was impossible to put into practice). By contrast, his last work, *The Laws*, appears to offer an intellectual compromise with the purity of his idealism which might be taken as a practical suggestion as to how an actual society might indeed successfully be formed. As Saunders (1970: 29) puts it, the guiding principles of this new utopia were:

(a) that certain absolute moral standards exist;

(b) that such standards can be, however imperfectly, embodied in a code of law;

(c) that most of the inhabitants of the state, being innocent of philosophy, should never presume to act on their own initiative in modifying either the moral ideas or the code of laws which reflect it; instead they must live in total and unconditional obedience to the unchanging rules and regulations laid down for them by the legislator.

---

31 In *Conditions of Liberty: civil society and its rivals*, Ernest Gellner (1994: 31–2) argues, generally speaking, that human societies maintain order by coercion and superstition. The enlightenment tried to replace this foundation by another wherein society was based on truth and consent. For Gellner–

'there are fairly good reasons why only coercion can constitute the foundation of any social order. Any system in operation must have possible alternatives, both of organisation as such and of the distribution of positions in that stable organisation. For a very significant proportion of the population these alternatives would always appear preferable, and these people cannot all be assumed to be fools. So it must be presupposed that they would endeavour to bring about that (to them) more favourable alternative, unless restrained by fear. The argument is, alas, cogent: the rather special conditions which may induce people to accept the social order even without fear, voluntarily, are indeed the preconditions of civil society, but these do not emerge easily or frequently. Only in conditions of overall growth, when social life is a plus-sum, not a zero-sum game, can a majority have an interest in conforming even without intimidation.

The reason why society must be based on falsehood is equally obvious. Truth is independent of the social order and is at no one's service, and if not impeded will end up by undermining respect for any given authority structure. Only ideas pre-selected or pre-invented and then frozen by ritual and sanctification can be relied upon to sustain a specific organisational set-up. Free inquiry will undermine it. Moreover, theories, as philosophers like to remind us, are under-determined by facts. In other words, reason on its own will not and cannot engender that consensus which underlies social order. The facts of the case, even if unambiguous (which they seldom are), will not engender a shared picture of the situation, let alone shared aims.'

Again Plato's idea is for a small state with adequate material resources, one in which there are no large discrepancies of wealth or status. When first founded the laws may need modification in the light of experience, but they will soon settle into a form that will be virtually unchangeable. Plato charges a Nocturnal Council with the task of overseeing research into the operation of the legal system and suggesting some changes. Rational obedience, rather than fear of sanctions, is the most effective method of gaining obedience, hence each section of the law is to be prefaced by a preamble explaining the rationality of the law and, hopefully, making the coercive element of the positive law redundant. It is better to refrain from crime, or pursue a certain course of action because one is convinced of the rightfulness of the action, than to be moved only by fear of the consequences.

CONCLUDING REFLECTIONS ON PLATO'S CONCEPTUALISM: DOES HE OFFER IDEALS OF REALITY, OR IMAGINATIVE CREATIONS?

To Karl Popper, Plato is dangerous since he presents the cosmos as if there is a realm of pure essences or ontological certainties which the elites can come to know. Natural law would then be man's obedience to the laws constructed in accordance with that knowledge. The just society is that which would be governed by such knowledge and hence the *polis* would be made rational and sober. In the properly organised *polis* every man would find happiness carrying out his natural tasks. The ruler returns from his encounter with truth to subdue the political chaos of the *polis* and creates the just state. The ruler is guaranteed to be legitimately exercising his power not through a political legitimacy – for example, democratic consent – but through his grasp of the mathematical nature of the ontology of the cosmos and his vision of that ontology. Popper reads Plato as a man of genius whose political and jurisprudential imagination was inspired by a fear of social chaos and the need for an ideology of 'truth' to guarantee social control. But there are occasions where we can also read Plato as suggesting that his theory of the ideas is a political and not an epistemological necessity.[32] The key passage is where Plato has Socrates finish his speech on the possibility of the just *polis* by an allusion to its impossibility:

> Perhaps it is a paradigm set up in heaven for him who wills to see and, seeing, founds a polis within himself. It makes no difference whether the polis exists somewhere or will ever exist. He will do only the deeds peculiar to that polis, and none else (*Republic*, 592b2 ff).

Socrates appears to argue that the 'true' *polis* of absolute justice will never be encountered in actual history, nor is it possible actually to encounter pure 'truth'; the rational person cannot claim to have total possession of the truth, but only an 'ideal' or

---

32 This reading would lead us to argue that Plato's image of justice is ultimately political and not metaphysical. This is in contrast to the dominant tradition of reading Plato is to see his conception as ultimately ontological; as reliant upon the claim that there is indeed a timeless realm of ideas or essences which constitute the ultimate 'truth' of existence.

concept. The rational person who seeks justice must turn to idealism, not because he wishes to escape from political commitment, but because he needs ideals – or mathematical models – in order to orientate himself in the otherwise disparate contingency of the empirical. His claim to the truth of natural law is a political commitment to certain rationally perceived ways of organising and expressing the meaning of human life.

PART FOUR
THE JURISPRUDENCE OF ARISTOTLE

ARISTOTLE AND THE ETHICS OF NATURAL ENDS

Whereas Aristotle (384–212 BC) is usually depicted as the originator of a more empirical approach in contrast to Plato's idealism, he nevertheless shares the belief that there is a certain ontological structure to human nature and the cosmos. Aristotle's writings are acutely logical, but work on the basis of classifying material provided by techniques of observation (empiricism) loosely based upon biological studies. Aristotle demands that we seek the essence of things, but that we do not do this by postulating that everything is a reflection of some pure idea or essence, rather we should try to ascertain the essential nature of things as they operate in the natural processes of the world. Our search for the essence of a thing is a search for the nature of that thing: what it is, and how it fits into the wider picture of this world's operation. Plato's theory of a timeless other world of pure essences seems to postulate that the actual 'reality' of things somehow existed outside the time and space structures we take for granted when we relate to things. But, for Aristotle, we are to turn our attention to the way things operate in this world around us. What guidelines are we to use? We have to look for the underlying similarities in the motion and change we see around us. Our basic assumption is that change is not random, that things develop in predictable ways, and that we differentiate between changes which are natural and those which are the product of human artifice. Natural changes are responses to the built-in ways of behaving that natural entities have; for example, plants grow into particular forms with distinctive ways of 'being'. Natural objects change towards their 'end', and it is through understanding this process that the 'good' of objects and actions is made visible: 'the end for which each action is done is the good, the good in each particular case, and in general the highest good in the whole of nature' (*Metaphysics*, 982b). The dominant process in life is change – development – not some static state of being. All Aristotle's writings upon human life are thus seen to be based upon a teleological or purposive account of human nature: everything in nature has a distinctive 'end' to achieve, or a function to fulfil. The cosmos is *teleological* in structure.[33]

Since social existence is natural and not some forced compromise, it is in the nature of humans to live in society. Aristotle argued that the contemporary Greek society was the result of a gradual process in which the nature of man was being realised.

---

33 While change for Aristotle appears to have included motion, growth, decay, generation, and corruption, he appears much more optimistic than Plato. For Popper (1945, vol II: 5), Aristotle remains within the sway of the Platonic idea of essences, but now the essence of something lies in its final stage of development, rather than in some original state. Teleology is the claim that *'the form or essence of anything developing is identical with the purpose or end or final state towards which it develops ...* The form or idea, which is still, with Plato, considered to be the good, stands at the end, instead of the beginning. This characterises Aristotle's substitution of optimism for pessimism.'

Historically, Aristotle narrates, the city-state is an organic result of the coming together of several villages into a state of 'self-sufficiency'. The city-state does not exist to merely satisfy material needs; it rather seeks to satisfy man's need for a satisfying existential life, and we need to strive to make this a way of life in accordance with man's nature.

> ... while [the city-state] comes into existence for the sake of life, it exists for the good life. Hence every city-state exists by nature ... [it] is the end of the other partnerships, and nature is an end, since that which each thing is when its growth is complete, we speak of this as being the nature of each thing, for instance of a man, a horse, a household. Again, the object for which a thing exists, its end, is its chief good; and self-sufficiency is an end, and a chief good. From these things, therefore, it is clear that the city-state is a natural growth, and that man is by nature a being inclined to a civic existence (politikon zoon) (Aristotle, *Politics*, 1.1).

Development occurs through *the dialectic of potentiality and actuality*. Everything in the cosmos has a power to become what its form has set as its end. The end of an acorn, for example, is to become an oak tree. At the present time its actuality is an acorn; its potentiality is an oak tree. The change from potentiality to actuality is a fundamental law of nature. For the acorn to become an oak tree the right conditions must exist; equally the right conditions must exist for the boy to become a man. The process is developmental and builds on the basic natural material of the entity; the boy must exist and possess a certain nature for the man to become. Every living thing has a different capacity for activity and organisation, and there are different elements with which bodies are constituted or *organised*: Aristotle called these different ways a body can be organised souls and he gave a hierarchy of purposes. The vegetative soul has simply the state of existing; the sensitive soul both exists and senses; and the rational soul combines the faculties of existence, sensing and thinking. The rational soul has the capacity for deliberation – it searches for the truth in the nature of things and discovers the underlying principles of human behaviour.

The *Nicomachean Ethics* begins with the premise that every art, every enquiry, and, similarly, every action and pursuit aims at some good. Thus the question for ethics is, 'What is the *good towards* which human behaviour aims?' Whereas Plato appeared to argue that man aims at a knowledge of the idea of the good (this supreme principle of good was separated from the world of experience and from individual men and arrived at by the mind's ascent from the visible world to the intelligible world), for Aristotle the principle of good and right was embedded within each man: 'Good is not a general term corresponding to a single idea' (*N Ethics*, 1096b). Aristotle argues that even if Plato were correct, it would be of little consequence to our practical life since the supreme good would be lost in mystery: 'If the goodness predicated of various things in common actually is a unity or something existing separately and absolute, it clearly will not be practicable or attained by man ... But the good we are now seeking is a good within human reach' (*ibid*, 1096b–1097a). We must search for conceptions of the good and the right that provide us with practical guidance for living the good life. While principles of ethics could be discovered by studying the essential nature of man, and attained through his actual behaviour in daily life, Aristotle warns, however, that the level of precision is not exact. But we should not imply from the variation and error inherent in ethics that ideas of right and wrong are purely conventional; Aristotle is certain that they exist 'in the nature of things'.

How can we know what are the ends for man? We need to reflect upon the way human life is lived, and come to understand the way that we need to live in order to bring out our human purposes. We can distinguish instrumental ends (acts that are done as means for other ends) and intrinsic ends (acts that are done for their own sake). Take the waging of war where various people and activities are involved jointly in an all-encompassing project. Carpenters build barracks and, when completed, they have fulfilled their function as carpenters. The barracks also fulfils its function when it provides safe shelter for the soldiers. The ends here achieved by both carpenters and building are not ends in themselves, but are simply instrumental in providing housing for soldiers until they move on to their next stage of action. Similarly, the builder of ships fulfils his function when the ship is built and successfully launched, and here again this end, in turn, is the means for transporting soldiers to the field of battle. The doctor fulfils his function to the extent that he keeps soldiers in good health, and the 'end' of health in this case becomes a 'means' for effective fighting. The officer aims for victory in battle, but victory is the means to peace. Peace itself, though sometimes mistakenly seen as the final end of war, is also the means for creating the conditions under which men, as men, can fulfil their function as men. When we discover what men aim at, not as carpenters, doctors, or generals, but as men – men in general – we will then arrive at action *for its own sake*, and for which all other activity is only a means, and this, says Aristotle, 'must be the good of man'. The good of man is something that exists distinct from the various tasks in which men engage. A person can be good at his profession without being a good man, and vice versa. Different levels of existence and functionality are present. To discover the good towards which man should aspire we must discover the distinctive function of human nature – the good man is the man who is fulfilling his function as a man.

As all parts of the human body have functions we can seek the overall function of the species – 'what is the function of man?' What is the distinctive mode of activity of man? The answer must come from empirically based analyses of man's nature and the needs of social life. The answer cannot be simply life, because that plainly is shared with all forms of living existence, even by vegetables. Nor is it the life of sensation, since that is the merely animal. Instead man's end lies in an active life involving rational reflection and action. The human good is the 'activity of soul in accordance with virtue'.

The most important aspect of the person is the human soul which has two parts, the irrational and the rational. In its turn the irrational part has two subparts, the vegetative and the desiring or 'appetitive' parts. Often the desires and the appetites act in opposition to 'the rational principle, resisting and opposing it'. Morality is the ongoing task of mediating the conflict between humans' rational and irrational elements.

Understanding and guiding action is a central responsibility for morality. Nothing can be called good unless it is functioning; one must be a participant in the game to claim a prize. Morality strives rationally to control and guide the irrational parts of the soul; the good man lives the life of virtue.

HAPPINESS AS THE FINAL END OF HUMAN LIFE

Human life is not a static but an active phenomenon – from birth the person strives to become fully human – to live a full life. How are we to lead the good life? All human action should aim at its proper end. But can we ascertain what this means by empirical observation? Everywhere we see men seeking pleasure, wealth and honour; is this all there is to human life? Aristotle says no. While these aims have value, none of them has the *self-sufficient* and final qualities – 'that which is always desirable in itself and never for the sake of something else' – *attainable* by reason, which would make it the true end of human action. Happiness is the end that alone meets all requirements for the ultimate end of human action;[34] indeed, we choose pleasure, wealth and honour only because we think that 'through their instrumentality we shall be happy.' Happiness is another word or name *for the good for humans*, since, like good, happiness is the fulfilment of our distinctive function. In fact, claims Aristotle, we experience happiness when we act virtuously: 'happiness is a working of the soul in the way of excellence or virtue'.

But this instantly appears strange. For the empirical world is full of people who are plainly not acting virtuously yet look happy; criminals who are not caught, politicians who lie and cheat to gain or hang on to power. Conversely, the virtuous man often seems deeply unhappy. How can we retain faith in the concept of the virtuous life?

Aristotle distinguishes between real happiness and mere pleasure. The temptations of the world move us with their promises of pleasure but these are only deceptions – there is a real, genuine happiness possible if we pursue virtue. We must not forget our divided selves – we are both rational and full of empirical appetites for physical and psychological pleasure. Although we should follow the general rule of morality, namely: 'to act in accordance with right reason' – and therein make the rational part of the soul control the irrational part – our appetites and desires are stimulated and aroused by the vast array of things outside the self, such as objects and persons.[35] Our passions, our capacity for love and hate, attraction and repulsion, creation and destruction, can quickly overwhelm us and pull us in a multiplicity of directions. By themselves they cannot offer any master principle or measure of selection. What should a person desire and how much? Under what circumstances? How should humans relate to material things, wealth, honour, and other persons? We have no automatic tendency to act the right way in these matters; 'none of the moral virtues arises in us by nature; for nothing that exists by nature can form a habit contrary to its nature'. The ethics of virtue demands that we develop habits; habits of right thinking, right choice, and right behaviour. Man is to be trained or formed for society by inculcation into virtue.

Since our passions make us capable of a wide range of action, from abstinence to excess, we must discover the proper meaning of excess or lack, and thereby discover the

---

34 'Happiness above all else appears to be absolutely final in this sense for we always choose it for its own sake and never as a means for something else' (*N Ethics*, 1097b).

35 Love and hate, or the concupiscent and irascible 'passions', provide the two basic ways in which the appetitive part of the soul reacts to these external factors. The concupiscent passion leads one to desire things and persons, whereas the irascible passion leads one to avoid or destroy them.

appropriate mean. Aristotle applies a dualist system of 'extremes' by which we can work through our empirical feelings. We understand that we sometimes feel emotions of fear, confidence, lust, anger, compassion, pleasure and pain, in extreme form; that is too much or too little, and in each case we understand we felt wrongly. Experiencing these emotions in the right degree and on the right occasions and towards the right subject; that is, to experience them as we should, is to experience the mean. To attain this state of equilibrium is to experience virtue. Again, vice is either extreme, excess or defect, and virtue is the mean. It is through the rational power of the soul that the passions are controlled and action is guided. The virtue of courage, for example, is the mean between two extremes: namely, cowardice (too little or lack) and foolhardiness or overconfidence (too much or excess). Virtue, then, is a state of being, but it is not that there is some simple formula that we must always adhere to, rather we are called upon to follow the 'right course' of action: ' ... It is the middle disposition in each department of conduct that is to be praised, but one leans sometimes to the side of excess and sometimes to that of deficiency, since this is the easiest way of hitting the mean and the right course' (*ibid*, 1109b).

Our actions are to be the result of 'deliberate choice, being in the relative mean, determined by reason, and as the man of practical wisdom would determine' (*ibid*, 1107a). Virtue is to act according to the mean, 'a settled disposition of the mind' but the mean is not the same for every person, nor is there a mean for every act. Each mean is relative to each person inasmuch as the circumstances will vary. In the case of eating, the mean will obviously be different for an adult athlete and a little girl. But for each person, there is nevertheless a proportionate or relative mean, temperance, clearly indicating what extremes – namely, gluttony (excess) and starvation (lack) – would constitute vices for them. Moreover, for some acts there is no mean at all; their very nature already implies badness, such as spite, envy, adultery, theft, and murder. These are bad in themselves and not in their excesses or deficiencies. One is always wrong in doing them.

How, asks the modern liberal (Popper, 1945 Vol II; Kelsen, 1957, Ch 4) are we to escape from social convention in identifying what is excess and lack? Is this whole system simply a working through of the conventions of society?[36] To a large extent this criticism cannot be avoided, however, Aristotle's concern is with the ethics of a situation or, in other words, with what has come to be called 'practical rationality'. All choice exists within some form of established social order: while the context for Aristotle is of a much greater closed order than that which the liberal desires, he is placing a large weight upon authentic choice. In this sense Aristotle's writings are timeless; we always exist in a social context and we have the weight of authentic choice inescapably upon us.

---

36 For Hans Kelsen (1957, 125), while Aristotle's ethics 'pretends to establish in an authoritative way the moral value, it leaves the solution of its very problem to another authority: the determination of what is evil or a vice, and consequently, also the determination of what is good or a virtue. It is the authority of the positive morality and the positive law - it is the established social order. By presupposing ... the established social order, the ethics of Aristotle justifies ... the established social order.'

THE SITUATION OF HUMAN CHOICE

We have two kinds of reasoning, theoretical (which provides knowledge of fixed principles or philosophical wisdom), and practical (which supplies a rational guide to a person's action under the particular circumstances in which they find themselves), or practical wisdom. The rational element enables man to develop moral capacity since, while he has a natural capacity for right behaviour, he does not act rightly by nature: reason is required to cope with the indeterminate number of possibilities in life. We are not destined by some inevitable force to the good; goodness is in man potentially but will not come to fruition without our deliberating about it, and then choosing in fact to do it. And against Plato and Socrates, who seemed to imply that once a man knew the good he would always do it, Aristotle did not believe that such knowledge made deliberate choice redundant. We can only have a moral action because of the capacity to choose – if we did things simply out of instinct, for example, we would not call them moral actions – moral choice combines a desire to do the right with reasoning about that end. Moral choice requires reason.

Human morality therefore is essentially linked to the structure of moral choices and this in turn implies human responsibility. If we are to praise or blame, praise virtue and blame vice, a person must be truly capable of making a choice. Aristotle held that an act for which a person could be held responsible must be a voluntary act. A genuine choice comprises a voluntary action. But not all our actions are voluntary. An involuntary act is one for which a person is not responsible because it is (1) done out of ignorance of particular circumstances, or (2) a result of external compulsion, or (3) done to avoid a greater evil. Voluntary acts are those for which a person is responsible because none of these three extenuating circumstances obtain.

In general, virtue is the fulfilment of man's distinctive function, and his experiencing of his feelings and emotions as the mean between extremes. Each virtue is the product of rational control of the passions. To live the life of virtue is not to negate or reject any of the natural capacities of man, but to control them. The moral man lives life to the full employing all his capacities, both physical and mental. While man can adopt intellectual virtues like philosophical wisdom and understanding through teaching and learning, moral virtue comes about as a result of habit, thence comes the name ethics (*ethike*), 'formed by a slight variation from the word *ethos* (habit)'. All the moral virtues have to be learned and practised, and they become virtues only through action, for 'we become just by doing just acts, temperate by doing temperate acts, brave by doing brave acts'. The 'cardinal' moral virtues are courage, temperance, justice, and wisdom.

JUSTICE AS A FUNCTION OF THE RELATIVE SIZE OF THE SOCIAL BODY

The term 'unjust' is held to apply both to the man who breaks the law and the man who takes more than his due, the unfair man. Hence it is clear that the law-abiding man and the fair man will both be just. 'The just' therefore means that which is lawful and that which is equal or fair, and 'the unjust' means that which is illegal and that which is unequal or unfair (Aristotle, *N Ethics*, 1129a).

Justice is 'the chief of virtue', but there are two senses of justice: a general and a particular sense.

In the *general sense of justice*, a man is acting unjustly when he breaches the law. Is this a purely legal positive sense of breach: is a man always unjust when he breaches every validly passed law? No. Some laws are bad laws and it would not be unjust to breach them. Although Aristotle believes that law is an instrument by which the city-state is directed towards the common good or through which an excellent ruling class guides the city, there may be laws passed which do not fulfil their purpose.

There are two kinds of *particular justice: distributive* and *corrective*. Corrective justice is 'that which supplies a corrective principle in private transactions' (*ibid*, 1131a), and is exercised by the judge in settling disputes and inflicting punishments upon offenders (Aristotle points out this is a complex matter. For example, he distinguishes between *formal* and *substantive* justice. A fine of a certain amount for a minor offence may seem to embody justice when applied equally to all offenders. However, the fine will affect the rich man much less than the poor man). Distributive justice is an entitlement to a share in social goods relative to a person's function in the social body. Commentators have called this *the principle of proportionate equality* (and, conversely, proportionate inequality): it is not a question of subjectively preferring one man to another and, therefore, rewarding him more, but of justifying preferences by means of identifiable, generally accepted criteria. The differing functions of men in the social body justifies a natural inequality – it corresponds to the nature of things. The structure of distributive justice is such that those who excel at their functions – for example, the excellent teacher – should receive greater rewards. The less deserving should receive lesser rewards. Much of this appears unproblematic; it enables, perhaps, a thesis of equality in so far as all are human, but an inequality insofar as each offers different skills and performs different tasks. It is these skills and tasks which determine differential distribution. If persons are equal they must have equal shares; if persons are unequal they must have unequal shares. Contravening this principle amounts to injustice, but what are to be the determining standards and criteria of equality and difference?

Drawing comparisons and agreeing criteria of judgment are, however, problematic issues. Even if the standard were to be 'contribution to the (true) interests of society', both the nature of the society's true interests and the nature of the contribution are deeply contestable. Aristotle suggests that in practice we can resolve this difficulty through exchange processes and social rules within which we calculate fair and equal deals (in Book V of the *Nichomachean Ethics* Aristotle enters into a discussion of the economics of transaction, taking into account the mechanics of money and demand). The legal system can create the normative structure for this process.

Once we place confidence in a fairly operating, open market process, what do people bring to the process of exchange and negotiation? What rewards do individuals deserve in their social roles? Aristotle suggests the criterion of *desert* is related to the overall conception of the purpose of society or the Greek city-state. Aristotle criticises Plato's assertion that every state is formed to supply the necessities of human life, asserting, by contrast, that the primary aim is 'to achieve the good' (*Politics* Bk IV, Ch iv, ss 11 ff). Thus Aristotle can rank the importance of trades and classes of worker depending on how they contribute to this end. The procedure underlying social justice is, therefore, the correct delineation of qualitative differences and differentiations in value of the various parts of the state, and even though the state is a communion (or fellowship) united by a common aim and by common action, it is composed of dissimilar members, distinct functions and policies, and diverse modes of life and excellence.

It is, however, only possible to work out a coherent sense of social desert if the state does not become too large. Furthermore, only within a relatively stable society can the mean of autonomy or self-government be achieved. To be free is 'to govern and to be governed alternatively ... to be under no command whatsoever to any one, upon any account, any other wise than by rotation, and that just as far only as that person is, in turn, under his also' (*Politics*, 1317b). The free man participates in the political creation of the laws, he is part of the living constitution of the state. The law is an instrument of command, but it is of free and natural command: 'all to command each, and each in its turn all'. Thus, we might say, law is ultimately a subsection of politics and jurisprudence a subsection of political philosophy. In *Politics* Aristotle was clear that, since the law was the order of the political community, justice was a function of the state and the task of law was to determine what is just. Justice, then, must be a part of the function of politics. The question of justice mediates between law and the political; it does not simply translate concerns from two distinct spheres, but conjoins related and interacting social phenomena. What is the end of the political association? To create the conditions of peace and enable human flourishing. If there were other means to achieve this then justice – in the sense of the laws and the structure of distribution thus enabled – would be redundant.[37]

THE EMPIRICAL MODE OF IDENTIFYING NATURAL LAW

Aristotle appeared to believe that there were natural laws governing moral and political life. The (positive) laws of the state are obviously a matter of convention – they are created and enforced by various civil institutions – and are mutable, while the laws which exist by nature are not derived from human action, but are unalterable, having the same force and validity throughout. He expressed this by way of an analogy with fire, which invariably burns the same way in both Greece and Persia, while men's ideas of justice, and other conventions, vary from place to place and from time to time. Behind the fire burning uniformly everywhere can be found law-like statements relating

---

37 Many commentators (for example, Popper, 1945) have seen in Plato and Aristotle the roots of the idea (given strong expression in Marxism) that a true social order would be 'beyond justice', where there would be no need for law in the spontaneous sociality of properly arranged human interaction. 'Friendship appears to be the bond of the state; and lawgivers seem to set more store by it than they do by justice; for to promote concord, which seems akin to friendship, is their chief aim; while faction, which is enmity, is what they are most anxious to banish. And if men are friends there is no need for justice between them; whereas merely to be just is not enough; a feeling of friendship is also necessary' (*N Ethics*, 1155a).

to the process of combustion, which we come to understand through reasoning upon what we observe. Aristotle seems to argue that a moral law must be as rational in its nature as a scientific one and that both can be revealed by a process of reason and observation; this basic idea, interpreted in various fashions, was to have a profound effect on all ideas that came after. But even for those who followed this early empirical approach, while it was all very well to agree that the world should be the site of rational analysis, agreeing, however, on what the world signified was a wholly different issue.

CHAPTER 3

THE LAWS OF NATURE, MAN'S POWER AND GOD:
the synthesis of mediaeval Christendom

And I saw a new heaven and a new earth: for the first heaven and the first earth were passed away; and there was no more sea. And I John saw the holy city, new Jerusalem, coming down from God out of heaven, prepared as a bride adorned for her husband. And I heard a great voice out of heaven saying, Behold, the tabernacle of God is with men, and he will dwell with them, and they shall be his people, and God himself shall be with them, and be their God. And God shall wipe away all tears from their eyes; and there shall be no more death, neither sorrow, nor crying, neither shall there be any more pain: for the former things are passed away. And he that sat upon the throne said, Behold, I make all things new. And he said unto me, Write: for these words are true and faithful. And he said unto me, It is done. I am Alpha and Omega, the beginning and the end. I will give unto him that is athirst of the fountain of the water of life freely. He that overcometh shall inherit all things; and I will be his God, and he shall be my son (*Revelation* 21: 1–7, AV (written by an old man in the evening of his life on the Isle of Patmos)).

As long as the priest is considered a higher type of man – this professional negator, slanderer, and poisoner of life – there is no answer to the question: what is truth? For truth has been stood on its head when the conscious advocate of nothingness and negation is accepted as the representative of 'truth' (Friedrich Nietzsche, *The AntiChrist,* in the Portable Nietzsche: 575).

That man is the product of causes which had no pre-vision of the end they were achieving; that his origin, his growth, his hopes and fears, his loves and beliefs, are but the outcome of accidental collocations of atoms; that no fire, no heroism, no intensity of thought and feeling, can preserve an individual life beyond the grave; that all the labours of the ages, all the devotion, the inspiration, all the noonday brightness of human genius, are destined to extinction in the vast death of the solar system, and that the whole temple of man's achievement must inevitably be buried beneath the debris of a universe in ruins – all these things, if not quite beyond dispute, are yet so nearly certain, that no philosophy which rejects them can hope to stand. Only within the scaffolding of these truths, only on the firm foundation of unyielding despair, can the soul's habitation henceforth be safely built (Bertrand Russell, *Mysticism and Logic,* 1929: 47).

THE RISE OF UNIVERSALISM WITH THE DECLINE
OF THE GREEK CITY-STATES

Socrates, Plato and Aristotle inhabited a specific social space. Their world was not to last. For a time its ending looked like success. But the conquests of Alexander the Great – which created a Greek empire – destroyed the boundaries giving intensity to Greek rationality.[1] The city-state provided only a temporary environment for the birth of Western philosophy; its passing created both a void and an opportunity. Simply put, while classical Greek philosophy was unavoidably the philosophy of a scene, of a boundary and its transgression – of the cave and its transcendence – subsequent philosophy must cope with universality. Post Alexander, to speak of man as a political animal could no longer mean 'in his relationships within the polis', but as an individual. In turn, to speak of an individual implied that man was also universal; whatever pertained to the individual must relate to mankind as a general species. While the abilities and duties of the Greek man pertained to his membership of the social order, of the polis, the stage was set for a new social entity – that of man as man.

THE PHILOSOPHY OF STOICISM

The philosophy associated with the last Greek school, the Stoic, provided some material to construct a bridge. Like other post-Aristotelian movements, it was orientated to producing self-sufficiency and individual well-being. Stoics sought happiness through the wisdom to ascertain what can be controlled by human power, and accept with dignity what lay beyond human control. The death of Socrates, in particular the way he faced death with courage and serenity, provided a fertile example of one man's control of emotion in the face of certain extinction. The Roman Epictetus (60–117 AD) argued that while one cannot escape death, one can escape the dread of it. Instead of demanding that events of the world occur as one wants them to, and experiencing a paralysing frustration when they do not, accept them for what they are. Moreover, positively wish them to operate as their natural processes require, and align oneself to that operation; peace of mind and serene happiness can be attained by acceptance of the way of the world.

Stoicism is an approach to life; controlling the emotions and accepting both life's forces and fate in an otherwise chaotic and unpredictable cosmos. This was not an irrational acceptance. Beneath the chaotic appearance of life, Stoics argued that the cosmos was an orderly arrangement where man and the cosmos behaved according to distinct principles of purpose. Reason and law operated throughout nature. Stoics reinterpreted pagan ideas of the prevalence of many Gods behind and influencing various events and happenings (the failure of crops, the weather, disasters of planning etc), substituting the idea of an all-encompassing rational substance pervading phenomena within the cosmos. The term God was used to conceptualise a unified form of reason which controls and orders the structure of nature, thus determining the course of events in the world.

---

1   Tan can even relate the change to a specific event: 'Man as a political animal, a fraction of the polis or self-governing city-state, had ended with Aristotle; with Alexander begins man as an individual. The individual needs to consider both the regulation of his own life and also his relations with other individuals who with him composed the 'inhabited world'; to meet the former need there arose the philosophies of conduct, to meet the latter certain new ideas of human brotherhood. These originated on the day - one of the crucial moments of history - when, at a banquet at Opis, Alexander prayed for a union of hearts (*homonoia*) and a joint commonwealth of Macedonians and Persians' (WW Tan, *Hellenistic Civilisation* (1955: 79) quoted in Sabine and Thorson, 1973: 141).

THE IDEA OF MANKIND AS PLAYERS IN COSMIC DRAMA

The reason that exists in all the entities of the cosmos lies in man: man has the 'spark of the divine within him'. The soul of man is both corporal (centred on the heart and spread throughout the body via the flow of blood), and reasonable (providing the uniqueness of man). Through their rational nature humans participate in the rational structure which underlies the vast forces of the cosmos. By the proper use of his reason, man understands the actual order of things and his place in that order; he comes to realise that everything obeys laws of existence. Man must, therefore, relate his behaviour to the order of 'natural' law. But how can we conceive of this entirety? In what way can we represent the whole of the cosmos, its activities, the flows of power through it, and its past, present and future (its history)? Epictetus stated it simply: we are actors in a vast cosmic drama. We cannot choose our own roles, but must act under the direction of the director/producer of the drama. A plot and various roles have been laid out by the writer and director; the producer has chosen different people to play various roles. The plot of this drama is provided by the intelligence or reason which pervades all entities, and the setting is the cosmos. We gain wisdom in recognising the role we are called upon to play, and performing that part to the best of our ability. While some of us have small roles, others have large ones, but all of us play a part. We cannot control things which have no relationship to our role, nor can we change the role of another. We should develop a positive apathy, or sense of detachment, in relation to those things which we cannot affect, and concentrate upon our own performance and the things we can do or influence.[2] We can be somewhat optimistic: after all, we can control our attitudes and enquire into the nature of the cosmos, but we cannot influence its outcome.

THE RETORT OF THE SCEPTICS TO THE CLAIMS OF KNOWLEDGE TO GUIDE HUMAN AFFAIRS

The Sceptics (from the Greek *skeptikoi*, seeker or enquirer) doubted that human knowledge claims could ever provide 'truth' about the whole of the cosmos. Plato and Aristotle had not discovered the truth about the world, they had merely provided differing conceptions of truth. The Sceptics proposed that most enquirers into truth soon became *dogmatists*, either proclaiming that they had found the truth, and thus there was no need for further enquiries, or announcing that truth could not be found, therefore there was no point in pursuing intellectual enquiries. Both denied the need to

---

2 A problematic point to this wisdom lies in the issue of freedom and determinism. If nature is fixed in its structures, and if there is a vast drama unfolding, then are not the parts fixed? Why bother? Is not the outcome already predetermined? Why should one be said to be free to decide the quality of one's performance if one cannot also be free to choose, or at least develop, the part one plays? Surely the freedom to choose the type of performance one gives is not radically different from asserting the freedom to influence the outcome? Which would amount to changing the role one played? The distinction which the Stoics made - that we were free to choose our attitudes and the quality of our performance, while we were not free to influence anything else - is unsustainable.

keep the process going. By contrast the Sceptics claimed the task was never-ending. Truth was the goal, but truth lay beyond human understanding.[3]

THE APPROACH OF THE ROMAN STATESMAN CICERO (OF ARPINUM, 106-43 BC)

The Roman orator and statesman Cicero was to combine the stoic idea of a universal law of nature directing the course of human conduct with the psychological attitude of the Sceptics. Cicero wrote many philosophical works during his (not infrequent) periods of enforced retirement from public life. A chronic insomniac, he often wrote through the night combining the ideas of the Stoics with other Greek influences. Believing that the Greeks had laid out the basic structures of all intellectual enquiries, Cicero's lasting impact lies in the clarity of his writing and the adaptations he made to the ideas of others. In particular, he believed philosophy and rhetoric were inseparable and blamed Socrates for separating them. Cicero believed the highest human achievement lay in an effective use of knowledge to guide human affairs. While philosophy and the other specialised disciplines supply knowledge, rhetoric makes it effective. A free society is a constitutional republic where persuasion, rather than coercion, is the instrument of political power. However, this is not easy to achieve, and the state needs great men to make this amalgam work. To be effective, the best men must unite knowledge with eloquence; a liberal education is an essential prerequisite. Eloquence and certainty of purpose shine though Cicero's stoic conception of an underlying law of nature:

> True law is right reason in agreement with nature, diffused among all men; constant and unchanging, it should call men to their duties by its precepts, and deter them from wrongdoing by its prohibitions; and it never commands or forbids upright men in vain, while its rules and restraints are lost upon the wicked. To curtail this law is unholy, to amend it illicit, to repeal it impossible; nor can we be dispensed from it by the order either of senate or of popular assembly; nor need we look for anyone to clarify or interpret it; nor will it be one law at Rome and a different one at Athens, nor otherwise tomorrow than it is today; but one and the same law, eternal and unchangeable, will bind all peoples and all ages; and God, its designer, expounder and enactor, will be as it were the sole and universal ruler and governor of all things; and whoever disobeys it, because by this act he will have turned his back on himself and on man's very nature, will pay the heaviest penalty, even if he avoids the other punishments which are adjudged fit for his conduct (*De republica*, 3.22.33, quoted in Kelly, 1992: 58–9).

All men are equal in the face of this eternal law, not in the outward artefacts of our property or social position, but in possession of reason. 'We are born for justice, and it is only bad habits and false beliefs which prevent us from understanding underlying human

---

3   Of course Sceptics allowed for different outcomes. Some said no final judgment is therefore possible, and one must refrain from denying or affirming anything. There is, however, always another perspective. The response might be that one must simply be very careful about the type of assertions made and the area which the assertion covers. This strain of scepticism distinguished between (i) the analysis of nature; (ii) the realm of human feelings; (iii) the traditions of laws and customs; (iv) the arts. In each area there are certain things we must simply accept.

equality and similarity' (*De Legibus*, 1. 10. 28–29). Against Aristotle, we are not fitted by nature for different tasks and to perform different functions; *it is the social order – NOT NATURE – which is the source of inequality.* Nature has commanded us to give each other equal respect and accord each other equal dignity in the very fact of our original human brotherhood. The state, therefore, must be(come) an ethical community – conscious of mutual obligations and mutual recognition of rights – bound together by a common agreement about law and rights, and the desire to participate to mutual advantage (*De Republica*, 1.25).

In *De Legibus*, Cicero presents Roman law as a near perfect realisation of Stoic theory. Nature is the source of precepts which any individual can access through use of his reason. The most learned men agree:

> Law is the highest reason, implanted in nature, which commands what ought to be done and forbids the opposite. This reason, when firmly fixed and fully developed in the human mind, is law. They believe that law is understanding; whose natural function it is to command right conduct and forbid wrongdoing ... The origin of justice is to be found in law, for law is a natural force; it is the mind and reason of the intelligent man, the standard by which justice and injustice are measured ... In determining what justice is, we may begin with that supreme law which had its origin ages before any written law existed or any state had been established (*De Legibus*, 1.6.18-19).

There is a law of nature independent of whether man-made (or positive) law exists or not. Thus even if there had been no written law against rape in the reign of Tarquin (the last king of Rome), Tarquin's son still violated 'eternal law' by his outrage on Lucretia:

> For reason did exist, derived from the nature of the universe, urging men to right conduct and diverting them from wrongdoing, and this reason did not first become law when it was written down, but when it first came into existence; and it came into existence simultaneously with the divine mind. Wherefore the true and primal law, designed for command and prohibition, is the right reason of the high God (*De Legibus*, 2.4.10).

The rest of the text continues the theme of the Stoic commonwealth of the world.

> The most foolish notion of all is the belief that everything is just which is found in the customs or laws of nations. Would that be true, even if those laws had been enacted by tyrants? ... [or if a law proposed] that a dictator might put to death with impunity any citizen he wished, even without a trial. For justice is one; it binds all human society, and is based on one law, which is right reason applied to command and prohibition (*De Legibus*, 1.15.42).

> If the principles of justice were founded on the decrees of peoples, the edicts of princes, or the decisions of judges, then justice would sanction robbery and adultery and forgery of wills, in case these acts were approved by the votes or decrees of the populace (*De Legibus*, 1.16.43-4).

> It is agreed that laws were invented for the safety of citizens, the preservation of states, and the tranquillity and happiness of human life, and that those who first put statutes of this kind in force convinced their people that it was their intention to write down and put into effect such rules as, once accepted and adopted, would make possible for them an honourable and happy life; and when such rules were drawn up and put in force, it is clear that men called them 'laws'. From this point of view it can be readily understood

that those who formulated wicked and unjust statutes for nations, thereby breaking their promises and agreements, put into effect anything but laws (*De Legibus*, 2.5.11).

THE AMBIGUOUS RELATIONSHIP OF MAN TO NATURE AND A GROWING DESIRE TO DEVELOP TECHNOLOGICAL POWER OVER NATURE

Who are we? What are the powers and limits of our world? Whereas Greek rationality ultimately favoured the path of practical reason over pure reason, the temptation to subject the world to an intense scrutiny loomed even larger. At what point did nature lose its power to dominate us, and become the site of our technologies? At what point did we begin to (co-)write the script?

The question existed as a latent possibility in the historical processes at work. Could man change his relationship to the cosmos by enlisting the support of the results of investigations into the nature of the world? Could it be that the relative size (not to mention the hierarchies) of social collectives will be profoundly modified by the intrusion of a new form of knowledge – technical power?

Let us turn to Plutarch (of Chaeronea, c 46–120, a Greek biographer and moralist, who was for 20 years or more a priest at Delphi). In *Marcellus' Life* Plutarch relates an (impossible) experiment which overturned the power relations within a particular society.

> Archimedes, who was a kinsman and friend of King Hiero, wrote to him that with any given force it was possible to move any given weight; and emboldened, as we are told, by the strength of his demonstration, he declared that if there were another earth, and he could go to it, he could move this one. Hiero was astonished and begged him to put his proposition into execution, and show him some great weight moved by a slight force. Archimedes therefore fixed upon a three-masted merchantman of the royal fleet, which had been dragged ashore by the great labours of many men, and after putting on board many passengers and the customary freight, he seated himself at a distance from her, and without any great effort, but quietly setting in motion with his hand a system of compound pulleys, drew her towards him smoothly and evenly, as though she were gliding through the water. Amazed at this, then, and comprehending the power of his art, the King persuaded Archimedes to prepare for him offensive and defensive engines to be used in every kind of siege warfare (Plutarch, *Marcellus' Life*, xiv, 7-9, trans Bernadotte Perrin, quoted Latour, 1993: 109).

Through the invention of the compound pulley, Archimedes changes the perception and reality of what can be done with the physical objects of nature; he also changes political relations by offering the king a real mechanism for making one man physically stronger than a multitude. At that time the rule of the king was unstable – sometimes relying on the myth of divine descent, sometimes ruling as spokesperson of the elites – lacking the means to achieve secure power. Archimedes' technical development changes the composition of political relations, which now can also be seen as a matter of technical power. Without geometry and statistics, Hiero had to reckon with social forces that by their nature infinitely overpowered him, hence he was always insecure, always facing the need to strike a balance. But now it appeared possible to add the (power) lever of technology to the plays of political manoeuvring, and the ruler becomes stronger than the multitude. The technology enabled new mechanisms of war and defence to be constructed – Plutarch relates that with the aid of this technology Hiero made his state secure from outside attack and thus increased its size and wealth. The consequences of this change in the relationship between man's intellect and nature were to prove dramatic – it is the necessary precursor for the development of modernity[4] – certainly, as Plutarch relates (more than 200 years after Aristotle), Hiero had good reason to be amazed at the power of technology.[5]

However, Plutarch does not advocate taking the path of increasing technical power. Although he relates how Archimedes successfully makes (physical) force now a factor commensurable with (political) force – and thus able to be its servant – owing to the relation of proportion between large and small, between the reduced model and the lifesize application, he fears such power would destroy human qualities:

> And yet, Archimedes [after equipping Syracuse with war machines] possessed such a lofty spirit, so profound a soul, and such a wealth of scientific theory, that although his inventions had won for him a name and fame for superhuman sagacity, he would not consent to leave behind him any treatise on this subject, but regarding the work of an engineer and every art that ministers to the needs of life as ignoble and vulgar, he devoted his earnest efforts only to those studies the subtlety and charm of which are not affected by the claims of necessity (Plutarch, *Marcellus' Life* xvii, 4-5, quoted Latour, 1993: 110).

Reducing the path of intellectual reflection to seeking knowledge that allowed technological application is to slide into the status of those who inhabit the lowly manual trades or engage in vulgar politics. By turning his back on this temptation, and remaining true to the pure pursuit of knowledge, Archimedes escapes to the platonic world outside the cave, leaving below the messy affairs of mortal men. But what if this movement beyond the cave was not engaged in? What if our intelligence remained within the cave, and men viewed the world as a mere collection of entities, somewhat contingently, or systematically, adhering? What if men looked on nature simply as the site to act out their intellectual powers, to uncover means to construct new natural-social technologies of control? Would not nature lose its 'otherness', and men become as God?

---

4   In *Natural Right and History*, Leo Strauss (1953: 23), observes that Aristotle 'could not have conceived of a world state. But why? The world state presupposes such a development of technology as Aristotle could never have dreamed of. That technological development, in its turn, required that science be regarded as essentially in the service of the 'conquest of nature' and that technology be emancipated from any moral and political supervision. Aristotle did not conceive of a world state because he was absolutely certain that science is essentially theoretical and that the liberation of technology from moral and political control would lead to disastrous consequences.'
     Strauss continues, no doubt thinking of the Nazi and Stalinist experiences: 'The fusion of science and the arts together with the unlimited or uncontrolled progress of technology has made universal and perpetual tyranny a serious possibility. Only a rash man would say that Aristotle's view has been refuted'.

5   Mechanics also rely upon a point of focus, and finding the Archimedean point has been a key ingredient. Translated into politics it is the place where real *justice* would be visible. The search is both necessary to engage in, and impossible to bring to a successful conclusion.

THE RETORT OF AUGUSTINE AND THE DEVELOPMENT OF A THEOLOGICAL NATURAL LAW[6]

There are some individuals who, having abandoned virtue and not knowing what God is nor the majesty of His eternal and immutable nature, suppose themselves to be engaged in a great enterprise when they busy themselves with intense and eager curiosity exploring that universal mass of matter we call the world. Such pride is engendered in them in this way, that they imagine themselves dwelling in the very heaven they so often discuss (Augustine, *The Catholic and Manichaean Ways of Life*, 1966: 32-33).

After a long personal and intellectual struggle, St Augustine came to believe that the path of true knowledge – real philosophy – love of wisdom, comes from the gift of moderation which protects us from the extremes of curiosity. The path of (pure) knowledge is not to explore the cosmos as if we were to be its rulers, but rather to inquire humbly into oneself as a limited and dependent being, and thereby ascend into knowledge of what is most true and pure: namely, God.

Augustine came to Christianise the Platonic structure by working through the dualist thesis of the Manichaeans – the world is comprised of the two forces of good and evil, of light and darkness in everlasting conflict – and the sceptical accusation of the academics – there is no way that a man can know the ultimate truth. Augustine found the solution to scepticism in faith. If the foundational entities cannot be discovered by man's powers of investigation, they must be accepted on faith, and the role of reason is to build structures based on a confluence of faith (and things presented to us through revelation) and reason.[7] God ultimately founds the cosmos and is the final stop in any

---

6   St Augustine (354-430 AD) is widely accepted as one of the key intellectual figures in the transition from the classical to the Middle Ages. He was born in the African province of Numidia of a pagan father and a devoutly Christian mother. At 16 years of age Augustine began a study of rhetoric in Carthage, a city renowned for its licentious ways. He cast off his Christian faith and morality, taking a mistress with whom he lived for a decade and fathered a son, until he moved to Italy where he adopted a new mistress. His interest in philosophy was stirred by reading the *Hortensius* by Cicero, with its exhortation to seek philosophical wisdom. His abiding interests were to understand how evil is possible and what is the role of both evil and love in human experience. To this end he turned to the doctrines of the Manichaeans, who preached a dualist ideology in which there are two basic principles in the universe: (i) the principle of light or goodness; and (ii) the principle of darkness or evil. These co-exist, are equally eternal, and are in conflict. The conflict is mirrored in the human body's struggle with the soul, comprising that of the soul representing light seeking goodness, and the body, comprising darkness easily swayed to evil. While this dualism solved some problems it raised others: why are there two conflicting principles in nature? How can we either trust, or hope accurately to find the truth of nature, if nature is always a conflict between opposing forces? Finally, Augustine resorted to a neo-Platonic view, wherein the search for knowledge entailed coming to know the ultimates; in his case this meant coming to know of God's existence and searching for God's will. Thus, he could make Platonism and Christianity virtually coextensive. After conversion to the status of a true believer in 386 AD he left his professional post as a teacher of rhetoric, and in 396 was appointed Bishop to Hippo, a seaport near the town where he was born. In his life he witnessed years of social upheavals and military disasters associated with the decline of the Roman Empire, as well as the transition from Roman paganism to Christianity.

7   For example, reason proved the principle of non-contradiction. We know that a thing cannot both be and not be at the same time. We can use the tools of reason to police and monitor assertions, revealing contradictions and inconsistencies. Thus the human mind is not lost in uncertainty; if we can find certain starting points or foundational entities, we can build structures of secure reason. But we need faith to provide a place to start from. 'Believe in order that you may understand; Unless you shall believe, you shall not understand.'

attempt to seek logical proofs of existence;[8] thus true wisdom is Christian wisdom. Reason must align itself with revelation and logically build arguments based upon the security of entities revealed to us. Philosophy is theology.

Not only would a philosophy which overlooked theology doom us to build structures founded on untruths, but a philosophical attitude which forgot the relationship of man and God, or which ignored the twin forces of good and evil, would invite the dangerous illusion that man was destined to use the power to reason only for good. Augustine interpreted the idea of original sin as the Christian acceptance of the coexistence of good and evil in man and, further, as indicating the falsehood of believing that man was destined for good alone, and that the pursuit of secular knowledge (and the creating of technology thereupon) was a method of achieving man's (earthly or secular) salvation.

THE NARRATIVES OF TRAVELLING AND PLATONIC ASCETICISM IN AUGUSTINE'S NATURAL ORDER

Augustine's account of his conversion to faith in God, although steeped in the language of the Bible, is a narrative of distress, intense longing and, finally, the discovery of a place for the tormented soul to rest. The *Confessions* begin by rejoicing at finding a place to rest; the main parts consist of accounts of the trials and terrors involved in attaining it, and the *Confessions* end with a prayer for rest, peace and fulfilment. With Augustine, the voyage of the self is a reflection of the journey of entire humanity. Whereas once, Augustine confessed, 'I thought I should be too miserable, unless folded in female arms' (*Confessions*, Bk VI, XI 20), and he had been kept from God through 'weight of carnal habit', he had ultimately found the true path, so must all find the true path of man's creation and destiny.[9] The world is best understood in terms of a Christian commonwealth, the culmination of man's spiritual development – whereupon we witness 'the march of God in the world'. What are we to make of the 'knowledges'

---

8   How does this work? Take the issue of knowledge of the truths of mathematics. Augustine differentiates between things we can touch and things which are independent of our senses, such as knowledge of numbers and their relations. Such knowledge cannot come from our senses nor can it depend upon the state of our minds, since they would then be only as stable as our minds. But we apprehend that '7 and 3 make 10 not only now but for ever; there was not a time when 7 and 3 did not make 10 and there never will be a time when they do not make 10' (*On Free Will*, 2, 12ff). Nor is it possible to criticise 3 and 7 for making 10, we simply 'rejoice in it like discoverers'.

What makes the truth of 3 and 7 making 10? Only the most excellent thing that could exist. Augustine is Platonic in arguing that mathematical truths are discovered and not invented by the mind. Accepting Plato's theory of ideas or essences Augustine states: 'Ideas are the primary forms, or the permanent and immutable reasons of real things, and they are not themselves formed; so that they are, as a consequence, eternal and ever the same in themselves and they are contained in the divine intelligence' (*Eighty-three Different Questions*, 46, 1-2). Augustine turns Plato's realm of pure ideas or essences into God's mind; it is because they are in the mind of God that the ideas are eternal and immutable. There is nothing outside of God which determines the way the cosmos is; when God created the cosmos he looked to nothing but himself.

9   We witness with Augustine the operation of a powerful drive: the desire to create a philosophy of history. A vast narrative of man's origins, his past and present, and an indication of his future, within which we banish unbearable mystery and know our essence and our destiny.

contained in his narratives? Augustine fought with his body and mind; he experienced the ups and downs of brothels, drink and mistresses. His writing, though subdued, resounds with the themes of longing, desire, and satisfaction which find their end – their telos – in the love of God; but what does the mind remember? Must it end in this particular version of Platonic success? For the Greek poet Cavafy, writing from North Africa in the 20th century, the body also remembers:

> Body, remember not only how much you were loved,
> not only the beds you lay on,
> but also those desires glowing openly
> in eyes that looked at you,
> trembling for you in voices ... (Cavafy, *Body, Remember* ... 1–5, 1984: 59)

Does a poet convey knowledge? The poet was an ambiguous figure in the Platonic scheme. Whilst, in the *Republic*, Plato banned poets from the ideal state on the grounds that their writing was irrational and antithetical to true knowledge, the poet provides visualisations of truths which are otherwise inexpressible. For Rosen (1985: 43): 'poetry is the visual effort to repair the gap between original and image'. Plato's emphasis upon sight (for example, in the narratives of the sun and of the cave) at the expense of the other senses (such as touch, the sense which provides the basis of the more empiricist legacy of Aristotle), leads him to a poetic recounting of ontological propositions which otherwise remain beyond our experience. But Plato distrusted the poet, since the poet allowed into our consciousness other experiences on the same level as the purity of reason. Listen to Cavafy again in a poem called *When they Come Alive*:

> Try to keep them poet,
> those erotic visions of yours,
> however few of them there are that can be stilled.
> Put them, half-hidden in your lines.
> Try to hold them, poet,
> when they come alive in your mind
> at night or in the noonday brightness (1984: 48).

Augustine's path for mankind is a narrative of asceticism and renunciation. We must renounce evil and struggle to overcome whatever elements in our lives are an obstacle to a higher, truer life.[10] The success of the journey depends upon our ability to focus on what is essential and to overcome distractions and impediments. Asceticism implies freedom from the life of the cave; from stagnation, entrapment, and imprisonment in the world of the body. It combines our manifold desires in the pursuit of our true ends. It is the essential method which allows a unity to our striving and overcomes that repose in pleasure which threatens to stop the dynamic of our highest activities. And in Augustine's story, faith is a bedrock. Faith allows us to believe in an overarching story. Faith enlightens and enables us to chose correctly between the various objects of desire,

---

10 Augustine's neo-Platonism is evident in the various discussions he entered into in the City of God. For example, in the resurrection we will come back with bodies but 'while all defects will be removed from those bodies, their essential nature will be preserved' (*City of God*, Bk XXII, Ch 17). Thus a woman's body, while preserving its sex, will not arouse any desire or lust in the beholder, it will be part of a new beauty, a pure beauty which transcends the body.

to replace our desire for earthly things (*cupiditas*), with the desire for the things of heavenly nature (*caritas*) – the essential things. To know God is to participate in the grand narrative of our creation, existence and our end – our eschatology.[11]

Moreover, belief that there is an overarching story amounts to faith in the possibility of reality being ultimately comprehensible, meaningful and acceptable – God reconciles the oppositions of good and evil in an ultimate structure which is good. The personal story of Augustine – his attempt to explain his beginning, middle and end, his attempt to interpret and shape his life-world – is subsumed in the telling of a more encompassing story; the story of God's intentions which, in the final analysis, only God can know. Although, of course, he can reveal some of it to us.

THE IDEAS OF LOVE AND GRACE

Man, having been created by God, is dependent, ultimately, upon the grace of God. Man may choose to do good, but he does not have the spiritual power to do the good he has chosen. He requires the help of God's grace. Whereas evil is caused by an act of free will, virtue is the product not of man's will but of God's grace. While the moral law may appear to tell man what he must do, in the end it really tells him what is wrong for him to do. Where the law commands, human weakness is most exposed: 'the law was given that grace might be sought; grace was given that the law might be fulfilled'. Sin threatens to engulf us, it is overcome by the love of God. This love is a gift of God and finds its greatest expression in the role of Jesus Christ, the mediator between God and man. Christ is the unique figure in that he is God made mortal, so that we might be made immortal.

JUSTICE AND NATURAL LAW

We have seen that with Augustine, the story of man's individual or personal life was a subset of the overall story of the final social order – God's story. Thus, a state's public or political life is under the same set of moral laws as those of the individual. Both spheres ultimately share a single source of truth; entire, inviolate, and not subject to changes in human life. Behind the entities and operations of the world order stands its author and ultimate ruler: God. All things are truly his creations and, correctly interpreted, reveal themselves as traces of his being (*vestigia*). All men can come to see and recognise this

---

11 The *Confessions* are an autobiography, which holds itself out as a true account of a person's life, and a story of finding truth. Augustine recounts the events and struggles of his own life, but presents this as the smallest intellectually discrete, and yet whole, unit of true experience he can convey to us. This is not a question of abstracting oneself from life in order to reach truth - God - since the life of the one, Augustine, occurs within the patterns and structures laid out by the other, God. The life-experience of Augustine is therefore not an account of the one meeting the other, ie the experience of Augustine coming to know of God, but a life-experience *with* God, even if the one did not initially recognise the existence of this 'other'. Humans live with God, even if they do not acknowledge God's existence. Similarly, the relationship of psychology (theoretical explanations of the self) to sociology (theoretical explanations couched in terms of the social phenomena), is not a coming together of distinct entities, but a relationship of each with the other.

truth, this structure of natural law or natural justice. Natural law is man's intellectual sharing in God's truth, or God's eternal law. Augustine draws upon the Stoic theory of the diffusion of the principle of reason which extends throughout all of nature, governing and ruling the proper functioning of everything. For Stoics, *nous* – the principle of reason – comprised the laws of nature. But, whereas for Stoics the laws of nature were the workings of the impersonal force of rational principles in the universe, Augustine interpreted the eternal law as the reason and will of the personal Christian God. Eternal law became the divine reason, the will of God, which commands the maintenance (observance) of the natural order of things, and which forbids its disturbance. *Eternal law* is God's reason commanding orderliness, and man's intellectual grasp of the eternal principles is called natural law. When the political state makes a law, said Augustine, for such laws to be fully just, the temporal laws should be in accord with the principle of natural law, which, in turn, is derived from the eternal law.

The political universe so envisaged has dramatically changed from the Greek *polis*. Augustine does not regard the political state as autonomous but as part of a larger whole. Therefore, the state does not merely express its power to legislate as it makes law; instead the state must also follow the requirements of a broader justice. This idea of justice, moreover, is a standard which precedes the state and is eternal. Augustine, thereby, drew upon the Platonic presupposition of prior essences to argue that justice is prior to actual social orderings. Whereas the practical problematic of Greek jurisprudence – locked into the pragmatic problem of how to construct an intellectual framework capable of rationally governing a society focused around participation in the polis – looked to justice to find a concept through which one could legitimately distribute the rewards due inside the variable participation in the polis, Augustine sought in the concept of justice a standard which transcended any particular social configuration, pertaining instead to the cosmos – to creation – as a whole. The terms of the previous Greek discussion provided a language and conceptual tools which became the material to construct a different constitutional imagination – Augustine accepted the formula of justice as the virtue of distributing to everyone his due – which, to an independent reader, now created new problems. Most particularly, how do we ascertain what is 'due' to anyone if we step outside the specificity of a certain locality? Is justice to be merely conventional; satisfaction with the distribution patterns which we experience because we have been socialised into a particular society? If so, justice will differ with each society. But then there will not be one justice, but as many 'justices' as there are societies. If we are to accept that, does it not mean we are accepting a concept that did not actually refer to anything, since how can X be just in society B, and at the same time unjust in society C? The logic of non-contradiction states that it cannot be both just and unjust at the same time. More correctly put, for Augustine, there can only be one justice, and while in actual societies there may be many perceptions of what is just and unjust, there is a reality to justice transcending these particular statements.

Augustine thought the reality of justice was to be discovered in the structure of human nature within its relation to God. Justice is 'the habit of the soul which imparts to every man the dignity due him ... Its origin proceeds from nature ... and this notion of justice ... is not the product of man's personal opinion, but something implanted by a certain innate power.' To require the state to follow such a standard was obviously to place heavy moral limitations upon political power. Indeed, Augustine argued, if the laws of the state were out of harmony with natural law and justice, they would not have the character of true laws, nor would there be a true state. Since he defined a commonwealth as an estate of the people, 'they be no people that are not united in one consent of the law: nor is that a law which is not grounded in justice: then it must follow, where no justice is, there no commonwealth is'. In this way Augustine appears to have found his answer for a justifying and critical concept to investigate the actual conventional legal order. The legal order must have a foundation, and this foundation cannot be the process itself; the mere creation of law through the organs of the state cannot confer the label just upon them. That appellation must come from some other act: here it is in accordance with the ultimate source of truth, God's will.

In relating justice to the moral law, Augustine argued that the primary relationship in justice is not the relation between man and man, but that between man and God: 'If man serve not God what justice can be thought to be in him? Seeing that if he serve not God the soul has neither lawful sovereignty over the body nor the reason over the affections.' Collective justice is impossible without the individual justice of the relationship with God, for 'if this justice is not found in one man, no more then can it be found in a whole multitude of such like men. Therefore, amongst such there is not that consent of law which makes a multitude of people.' Again, 'Is he not [unjust who] takes himself away from his Lord God, and gives himself to the service of the devil?' To serve God is to love God, but this means also to love one's fellow man. Still, 'what justice is that which takes man from the true God ... ?' To serve God and to love one's fellow man are, among other things, to recognise that all men should also have this inviolate right and opportunity to love and serve God. All of ethics, then, is based upon man's love for God and his love for his fellow man. Love precedes justice.

Having raised Church and religion to a position of superiority over the temporal state, Augustine accedes to the state the right to use coercive force. The state is the product of man's sinful condition and, therefore, exists as a necessary agency of control. Even so, Augustine does not concede that the principle of force is higher than the principle of love. For Augustine, the foundation of the ideal society is faith and the 'strong concord' which occurs when the object of love is the universal good which in its highest and truest character is God himself, and where men love one another with complete sincerity in their confidence in God. The foundation of this social love is the 'love of Him from whose eyes they cannot conceal the spirit of love'. The earthly state still has a function (even though its force cannot match the creative power of love), for the state's action can at least lower some evils: 'When the power to do hurt is taken from the wicked, they will carry themselves better being curbed ... The state had not been designed in vain.' But the state that used its coercive power to enforce laws without justice was the empirical occurrence of an imperfect state.

AUGUSTINE'S IDEA OF SOCIAL EXISTENCE AS DIVIDED BETWEEN 'TWO CITIES' AND HIS PHILOSOPHY OF HISTORY

In his major work, *concerning* **The City of God** *against the pagans*, Augustine set out to defend Christianity against the charge that the Church's refusal to make offerings to the pagan gods of Rome – as the Christian faith became the major religion – led to the collapse of the Roman Empire and the sacking of Rome. Why, if Christianity were true, had (this new) God not defended Rome against the Goths? His answer was to divide humanity into two, with two kinds of interests and energy, two kinds of love, inhabiting two cities:

> the one consists of those who live by human standards, the other who live according to God's will ... By two cities I mean two societies of human beings, one of which is predestined to reign with God for all eternity, the other doomed to undergo eternal punishment with the devil (Bk XV, 1).

Mankind experiences two kinds of love: some love God, others love themselves and the world. Rome was lost because of the vices of its inhabitants. The old republic lacked true depth, since it lacked real justice, only possible if united in the love of God. As Augustine asked in a famous passage:

> Remove justice, and what are kingdoms but gangs of criminals on a large scale? And what are gangs but petty kingdoms? A gang is a group of men under the command of a leader, bound by a compact of association, in which the plunder is divided according to an agreed convention.

> If this villainy wins so many recruits from the ranks of the demoralised that it acquires territory, establishes a base, captures cities and subdues peoples, it then openly arrogates to itself the title of kingdom, which is conferred on it in the eyes of the world, not by the renouncing of aggression but by the attainment of impunity.

> For it was a witty and a truthful rejoinder which was given by a captured pirate to Alexander the Great. The king asked the fellow, 'What is your idea, in infesting the sea?' And the pirate answered, with uninhibited insolence, 'The same as yours, in infesting the earth! But because I do it in a tiny craft, I'm called a pirate: Because you have a mighty navy, you're called the emperor.' (Bk IV, 4)

A true society is an association of rational beings united by unanimous agreement upon the things they love. The destiny of the world lay in the conflict between two kinds of love, and two kinds of cities. Ultimately, with the grace of God, true love would win. If Augustine's language breathes an eloquent vagueness it could have coercive bite.[12] For if one could be certain of the truth of one's essential being, it is a perversity to turn away

---

12 To liberal conceptions this belief in one truth may prove authoritarian. Two events relating to Augustine may serve as examples. The first concerns his role as Church administrator, the second, the force given to a text when the institutional structure holds to it as consecrated truth. As regards the former, in the course of the struggle with the Donatist movement in North Africa - a dissenting movement increasingly repressed by the authorities - Augustine gradually, and at first reluctantly, consented to coercive measures used against the movement. His endorsement of these repressive measures appeared to constitute a political action running counter to the fundamental direction of his [cont'd]

from that 'natural' being.[13] The relationship between God's love and God's power, and man's relationship to both, was never fully settled. Augustine refers constantly to 'a sickness of the soul' which keeps one from God, 'disobedience' to God's will coming from 'insufficiency of the will', or 'the iron bondage of my own will ... which held me fast in a hard slavery'. Perhaps Augustine was right to speak of the weight of this world's concerns, and bemoan that many would find 'the pack of this world was a kind of pleasant weight ... as happens in sleep', for while he awaited a Platonic enlightenment for the masses, the beliefs underlying his hopes were soon to be sorely tested. The wisdom of the ancients as general learning was almost lost in the 'dark ages' which came after the fall of the Roman Empire in 476 AD, only kept alive by Christian scholars who struggled in pursuance of its 'truth'. Legal scholarship was to be given secular roots in the pioneering Law School of Bologna in the papal territory of north central Italy (beginning around 1100). There the study of Justinian's *Digest* – which together with Justinian's *Institutes, Codex,* and *Novellae* (students' textbook and collection of late imperial Roman law) made up what was called the *Corpus Iuris Civilis* – founded a tradition of the study of Roman law which still persists. Viewed as the classical embodiment of legal and political reason, the study of Roman law provided a basis for civil administration. Nevertheless, most legal theory continued to be proposed by churchmen – rather than lawyers – whose interest was in maintaining a synthesis of the relations of man and God. A synthesis which was to receive its most advanced form in the writings of St Thomas Aquinas.

ST THOMAS AQUINAS: THE THOMISTIC DOCTRINE AS THE HIGH POINT OF THE SCHOLASTIC SYSTEM OF MEDIEVAL PHILOSOPHY[14]

Primarily a theologian, Aquinas 'Christianised' Aristotle. Aquinas did not so much write a theological philosophy, but delineated theology and philosophy as different ways of approaching the enormity of God's creation. While Aquinas agreed with Augustine that true happiness lay in our coming to know God, he stressed that errors in our basic starting positions could radically affect our life, and thus lead us into false relationships with God. Theology begins with the truths of God's will, as revealed through divine

---

12...thought but they make sense in the context of the threat they posed to unity and the necessity for the one vision of love which underlay Augustine's system. The latter refers to the interpretation that later officials of the Christian bureaucracy gave to his use of the gospel phrase 'compel them to come in' (*Coge intrare,* Luke, 19.23), an interpretation which legitimated the use of persecution, repression and violent conversion, in which processes the tragic events of the Inquisitions are the best known.

13 ' ... it is not a substance, but a perversity of the will turning away from you, God, the supreme substance, toward lower things' (Confessions, VII, 5).

14 St Thomas Aquinas (1225-1274), widely recognised as the greatest Catholic thinker of the middle ages, synthesised classical Greek - particularly those of Aristotle - and Christian ideas. Other influences were Arabian and Jewish writers. The dispute between Augustinians and Thomists came to dominate Christian philosophy in the Middle Ages, the distinction being that between neo-Platonic and neo-Aristotelian views, between using faith or empirical reasoning on the world as the foundation of knowledge, between reaction to the body or working through the body.

revelation, while philosophy begins with the world as revealed to our senses and analyses it to discover principles. Philosophy concerns itself with immediate objects of sense experience and reasons upwards to more general conceptions; ultimately the mind comes to the end of the first principles of original causes of being and thus arrives at proof for the existence of God. Theology, conversely, begins with a faith in God and comes to interpret the life of all things as deriving from their existence as creatures of God. The philosopher decides upon his conclusions – his truth – through analysing the rational descriptions of things; whereas the theologian works from the security of an absolute faith in the bedrock of revealed knowledge. Philosophy can offer five ways of reasoning to conclude that God exists. These are proof from motion; proof from efficient cause; proof from necessary, as opposed to possible, being; proof from degrees of perfection; proof from the order of the universe (*Summa Theologiae* q II, a. 1, 2, 3).

The cosmos is a hierarchy of different things conjoined in a great *chain of being*. Everything belongs to one or other species, and variation in the cosmos demonstrates the range of God's perfection, from angels down to the elements of fire, earth, water and air. Each level of being has a particular composite nature; for man, the soul is the form, and the body is the material substance.

AQUINAS' IDEAS OF THE ENDS OF MAN AND THE NATURAL LAW

The Thomistic conception of natural law presupposes a teleological view of human nature. Man is naturally orientated to certain ends; happiness lies in attaining man's end or purpose. Conversely, to sin is to fail to act perfectly. The power to sin is the ability to fail to act according to the ends we ought by our nature to be achieving. These ends lie on different levels, as is the case with man's various tendencies. Whereas Aristotle had offered a naturalistic morality in which men could achieve virtue and happiness by fulfilling their natural capacities or ends, Aquinas added the Christian concept of man's supernatural end. For Augustine, both the source and ultimate end of man's existence lay with God. Human nature is not self-sufficient with its own standards of fulfilment; instead mankind must combine the ends of natural functioning with supernatural ends. Conversely, Aquinas argued the body could not be rejected.[15] It instigates certain kinds of acts, appetites and passions. The senses enable a level of knowledge about sensible objects, and man is attracted to some objects perceived as pleasurable and good (concupiscent appetite), and repelled by others perceived as harmful, painful, or bad (irascible appetite). This attraction and rejection are the basic rudiments of man's capacity for love and pleasure, hate and fear.

---

15 In developing a conception of human nature we cannot ignore the fact that man is a physical substance. Whereas Plato had talked about the soul as being imprisoned in the body, and Augustine considered the soul as a spiritual substance independent of the body, they neglected the fact that the soul of man is as dependent upon the body as the body is upon the soul. For Aquinas, *man is a unity of body and soul*. Without the soul, the body would have no form. Without the body, the soul would not have its required organs of sense through which to gain its knowledge. As a physical substance, man is a composite of soul and body; as a rational creature, man exists and functions as man only when unified as body and soul.

While animals are under the control of these irascible and concupiscent appetites, man escapes such dependency and becomes a free subject through the power of will and reason. The intellect can rank the goods of existence. Riches, pleasure, power, and knowledge are all goods – legitimate objects of the appetites – but they cannot produce man's deepest happiness. They do not possess the character of the universal good that man's soul seeks. Aquinas believes this is not found in created things but in God; the supreme good.

Man is a mixture of sensuality, appetites, will, and reason which enables him to exercise moral choice in constructing his life-course. Man creates his life out of *free* acts. If physical determinism rules over man, no freedom of action, and thus no morality, is possible. Freedom is an absolute prerequisite for any act to be considered moral; Aquinas states that an act is human only if it is free. Freedom entails knowledge of alternatives and the power to chose between them. Virtue, or goodness, consists in making the right choices, the mean between extremes. Virtue comes through control of the appetites by exercise of the will and reason. There are certain natural virtues – courage, temperance, justice, and prudence – which are complemented by man's knowledge of natural law or moral law.

The basis of moral obligation is to be found, first of all, in the fundamental nature of man. Built into man's nature are various imperatives, such as the need to preserve his life and propagate his species, also, because he is rational, an imperative directed toward the search for truth. The elemental moral truth is simply to 'do good and avoid evil'. When, therefore, we analyse our condition certain things appear reasonable:

(i)   man is under a natural obligation to protect his life and health, hence suicide and carelessness are wrong;

(ii) the natural need to propagate the species provides the fundamental necessity for the union of man and woman (husband and wife);

(iii) because man seeks for truth, he can best achieve this by living in social harmony with his fellow men who are also engaged in this quest. To ensure an ordered and harmonious society, human laws are fashioned to direct the community's behaviour.

These factors: preservation of life, propagation of the species, formation of an ordered society under human laws, and pursuit of truth, all pertain to man's natural state. The moral law is founded upon reason's ability to discern the right course of conduct in the light of human nature; that is, after considering humanities' natural inclinations toward specific modes of behaviour.[16] Because human nature has certain fixed qualities, rules for behaviour that correspond to these qualities are called natural law.

What then is justice? 'Justice is the constant and lasting will to give each one his due' (S T q 58, a 1). One's due is that to which one is ordered, according to one's natural tendencies, towards the perfection of one's end. One's due is not conferred by positive law but by natural tendencies of human nature. It follows, thereby, that if positive law

---

16 'Moral virtue derives its goodness from the rule of reason, while its matter consists in passions or operations ... It makes the passion conform to the rule of reason' (S T q 64 a 1).

violates what is naturally due to man, then such a (positive legal) order can be called unjust on the basis of the natural law.

Much of the impetus for this theory of natural law was already developed by Aristotle. In the *Nicomachaean Ethics* Aristotle distinguished between natural justice (*physikon dikaion*) and conventional justice (*nomikon dikaion*). The first he saw as immutable, and the second mutable or changeable. Some forms of behaviour, he said, are wrong only because, and only after, a law has been made to regulate such behaviour. To use a modern example, it is wrong to drive a vehicle at certain speeds only because a speed limit has been set, but in nature there is nothing requiring vehicles to travel at that speed. Such a law is therefore not natural but conventional, because before the law was passed, there was nothing wrong with travelling at speeds exceeding the new limit. On the other hand, Aquinas would argue, there are some laws the precepts of which are derived from nature, so the behaviour they regulate has always been wrong, as in the case of murder. But Aquinas did not limit his treatment of natural law to the simple notion that in some way man's reason is able to discover the natural basis for human conduct. Instead, he reasoned, if man's existence and nature can be fully understood only when seen in relation to God, then natural law must be described in metaphysical and theological terms; as the Stoics and St Augustine had done.

Law, says Aquinas, has to do primarily with obligations ultimately imposed by reason.

> It belongs to law to command and forbid ... Law is a rule and measure of acts, whereby man is induced to act or is restrained from acting; for lex [law] is derived from ligare [to bind], because it binds one to act. Now the rule and measure of human acts is the reason ... for it belongs to the reason to direct a man's whole activity toward his end' (S T q 90 a 1).

Law involves power, it imposes obligations. But behind this exercise of power in law lies reason. It is not simply that 'whatsoever pleaseth the sovereign has the force of law', since law should 'move those who are subject to it to act rightly'. The sovereign may command through the positive law things which are not reasonable, may command man to act in ways which are not right, but this is not law operating in accordance with nature. Natural law is dictated by reason.[17] And since God created all things, human nature and natural law are best understood as the product of God's wisdom or reason. What then is a simple definition of law?

> Law is nothing else than an ordinance of reason for the common good, promulgated by him who has the care of the community (S T q 90 a 4).

Ideally law springs from the power to order for the common good, which 'belongs either to the whole people, or to someone who is the vice-regent of the whole people. The making of the law belongs either to the whole people or to the public personage who has care of the whole people'. Moreover law is something which lives, which exists, internally in the people: 'A law is in a person not only as in one that rules, but

---

17 'Accordingly, the order of precepts of the natural law follows the order of natural inclinations' (S T q 94 a 2).

also, by participation, as in one that is ruled'. The proper work of law is written in the hearts and will of the people, since human nature is, ultimately, rational nature. From this standpoint, Aquinas distinguishes four kinds of law (see *Summa Theologica*, Questions 90–95).

THE INTERCONNECTION OF ETERNAL, NATURAL, HUMAN AND DIVINE LAW

Eternal law

> ... Law is nothing else but a dictate of practical reason emanating from the ruler who governs a perfect community ... granted that the whole community of the universe is governed by Divine Reason. Therefore the very idea of the government of things in God the ruler of the universe, has the nature of a law. And since the divine reason's conception of things is not subject to time but is eternal ... therefore it is that this kind of law must be called eternal (S T q 91 a 1).

In God's intellect there exists a plan expressing the order of all things to their ends; this plan we can refer to as eternal law. All creatures bear the imprint of this eternal law, and for man this imprint has a special bearing due to his rationality.

Natural law

Natural law consists of that portion of eternal law that pertains particularly to man. While man cannot know the entirety of God's plan, man's rationality ensures he has a share of eternal reason, whereby he can recognise a (normative) natural inclination to proper acts and ends.[18] 'Natural law is nothing else than the rational creature's participation of the eternal law' (S T q 91 a 2).

The basic precepts of natural law are the preservation of life, propagation, education of offspring, the pursuit of truth and the construction of a peaceful society. Thus natural law consists of broad general principles reflecting God's intentions for man in creation.

Human law

The specific statutes of governments, or human laws, ought to be derived from the general precepts of natural law. Law being 'a dictate of the practical reason', the process of drawing conclusions for law is much the same as for 'speculative reason' (the sciences). Just as 'we draw conclusions of the various sciences' from 'naturally known undemonstrable principles', so also 'from the precepts of the natural law ... human reason needs to proceed to the more particular determination of certain matters'. And 'these particular determinations, devised by human reason, are called human laws ...'

---

18 'Hence we must say the eternal law as it is in itself cannot be known by anyone except God and the blessed who see God in his essence. But any rational creature knows this law by a stronger or weaker 'irradiation" (S T q 93 a 2).

Man has a natural aptitude for virtue; but the perfection of virtue must be acquired by means of some training. A law is not 'just' simply from the fact that it was decreed by a sovereign. Aquinas argued that what gives a law the character of law is its moral dimension, its conformity with the precepts of natural law, its agreement with the moral law. Taking St Augustine's formula, namely, 'that which is not just seems to be no law at all', Aquinas argues: 'every human law has just so much of the nature of law, as it is derived from the law of nature', but adds, 'if in any point it deflects from the law of nature, it is no longer a law but a perversion of law'. While such laws no longer bind in conscience, they are sometimes to be obeyed to prevent an even greater evil. Aquinas went even further than to deny the character of law to any command of government that violated the natural moral law; such a command, he stated, should not be obeyed. Some laws may be unjust through being opposed to the divine good: such are the laws of tyrants inducing to idolatry, or to anything else contrary to the divine law. Laws of this kind must 'nowise be observed, because ... *we ought to obey God rather than men*'. Human reason is fallible and prone to mistakes; human law 'cannot have that inerrancy that belongs to the demonstrated conclusions of the sciences'.

Divine law

The function of law is to direct man to his proper end. Since man is ordained to an end of eternal happiness, in addition to his temporal happiness, there must be a kind of law that can direct him to that supernatural end. Aquinas here goes beyond Aristotle, since he states that Aristotle knew only about man's natural purpose and end, and for this purpose the natural law, known by man's reason, was considered a sufficient guide. But the eternal happiness to which man is ordained, makes it 'necessary that besides the natural and the human law, man should be directed to his end by a law given by God'. *Divine law*, then, is available to man through revelation and is found in the Scriptures. It is not the product of man's reason, but is given to man through God's grace to ensure that he should know what he must do to fulfil both his natural and, especially, his supernatural ends. The difference between natural law and divine law is this: natural law represents man's rational knowledge of the good, operating by the intellect directing the will to control his appetites and passions, leading him to fulfil his natural end by achieving the cardinal virtues of justice, temperance, courage, and prudence. Divine law, on the other hand, comes directly from God through revelation, a gift of God's grace, whereby men are directed to their supernatural ends; having obtained the higher, or theological, virtues of faith, hope, and love, these virtues are 'infused' into man by God's grace. In this way, Aquinas Christianised and surpassed the naturalistic ethics of Aristotle, by supposedly demonstrating how the natural desire of man to know God can be assured, indicating how revelation becomes the guide for reason, and describing the manner in which man's highest nature is perfected through God's grace.

THE THOMISTIC CONCEPTION OF THE STATE

Building upon Aristotle's definition of man as a social animal born for political society, Aquinas agrees that the state is a natural institution derived from the nature of man, but postulates that the state also has a duty imposed upon it to help man fulfil his supernatural end. Since the state is not equipped to deal with this more ultimate end of man, it must acknowledge limitations upon its functions; it is the role of the Church to direct man to this end. Aquinas did not simply divide authority into these two realms of human concern, giving authority in one area to the state and authority in the other to the Church, he rather looked at the state, and explained its origin, in terms of God's creation.

The state, in this view, is willed by God and has as its God-given function to cater for the social nature of man. Contrary to Augustine, Aquinas does not see the state as a product of man's sinfulness: even 'in the state of innocence man would have lived in society'. But even then, 'a common life could not exist, unless there were someone in control, to attend to the common good'. The state's function is to secure the common good by keeping the peace, organising the activities of the citizens into harmonious pursuits, providing for the resources to sustain life, and preventing, as far as possible, obstacles to the good life. This last item, concerning threats to the good life, gives to the state not only a function tied to man's ultimate end; it also accounts for the state's position in relation to the Church.

The state is subordinate to the Church. It is not that the Church is a superstate; simply that the state has its own sphere of legitimate functions as does the Church. Within this sphere the state is autonomous. But, insofar as there are aspects of human life that bear upon man's supernatural end, the state must not put forward arbitrary hindrances to frustrate man's spiritual life. Within its own sphere, the state is what Aquinas calls a 'perfect society', having its own end and the means for achieving it, but the state is like man; neither the state nor man is limited to a natural end. Man's spiritual end cannot be achieved 'by human power, but by divine power'. Still, because man's destiny includes attaining the enjoyment of God, the state must recognise this aspect of human destiny: in providing for the common good of the citizens, the sovereign must pursue his community's goal with a consciousness of man's spiritual end. Under these circumstances, the state does not become the Church, but it does mean that the sovereign 'should order those things which lead to heavenly beatitude and prohibit, as far as possible, their contraries'. In this way, Aquinas affirmed the legitimacy of the state and its autonomy in its own sphere, subordinating it to the Church only to ensure that the ultimate spiritual end of man be taken into account.

As the state rules the behaviour of its citizens through the agency of law, the state is in turn limited by the requirements of just laws. Nowhere is Aquinas' rejection of the absolute autonomy of the state so clearly stated as when he describes the standards for the making of human or positive law. We have already analysed the different types of law, eternal, natural, human and divine. The state is particularly the source of human law. Each government is faced with the task of fashioning specific statutes to regulate the behaviour of its citizens under the particular circumstances of its own time and place.

Lawmaking, however, must not be an arbitrary act but be enacted under the influence of the natural law, which is man's participation in God's eternal law. Positive laws ought to consist of particular rules derived from the general principles of natural law. Any positive human law that violates the natural law loses its character as law, is 'a perversion of law,' and loses its binding force in the consciences of men. The lawmaker has his authority to legislate from God, the source of all authority, and to God he is responsible: ' ... in human affairs superiors move inferiors through their will by virtue of their divinely ordained authority' (S T q 104 a 1).

The purpose of political authority is to provide for the common good; authority is never to be used as an end in itself, or for selfish ends. Nor must the common good be interpreted in such a way that the individual is lost sight of in the collective whole. The common good must be the good of concrete persons. Thus Aquinas says that 'the proper effect of law is to lead its subjects to their proper virtue ... to make those to whom it is given good'. The only 'true ground' of the lawgiver is his 'intention to secure the common good regulated according to divine justice', and hence it follows that 'the effect of the law is to make men good'. This is to say that the phrase *common good* has no meaning for Aquinas except insofar as it results in the good of individuals. At the same time, Aquinas says that 'the goodness of any part is considered in comparison with the whole ... Since then every man is a part of the state, it is impossible that a man be good unless he be well proportionate to the common good.' The entire scheme of society and its laws is characterised by the rational elements in it Thus, although the sovereign has authority and power, law must not reflect this power in a naked sense but as domesticated by reason and aimed at the common good. All rationality, all areas of regulation, must consider the operation of the whole. Balance and harmony reign according to right reason founded ultimately upon the security of God's existence. But what would happen if that security was destroyed? If the close bond between heaven and earth were to be severed and man was to be alone upon the earth? What would happen if philosophy resisted its incorporation with theology and demanded the right to scrutinise all claims to know?[19] Could theology survive such a critical interrogation? Or would it deconstruct? What then would supply the reason behind the power of law to command?

---

19 As Leo Strauss (1953: 74) puts it, the medieval reconciliation of faith and reason was unsustainable:

'Man cannot live without light, guidance, knowledge; only through knowledge of the good can he find the good that he needs. The fundamental question, therefore, is whether men can acquire that knowledge of the good without which they cannot guide their lives individually or collectively by the unaided efforts of their natural powers, or whether they are dependent for that knowledge on divine revelation. No alternative is more fundamental than this: human guidance or divine guidance. The first possibility is characteristic of philosophy or science in the original sense of the term, the second is presented in the Bible. The dilemma cannot be evaded by any harmonisation or synthesis. For both philosophy and the Bible proclaim something as the one thing needful, as the only thing that ultimately counts, and the one thing needful proclaimed by the Bible is the opposite of that proclaimed by philosophy: a life of obedient love versus a life of free insight.'

A CRITICAL NOTE ON THE MYSTIFICATION OF NATURAL LAW AND ITS RELATIONSHIP TO EXISTENTIAL SECURITY

Thomistic natural law has a critical edge. It makes it difficult for rulers to appeal to God in order to assume absolute power since the ruler has authority only to the extent that it has been granted by the natural law. If the ruler goes beyond his competence and tyrannises the people, he oversteps his legitimate authority. As the rulers are also subject to the natural law, the subjects can refuse obedience and may even be justified in starting a rebellion (S T I-II, q 96 a 4).

But how is this law of nature to be 'truthfully' known if we cast out faith in revelation, and allow doubts as to the ability of man's natural reason to uncover sufficient areas of God's plan for the cosmos to be faithfully revealed? Would the results stand scrutiny as natural correlations or would they be simply ideological assertions? Several examples:

(i) Aquinas clearly accepted slavery, defending it on the basis that it simply reflected the natural order and the natural end of certain things:

Slaves do not form part of the people or of the state (S T I-II, q 98 a 6).
The slave is something belonging to his master because he is his instrument (S T I, q 97 a 4).

Whence it is proved that some are slaves according to nature (*De regimine principum*, Bk I, Ch 10).

The state is to reinforce this natural order: ... to everyone is due what is his. Now a thing is said to be his when it is ordered to him, as a slave is to his master (S T I, q 21 a 1).

(ii) Political elitism is naturally ordained. 'Men of superior intelligence are naturally the rulers and masters of others' (*In metaphysicam Aristotelis commentaria, prologus*).

(iii) Women are naturally inferior to men. 'By nature the masculine is better and the feminine worse; and the male rules while the female is subject' (In *IV libros politicorum commentaria*, Lib I, Lect 3, Parma edn vol IV: 377).

To modern sensibilities, Aquinas is investing the empirical order of things with a metaphysical certainty, and a divinised bedrock, it has no 'right' to. Once we see this, the specific contents of these theories of natural law no longer look like revelations of eternal wisdom, providing being and order to creation, but, rather, a rationalisation of those aspects of the contingent order which are currently accepted and a distancing from those that are objected to. In this way, the recourse to a God-given order serves to quell the mystery at the root of this vast contingent world while stilling the philosophical desire to continue on the quest for knowledge. To many moderns – and the second quote at the beginning of this chapter from Nietzsche is a fine example – the theological doctrines of natural law may have served to free men from fear of the cosmos, but subjected them to the power of organised untruth. The thesis of natural law and the natural order offered existential security by refining and domesticating enchanting mystery; modernity was soon to call upon humanity to travel another path – that of separating man from nature and changing mankind's perception of the relationship of nature and law. Instead of law becoming the bridging mechanism joining man's capacity for relative autonomy and self-determination to natural functioning and natural ordering, the jurisprudence of the modern – that of legal positivism – offered mankind the mechanism by which to order social relations on the basis of their modernness – that is, their unnaturalness. The story of that development will occupy much of this text, but suffice to say at this point that the freedom of the modern comes with a price, that of a growing disenchantment and realisation of contingency.

It is true that to call our position in the cosmos contingent is to speak in a modern language and denotes a remarkable transformation. This chapter began with three quotes; the first was an extract from the Book of Revelations, written in a time when the prospect of death weighed heavily upon the author and calling upon us to believe in religion and hope for reconciliation; the second is from the modernist anti-religious writings of Nietzsche blaming religion for subjecting man's desire for truth to the confines of religious ideologies; the final quote offered was from Bertrand Russell advocating contingency. In modernity the unresolved tension in medieval theology between the idea that 'God is the lord of history', and the freedom of the individual to shape his destiny widened as God 'dies the death of a thousand qualifications' (Flew, 1971: 14), to the point where man became the engine of history. Russell called upon us to face a new sense of responsibility, but contemporary scientists, such as the molecular biologist Jacques Monod (who entitled his book *Chance and Necessity*), also call upon us to be aware of the existential price to be paid for the passing of the solace of God's love.

> Man must at last fully awake from his millenary dream; and in doing so, awake to his total solitude, his fundamental isolation. Now does he at last realise that, like a gypsy, he lives on the boundary of an alien world. A world that is deaf to his music, just as indifferent to his hopes as it is to his suffering or his crimes (1972: 172-3).

But, as humanity came out of the middle ages, jurisprudence was to defuse the tension between God's love and God's power by sidelining love to metaphysics and secularising power. The key figure in that transition was to be the Englishman Thomas Hobbes.

CHAPTER 4

THOMAS HOBBES AND THE ORIGINS OF THE IMPERATIVE THEORY OF LAW:
or *mana* transformed into earthly power

From harmony, from heavenly harmony,
This universal frame began:
When nature underneath a heap
Of jarring atoms lay
And could not heave her head,
The tuneful voice was heard from high:
Arise, ye more than dead.
Then cold and hot and moist and dry
In order to their stations leap
And music's power obey.
From harmony, from heavenly harmony,
This universal frame began;
From harmony to harmony
Through all the compass of the notes it ran,
The diapason closing full in man (Dryden, 1687).

What a piece of work is a man: how noble in reason; how infinite in faculty; in form and moving how express and admirable; in action how like an angel; in apprehension how like a god; the beauty of the world, the paragon of animals (Shakespeare, Hamlet, 1604).

THE DIVIDED ATTENTION OF MAN IN THE MEDIAEVAL TRADITION: SHOULD MAN LOOK TO CONTROL THE EVENTS OF THIS WORLD OR SEEK SALVATION IN THE 'OTHER' WORLD OF GOD'S LOVE?

Shakespeare, writing with the rhetoric of the medieval tradition, yet facing the developing humanist ethics of self-expression, gave us a dual image of man. On the one hand man, created in the image of God, was a wondrous being in his natural and uncorrupted state. Rejoice in what man can do; despair at how circumstances abuse him. On the other hand, man was often the victim of a radical inability to choose. How could Hamlet succeed if it was man, and man alone, that was to be asked to restore the balance of the cosmos? Medieval Europe, for all its divisive forces, was united in a theological conception of the cosmos bound together, the world and heaven linked in an unbroken chain of cause, effect and consequence. But while Dryden, as late as 1687, could depict the cosmos joined in musical harmony, worldly events often sounded shrill upon man's ears. Both Platonic and Christianised Aristotelian intellectual structures led man's attention to be torn between the existing world and the other world; while man was told salvation lay outside the cave, he wished to humanise the conditions of the present life. The struggle between the two worlds was intellectual, practical and deadly. Even as the Duke implored Claudio in *Measure for Measure* to remember eschatological reality when faced with temptation – 'Be absolute for death' – death was an all too present feature. Niccolo Machiavelli, an Italian political thinker, was perhaps the first to disregard the spiritual world of eschatology and redemption and to argue that we should concentrate upon avoiding death in the existing world.

THE USURPER MACHIAVELLI: AN EARLY ATTEMPT TO BREAK THE RELIGIOUS CONCEPTION OF NATURAL LAW

Machiavelli (1469–1527) is famous for two, somewhat contrasting, works: *The Discourses* and *The Prince*. In *The Discourses* (now read by several commentators as the first text laying out the ideas for a modern 'civic humanism' or 'civic republicanism') the Roman republic was portrayed approvingly, and rather idealistically, as championing self-government and liberty. *The Discourses* advocated a free republican organisation in which a unifying spirit of purpose was evident which would produce a new individuality – virtu – an ethics free from traditional morality. By contrast, *The Prince* recommended that an absolute monarch be capable of gross deception in order to hang onto power and make his wishes effective; *The Prince* stressed the inevitability of social conflict and the impossibility of removing the division between friend and foe. Weak government was partly a reflection of the types of moral obligations, or normative imagination, official religion encouraged. Christianity placed supreme happiness in humility, lowliness, and contempt for worldly objects, whilst the religions of antiquity (or so Machiavelli argued) had stressed grandeur of soul, strength of body, and various qualities which rendered men formidable. Christianity had made men feeble, causing them to become easy prey to evil-minded men: 'we Italians owe to the Church of Rome and to her priests our having become irreligious and bad ...' While religion was necessary to bind together the common people, to ensure peace and order by placing them in fear of the consequences of disobeying authority, the ruler must not be taken in by religious myths. Religion was really a 'civil' phenomenon, something which should be discussed freed from mythology. The ruler should disguise his true beliefs and intentions, 'to be a great feigner and dissembler ...' The prince must disregard consideration of whether his actions could be called virtuous or vicious, and instead do whatever is required – whatever is appropriate – to the situation he found himself in and which would most quickly and effectively lead to success. Machiavelli's picture of men was harsh and drew upon bitter personal experience.[1]

> ... the question arises: is it better to be loved than feared, or vice versa? I don't doubt that every prince would like to be both; but since it is hard to accommodate these qualities, if you have to make a choice, to be feared is much safer than to be loved. For it is a good general rule about men, that they are ungrateful, fickle, liars and deceivers, fearful of danger and greedy for gain. While you serve their welfare they are all yours, offering their blood, their belongings, their lives, and their children's lives ... so long as the danger is remote. But when the danger is close at hand, they turn against you. Then, any

---

1   Machiavelli was writing in 1513 and until 1512, when the Medici family regained control of Florence and ended its short republican experience, Machiavelli had been one of the leading officers of the republic, working on domestic concerns and the relations with other states.

prince who has relied on their words and has made no other preparations will come to grief; because friendships that are bought at a price, and not with greatness and nobility of soul, may be paid for but they are not acquired, and they cannot be used in time of need. People are less concerned with offending a man who makes himself loved than one who makes himself feared: the reason is that love is a link of obligation which men, because they are rotten, will break any time they think doing so serves their advantage; but fear involves dread of punishment, from which they can never escape ([1513] 1977: 47–8).

Cruelty, leniency, loyalty, all have a place, are valid tactics, or can equally easily be disregarded, depending upon the circumstances. Law does not transcend the nature of man; it is a mere technique of ruling. Social relations are essentially struggles for power:

... there are two ways of fighting, one with laws, the other with force. The first is properly a human method, the second belongs to beasts ... a prince must know how to use both of these two natures, and that one without the other has no lasting effect (*Ibid*: 49–50).

Machiavelli grounded his rejection of theology and Aristotelian philosophy as guides for politics, in a vision of humanity where the products of human activity were seen as natural phenomena subject to laws of nature. Laws, which are sought on their own terms, rather than through methodologies subordinated to religion.[2] The world moves according to laws of birth, growth, change and death. All living things – plants, animals, humans and states of political association – die. Well-organised associations may live longer than disorganised associations but death comes inevitably. Sustainable political associations, however, may be developed if based upon knowledge of natural laws of association, growth, change and decline, and the instability and impermanence, which is the essence of life, thereby partially subdued. Although some guidance from these laws could be relied upon, and thus a technology of ruling could be developed, chance, accident and good fortune all played a part in social relations. The prince requires an uncompromising craft, or *virtu*, to succeed. Unrelated to the Christian virtue, virtu is that self-reliance and firmness of conviction which enables the prince to seize opportunities even when unexpected contingency surprises him; it enables *fortuna* to be subdued.[3]

Fortune is a woman, and if you wish to master her, you must strike and beat her, and you will see that she allows herself to be more easily vanquished by the rash and violent man than by those who proceed more slowly and coldly (*Ibid*: 114).

---

2   Machiavelli's twin foundation was a harshly negative anthropology depicting men and women as steeped in egoism, deception and trickery, combined with a mostly secular conception of government.

3   *Machiavelli's radicalism lies in the fact that he symbolically reduced God to fortuna (or chance)*, which appears as a foe to be conquered. As Leo Strauss reads his message (*Thoughts on Machiavelli*, 1958: 218–223) nature becomes roughly equivalent to a mysterious order, only relatable to as fortuna. One never conquers her, but the wise man appreciates her character. Strauss argues that Machiavelli 'abandoned the teleological understanding of nature and natural necessity for the alternative understanding. He speaks very frequently of 'accidents' but never of 'substances''. Thus Machiavelli warns that although the modern person desires to place the cosmos under human control, the cosmos's nature is unpredictable; thus we must learn to live with 'chance understood as a non-teleological necessity which leaves room for choice and prudence and, therefore, for chance understood as the cause of simply unforeseeable accidents'.

THE ELIZABETHAN IMAGE OF THE COSMOS AS A SETTLED CHAIN OF BEING

Most contemporaries (and indeed the majority of establishment figures for several centuries thereafter) were shocked by Machiavelli's writings. They were taken to advocate a politics of evil: Cardinal Reginald Pole claimed Machiavelli wrote 'with the finger of the devil'.[4] Machiavelli upset the settled (official) image of the cosmos; the picture of a naturally ordered universe arranged in a fixed system of hierarchies, through which the idea of man's original sin, and the hope for his redemption, appeared as poles of darkness and light. Perhaps the real challenge Machiavelli posed was the necessity to face up to the role of force and coercion in politics. If there is no natural harmony in the world, what guarantees that good will win over bad, what ensures ethical politics is correct? Indeed how does one recognise good as opposed to bad? But, to many, questioning assumptions that harmony, balance, and unity underlie the cosmos amounted to courting chaos.[5] Elizabethan literature, for example, the words on 'degree' Shakespeare places in the mouth of Ulysses in Troilus and Cressida, presented images of the great chain of being, so familiar to Aquinas. All the entities of the cosmos are interconnected – the sun, the king, the household, the crops, primogeniture. Chaos is kept at bay by the operation of a superior power; religion dominates the consciousness. Awe and wonder at the mystery of the cosmos and our roles in it find expression in

---

4 Subsequent writings, even if Machiavelli received no mention, were in large part a response to his implication that political association amounted to the coming together of nasty people into unstable and essentially fragmented bodies. Classical Greek writings and the Christian tradition of Augustine and Thomas Aquinas had invested human interaction in political associations with an almost mystical significance. Ernst Kantorowicz identifies a process in the middle ages whereby the religious concept of *corpus mysticum* was transferred from the Church to the idea of empire and then generally to any 'body politic' (1957: 193–272). This process was the work of professional legists centred on the universities in their reading and commentaries focusing upon the *Digest* of Justinian. Political association requires a myth of being; and an appeal to believe in something transcendent is part of the very concept of a mystic body. The supernatural and mystic character which the religious body requires was transferred to ideas of political community. The celebrants of this ritual were legal and jurisprudential experts who delivered 'to the secular polity, as it were, a whiff of incense from another world' (Kantorowicz 1957: 210).

5 The choice is between accepting the Aristotelian thesis of the unity of the good and the indivisibility of ethics and politics, or following Machiavelli in sharply separating these domains and stressing the central role of managing and relating *conflict* in social order. In reality, the two images were not entirely separate. Pocock (1973, 1975, 1985) argues that modern political thought contained both styles of political language, one of which succeeds in imposing itself over time. The language of virtue lost out to the language of *rights*, developed a paradigm of natural right and became expressed in an emerging jurisprudence. Freedom and liberty were expressed in the term *libertas*, but in the new language of the jurists, libertas meant imperium, the freedom to carry out their own laws. The liberty of the citizen consists therefore in the freedom to go about one's business under the protection of the law; conversely, in the republican language, one insists upon liberty in the sense of participation in the government of the state, tied to a conception of man as a political animal who only realised his nature through his activities in the public domain. The historian Quentin Skinner (1978) relates how both the language of the jurists, and the republican language, coexisted in the Italian republic's development, but the language of natural rights came to supplant that of virtue as a tradition of liberalism, emerging with ideas of law conjoined with rights and the subjectivity of individualism, rather than that of the virtuous citizen, took root. Skinner sees Hobbes as the major figure in creating a mode of political reasoning whereby liberty becomes the defence of individual rights.

institutionalised language provided by organised religion, linking awe and fear with a law underlying the structure of order.[6]

THE DIALECTIC OF FEAR AND POWER WHEN THE MEDIAEVAL VIEW WAS UNSETTLED

The earthly order of the Elizabethan synthesis was precarious. On 5 April 1588 came the news that the Spanish Armada had set sail. The shock sent the heavily pregnant wife of Thomas Hobbes, drunkard vicar of Westport, into labour. A son, a new Thomas Hobbes was born (1588-1679). As that Hobbes was later to express it: 'My mother dear did bring forth twins at once, both me, and fear'. Philosophical liberalism was in a real sense founded upon this emotion, and upon Hobbes's desire to preserve his earthly domain against the prospect of death.[7] Hobbes was to develop the perspective running as a submerged intellectual current – that of law as convention, and society as an artefact – in previous writings and give it a new powerful meaning. In the midst of a social order facing the chaos of the English Civil War, Hobbes penned the foundational text of British political philosophy the *Leviathan* (1651), and founded both a dominant political philosophy for modernity, political liberalism, and a new social ethic, self-assertion. The world was to become a site for individuals to follow their desires, to plan their personal and social projects, and to realise their power. Whatever the final power in the cosmos, it was certain, Hobbes stated, that we are in charge of civil society, we could fashion a political instrument to allow us to pursue our ends, our interests. Expansion and progress were possible; but only if we could first create the framework of a stable social order. His

---

6   The Protestant legal writer, Hooker, was a prime example of this thinking. Richard Hooker (1553-1600) was an English theologian and social and political philosopher. His *Laws of Ecclesiastical Polity* are the direct application of the Aristotelianism of Thomas Aquinas to Elizabethan society. Although he enlivened the discussion with picturesque turns of phrase and strong emotions, he was convinced that Aristotelianism was the only path for Christian humanism. By contrast the new natural law of the 17th century (of Grotius, for example) was to found itself upon calculations of enlightened self-interest. Natural law came to lose its association through structural interconnection with the rules laid down by God. But for Hooker, when we look at the world we look through eyes which see all things as signs to our place in the chain of being. The world reflects an underlying order of things which we ought not disturb, for if the harmony of order is disrupted then chaos and destruction will result. 'For we see the whole world and each part thereof so compacted that, as long as each thing performeth only that work which is natural unto it, it thereby preserveth both other things and also itself. Contrariwise, let any principal thing, as the sun the moon any one of the heavens or elements, but once cease or fail or swerve; and how doth not easily conceive that the sequel thereof would be ruin both to itself and whatsoever dependeth on it? And is it possible that man, being not only the noblest creature in the world but even a very world in himself, his transgressing the law of his nature should draw no manner of harm after it?'

7   Most of Hobbes' adult life was spent as tutor and secretary to the Cavendishes, Earls of Devonshire. Scholars have noted how the life experiences of Hobbes (as with John Locke) were exempt from the customary familial relationships; Hobbes lived a life more of contract than affection. Although he was courageous in the writing of unpopular ideas, Hobbes took pride in his efforts to escape any form of physical danger. As well as his self-imposed exile in France while the civil war raged in England, he regularly took large quantities of spirits and threw up to cleanse the system (although he despised drunkenness), played tennis, sang at the top of his voice to exercise his lungs and exorcise the spirits, and even washed regularly. He gave up eating red meat in middle age ... And in an age not noted for the length of the average life expectancy, he lived to be 91.

secret was calculation, the rational calculation of individual humans based on their experience of the human condition. Hobbes agreed with Machiavelli that there are certain rules of nature which must be followed in the making of successful political society – or commonwealth, as Hobbes calls it – and it is through following these rules, as in geometry, and not just practising one's practical skills, as in tennis, that made for success. No one, however, until then, had had enough curiosity or method to ascertain them.[8] But with this knowledge, one could take charge of social organisations and fashion and refashion them as one pleased.[9]

THE POWER RELATIONSHIP INHERENT IN NATURAL RELIGION CONTRASTED WITH THE POWER OF KNOWLEDGE

Machiavelli had upset many by appearing to suggest that religion had a set of natural functions; that religion was, in other words, an ideology, a way of thinking which had positive and negative outcomes, positive and negative effects. This growing 'naturalism' came in time to be the basis of sociology (à la Comte), but in Hobbes's time we witness an infiltration of naturalist views into intellectual structures. Naturalism accepts that there is something to the religious experience, but denies that there is anything over and above nature; and that thus there is no basis for belief in the supernatural, such belief was really a condition of the mind which performed a function in sustaining power in society. Traditional Christianity held that God was ultimately capable of rational proof. God was the site and being of all that we could not know but could understand as power: God was the first designer, whose existence must follow from the fact that the cosmos is ordered; the first cause, since we realise that everything that is has a cause; the first motion; the source of goodness – the site of absolute worth; the totality of perfection; the source, indeed the power, of creation; the being greater than anything we can think of (St Anselm's so-called ontological proof); the goal, or end, of the created order (Erigena's proof); and so forth. In the naturalist perspective, however, it is only an historical contingency that mankind's contemplation of these mysteries – or limits to his knowledge – turned into forms of organised religions, each with particular creeds and 'truth tellers'.

Naturalism accepts a religious orientation as part of human psychology: Hobbes believed it to be founded upon the recognition of the existence of a first cause, and a

---

8   'The skill of making, and maintaining Common-wealths, consisteth in certain Rules, as doth Arithmetique and geometry; not (as Tennis-play) on Practise onely; which Rules, neither poor men have the leisure, nor men that have had the leisure, have hitherto had the curiosity, or the method to find out.' (*Leviathan*, Tuck edn 1991, Ch 21: page 145; further references to this text annotated as L, Ch no: then page no of the Tuck edn).

9   'Though nothing can be immortall, which mortals make; yet, if men had the use of reason they pretend to, their Common-wealths might be secured, at least, from perishing by internal diseases. For by nature of their Institution, they are designed to live, as long as Mankind, or as the Laws of Nature, or as Justice it selfe, which gives them life. Therefore when they come to be dissolved, not by externall violence, but intestine disorder, the fault is not in men, as they are *Matter*, but as they are the *Makers*, and orderers of them. (L 29: 221)

feeling of awe and wonder at the power of such a cause to produce the universe. In the *Leviathan*, Hobbes shocked his readers as he appeared to argue that no inevitable or logical tie exists between this natural religious orientation – feeling awe and dread in the face of our lack of knowledge and power in the face of the absolute – and conventional theism. We cannot know the nature of the first cause, and, when we look at different societies, we note different conventions as to the expression of awe and wonder, in other words different institutionalised structures for adjudicating the meaning given to our natural religious feelings. We see sets of theological language, which, however, are not true beyond an expressive sense: such language is purely emotive in character, and contains no truth values other than those reflecting the position of the speaker(s) (see Ch 31 of the *Leviathan*). The dramatic consequences of this naturalist infiltration into the positioning of law and political organisation can be gauged by ascertaining the phenomenological reality expressed in the religious experience.

First consider Augustine, on his discovery of God as truth:

> Eternal Truth, true love, beloved Eternity – all this my God, you are ... I gazed on you with eyes too weak to resist the dazzle of your splendour. Your light shone upon me in its brilliance, and I thrilled with love and dread alike' (*Confessions*, VII, 10).[10]

God is the only true being, all else can be doubted:

> Far off, I heard your voice saying: 'I am the God who IS' ... and at once I had no cause to doubt. I might more easily have doubted that I was alive than that Truth had being (*St Augustine's Confessions: The Odyssey of Soul*, 1969: 1-3).

Two methodologies were, however, developing which provided the material for Hobbes to counter this experience: the empiricism of Francis Bacon and the rationalism of Rene Descartes.

THE ROLE OF POWER AND KNOWLEDGE IN THE WORK OF FRANCIS BACON:[11] KNOWLEDGE GIVES POWER, BUT REAL KNOWLEDGE ONLY COMES FROM THE EMPIRICAL METHOD

Francis Bacon was the forerunner of the British empirical tradition. Bacon distinguished firmly between knowledge inspired by divine revelation, and knowledge which arose from the senses; only the latter kind of knowledge was truly suitable for bettering conditions in this world. Detached, speculative thought was downplayed in favour of collecting facts through organised and systematic observation and from there deriving

---

10   Also 'What is that light whose gentle beams now and again pierce straight through to my heart, causing me to shudder in awe yet firing me with their warmth? I shudder to feel how different I am from it: yet in so far as I am like it I am aglow with its fire. It is the fire of Wisdom.' (*Confessions*, XI, 9).

11   Born in 1561, the son of Sir Nicholas Bacon, the Lord Keeper of the Great Seal, Bacon entered Cambridge at the age of 12, and was admitted to Gray's Inn at 16. He became a member of Parliament, then of the House of Lords, in time becoming Solicitor General and finally Lord Chancellor. He wrote philosophical works of considerable scope as well as carrying out a full legal and political career.

theories. Bacon's anti-scholasticism led him to reject traditional syllogistic logic as a means of empirical discovery. While inheriting from Plato and Aristotle the notion that the mind is tainted by error and false belief, Bacon held that the source of true knowledge was nature itself, which does not lie. Consequently, the mind has to be purged from all anticipations, conjectures and guesses which are sources of error and impurity. The scientist is to observe the world around him in order to prepare his mind for unbiased interpretations of nature. Nature, according to Bacon, 'bears the signature of God, and it is these, the true forms of things, which are the goal of natural philosophy, and not the false images imposed on things by man's mind' (Hesse, 1964: 143). Thus, Bacon argued for 'the total reconstruction of the sciences, arts and all human knowledge', replacing the authority of religious or philosophical conviction based on the study of the texts of Aristotle, Plato or the Bible – which gave either external authority of revelation or internal authority of reason – with the authority of the senses. We must get rid of all our preconceptions – the idols of the cave, the tribe, the market place, and the theatre[12] – and concern ourselves with 'facts' and facts alone. Facts can be developed from 'experiments', and knowledge inductively built from simple observations of particulars and their series and order. Bacon's method, however, failed to understand the role of an hypothesis, and placed a naive trust in 'facts' as indisputable building blocks. Nevertheless, he dislodged the hold of scholasticism as a scientific methodology by arguing that the only way to improve the conditions of man on this earth was through attainment of real knowledge of empirical natural processes.

THE CONTRASTING APPROACH OF DESCARTES:[13] THE TEST OF SCEPTICISM AND THE TASK OF BUILDING A RATIONALIST STRUCTURE UPON INDUBITABLE TRUTHS

Descartes proposed a new beginning and a new methodology for gaining secure knowledge; we were to build structures of knowledge upon the foundations of those entities which survived the test of thoroughgoing scepticism. Descartes's scepticism was uncompromising. Neither mystical experience nor any apprehension of the 'other' was allowed. In Descartes's narrative, when we doubt everything around us, we go on an introspective voyage in search of that which cannot be doubted to exist, the Archimedean point of the absolute, the source of certainty, and we ultimately reach the bedrock of our own consciousness: 'I think, therefore I am'. Everything else can be

---

12 The *idols of the cave* refer to the limitations of the untrained mind shut in the cave of its own environment of customs and opinions; the *idol of the tribe* is man's preoccupation with the opinions of others; the *idols of the market place* are the words of everyday life which men tend to invest with undue significance; the *idols of the theatre* are grand systematic dogmas of long philosophical treatises wherein we study concepts created by the philosophical system rather than the real world. We must destroy all idols and rebuild on the security of the facts of the world and the world alone.

13 Rene Descartes, often called the father of modern philosophy, was born in Touraine in 1596. Educated in a Jesuit college, he was extremely impressed by the certainty and precision of mathematics as contrasted to the vagueness of philosophy. Descartes, like Bacon, believed it was necessary to destroy much received opinion and start again. But Descartes believed the senses could not be trusted and resolved to build intellectual certainty upon the basic truths of his own reason.

doubted, the only certainty is my consciousness of my own existence. The pure knowing *ego*.[14] Upon this foundation a structure of rationalist certainty can be built.[15]

THE POWER THESE APPROACHES GAVE TO THE HUMAN AGENT WAS IN SHARP CONTRAST TO THE IDEA OF DEPENDENCY INHERENT IN THE MYSTICAL EXPERIENCE OF THE SACRED

Religious experience, by contrast, is based on the presence of something that is more real than I myself and the world of my immediate experience. I, therefore, become relative. The other, God, is the thing to which all else is relative. What is the effect of this upon our human goal, or end, to life, our *telos*? In the sacred consciousness, the end, set by the other, is the reality of existence; while for the profane consciousness, the self is the *ens realissimum*: the self becomes its own end. The world is of interest, not in so far as it can reveal God's plan for us, but so that we can identify opportunities for self-advancement. Profane consciousness sees itself as the centre, the focus of truth, of being; exactly what the religious mode of consciousness believes itself not to be.

The nation state is a specifically modern phenomenon. It is a social arrangement created by man, which takes charge of the affairs of a given geographical area and organises itself upon grounds which it rationally chooses. For the nation state to come out of the consciousness of Christendom, to develop beyond anything the Greek city-states could picture, that sense of human nothingness before the being of God, before the sacred, needed to be abandoned. As the Book of Isaiah described it:

Why, to him nations are but drops from a bucket,
no more than moisture on the scales;
coasts and islands weigh as light as specks of dust ...

---

14 Descartes sought to provide a secure foundation for reason independent of tradition, custom and the vagueness of experience. The new basis was to be man's own reason; only those truths he could know through his own powers. The structure was a system of thought whose various principles were thus true and related in such a way that the mind could move easily from one true principle to another. Mathematics (with the mind's ability to apprehend certain basic truths, for example that $2 + 2 = 4$), intuition (an intellectual vision of such clarity that no doubt is possible) and deduction (the process of reasoning by necessary inference from facts that are known with certainty), provided the methodology. The foundation point - the point which was irreducible after doubting all things - was *cogito ergo sum*, 'I think· therefore I am'. On the basis of this we can deduce that other ideas which we can conceive clearly and distinctly are also true. But what guarantees are there that these ideas are actually true? Ultimately, Descartes has to bring in God as the final guarantee. But this is a defensive, albeit rational, belief necessitated by the need to put some stop to an infinite regression in positing a definite guarantee, otherwise there would be no foundation, no beginning to reason.

15 Note also another consequence of the Descartean methodology: it is anti-historical. The search for absolute certainty is not conducted through an historical analysis of the rise and decline of forms of thinking and substantive beliefs, but by analysis of the abstracted subject engaged within patterns of rational self-assertion. These are the beginnings of a specifically modern consciousness *AND* an abstracted analytical method. Rational thought can be satisfied with an analytical rather than an historical methodology. The current text asserts in contrast to much of modern philosophy, and jurisprudence, that all analysis takes place within, and can only be fully understood as developing out of, a prior synthesis. All thought is contextual.

> All nations dwindle to nothing before him,
> he reckons them mere nothings, less than nought (*Bible*: Isa 40: 15 and 17).

And the Israelites, while promised the status of nationhood, of a future destined for greatness, were also reminded of their dependency ... of the fact, the incontestable reality, that they were as nothing in the face of a power which loomed above all. Which created all ...

> I am the Lord, your Holy One,
> the creator of Israel, your King ...
> I, I am He
> who blots out your transgressions for my own sake,
> and I will not remember your sins ...
> Remember these things, O Jacob,
> and Israel, for you are my servant;
> I formed you, you are my servant;
> O Israel, you will not be forgotten by me.
> I have swept away your transgressions like a cloud,
> and your sins like mist;
> return to me, for I have redeemed you (Isa 43:15, 25, 44:21-22).

How is man to address God? Will the language of Abraham, as he asks permission to pray for the wicked Sodom, suffice: 'May I presume to speak to the Lord, dust and ashes that I am?' And Job,[16] he who was so put upon that he dared question God's reasons and God's power?[17] Job was a good man who sought God, but was nonetheless persecuted and injured by him. Surely God rewards goodness and punishes wickedness; why then was Job subjected to repeated and horrible torments despite his goodness? Job, who had seen the wicked prosper and the virtuous fail, began to doubt God's concern, and dared to ask 'why'? Finally, God broke his divine silence and, employing an ironic, but angry mode, denied Job any right to question how he exercised his power. Hobbes read the passage with a renewed interest, realising there is a vital message conveyed.

> And how bitterly did Job expostulate with God, that being just he should yet be afflicted with so many calamities! God himself with open voice resolved this difficulty in the case of Job and hath confirmed his right by arguments drawn not from Job's sin but by his own power (*The Citizen*, Ch 15 293).

God can command obedience and punish wrong, because of his power rather than because wrong pre-exists God's power; his right is 'drawn not from Job's sin but by his own power'. We cannot resolve the problem of defining evil, of demarcating the legal from the illegal, crime from good, normality from deviancy, by intellectual discussion or uncovering the world's natural structure. Equally, we cannot work out our destiny by following the dictates of our ontology; for our epistemology cannot uncover an ontology that tells us our telos. Our words are but human artefacts, thus, so too are our

---

16 The Hebrew name Job means, equivocally, 'the hated, persecuted one', and 'where is the divine father?'

17 The importance of Job for Hobbes's thought can be seen by recalling that two of his own texts are named after monsters introduced in it: *Leviathan*, the powerful ruler of the sea who 'beholdeth every thing that is high' and is 'king over all the sons of pride', and *Behemoth*, the monster of the land.

demarcation procedures. Are we doomed to epistemological anarchism? Hobbes resolved the disputes as to the nature of being by appealing to a mysterious, omnipotent God, whose power and purposes are simply beyond our finite powers of understanding. God ultimately demands of Job: 'Where wast thou, when I laid the foundation of the earth?' Job is reduced to a state of pathetic dependency:

Naked I came from the womb,
naked I shall return whence I came.
The Lord gives and the Lord takes away;
blessed be the name of the Lord.

Hobbes understood that obedience is founded upon God because he 'hath a right to rule and punish those who break his laws, from his sole irresistible power'.

What was the lesson? God, the mysterious creator of the world, is master of the world he created. Where were we when he created it? Could any of us accomplish that feat? We pale into nothingness by comparison. God's power is irresistible, because (i) we properly fear a being so superior to us that it created the entire world (and could recreate it along entirely different lines if it wished), and (ii) while we cannot understand the point of everything created by God, or every injunction he established to deal with the exigencies of common life between finite and prideful beings, we must, nevertheless, have faith that there is a point to the rules established by such an all-powerful being; (iii) as he will eventually have his way in any event, we might as well follow his word from the start; (iv) we naturally stand in awe of such mystery and invest it with benign qualities to lower our fear.

But what if power transcends all qualities, is neither moral nor amoral, neither kind nor cruel ... what if ... it simply is?

Thus the lesson to be drawn from Job's experience was simple: pure power. It was God's power that determined the way of the cosmos; that determined truth. But what if God's power was simply the workings of nature? Again, what if God's power (the positive, the light, the truth) was the inverse of our lack of power (the absence, the darkness, ignorance)?[18]

Hobbes, that man of fear, is suddenly unafraid ... He will call his master-text *Leviathan* ... by understanding Job's position, Hobbes has answered God back: we can do a deal.

---

18 As Nietzsche's Zarathustra confided: 'But let me reveal my heart to you entirely, my friends: if there were gods how could I endure not to be a god! Hence there are no gods' (1954: 198).

HOBBES CONCEIVES OF A DEAL WITH GOD WHEREBY THE COSMOS IS DIVIDED INTO THE REALMS OF AN EARTHLY SOVEREIGN AND AN ECCLESIASTICAL SOVEREIGN

Hobbes realises that the underlying core of man's relationship with religion is *mana* or *fear of power*.[19] The power of the unknown, the power of the mysterious, the power ... the sheer unknowable power that renders all else a pale being. We have constructed official religions with their elaborate doctrines and chains of authority – and their right to confer authority on the distinctions of the earthly world – out of fear of this power. Out of awe at the mystery of being. We can become modern only by seizing the power which gives rise to awe, by turning it into a power in ourselves.

Who can organise this *mana* in civil society? Not all of us, since we could only contradict each other and chaos result. We need a decision-maker to represent us. The *Sovereign* is the key figure in deciding how this awe should be expressed, and thereby all religion is, in principle, 'civil'. The mystery underlying natural religious experiences requires understanding; to create the knowledge necessary for understanding we need epistemological imagination, and the products of this epistemological methodology include social order. While Hobbes reserves his full epistemological statement for the *Leviathan*,[20] in *De Cive* he held onto the institutional role of faith, claiming that if one had faith in the principles of Christianity, then one accepted the special character of the messages which have been passed down from Christ, via apostolic succession and the official priesthood. Even the sovereign must 'interpret the Holy Scriptures through

---

19 Max Muller was the first to use the term *mana* in European scholarship, referring to a concept at the basis of much of Melanesian and Polynesian life. Muller quoted a letter from the missionary RH Codrington. 'The religion of the Melanesians consists, as far as belief goes, in the persuasion that there is a supernatural power about belonging to the region of the unseen; and, as far as practice goes, in the use of means of getting this power turned to their own benefit. The notion of a Supreme Being is altogether foreign to them, or indeed of any being occupying a very elevated place in their world ... There is a belief in a force altogether distinct from physical power, which acts in all kinds of ways for good and evil, and which it is of the greatest advantage to possess or control. This is *mana* ... It is a power or influence, not physical, and in a way supernatural; but it shows itself in physical force, or in any kind of power or excellence which a man possesses. This *mana* is not fixed in anything, and can be conveyed in almost anything, but spirits, whether disembodied souls or supernatural beings, have it and can impart it; and it essentially belongs to personal beings to originate it, though it may act through the medium of water, or a stone, or a bone. All Melanesian religion consists, in fact, in getting this mana for one's self, or getting it used for one's benefit - all religion, that is, as far as religious practices go, prayers and sacrifices' (RH Codrington, *The Melanesians: Studies in Their Anthropology and Folk-Lore* (Oxford, 1891: 118-19)).

20 Tuck (1991: xvii) considered the central issue for Hobbes was not that in some state of nature our wants and needs were necessarily in conflict, rather: 'The problem which exercised Hobbes, almost alone among theorists of his time, was that even if men are basically self-protective and therefore in principle pacific towards one another, their independence of judgment about the world will lead to conflict. His proposed solution was therefore to eliminate independent judgment about most matters of fact. Natural man, he argued, would see the necessity for everyone to transfer their individual judgment in cases of uncertainty to a common decision-maker, whose opinion about what constitutes a threat would be conclusive ...

The power of Hobbes's sovereign was thus above all an epistemic power, to determine the meanings of words in the public language, and to induce his subjects to agree on what they termed 'good' and 'bad'.'

properly ordained Clergymen' (XVII 28). But man has power in the world. The harmony of mediaeval Christendom is both a bureaucratic structure, made possible by the interpretative power of the organised clergy, and an enchantment, wherein the world is a text in which the signs of God are inscribed. Following Bacon,[21] Hobbes transfers the light of truth from revealed truth to empirical investigation of the natural condition. The idea of guidance, the methodological security, however, is not abandoned. Hobbes finds metaphors from Parmenides and Plato onwards, in which truth gives 'light' and a confidence to act, reasserted in biblical phrases.[22] In transferring the source of light from God's revelation onto reason and nature, Hobbes tries to keep the authority of a single source, while changing the domain. We no longer need to leave the cave, since we are now able to enquire into the shadows and forms, into the deceptions and processes of the shapes of this life. And the chief source of the shapes and images of this world is language.

Hobbes is a nominalist.[23] Words do not have a pure essence, or natural coherence with certain entities in the world. Instead language is a tool, its creations, its structures of meaning, are human artefacts. Hobbes is clear: the moral world is a product of human artifice or creation. Language makes possible a complex culture. But how can a disorganised, confused and chaotic assemblage of signs and significations, a babble of discourses and meanings, a veritable civil war, be avoided? Language reveals itself as a progressive tool, enabling us to create definitions and social artefacts – thus the Sovereign has free rein to define the common rules, the positive law[24] – but can also open itself up to the reflexive analysis which says that because all meaning is humanly created it is actually 'meaningless'. Understanding the nature of language, and its creations, for example texts, offers the hope of progress in that we can fashion texts using them as the basis of constructing a new order. This, however, is a foundation for order that is liable to self-destruction, to auto-deconstruction; texts are not stable entities with fixed meanings, but rather phenomena open to interpretation(s). Additionally, what would prevent attempts by discontented subjects to appeal above the sovereign to a higher power, in the hope that this would guarantee the true or proper meaning to words such as 'right' or 'justice'? Hobbes walked a tightrope: to keep his balance he needed to overcome anarchic tendencies in nominalism and Protestantism, without falling back into the net of Aristotelianism, scholasticism, or 'Popism.' If the meanings given to words are human artefacts, fixed by definition, then our knowledge itself is

---

21 As a young man Hobbes worked for a time inscribing Bacon's dictation. The guarantee for Bacon that the fruits of his observational methodologies were to be accepted as true 'facts' was that God had written his will into the natural process of the world, and he would not deceive us. Late-modern science, even empiricism, is not so trusting.

22 Hobbes quotes phrases such as 'the commandment of the Lord is pure, and giveth light to the eyes'; 'thy word is a lamp unto my paths'; he refers to Christ as 'the true light, that lighteth every man that cometh in the world' (*The Citizen*, Ch 4).

23 '... names have arisen from human invention ... (Hobbes, *On Man* 1991: 38).

24 'We ourselves make the principles - that is, the causes of justice (namely laws and covenants) - whereby it is known what justice or what equity, and their opposites in justice and inequality, are. For before covenants and laws were drawn up, neither justice nor injustice, neither public good nor public evil, was natural among men' (Hobbes, *On Man*, 1991: 42–3).

language-bound and does not reach to the essence of the world; it is created by humans and resides in various theories which meet the requirements of logic and strict definition. Knowledge of moral rules, like knowledge of mathematics, is a consequence of previous stipulations:

> That five shall be the name of so many unities as are contained in two and three taken together ... this assent shall be called knowledge ... In like manner if we remember what it is that is called theft, and what injury; we shall understand by the words themselves, whether it be true that theft is an injury or not (*The Citizen*, 1991: 373–4).

Whatever power of reason we use it cannot penetrate the mystery of God:

> No shape therefore must be assigned to God, for all shape is finite; nor must he be said to be conceived or comprehended by imagination, or any other faculty of our soul; for whatsoever we conceive is finite. For when we say that a thing is infinite we signify nothing really, but the impotency of our own mind (*ibid*: 298–9).

But this may go too far. If we can have no knowledge of God, if all talk of God is empirically meaningless, then there may be no way we can create a secure basis, a legitimation, for drawing the distinctions civil society requires. The positive law would be merely arbitrary. How could it then command respect? A command, by definition, must come from a source authorised to issue it, otherwise it is not a command but a mere demand. We need religion, the task is to reposition its sphere of concern, rather than destroy it completely. Religion provides a form of security. Through God's word as revealed in scripture, and through natural reason, we gain some knowledge.

> It can further be asked how one can know what things God hath commanded. To this question it can be replied, God himself, because he hath made men rational, hath enjoined the following law on them, and hath inscribed it in all hearts: no one shall do unto another that which he should consider inequitable for the other to do to him (*On Man*, 1991: 73).

And how can man know what is natural? Hobbes continues:

> Natural is that which God hath declared to all men by his eternal word born with them, to wit, their natural reason (*ibid*).

Man can use his reason to take command of the conditions of human life. Man must divide his attention between two worlds, represented by the ordinary life of the cave and the transcendent. The latter is to be God's world, the 'other' aspect of existence, while the life of the cave, our reality, is now ours to understand, and to build a secure social order within. Faith cannot be neutrally analysed, hence let it be; social arrangements, on the other hand, can. Thus, build social order upon natural reason.

IN THE *LEVIATHAN*, HOBBES PROPOSES THAT POWER GIVES KNOWLEDGE, AND THE SECRET OF SOCIAL ORDER IS TO CONTROL THE INTERPRETATION OF THE SOCIAL BODY

In the *Leviathan*, Hobbes reneges upon aspects of the deal worked out so carefully in *Elements of Law* and *De Cive*. Whereas faith has a role to play in his earlier work, in which he supports the role of officials of the Church in determining how the impulses of natural religion are to be understood and institutionalised in society, in the *Leviathan* it is the sovereign who has the power to determine the nature of religious belief in society. The crucial development is the clarity with which we now see that *power is the object of natural religion.*[25]

Hobbes begins the *Leviathan* with a description of the basis of natural religion. At first, his discussion appears a mundane rendition of the faculties of man. Chapter 1 concerns sense, and moves on to the imagination – the credentials of empiricism are established, but the stakes are higher. Hobbes's target is the experience of the sacred, of the holy; that mode of apprehension that evokes the consciousness of creaturehood, or of ontological deficiency, in the face of the experiencing of awe and fascination in mystery. The holy is a mystery; it is not some puzzle to be solved but an existential experiencing of the other world, of something so far beyond the ordinary that it can only be a sign of the impregnable other.[26] The creeds of organised religion combat this mystery and tell us its 'truths', but Hobbes is scathing. Instead of the experience being that of transcending the mundane world of the senses and the normal into real truth, the experience is simply the result of forgetting the difference between being awake and dreaming:

> From this ignorance of how to distinguish Dreams, and other strong Fancies, from Vision and Sense, did arise the greatest part of the Religion of the Gentiles in time past, that worshipped Satyres, Fawnes, Nymphs, and the like; and now adayes the opinion that rude people have of Fayries, Ghosts, and Goblins; and of the power of Witches. For as for Witches, I think not that their witchcraft is any real power; but yet that they are justly punished, for the false belief they have, that they can do such mischief, joined with their purpose to do it if they can: their trade being nearer to a new Religion, than to a Craft or Science. And for Fayries and walking Ghosts, the opinion of them has I think been on purpose, either taught, or not confuted, to keep in credit the use of Exorcisms, of Crosses, of Holy Water, and other such inventions of Ghostly men. Nevertheless, there is no doubt but God can make unnatural Apparitions; but that he does it so often, as men need to feare such things, more than they feare the stay, or change, of the course of Nature, which he can also stay, and change, is no point of Christian faith (L, 2: 18).

---

25 This is even more apparent in *On Man (De Homine)* written in 1658 (seven years after *Leviathan*). There, while we still keep a public faith, and thus have a foundation to the cosmos, it is law which guarantees religion, rather than religion which guarantees law. Hobbes is clear that if religion was purely a question for private persons epistemological anarchy would reign, thus 'if religion ... doth not depend on private persons ... it must depend on the laws of the state. And so religion be not philosophy, but rather in all states law; and on that account it is not to be disputed but observed.' Disputes need to be regulated since if we were to seek the answer through scientific knowledge: 'while we are seeing scientific knowledge of those things which do not belong to science, we are destroying faith in God, as much as we have in any of us' (*On Man*, 1991: 72-3).

26 By contrast, in his discussion of religion (L, Ch 12) Hobbes will assert that: 'Seeing there are no signes, nor fruit of religion, but in Man onely; there is no cause to doubt, but that the seed of Religion, is onely in Man ...' Namely, (i) to be 'inquisitive into the cause of events'; (ii) to think that there must be some cause which gives beginning to things; (iii) the faculty of the imagination causes men to create images and entities beyond what he can with sense understand. Man suffers 'anxiety' and 'perpetual feare' where he is ignorant of causes. He feels the 'dark' and invents things to bring light; he creates 'objects', of which there can be no proof.

By laying bare and criticising previously authoritative beliefs, *Leviathan* proposes to offer a true and final understanding of political life. In it, Hobbes discovers the crucial modern truth that no essential order binds men from the origin to the end of all things. For Hobbes, the proof of this truth lies in the evidence of progress itself:

> Time, and Industry, produce every day new knowledge. And as the art of well building, is derived from Principles of Reason, observed by industrious men, that had long studied the nature of materials, and the divers effects of figure, and proportion, long after mankind began (though poorly) to build: So, long after men have begun to constitute Common-wealths, imperfect, and apt to relapse into disorder, there may, Principles of Reason be found out, by industrious meditation, to make their constitution (excepting by externall violence) everlasting. And such are those which I have in this discourse set forth (L, 30: 232).

Hobbes creates his world view piece by piece. The analysis of language in Chapter 4 warns us not to lose ourselves in a false discussion of language forms alone; our concern must be with the world, rather than with modes of representing it. 'There being nothing in the world Universal but names' (L, 4: 26). We need to agree precise definitions and build structures upon them. Above all it is ourselves that we need to understand.[27] When we define actions as good or bad it is a human process at work, a matter of our sociality, rather than our movement to fulfil a natural ordering of the cosmos.

> But whatsoever is the object of man's Appetite or desire; that is it, which he for his part calleth Good: And the object of his Hate, and Aversion, Evill; And of his contempt, Vile and Inconsiderable. For these words of Good, Evill, and Contemptible, are ever used with relation to the person that useth them: There being nothing simply and absolutely so; nor any common Rule of Good and Evil, to be taken from the nature of the objects themselves (L, 6: 39).

How are we to understand our place in the cosmos? What does history tell us? Hobbes calls upon us to reject all traditional forms of natural law; we replace the traditional ideas of a *summum bonum* or *telos* in favour of our own self-assertion and creativity: 'there is no such *Finis ultimis* (utmost ayme) nor *Summum bonum* (greatest Good) as is spoken of in the books of the old Morrall Philosophers' (L, 11: 70). Motion, process, rather than essence, underlies nature. The passions of man, for example, are springs of voluntary motions. Passions are of two kinds: appetite or desire (love), as contrasted to aversion (hate). Deliberation controls our natural appetites and aversions by alerting us to good or bad consequences, or sequels, to our actions. We have a natural criterion of happiness – *felicity*.

> Continuall success in obtaining those things which a man from time to time desireth, that is to say, continuall prospering, is that [which] men call Felicity.

---

27 Hobbes is clear in his discussion of 'the virtues called intellectual, and their defects', that men put together discourses which do not signify any real entities but only the creations of the texts. This may be done in ignorance or by conscious purpose to deceive. Power over others is the result. An example is the scholistic tradition with its doctrines which only the church powerful are supposed to be able to interpret, such as transubstantiation. 'When men write whole volumes of such stuffe, are they not Mad, or intend to make others so?' (L, 8: 59)

Hobbes tells us we are doomed to desire continually:

> For there is no such thing as perpetual Tranquillity of mind, while we live here; because life it selfe is but Motion, and can never be without desire ... (L, 6: 46)

Success is, however, attaining 'power'; 'Good success is Power ... which makes men either feare him, or rely on him' (L, 10: 63). All men share a relentless desire for power: 'a perpetual and restless desire of Power after Power, that ceaseth only in Death'. The process is without end; attaining worldly goods does not satisfy us, as they are the vehicles of power. Attaining a level of power causes the desire for more to develop. This is partly a defensive measure, in that a man requires greater power to guarantee the enjoyment of the goods his past power has brought him. Thus kings need to create laws at home to ensure that their power is safe, and to engage in wars abroad to protect their power and enlarge it (Ch 11). The powerful use religion to create images of 'Lawes', to which they add invented narratives of the future of the world and personal destiny as 'they thought they should best be able to govern others, and make unto themselves the greatest use of their Powers' (Ch 12). To counter this history we need a new beginning; a beginning based on the foundations of 'the natural condition of mankind'.

HOBBES'S SECULAR NATURAL LAW OR 'THE NATURAL RULES OF THE HUMAN CONDITION'[28]

Nature has made (i) men approximately equal in the 'faculties of body and mind'; the differences between men are not so great that one can claim a natural benefit: 'the weakest has strength enough to kill the strongest ... ' (ii) men are equal in their 'hope in the attaining of our Ends'. Men desire the same things, but there is (iii) a relative scarcity of goods. Thus (iv) from the equality of men's abilities and desires, there comes difference, namely, competition, civil war, and pursuit of glory. Men resort to violence and trickery, fraud and deceit, to satisfy their wants and desires. Hobbes draws a telling image of the natural state:

> Hereby it is manifest, that during the time men live without a common Power to keep them all in awe, they are in that condition which is called Warre; and such a warre, as is of every man against every man ... the nature of War, consisteth not in actual fighting; but in the known disposition thereto, during all the time there is no known assurance to the contrary. All other time is Peace (L, 13: 88).

In the natural state, the very fact of the approximate equality of mankind, situated in a world of scarce resources, results in a continual tension, a war of all against all – this situation must be constrained. Since:

> In such a condition, there is no place for Industry; because the fruit thereof is uncertain; and consequently no Culture on the earth; no Navigation, nor use of commodities that may be imported by sea; no commodious Building; no Instruments of moving and

---

28 Hobbes's analytical construction of a picture of man in 'meer Nature' is to provide a foundation for liberal thought through Locke, through Austin's contrast of 'natural association' and 'political association', and is given its modern formulation in HLA Hart's minimum conditions of natural law (*Concept of Law*, 1961: see Chapter 13 of this text).

removing such things as require much force; no Knowledge of the face of the earth; no account of Time; no Arts; no Letters; no Society; and which is worst of all, continuall feare, and danger of violent death; And the life of man, solitary, poore, nasty, brutish, and short (L, 13: 89).

Hobbes argues that the current situation of the Indians of America provides examples of what we once were like. Creating government leads us out of that natural condition, resulting in civilisation and preventing us descending into chaos.[29] It is not that we are born into sin, for without the power of a sovereign, a God, to define sin, nature knows no such thing:

> The Desires, and other Passions of Man, are in themselves no Sin. No more are the Actions, that proceed from those passions, till they know a Law that forbids them: which till Lawes be made they cannot know: nor can any Law be made, till they have agreed upon the person that shall make it (L, 13: 89).

This is a radical claim: before the power to govern there was no justice, no way of demarcating right from wrong, evil from good. In the natural state:

> ... nothing can be Unjust. The notions of Right and Wrong, Justice and Injustice have there no place. Where there is no common Power there is no Law: where no Law, no Injustice. Force, and Fraud, are in warre the two Cardinall vertues. Justice, and Injustice are none of the faculties neither of the Body, nor Mind. If they were they might be in a man that were alone in the world, as well as his Senses, and Passions. They are qualities that relate to men in Society, not Solitude (L, 13: 90).

The passage is of vital importance. It is easily misinterpreted. It has been taken to imply that everything that is legislated by the proper authority, recognised as valid law, is thereby just. That there is no standard outside of legal positivism that can question the justice of valid law. This is nonsense. Hobbes deconstructs the idea of some independent standard to man's social thought which can provide a natural reference to guarantee the validity of our claims as to justice and injustice.[30] There is no such standard. Or, more correctly, the natural state does not provide one, but our understanding of that fact may

---

29 Compare the English writer Locke's image. In Locke's *Two Treatises of Government* (1690) and in his various *Essays* and *Letters* (written between 1667 and 1692), man is viewed as inhabiting a state of nature where he is in full possession of certain basic natural rights (for example, he has the natural right to possess whatever fruits of the earth he comes across) and the compact of government is necessary to secure those rights. The compact of government therefore reinforces naturally existing property rights and protects the rights of 'life, liberty and possessions'. Government is necessary to prevent us falling into chaos. Since the 'pravity of mankind is such that they had rather injuriously prey upon the fruits of other men's labours than take pains to provide for themselves'. Given this natural tendency it is necessary to construct laws to protect property and to encourage the creation of property. 'The necessity of preserving man in the possession of what honest industry has already acquired, and also of preserving their liberty and strength, whereby they may acquire what they further want, obliges men to enter into society with one another; that by mutual assistance and joint force, they may secure unto each other their properties, in the things that contribute to the comforts and happiness of this life.' Thus the major purpose of government is to preserve what we have come to call the operation of civil society: the small scale series of interactions throughout the social body. Government constructs laws 'for the defence of temporal goods', protecting man from 'the rapine and fraud of their fellow citizens ... and from the hostile violence of foreigners' (First Letter, *The Works of John Locke in Ten Volumes*, 1823: 45).

30 I use the phrase deconstruct precisely. As we shall see in later discussion, the work of Hobbes and Hume in this area prefigures the radical deconstructive energies of Jacques Derrida.

itself be such a guiding standard. Our reasoning upon the human condition – a reasoning conducted after the false images and promises of religion have been deconstructed – gives us a frame of reference within which we have criteria of justice and injustice. But there may be others ... Although Hobbes is sceptical of all claims which do not follow the Baconian route, this does not mean that, as society progresses, an increase in the quality and range of human arguments will not ensue. In fact, this is a consequence of Hobbes's theory. All claims to law, all claims to justice, are human, are social; for the purpose of organising society we shall assume there is no world outside of the sociality of the cave. And the justice of our world inside the cave is founded upon an original act of power, on the violence which constrains and keeps in check that other violence which always resides in the absence of violence.[31] The peace of the civilised civil society is based on our understanding of the ever-present potentiality of the violence of civil society.

> The Passions that encline men to peace, are Feare of death; desire of such things as are necessary to commodious living; and a Hope by their Industry to obtain them. And reason suggesteth convenient articles of Peace, upon which men may be drawn to agreement. These articles are they, which otherwise are called the Lawes of Nature ... (L, 13: 90)

Natural law actually consists of a natural right in the natural condition to exercise basic power and preserve life and liberty. The right of nature 'is the liberty each man hath, to use his own power, as he will himselfe, for the preservation of his own Nature ...' Liberty is 'the absence of external Impediments' which hinder a man using his power 'according as his judgment, and reason shall dictate to him' (L, 14: 91). But man realises that part of his natural liberty needs to be given up to avoid the war of the natural state. Reason tells us the first natural law: '*to seek peace, and follow it*'. Then we discern a second natural law: a man is willing, as long as all others are also willing: 'to lay down this right to all things; and be contented with so much liberty against other men, as he would allow other men against himself' (L, 14: 91).

Hobbes's third law of nature concerns contracts. Hobbes appears to argue that a primitive sense of contractual negotiation inheres in individuals in the natural state. This becomes the method by which peace is ensured since there is a third law of nature: 'That men performe their Covenants made without which Covenants are in vain, and but Empty words ...' (L, 15: 100) But this is both natural and unnatural. Nature provides a way of making social links, 'Bonds, by which men are bound, and obliged'; but these bonds need some external force, or evil consequences, to ensure that they are not broken.[32] Men can mutually transfer their rights by contract; contracts provide the

---

31 Hobbes links intimately together the creation of law and its enforcement. Since the legal order begins with the sovereign, justice means the administration of the legal order. *Justice cannot precede the creation of the legal order and retain its meaning as a 'thing of empirical substance'. Put another way, to make an appeal to a justice which is beyond the cave is to invoke metaphysics, now ruled out of the bounds of natural reason.* Although there cannot be a transcendental appeal to such a non-empirical justice, there can be good and bad laws, since the purpose of the legal order is social protection and setting out the conditions for the pursuit of felicity. (The reading of Derrida (1992) on justice follows Hobbes exactly; *cf Force of Law: the 'Mystical foundation of Authority'*.)

32 'Bonds, that have their strength, not from their own Nature, (for nothing is more easily broken than a man's word,) but from Feare of some evill consequence upon the rupture' (L, 14: 93).

methodology for attaining goods, for achieving power. But contracts need a regime of power to be effective. Contracts need the power of a law – and this law needs a fountain of power to exist – to define that justice is the keeping of the contract and injustice the breach of the contract.[33] This is a witches' circle of foundation – legitimation – constitution. Although there may be some natural tendency to use contracts, contracts are of no use unless some power is in existence to enforce them – to punish for breach – but this power is itself created by covenant.

> ... before the names of Just, and Unjust can have place, there must be some coercive Power, to compell men equally to the performance of their Covenants, by the terrour of some punishment, greater than the benefit they expect by the breach of their Covenant; and to make good that Propriety, which by mutuall Contract men acquire, in recompense of the universal Right they abandon: and such power there is none before the erection of a Common-wealth (L, 15: 100–101).

This is also the point where property begins; property is only made possible by the rules of law. There is no natural right to property, since property is a function of legality; hence property is not something which stands against the state, but is created by the state (taxation is not theft in other words!)[34] Property is the artificially conditioned abstinence from interfering with the enjoyment of others over their possessions. But all the habitual restraints that civil society relies upon are created by discipline and the operation of the law.[35]

Hobbes articulates some 19 laws of nature – more properly conclusions concerning what is appropriate to the preservation and defence of man in society[36] – including that no man is his own judge. A mechanism for judging must be constructed: a science, and a power, of 'guilt and innocence'.

---

33 Hobbes calls the natural law of obligation to perform contracts the 'fountain and originall of JUSTICE. For where no Covenant hath preceded, there hath no Right been transferred, and every man has right to everything; and consequently, no action can be Unjust. But when a Covenant is made, then to break it is Unjust: And the definition of INJUSTICE, is no other than *the not performance of Covenant*' (L, 15: 100).

34 A favourite tactic of the new Natural Rights theorists, such as the French political theorist Bodin (1530–1597) before him and Locke (1632–1704) afterwards, was that a natural right to property existed which the state comes into existence to defend. Hobbes argues such a right would be incompatible with the aim of achieving good order underlying our giving up power to the sovereign: 'A fifth doctrine, that tendeth to the dissolution of a commonwealth, is, that every private man has an absolute propriety in his goods; such, as excludeth the right of the sovereign. Every man has indeed a propriety that excludes the right of every other subject: and he has it only from the sovereign power; without the protection whereof, every other man should have equal right to the same. But if the right of the sovereign also be excluded, he cannot perform the office they have put him into, which is, to defend them both from foreign enemies, and from the injuries of another, and consequently there is no longer a commonwealth' (L, Ch 29: 224–5).

35 'So that the nature of Justice, consisteth in keeping of valid Covenants: but the validity of Covenants begins not but with the Constitution of a Civil Power, sufficient to compel men to keep them: And then it is also that Propriety begins' (L, 15: 101).

36 These dictates of reason, men use to call by the name of Lawes; but improperly: for they are but Conclusions, or Theoremes concerning what conduceth to the conservation and defence of themselves: whereas Law, properly is the word of him, that by right hath command over others. But yet if we consider the same Theoremes, as delivered, in the word of God, that by right commandeth all things; then they are properly called Lawes' (L, 15: 111).

HOBBES'S SOLUTION TO THE PROBLEMS OF THE NATURAL CONDITION: THE CREATION OF THE SOVEREIGN: AN ARTIFICIAL BEING, A MORTAL GOD

Men can make themselves into one body – an institution – capable of judging.

> A multitude of men, are made One person, when they are by one man, or by one Person, Represented; so that it be done with the consent of every one of that Multitude in particular. For it is the Unity of the Representor that beareth the Person, and but one person: And unity, cannot otherwise be understood in Multitude (L, 16: 114).

The sovereign will be one institution, one body, but this oneness is artificial – a creation – in reality the sovereign is an institution comprised of the powers given up by the individual members of the society, to act as allowed by the powers given up.[37] The sovereign is created by the event of the social contract. The social contract is the methodology which erects a 'common power' which pacifies the social body and reduces:

> all their Wills, by plurality of voices, unto one Will: which is as much as to say, to appoint one Man, or Assembly of men, to beare their Person ...
> this is more than Consent, or Concord; it is a real Unitie of them all, in one and the same Person, made by Covenant of every man with every man, in such manner, as if every man should say to every man, *I authorise and give up my Right of Governing my selfe, to this man, or to this Assembly of men, on this condition, that thou give up thy right to him, and Authorise all his Actions in like manner.* This done, the Multitude so united in one person, is called a COMMON-WEALTH, in latine CIVITAS. This is the generation of that LEVIATHAN, or rather (to speake more reverently) of the Mortal God, to which we own under the Immortal God, our peace and defence (L, 17: 120).

The essence of the commonwealth is:

> *One Person, of whose Acts a great Multitude, by mutuall Covenants one with another, have made themselves every one the Author, to the end he may use the strength and means of them all, as he shall think expedient, for their Peace and Common Defence* (L, 18: 121).

The relationship of sovereign and subject is thus established. As power is the core, the sovereign cannot bind himself by law, only by some other means. Hobbes is specific:

> The Sovereign of a Common-wealth, be it an Assembly, or one Man, is not Subject to the Civill Lawes. For having power to make, and repeals Lawes, he may when he pleaseth, free himselfe from that subjection, by repealing those laws that trouble him, and making of new; and consequently he was free before. For he is free that can be free when he will: Nor is it possible for any person to be bound by himselfe; because he that can bind, can release; and therefore he that is bound to himself onely, is not bound (L, 26: 184).

---

37 'And because the Multitude naturally is not One, but Many; they cannot be understood for one; but many authors, of everything their representative saith, or doth in their name; Every man giving their common representor, Authority from himselfe in particular; and owning all the actions the representor doth, in case they give him Authority without stint: Otherwise, when they limit him in what, and how farre he shall represent them, none of them owneth more, than they give him commission to Act.

And if the Representative consist of many men, the voyce of the greatest number, must be considered as the voyce of them all' (L, 16: 114).

The sovereign is the social point wherein power resides – power cannot bind itself. If a superior power were to exist, then it would be the sovereign. The sovereign is absolute.

LAW AS THE COMMAND OF THE SOVEREIGN REINFORCED BY POWER

There is no natural moral sense to obey law. Natural law does not guarantee civil law since natural law is but a general tendency; 'qualities that dispose men to peace, and to obedience' (L, 26: 184). Left to their own devices men differ in those substantive qualities they present in their appeals to equity or justice. The moral sense of men is diverse and individualist. However, men have covenanted to obey the power of the sovereign and this power 'obliges men to obey'. Hobbes differentiates between 'commands' 'when a man saith, do this, or do not this, without expecting other reason than the will of him that says it', and 'counsell', 'where a man saith do, and do not do this, and deduceth his reasons from the benefit that arriveth by it to him whom he saith it' (L, Ch 25: 176). While a man 'may be obliged to do what he is Commanded', he cannot be forced to obey counsel (unless through agreement this is turned into the province of command), since the harm or benefit is solely his own. Ultimately 'Law is a Command', and the sovereign has the sole power to determine what is in the interests of the society.[38] It is a declaration or manifestation of the will of him who commands.

Hobbes (Ch 26) then brings in an analysis which prefigures that of the American Legal Realists in the 20th century. First, he recognises the power that the legal officials have in determining the empirical nature of law. 'All laws', for example, 'written, and unwritten, have need of interpretation' (L, Ch 26: 190). This is not a process which can be governed by the books of moral philosophers, but is ultimately the arena of the judge in the particular case. Second, Hobbes differentiates 'human positive laws' from distributive laws (those which determine the rights of every subject) and penal laws. The penal laws lay out the penality, and here Hobbes anticipates the arguments which Kelsen was to give some three centuries later: namely, that the key figures to whom the laws are addressed are actually the legal officials, who have to determine whether breaches have occurred and apply sanctions.

> Penal are those, which declare, what penality shall be inflicted on those who violate the law; and speak to the ministers and officers ordained for execution. For though every one ought to be informed of the punishments ordained beforehand for their transgression; nevertheless the command is not addressed to the delinquent, who can not be supposed will faithfully punish himself, but to public ministers appointed to see the penalty executed (L, Ch 26: 197).

Third, the methodology of command in the commonwealth must obey certain precepts, otherwise it would be contrary to the law of nature (for example, the civil law must be articulated, published – a secret law is not proper).[39]

---

38 To the Christian who believed that the command of the sovereign was against the law of God, Hobbes offered scant comfort: 'go to Christ in martyrdom'.

39 'No Law, made after a Fact done, can make it a Crime ... a Positive Law cannot be taken notice of, before it be made; and therefore cannot be obligatory' (L, 27: 203).

Law must be written, published and exhibit signs that it came from the will of the sovereign; there must be some procedure for recognising proper laws, of distinguishing law from the commands of those not authorised. Law can come about by the tacit adoption of local customary rules by the sovereign, otherwise the law is clearly established by the decree of the sovereign in legislative function or through the judges (Ch 27). Civil laws are a species of rules. Rules enable certainty of expectation, they enable promises to be relied upon, they create social artefacts, they create the sphere of tenable relationship to things we call property. Sovereignty is 'the whole power of prescribing the Rules'.

> Rules, whereby every man may know, what Goods he may enjoy, and what Actions he may doe, without being molested by any of his fellow subjects: And in this men call *Propriety*. For before constitution of Sovereign Power ... all men had right to all things; which necessarily causeth Warre: and therefore this proprieties, being necessary to peace, is the Act of that Power, in order to [ensure] the publique peace. These Rules of Propriety (or *Meum* and *Tuum*) and of *Good, Evil, Lawfull,* and *Unlawfull* in the actions of Subjects, *are the Civill Lawes* (L 18: 125).

Thus the sovereign will is in a sense general, formal – non-substantive. The rule-bound nature of the laws implies that they are no mere expressions of the whim of a personal sovereign (although rules may be created which have very specific effects), rather, we are looking at the creation of a social space for individual activity. The rules enable individuals to create contracts, act out their desires for advancement, for power, for reward, for goods, as long as they operate according to the rules. The sovereign provides the foundation, the Archimedean point whose creation allows a new form of social power – predictability of action amidst strangers, in a new, a modern, civil society – to be evolved. But what does the power of the sovereign depend upon?

Hobbes offers two answers: (i) it depends upon the successful operation of the system which, once constituted, needs to run smoothly. The smooth operation of justice ensures that men do not abandon the condition of civil society and return to the natural state; they do not because it is recognised as not in their self-interest to do so; (ii) it depends upon the populace understanding the rational basis for the sovereign's existence and rights. 'The grounds of these Rights, have rather the need to be diligently, and truly taught; because they cannot be maintained by any Civill Law, or terrour of legall punishment' (L, 30: 232). Modern society is like a house which will only last as long as the materials last; coercion is essential but it needs support, the materials of coercion need to be secured by 'the Principles of Reason'.[40] The foundation of modern sovereignty is the ability of intellectuals to discover and articulate principles of reason,

---

40 Thus the social development of the *Leviathan* is two-fold: the power of the sovereign determines the truth of the competing claims for knowledge, but then accepted knowledge determines the truth sovereignty is founded upon and the power of sovereignty. We have, therefore the beginnings of a power - knowledge, knowledge - power, spiral. The image of the social, the self-image of the society - provided by philosophy, by jurisprudence, by 'sociology' - is a contributing element to control of the social. Not only does it enable a 'purpose' to be installed, it enables the 'normal' to be identified as distinct from the 'deviant'. From Hobbes onwards this is a submerged thread running through the writings of Bentham, Austin, Weber, Kelsen, HLA Hart, and given a reinterpretation in the work of Foucault. It is the foundation of what Gramsci was later to call hegemony, and which the Critical Legal Studies movement identifies as the secret to social control in the modern West.

structures of political philosophy, to create modern jurisprudence, and instruct the populace in its use and rationality. The greatest battle for social stability concerns social opinion. And Hobbes argues that since it has been possible to teach nations the 'great Mysteries of Christian Religion, which are above Reason, there is no difficulty (whilst a Sovereign has his Power entire)' in believing that such a process of education will not succeed (L, 30: 233). But the sovereign must live up to his word: not only is the punishment of innocent subjects against the law of nature, but 'the most common Soldier, may demand the wages of his warrefare, as a debt' (L, 28: 220). If the subjects are to act in a rule-bound and predictable way then the sovereign should see himself in like light.

TO FOUND MODERNITY, MANKIND'S ATTENTION MUST BE FOCUSED UPON PROGRESS AND FEARS OF THIS WORLD, OR *THE NEED TO CONTROL ESCHATOLOGY*

The *Leviathan* has a natural division; the first part consists of discussion of the secular world; the second the nature of a Christian commonwealth. The entire basis of the first section, the creation of the sovereign and subject relation is 'from the principles of nature onely'. But before Hobbes turns to his discussion of Christianity he feels the need to end his secular section with an eschatological image of natural punishment (Ch 31). The secular images of the past (even if we interpret his state of nature as an 'as-if' narrative) need reinforcement; the eschatological narratives – common to religious discourse – must be faced up to and properly understood.

Eschatology is the discourse which offers the final account of life and death; Hobbes is clear that since the effectiveness of the power of the sovereign requires that he has power over life and death, if there were a promise, a reward, of eternal life to come for those who opposed the sovereign, worldly power would be compromised.[41] Thus the promises and hopes for a society founded upon natural reason must be clearly distinguished from those of scripture. Hobbes turns to a detailed argument, the effect of which is to demonstrate that there is no contradiction between the interpretation of scripture and the necessity of civil obligation. Religious belief ultimately becomes a personal matter, insofar as it does not disturb the commonwealth. Hobbes presents an historical narrative in which the English Civil War, although a thing to be feared, had the positive effect of breaking the hold of the dominant religious doctrine and church power. Henceforth, morality was to become a matter of reasoned argument, and faith an inward matter. *Leviathan* is thus a text written full of the hope of a new dawn: a modernity founded upon confidence in the power of reason and the liberality of private faith.

---

41 'The maintenance of Civill Society depending on Justice; and Justice on the power of Life and Death, and other lesse Rewards and Punishments, residing in them that have a Soveraignty of the Common-wealth. *It is impossible a Common-wealth should stand, where any other than the Sovereign, hath a power of giving greater rewards than Life; and of inflicting greater punishments than Death*' (L, 38: 306-7).

CONCLUSION: UNDERSTANDING THE DILEMMA AND THE LEGACY HOBBES LEAVES US WITH

Bacon's message was simple, knowledge can give power – with real knowledge of the empirical conditions of nature's operation, man can effectively intervene and create a new social order. But what if knowledge was determinate upon methodology? Would not different scientific methods – as with the Protestant argument that the individual can bypass the Church hierarchy by personal petitions to God – lead to different results? The Protestant ethic destroys the effectivity of the settled chain of being, even if the image was still retained by popularist legal scholars (such as Hooker) and others, in that God becomes an entity that citizens feel they have the right individually to petition when they are persecuted by the authorities of this world. The loyalty of medieval society – set in chains of reciprocity and hierarchies of being – to lords, king and God, is upset if people can key into a relationship with God directly, or designate their own king. Hobbes constrains the Protestant desire towards subjective knowledge – he retorts that power gives knowledge.

The jurisprudential task was to modernise natural law and stabilise social order in the face of pressures resulting from the decline of mediaevalism. Hobbes ushers in the modern subject-sovereign relationship and provides a new epistemological configuration and legitimacy for the power to command. Positive or human law replaces natural law as a result of the process of naturalisation. The naturalist perspective has disrupted the ontology of God, who has been transformed into an idea which was important for man, and fear of God into a natural function, reflecting the hold of *mana*. When we, as moderns, look at the cosmos it no longer contains a natural message of harmony and position; it is simply a mass of materiality. Who then are we? We are rationally willing subjects (citizens of a commonwealth); the basic building blocks of the social world, who can now look upon the world as the site for our creativity to work upon. But if we break the hold of the Church, of faith in the Great One (God) as the point of focus, we face a disconcerting multiplicity of perspectives. The same process of visualisation which opens up the world as a space for transformation from within, also denotes that the world is not governed by any naturally authoritative perspective or controlling point of view. Hobbes has stabilised this disconcerting multiplicity through the formation of an earthly power – the sovereign – who has taken on the *mana* and roles of the transcendental object as guarantor of the framework of the world view. A new triangle of understandings and concepts has replaced the idea of seeking truth by moving outside the cave to a secure position of truth; these understandings now provide a methodology for transforming life within it. The triangle is (i) the cosmos is now a world of represented objects; (ii) truth is the organising point, but truth cannot be guaranteed by some point outside the cave, other than as an empty transcendental signifier; instead truth is to be gauged by reference to (iii) its adequacy to a subject (for Hobbes, its ability to ensure social order for the sovereign) in the light of its pragmatic performance.[42]

---

42 If scripture is so open to interpretation that order needs to be imposed then what of statutes? The statute is a paradigm of will; of the express will and intention of a sovereign body. But what reason founds this will? Or is it mere power that founds a statute? Can the process itself provide enough foundation? If that is the outcome witnessed in the 20th century, whereby the democratic processes have come to legitimate the power of statute, it was by no means self-evident.

Hobbes substitutes a natural claim or right in place of a natural law, and substitutes will for law, as the starting point of political philosophy and the jurisprudence of modernity.

The solution of the old problems is the beginning of new problems. What will make modernity a success? If 'we' are no longer a natural whole (God's creation) how will 'we' be able to know the difference between success and failure? Hobbes might answer that success will be its own success; once established the state's continual existence will provide its own validity. The actual empirical/historical evolution of the state is of less importance than a rational account of why we need to accept its creation and form. The foundation for authority of the sovereign lies in the covenant of those isolated, calculating individuals who create a Leviathan, a mortal god, an artefact. The strength of the *Leviathan*, the sovereign, is derived from the consent of that multitude which, once given, cannot be revoked – there is no retreat from modernity. Legal relations have come to replace pre-legal social norms (which are themselves materially linked within relations of social hierarchies). We have witnessed a social and ethical transformation: the birth of a liberal society, and the transformation of ethics into legality. Who then is commanding, and who is acting in obedience, when the *sovereign* commands? We all are, in that we have all delegated our power to him. In whose name does the sovereign speak? In the subjects, ours ... or does he?[43] Modern jurisprudence is, in considerable part, an attempt to find and understand sovereignty. Through philosophy, it is made visible. But no sooner is one model created, than it is destroyed through analytical investigation. For, while there are those who define it as a matter of thinking about social facts and pragmatic success (Hobbes, John Austin), later jurisprudential writers (for example HLA Hart) will claim they are either not pure enough in their philosophy, or they are engaged in sociology. While those who seek it in sociology, will criticise the efforts of earlier writers as mere ideology and may be moved to despair of the sovereign ever speaking in the people's name (as with the mature Marx), or will be forced to invest it with a psychology reminiscent of God (as was the case with the French sociologist Emile Durkheim).

Hobbes opens up space for law to become the norm, and legal relations to become implicated into the structure of the state. In time, the state will take on the tasks of administration, enforcement, compliance, and regulation of the social body. Many will dispute its reach; some will despair at its discipline.[44] In the post-modern condition we wonder if the advance of law has rendered the ethical structures of the social body so

---

43 As a contemporary writer expresses it, then is no answer to these issues. 'The republic is a paradoxical artificial creature composed of citizens united only by the authorisation given to one of them to represent them all. Does the sovereign speak in his own name, or in the name of those who empower him? This is an insoluble question with which modern political philosophy will grapple endlessly. It is indeed the sovereign who speaks, but it is the citizens who are speaking through him. He becomes their spokesperson, their persona, their personification. He translates them; therefore he may betray them. They empower him: therefore they may impeach him. The Leviathan is made up only of citizens, calculations, agreements or disputes. In short, it is made up of nothing but social relations. Or rather, thanks to Hobbes and his successors, we are beginning to understand what is meant by social relations, powers, forces, societies' (Latour, 1993: 28).

44 The entire body of the oeuvre of the recent French social theorist Michel Foucault, for example, is a debate concerning the role of law and discipline. For Hobbes, man is fitted for society by discipline, not by nature.

weak as to severely limit their capacity to offer us anything other than a law-and-order society.[45] And, if in searching for guidance we have come back to Hobbes in our current – post-modern – era this may be a direct consequence of the advances Hobbes achieved with his epistemology. Yet he was but a beginning for modernity. Hobbes could not openly state that we were alone in the cosmos; he had still to speak the language of some faith in God. If faith is left out of the Hobbesian system altogether, then order is based upon commands, upon the will of the sovereign, but the Hobbesian sovereign has no rationality – other than the calculating self-interest of the subjects – to confer the intrinsic, obligatory status Hobbes appears to think needs investing in these commands or laws.[46] They can be guaranteed only by coercion, by power. And Hobbes does not totally face up to this tension, for he still bows to the rhetoric of God's existence.[47] But, if we were to lose all faith in God, would not power be stripped of all moral value whatsoever? Would it not simply become the principle of the dynamic, and, thus, the world in no way be naturally ethical or spiritual? Hobbes has torn asunder the chain of being, he has seized mana from the other world – what happened, then, to

---

45 Another way of asking this question is to ask what sort of freedom is the West heading into. The liberty of the 'modern' - since Hobbes - is read as the freedom to enjoy the pursuit of his private goals and gains in material possessions, safe from interference by 'others', and structured by the law (commercial, civil, criminal). The price is to renounce the ideal of freedom of the ancients, that of active participation in collective power (no matter how elitist in practice), since that implies that the person is only an element in the community (rather than a self-sustaining individual). The liberal writer Isaiah Berlin (1969) distinguished between a 'negative' conception of liberty (simply the absence of external controls or coercion), and a 'positive' conception of liberty (the idea of the realisation and accomplishment of a true human nature). To Berlin, the second conception is anti-modern, potentially totalitarian, and cannot be accepted by a true liberal since it requires from man the postulation of the existence of an objective notion of the good life. Thus, the interpretation of the classical republican ideal of liberty as participation in the reality of a communal government cannot be accepted. The historian Quentin Skinner (1978) argues against this conclusion, believing that it is possible to construct an idea of liberty which, while still being negative (in that it rejects a substantive definition of *eudiamonia*), includes the ideals of participation and civic virtue. He re-reads Machiavelli's *Discourse* as proposing a conception of liberty entailing the capacity of men to pursue their proper objectives (their *humori*), at the same time as acknowledging that in order to secure the proper conditions for avoiding coercion and servitude (which make it impossible to exercise individual liberty) it is necessary to practise civic virtue and serve the common good. We are required to practise civic virtue and serve the common good so that we can guarantee the degree of personal liberty which enables us to pursue our personal ends (our personal life-projects); rather than seeing a contradiction between negative and positive liberty Skinner is pointing to their necessary coexistence. Without an idea of the common good and civil participation we are condemned to see the law as a structure without positive meaning; a structure which differentiates us as individuals from each other, but which imprisons as well as it separates. Our accumulation of material success - our felicity - is achieved at the price of imprisoning those who cannot be successful and break the law in the pursuit of their (illegal) felicity.

46 This is precisely the complaint that HLA Hart made against the model of the Imperative Theory he loosely based upon Austin in the opening chapters of the *Concept of Law* (1961). As we shall later argue, Hart's criticism is misplaced in that it neglects the inescapable element of politics which flows as an indivisible chain through Hobbes, Bentham and Austin. Nevertheless, the question remains - what can found authority and survive reflexive analysis?

47 The contrast of the chain of being, of classical and theological tradition, with that of pure individualism is striking. For Oakeshott (1975), the natural law tradition did not completely die, and Hobbes never had a satisfactory or coherent theory of volition. The compromise solution which trends in political philosophy adopted was the union of a reconstituted natural law theory with the 'will' ideas of Hobbes. A union indicated in phrases such as Rousseau's *General Will*, Hegel's *Rational Will*, and Bosanquet's *Real Will*. A revivification of the Stoic natural law theory by grafting onto it a will theory.

nirvana?[48] If, with time, the modern age finds itself disenchanted, perhaps in part it is because the enlightenment seized mana without understanding the (non-understandable) mystery that gave it meaning.

48 While Hobbes lays out the grounds for legal positivism through his use of a naturalist scientific account and his firm championing of positive law (at the expense of the common law), it is too early to call him a legal positivist. He cannot breath the air which Comte (in the 19th century) creates with his total confidence in the power of positive, or scientific, knowledge to find the methods and conditions for a future paradise on earth, nor can Hobbes make a religion of humanity.

CHAPTER 5

DAVID HUME – DEFENDER OF EXPERIENCE AND TRADITION AGAINST THE CLAIMS OF REASON TO GUIDE MODERNITY

Let us become thoroughly sensible of the weakness, blindness, and narrow limits of human reason; let us duly consider its uncertainty and endless contrarieties, even in the subjects of common life and practice; let the errors and deceits of our very senses be set before us; the insuperable difficulties which attend first principles in all systems ... when these topics are displayed in their full light ... who can retain such confidence in this frail faculty of reason as to pay any regard to its determinations in points so sublime, so abstruse, so remote from common life and experience (Philo (the character Hume has represent his own views), in Hume, *Dialogues Concerning Natural Religion*, 1957: 6).

The existence of any being can only be proved by arguments from its cause or its effect; and these arguments are founded entirely on experience ... It is only experience, which teaches us the nature and bounds of cause and effect, and enables us to infer the existence of one object from that of another ... When we run over libraries, persuaded of these principles, what havoc must we make? If we take in our hand any volume – of divinity or school metaphysics, for instance – let us ask, Does it contain any abstract reasoning containing quantity or number? No. Does it contain any experimental reasoning concerning matter of fact and existence? No. Commit it then to the flames, for it can contain nothing but sophistry and illusion (Hume, *Enquiries Concerning Human Understanding*, [1777] 1975: 164-5).

UNDERSTANDING HUME: A NOTE ON THE LITERATURE

The Scottish philosopher/historian/writer David Hume[1] has been revered as perhaps the most eloquent philosopher of the English language, and the man who exposed the

---

1   David Hume was born in Edinburgh in 1711, and his early love of literature indicated to his family that he would not follow their plan for him to become a lawyer. Though he attended the University of Edinburgh, he did not graduate, preferring free study across a range of subjects. His abiding passion lay in literature, philosophy and general historical learning. He spent the years 1734-1737 in France, under conditions of 'rigid frugality,' composing his *Treatise of Human Nature*. When this book appeared in 1739, Hume was disappointed in its reception, remarking later that 'never a literary attempt was more unfortunate', for the book 'fell deadborn from the press ...' His next book, *Essays Moral and Political*, published in 1741-1742, was an immediate success.

Hume then revised his *Treatise*, simplifying or popularising the arguments for the general public, and published it under the new title *An Enquiry Concerning Human Understanding*. Besides his extensive books on the history of England, Hume wrote three other works that were to enhance his fame, namely, *Principles of Morals and Political Discourses*, and, after his death, Adam Smith brought out the book which Hume's friends had advised him not to publish during his lifetime, *Dialogues on Natural Religion*. Smith received more criticism for allowing this book to be published than he did for anything that he himself wrote.

Hume went to France in 1763 as secretary to the British ambassador. His books had given him a substantial reputation on the Continent, and Hume had a mixed relationship with Rousseau, whom Hume later invited to come to live in England when Rousseau was facing hostile criticism in France. The stay was not a very pleasant one, with Rousseau displaying suspicion at every arrangement Hume made for him. For two years, 1767 to 1769, Hume was Under-Secretary of State, and in 1769 he returned to Edinburgh, where his house became a centre for literary and philosophical conversation. He died in Edinburgh in 1776.

pretensions of reason to become the foundation and guide for developing the new society (thereby destroying the ontological thesis of natural law[2]), rather than proposing anything positive for modernity.[3] A radical sceptic in his philosophy, and a conservative in his political and social views, Hume appears at odds with the optimistic trend of the enlightenment.[4] Refusing to build speculative images of future utopias, he turned to history to depict what we are and how we got here (in his lifetime he was recognised as an historian first, a philosopher second). In the tradition of Humean scholarship bequeathed by Kemp Smith (1941), Hume so 'empiricises' man that the scope of knowledge relevant to our concerns (and thus capable of guiding action) should be confined to understanding the sentient and emotional side of man, and we must be suspicious of claims made in the name of reason. Kemp Smith summarises key statements, such as 'Reason is and ought to be the slave of the passions', to depict Hume as arguing that we are truly only within 'Nature's guidance, operating ... not through reason but by way of feeling ...' Hume is seen to present a thoroughgoing naturalism, reducing man to a mere bundle of cause and effect from which all transcendental ideas of morality or the human soul are banished. For Barry Stroud, Hume's central claim is that 'reason, as traditionally understood, has no role in human life' (1978: 14), placing Hume in the conservative strain of common sense philosophers.[5]

These views have become complicated by a mushrooming of Humean scholarship. Many recent interpretations are openly concerned, not with breaking down the texts of Hume — as the analytical tradition has historically done — but with contextualising and understanding the import of his work.[6] Read as a contributor to the jurisprudential

---

2   Hume argued that whatever knowledge we could gain from how things operated - matters of fact - we could not infer directly from that knowledge an answer to the question 'how ought things to be?'

3   As David Faith Norton put it: 'David Hume's philosophy has been exciting responses for nearly 250 years. The overwhelming majority of these responses have been negative, based on the understanding that Hume's philosophy is itself negative, a dogmatically sceptical denial of man's knowledge of truth and value.'

4   Hume has recently been the target of a writer from the Critical Legal Studies movement. In *Legal Theory, Political Theory, and Deconstruction*, Matthew Kramer (1991: 145-6) argues 'conservatism looms as the ideology of particulars. With rage and often with eloquence, conservative thinkers have derided the grand schemes of visionaries who seek to turn politics into an arena of experimentation ... Hume was the philosopher of particularities par excellence.'

5   A position later subjected to criticism by Hegel: 'since the man of common sense makes his appeal to feeling, to the oracle within his breast, he is finished and done with anyone who does not agree; he only has to explain that he has nothing more to say to anyone who does not find and feel the same in himself. In other words, he tramples underfoot the roots of humanity. For it is the nature of humanity to press onward to agreement with others; human nature only really exists in an achieved community of minds. The anti-human, the merely animal, consists in staying within the sphere of feeling, and being able to communicate only at that level.' (*Phenomenology of Spirit*, para 69).

6   To the names of Kemp Smith, or alternatively those who saw only the classic sceptic, recent names have been added such as Duncan Forbes (1975), Donald Livingstone (1984), David Faith Norton (1982), Frederick Whelan (1985), and Alisdair MacIntyre (1988). The result is an increase in perspectives and modalities of understanding, the effect of which is to enrich, as well as make more difficult, the task of coming to grips with Hume. Hume was always a synthesiser in each and every one of his texts, whether they be properly philosophical, for example the *Treatise on Human Nature* (1978 [1739-40]) (all further references to this text annotated as (T, page number), or the *Enquiries* (1975 [1777] (all further references to this work annotated as (E, page number); or essayist, for example The *Histories*, the *Dialogues* (1957) and the *Essays*.

imagination, Hume offers us a way of implicitly understanding why two key underpinnings of the common law – experience and tradition – could survive in the face of the growing potentiality of legal positivism – a developing idea of law as the instrument of rational command, or the structuring of social order via a rational and logical code. In undercutting claims for reason, Hume allows claims for experience and tradition to survive and be 'rationally defended'.

HUME'S RELEVANCE FOR JURISPRUDENCE LIES PARTLY IN HIS DEFENCE OF TRADITION AND EXPERIENCE WHICH WERE IMPLICITLY UNDER ATTACK BY THE HOBBESIAN LEGACY

Hobbes replaced God with the concept of the calculating individual as the natural basis of social order. Modern social order was to be a structure made possible by law – by the commands of the sovereign – authorised by the rational understanding of individuals that such a focus of secular power was required by the indeterminacy of subjectivity facing the 'natural' human condition. In this secular world, the basic unit is the rationally calculating individual who becomes master of his existence and all that he owns. Law is the instrument of human power, the tool of a human subject who begins to loom over the world, subjecting the world to rational analysis, confident in his powers of reasoning, able to build a social structure, a society, through types of law – private and public, civil and criminal – all interconnected. The world becomes a domain of boundless opportunities to be mastered by legality: specifically, contract, property, individuality, and the defence of legal relations via criminal sanction.

Modernity will take its bearings by the desires, reasoning and happiness of individuals who comprise the social body. Law will serve to pacify internally and structure a set of localities – emerging nation-states – by providing a constitutional foundation, a social contract, and through the sovereign so constituted – the constitutional state – law will set out the conditions for social interaction within that terrain.

Hume, however, problematises confidence and optimism in this idea of an emerging modernity which will be both the realm of possibility for the self's desires, and able to be ruled by the free rational self. Although Hume further undermines any remaining link between human reason and faith in God – and thereby aids the process of modernisation – he also undercuts hope in a secure home based upon the structures of Descartean rationality. Hume asks what sort of foundation underpins the idea of a free, rational self who comes to know truths of reason in morals and ethics, and who will create a new social order.

This chapter follows the path of Hume's reasoning in the *Treatise*, specifically, in outline:

(i) Hume attempts to follow strictly the Baconian and Descartean dictates to undercut sceptically all religious or metaphysical idols and replace them with certain truths;

(ii) but he then asks: where are these truths to come from? Hume cannot trust pure reason; he argues that pure reason can tell us nothing of importance about the world; what then are we to use as the foundations of our knowledge of the world? Only facts of observation and experience of the empirical self – but can we trust the security of this basic 'self'?

(iii) Hume seeks a 'self' which is both atomistic and whole, but finds only a confused and confusing mass of impressions and emotions – what is called the self is only an imaginative perception of identity, constructed in symbolic interaction with a whole host of entities in society. Since it cannot offer us security, we must trust the facts of the world. But:

(iv) if the self cannot be trusted, then we cannot trust facts gathered via our sense perceptions either, since it is the self that organises these perceptions. This means we have no way of gaining a sense of certainty – everything is deconstructable – nothing is certain. How are to cope with this understanding?

(v) Hume suggests we have a choice – (a) to retreat to nihilist passivity, and nervous and social breakdown, or (b) to work through the common sense narratives and categories presented by the 'common life'. Hume proposes the second; but in what sort of mood should we locate ourselves in the 'common life'? Hume suggests a mood of mitigated scepticism. Thus:

(vi) we must work within a tradition. All human endeavour, all knowledge, comes out of a social tradition. However, we must also understand that the tradition does not bring us 'truth', in the sense of absolute and undeniable entities of the purity and certainty we desire. We are doomed to exist only with conjectures and guesses, with accepting the tools and methods of our traditions; moreover, it is only by remembering and thinking through our tradition-bound methods and the concepts of our traditions, that we gain an idea of our identity (as people, as individuals, as lawyers, as judges);

(vii) thus, Hume asserts, the rules of justice, the rules of the legal order, are the result of historical processes, of traditions and experiences, and we should hesitate to make dramatic changes merely because we create thereby some appealing logical argument (based, for example, on 'equality'). We need to understand the kinds of knowledge involved in rational arguments, and the limits of such arguments. Conversely,

(viii) if we search for knowledge of the actual operation of the world we may gather empirical facts and use them to guide our process of social construction.

EMERGING METHODOLOGICAL CONCEPTS FOR UNDERSTANDING HUMAN SOCIALITY: INDIVIDUALISM VERSUS HOLISM

As a consequence of this project, Hume offers an imaginative reconstruction of the modern subject which pragmatically straddles the divide between methodological individualism and social holism.

Methodological individualism

The Hobbesian legacy offers social theories built upon methodological individualism, or taking as the basic building block individuals, rather than some collectivity – for example, the *polis* – or a totality – such as seeing the cosmos as the product of God's will. Individuals are deemed to be independent from each other and there is no natural social order. The problem is then *how to harmonise individual wills into a social whole?* Hobbes solves this – intellectually – through the image of the original social contract whereby rational individuals set up a sovereign as the central focus of legitimate power. Yet if religious tradition, myth, and custom, are undercut in favour of a new scientific approach to the basis of the social order, can a rationality be developed to sustain authority, or must naked power be its foundation? Hobbes solves this by postulating that the social order should be based upon individual consent, or, at least the rational understanding that each and every individual would have consented (since the alternative is a war of all on all).[7] The social contract intermixes natural freedom (liberty) with legitimacy, providing us with a narrative of methodological individualism: modern society is created out of the mass of individuals and their wills.

How are we to relate to this artefact?[8] Is the socio-legal constitution merely an instrumental form of social ordering of no value in itself, simply embodying our fears of life without it? Or does this modern socio-legal constitution express societies' morality?

First the *instrumental account*. In the instrumental account the role of law in constituting the social body lies in the creation and thereafter the maintenance of rules (any rules; their moral content is of lesser importance than their effectiveness); the rules stand between the subjects and the social chaos which would result from individual subjectivism. Since the object of this system of rules is the preservation of order, as modernity takes organisational form, the fear of some critics is that those subjected to the rules will lose their individual creativity and become 'mere objects of the administered life' (Adorno and Horkheimer, 1972: 32; more generally Weber, 1984).

The instrumental account – while claiming to be a realistic narrative – was weak in drawing upon the traditions of the past. It overlooked a fundamental aspect of religious experience: the *expressive*. The instrumental account did not provide a significance wherein each person could identify the social body. Would naked calculation prove enough? Or would that mean that a man owed allegiance to his society only if, and as long as, society provided satisfactions for man's needs? What of the position of all those – the majority in early modernity – who were excluded from real participation in the social constitution (women, the property-less, slaves, the 'others'); what would make them accept the position of those more fortunate?

---

7   To repeat the legitimation strategy contained in the Hobbesian social contract: 'every subject is Author of every act the Sovereign doth ... the Consent of a Subject to Sovereign Power, is contained in these words, *I Authorise, or take upon me, all his actions*' (*Leviathan*, Ch 21: 265, 269).

8   Put another way, if through law modern society is constituted (either through some founding document in an act of political will, such as a declaration of independence and written constitution, or slowly, as in the British Constitution) what is our relationship to this constitution?

The beginnings of the expressive tradition

Thus a path was set for an alternative tradition – evolved by the romanticism of Rousseau, joined by Hegel (both discussed in Chapter 7 of this text), and inherited by Marx (discussed in Chapter 10 of this text). In this tradition, the circumstances that man finds himself in belittle him; mankind must aspire to become more than the sorry creatures their behaviour indicates they are. This tradition keeps alive the idea of transcendence; in the name of our 'humanity' we demand that our 'essence' is destined for something other than the empirical context of our arbitrarily restricted lives.

Alternatively we might find grounds for identifying ourselves with society and giving allegiance to it, when it is ours in the sense that it is our creation; that is, when we can see society as the outcome of uplifting desires and senses of ourselves pertaining to our spiritual nature. As Charles Taylor (1979: 113) put it: 'Only a society which was an emanation of free moral will could recover a claim on our allegiance comparable to that of traditional society. For once more society would reflect or embody something of absolute value ... only this would no longer be a cosmic order.'

HUME DENIES THAT WE CAN UNDERSTAND THE TOTALITY OF EXISTENCE THROUGH OUR USE OF REASON ALONE, AND HINTS AT A STRUCTURAL-FUNCTIONAL ACCOUNT OF THE SOCIAL BODY IN WHICH TRADITION AND EXPERIENCE ARE THE IMPORTANT ASPECTS OF SOCIAL PROGRESS

Hume takes three major steps:

(i) he demarcates knowledge of facts from knowledge of ideas and the relations of ideas;

(ii) he deconstructs the claims of 'reason', showing that the only true knowledge we can have of the human condition is gained from observation and experience;

(iii) he proceeds to deconstruct the idea of the self, thereby demonstrating that we have to rely upon a 'social' experience and tradition instead of methodological individualism.

Step one: demarcating knowledge of facts from knowledge of ideas

This was a key idea of the *Treatise* which Hume realised had not come across as clearly as he intended; he therefore stated it more clearly in the *Enquiries*:

All the objects of human reason or enquiry may naturally be divided into two kinds, to wit, *Relations of Ideas*, and *Matters of Fact*. Of the first kind are the sciences of Geometry, Algebra and Arithmetic; and, in short, every affirmation which is either intuitively or demonstratively certain. That *the square of the hypotenuse is equal to the square of the two sides*, is a proposition which expresses the relation between these two figures. That *three times five is equal to the half of thirty*, expresses a relation between these numbers. Propositions of this kind are discoverable by the mere operation of thought, without dependence on what is anywhere existent in the universe …

Matters of fact, which are the second objects of human reason, are not ascertained in the same manner; nor is our evidence of their truth, however great, of like nature with the foregoing. The contrary of every matter of fact is still possible; because it can never imply a contradiction, and is conceived by the mind with the same facility and distinctness, as if ever so comfortable to reality. That the sun will not rise tomorrow is no less intelligible a proposition, and implies no more contradiction than the affirmation, that it will rise (E, IV, pt I: 25-6).

Later commentators refer to this as 'Hume's fork'. Hume asserts that all knowledge falls into one or other of these two mutually exclusive and separate categories. Moreover we should always be clear as to what type of knowledge we are claiming.

First, *knowledge of ideas and of the relations of ideas*, concerns the construction of concepts and the logical relations between concepts; this knowledge of relations of ideas is built on the foundation of propositions which are necessarily true or express necessary truths (such as, a bachelor is an unmarried man), and we test such a structure by asking what follows or what does not follow, what is or is not logically compatible with that statement. The fundamental logical rule is the law of non-contradiction; a thing cannot be both 'A' and 'non-A' at the same time. One cannot both assert 'B' and then build a logical argument in which 'non-B' is asserted; and if you find such an argument it is clear that an internal contradiction has occurred. If so, the argument is clearly flawed. The problem with claims made for this type of knowledge, Hume saw, was that it was very limited in its ability to tell us anything new about the world; since the structure was constructed through a process of logical deduction and avoidance of self-contradiction, valid deductive arguments could never tell us anything more than what was already inherent in the premises of the argument. We assert and build upon such propositions by engaging in detailed logical argument and constructing logical models, but it is difficult to see how the enterprise elucidates anything substantial concerning the world around us. A great number of claims are made, however, for such knowledge, which are in reality either examples of 'reason overstepping its limits', or mere tautologies.

Second, *knowledge of facts* concerns statements relating to the way things actually are in the world, and these can be tested (or attempts made to test them) through checking how they correspond to the state of affairs they purport to represent. This type of knowledge reveals to us how things actually are in the world, but verifying this knowledge is difficult. Hume will demonstrate that the major problem lies in the relationship between observation, the construction of facts, and the logical impossibility of constructing 'laws' based on recurrence of the things we observe (for example, simply because we have never seen a black swan does not mean that tomorrow a black swan will appear; we cannot logically announce a natural physical law that 'all swans are white', all we can say is that 'in our experience – ie as a result of our observations – swans are coloured white'. The fact that the sun has always risen in the morning does not logically determine that the sun will thereby rise tomorrow morning). Hume relied upon this distinction to undercut sceptically many claims to knowledge he saw other writers making.

Step two: deconstruction of the claims of 'abstract reasoning', or pure philosophy, to found the new society

A third of the way through the *Treatise* Hume begins to use the test of scepticism. In introducing 'The sceptical and other systems of philosophy', Hume argues that while 'reason' presents itself as a new dominant system of truth, we can enter inside its structure and show up internal contradictions and the extent to which it takes its foundations on non-rational grounding.

> Reason first appears in possession of the throne, prescribing laws, and imposing maxims, with an absolute sway and authority. Her enemy, therefore, is oblig'd to take shelter under her protection, and by making use of rational arguments to prove the fallaciousness and imbecility of reason, produces, in a manner, a patent under her hand and seal. This patent has at first an authority, proportion'd to the present and immediate authority of reason, from which it is deriv'd. But as it is suppos'd to be contradictory to reason, it gradually diminishes the force of that governing power, and its own at the same time; till at last they both vanish away into nothing, by a regular and just diminution (T, 186-7).

This is what has come lately to be fashionably called deconstruction. Hume's tactic is to infiltrate and internally dismantle the very structure which grants rationalism its strength.[9] Hume had earlier warned that there were many writers who appealed to reason to invoke an image of expertise and trust, to claim that reason replaces ignorance and mythology, thus:

> disputes are multiplied, as if everything was uncertain; and these disputes are managed with the greatest warmth, as if everything was certain.

Instead of a real advance in knowledge, rhetoric is actually the victor:

> Amidst all this bustle 'tis not reason that carries the prize, but eloquence; and no man needs ever despair of gaining proselytes to the most extravagant hypothesis, who has art enough to represent it in any favourable colours. The victory is not gained by the men at arms who manage the pike and the sword; but by the trumpeters, drummers, and musicians of the army' (T, xi – xiv).

By contrast Hume asks us to:

> ... march up directly to the capital or centre of these sciences, to human nature itself; which being once masters of, we may every where else hope for an easy victory ... [Through the exposition] of the principles of human nature, we in effect propose a compleat system of the sciences, built on a foundation almost entirely new, and the only one upon which they can stand with any security.

---

9   The Introduction (T, xiii) begins: 'Nothing is more usual and more natural for those, who pretend to discover anything new to the world in philosophy and the sciences, than to insinuate the praises of their own systems, by decrying all those, which have been advanced before them.' [If we, 18th century men, were] 'content with lamenting that ignorance, which we still lie under in the most important questions, that can come before the tribunal of human reason, there are few, who have an acquaintance with the sciences, that would not readily agree with them.' [But] ''Tis easy for one of judgment and learning, to perceive the weak foundation even of those systems, which have obtained the greatest credit, and have carried their pretensions highest to accurate and profound reasoning. Principles taken on trust, consequences lamely deduced from them, want of coherence in the parts, and of evidence in the whole, these are everywhere to be met with in the systems of the most eminent philosophers, and seem to have drawn disgrace upon philosophy itself.' Hume decries the use of rhetoric by using rhetoric.

Hume here appears to obey all the dictates of enlightenment subjectivism, moving the basis of epistemology onto the shoulders of the subject, man, viewed as a self-contained entity. Moreover:

> as the science of man is the only solid foundation for the other sciences, so the only foundation we can give to this science itself must be laid on experience and observation (T, xvi).[10]

Step three: the deconstruction of the self

If the only real foundation we can trust is one of observation and experience can we trust the self to provide a secure point of reference, and thereby guarantee the process of observation and experience? To ascertain Hume's answer we shall concentrate upon a small passage of the *Treatise*; namely Section VII of Book I; the Conclusion to that book entitled *Of the Understanding*.

Hume begins these pages as if pausing for a momentary breath in the midst of a grand enterprise; it is a moment of reflexivity – of turning the action of critical examination away from the observed world to the subject doing the observing.[11]

> But before I launch out into those immense depths of philosophy, which lie before me, I find myself inclin'd to stop a moment in my present station, and to ponder that voyage which I have undertaken, and which undoubtedly requires the utmost art and industry to be brought to a happy conclusion (T, 263).

Hume began, as usual, with a rationalist conception of the self, but this time he presented the fact of our reliance upon the idea of a coherent 'self' in such a way that we are fully conscious that Hume is not one of those 'certain, beyond the evidence of a demonstration, both of its perfect identity and simplicity' (T, 251).

Hume subjects the concept of the self to the test of experience and observation; he tries to catch his own self through his powers of observation, but finds that he cannot – no distinct impression corresponding to the notion of the 'mind' or the 'self' is encountered. Instead, Hume tells us 'when I enter most intimately into what I call myself ... I can never catch *myself* other than those series of perceptions which are present at that time (T, 252). Thus:

> the mind is a kind of theatre, where several perceptions successively make their appearance; pass, re-pass, glide away, and mingle in an infinite variety of postures and situations ... there is properly no simplicity in it at one time, nor identity in different (T, 253).

---

10 Furthermore, there are certain preconditions, or structural frameworks for the freedom to engage in such 'experience and observation', namely as Hume witnesses from the predominance of Scottish and English writers in the recent rise of scientific studies of human nature, 'a land of tolerance and of liberty'. What this implies is that not only is there the probability of a direct link between metaphysical systems of absolute certainty and intolerant politics, but that the socio-political world may strongly constrain the activities of thought and discussion within it.

11 Having finished his 'examination of the several systems of philosophy, both of the intellectual and natural world', it is 'now time to return to a more close examination of our subject, and to proceed in the accurate anatomy of human nature, having fully explain'd that nature of our judgment and understanding'.

The self is not some secure unified entity, rather it is a site where various messages and impulses pass and re-pass: it cannot serve as secure grounding.

THE RESULT OF OUR SEARCH FOR THE BASIS OF THE MODERN INDIVIDUAL SUBJECT IS UNCERTAINTY AND CONFUSION, RATHER THAN A SECURE FOUNDATION

The absence of this secure grounding in a coherent autonomous self spells trouble; political, personal and epistemological.

Politically, if liberalism, for example, is to be seen as beginning with the work of Locke and Hobbes, both roughly labelled as empiricist, its beginning placed great reliance upon a notion of the individual's private consciousness (a conception of the self) as the foundational basis upon which the political entity of the autonomous individual could be fashioned.[12]

In the absence of such security how can individuals attain authenticity of opinion or desire? Hume explains his own experience:

> I am first affrighted and confounded with that forlorn solitude, in which I am placed in my philosophy, and fancy myself some strange and uncouth monster, who not being able to mingle and unite in society, has been expelled from all human commerce and left utterly abandoned and disconsolate ... When I look abroad, I foresee on every side, dispute, contradiction, anger, calumny and detraction. When I turn my eye inward, I find nothing but doubt and ignorance ... such is my weakness, that I feel all my opinions loosen and fall of themselves, when unsupported by the approbation of others. Every step I take is with hesitation, and every new reflection makes me dread an error and absurdity in my reasoning (T, 264).

As with Plato's allegory of the cave, Hume feels he can only describe the problem through the narrative form asking:

> Can I be sure, that in leaving all established opinions I am following truth; and by what criterion shall I distinguish her, even if fortune shou'd at last guide me on her foot-steps?

---

12 The extent to which this interpretation of Hume's deliberations upon the self undercuts the liberalism of the Lockean legacy can be seen by contrasting its effects with MacPherson's classic summary (1962: 3): 'The possessive character of individualism in the 17th century was found in its conception of the individual as essentially the proprietor of his own person or capacities, owing nothing to society for them. The individual was seen neither as a moral whole, nor as a part of a larger social whole, but as an owner of himself. The relation of ownership, having become for more and more men the critically important relation determining their actual freedom ... was read back into the nature of the individual. The individual, it was thought, is free inasmuch as he is proprietor of his person and capacities. The human essence is freedom from dependence on the wills of others, and freedom is a function of possession.'

Let us remember that John Locke places the reason for men forming society as the protection of their property and yet the basis of private property was the interaction of a self-enclosed 'self' and the objects of the world: 'Though the Earth, and all inferior Creatures be common to all Men, yet every Man has a *Property* in his own *Person*. This no Body has a right to But himself. The *Labour* of his Body, and the *Work* of his Hands, we may say, are properly his. Whatsoever then he removes out of the State that Nature hath provided, and left in, he hath mixed his *Labour* with, and joined to it something that is his own, and thereby makes it his *Property*' (Locke, *Second Treatise*, sec 27).

Hume's narrative does not depict a process where we are guided by an emancipator – the sun goddess or the emancipator from the chains of the cave – who leads us to encounter the being of truth; Hume offers only the companionship of sceptical doubt. As a result:

> After the most accurate and exact of my reasonings, I can give no reason why I shou'd assent to it; and feel nothing but a strong propensity to consider objects strongly in that view under which they appear to me. (T, 266)

The only guide is experience and habit. But this guide upsets us, it causes us to perceive as ridiculous our desire to encounter 'the original and ultimate principle', which has been 'our aim in all our studies and reflections'.

> How must we be disappointed, when we learn that this connection, tie, or energy lies merely in ourselves, and is nothing but the determination of the mind, which is acquired by custom ... (T, 266)

We want to believe that there exist ultimate principles which reside in some realm external to ourselves; but when we analyse this belief 'we either contradict ourselves or talk without meaning'. The meaning we find in the world comes not from some pure realm of Platonic essences, or from God's mind, but from our own intellectual struggles.

This is an amazing assertion. It threatens to overturn whole traditions by stripping them of their foundations. Hume says the difficulty is not perceived in the common life; rather we find the difficulty in 'understanding when it acts alone and according to its most general principles'. When we are absolute in the pursuit of rationality, rationality 'entirely subverts itself, and leaves not the lowest degree of evidence in any meaningful proposition, either in philosophy or in common life'. Ultimately:

> We have, therefore, no choice left but betwixt a false reason and none at all ... I know not what ought to be done ... I can only observe what is commonly done; which is that this difficulty is seldom or never thought of ... (T, 268)

The twin factors of subjectivism and a thoroughgoing search for a rational foundation to our beliefs have now wrought their revenge. The result is intellectual chaos, a multiplicity of impressions without any semblance of sense.

> I am ready to reject all belief and reasoning, and can look upon no opinion even as more probable or likely than another. Where am I, or what? From what causes do I derive my existence, and to what condition shall I return? Whose favour shall I court, and whose anger must I dread? What beings surround me? and on whom have I an influence, or who have any influence upon me? I am confounded with all these questions and begin to fancy myself in the most deplorable condition imaginable, inviron'd with the deepest darkness, and utterly deprived of the use of every member and faculty (T, 269).

CLIMBING OUT OF THE VOID UNDERLYING THE NEW START OF MODERNITY

Thus Hume graphically describes the crisis of grounding or foundationism. We search for an absolute position to secure those calculations which will constitute the intellectual foundations of truly modern institutions but cannot find certainty. Are we doomed to failure? Hume can only sum up:

'Tis happy, therefore, that nature breaks the force of all sceptical arguments in time, and keeps them from having any considerable influence upon the understanding (T, 186-7).

'Nature' intervenes at the ultimate moment of metaphysical absurdity, dispelling the tension by either weakening the intensity of the dilemma or transferring attention to more practical concerns. Hume returns to dining, backgammon, and conversing with friends. He finds himself 'absolutely and necessarily determined to live, and talk, and act like other people in the common affairs of life'.

This return to the common life, and the psychologism which appears to underpin it, provides the point of departure at which Hume is believed by many to despair of reason and to reduce the hopes for a new social order to hope in 'the current of nature', or the natural flow of man's unintended interactions. Hume appears to say that, if we attempt to take control of the world rationally and plan future utopias, or the just society, we are doomed to intellectual incoherence; instead our designs ought to be limited and based upon experience and observation, themselves reliant upon a (non-rational) confidence in the natural operation of the world.

This founds a conservative tradition in that it appears to offer a faith in natural functionalism, wherein the metaphysical faith in God is replaced by faith in the natural operation of institutions and progressive interaction. Politically and economically, the world is better left to spontaneous ordering or the hidden hand of the market to work out the weight of values, rather than attempts to impose our structures of rationality. In philosophy, the subsequent development of epistemology consists, in large part, of of responses to Hume, which attempt to counter the idea of a void or abyss underlying our attempts to find secure intellectual grounding for modernity. Those who believed in the powers of pure reason found champions in Kant[13] (see chapter 6 of this text), and Hegel

---

13 For Kant, Hume had failed by not suspecting the existence of a pure science of reason he 'ran his ship ashore, for safety's sake, landing on scepticism, there to let it lie and rot; whereas my object is rather to give it a pilot, who by means of safe astronomical principles drawn from a knowledge of the globe, and provided with a complete chart and compass, may steer the ship safely, whither he listeth' (1902: 9).

Kant's narrative follows the terminology of Hume, transforming, however, the barren rock of scepticism into 'an island, enclosed by nature itself within unalterable limits. It is the land of truth - enchanting name - surrounded by a wide and stormy ocean, the native home of illusion, where many a fog bank and many a swiftly melting iceberg give the deceptive appearance of farther shores, deluding the adventurous seafarer ever anew with empty hopes, and engaging him in enterprises which he can never abandon and yet is unable to carry to completion' (1965: 257). Kant's own system must also inevitably encounter crises, the occasion which 'we cannot put aside and yet cannot endure. All support here fails us and the greatest perfection, no less than the least perfection, is unsubstantial and baseless for the purely speculative reason, which makes not the least effort to retain either the one or the other and feels indeed no loss in allowing them to vanish entirely' (1965: 513). Ultimately: 'the thing itself is indeed given, but we can have no insight into its nature' (1965: 514).

(see chapter 7 of this text), whilst Nietzsche[14] (see chapter 11) placed this crisis at the very centre of his work.

This problem is at the centre of the so-called crisis of social sciences in late- or post-modernity. It was recognised in Hume's time as the argument that without God there would be no way of guaranteeing our demarcation of good from evil, and ultimately nothing to give human life secure meaning; nihilism threatened.[15] It continues to do so; how is it countered? Hume appeared to advocate a stoic acceptance of some natural flow underlying life's ultimate mystery. The converse argument of Nietzsche – to take courage and create our own 'truths' – has been seen to lead to irrational programmes. An alternative pragmatic solution is that of the later Wittgenstein, who accepts that we will never reach a foundation of absolute truth, thus we simply should work on the basis of one or other system. In *On Certainty* Wittgenstein holds:

> All testing, all confirmation and disconfirmation of a hypothesis takes place already within a system. And this system is not a more or less arbitrary and doubtful point of departure for all our arguments: no, it belongs to the essence of what we call an argument. The system is not so much the point of departure, as the element in which arguments have their life (1969: 16).

THE PRAGMATISM OF HUME'S RETURN TO THE COMMON LIFE

Such a maxim appears very close to Hume's return to the common life. Hume's dictum that philosophy must have stock with the 'gross earthy mixture' of the common life, does not mean, however, that all we can do is analyse the rules and live by them, as Wittgenstein appears to offer (and, it must be admitted, the conservative politics of which Hume claimed 'justice' consisted). For although thought, philosophy, must begin within the common life, after the return to the common life we must recognise:

> ... we can give no reason for our most general and most refined principles, besides our experience of their reality; which is the reason of the mere vulgar, and which required no study at first to have discovered (T, xviii).

---

14 Nietzsche's implicit retort to Hume was that the desire to return to the common life from the crisis was no more than one of the many symptoms of human weakness; a symptom of our inability to rely upon ourselves, a denial that we are alone as individuals and thus must carry the burden of our solitude; a failure to assert our individual will as the ultimate ground for everything, and to realise that we are self-grounded and not constrained by any external order of things. The Nietzschean solution transforms Hume's current of nature into 'an inner will' which he 'designate(s) as "will to power"'. Basing himself upon a critique of Kant, Nietzsche tells us: 'The sore point of Kant's critical philosophy has gradually become visible even to dull eyes: Kant no longer has a right to his distinction "appearance" and "thing-in-itself"' (1967: 300). Pragmatically, Nietzsche holds: 'the categories are "truths" only in the sense that they are conditions of life for us: as Euclidean space is a conditional "truth"' (1967: 278). The image of the abyss is ever present with Nietzsche - it is the remembrance which stimulates Zarathustra in his message that the play of life must continue over this suspension. A message which continually breaks the impasse of the lack of grounding in the 'fact' that 'the criterion of truth resides in the enhancement of the feeling of power' (1967: 290).

15 As Hume lay dying from bowel cancer, the essayist Boswell visited him hoping to find him finally ready to accept God's existence. The patience and stoic resilience with which Hume refused to compromise his position in the face of death greatly depressed Boswell. Not even several bottles of port and visiting a prostitute could lift Boswell's mood!

But our acceptance of the natural ways of the world is mitigated; David Faith Norton calls this a mitigated naturalism to accompany Hume's mitigated scepticism. Scepticism is a moral decision; we need to develop a critical distance from the claims of power. As Hume states in the introduction to the *Treatise*, this decision is not made by those who hold to the 'modern systems of philosophy' – for they instead impose 'their conjectures and hypotheses on the world for the most certain principles' (T, xviii). The proper attitude to such claims is the sceptical one – but the sceptical attitude must itself be guided by an understanding of its social role. That is to say, epistemological scepticism must be socially responsible. It must coexist with social belonging.[16] This return to the common life is not irrational, but eminently rational; it is rational to base one's life and intellectual arguments within the narratives of the social world, exemplified, for Hume, by moral belonging. But the claims of participants in the common life can themselves be subjected to a mitigated scepticism proper to such life.

Thus, we must enjoin the narratives of the social world, for they should serve both as the framework for our aspirations and for the dialogical opponents of our activities. My social existence not only puts me into social interaction with a co-existing range of contemporaries in a geo-economic position, it also connects me with a peculiar form of temporal continuity, an existence in time/space co-ordinates, mediated by recall of the past, strongly felt for Hume in custom, which runs from predecessors to successors. It is a sequence which extends beyond the boundaries of my life, both into the past before my birth and into the future beyond my death.

THE ROLE OF MEMORY AND OF THE NARRATIVES OF SOCIAL LIFE

Hume resolved this instability of the self through postulating an active role for the memory. The memory allows the imagination to shape a series of somewhat related perceptions into a unity to create a fiction of the self, through which order can be made of otherwise chaotic presentations. The fiction of the self is a product of memory, via the faculty of recall and reflection on our past perceptions, which represents them as linked together in a network of relations. The memory, via this act of recall and fictional creation, transforms a 'bundle or collection of different perceptions' into the fiction which provides us with a notion, an idea, representing diverse perceptions into a patterned entity which is the only possibility of continuous identity that there is. What sort of presence then does the self have? Hume stresses that although the belief in the self is a 'natural belief', and thus demanded by the functioning of nature, it is a 'confusion and mistake' to claim it amounts to a real personal identity (T, 254). Moreover, the fiction of the self has another function. For when we do not utilise this fiction 'we are apt to imagine something unknown and mysterious'. In other words use of the fiction of the self, and the reflexive acknowledgment that it is a fiction, saves us from the trap of

---

16 Here Hume is rather conservative seeing the ongoing journey of the intelligent individual as one who defends the ongoing traditions of the time, his non-sceptical moralist positions likewise participate in what Hume presents as the proper narrative of intellectual progress.

metaphysics, that is from the enthusiasm of building a structure upon a falsely asserted true foundation.

Hume is sometimes taken as seeing memory as a passive process – as a mere set of weakened impressions of objects – but Hume makes extensive use of the active process of narration, and the memory as an interactive facility. To narrate is to make sense of entities in life via giving meaning to events, as in the presentation of a story, containing, perhaps, an imposition on the events of the past of a form which they otherwise do not have. Narration is essentially an active process. Hume uses narration in two ways.

First, he uses narration as an essential element of small-scale social interaction, whereby meaning is given to impressions which would otherwise just be relations of quantity, indeed, as the precondition for much of the causation of those quantitative ascriptions. Thus, the receptivity of the individual to his social environment is bound up with his concept of his 'self' and of 'others' which are products of his social and other memories, and of the sets of meaningful behavioural patterns he has absorbed from communication with other people. These include the ideas that a person receives regarding other people's opinions of him and his actions – a feature Hume makes centrally to the notion of reputation. Reputation is, for Hume, a cause of the passions of pride and humility; he calls it a secondary one but in practical terms it is the most important (T, 316-7).[17] Outside of society, and within the context of isolated metaphysical speculation, the scientific methodology of subject-objectification makes the self without meaning. Being inside society means, however, being susceptible to other causalities (influences) not capturable in the terms of an isolated object-subject relationship. Moreover, these reinforce, rather than go against, the skeletal findings of human nature. For since there is no distinct human self there can be no pre-social humanity – since there is no distinct individual mind, but only perceptions associated in various patterns, individual identity is something which is strongly determinate upon social experience, including socially instilled habits of thought and of interpretation of action, ie forms of narrative understanding of relationships in the social world.[18]

---

17 The notion of reputation is placed alongside the notions of character and name, all of which as Hume uses them in the context of his moral psychology, imply a strong concept of self-identity. But the context of these considerations, as opposed to the context of the destructive analysis in the early parts of Book I, is social life.

18 The social reality of identity, contained in the social existence of character and name, of virtue, of pride and humility, is something whose present existence depends upon the understanding derived from the interpersonal associations and interactions of the relationships of life. The individual keeps his character, his name, by behaving in his habitual manner. Through his customary activity, through his conditioned sentiments, his reactions to stimuli, his ongoing social reputation is continued as ascribed identity. The 'heaps and bundles' of the impressions of his activity, are constituted either into the character of an honest man, a man of integrity, or alternatively, by the acts of social memory received and constituted by testimony, precept, habitual understanding, and other modes of social communication. The testimony and opinions of others, are part of the general 'bundle of perceptions' but they also help structure this bundle into coherence. Via sympathy, understood communicatively, the individual stands always within interpersonal relationships which allow him to relate to himself as a participant in those relationships, the essential meanings of which cannot be fixed either from the perspective of some exteriority or from some absolute intuition, but depend themselves upon the performability of their interaction. Prevalent throughout Hume's writings is the absurdity of absolutely new conceptions making sense in social relationships. The mind simply rejects them. So it is that the ascriptions of character draw upon, and are dependent upon, elements of already existing ...

Second, the structure of his writings is usually in narrative form. The central metaphor is that of a voyage. Hume consistently offers more than mere chronicling, rather he puts forward an active narrative implying that all 'events', even when they are considered to be real occurrences of the past, disclose their lack of self-interpretation. We cannot refer to events as such, but only to events under a description, and the description is a function of the narrative the events make up. Hume, after all, begins his various examples with meaningful descriptions which set a coherence to everyday reality by permeating it with narrative – it was, for instance, 'a person who stops short in his journey upon meeting a river in his way' who was the subject of a crucial example. Hume's authenticity lies in his developing and refining narratives which present the process of doing philosophy and analysing the role of understanding in human affairs.[19]

THE ARGUMENT FOR DEMARCATING FACTS AND VALUES, AND BUILDING AN IDEA OF MORAL RELATIONS UPON OUR KNOWLEDGE OF THE REAL FACTS OF NATURAL HISTORY AND THE OPERATION OF THE WORLD

In every system of morality, which I have hitherto met with, I have always remark'd, that the author proceeds for some time in the ordinary way of reasoning, and establishes the being of a God, or makes observations concerning human affairs; when of a sudden I am surpriz'd to find, that instead of the usual copulations of propositions, is, and is not, I meet with no proposition that is not connected with an ought, or an ought not. This change is imperceptible; but is, however, of the last consequence. For as this ought, or ought not, expresses some new relation or affirmation, 'tis necessary that it shou'd be observ'd and explain'd; and at the same time that a reason should be given, for what seems altogether inconceivable, how this new relation can be a deduction from others, which are entirely different from it. But as authors do not commonly use this precaution, I shall presume to recommend it to the readers; and am persuaded, that this small attention wou'd subvert all the vulgar systems of morality, and let us see, that the distinction of vice and virtue is not founded merely on the relations of objects, nor is perceiv'd by reason (T, 469).

So Hume undercuts the ontological thesis of traditional natural law. Hume's message is simple – matters of fact and matters of value are distinct spheres. One cannot deduce an 'ought' from an 'is'. Knowledge about the actual state of affairs of something does not tell us how it ought to be. However, Hume argues, this distinction is not usually drawn.

18...social understanding. This we can call the narratives of social life - those conjunctions of words and expressions that tell us that such and such an activity is fit for such and such an occasion, that present us with images and expectations of behaviour for character and situations, and which mean that the mind has only comfortable impressions when the narratives are followed, and upsetting ones when the narratives break down or when the behaviour we encounter is at odds with the narrative expectation.

19 In *After Virtue*, Alasdair MacIntyre, having introduced the perspective of the human agent as both actor in, and author of, his own story, immediately states the essential sociality of this phenomenon: 'We are never more (and sometimes less) than the co-authors of our own narratives' (1982: 199).

Hume held it was possible to replace the existing transcendental and religious basis of obligation with a 'natural basis', or understanding of the natural operation of the sentiments.[20] In time *scientific knowledge of moral sentiments*, ie a knowledge of psychology and the natural composition of man and his environment, could rationalise and replace the power of religion over public opinion. Man should not look to abstract reason, but recognise the guidance inherent in his passions and natural desire. These, after all, have moulded civil society, and we need a proper understanding of them and use this understanding to guide the institutions of civil and political society.[21]

Thus empirical analysis should structure the imaginative domain: moreover, the enquiries of man should not be directed to obtaining conceptions of the 'whole', but focus instead upon situations of common life and seek knowledge of its guidance. 'True' philosophy is not concerned to give totally encompassing theories, indeed it can only focus upon the empirical appearance and does not plan to tell the whole story; it claims to leave the world ultimately a mystery. As he put it in the conclusion to the *Natural History of Religion*:

> The whole is a riddle, an enigma, an inexplicable mystery. Doubt, uncertainty, suspense of judgment, appear the only result of our most accurate scrutiny concerning this subject.

Yet, in a sense, this is a false 'mystery' — for Hume provides a notion to fill this void: it was 'nature' herself that broke out of the trap of reflexivity in approaching the abyss of reason — what then is this 'nature' and how is it so powerful?

THE SUPPOSITION OF A BENEFICENT NATURE WHICH WORKS BY GRADUAL ACCUMULATION

The idea of 'secret springs and mechanisms' of social life implies we can potentially uncover the operative forms of an underlying determinism[22] and this conception evokes a change in our attitude towards the world — our previous superstitious 'admiration' for the natural order of things is replaced by a more mundane relationship, which sees all objects merely as items governed by relations of cause and effect. Respect, or religious

---

20 Hume is clear that this enterprise implicitly goes against certain forms of power, specifically the religious. In the *Dialogues* he holds that the true use of religion was to take advantage of the psychological situation where 'motives of morality and justice [need reasoned support] but nature compels man to set religion up as a "separate principle"', which inevitably becomes 'only a cover to faction and ambition' (D, 114-5).

21 In the terms of Hume's friend, Adam Smith, both our survival and potential for happiness have not been 'entrusted to the slow and uncertain determinations of our reason ...[but to] original and immediate instincts'. The science of moral sentiments can put the question of obligation on a grounding which is strictly 'empirical'. As Adam Smith specifies it, the question now 'is not concerning a matter of right, if I may say so, but concerning a matter of fact' (1976: 114-5).

22 'The actions of matter, are to be regarded as instances of necessary actions: and whatever is in this respect on the same footing with matter, must be acknowledged to be necessary' (T, 410). Moreover, 'in the communication of their motion, in their attraction and mutual cohesion, there are not the least traces of indifference or liberty. Every object is determined by an absolute fate to a certain degree and direction of its motion, and can no more depart from that precise line, in which it moves, than it can convert itself into an angel, or spirit, or any superior substance' (T, 400).

fear, in the face of mystery is overturned; it is only the weakness of our conceptual and investigative tools which prevent us from uncovering the operative mechanisms of nature.[23]

What then is man? Is man a naturally determined entity? What of free will? Liberty and necessity are reconciled as different sides of the same coin: the determination of the will by motives. Motives, for their part, are presented as causal entities operating within the reality of events. Motives are factors within the pattern of empirical causality; man is part of the flow of the world and the world is to be conceived of naturalistically.[24] There simply is nothing outside the world which can be kept steady and thereby constitute the ultimate frame of reference to understand and rank particulars; instead, the principles of science, for example, the causal principle, perform this function, and sense is made of the world through observing the phenomena of the world with this principle kept constant. This conclusion to modernity's problem of grounding – scientific naturalism – should lead men towards valuing intellectual modesty, encouraging them to moderate their enthusiasms and temper their expectations; expectations otherwise unduly aroused by fictions.

As Livingstone (1988) summarises, Hume presents a picture wherein authority, and in turn social order, is held together by the many and various manifestations of the social consciousness of individuals and the narrative structure of the social whole. Thus, social and political standards exist as a temporal conflux between future and past experiences and ambitions. Ideas and motifs are positioned by narrative recall of the past. As opposed to arguments for the timeless essences of the natural law and social contract positions then current, Hume sees the narrative standards constituting present political and social order as a mixture of the traditional and the contingent; they are not the objects of 'autonomous' reason.

---

23 In applying this to the human personality, Hume appears confident 'of an entire victory ... having proved, that all actions of the will have particular causes' (T, 412). An understanding of human nature is seen as applying the lessons of the physical sciences which Bacon had provided. The causal principle is thus central and if there is a mistake in the causal principle then we have no certainty of knowledge, but if the causal principle is independent of subjective desire we can look forward to an expansion of knowledge and sound improvement in the ordering of human affairs. Hume first subjects the causal principle to sceptical attack but ultimately holds that the causal principle is secure from scepticism because it is not founded in reason but in 'nature'; the structure of the world is not built upon truths of reason but is a variable mass of entities in interaction obeying ultimately only the flow of causality.

24 Donald Livingston observes that 'the ultimate system which Hume officially adopts is pure theism'. Livingston points out, however, that this is no traditional religious theism. (*The Natural History of Religion*, HE Root (ed), Adam and Charles Black, London, 1956 – referred to in the text as *Natural History*, page no – had given a naturalist explanation for man's religious belief, seeing such belief as the result of psychological need.) From observation of the complexity of the world we are led to suppose there is some purpose or design, and from this we are led to the idea of an intelligence which is 'single and undivided'. Thus: 'Even the contrarieties of nature, by discovering themselves everywhere, become proofs of some consistent plan, and establish one single purpose or intention, however inexplicable and incomprehensible' (*Natural History of Religion* p 74, quoted in Livingston (1988). Livingston contends that 'advanced scientific knowledge might well collapse without this belief' seeing this as 'a new and specifically Humean insight'. Whereas 'Newton, Boyle and others had argued that scientific reasoning can provide independent grounds for the belief in a supreme intelligent author, Hume is arguing the other way, that belief in a supreme intelligent author is a ground for scientific thinking' (*ibid*: p 179).

This reliance upon the narrative technique means that Hume is often mixing the descriptive with a confidential prescription.[25] Individual man has only a limited sphere of political interest; the model of the ancient *polis* is not one to which we could aspire. Hume's critique of the arguments for a reconstituted *polis* are presented as fundamentally epistemological: those who recommend it produce ideal visions, produced out of the abstract flight of reason where:

> every man framed the model of a republic; and, however new it was, or fantastical, he was eager in recommending it to his fellow citizens, or even imposing it by force upon them (*The History of England*, Oxford, 1826, vol vii: 136).[26]

Thus Hume refers to the Levellers in the *Enquiry* as 'a kind of political fanatics, which arose from the religious species'. We need a political awareness based upon a proper study of natural history. Not all can personally participate in the political process – instead, we should look to constitutional representation – and we need encompassing rules of justice (law) that establish good authority. The passions of man are capable of moving man with many conflicting feelings requiring subjection to ordered repetition (the control of law). Law, in its turn, is most just when reflecting its growth from the structures of habit and custom – its primary role in normal life is the protection of the rules of property and reinforcement of mutual respect and reciprocity. As man moves away from the restraint of custom and tradition the restraint of law is vital. As Hume expressed it in the *Enquiries*:

> good laws may beget order and moderation in government where the manners and customs have installed little humanity or justice in the tempers of men.

Only in the orderly state, made possible by laws of justice which support the authority of government and which incorporates the natural loyalties of the people, can liberty, commerce, and progress in the social 'ease' of arts and science be possible. Moreover, private happiness, secured through cultivation of private virtues, could only be enabled via such civic foundations. However, the stability of politics was, for Hume, being put at risk by exposure to metaphysical social currents which were at odds with maintaining political stability and the rules of justice.[27]

---

25 The programme for political moderation, a programme for some reliance upon habit, custom, caution and diffidence in reasoning and a critical stance toward all non-evident contentions amount to a programme derived from Hume's analysis of the way the world is. Either that is the case, or Hume's normative stance is but the beginnings of a tradition for modernity, the ultimate foundation of which is a considered act of philosophical choice. Note that Hume does not fall into the logical premises of his 'is'-'ought' trap. He does not base his normative stance upon his possession of a certain number of absolute truths in a positive sense. Indeed his position derives from the sceptical crisis entailing the absence of such truths, but out of this he provides a solution which in itself must amount to some form of claim to a 'truth of Hume's empiricist meta-narrative'.

26 The substance of this argument is reproduced by Popper (1945) in his *The Open Society and its Enemies*.

27 Individual freedom can be best ensured by making clear the relationship between the public and the private worlds in which individuals find themselves. We must not expect too much from the promises of the public, for if we were to commit the fallacy of pinning our hopes and fears upon the external public realm of the politics of state, we would risk losing the moral control we have over our own lives and happiness. It was not the role of government to instruct as to the proper ethical formulation of social order, instead the proper role of the state should be to react to and help further the functional needs of the natural social body - to obey the imperatives of empirical operation and naturalist desire.

OUR VIEW OF JUSTICE OUGHT TO BE BUILT UPON THE CONDITIONS NECESSARY TO DEVELOP SOCIETY GIVEN THE NATURAL CONDITION OF MAN

Ought mankind to dream of a perfect society? Again Hume demands modesty. Movement and gradual reform are possible, perfection through revolution or other events is not; thus 'men must, therefore, endeavour to palliate what they cannot cure'. The framework of contemporary social order, ie the rather rigid rules of justice, is necessary because of certain empirical features of the human condition. Notably, the paucity of nature's means for man's provision; the fact that man is of limited generosity; the harshness of social life, however, is tempered by emotions of sympathy.

> If every man had a tender regard for another, or if nature supplied abundantly all our wants and desires [then] the jealousy of interest, which justice supposes, could no longer take place; [nor says Hume would there be need for the rules of property *per se*] ... increase to a sufficient degree the benevolence of men, or the bounty of nature, and you render justice useless, by supplying its place with much nobler virtues, and more valuable blessings (T, 494).

If we could replace material scarcity with plenty:

> ... or if everyone had the same affection and tender regard for everyone as for himself, justice and injustice would be equally unknown among mankind (T, 485).

The rationalist solution to the problem of justice was simply to produce solutions out of the 'fancies of the imagination', but thereby man would have neither security nor reality. We should turn away from the constructs of the rationalist, instead 'look abroad into the world' and base political and social aspirations upon the real, empirically operative foundations of authority. Authority cannot claim justification by evoking a rationalistically defined essence, but by observable actions in the natural movement of society. We require knowledge of functional integration, wherein:

> ... the happiness and prosperity of mankind [is as] a wall built by many hands, which still raises by each stone which is heaped upon it ... [Society is to be an edifice of happiness] raised by the social virtue of justice ... the building of a vault where every individual stone would fall to the ground [without] the mutual assistance and combination of its corresponding parts (E, 304-5).

This slowly constructed building, the proper societal existence for man, is fragile and constructed over time. Life in it, the progressive social life of modernity, is not so much a question of 'ethical' participation in a common, overarching framework of social identity, but rather a process of studied indifference by individuals which avoids grand universal claims and similar styles of politics. Social movements such as the Levellers – who proposed state intervention over the question of the allocation of property and a politics modelled on participation in a reconstituted *polis*-type republic – offered utopian visions of radical democracy deeply repugnant to Hume. First, Hume felt, their epistemology was wrong; and not only wrong, but unnecessary. We ought to throw out the motif of rationalism from any legitimation strategies. Second, we ought to be cautious in the face of the rhetoric of progress and utopia. Even if some 'progressive' faith in man could be shared in moments of optimism, there was great danger in change; we need tradition and authority.

Rather than optimistic and heady calls for participation and freedom, Hume's response can, retrospectively, be summed up in one word: institutionalism. Institutionalism represented the gradual victory of political moderation; the denial of party political fanaticism and a process which retained certain of the mechanisms of past legitimation strategies for authority in that it placed the citizen's primary duty solely in terms of maintaining the rules of justice: in particular the rules of property and the established legal rights of citizens.

SOCIAL INSTITUTIONS DISCIPLINE MANKIND INTO SETTLED HABITS OF BEHAVIOUR

Human actions, beliefs, and political power need to be regulated, positioned, engaged in frameworks and located amidst rules and patterned expectations. In a broad sense, acceptable ('moral') behaviour is only possible within a structured society, and, combined with what Hume terms 'the principle of parsimony' (which here means that we have a natural disposition to respect established authority and be economical with our political enthusiasm) providing systematic frameworks for social life will enable social stability.

Hume claims that history, as Book III of the *Treatise* outlines, demonstrates that liberty, commerce, refinement and progress in the arts and sciences have arisen only in countries with good laws and constitutions; thus there is an historically demonstrable relationship between these two variables.[28] The free society will be the society of good laws and disciplined citizens who have learnt to control their passions and desires.

One current of the 18th century was to use history to bring about societal changes, to help generate the kinds of upheaval of which the French Revolution stands as the supreme example. Hume labelled this use of history a branch of polemics giving sanction to political conflict, a fictitious history which wove webs of dreams and utopias. History 'ought' to be 'scientific', and real historical analysis, conceived as a study of growth and development, could in turn become a counter-revolutionary force; a 'philosophic history' in the service of a politics of moderation. Here Hume, as Duncan Forbes brings out, differed from the other key writers of the Scottish enlightenment in appearing to lack a degree of 'sociological sophistication'. Hume allowed a greater role for chance,

---

28 Duncan Forbes reads Hume as offering the contrast between 'modern regular government and medieval irregular government, where the personality of the king was all-important, and respect for the rule of law, as such, weak or non-existent. In such circumstances men who would have made excellent kings in a modern monarchy were bad kings'. Forbes (1979: 94–109) suggests Hume as 'a remote ancestor, in a general sort of way, of Max Weber's essentially bureaucratic modern state'.

accident, and the intentions of key actors in politics than a structuralist sociology, ie a thoroughgoing in-depth deterministic approach, would have allowed.[29]

Man's choices are empirically explicable within the 'natural' product that is society. Moreover, although the rules of justice are 'artificial', this is an artificiality that has 'naturally' come about and owes its necessity to natural processes. The necessity for the rules of justice is not a rationally consequentialist argument, whereby man chooses, as in a contract, as a mass act of will, but rather as a participant in the machinery of social change. However, this understanding of participation in natural depth can itself be conservative. If the constitution of the rules of justice was a process of utility, then man could freely change the rules of justice as his abstract arguments from utility led him, but there is an almost unchangeable image to Hume's conception of the rules of justice. Nihilism is denied but the price is a recourse to an ideology of assumed function for the affairs of the world. Since society has come about as a natural product, its structure is essentially superior to those ideas of social organisation which any rationalist approach could give us.[30]

What then are we to be guided by? The natural bonding of society flows out of the interaction of everyday life, and operates best when the naturalness of sympathy is undistorted by rationalist speculation. 'The question of government' is not the arena of pure reason, 'vulgar sense and slight experience are sufficient' (E, 195). Social justice is

---

29   This difference is ambiguous, for, on the one hand, Hume appears to have had some aversion to the very idea that sufficient knowledge of the 'reality' of determinism could ever be arrived at, that would enable such a structural analysis of history as Marx was later to provide, and yet, on the other, he feels the need to state that there must be some scheme of natural flow, even if we are never to be a party to it. The first can give us a notion of history as resulting from decisions that men, both as individuals and temporary groupings, have carried out, rather than presenting these men as arriving at decisions resulting from intentional states implicit and understandable in their nature as objects where these intentions result from causal conditions - which must be carried out and are inexorably fulfilled by man. Man thus becomes the tool of other forces. Hume cannot, however, be seen as a champion of radical openness in human affairs, as an early proponent of the 'pragmatic' contingency of human affairs - the demand to give a proper foundation inherent in empiricism becomes too strong.

30   A key example is the idea of distributing property according to the principle of desert, as opposed to the Humean defence of present possession (lawful possession, that is). In the *Treatise*, Hume had suggested that the sentiment of sympathy would lead men to consider equality-type considerations (his own version was that a deserving man would be given goods over an undeserving man), however, this appears as an anomaly to the rigidity of the rules. In the *Enquiries* Hume considered the rationalist imagination as giving rise to social change by inducing men to pursue an abstract ideal - again that of distribution by desert. 'A creature, possessed of reason, but unacquainted with human nature, deliberates with himself what rules of justice or property would best promote public interest, and establish peace and security among mankind: His most obvious thought would be, to assign the largest possessions to the most extensive virtue, and give everyone the power of doing good, proportioned to his inclination. In a perfect theocracy, where a being, infinitely intelligent, governs by particular volitions, this rule would certainly have place, and might serve to the wisest purposes: but were mankind to execute such a law: so great is the uncertainty of merit, both from its natural obscurity, and from the self-conceit of each individual, that no determinate rule of conduct would ever result from it: and the total dissolution of society must be the immediate consequence' (E, 192-3). Hume thus gives some recognition to the argument from desert, but counterposes arguments based upon his 'empirical' knowledge of human nature and the events of history - his overturning of the *Treatise* position, where in the conflict between sympathy and justice, justice wins, may reflect his growing concern with historical analysis. It can also be seen as an argument showing that the use of reason must necessarily take place in an imperfect world and be combined with the evidence of empirical investigations.

not something which has its foundation in a body of first principles, but is basically adherence to the evolved rules of social life, in particular the 'abstaining from the possessions of others' (T, 489), and adjudicating questions of justice is to concern oneself with pragmatic issues of social behaviour.[31] Although the 'remedy' to the problem of 'justice … is not deriv'd [directly] from nature, but from artifice', the reality is that:

> nature provides a remedy in the judgment and understanding for what is irregular and incommodious in her affections (T, 489).

As opposed to social contract theorists, the 'convention [of justice] is not of the nature of a promise' but comes out of 'a general sense of common interest': the actual mutual expression of which may produce resolutions in the nature of a promise, but any conception of a 'state of nature' out of which man contracted 'is to be regarded as a mere fiction' similar to the notion of 'the golden age' which Hume refers to as an invented poetical notion. Reliance upon the notion of an original state, or state of nature is, for Hume, an alternative usage of the golden age motif.[32]

We have seen that to those 'liberal' writers of the 17th century who are often thought of as Hume's predecessors, 'civil society' – modernity's early presentation of a concept for self-understanding – came about as a sudden act of individuals in pursuit of

---

31 Justice, 'a general peace and order' or 'a general abstinence from the possessions of others', reflects the self-interest of each person who desires to be secure in person and property. This security and happiness can be achieved only in society in an arrangement of justice and, to an extent, justice is a reflection of self-interest. The usefulness of justice is that it satisfies self-interest. Thus, Hume claims, public utility is the sole origin of justice, and that reflections on the beneficial consequences of this virtue are the sole foundation of its merit. But although social utility or self-interest drives men into society or into a scheme of justice, it is something besides self-interest which provides the moral basis for justice. The moral quality of justice is not founded on self-interest but rather the sentiment of sympathy. We condemn injustice not only when our own personal interests are involved but also whenever it produces pain or disagreeableness in others which we can share through sympathy. 'Thus, self-interest is the original motive to the establishment of justice: but a sympathy with public interest is the source of the moral approbation which attends that virtue.'

32 Hume draws us into a distrust for rationalist approaches to the notion of justice by the rhetorical use of a social principle of parsimony – he states that if the 'rule' of justice 'be very abstruse, and of difficult invention' then society must 'be esteem'd in a manner accidental, and the effect of many ages'. Hume's position is that a low degree of rational speculation is required to grasp the concept of justice, for the rule of justice is nothing other than 'the rule for the stability of possession'; a 'simple and obvious' position such 'that every parent, in order to preserve peace among his children, must establish it; and that these first rudiments of justice must every day be improved, as the society enlarges' (T, 489). Man's natural condition requires such rules of justice, since what is 'to be regarded as certain, is that it is only from the selfishness and confin'd generosity of men, along with the scanty provision nature has made for his wants, that justice derives its origin' (T, 495). Although the operation of justice may involve articulation of those principles which assume the character of universality and generality, these, important as they may become for the continual operation of the system of justice, cannot be considered essential to its origins or its actual binding force: since "tis certain that the imagination is more affected by what is particular than by what is general: and that the sentiments are moved with difficulty, when their objects are, in any degree, loose and undetermined' (T, 580). Defence of the institution of justice is essential and this is superior to the possible wrongness of the particular: 'Whereas a single act of justice, considered in itself, may often be contrary to the public good … 'tis the concurrence of mankind, in a general scheme or system of action, which is advantageous'. Thus 'before any tribunal of justice' it may be 'an instance of humanity to decide contrary to the laws of justice … the whole scheme, however, of law and justice is advantageous to the society' (T, 589). Further, once the rules of justice have been established they are 'naturally attended with a strong sentiment of morals; which can proceed from nothing but our sympathy with the interests of society' (T, 579–80, emphasis in the original).

individual ends. But for Hume there is no sudden decision – no break with the slow and gradual processes of nature. Instead the performance of the virtue of justice, ie obedience to the rules of justice, is best conceived of as lying inside the gradual flow of nature which has operated through a vast amount of individual human actions. Nature has performed the task with great subtlety since these 'rules by which property, right and obligation are determined, have in them, no marks of a natural origin, but many of artifice and contrivance'. They appear 'too numerous to have proceeded from nature' and 'are changeable by human laws', yet 'all of them have a direct and evident tendency to public good, and the support of society'. Hume states that 'this last circumstance is remarkable upon two accounts' and it is illuminating to follow his statement through. We read:

> First, because, though the cause of the establishment of these laws had been a regard for the public good, as much as the public good is their natural tendency, they wou'd still have been artificial, as being purposely contriv'd and directed to a certain end. Secondly, because, if men had been endow'd with a strong regard for the public good, they wou'd never have restrained themselves by those rules: so that the laws of justice arise from natural principles in a manner still more oblique and artificial. 'Tis self-love which is their real origin; and as the self-love of one person is naturally contrary to that of another, these several interested passions are oblig'd to adjust themselves after such a manner as to concur in some system of conduct and behaviour. This system, therefore, comprehending the interest of each individual, is of course advantageous to the public; tho' it be not intended for that purpose by the inventors (T, 528-9).

Thus the intentions of the 'inventors' – judges, legislators, 'class-interests' and so forth – are not sufficient as causal entities truly to explain the evolution and operation of the system of justice. Even when we may observe evidence that law-makers create law for their own interest, for their own 'interested passions', they are within the flow of nature with the result that they 'adjust themselves' to 'a system of conduct and behaviour': the whole of which gives a social benefit 'not intended ... by the inventors'. Stripped of the justifications of abstract reason, the rules of justice still bind, and the foundation of their hold can be demonstrated by the proper investigation of 'natural history'.[33]

This knowledge of natural history and the operation of the passions can be used against ideas of radical revolutionary change or the arbitrariness of the simple 'command version' of legal positivism. By contrast, we have a grand narrative of an evolutionary 'empirical natural development of law'; this preserves the strength of law from easy change and defends it against charges of arbitrariness or partiality. There is no need for some fundamental set of innate ideas or external reference point, such as the existence of God, to give a basis to the moral sense of man. The growth and operation of natural justice can be accounted for by the facilities of human nature (self-love and some

---

33 In *The Wealth of Nations* Smith presents arguments for increasing the general level of prosperity of all citizens - while minimising the role of politics. The growth and extension of the middle classes is crucial for social order since 'no society can surely be flourishing and happy, of which the far greater part of the members are poor and miserable'. Smith related the condition of individual men to their experience of the division of labour and the environment they experienced.

benevolence), the capabilities of human action (communication via sympathy, and restraint from seizing the possessions of others) and the entirety of social interaction (mutual recognition).

The search for knowledge is guided by our belief that it will aid natural social change. While Hume's implication is clear – we need empirically to analyse our legal institutions and come to a real understanding of their operation – Hume appears confident that such analysis will aid cultural changes already taking place. In the penal system, for example, Hume notes a growth away from the 'unnaturalness' of the religious notions of equivalence to a growing system of natural responses made possible by sentience – the response to offenders is becoming 'more natural' as the hold of religion decreases. Law should be structured to enable the proper operation of the social body, and the modern creation of 'civil law' is an advancing product of the stream of nature which places together 'industry, knowledge and humanity ... by an indissoluble chain' (1966: 278). Social control is linked to social relationships and the interaction of the individual with his fellows, the risks in social change can and will be contained through the expansion of the middle class, that 'middling rank ... who are the best and firmest basis of public liberty' (1966: 284). Through their participation in industry, and the indulgence in the 'luxury' which follows, men are socialised for peaceful cohabitation even in the face of the greater pressures and opportunities allowed by the increasing division of labour.

The power of government can only provide a crude instrument for social control; naked force, the visible coercive instrument at a government's disposal, is limited in its scope; instead custom and habit are the true restraining forces on man's rather asocial tendencies. Various restraints on man's conduct operate in the micro-situations in which man interacts with his fellows; individual man feels the need to preserve his reputation, and relate to the reactions of others to his actions. Effective control lies in influencing 'opinion'. Adam Smith was even more specific; knowledge of the 'natural sentiment of justice' (ie psychological impulse), could in time substitute for either clear coercion, or the hold of religious belief and the transcendental idealism thereby associated. For both men, the key to social progress lay in influencing the 'collective judgments' of society. Indeed, both Hume and Smith saw decline in the power of religion as giving a more 'natural' bent to social 'opinion', or in Smith's phrase the 'moral sentiments' of society.[34] Hume holds that moral sentiments are common to all humanity and are empirical instincts 'absolutely universal in all ages and nations'. Most men did not engage in reflexivity. They were moved by unexamined feelings owing much to unexamined religious ideologies; moral sentiments are truer since they are a consequence of our active engagement with the reality of our social and material world. An engagement which allows us 'little leisure or inclination to think of unknown invisible regions'.[35]

---

34 Smith's jurisprudential project was to create a *Theory of Moral Sentiments* (to use the title of his major work on jurisprudence, 1976) without foundational reference to the grid templates of theology. Moral sentiments differ from religious because they are direct passions, while religious conceptions are secondary effects of such passions.

35 *Natural History*, pp 21 and 31.

IS PHILOSOPHY OR MORAL THEORY REDUNDANT? OUGHT THE PHILOSOPHY OF RIGHT AND WRONG TO BE REPLACED BY THE EMPIRICAL ANALYSIS OF NATURAL UTILITY?

The whole enterprise of 'moral theory' is thrown into question by Hume's analysis. What then is the role of philosophical discussion concerning moral distinctions under Humean empiricism?[36]

The issue has dramatic considerations: how can we build a system of ethics based upon the faculty of feeling, sentiment, or sympathy, without reducing ethics to a matter of taste, where moral judgments are subjective and relative? Hume argues that moral sentiments are found in all men, that men praise or blame the same actions and that praise or blame are not derived from a narrow self-love. Instead, we have a natural process of sympathy. Again, Hume's target in describing morality is a pure model of rationalism: a model whereby morality is the subject for reason alone to tell us its nature producing a table of 'abstract rational difference[s] betwixt moral good and evil' (T, 466). By contrast, Hume's primary argument is that, as morals have to do with practical life, as a consequence 'moral philosophy' must be something which will:

> influence our passions and actions, and go beyond the calm and indolent judgments of the understanding, [and] ... since morals have an influence on the actions and affections, it follows, that they cannot be deriv'd from reason; and that because reason alone, as we have already prov'd, can never have any such influence. Morals excite passions, and produce or prevent actions. Reason of itself is utterly impotent in this particular. The rules of morality, therefore, are not conclusions of our reason (T, 457).

The role of reason is secondary to the empirically operating mechanism of the world – reason must serve only to bring to light what nature has decreed.[37]

Hume now makes a further claim, for not only is the distinction between good and evil not something that exists in the categories of reason, it is not even something that depends upon 'any matter of fact' discoverable by a simple positivistic investigation:

> Take any action allow'd to be vicious: wilful murder, for instance. Examine it in all lights, and see if you can find that matter of fact, or real existence, which you call *vice*. In which-ever way you take it, you find only certain passions, motives, volitions and thoughts. There is no other matter of fact in the case. The vice entirely escapes you, as long as you consider the object. You never can find it, till you turn your reflexion into

---

36 In the *Enquiries* (E, 170) the problem is set out thus: are morals 'derived from Reason, or from Sentiment; whether we obtain the knowledge of them by a chain of argument and induction, or by an immediate feeling and finer internal sense; whether, like all sound judgments of truth and falsehood, they should be the same to every rational intelligent being; or whether, like the perception of beauty and deformity, they are founded entirely on the particular fabric and constitution of the human species'. Hume's aim is to achieve a 'reformation in all moral disquisitions and reject every system of ethics, however, subtle or ingenious, which is not founded on fact and observation' (E, 175).

37 Thus, for instance, Hume declares the reason incest is allowed in the animal kingdom and not in human culture looks as if, through his use of reason, man has declared its 'turpitude', passing laws against it. But the moral explanation lies not in our rationality, since that is to argue in a circle: 'For before reason can perceive this turpitude, the turpitude must exist; and consequently is independent of the decisions of our reason, and is their object more properly than their effect' (T, 467).

your own breast, and find a sentiment of disapprobation, which arises in you toward this action. Here is a matter of fact: but 'tis the object of feeling, not of reason. It lies in yourself, not in the object. So that when you pronounce any action or character to be vicious, you mean nothing, but that from the constitution of your nature you have a feeling or sentiment of blame from the contemplation of it (T, 468-9).

Moral theory is only talk, its elements of 'reason' a superstructure which fits over the true, subjectivist economy of 'certain passions, motives, volitions and thoughts' which run throughout and structure the reactions of the self. In reality:

> ... virtue [is] whatever mental action or quality gives to a spectator the pleasing sentiment of approbation; and vice the contrary (ibid).

The sentiment of sympathy, or fellow-feeling, is a 'principle in human nature beyond which we cannot hope to find any principle more general.' Thus we 'bestow praise on virtuous actions, performed in very distant ages and remote countries; where the utmost subtlety of imagination would not discover any appearance of self-interest, or find any connection of our present happiness and security with events so widely separated from us'. Similarly, 'a generous, a brave, a noble deed, performed by an adversary, commands our approbation; while in its consequences it may be acknowledged prejudicial to our particular interest.' Hume's idea of moral sentiment and sympathy opposes the traditional ethical theory which holds that morality consists in the relation of actions to a rule of right and an action as good or evil depending upon whether the action agrees or disagrees with the rule. Hume rejects the hypothesis that there are moral rules, saying that such a thesis is 'abstruse' and 'can never be made intelligible'. Among those qualities which give the spectator the pleasing sentiment of approbation are 'discretion, caution, enterprise, industry, economy, good-sense, prudence and discernment'. There is also virtually universal agreement – even among the most cynical of men – concerning 'the merit of temperance, sobriety, patience, constancy, considerateness, presence of mind, quickness of conception and felicity of expression'. What is there about these qualities which generates our praise? The fact that these qualities are both *useful* and *agreeable*. Useful for what? Hume replies:

> for somebody's interest, surely. Whose interest then? Not our own only: For our approbation frequently extends farther. It must, therefore, be the interest of those, who are served by the character or action approved of.

Usefulness is 'a tendency to a natural end.' Thus the essential moral distinction is really that between what is useful and what is pernicious:

> if usefulness ... be a source of moral sentiment, and if this usefulness be not always considered with reference to self; it follows, that everything which contributes to the happiness of society, recommends itself directly to our approbation and goodwill. Here is a principle which accounts in great part for the origin of morality: And what need we seek for abstruse and remote systems, when there occurs one so obvious and natural?

We thus return to where this chapter began; into considerations of the grounding of the modern self and the interactions between social theory, conceptions of self, and the interdependent structuring of social relations. Hume warns us that, just as the search for the self causes us to experience chaos in moving beyond the rules of everyday life, so too does the justice of the social needs adherence to the settled rules of the social in order to prevent chaos. The rules of the self and the rules of the social reflect the precepts of that epistemology. The foundations of modernity are tradition(s) modernity thought its rationality had left behind. If law is to be the instrument of the sovereign's will, he had better watch his back, for fear his instrument deconstructs. For, unless positioned within a tradition, there is no presence or absence, no particularity or difference, no justice or injustice, no grounding for meaningful expression.

CHAPTER 6

IMMANUEL KANT AND THE PROMOTION OF A CRITICAL RATIONAL MODERNITY

The greatest problem of the human race, to the situation of which nature drives man, is the achievement of a universal civic society which administers law among men (Kant, *Idea for a Universal History*, 1963: 16).

... if the freedom of man were not kept within bounds by objective rules, the result would be the completest savage disorder (Kant, 'Duties to Oneself', in *Lectures in Ethics*).

The rights of man must be held sacred, however great a sacrifice the ruling power may have to make. There can be no half-measures here; it is no use devising hybrid solutions such as a pragmatically conditioned right halfway between right and utility. For all politics must bend the knee before right, although politics may hope in return to arrive, however slowly, at a stage of lasting brilliance. (Kant, quoted by Williams, 1983:42.)

PURITY AND AUTONOMY AS THE PRINCIPLES OF THE MODERN

The son of simple, but rigorously pious, parents of Scottish extraction, the German academic philosopher Immanuel Kant (1724–1804) laid out the structure of what has come to be called deontological (or absolutist) liberalism.[1] His philosophy differentiates conceptions of the *right* (based upon the idea that one can assert that something is right, clearly and independently of consideration of its social effects or other value) from the good (where value is identified in relation to worthwhile consequences of other effects), and stresses the primacy of the right over the good. Kant's deontological liberalism asks us to consider mankind as comprised of separate, moral individuals able to orientate themselves rationally through life's trials.

---

1   Kant spent all of his life in the small provincial town of Königsberg in East Prussia. The idea of personal duty dominated his thought and personal life. His education began at the local Collegium Fredericianum, whose director was also a Pietist, and in 1740 Kant entered the University of Königsberg. Kant's university training laid much emphasis upon the power of human reason to move with certainty in the realm of metaphysics. He developed an interest in Newtonian physics, an interest that played a very important part in the development of Kant's original and critical philosophy. Upon completion of his university course, Kant spent about eight years as a family tutor, and in 1755 became a lecturer at the university. He was appointed to the chair of philosophy in 1770.

While Kant's personal life contains no remarkable events – he did not travel and developed no notable political or social connections – he was a highly successful lecturer and an interesting conversationalist. He is often pictured as an old bachelor whose every activity was scheduled with such precision that neighbours could set their watches when he stepped out of his house each day at half past four to walk up and down his small avenue eight times. His discipline was matched by a mind which sought the universality of reason, and late in life he produced an array of work which has set much of the contours of the intellectual development of modern liberalism. This stream began with the monumental *Critique of Pure Reason* in 1781, and moved onto the *Prolegomena* to any Future Metaphysics in 1783, *Principles of the Metaphysics of Ethics* in 1785, *Metaphysical First Principles of Natural Science* in 1786, the second edition of the *Critique of Pure Reason* in 1787, the *Critique of Practical Reason* in 1788, the *Critique of Judgement* in 1790, *Religion within the Limits of Mere Reason* in 1793, and the small work *Perpetual Peace* in 1795.

In the *Prolegomena*, Kant acknowledges that the writings of David Hume 'interrupted [his] dogmatic slumber' and set his thoughts off in a new direction. Kant read Hume as declaring that the only possible knowledge was either of relations of ideas or empirical observations. Philosophy comprised the first, which, according to Hume, amounted to various discussions in danger of moving in tautological circles. By contrast the developing empirical sciences appeared to offer real knowledge; however, they were themselves based on non-rational foundations. Kant had been trained to believe in *reason* and to hope that through the use of reason men would know the duties expected of them and what was right to do in life. Hume appeared to undercut these beliefs; additionally a host of questions now appeared. What was man's relationship to 'nature' and the common life of the market and his sentient needs and psychological desires? What happened to our ideas of morality and of God if it were only the empirical sciences that provided knowledge about the world? Were we doomed to relegate ideas of God and morality to the status of the non-rational? Did morality really consist of feeling, emotion and natural sentiment? Did man need to follow nature, or could man take rational charge of building a new social and world order? If so, what principles of reason could he rely upon?

ANSWERING HUME

Could Hume's sceptical challenge be answered through reason? Kant's answer involved both an epistemological (concerned with the truth claims for knowledge), and social project. The epistemological project followed Hume's quest for the foundations of knowledge, but, instead of deconstructing the ideas of pure reason or of the experiencing self, and then turning back to working within the narratives of the common life, Kant first analysed the purely formal sciences of reason purified of empirical content looking for *a priori* understandings,[2] and then turned the same methodology onto our everyday moral sentiments looking for the rational presuppositions which underpinned them. The aim was to keep both philosophy and morality as realms where reason, and not custom or empirical analysis, ruled. Against Hume, Kant argued that it was possible for pure reason to convey real knowledge about the world,[3] and that our everyday moral conceptions rationally presupposed that some things were purely right in and of themselves, while others were wrong.[4] And this was irrespective of our emotional desires or consideration of what was socially useful.

---

2   Kant distinguishes theoretical reason – the reason of what we normally call science, practical reason – the reason of morality, and aesthetic judgment – or questions of beauty and artistic interpretation. The key methodological principle for Kant is to distinguish between the purely formal or logical and the sensory; he claims the former is universal and necessary in its principles, while the latter is incidental and concrete or particular.

3   Kant called these propositions 'synthetic a priori', or knowledge which applied to the world but was not derived from observation of the world.

4   Behind these distinctions Kant makes a rationalist distinction between what he calls 'things-in-themselves', or the world as it is 'in itself', and 'appearances'. Our empirical knowledges are of the world of appearances, while pure reason seeks knowledge of things 'in themselves'.

Kant's social project worked through his epistemology; specifically, he asks the modern person to: (i) adopt a critical rationality instead of scepticism; (ii) undertake a vigorous separation of the types of knowledge; and (iii) ask what are the foundational presuppositions which make these knowledges possible, and search for the rational principles inherent in these propositions; and then combine these analyses into (iv) a philosophic history that provides a goal for human endeavours, in the course of which we will in turn be guided by the pilot of critical rationality.

THE PRINCIPLE OF RATIONAL AUTONOMY WOULD BE THE GUIDE FOR MODERNITY

Kant was perhaps the first writer to define modern man as self-defining, rather than as reading sets of meanings from where things empirically are positioned in the cosmic order. Modern man could escape from the binds of the past and uncover his true 'humanity' by developing self-imposed, rather than naturally conditioned, ends and activities. Modern man should not be:

> ... guided by instinct, not nurtured and instructed by ready-made knowledge; rather he should bring forth everything out of his own resources. Securing his own shelter, food and defence ... all amusement which can make life pleasant, insight and intelligence, finally even goodness at heart – all this should be wholly his own work (1983: 14).

Man's dignity and uniqueness lie in his capacity to use reason;[5] this is a capacity which all men share as rational beings and which enables men to step outside the confines of their local or communally based patterns of socialised beliefs.[6] Reason must itself be the

---

5 Use reason and use it direct your will-power can be taken as Kant's key message. As with Hobbes (see Chapter 4 of this text) Kant looks to the story of Job to interpret religious truth. After experiencing extreme misfortune Job turns to his friends for advice; they offer a doctrinal interpretation of his suffering, stating it must represent God's punishment of Job's past sins which Job is not conscious of. They recommend Job to plead for God's forgiveness. Job refuses, indicating that his own conscience is clear and does not warrant him repenting. In the end he confronts God and God displays his ultimate power. How do we understand the outcome? Kant argues that Job is vindicated in ignoring his friends' doctrinal interpretation, since God demonstrated 'an ordering of the whole which manifests a wise Creator, although His ways remain inscrutable for us'. We cannot know all, therefore doctrinal interpretations will be inexact. How can we orientate ourselves? We need 'only the uprightness of the heart, not the merit of one's insights, the sincere and undisguised confession of one's doubts, and the shunning of feigned convictions which one does not really feel' (*On the Failure of all Attempted Philosophical Theodicies*, 1973: 292-3). We need a general understanding of the tone or shape of the totality, but we cannot know the totality. Our moral relation to God depends not on the actuality of experience, but on the uprightness of the heart and genuine morality.

6 Both Hume and Kant wished to escape the confines of locality, the conventions of the platonic cave, or the security of community based systems of morality. Hume escaped by postulating a universal empirical basis to human nature. His historical reading – focusing upon the classical Greeks and Romans – indicated to him that there was a constant to human nature throughout the centuries. In opposition to the romantic tendency of the enlightenment, which saw great potential in education to change human behaviour (John Locke saw human beings born as a blank sheet which thereafter was written on by their experiences and education), Hume thought the classical Greeks and Romans were driven by the pursuit of sex, power, and self-esteem, much the same as the people he saw around him. It was the role of institutions to keep these universal desires in check and social reform could be achieved by understanding the universal characteristics of the human condition. Kant sought for the rational presuppositions which transcended the conventions of our everyday beliefs and intuitions.

subject of rational analysis.[7] There was no point in relying upon our moral intuitions as if an appeal to intuition answered the appeal of our opponents to feeling;[8] intuition must be rationally analysed:

> reason does not work instinctively but requires trial and instruction in order to gradually progress from one kind of insight to another (1983: 13).

Whereas Hume collapsed his hopes for secure knowledge into social interaction and a thesis of common empirical faculties of mankind, Kant argues for the existence of 'pure reason ... a sphere so separate and self-contained'. Reason is not liable to subjective contamination or arbitrary desire, but we must understand its interrelational nature:

> We cannot touch a part without affecting all the rest. We can therefore do nothing without first determining the position of each part, and its relation to the rest; for as our judgment cannot be corrected by anything without, the validity and use of every part depends upon the relation in which it stands to all the rest within the domain of reason ... In the sphere of this faculty you can determine either everything or nothing (1902: 10-11).

Mankind is on a journey of discovery. The circumstances of the modern person are similar to being on a ship embarking on a voyage across an unknown sea. Hume, Kant argued, was forced to leave his ship adrift on the current of nature but Kant's analysis can provide us with:

> ... a pilot, who, by means of safe astronomical principles drawn from a knowledge of the globe, and provided with a complete chart and compass, may steer the ship safely, whither he listeth (1902: 9).

The key was to develop a critical rationality based upon the rational foundation underpinning the items of everyday life – such as our belief in God and our treatment of each other as free-willing individuals. The preface to the first edition of the *Critique of Pure Reason* had set this out clearly:

> Our age is essentially an age of criticism, to which everything has to submit. Religion, on account of its sanctity, and legislation on account of its majesty, both try to withdraw themselves from it. But they then straightaway arouse just suspicion against themselves and cannot claim that sincere respect which reason grants to whoever has been able to withstand its free and open examination.

Critical understanding also addressed the question of what, and how, understanding and reason can know, apart from experiences.[9] In this way critical understanding did not

---

7   As Kant suggested in his own analysis of religious practices: 'Kneeling down or grovelling on the ground, even to express your reverence for heavenly things, is contrary to human dignity; as is also invoking heavenly things in actual images, for you then humble yourselves not to an ideal which your own reason sets before you, but to an idol which is your own handiwork' (*The Metaphysical Principles of Virtue*, 1964: 99).

8   Moral intuition alone is not enough. Kant's argument is that pure moral intuition amounts to 'merely an inner feeling' aroused by the situation or the material being read or discussed. As with scripture (discussed in *Religion within the Limits of Reason Alone*, 1960: 100ff).

9   Philosophy was asked to turn its critical attention to the constitution, power and structure of human reason itself – to perform a 'Copernican' reversal of perspective (*Critique of Pure Reason*, 1949: 2nd Preface). The primary examination of science was the scope of the *Critique of Pure Reason*, and the handling of this knowledge of the nature of the world, and man's moral responsibilities and social obligations which constituted his special 'humanity', that of the *Critique of Practical Reason* and the *Groundwork of the Metaphysic of Morals*.

destroy metaphysics, but provided a 'single and sudden revolution' which cleared the way for true metaphysical understanding (1965: 21-22).

RECOGNISING THE TYPES OF KNOWLEDGE, EACH WITH DIFFERENT FUNDAMENTAL PRESUPPOSITIONS

The first step was to save the claims of philosophy to tell us things of real importance about the world. Following Hume's division between relations of ideas and relations of facts, Kant claimed:

> ... all rational knowledge is either material and concerned with some object, or formal and concerned solely with the form of understanding and reason themselves – with the universal rules of thinking as such (*Groundwork of the Metaphysic of Morals*, 1964: 53).

Kant distinguished 'a priori' forms of the understanding from the 'a posteriori' sensuous content of experience. Each relies upon certain features which structure our human capabilities for understanding. All knowledge is human knowledge, it is a function of what and how it is possible for us to know. The human subject can never see the world as the world was in its purity, but brings to the interaction of an (essentially mysterious) world certain ways of perceiving, certain presuppositions, and it is only through these ways of perceiving, and by the use of these presuppositions, that knowledge is possible. Knowledge is a function of the faculties we bring to bear. As Kant put it in a witty example, we often attempt to gain a type of knowledge our faculties are incapable of:

> This would be similar to the experiment that someone attempted by standing before a mirror with closed eyes and, when asked what he was doing, replied: 'I just want to know what I look like when I am asleep' (1983: 153).

The necessity of working through ways of perceiving and presuppositions

We accept that we cannot help but make use of certain fundamental features in the epistemological process. The trick is to understand how exactly we actually use them and how they serve to structure human knowledge. It is only after this knowledge is obtained that we may properly apply our critical orientation. Our questioning is firstly – how is pure mathematics possible? How is the pure science of nature possible?[10] We then apply this understanding to analyse candidates for inclusion in a 'pure' system of reasoning. The process is repeated in the *Critique of Practical Reason* to analyse critically the rationality inherent in our moral belief systems. We start from the fact of our actual use of morality; we do not wish to come out with the concept of 'morality' as our final product but its reality is accepted or 'presupposed' – from our recognition of moral

---

10 See *Prolegomena: To Any Future Metaphysics That Can Qualify as a Science*, Paul Carus trans, Open Court, La Salle (Illinois), chapters of which bear these titles.

demands and duties. We then move, via the assumption that we must be free to fulfil them, to the conditions of their operation.[11]

Our rational behaviour does not occur passively, but is the result of the active participation of the mind acting according to what Kant calls *regulative ideas*. Our moral interactions are governed by *practical reason*; in practical reason the connection between 'will' and 'reason' is such that the will is the faculty of acting according to a regulative ideal called 'law'. This regulates and distinguishes human will from the capacity of acting according to desire, which Kant views as essentially a passive and reactive activity. The operation of the will *vis-à-vis* 'law' is the active engagement in the realm of practical action of our rational capacity with regulative ideas.

The foundational categories of science and the division of the world into realms of the intelligible and the empirical

In analysing how science is possible, the justification for those ideas which we rely upon as providing the foundations of scientific knowledge (the '*a priori*' concepts) comes from our recognition of them as the basic conditions of thought – they are the 'categories' of thought.

> Now I maintain that the categories ... are nothing but the conditions of thought in a possible experience, just as space and time are the conditions of intuition for that same experience. They are fundamental concepts by which we think objects in general for appearances, and have therefore *a priori* objective validity. (1965: 138; the passage continues: 'this is exactly what we desired to prove'(!)).

The function of foundational categories is dual: both bedrock and limit. Efforts to obtain knowledge unconditioned by the categories of the understanding – as with traditional metaphysics – are to be rejected as dogmatic and self-contradictory. We cannot get at the 'pure' world and grasp things as they are in themselves apart from the categories of the mind; however, we can be aware of the limiting character of these categories and so we can meaningfully conceive of concepts of reality and knowledge beyond human understanding. What is on one side made understandable through the categories, Kant calls the 'phenomenal' world, and what is on the other he calls the 'noumenal'. In this way Hume's empiricist outcome, whereby the concepts which provide epistemological bedrock ultimately derive from the custom of repeated association in experience, is transformed into a solid objectivity providing legitimate foundation. As a consequence, however, the world divides up into that about which we can have knowledge and that about which we can never have knowledge.

---

11 The method for locating these 'conditions' Kant terms 'transcendental analysis' – it is a process of elimination in which one accounts for all those aspects of experience derived from terms of sensation, and the residue is explainable in terms of the structure of the mind, or what he calls the 'categories of the understanding'. Thus the content, or the 'matter', of experience, the '*a posteriori*' sensuous content, is supplied by sensation, and the 'form' of experience, what enables us to understand it, is supplied by the mind. This last feature is the formal component which comprises the conditions of knowledge, and its members are universal, conceptual, and '*a priori*'. *Cf Critique of Pure Reason*.

THE RATIONALITY OF MORALITY AND THE DEFENCE OF THE VIEW OF MAN AS A FREE INDIVIDUAL, PRESUPPOSED IN LAW

What are we to make of our language of morality? What is the basis of our ideas on moral or legal duties, or of God? Are these to be reduced to mere questions of feeling? To emotive needs? Kant asks us to use the language of our everyday social life as a starting point and seek the rational underpinnings of our language use.

What is an individual human being? A section of reality; but by which perspective, and what are the limits to the identification of reality that any concept used about him attains? In the discourse of the developing empirical sciences we assume cause and effect; the implication is that every act of man is that of a determined entity in the spatial, temporal world. But we do not act as this was the case; in the morality of everyday life we treat others as capable of making promises, of making choices, and we hold them responsible for their actions. Many concepts which we use in practical life imply that a person is to be treated as an autonomous being which continually motivates him/herself. Does this deny his links to physical reality, and thus already assert an '*a priori*' to which we have no right? Or, are we highlighting 'another reality'?

The partiality of empirical science

Kant regarded Humean-style empiricism as being correct in many aspects. Thus, it was correct and proper to think of a human being as a finite, contingent, complex mind-body of actual physical substance, and hemmed in on all sides by the physical world. What could we know about the person? We could observe him interacting with other objective particulars in a 'reality' which was observable and where things acted in obedience to the principle of causality and thus necessity. Under these regulatory ideas, we could only discuss humanity in the language of empirical science. Nevertheless, for Kant this was in a sense an abstract view of the individual.

> [There are] two points of view from which he can regard himself and from which he can know laws governing the employment of his powers and consequently governing all his actions. He can consider himself first – so far as he belongs to the sensible world – to be under the laws of nature (heteronomy), and secondly – so far as he belongs to the intelligible world – to be under laws which, being independent of nature, are not empirical but have their ground in reason alone. (quoted in Williams 1964: 120)

When the actions and choices of men are regarded as events in the spacial-temporal world then they must be subject to the laws of empirical necessity. Take the area of criminal law. When we begin as independent observers to explain men's actions, we may trace the commission of crime to factors such as heredity, education and environment. We create an effective explanatory scheme. A scheme which is so effective it begins to look as if it were impossible for the person not to have acted in this way; there is an inevitability of action imposed upon us. What happens to our everyday ideas of free will? It seems that we only use such ideas because of a lack of information as to all the conditions, circumstances, factors and degrees of influence that prevent us from a total knowledge of a person's action – and hence from predicting exactly what he would do in the circumstances. By implication, as science proceeds we will have less confidence in the reality of morality. The criminal law, for example, will become redundant, replaced by measures of social protection (which aim to prevent the undesired conduct deterministically).

Man transcends his empirical nature and is capable of a course of action governed by practical reason

However, Kant notes that even in the light of this potentiality we persist in holding man responsible for his actions and we join in the general social practice of attaching appropriate blame or reward. When we use *theoretical reason* we adopt a stance which has developed into the various roles of criminologist, sociologist, psychologist and so forth, whilst in our everyday role in civil society we attribute praise and blame, we consider the situation in the light of practical reason. It is in the light of *practical reason* that we hold moral feelings and legislate laws which have as their presupposition the fact that people need not breach them. In fact, we are saying that a person *should* not do certain things, and if he should not have done an action but actually did, then we are saying that it must have been possible for him not to have done it. But we as psychologists etc, have the potentiality to offer a complete explanation in such a way for there to be simply nothing visible to us that could have enabled the person to have refrained from the action. It is in this quandary that Kant introduces a strange concept peculiar to human action. He calls this 'another causality', that of 'freedom'.

This is one example of what Kant termed 'transcendental objects'. These are objects that transcend experience and sensation-based systems of description. The criminologist who bases his approach upon the foundations of empiricism will never be able to consider the operation of this 'causality'. However, by the use of transcendental objects we may regard the offence in question (he uses an example of lying) as completely undetermined in relation to the man's previous condition. It is 'as if the offender started off a series of effects completely by himself'. Kant goes on to say that when we are faced with a situation where our theoretical reason tells us empirical conditions have determined a person's actions, we may still legitimately hold that person responsible and blame him. We are, thus, justified in holding a man responsible for his actions, even if we as (future) criminologists can also say that 'before ever they have happened, they are one and all predetermined in the empirical character'. How are we justified in this? Kant states:

> this blame is founded on a law of reason by which we regard the reason as the cause which, independently of all the above mentioned empirical conditions, could and should have determined the man's actions in another way. We do not indeed regard the causality of reason as something that merely accompanies the action, but as something complete in itself, even if the sensible motives do not favour but even oppose the action; the action is imputed to the man's intelligible character and he is wholly guilty now, in the very moment when he lies; therefore the reason was wholly free, notwithstanding all the empirical conditions of the act, and the deed has to be wholly imputed to this failure of reason (*Critique of Practical Reason*, A 555, quoted and commented upon in Acton, 1970: 45–46).

As well as the closed and determined grip that the empirical observer hopes to identify, there is always 'another causality' operative which can ensure a different action, and this 'other' is of its nature not able to be located in any spacial-temporal causal series. Man participates in both an empirical and a moral realm. The ability to partake of this other realm of causalities is, moreover, that aspect of man which makes him the fit subject for moral praise and condemnation which accompany participation in the linguistic and practical arrangements of our world. Furthermore, it is upon the supposition of the operation of man's 'will', and the concepts associated with it, that practical, free and rational life is possible. This rational, free life comes from the interaction of the will with an 'a priori' law essential to the operation of morality. Kant held:

> These categories of freedom – for we wish to call them this in contrast to the theoretical concepts which are categories of nature – have a manifest advantage over the latter. The latter categories are only forms of thought, which through universal concepts designate, in an indefinite manner, objects in general for every intuition possible to us. The categories of freedom, on the other hand, are elementary practical concepts which determine the free faculty of choice. Though no intuition exactly corresponding to this determination can be given to us, the free faculty of choice has as its foundation a pure practical law a priori, and this cannot be said for any of the concepts of the theoretical use of our cognitive faculty (*Critique of Practical Reason*, quoted in Beck, 1960: 139).

These concepts, which Kant holds as the foundation of practical life, however, present a terrible morass, for they are 'beyond the limits' of scientific reason.[12] We can therefore appreciate that the laws of morality are laws of pure reason.

A boundary is drawn beyond which empirical scientific knowledge cannot aspire, and we are free to argue that laws of nature are not the only formula of causality; there is another approach to understanding what it means to be human that is based on this 'rational faith'. This 'faith' preserves morality against the dictates of scientific knowledge

---

12 In the structure of the Kantian project they constitute Kant's 'third antinomy'. An antinomy is a pair of contradictory statements both of which may be validly proved, and both of which represent a crucial and essential interest of reason. They are enabled by the possibility of making 'synthetic a priori' judgments (statements in which the predicate is not logically included in the concept of the subject, ie this man is a thief – an assertion the truth of which is only establishable in experience – is an example of a synthetic judgment. Kant holds that there are some synthetic judgments that are logically true, a crucial one is 'every event has a cause'). In the third antinomy conflict arises out of the concept of causality. The statement that everything has a cause serves to bring the elements of causality within time and under the laws of nature: but if everything must have a cause then there must be a cause that is not an event in time under the law of nature. Further, both of these considerations are necessary to give absolute validity to the principle of causality; but both cannot, it appears, be true. The resolution of this antinomy relies, to use the title of Strawson's book on Kant, on a division of 'the bounds of sense' (1966: 12). The thesis, which asserts the reality of cause not contained within the limits of the laws of nature, and the antithesis, which asserts that all causation lies within the limits of the laws of nature either now known or potentially to be uncovered, may both be true if their respective areas are distinguished. The areas of each are confined to their specific realms and cannot validly cross the limits or boundaries of their domain. Thus the thesis is applied to the relationship between *noumena* (being 'things-in-themselves', and here containing the idea of a sufficient cause) and phenomena, whilst the antithesis is restricted to relations among phenomena. In this way, separate and distinct applications of human understanding which are compatible in existence are legitimated; the legitimation of this state of affairs is occasioned by the distinction between the world of appearance and the *noumenal* world. This dualism limits science and re-establishes mystery, but this is not a superstitious or dogmatic mystery but a mystery based on rationally argued grounds.

claims. There can be no knowledge of this other causality, although, we are told, the general concepts relating to these aspects beyond the bounds of knowledge are meaningful. Indeed, theoretical reason needs the existence of this other realm for its own completion, but can never establish the nature of it.[13] However, without it, the very being of theoretical reason is endangered and if we attempt to do without the realm of the 'other', we 'plunge it [theoretical reason] into an abyss of scepticism'.

The categorical imperative

For its part, the operation of human freedom is subject to the rules of the intelligibles.[14] We can create rules of the right; we can lay down what reason demands of us. The essential requirements of morality are built into the structure of rationality itself; hence moral requirements must, *a priori*, be acknowledged by all rational beings as binding. The role of the moral philosopher is to seek axioms of the right and principles of action corresponding to principles of morality. Kant's most famous rule is the *Categorical Imperative*:

> Act only according to that maxim by which you can at the same time will that it should become a universal law.
> Act as if the maxim of your action were to become through your will a universal law of nature (*Groundwork of the Metaphysics of Morals*, 1981: 421; 30).

Kant argues that the only acceptable moral rules are those which everyone could adopt. Morality imposes upon us principles and conditions of action that – once understood – are rationally entitled to the assent of any possible community, moreover, Kant implies that there is at the basis of our moral positions ultimately only one set of such principles and conditions that will pass the test of critical rational acceptability. The task of moral philosophy is to strive to uncover that set of principles.

We implicitly recognise the foundations of practical reason and our free will in our everyday activities of praise and blame

When an offence is committed in this Kantian-reconciled world, what is actually having the linguistic utterance of condemnation attached to it is not the immanent

---

13 'Thus the question as to how a categorical imperative is possible can be answered to the extent that there can be supplied the sole presupposition under which such an imperative is alone possible – namely, the idea of freedom. The necessity of this presupposition is discernible, and this much is sufficient for the practical use of reason, ie, for being convinced of the validity of this imperative, and hence also of the moral law; but how this presupposition itself is possible can never be discerned by any human reason' (Kant, *Grounding for the Metaphysic of Morals*, 1981: 461; 60).

14 Remembering that Kant held that 'the true method of metaphysics is fundamentally the same as that which Newton has introduced into natural sciences and which has there yielded such fruitful results', a statement such as 'psychological causality subjects man to natural necessity as much as "mechanical causality" does' reflects Kant's desire to assert the law-abiding operation of the realm of the intelligibles. Interestingly, in the chronology of Kant's output the earlier *Critique of Theoretical Reason* is often read as leaving an unrestricted freedom to this other realm, whereas in the *Critique of Practical Reason* this other realm is held subject to its own species of causality. The operation of this realm is devoid of spacial-temporal matrices, and thus is outside of time, which means that in a crucial sense morality is also timeless. We see, therefore, that, in the totality of Kant's reconciliation, contingency and eternity coexist.

phenomenal-bound character of the activity, but the intelligible. Here guilt is complete when the person commits the crime, and nothing that went before can alter his guilt. Whatever the life-form patterns of the phenomenal world, which constitute a person's sociological or psychological (in the behaviourist as opposed to the looser Kantian sense) position, these do not affect the evil of his deed, an evil which is his evil, introduced into the world by him in his exercise of freedom. A wrong is not converted into a non-wrong on account of the activities which preceded it, nor can it be dissolved by what comes afterwards.[15]

For Kant the categories of practical reason – the operation of the moral law – provide a mechanism which stabilises the conflicting desires and empirical pulls of the spatial-temporal world and the moral law is the operation of the 'I' that is truly 'my self'. This is, however, a difficult task and Kant places the nature of the 'will' as central to its resolution. Here he distinguishes between desire in the animal, Humean form which subjects reason to the passions, and the higher form of desire that not only subjects the passions to reason but is itself subjected to the power of reason. Rational men are a part of a rational universal. But here we have a fundamental problem – that of the relation of the will to the world of appearances. How does the moral decision, the activity of the will, moral thought, interact with the phenomenal world? How in effect is it to control, or even to be relevant? Kant argues:

> It is man's duty to strive for this perfection, but not to reach it (in this life), and his compliance with this duty can, accordingly, consist only in continual progress (*ibid*, VI: 446; 241).

The moral law can only exist in the phenomenal realm as an act of will, of conscious striving, by real people. We can reflectively evaluate possible actions. Kant's two-fold categorising of 'desire', so different from the empiricist reading of Hume, entails our ability to evaluate our desires, to regard some as qualitatively 'desirable' and others as qualitatively 'undesirable'; action upon some 'acceptable', others not; and this is to acknowledge that the crucial difference between man and sentient animal is the moral law within.

Action under the moral law is linked to our capacity for self-evaluation and the distinguishing feature between the Kantian agency and the Humean lies not in that we are conscious of our capacity for making decisions about desired actions but on two differing kinds of evaluation of this consciousness. The Humean is subject to a realm where evaluation is, and cannot fail to be, a mode of quantitative analysis. The individual is linked to feelings as to the most desirable upon a plane of sentience and eventual satisfaction. In the act of deciding between two possible courses of action the Humean is attempting to make different desires commensurable under instrumentality, functionality and systematisation by usefulness. By contrast the Kantian claims to

---

15 Kant holds that we demonstrate our recognition of this in our experiencing of remorse. Remorse, he declares, even when it takes the form of labelling an event an accident or mistake, by its nature can only have one true cause. Remorse, as opposed to regret (which is the simple reflection on outcome), is reflection on the evil brought into the world. Remorse is not atonement, it cannot achieve the undoing of what has been done, but is simply the painful recognition that we, in our freedom, did wrong.

transcend quantitative weighing by imposing qualitative evaluations. The moral law is contingent upon the ability to rank, classify and categorise the qualitative worth of different desires as they are judged by moral principle.

The ambition of the empiricist construction of knowledges was to turn practical reason as much as possible into calculation, an ambition whose major expression has been in the doctrine of utilitarianism. Kant moves against this and declares that to engage in qualitative evaluation of our desires is to engage in a qualitatively different mode of life – one he calls truly free – expressive of the distinctive quality of being human. The domain of this judgment, the domain of the ought, cannot exist in purely material nature, it is dependent upon beings who are apart from material nature.[16]

The Kantian transcendence of the cave, and the visualising of the true nexus of humanity, comes from facilities inherent in man himself – in his reason which gives the *ideal* of humanity. The moral law, which corresponds not to any particular regime of morality (which although customary may be regarded as unjust or tyrannical) but the constraint of morality itself, is ingrained in the person because of his humanity; it is not a mere calculus of self-interest, but lies in the obedience to that which is a part of oneself – not to an external force.[17] Man as subject draws the precepts of action out of his own will and not from any external empirical source: man in empirical circumstances may feel passions and desires inclining him to act in a certain way – but he has the capacity of will to substitute these desires for will to do other than the desired activity. On reflection:

He must unhesitatingly admit that it is possible for him. He judges, therefore, that he can do a thing because he is conscious that he ought to do it, and he recognises in himself the freedom which, but for the moral law, would have remained unknown to him (1949: 30).

As Acton summarises:

A man who tries to excuse a wrong act by reference to his heredity and circumstances is, so to say, rationally abandoning his rationality ... to argue that one could not help it is to say that one is a passive subject of external stimuli in the very breath in which one shows that one is not ... If we recognise the obligations that morality places upon us we *ipso facto* regard ourselves as free, for we accept the moral law as consonant with our practical reason, and we presuppose our ability to conform to it (1970: 51–52).

---

16 The bent of utilitarianism has been to do away with qualitative distinctions of worth on the grounds that they represent confused perceptions of the real bases of our preferences which are sentient and quantitative; the hope being that once we have done away with strong evaluation we will be able to calculate – but the Benthamite basis of calculation was prefaced upon the commensurability of the units totalling up the significant units of pain and pleasure. Utilitarians are right to see their enemy as the mechanism of strong qualitative evaluation, for the mechanism of the Kantian *Practical Reason* simply cannot be reduced to mere calculation. Moreover, it is more than the difference between quantitative and qualitative evaluation, or the presence, per se, of higher desire, but is the ability of desires to be distinguished as to worth – and thus the idea of a table of values. The Kantian individual refrains from lying, not because that will have such or such a consequence, but because that simply is base.

17 Kant holds: 'Man is a being who has the power of practical reason and is conscious that his choice is free (a person); and in his consciousness of freedom and in his feeling (which is called moral feeling) that justice and injustice is done to him, or by him, to others, he sees himself as subject to the law of duty no matter how obscure his ideas may be' *Anthropology*, 1974:185.

DEFINING THE ONTOLOGY OF THE RATIONAL AGENT

Man is constituted both in the phenomenological realm and in the transcendence of this, the noumenal; thus the absolute truth of man – man's 'essence' – is beyond the trap of empirical contingency, beyond time, beyond temporal expression. Man straddles and is genuinely apart from the natural empirical world of appearances or the political world dealing with the material desires of humankind. He is of two domains – the empirical and the moral/ethical.[18]

Man's reflection upon the forces he mediates takes him both to 'the starry heavens above … [and] to the moral law within'. Man, in practical action, continually synthesises the '*a priori*' and universalistic concepts of the moral law with his active interpretation of social existence. The application of the transcendental principles is the active task of the moral life.[19]

CONTRASTING THE RIGHT TO THE GOOD

The central doctrines of Kant's later work on law *The Metaphysics of Morals* (which contains *The Metaphysical Elements of Justice*) appears to universalise moral claims away from their location in any particular community and presents moral reasoning as universal to all men (rational beings). The *Metaphysics* is preceded by a work entitled *Grounding of the Metaphysic of Morals* (various translations referred to as 1959, 1964, 1981), a work Kant directs at the general reader who possesses 'common rational knowledge of morality'. It is to operate 'within the moral knowledge of common human reason', and to unpack the essential conditions of the commonly held ideals of the time, the rational constitution of the *sensus communis*. The essential precondition is that there are the situations where people do know full well in practice right from wrong, good and evil, obligation and response, and our task is to discover the rational basis of these configuration.

Kant's work seeks to found modernity in universality, in that it is concerned to destroy the limited substantive conceptions of conditioned moral responses coming from socialisation in a sensus communis by the rhetorical force of the universal rationality of

---

18 It is a standing objection that Kant gives us a theoretical situation inhabited by very abstract or empirically 'irrelevant' 'persons', who preserve a dignified separateness, or autonomy, at the expense of denying their very reality as actual, empirical individuals (ie of their 'real' individuality). This was noted early: Hegel saw in Kant the mistake of idealism in separating itself from the world and held the critical philosophy of Kant as creating a dilemma where it seeks to provide the existence of God (the absolute foundation of good in the world) via the science of reason, but this being unsatisfied it is handed on to faith in the *Critique of Practical Reason* which presupposes God as the practical supposition. For Hegel Kant is forced to realise the failings of critical philosophy; a failure centred around the impossibility of knowing the 'thing-in-itself' (Hegel, *History of Philosophy*, Vol 3, 428-30).

19 The Kantian actor is one freed from a cosmos of set meaning, confronting the world instead on his or her own terms – a moral freedom to act which is governed transcendentally. The actor having confronted the dehumanised natural world, operates in a denaturalised social-moral world governed through the principles of the transcendental 'other'. The operations of man in society are dictated by the primacy of practical reason over the theoretical – practical reason exists two-fold: both in the publicly created and open political-social situation and in a private yet universal grounding.

man. Kant is not concerned to unpack the beliefs of any one particular area, of one community, but to formulate for all and any 'man': metaphysics is the science which exhibits in systematic connection the whole body (true as well as illusionary) of philosophical knowledge arising out of pure reason' (*Critique of Pure Reason*, A 841–B 869, quoted in Acton, 1970). Men share a rational nature and are capable of self direction: 'rational nature is distinguished from others in that it proposes an end in itself' (1959: 56). The central feature of man, social man, is that he involves himself with a 'realm of ends', in which 'everything has either a price or a dignity. Whatever has a price can be replaced by something else as its equivalent; on the other hand, whatever is above all price, and therefore admits no equivalent, has a dignity.'

That which is related to general human inclinations and needs – we can call this the *good* – has a market price. That which, without presupposing any need, accords with a certain taste, ie with pleasure in the mere purposeless play of our facilities, has an effective price. But that which constitutes the condition under which alone something can be an end in itself does not have mere relative worth, ie a price, but an intrinsic worth, ie dignity. We can call this the *right*.

> Morality is the condition under which alone a rational being can be an end in itself, because only through it is it possible to be a legislative member of the realm of ends. Thus morality and humanity, so far as it is capable of morality, alone have dignity. Skill and diligence in work have a market value ... but fidelity in promises and benevolence on principle (not from instinct) have intrinsic worth.
>
> [Moral] actions need no recommendation from any subjective disposition or taste in order that they may be looked upon with immediate favour and satisfaction, nor do they have need of any immediate propensity or feeling directed to them. They exhibit the will which performs them as the object of an immediate respect, since nothing but reason is required in order to impose them on the will (1959: 53).

Society must never fall into 'market' mentality in questions of punishment – dignity does not allow the calculations and administrative ethos of 'prices', but the absolute bindings of deontological reasoning.[20]

Contrasting the right and the good: the critique of utilitarianism

The deontological legacy of Kant has provided a central attack on utilitarianism. Bentham (see discussion in Chapter 8 of this text) offered utility as the master principle to overcome, in part, subjectivist accounts of moral intuitionists as to what the right and good in morality was. Moral intuitionists could respond to Bentham by arguing that the principle of utility appeals because, apparently, this is what man wants inherently – happiness and not pain – moreover we intuitively believe that we should have more pleasure in the world and less unhappiness and pain. In this reading, Bentham simply takes hold of this intuition and turns it into a general theory. The utilitarianism suggests

---

20 In effect Kant recognises 'market mentality' as an entirely different species of social ordering – one determinate upon sensual gratification and payment for compliance (commodity fetishism). Its structure is opposite to that of a truly rational and universal *sensus communis* and thus lacks the resources to enable reason to bind.

we should concentrate on the consequence of any act – there is nothing inherently good or right about an act; the good act is the one that produces the most consequences for happiness and pleasure or has the consequence of satisfying people's preferences.

However, utilitarianism often runs up against a set of objections we can call *moral monstrosity*, where the outcome which appears most good in consequential terms runs directly counter to our intuitive reasoning and the idea of the right. We can approach this by engaging in various thought experiments.[21]

A common set of examples is called doctors' dilemmas. In the first example we imagine it is wartime. A doctor is tending a badly wounded man in conditions where the doctor's life is actually at risk. To save the man the doctor needs all his time and attention: he cannot afford to be distracted. If he attends to anything else but this one man the man will die. Our doctor is at great risk but he acts oblivious to it all. Ultimately, he survives and the man is saved. We would say not only is the doctor very brave, but he is a hero. At risk of his own life he kept to his goal. He should be rewarded. But what if the possible distraction were the fact that there was not one man that was wounded but several. Imagine that there are five other wounded men: they are not actually as badly wounded as the first, but if they do not receive attention they will die. If the doctor concentrates upon the most badly wounded man the others die. Imagine that he does and the five others die – is he still a hero? Do we reward him or think he made a bad decision? What if he turns away from the first to tend to the others, and the first dies? We have already recognised that if the doctor stays tending to him then he does a morally praiseworthy act – would he be justified in letting the one die for the others? What if some of the wounded are officers and some ordinary soldiers – should he try harder with the officers? What if some of the wounded are actually captured enemy, who only a short time previously were trying to kill the company with which the doctor is stationed?

The second example is a related doctor's dilemma: we can call it *the patient in room 306*. Our doctor is in a hospital where there are six patients awaiting organ transplants; one a liver, the other a heart, another a kidney etc. Without the transplants these six will die. Supplies of organs have run out. A patient is in room 306 and has booked in for a routine operation. His organs are all healthy. What if the doctor actually uses the patient in room 306 as a supply of organs? The one patient dies but is the source of life for six others – would not that be a noble thing for the doctor to do? To create the conditions wherein human life flourishes ...

A third, and favourite, example is that of punishing the innocent for the sake of doing greater overall good. Utilitarianism justifies punishing people only if punishment

---

21 Offering anti-utilitarian thought experiments is a common tactic which some writers attempt to defuse by distinguishing between act-utilitarianism (considering the action independently), and rule-utilitarianism (considering the action as a species of general rule and considering the effects of the general observance or non-observance of the rule). A common defence is that if we acted in the 'inhuman' way that utility seems to suggest there would be a general loss of confidence in our social institutions and general social happiness would decline. For example the level of trust would decline. This sort of argument is, in theory at least, easy to dispose of – simply consider the acts such that no publicity is given and therefore no decline in confidence takes place.

produces the best consequences. Under a deterrent theory of punishment, punishment is not inflicted because it is right and just that certain persons be punished, rather they are punished so that, as a result of the act of punishment, social pain is reduced because crime is deterred. But take the following example usually referred to as *the sheriff's dilemma*. We are in a small town in the Southern States of the United States of America and a story gets about that a black man has raped a white woman. The local sheriff is basically a good man; he realises a heavily armed lynch mob is preparing to go down to the black area of town which would result in a host of beatings and lynchings. Understanding that a number of people are going to suffer, the sheriff goes down to the black part of town before the lynch mob gets there and takes a black man who is quite a simple, nice and decent fellow and entirely innocent. The sheriff takes him back to the jail, gives him a quick mock trial and hangs him. He tells the lynch mob: 'it's okay, I have got the rapist; he admitted the crime and I have strung him up around the back – you can go and have a look.' The lynch mob no longer has a reason to go into the black part of town and have a lynching. As a result many lives are saved. Is this action of the sheriff justified? Mostly we say 'no, because it is punishment of the innocent'. But the sheriff can reply that the person concerned died quickly, almost painlessly, and although his suffering was unfortunate because he was innocent, his suffering was as nothing compared to the suffering that would have taken place had the lynch mob attacked a bunch of innocent people.

Most people believe utilitarianism is wrong in these situations and runs counter to strong intuitions we have concerning the priority of the right over the consequentialist accounting.

The fourth area is more subtle (it has some overtones of the doctors' dilemmas) and it is expounded by Bernard Williams (1973). We are asked to imagine an English explorer who comes to a South American town to find a firing squad about to shoot 20 Indians as a reprisal for acts of protest against the government. The captain of the militia offers the visitor a 'guest's privilege' of shooting one Indian on the understanding that if he does so the rest will be set free, but, if he does not, all 20 will be shot. There is no chance of the visitor overwhelming the captain by force, so what should he do? Utilitarianism answers that he should kill the Indian and Williams comments on the fact that utilitarianism not only gives this answer but gives it as the obvious answer. Williams does not find it so obvious for a number of reasons, including the wrongness of the killing and the fact that the utilitarian argument appears to put the visitor under a duty to do the killing. Utilitarianism does not bring out the wrongness of forcing a person to do something which is against his values. Here the visitor is expected to do something which his whole being, his integrity, is against. Utilitarianism just cannot account for this concept of dignity, or the idea of a person having a transcendent moral personality.

Contrasting the right and the good: the example of sentencing and punishment

Punishment is the deliberate infliction of pain, and we normally hold that consciously to inflict pain, loss, misery, deprivation on a person is to do what is morally wrong; how then is this deliberate action justified? Utilitarianism holds that the only good reason for punishing is the hoped-for good consequences of doing so, while retributionism holds that punishment is only justified as the giving to the offender of his just deserts. These two theoretical positions are contradictory; one looks to the future while the other looks to the past.

The classic utilitarian position, the position of philosophers and legal reformers in the tradition of Beccaria, Jeremy Bentham and William Paley (1743–1805), can be summarised in the following propositions:

1   The only acceptable reason for punishing a person is that punishing him will help prevent or reduce crime.

2   The only acceptable reason for punishing a person in a given manner or degree is that this is the manner or degree most likely to reduce or prevent crime.

3   People should be punished only if punishing is the best way to prevent or reduce crime.

A utilitarian judge in sentencing looks to the future. He is concerned with what good punishment is likely to do for everyone concerned. The overall aim is to maximise the happiness of the totality. Crime is a reduction in happiness. Utilitarian judges and legislators consider punishment as only one of the measures for dealing with crime. The chief value of punishment consists in its deterring or preventing crime. Punishment is a general deterrent if it deters other potential criminals from crime, for fear they will suffer what the convicted criminal suffers. It is a specific deterrent if it discourages the criminal himself from committing a crime.

Punishment, by its nature, causes some misery, the misery of the criminal. A good utilitarian has to show therefore that punishment is preferable to crime-reducing measures that cause less, or no, misery. Among other ways of preventing or reducing crime, classic (and modern) utilitarians consider means of reducing temptations to crime. Examples of such means are legislation controlling the sale of explosives or of easily concealed arms, warnings against leaving portable property unwatched or unlocked, or the printing of difficult-to-reproduce currency. In designing a criminal code, utilitarians consider such matters as motivating the criminal contemplating a crime to commit the less serious of the alternative crimes he may have in mind. For example, if the penalty for rape as well as for murder is execution, the rapist will have no incentive, so far as the criminal code is concerned, not to murder his victim.

From the utilitarian point of view, no penal legislation is warranted that is ineffective, that is, if it cannot serve to prevent crime. This rules out *ex post facto* laws, laws that are not adequately promulgated, and the punishment of infants, insane persons, or persons who were physically compelled to do what they did. Penal legislation must also not be unprofitable or needless. It is unprofitable if it would produce worse consequences, with respect to the general happiness, than the offence it is meant to prevent – for example, the 18th-century penalty of execution for stealing bleaching goods from the bleaching grounds. It is needless if the crime can be prevented or discouraged at a lower cost in misery than punishment – for example, by early childhood instruction.

To be guided by what the criminal deserves is, from the classic utilitarian point of view, to be confused or misled. Paley puts the point clearly:

> The crime must be prevented by some means or other; and consequently whatever means appear necessary to that end, whether they be proportional to the guilt of the criminal or not, are adopted, rightly, because they are adopted upon the principle which alone justifies the infliction of punishment at all ... The very end for which human government is established, requires that its regulations be adapted to the suppression of crimes. This end, whatever it may do in the plans of infinite wisdom, does not in the designation of temporal penalties, always coincide with the proportionate punishment of guilt (Paley, Vol II, Book VI, Ch 9).

For every proposition in the classic utilitarian position, there is a classic retributionist counter-proposition:

1   The only acceptable reason for punishing a person is that he has committed a crime.

2   The only acceptable reason for punishing a person in a given manner and degree is that the punishment is what he deserves.

3   Whoever commits a crime must be punished in accordance with his desert.

Retributionism asks the judge to look back to what the criminal has done, ie, the offence. What the offender deserves is linked to what he has done, the seriousness of the crime. The possible or probable consequences of punishing the criminal are irrelevant. Kant's theory on punishment is a rationalist argument and has come to be known as a natural rights theory. In *The Metaphysical Elements of Justice* (1965), Kant rejects the utilitarian arguments of Beccaria while strengthening his 'rights' approach into the absolute binds of deontological reasoning. He argues that we cannot look to calculations as to the effects of punishment, or non-punishment, upon the sum of goodness in the world (whether we define that goodness as pleasure, satisfaction of desire etc), but must relate punishment to the test of whether it satisfies the person's capacity for *autonomy*. Thus, individuals are assumed to have the capacity to determine their own ends as free and rational creatures and to live their life acknowledging this capacity in all the other members of their society of mankind. Punishment is thus done to an individual for his intrusion into the autonomy of the other, and that punishment is to be related to the degree and quality of that disrespect and intrusion. Punishment is then to be strictly limited in kind and duration to the moral gravity of the actions which the offender has performed; the purity of this linkage, however, is such that it must not only be limited in extent and duration, and hence to overpunish is wrong, but that punishment must always be undertaken, for not to punish is wrong (it does not respect the autonomy of the offender). Kant is the paradigm of the classic retributionist:

> Judicial punishment can never be used as a means to promote some other good for the criminal himself or for civil society, but instead it must in all cases be imposed on him only on the ground that he has committed a crime; for a human being can never be manipulated merely as a means to the purposes of someone else .:. The law concerning punishment is a categorical imperative, and woe to him who rummages around in the winding paths of a theory of happiness looking for some advantage to be gained by

releasing the criminal from punishment or by reducing the amount of it – in keeping with the Pharisaic motto: 'It is better that one man should die than that the whole people should perish.' If legal justice perishes, then it is no longer worth while for men to remain alive on this earth (Kant, 1797: 331-332).

In deciding how and how much the offender is to be punished, Kant insists that the only thing able to be considered is the act the offender has done. The system of punishment is to be formulated strictly and solely based on the nature of the crime. And punishment is to be ranked in seriousness equal to the seriousness of the offence. Under this principle of equality:

... any undeserved evil that you inflict on someone else among the people is one that you do to yourself. If you vilify him, you vilify yourself; if you steal from him, you steal from yourself; if you kill him, you kill yourself. Only the law of retribution (*jus talionis*) can determine exactly the kind and degree of punishment ... All other standards fluctuate back and forth, and, because extraneous considerations are mixed with them, they cannot be compatible with the principle of pure and strict justice (Kant, *ibid*: 332).

Kant thus tells us how and how much we must punish, if we punish. But this is no light burden, crime must meet its desert. We have an absolute obligation to punish crime in accordance with its desert:

Even if a civil society were to dissolve itself by common agreement of all its members (for example, if the people inhabiting an island decided to separate and disperse themselves around the world), the last murderer remaining in prison must first be executed, so that everyone will duly receive what his actions are worth and so that the blood-guilt thereof will not be fixed on the people because they failed to insist on carrying out the punishment; for if they fail to do so, they may be regarded as accomplices in this public violation of legal justice (Kant, *ibid*: 333).

To utilitarians this is pure moral rigidity. However, classic retributioniism and classic utilitarianism are polar opposites.

KANT ON DESCRIBING THE JOURNEY OF MANKIND

Kant surrounds his various discussions on morality and political philosophy with a particular vision of the nature of progress and the role of man. Progress for man is movement towards the highest good. Man in society considered phenomenally is subject to the laws of nature, and in his rational existence in the social body he is subject to laws which apply both externally and internally (ourselves considered both phenomenally and noumenally). The laws of our free state:

... insofar as they are only directed at external actions are called judicial, but when they also demand that they [the laws] should themselves be the determining grounds of the action then they are ethical.

Man can use the structures of human cognition, the structure of humanity's linkage to reason, to open up the task of social life to reason. Mankind:

... cannot do without associating peacefully and yet cannot avoid constantly offending one another. Hence they feel destined by nature to create through mutual compulsion under laws which proceed from themselves, a coalition which, though constantly threatened by dissension, makes progress on the whole (*Anthropology*, 1974:191).

Kant states that if a man acts in accordance with the law out of terror or coercion it is a mere hypothetical motive, but when he is motivated by an acceptance of the law itself it is an act in line with the categorical maxim. Freedom exists only in the second case and comes from 'the autonomy of the will', as opposed to the 'heteronomy' of the agent who acts in obedience not to the commands of his rational reflection but out of passion, fear or hope of reward. The heteronomous agent is truly the 'slave' agent and although in his lack of strength he performs the observable actions of morality, he has taken refuge in this subjection to 'nature' and/or to 'superior force'. He may disguise his slave mentality, his amorality, in a confusion of discourse, but this needs to be subjected to critical examination and this critical orientation is necessary to achieve the autonomy which will enable him to act as rationally autonomous and in so doing command the respect of other rational beings.

In *What is Orientation in Thinking* (contained in Kant, 1949), Kant appears to argue that the guarantee of progress is reason's own ability to point itself in the proper direction, to determine for itself the correct use of the transcendental procedure. This is the full confidence of the rationalist imagination – the true metaphysical faith. Seen in this way, the progress of man is, in effect, part of the journey of reason: one which is also an historical journey in which are tied together the diverse strands of man's existence. The backdrop of man's phenomenal positioning is the metaphysical aspects of practical reason in the suppositions of God, immortality, freedom, and their interactions within the life of rational coexistence and co-operation with fellow rational human beings. Man considers himself first, and insofar as he belongs to the sensible world, to be under the laws of nature (heteronomy), and second, insofar as he belongs to the intelligible world, to be under laws, which being independent of nature, are not empirical but have their ground in reason alone. Out of this interface frames of reference for social life develop, and thus the limited potentiality of the sentient life of the cave, or alternatively as Plato also put it, the life of the city of pigs, is enabled to be transcended and guided by the transcendental procedure. In this, 'man as a rational being' can never exist in a system governed by the operation of his will except under the idea of freedom, attached to which is the concept of 'autonomy', and it is from this that the 'universal principle of morality', the 'categorical imperative', issues.

What is this freedom to consist of? Freedom is not lack of constraint, but is a particular form of constraint. The true state of freedom for man lies in his subjection to the moral law of which man himself is the giver to man, and is at its highest when man recognises the necessity of that law and its absolute authority over the actions of the rational agent. Social progress, what appears as the teleological realisation of social man, is effected through the mediation of judgment as it transforms people from pre-rational to rational beings. Man is to be the creator of the progressive social, and of his individual character 'insofar as he is capable of perfecting himself according to ends he himself adopts'. The construction of the social is a distinctly moral-ethical problematic and is the true activity of the 'human' enterprise (1974: 183).

The progress of the social can only be structured by the declaration of regulative ethical norms – in the acceptance and communal articulation of these norms the rational guidance of man as social being is affected and the resulting expression conveys the expressive realisation of the dignity of man. The laws man forms in social life are to:

> ... proceed from themselves, a coalition which, though constantly threatened by dissension, makes progress on the whole (1974: 191).

The political-ethical life of the modern state is to be constitutional, bound by those public laws created under the guidance of:

> an idea of reason, which nevertheless has undoubted practical value; for it can oblige every legislator to frame his laws in such a way that they could have been produced by the united will of the whole nation, and to regard each subject, insofar as he can claim citizenship, as if he had been represented within the general will. This is the test of rightfulness of every public law ('*Theory and Practice*', p 74).

THE JOURNEY OF THE WHOLE

> Individual men and even entire peoples give little thought to the fact that while each according to his own ways pursues his own end – often at cross purposes with each other – they unconsciously proceed toward an unknown natural end, as if following a guiding thread; and they work to promote an end they would set little store by, even it they were aware of it (Kant, *Idea for a Universal History with a Cosmopolitan Intent*, 1983: 29).

Kant postulated that society is progressing towards the constitution of a world-wide ethical commonwealth in which the process of creating a political commonwealth is the first step. There are two areas where progress must occur: (i) progress in politics and in the development of a world-wide legal system; (ii) progress in ethics and in the correspondence of the internal (ethical) law-making to the external. There are two stages of association.

> A juridico-civil (political) condition is the relation of men to each other in which they are all alike and stand socially under public juridical laws (which are as a whole coercive laws). An ethico-civil condition is that in which they are united under non-coercive laws, ie laws of virtue alone (1960: 87).

The judico-civil condition presents an external framework, creating assurances demonstrated in the formal coercive instruments of the state that individuals will act in a lawful way. Kant saw this society as, however, a rather fragile structure and one that was dependent upon this 'artificial' law to unite the various pulses, desires, and projects which otherwise threaten to tear it apart. The operation of law at this stage was to hold together a socially disunited group of people through moderating and controlling individual claims. The otherwise rampant subjectivism of man's contingent and historical attitudes needed to be brought under a system of state laws, and the operation of these coercive laws was based upon the principle of strict reciprocity in the treatment of others since no individual is prepared to give to others any more than the freedom which he enjoys. This is not a state of social peace. In our present political condition (*judicio-civil*) we are internally in a state of nature, for no one accepts the public, general authority as having the power to judge 'what is each man's duty in every situation.' The state cannot tell man how he ought to live, it can only tell him how he can and must live. Civil society is the product of the 'political' dimension of man, and the realm of civil society is divided into two realms, the public and the private, a demarcation which has proved basic to liberalism; the private domain of liberal virtue, and the public domain of political, lawful 'right'. The legitimation of the inner continues directly the tradition of the religious, the outer becomes the institutionalised order legitimated through the political constitution and the formal laws of the state. The ethical community, which will in time, Kant hopes, come to replace the political, cannot be based upon coercive laws such as those of the political situation since with the ethical community 'the very concept involves freedom from coercion' (1960: 87). Man progresses by leaving the ethical state of nature and thus frees the state from the existence of coercive laws in the adoption of virtuous motives and the performance of action under the idea of achieving the highest social good, which is the ultimate social goal.[22]

> Here we have a duty which is sui generis, not of men towards men, but of the human race towards itself. For the species of rational beings is objectively in the idea of reason, destined for a social good, namely, the promotion of the highest good as a social goal (1960: 89).

Thus we can postulate a goal to history: 'the sublime, yet never wholly attainable' idea of an ethical commonwealth (1960: 91), and we can place our trust in reason: 'The universal religion of reason' (1960: 113) can lead us onto 'a (divine) ethical state on earth'. The moral law of reason is 'erecting for itself ... a power and kingdom which sustains the victory over evil and under its own dominion, assures the world of an eternal peace' (1960: 114). Our commitment to reason will overcome the dehumanising state of the political commonwealth, transform the epoch, and overcome the political providing the space of the ethical. The spirit and constitution of modernity will be transformed into the 'peace' of the universal ethical spirit. A system of comprehensive and enforceable law is therein not the goal of human ordering, nor is it a sufficient condition for the good society, but it is a necessary condition. Ultimately, Kant's message is simple: we must be subjects of law before we can be creatures of peace.

---

22 This concept, although central, is ambiguous. As Beck (1960) identifies it, the concept of the highest good is also described variously as the kingdom of God, the intelligible world, the existence of moral beings under the moral law, the moral vocation of man, the regulative 'ideal of reason' (with an ideal being 'the concept of an individual object completely determined through the mere idea'), and also as the greatest happiness combined in the most perfect proportion with the highest degree of moral perfection, and the statement of the *Grounding for the Metaphysic of Morals* that 'two things constitute the *summum bonum* – the moral perfection of the person and the physical perfection of his state'.

CHAPTER 7

FROM ROUSSEAU TO HEGEL:
the birth of the expressive tradition of law
and the dream of Law's Ethical Life

PART ONE
THE AMBIGUOUS ROMANTICISM OF
ROUSSEAU AND THE EXPRESSIVE IDEA
OF THE SOCIAL CONTRACT

The passage from the state of nature to the civil state produces a very remarkable change in man, by substituting justice for instinct in his conduct, and giving his actions the morality they had formerly lacked. Then only, when the voice of duty takes the place of physical impulses and right of appetite, does man, who so far had considered only himself, find that he is forced to act on different principles, and to consult his reason before listening to his inclinations ... What man loses by the social contract is his natural liberty and an unlimited right to everything he tries to get and succeeds in getting; what he gains is civil liberty and the proprietorship of all he possesses. If we are to avoid mistakes in weighing one against the other, we must clearly distinguish natural liberty, which is bounded only by the strength of the individual, from civil liberty, which is limited by the general will ... We might, over and above all this, add, to what man acquires in the civil state, moral liberty, which alone makes him truly master of himself; for the mere impulse of appetite is slavery, while obedience to a law which we prescribe to ourselves is liberty (J-J Rousseau, *The Social Contract*, [1762] 1973: 195-6).

[While] money buys everything else, it cannot buy morals and citizens (J-J Rousseau, *Discourse on the Arts and Sciences*, [1750]).

MODERNITY: AN UNCERTAIN CONTEXT FOR
LEGITIMATING SOCIAL INSTITUTIONS

An ambiguous writer, who internalised the enlightenment's conflicting trends of optimism and pessimism, Rousseau (1712–1778)[1] appreciated that the process of

---

1   Rousseau was born in Geneva in 1712; his mother died soon afterwards, and his father, a watchmaker, left him from the age of 10 in the care of an aunt who raised him. After a short period in a boarding school where he learnt 'all the insignificant trash that has obtained the name of education' (as he put it in his Confessions) his formal education finished at 12. However, he was an avid reader. After being an apprentice to an engraver of watchcases, he left Geneva and wandered from place to place, meeting a series of people who alternately helped him make a meagre living, or referred him to still other potential benefactors, finally settling in France. His most consistent work was copying music, though he was for a while tutor to the children of M de Mably, grand provost of Lyons, and later secretary to the French Ambassador to Venice. The most obvious influence upon him was his imaginative readings of the 'classics' of Plato, Virgil, Horace, Montaigne, Pascal, and Voltaire. In Paris he moved in literary circles but was struck by the great extremes of wealth and social existence, the majesty of cathedrals and the desperate poverty of slums, the gaiety of salons and the tragic themes of Racine's plays. Although moving increasingly within upper social circles he never felt at home in them and, in 1746, he formed a lifelong relationship with an uneducated young servant girl, Thérèse Levasseur, whom he finally married in 1768.

modernisation was creating a radically different context for humanity. In that modern society transgressed – or moved beyond – any natural state, a basic question becomes that of legitimation. What could make the differences in power and reward in the modern social structure acceptable?[2]

Rousseau was no social insider; his literary career began with his prize-winning essay entitled *Discourse on the Arts and Sciences* (1750). This was a work of tremendous rhetorical power which argued that morals had been corrupted by the replacement of religion by science, by sensuality in art, by licentiousness in literature, and by the emphasis upon logic at the expense of feeling. It made Rousseau instantly famous and his later writings received wide recognition.

The context of the modern subject – new organisations, procedures and new powers – threatened to prevent freedom, or *autonomy*. The themes of powerlessness, alienation and purity underpin Rousseau's concerns. Modernity forces upon the subject the questions 'who am I', and 'where am I?' But the subject is racked with conflicting emotions, hopes and fears and can hardly cope with understanding his/her personal position; how then can the social be judged? Understanding this weakness was itself a start, proposing a first principle, namely, that the personal and the social were intertwined. Our personality – our personhood – is a function of the social and historical context we find ourselves in. What then of the new society of the Enlightenment? How is this context to be understood and what was the impact of emerging modernity upon the human condition? Rousseau was convinced that a new form of human existence had been created. In opposition to Hume, Rousseau suggested that human nature was not a constant but had been changed through involvement in society. As a consequence, self-criticism is a form of social criticism, and social criticism is self-criticism. The new 'modern' self is a social self, made possible by a new social order, but that social order needs the self to recreate itself, modernity demands that the (pre-)modern social subject transform itself into a new social self.[3] But, in socialising humanity for this new order, what is gained and what lost? Is the civilising process the progressive and irreversible development of a fully modern individual, or the sublimation of aspects of human nature by a facade of inhuman constraints in the name of proper socialisation?

In what way do our emerging modern institutions express the truth of mankind's natural condition? Does the 'escape' from the domination of religion, tradition, custom and 'natural ordering' in favour of modernity, make mankind more free, or simply the servants of a new master? Does freedom allow us to become fully human – in that we develop our own ends and desires as opposed to those imposed upon us by nature? If we

---

2   In 1755 Rousseau identified the problem of social order in terms of a paradox: 'Man is born free, and everywhere he is in chains ... How did this change occur? I do not know. What can make it legitimate? I believe I can answer this question ... the social order is a sacred right that serves as the basis for all others. However, this right does not come from nature; it is based on convention. The problem is to know what these conventions are' (opening sentence of Book I of *The Social Contract*). Man desires freedom but delivers himself into chains; a subjection legitimated by the conventions of the social order. The social order, however, is not a mere reflection of a natural order, it is an artifice created by man.

3   The context of this social order is the city. The city stands for both the new freedom, a freedom in anonymity, and terror, the terror of uncontrollable (un)sociality.

follow the projects of our 'self-assertion' are we engaging in a more fully 'human' behaviour, as opposed to following the impulses of our nature, no matter how satisfying the latter are?

The idea of a fundamental disjunction between the social and the natural condition provides the basis of all Rousseau's work serving as the backdrop to his writings on law and politics (the classic text is *The Social Contract*; references given as SC). Through socialisation man is transformed 'from a stupid, limited animal into an intelligent being and a man ... [to obey] the impulse of appetite alone is slavery'. The political and legal constitution effects a creative 'denaturing' of man. Thus, modernity could offer scope for the radical development of a new kind of humanity; conversely, it could subject us to confining practices and turn us into mere objects of rule. We need moral concepts to judge the transformations of modernity. Rousseau suggests that institutions that do not in some way embody our freedom to define our own ends, strip us of our humanity. Moreover, if our institutions do not recognise and incarnate our humanity they are an obstacle to freedom. Humans have many contradictory impulses; our institutions ought to allow complexity, but aim to overcome contradiction: 'all institutions which put man into contradiction with himself are worth nothing' (SC, 3: pp 464 and 128 of the *Complete Works*). Social institutions should express and reconcile the truths of the human self, else we are doomed to inhuman contradictions and incoherences. The sources of dissatisfaction lie in both the social order *AND* the composition of the human self. There can be no retreat to an analysis of either the social without the personal, or the personal without the social. The personal is created by the social, and the social is the realm where the personal takes its life.

The emerging discourses on law and society tended to deny this interrelationship. 'Modern' discourses separated realms of analysis, compartmentalising the human condition; in discussing politics, for example, they stressed effectivity rather than the affectional.[4] The proto-liberalism of the day stressed that the legal structure will only lay out tools of impersonal social interaction – the realm of the abstract citizen entering into contracts. As a consequence, the (social) 'meaning' of life will become a private pursuit. Rousseau imagined that the past held a greater social belonging and purity; as he put it in *Discourse on the Arts and Sciences*: 'Ancient politicians spoke incessantly about morals and virtue, ours speak only of business and money' ([1750] 1973: 19). The ancient pagan republics of Athens and Sparta seemed to offer examples of social belonging; a way of life and political discourse where the social constitution provided a home for the persons who made it up, in contrast to an empty individualism increasingly espoused in the name of modern freedom. Classical republics were inhabited by strong men who were

---

4   The new discourses of modernity were stressing distance and control. Man was taken out of his 'natural' position in the name of freedom; but this increased the need for a discourse and a technique for creating a new order which would command the (new) individual's allegiance. The traditional form of legitimation and allegiance, that of the 'natural law' was fractured: 'I observe that in the modern age men no longer have a hold on one another except by force or self-interest; the ancients, by contrast, acted much more by persuasion and by the affections of the soul because they did not neglect the language of signs ... The face of the earth was a book in which their archives were preserved' (J-J Rousseau, *Emile*, 1979: 321).

bursting with pride; their plays reflected the heights of tragedy and comedy. Looking at his fellow citizens, Rousseau could only see the Hobbesian quest for felicity:

> You are neither Romans nor Spartans; you are not even Athenians. Leave aside these great names that ill suit you. You are merchants, artisans, bourgeois, always occupied with private interest, work, business, and gain; people for whom freedom itself is only a means of acquiring without obstacle and possessing without security (*Letters from the Mountain*, 3: 881).

How could men become as good as those of the ancient past in the conditions of early modernity? Rousseau's answer was in a just social order. How would this be made possible? Only if the social contract founding the new society expressed the *general will*.[5]

THE SOCIAL CONTRACT

Rousseau does not use the social contract idea to describe the transition from the state of nature to civil society, rather the social contract provided an answer to the question 'why should a person obey the laws of a modern society?' *The Social Contract* is an extended essay upon the *legitimation of modernity*. It is an attempt to transform an instrumental idea into an expressive phenomenon.

Note that the expressive tradition is also normative. Rousseau's essays are not dryly descriptive of the historical development of modernity, rather they are *aesthetic* readings of the conditions for ascertaining legitimacy in early modernity. Rousseau creates his essay on justice, for example, to enable us to criticise the social from a 'provisional' point of view. We need to attain a site, a distance from our context, wherefrom we may better understand and critically judge our conditions. But we can never transcend our context; the Platonic simile of the cave cannot be experienced in real life; how then can we escape from our immersion in convention? We do this by 'setting all the facts aside' and creating hypothetical models and images in comparison to which we may better understand our present: 'The researches concerning [the origins and foundations of inequality among men] must not be taken for historical truths, but only for hypothetical and conditional reasoning, better used to clarify the nature of things than to show their true origin' (*Discourse on the Origins and Foundations of Inequality among Men*, 1964: 103).

The *Social Contract* intermixes the historical, the theoretical, the fictive and the hypothetical; while we may be dissatisfied by the impurity of this methodology, it may also reflect Rousseau's recognition of the inherent impossibility of telling the 'truth' of the human condition. Rousseau refers to a discourse which lays out a genealogy of the modern individual, while providing a discourse of speculative truths on mankind. We cannot have a total or absolute science of the modern subject since the modern subject is no longer natural, but rather social-cultural: 'The passage from the state of nature to the civil state produces a truly remarkable change in the individual. It substitutes justice for

---

5   This answer is open to varying interpretations. Each idea can be analysed and deconstructed and repositioned in varying schemes. Rousseau has been seen as the theoretical instigator of the French Revolution, as the rhetorical father figure of Marxism, as a defender of the rule of law, and as leading to totalitarian results.

instinct in his behaviour, and gives to his actions a moral basis which formerly was lacking (SC, i, viii, 1973: 177).

How does the social contract found justice? Man was happy in the state of nature in that he enjoyed an absolute independence and obeyed only the laws he gave himself. Although he was primarily motivated by the desire for self-preservation, this desire led him to recognise the need for virtue and his common humanity. His natural innocence became corrupted: through social contacts man developed vices and was motivated to raise himself over his fellows. The competition to succeed and dominate others was the source of the crimes and evils men perpetrated upon each other. How could a social association be created which reconciled the independence which men naturally had with the necessities of social life? The task was to develop an 'association which will defend and protect with the whole common force the person and the goods of each associate, and in which each, while uniting himself with all, may still obey himself alone'. To solve the problem of the tension between the individual and the social, the social must become the embodiment of the personal; the laws will command obedience because they are what we have commanded to ourselves and express our general will.

The social contract was not some event of the past but a living reality present wherever there was legitimate government. This living contract is the fundamental principle underlying a political association in that it provides a mechanism whereby everybody adjusts their individual conduct to harmonise with the legitimate freedom of others. Man trades his 'natural liberty' for a 'civil liberty' and the enforcement of property 'rights'.[6] In a famous phrase Rousseau defines the social contract in terms of each individual putting his person and power into a common holding under the supreme direction of the *general will*, whereby we relate to each other as constituent parts of an 'indivisible whole'.[7] Moreover, by the terms of the contract, those who refuse to obey the general will can be compelled to do so; men can be compelled to be free. The social contract is the mechanism by which the problem of constructing the modern is solved, namely the constituting force of law.[8]

---

6   What is this civil liberty to consist of? In the terms of our earlier discussion derived from Hobbes it looks as if it will be a negative liberty (defined by Hobbes when he refers to 'natural liberty', and which carries over to liberalism's idea of freedom from restraint, as 'Liberty, or freedom, signifieth, properly, the absence of opposition; by opposition I mean external impediments of motion' (L, Ch 21)), or *freedom from* constraint, etc. Rousseau appears to be searching for a new form of civic freedom, or *freedom to* live as a more fully human being than allowed in the past, without being destroyed by personal and social conflict.

7   'The problem is to find a form of association which will defend and protect with the whole common force the person and goods of each associate, and in which each, while uniting himself with all, may still obey himself alone, and remain as free as before ...
     The clauses of this contract ... are everywhere the same and everywhere tacitly admitted and recognised ... These clauses, properly understood, may be reduced to one – the total alienation of each associate, together with all his rights, to the whole community ... for, if the individuals retained certain rights, then there would be no common superior to decide between them and the public, each, being on one point his own judge, would ask to be so on all, and the state of nature would continue' (SC, 1973: 174).

8   For Rousseau the central problem of politics was how 'to place law above man'; this he compared 'to the squaring of the circle in geometry'. Modern freedom was tied to the project of coming to obey laws and not men.

The social contract gives 'the body politic existence and life', but legislation gives it 'movement and will'. The idea of the general will solves a pressing problem. Namely, Rousseau wants the law to be free from the domination of a small elite and express the will of the people as a whole – whereby the citizen who can be compelled to obey the law, obeys not an instrument of specific domination, but of general value.

> That all should obey, yet nobody take upon him to command and that all should serve and have no masters? ... These wonders are the work of the law. It is to law alone that men owe justice and liberty. It is this salutary organ of the will of all which establishes in civil right the natural equality between men ... The first of all laws is to respect the laws (*A Discourse on Political Economy*, 1973: 124).

THE IDEA OF THE GENERAL WILL

How can the diverse groupings and subjective wills of the population be linked together into a rational system?[9] Only if the law is the product of the general will, and this general will is the will of the 'Sovereign', then the law speaks for the rationality of the whole social body. The will of the Sovereign is not the arbitary will of an individual or groups of individuals; the prince, or the elite body of men who make up the Sovereign, is a distinct body from the jurisprudential entity of the Sovereign. The Sovereign is the centrality of power and the general will which directs that power through law.[10] In ideal form, the Sovereign would consist of the total number of the citizens of the society; the general will is therefore the single will of the total of the citizens. The many and diverse wills of the population can be considered a single will because everyone is a party to the social contract and in that contract they have agreed to direct their actions to achieving the common good. Each citizen understands that he should refrain from any action which would cause the others to turn upon him; in this way each realises that his own good and the common good are intertwined.[11] Ultimately, through the contract, each individual's will becomes merged with others in that all are directed to the same purpose, namely the common good.

---

9   'How can a blind multitude, which often does not know what it wills, because it rarely knows what is good for it, carry out for itself so great and difficult an enterprise as a system of legislation?' (SC, 1973: 193)

10 In the original sections which were in the *Geneva Manuscript of the Social Contract*, (contained in 1973: 281) Rousseau defines sovereignty as follows: 'There is ... in the State, a common force which sustains it and a general will which directs this force; the application of the one to the other constitutes sovereignty. From this it becomes clear that the sovereign is, by its nature, only a corporate entity, that it has only an abstract and collective existence, and that the idea which is attached to this word cannot be united to that of a single individual.'
    This means that the actual body of men exercising sovereign power can be constrained by the jurisprudential imagination. Thus: ' ... the dominant will of the prince is, or should be, nothing but the general will or the law; his force is only the public force concentrated in his hands, and, as soon as he tries to base any absolute and independent act on his own authority, the tie that binds the whole together begins to be loosened. If finally the prince should come to have a particular will more active than the will of the sovereign, and should employ the public force in his hands in obedience to this particular will, there would be, so to speak, two sovereigns, one rightful and the other actual, the social union would evaporate instantly, and the body politic would be dissolved' (SC 1973: 211-212).

11 Thus 'whoever refuses to obey the general will shall be compelled to do so by the whole body. This means nothing less than he will be forced to be free; for this is the condition which ... secures him against personal dependence' (1973: 107).

The general will is a specific concept; it is not the simple mathematical calculation of the 'will of all', such as a mere empirical manifestation of the votes in some simple voting system. The will of all becomes the general will only when it is in accordance with the purposes of the common good; often it is simply the will of a majority or a minority who have the vote. A society may not have a general will; instead its 'will of all' may be that of a political faction, and its purpose only the expression of dominant interest groupings[12] Rousseau appeared to believe that a diffusion of adequate knowledge concerning particular social problems would enable the opinions of the citizens to be shaped into a general will.[13] Knowledge concerning the social problem leads to a consensus and the wills of all are directed to the common good; the general will thereby directs us to social justice.

On what grounds can obedience be compelled? Only when we are operating under the idea that the law was made with the common good or social justice in mind; in which case the law expresses the general will, as opposed to being the instrumental outcome of special interests.[14] In this case the person who goes against the law is going against his own best interests; he is in error in that he is misguidedly putting his subjective desires in opposition to the just state of which his will, objectively, should be part. Politically, the voting system and the passing of law should be guided by the overriding purpose of the common good or social justice. It is only when the whole system is directed to the attainment of social justice and the laws and institutions express that commitment that we can be sure that the laws passed are actually in line with the general will.

Can we be sure that the idea of the general will is of actual use? How could an actual general will, a just political system, be established? What would provide the foundational point for this vehicle of pure modernity? The answer Rousseau gives in a chapter entitled 'The Law-giver' or 'The Legislator' (SC, 1973: 194-197) demonstrates the impossibility of modernity founding itself.

---

12 For Rousseau limited sovereignty is a contradiction in terms. The sovereign has the right to enforce whatever the common good requires. How then does he establish 'the limits of sovereign powers'? (SC, Bk II, Ch 4). Quite simply, the limits are those of justice. The state has the unlimited right to intervene for the common good of the whole when it needs so to intervene, but has no right to intervene when this condition is not satisfied. 'The sovereign cannot impose upon its subjects any fetters that are useless to the community, nor can it even wish to do so.' Of course, empirically, it has done so: often in countries that might trace their history of revolutionary fervour and ideas of enforcing the common good back to Rousseau.

13 This requirement probably limits the scope of legislation that Rousseau envisaged a rational state engaging in. He clearly states that 'no function that has a particular object belongs to the legislative power' (SC, 1973: 192). Rousseau distinguished 'magistracy' from the marks of 'sovereignty'. Making particular decisions, or creating specific 'commands' which affect only 'a particular matter', fall into the first category rather than being proper activities of law. Rousseau blamed the decline of democracy in ancient Athens upon the Greeks passing laws to satisfy personal whims, and creating particular favours (see discussions in Discourse on Inequality; also SC, 1973: 187, and on social decline through not understanding the role of law Bk III, Ch 11).

14 Let us remember that these laws are for Rousseau small in number ('a state so governed [according to Rousseau's principles] needs very few laws' SC, 1973: 247), and the political process is open to scrutiny, ensuring that the necessity for a particular law is easily recognised.

> In order for an emerging people to appreciate the healthy maxims of politics, and follow the fundamental rules of statecraft, the effect would have to become the cause; the social spirit, which should be the result of the institution, would have to preside over the founding of the institution itself; and men would have to be prior to laws what they ought to become by means of laws.

We find ourselves in a vicious theoretical circle where the effect must precede the cause! The social consciousness which would be the product of modern institutions would have to be in existence to produce modern institutions. Free institutions will only work if the citizens are free men; but only free men can (freely) bring about free institutions. Thus we must have some form of founding moment and founding mechanism which sets in place the conditions by which a free system can take life. The free state needs a *deus ex machina*, a 'law-giver', to found its institutions:

> The discovery of the best rules of society suited to nations would require a superior intelligence, who saw all of men's passions yet experiences none of them; who had no relationship at all to our nature yet knew it thoroughly.

No one body has this disinterested prescience, but the elites must try to recognise the path to a just social order in an essentially corrupt society, proposing laws by arguments addressed to the populace in such a form as would make them acceptable to a people not yet ready for the demands of pure freedom. The usual tactic historically, Rousseau notes, had been 'to have recourse to the intervention of heaven and to attribute their own wisdom to the gods', and thereby 'convince by divine authority those who cannot be moved by human prudence' (in *Complete Works* references at SC, 3: 381, 383–4; 67–68, 69–70). Rational discourse is grounded on the irrational; modern truth upon a falsehood. Modernity is founded on the lie that it is modern; the modern needs the tactics of the pre-modern to be effectual.[15]

INTERPRETING ROUSSEAU'S MESSAGE

What are we to make of Rousseau's bluntness? Is he telling the rulers that they can successfully rule only by fraud and trickery? Or is he cautioning the people to be wary of the promises and illusions that their rulers would impose upon them? And what of the *general will*? That regulative idea which, because it is easily misunderstood as if Rousseau were describing a reality, all too easily becomes the excuse for a totality? Does Rousseau, albeit in his desire to ensure that the social constitution does not lose its expressive nature, sacrifice the individual to the totality? In Rousseau's system the modern citizen is meant to be the fully social man, a man so conscious of his social

---

15 Rousseau did not appear to realise that the processes he was witnessing at the birth of modernity would speed up rather than stabilise over time. His entire work was a project in setting out the framework for modernity to establish and stabilise into a coherent form. He looked to the power of custom to establish practical allegiance. The new society, based on reasoned discussion, social justice and transparency, would be stable.

interdependency that he will not risk destroying the social bonds by retreating into his arbitrary subjectivity.[16] But, in describing how our rulers will need to convince us that it was not they who created our new laws but that the laws flowed from some form of God's will or functional necessity, Rousseau holds up both the image of a weapon for our subjection and the possibility of our demystifying such domination. Whether awareness of the tactics for creating legitimacy works to mystify us, or to offer us greater transparency concerning our social existence, may lie with our social imagination and willingness to create and defend our liberties.

Rousseau speaks of the inherent tensions of social life highlighted by modernity; law is interlinked with social institutions and cultural understandings. A law which forgets to express the culture of the people will be bad law.[17] We need each other as we fear each other; through the alienation of the individual to the community (the theoretical incorporation of the individual in the *general will*). Rousseau tries to legitimise and make bearable the chains of dependency we bear in civil society. We justify our loss of self-sufficiency and self-regarding happiness only by creating a political freedom wherein we make of ourselves something greater than we are in any natural state and create a new individuality worthy of respect. For several commentators this is the central political tension in Rousseau's position: he demands the complete subordination of the individual to the social for the sake of the individual, and in order to create an individuality that is more fully human than a non-social individuality. Political institutions not only secure the conditions through which the individual seeks satisfaction, but should ennoble his character and reconcile the conflicting demands of socialisation. The legitimate state is to produce healthy individuals as well as secure property.[18] What is the point of living in a 'law-and-order' society, in which one is free to accumulate property and engage in contracts secure in one's right to enforce them, if one's humanity is debased in the struggle and pulled apart by internal struggles and contradictions? The question raises itself in our own times with renewed force; not only have we come to appreciate Rousseau's contention that the cultural underpinnings of legal order are of vital importance in determining the 'kind of law' we have, but the fact that the idea of inherent contradictions as defining the human condition in (liberal) modernity is central to the Critical Legal Studies movement (see chapter 16 of this text)

---

16 'The legislator must take away from man his own resources and give him instead new ones alien to him, and incapable of being made use of without the help of other men. The more completely these natural resources are annihilated, the greater and more lasting are those which he acquires, and the more stable and perfect the new institutions; so that if each citizen is nothing and can do nothing without the rest, and the resources acquired by the whole are equal or superior to the aggregate of the resources of all the individuals, it may be said that legislation is at the highest possible point of perfection' (Rousseau, SC 1973: 194).

17 In SC, Bk II, Ch 12 (1973: 206-7) Rousseau stresses that the 'real constitution of the State' is 'not graven on tablets of marble or brass, but on the hearts of the citizens'. That is, morality, custom, and public opinion form social powers 'unknown to political thinkers, on which nonetheless success in everything else depends'.

18 The fact that the emerging modernity had not made people into better individuals was his chief ground for rejecting the form that modernity was taking. Thus, modern institutions had deformed mankind; they had made humans weak and miserable creatures.

is only one contemporary manifestation that Rousseau's dilemma has not been overcome. Rousseau's message to us may well have been simple: beware of all social theories which purport to make modernity appear natural![19]

---

19 But at the same time we have a desperate need to feel that the world makes sense. The tension has only increased since Rousseau's time.

PART TWO
FREDERICK HEGEL: THE PHILOSOPHY OF
TOTAL RECONCILIATION AND THE SEARCH
FOR LAW'S ETHICAL LIFE

The silent acquiescence in things as they are, the hopelessness, the patient endurance of a vast, overmastering fate, has turned to hope, to expectation, to the will for something different. The vision of a better and a more just time has entered alive into the souls of men, and a desire, a longing, for a purer, freer condition has moved every heart and has alienated it from the existing state of affairs ... Call this, if you like, a fever-paroxysm, but it will end either in death or in eliminating the cause of the disease ...

How blind are they who can imagine that institutions, constitutions, and laws can persist after they have ceased to be in accord with the morals, the needs, and the purposes of mankind, and after the meaning has gone out of them; that forms in which understanding and feeling no longer inhere can retain the power to bind a nation (Hegel, *Werke*, 1798: 150-151; quoted in Sabine and Thorson, 1973: 574-575).

HEGEL: RECONNECTING THE DUALISM OF THE HUMAN CONDITION INTO THE TOTALITY OF THIS WORLD

While Rousseau argued that only the state that attained perfect social justice could resolve the contradictions of the human condition, and Kant appeared to leave us suspended into two divided worlds, Hegel argued that reconciliation was, at least theoretically, possible.[20]

---

20 Kant's implication is that metaphysics is beyond science, that it is impossible for the human mind to achieve theoretical knowledge about all of reality. But Hegel began from the assumption 'what is rational is real and what is real is rational', and therefore everything that exists is knowable and furthermore has a rational construction. This was a total conception which provided a new basis for thinking about the very structure of reality and about its manifestations in morality, law, religion, art, history, and, above all, thought itself. His ideas have had a substantial impact. Much of 20th century philosophy represents revisions or rejections of aspects of his absolute idealism.

Hegel was born in Stuttgart in 1770 and the young Hegel was influenced both by the romantic movement in poetry and the writings of Plato and Aristotle. He attended the theological school at the University of Tübingen, was caught up in lively discussions over the issues of the French Revolution and his interest gradually turned to the relationship between philosophy and theology. In a sense Hegel developed Christian eschatology, where man meets his destiny with the final judgment and the life hereafter, into a philosophy of history where the development of the totality of human knowledge is essentially the same as the rational ordering of history, and so (replaces) our destiny with God.

In 1801, Hegel was appointed to the faculty of the University of Jena, and his first major work, *The Phenomenology of Mind*, was finished at midnight before the Battle of Jena in 1807. As this battle closed his university, Hegel supported himself and his wife, whom he married in 1811, by becoming rector of the secondary school at Nuremberg, where he remained until 1816. There he wrote his influential *Science of Logic*, which brought him invitations from several universities. In 1816 he joined the faculty of Heidelberg, where in the following year he published his *Encyclopedia of the Philosophical Sciences in Outline*, the work in which Hegel presents the grand structure of his philosophy in its three-fold aspect, namely logic, philosophy of nature, and philosophy of mind. Two years later, Hegel was given the chair of philosophy at the University of Berlin, where he remained until his death from cholera in 1831 at the age of 61. At Berlin Hegel's writings were massive, although most of them were published after his death. His works during this period included his *Philosophy of Right* and lectures, posthumously published, on *Philosophy of History, Aesthetics, Philosophy of Religion,* and *History of Philosophy*.

His message is, however, deeply ambivalent. While Hegel appeared to lay out the philosophy of the perfect social justice – the social totality of the ethical community – he did so within a philosophy of history and social development capable of multiple interpretations. Hegel gave us the image of social development as driven by dialectics (the clash of opposites); history was moved by the clash of opposing tendencies. Any static position contained conflicting – apparently contradictory – tendencies, and as apparent contradictions clashed and worked themselves into a new position (a temporary synthesis of the best elements in the two opposing positions), new conflicts and apparent contradictions became visible. Could we ever overcome social conflict and contradictions? Or is human history an inescapable process of continual movement wherein conflict and opposition is negotiated, compromises worked out, only for these in turn to be immediately rendered the subject of new conflicts?

FREEDOM AS A KEY CRITERION FOR MODERNITY

Influenced by Kant, Rousseau and others, Hegel accepts the principle of autonomy and the social project of realising freedom as the core of modernity, but argues that a new relationship of happiness and freedom was made visible when we situated what we empirically observed around us within the totality of philosophic history. The traditional aim of happiness as the end of human existence transposed to this world implied that man could only be happy when he was free. While freedom should be the regulative principle for guiding the historical destiny of mankind, Hegel argued freedom should be read in the widest, most expressive sense. Freedom ought to be the freedom to become; man must develop a consciousness of himself as a part of a socio-historical process moving towards the goal of absolute freedom. We must not rest an analysis of society upon static conceptions, or any philosophical analysis that proposes its analysis as if the truth of social existence could be divorced from the social-philosophical context; an essentially historical context.[21] Freedom is a historical process; the freedom which man

---

21 In essence for Hegel:

1 Reality is an historical process.

2 The historical process determines factors within it, for example, how humans behave. Human nature is not a constant but is embedded in ways of life, in societies.

3 There is a development discernible in history; history 'progresses' and this development is dialectical.

4 The aim of humanity is happiness but happiness is to be found in freedom; history is a movement towards realising human freedom; this process is reflexive, ie it involves our awareness of freedom and of increasing knowledge of ourselves.

5 The danger to freedom is *alienation*; alienation is the situation where part of ourself appears foreign to our real self – where humanity is at odds with itself. Alienation will be overcome when both social reason and personal reason are understood to be one and that this one is truly rational.

6 Knowledge brings freedom. In previous stages of world history we have not been in control, since things have been happening to us without our realising why they were happening nor understanding fully what they were. But, in that we now realise that the social world is our creation, our own reason can lay out its laws.

7 We seek life in a rationally ordered society. To achieve this society we should not impose some template of rationality upon it but bring out the rationality in the processes which have historically constituted it and build upon these. The technique is to find what is rational in the real, enhance it and develop it so as to allow it to fulfil itself.

seeks in modernity is to be realised through a normatively based society. A society which recognises individual autonomy and particularity, while its structures mediate individuality into an ethically constituted whole. The just society combines personal particularity and substantive unity within the objective forms of civil sovereignty.

THE STATE MUST REFLECT OUR NEED FOR A MORAL SOCIAL ORDER

If happiness is a question of living the truly free life, the social constraints that one is subjected to ought to be morally defensible. Law, as a regime of coercive power, must reflect the moral striving of the society. In pursuit of this aim, Hegel appears to remove any distinction between right and morality – between human law and morality – situating them instead within the context of an ethically constituted social order. In the *Philosophy of Right*, Hegel explicitly rejected the idea of the social contract as a basis for the explanation of the nature of political obligation. In contrast to Hobbes and Locke, where the legitimacy of civil government was rooted in the consent of its subjects, Hegel argued that the legitimacy attaching to governmental institutions of the state was grounded in principles of political morality immanent in the pre-legal norms, customs and practices which comprised what he called civil society. The dominant utilitarian trend to enlightenment thought saw in civil society the grounding of a form of association in which the contractual nexus – the coming together of essentially separated and atomistic individuals for mutual profit and security – predominated. Hegel's idea of community was much greater:

> If the state is confused with civil society, and if the state's specific end is laid down as the security and protection of property and personal freedom, then the interest of the individuals as such becomes the ultimate end of their association, and it follows that membership in the state is something optional. But the state's relation to the individual is quite different from this. Since the state is spirit objectified, it is only as one of its members that the individual himself has objectivity, truth (*Wahrheit*), and ethical life ... The individual's calling (*Bestimmung*) is to live a universal life. His further particular satisfactions, activity, and mode of conduct have this substantial and universally valid life as their starting point and their result (*Philosophy of Right*, para 258).

The so-called modern 'free' citizen of civil society, liberated from tradition and custom, is not free enough. He becomes immersed in the play of economic forces; following the contingent content of his desires he seeks out pleasures and lives a fate generated by the decisions of others in the market. A new form of objectivity is required to provide the modern with a rationally valid, yet free way of life. The aimless strivings of 'economic man' must be directed into a striving for the common good.

> The state is the actuality of concrete freedom. But concrete freedom consists in this, that personal individuality and its particular interests not only achieve their complete development and gain explicit recognition for their right ... but, for one thing, they also pass over of their own accord into the interest of the universal, and for another thing, they know and will the universal ... They take it as their end and aim and are active in its pursuit. The result is that the universal does not prevail or achieve completion except along with particular interests and through the co-operation of particular knowing and willing; individuals likewise do not live as private persons for their own ends alone, but in

the very act of willing these they will the universal in the light of the universal and their activity is consciously aimed at none but the universal end (*Philosophy of Right,* para 260).

For Hegel, however, civil society was made up of forms of human association, like the family and the household, which were essentially non-contractual in nature, and which, in consequence, generated principles of legitimacy and obligation that were binding irrespective of the consent or voluntary agreement of their members. Hegel insisted that such forms of association were metaphysically prior to the individual, in the sense that the family, the household and the other institutions constitutive of civil society could not properly be understood as instrumental associations – that is, as associations which existed merely to promote the realisation of the private aims and objectives of their members. Thus, Hegel characterised the true state as an ethical community, or more precisely as a form of Sittlichkeit, which embodied moral goods and values that were internal to its formal system of rules, laws and institutional procedures.[22]

THE CONSTITUTIONAL STATE IS AN HISTORICAL DEVELOPMENT WHICH MUST BE UNDERSTOOD AND CONTROLLED BY REFERENCE TO THE CONCEPTUAL TOOLS OF HISTORICAL UNDERSTANDING AND OUR READING OF HISTORY AS THE UNFOLDING OF AN ETHICAL SOCIAL LIFE

The state is the actuality of the ethical Idea. It is ethical mind qua the substantial will manifest and revealed to itself, knowing and thinking itself, accomplishing what it knows and in so far as it knows it (*Philosophy of Right,* para 257).

The true or ideal political constitution, the ideal society, the just state, is to reflect the progressive dialectical arguments concerning the social position and recognition of the worth of individual human dignity. The state is fully rational when it organises itself according to the totality of knowledge of the human condition and develops its substantive arrangements to reflect this knowledge. The state cannot abandon the question of justice, of the right, to some hidden hand of the market or other underlying 'natural' mechanism of civil society, rather, the idea of the general will is to be given substantive content. Hegel argues that social contract theorists, with their ideas of natural liberty, ignore the historical fact that human liberty is dependent upon social belonging. Hegel finds even Rousseau's idea of the social contract unacceptable, since he believes it:

---

22 Hegel's work has had a huge influence far beyond the usual identification with Marxism. In the British tradition Hegel's communitarian view of political association was taken up and restated by the influential philosopher Green in the posthumously published *Prolegomena to Ethics* (1883) and *Lectures on the Principles of Political Obligation* (1886), as well as by Bradley in his *Ethical Studies* (1876). In contemporary times the conservative scholar Michael Oakeshott followed Green and Bradley in acknowledging no absolute distinction between the legal and constitutional arrangements of the state and the cultural, economic and religious practices which made up the sphere of civil society. It was a mistake, he contended, to conceive of the state as merely 'a collection of persons', whether organised for legal, economic or political purposes, or to conceive the state as merely a physical territory subject to the jurisdiction of a particular system of law and civil administration. The authority exercised by the formal institutions of state government, he insisted, always presupposed the context provided by the social whole which satisfies the whole mind of the individuals who comprise it' (*The Authority of the State*: 10). Instead of the authority of the state arising from the voluntary consent or promissory agreement of its subjects, it lay solely in the completeness of the satisfaction which the state itself affords to the needs of concrete persons.

... reduces the union of individuals in the state to a contract and therefore to something based on their arbitrary wills, their opinion, and their capriciously given express consent; and abstract reasoning proceeds to draw the logical inferences which destroy the absolutely divine principle of the state, together with its majesty and absolute authority. For this reason, when these abstract conclusions came into power, they afforded for the first time in human history the prodigious spectacle of the overthrow of the constitution of a great actual state and its complete reconstruction *ab initio* on the basis of pure thought alone, after the destruction of all existing and given material. The will of its re-founders was to give it what they alleged was a purely rational basis, but it was only abstractions that were being used; the Idea was lacking; and the experiment ended in the maximum of frightfulness and terror (*Philosophy of Right*, para 258).

In their desire to universalise the freedom and liberty which they thought to underpin the French Revolution, the actors ignored social wisdom; Jacobean terror sprang from unbridled freedom. The multitude of individual actors and groups championed subjective rationality without incorporating and constraining the principle of individual autonomy within the objectivity of historical consciousness. Conversely, the fully modern state must be aware of the dialectics of history.

The state needs to be a legally constitutional state in the broadest meaning of the term. It needs to be an *imperium* of law's dominion. But this power must be ethical; law's imperium was to build Law's *Ethical Life*.[23] The French Revolution demonstrated that the divisions between social classes, between the rural and the urban, between the various groups, factions and individuals, ran so deep that some superior mode of attaining unity was required. Hegel refused to retreat to the tradition of patriarchal absolutism, or to turn to the vague imagery of some pure Germanic, organic *Volksgeist*. Instead the goal is for humanity to attain a perfect self-consciousness about the whole of its being; modernity was to be provided unity in the social power of knowledge itself and the social commitment to create a rational state obeying the dictates of that knowledge. 'The rational state', the living substantive incarnation of rationality, would provide the unifying mechanism and a site fit for mankind's fully modern life. But unity must not destroy individuality; the state must resolve the divisions of civil society without abandoning the principle of liberty. The individual was to be preserved by positioning individuality through the development of a jurisprudence of individual rights (property rights, contractual rights, recognition of being rights) into an objectively given historical reality of the state. The individual can only be preserved as a real living life-force if individuality is recognised as dependent upon a social totality organised around the dialectical progression of the particular and the universal, the individual and the social.

Individuality and sociality were not poles that cancelled each other out, they were rather conceptual tools whereby we recognised different sites of historical movements. When we recognise that individuality can only exist as part of a totality we understand that desiring the universal is both a movement of 'overcoming and preserving' the individual (the particular) in favour of the universal, and the safeguarding of individuality against the danger of a non-ethical totality. The development of law, the development

---

23   To give the title of the Third Part of Hegel's *Philosophy of Right* (law).

of the rational constitutional state, was the centre of Hegel's social theory; it depicted how the primary social institution was constructed through social dialectics (Aughebung), or the processes whereby the opposing sides of rational argument clashed and the best aspects of both were incorporated in the new position.

THE AMBIVALENCE OF HEGEL'S PICTURE: ROMANTICISM AND WARNING

Hegel has given inspiration to both the right and the left of the political spectrum. In part he reads like an historical romantic offering uplifting images, but while we can only make sense of our identity through history, and appreciate the glories of the past, we should neither underestimate nor overestimate the progressive and accumulative effects of our social development. We need a motivating spirit to guide social development, a Geist, which can enthuse us and be incorporated into all our social institutions. But what can provide this Geist? How can we be sure that this philosophy has any grounding in real history?

Hegel offers a reading of the history of the world in terms of the tensions between individual subjectivity and ideological totality. The ancient city states of Greece offered visions of strength and purpose but could not withstand the challenges of individuality. In the *Phenomenology of Spirit* Hegel abandons the spirit of the *polis* as the standard by which to measure modern social life, while Greek culture may offer us a beautiful unity, by contrast with which we often become ashamed of our divisions, the freedom of the modern outweighs what we have lost. Hegel depicted early Greek culture as exhibiting a basic contradiction, in that Greek life did not have the intellectual resources to sustain subjectivity but could not prevent subjectivity from coming into play. The society could only progress through bringing subjectivity to light, but once effective, subjectivity disturbs the equilibrium of Greek rationality. It disrupts its patterns and a new equilibrium is only possible on the basis of the principle of the self as a free independent subject. This individuation must, however, be sound; it must exist within a way of life which sets just limits to subjectivity and harmonises it within a larger, institutionalised ethical life.[24] For Hegel, this is the foundational problem of social existence. He appears to have feared that the world requires subjectivity but that no way of life could accommodate it effectively. His official position, though, is that the modern state, with its complex layering of the independent agent, the family, together with the mechanisms of market society, the universal orientation of the civil service, the will of the monarch and the unifying power of rational identification within this totality, is capable of housing each of these elements in a common life which harmonises them together. Modernity will transcend the tragic character of Greek life – hopefully ... The legal order, however, was in danger of ignoring the need for expressive unity:

---

24 Hegel viewed pre-Socratic Greek society as exhibiting a harmony between reason, desire and action. Socrates disrupted this simple harmony by asking 'what is justice? Why obey the law? What is the meaning of life?' Socrates subverted the social order by encouraging individual thought. Once in movement, subjectivity can only find a home in a social environment which allows individual conscience.

The statues are now mere corpses from which the living soul has flown, just as the hymns are words from which belief has gone. The tables of the gods provide no spiritual food and drink, and in his games and festivals man no longer recovers the joyful consciousness of his unity with the divine. The works of the Muse now lack the power of the spirit, for the spirit has gained certainty of itself from the crushing of gods and men. They have become what they are for us now – beautiful fruit already picked from the tree, which a friendly fate has offered us, as a girl might set the fruit before us ... But, just as the girl who offers us the plucked fruits is more than the nature which directly provides them – the nature diversified into their conditions and elements, the tree, air, light, and so on – because she sums all this up in a higher mode, in the gleam of her self-conscious eye and in the gesture with which she offers them, so, too the spirit of fate that presents us with those works of art is more than the ethical life and the actual world of that nation, for it is the inwardising in us of the spirit which in them was still outwardly manifested.

The message is simple – we moderns are in danger of losing our intellectual imagination to the dry writings of utilitarianism – but response is difficult. In part, Hegel contrasted utility to romantic passion,[25] and created a philosophical reading of the world which provided the state with an abstract purpose to give social life expressive meaning. For without expressive unity we could soon be lost in Hobbesian felicity, the pursuit of individual pleasure via playing the games of bourgeois life; our daily life more a reflection of our capital. Modernity would turn humans either into petty conformists without any sense of personal mission,[26] or alienated individuals incapable of finding meaning for life.[27]

THE SOVEREIGN WILL, OR THE NATURE OF THE WILL OF THE SOVEREIGN

Hegel argues that the legal order of the rational state comprises three elements: (i) the constitutional nature of sovereignty; (ii) the basic nature of law as principles which strive for universality – each 'idea' of spirit at any one time is undeveloped and must be

---

25 ' ... we may affirm absolutely that nothing great in the world has been accomplished without passion' (*Philosophy of History*, 163).

26 Hegel's image of the modern social subject was that of the bourgeois: 'The subject sows his wild oats, builds himself with his wishes and opinions into harmony with subsisting relationships and their rationality, enters the concatenation of the world, and acquires for himself an appropriate attitude toward it. However much he may have quarrelled with the world, or been pushed about in it, in most cases at last he gets his girl and some sort of position, marries her, and becomes as good a Philistine as others. The woman takes charge of the household management, children arrive, the adored wife, at first unique, behaves pretty much as other wives do; the man's profession provides work and vexations, marriage brings domestic affliction' (*Aesthetics*, 593).

27 For Hegel the ancient Greek worked with substantive ideas as to what the good life was. Everyday practices acknowledged and recognised the person according to the social roles and the place of those roles in the overall totality. But while each role took its meaning from its place and operation in the whole, it was open to the possibility of disagreement as other roles interact. As societies mature, a greater differentiation in roles and social knowledge occurs; this division can be interpreted as disintegration and social opposition, but is essential to the development of greater levels of social knowledge and perspectives. In short to the development of *Geist* or spirit. But the individual may find the development of differentiation too great to comprehend. While the complexity of modernity allows the individual to assert him/herself, and begin to choose a personal identity for him/herself (as opposed to an ascribed one), this may result in the failure of freedom, and personal meaninglessness: the only hope is for the individual to understand that they only gain their recognition as an individual by participating within a larger community (see discussions in Taylor, 1975: 433-36, 487-88; Kolb, 1986: ch 2).

constantly worked further; (iii) the need to contrast legal principles with empirical reality – the purity of the idea of law must face knowledge of its actuality in concrete situations.

Constitutionality

> The fact that the sovereignty of the state is the ideality of all particular authorities within it gives rise to the easy and also very common misunderstanding that this ideality is only might and pure arbitrariness while 'sovereignty' is a synonym for 'despotism'. But despotism means any state of affairs where law has disappeared and where the particular will as such, whether of a monarch or mob (ochlocracy), counts as law or rather takes the place of law; while it is precisely in legal, constitutional, government that sovereignty is to be found as the moment of ideality (*Philosophy of Right*, para 278).

The constitutional state – legality – is the answer to the question 'how can a rational modernity be organised?' The early modern freedom of philosophy needs to find empirical recognition and a medium through which it can achieve results. Law is to be the medium which recognises and responds to the rational necessity of the *spirit of humanity*. But Hegel goes further: because he argues that law already does this, he can present law as the medium that will articulate and concretise this rational necessity. We can see this when we seek a general understanding of law's operationality. Our analysis of law must be socially aware and historically located in the full knowledge that law mediates intrasubjective relations in an unequal division of roles. We must separate legality from despotism and read in the historical development of the progressive unfolding of the spirit of modernity that the key to harness power is constitutionality. In a sense we build upon the undeveloped rationality bequeathed by Hobbes. The Hobbesian image is the incorporation of mana into the reality of power within the centrality of the will that is the power of the state. Hobbes centralises the otherwise diverse wills of a naturally chaotic array of subjectivity – for social peace it is in crucial respects the sovereign's will which is to count, and his power makes that will the organising point for social progress. The absence of a generally operative social will – a whole will – necessitates that a single will be produced and buttressed by force. For Hegel, conversely, society is the ground for the articulation and actualisation of reason, this can only take place when the members of society are integrated with, and identify with, the social project of reason; they cannot be forced successfully to act against the path of reason. An example is the history of the master–slave relationship.

Legal identity and the contingency of the modern: the example of the master–slave relationship

History is founded on the domination of men over men. Law reflects this. The relations of master and slave manifest an historically accepted division of roles; what consciousness makes this possible? Consider Aristotle:

> ... is there anyone thus intended by nature to be a slave, and for whom such a condition is expedient and right, or rather is not all slavery a violation of nature?

> There is no difficulty in answering this question, on grounds both of reason and of fact. For that some should rule and others be ruled is a thing, not only necessary, but expedient; from the hour of their birth, some are marked out for slavery, some for rule (Aristotle, *Politics*, 1, 4–5).

Aristotle 'trusted' nature. Aristotle was deeply embedded in the network of social relations in which he lived. He could not perceive these – as the modern does – in terms of contingency or social construction, but saw them as 'natural'.[28] However, as individuals break free of the totality of the ideology that comprised the socially accepted mode of life, 'existential trust' disappears.[29] This comes about because no matter how strong the dominant image of the world, and the naturalness of the 'roles' that are on offer, conflicting social perceptions, and contradictions of interest, exist. The master-slave relationship is one of domination, and no matter how 'natural' this domination can look, the master and the slave occupy different social locations which contain – at least potentially – a conflict (see discussion, Taylor, 1975: 153–7). And whatever the dominant social consciousness which legitimates the master-slave relationship, there is the possibility of another concept – such as that of 'natural equality' – which calls it into question.

As Hegel describes it, the master, the 'superior' subject, holds off the upsetting idea of equality by interposing upon the 'other' the status of inferior, and using the 'inferior' subject as a means of procuring achievement. The slave is compelled to labour in order to procure freedom for the 'superior' subjectivity of the master. But in this labour the 'inferior' engages his own subjectivity in the world of the real, and develops a subjectivity independent of, although related to, the subjectivity of the master. Domination invites resistance, both in physical and intellectual terms; the conflict results in the development and articulation of new norms of conduct, and new ways of perceiving of the relationship. The slave negates the domination of the master, an activity which signifies the capacity for self-creation and expresses the search for freedom which transforms nature into culture. We 'moderns' understand that the difference between the slave and the master cannot be found at the level of nature, rather it is located in the history of the institutionalisation of social relationships. A history in which the concrete history of domination and subjugation is encoded in legitimate social categories – laws of the society. The search for freedom involves a struggle against these forms of 'legitimacy' – against the jurisprudence which provided intellectual weight to these social institutions. As jurisprudence becomes 'modern', it invalidates the reason embodied in pre-modern social institutions – this struggle is the constituting force of freedom.

---

28 Aristotle can be described as preparing an inventory of the ethics, the duties, and the modes of perception of the Greek world. Aristotle – unlike Plato, who was originally a slave – 'settled into' his empirical world. Aristotle's 'subject' was not a contingency. The 'Greek master'-'barbarian slave' relationship was not an 'accident' in the sense of an historical creation – and thus might as easily have been something else – instead it appeared as if it were 'natural', ie simply the performance of each one's respective role and purpose.

29 'The single, individual consciousness as it exist in the real ethical order, or in the nation, is a solid unshaken trust in which Spirit has not, for the individual, resolved itself into its abstract moments, and therefore he is not aware of himself as being a pure individuality on his own account. But once he has arrived at this idea, as he must, then this immediate unity with Spirit, his trust, is lost. In thus establishing himself ... the individual has thereby placed himself in opposition to the laws and customs. They are regarded as mere ideas having no absolute essentiality, as abstract theory without any reality, while he as this particular 'I' is his own living truth' (*Phenomenology of Spirit*, 1977: 259).

But if this freedom becomes rampant subjectivity – if, in other words, modernity becomes only a mass of individuals with their differing perspectives – then no real freedom is possible. No real freedom is possible because there would be no way of coming to agreement on what constituted the moral facts of modernity, and no absolutely guaranteed way of demarcating the good from the bad, the moral from the immoral. In that case, law could neither guarantee freedom or be the facilitating mechanism of a free modernity.

Jurisprudence also must be provided with an historical consciousness in which we tell ourselves we are progressing, otherwise jurisprudence could not serve as the record of our progressive institutional imagination. Thus, Hegel assures us, we should treat history as the progress of reason becoming self-conscious.

In the light of this, we read the changing forms of the master-slave conflict as the development of the consciousness of freedom through which mankind is established as an object for itself. Interpreting this tangible situation, we witness not only reason's historical development, but the real embedment of reason in a normative institutionalisation within the world reality of domination and subjugation, of blood and despair. Hegel assures us that *reason has three sites in the world*: language (representation), fighting (the struggle for the norm of recognition; the province of politics) and work (labour; the province of the economy). At the beginning of the master-slave conflict two opposing subjective positions were in contradictory relation, in the course of the conflict each opposing subjectivity supersedes their particularity, and both the identity of the slave and the master are transformed, with each becoming a modern free human being. Each now must grant mutual (self-)recognition of each as (an)other, a real human being. This is only possible through the mediation of (modern) law which constitutes the state of freedom and guarantees to the (past) slave modern rights. Through being granted rights, the slave is brought out of nature and turned into a modern person; similarly, the master is humanised.

Human history is a rational process working through the irrationality of individual's unconscious social projects

At any one time individuals and groups, their writings and concepts, are in a conflict which drives historical development, although individuals are not consciously striving to create progressive history. However, through their interaction and the social communication of knowledge, out of their various, multi-layered struggles, the reason of modernity emerges and becomes institutionalised in a political-legal constitution.[30]

---

30 There is a sense in which Hegel takes the idea of the underlying natural functioning of the world – put forward by Hume and Adam Smith – and treats this as the progressive unfolding of reason. Whereas, however, Smith founds a policy tradition in which this rationality must – absolutely must – be left to the hidden hand of nature to develop (the major expression of this being the hidden hand of the market), Hegel is replying that we take charge of this process and make sure that the interactions recognise *significant* action. By contrast liberalism will have doubts as to any overriding scheme of historical interpretation which claims, by reference to a total vision, to discern the truly significant basis for human community.

Law is the medium which both records this ethical progress of concrete humanity, and structures the conditions for the next stage. The activities of state officials, the living reality of the constitution, the operation of the legal system, are a series of institutional reference points for collective and individual identity and will-formation. The development of the legal system must serve as the development of the representation of humanity.

The particularities of legal development

> Principle – plan of existence – law – is a hidden, undeveloped essence, which as such, however true in itself, is not completely real (*Philosophy of Right*).

At any one time, law is a both a present and hidden phenomenon. It is always a possibility, a potentiality, which emerges through human endeavour. Law emerges through will, through the passion of man to make principles come to light.[31] The individual passion of the legal actor must be fused into duty, into an ethical appreciation of his task. The actor – the judge, the advocate – cannot escape his personal desires and aims, but these need to be fused into conceptions of justice and duty to transcend arbitrary desire.[32] Above all we need to see the law as a 'whole' – the particularity of any law and of any decision, is an expression of *LAW* as it works itself pure in the (historical) dialectical progression of the rationality of man's nature.

The direction of the law?

Legal development in its totality is the state pursuing the universal interests of humanity as these gradually become known. The operation of the institutions of the state offers 'the firm foundation not only of the state but also of the citizen's trust in it and sentiment towards it. They are the pillars of public freedom since in them particular freedom is realised and rational' (*Philosophy of Right*, para 265). Universal lessons are drawn from the particularity of social conflicts. Through this history of social conflict, through the realisation of the interdependency of the particular and the general, of the individual and the social, the state is 'educated' and develops institutions which 'actualise' rationality. By a rigorous analysis of its laws, of their development, and the social effects of these laws, the state comes to a consciousness of its operation and refrains from serving only particular or vested interests.

> The abstract actuality or the substantiality of the state consists in the fact that its end is the universal interest as such and the conservation therein of particular interests since the universal interest is the substance of these ... [The state] works and acts by reference to

---

31 In language remarkably similar to the discourse of legal integrity invoked by Ronald Dworkin nearly two centuries later (see Chapter 15 of this text) Hegel argues that it is 'the absolute right of personal existence – to find itself satisfied in its activity and labour. If men are to interest themselves in anything, they must have part of their existence involved in it; find their individuality gratifying by its attainment' (*Philosophy of History*, 163).

32 'The aims which the agents set before them are limited and special ... [but in their rationality] the purport of their desires is interwoven with general, essential considerations of justice, good, duty, etc, for mere desire, volition in its rough and savage forms falls not within the scene and sphere of universal history' (*Philosophy of History*, 166).

consciously adopted ends, known principles, and laws which are not merely implicit but are actually present to consciousness; and further, it acts with precise knowledge of existing conditions and circumstances, inasmuch as its actions have a bearing on these (*Philosophy of Right*, para 270).

The ambition of law

What drives law is an ambition: the ambition to develop 'the principle of rational being and knowing, ie into the rationality of right and law'. Law is the instrument by which men's will is expressed – a social will – but law can only be rational law where it refuses to be merely a matter of plain facts or an empty instrument of the chaotic or arbitrary will(s) of the powerful. Hegel (romantically) tells us that law has indeed become free of its merely arbitrary positivity, it has refused barbarity and entered into the service of truth, while knowledge has ceased to be tied to extra-worldly concerns and come to focus upon the actuality of the world.[33] As a result the legal system has come to express the development of social reason – it is the path by which the ideal world becomes the real world. Hegel thus calls upon the legal actor to dream the full dream of the enlightenment wherein the world becomes knowable and to pursue the rational reconciliation of universal and particular interests through the forum of laws' 'ethical life'.

THE SOCIAL ROLE AND LIMITS OF MODERN KNOWLEDGE

In modernity mankind agrees to go where knowledge leads without hesitation. Knowledge makes both goodness and evil possible. Before humanity came to know – epitomised in the biblical story of the fall from the garden of Eden – humanity could do neither good nor evil.

> What [the fall] really means is that humanity has elevated itself to the knowledge of good and evil; and this cognition, this distinction, is the source of evil itself. Being evil is located in the act of cognition, in consciousness (*Lectures on the Philosophy of Religion*, III: 301).

We can only know sin through knowledge; thus we can only know true salvation through knowledge. This is not to be a negative knowledge, not a realisation of what we do not know, or of the insurmountable reality of mystery, but the full confidence in the realisation of Absolute Spirit, or a coming to that stage where we have total self-consciousness and reflexivity.

By contrast Hobbes's social contract and defence of sovereignty is constructed through knowledge of our weakness; the sovereign makes possible the conditions wherein our pursuit of felicity is equivalent to our pursuit of 'happiness'. Ultimately we pursue happiness through the market protected by civil and criminal law. Behind the law lies the absolute power necessary to *save us from our weaknesses and death*. But how are we to be legitimated to *live*?

---

33 'The realm of fact has discarded its barbarity and unrighteous caprice, while the realm of truth has abandoned the world of beyond and its arbitrary force, so that the true reconciliation which discloses the state as the image and actuality of reason has become objective' (*Philosophy of Right*, para 360).

Hegel is specific: we must construct a knowledge capable of recognising our social totality.

But how is this total representation possible? Hegel turns to the desire at the basis of religion asking what is our science – indeed the totality of our science(s) – to look like if we convert the spirit of religion – God – into a spirit that pervades this world? If instead of dreaming the religious dream of an eschatology of a final judgement, an all powerful observer who gained full knowledge of our human weaknesses and projects – the God which is above this world – we converted the ideas of right and wrong, the just and the unjust, the present and the future, the immanent and the transcendent into sub-concepts of a human knowledge of the whole of human existence. But even if we were to create a philosophical understanding which worked this way, what guarantees the actual coincidence of the totality of what happens, history, human knowledge and our attainment of 'true' existential happiness?

Perhaps nothing but the desire to believe in the project of modernity. In a sense Hegel is saying that all the efforts of the medieval tradition were correct, but the target was wrong. Christian theology was right, provided that it is read as applying not to a transcendental and imaginary God but to man himself, living in the real world. The basic problem is man's inability to find a home for himself in the world; man's alienation from existence. The goal of philosophy should be not particular knowledge, but knowledge of the totality – in short the state of complete wisdom.[34]

THE DIALECTICS OF MODERNITY: ACTION, HOPE AND DESTRUCTION

The progress of knowledge serves as a model for social advancement. Thus, Hegel assures us we can to look to science as our model. The error of the mediaeval tradition –

---

34 We need not go into the complicated and often obscure writings where Hegel tries to follow through these ideas. Suffice to say that Hegel draws our attention to various, perhaps paradoxical, features of the drive to total knowledge; specifically: (i) the unreasonable origins of reason, or the unjust origins of the just; (ii) the dialectics of destruction and construction: all epochs are the dialectic of the desire for freedom and the terrorism of the (de)struction of the present; (iii) the inevitable of the friend-other relationship in human affairs. The other – the enemy, the error, the unforeseen, the yet-to-be, – is the opposite of the same – the friend, the conformation, the repetition, the rediscovered, the similar; (iv) the continual question: how are we to conceive of the totality of existence? The ultimate is the presentation of God as he is in his eternal being before the creation of nature and of a finite mind. If, however, the grounding of the search for knowledge was the unreasonableness of myth, turned into a faith in God, then the course of modern knowledge is faith in the absolute reach of the sum of man's knowledge(s). And this is dangerous. For what if we were to lose this faith – as many would define the post-modern condition as demonstrating? Then nihilism threatens. If we lose our faith in the possibility of mankind coming to a full knowledge of eternity then why believe anything? What then of the project of social constructionism? For, as Hegel has defined it, the goal of politics, of writing, of struggle, is the creation and reproduction of a stable normative order that facilitates the universalisation of social individuality – an ethical individualism which owes the truth of its (legitimate) existence to its indivisible particularity of a social whole. A whole whose legitimacy is founded upon the guarantee of total knowledge. Put another way, what prevents nihilism for Hegel, is not the fact that God lives on but that we humans will not be affected by the death of God, since man always desired to be God. And modern law will be the instrument by which God's creation is turned in law's (human) empire. But this must – absolutely must – be saved from the institutional imagination of mere positivity; we must believe in the dream of ethical totality – in law working itself pure, and in the existence of 'right answers' to legal and ethical questions.

a tradition in which religion defined what was the rational, the real and the truth – has been converted into the truth of today. Similarly, with the ethical, we can only judge the truly just at the end of history.[35] The bad can be converted into the good, sin can be forgiven. Since, if it is successful, it becomes the new order; it becomes the real, the rational, the structure of the good. The future good is always something that transcends the structure of the good of the present. The revolution is always to be feared, but it is also the deliverer of the (future) good.

Critics point to the absence of any encouragement by Hegel for widespread public discussion affecting the state's operations. Since the state is required to follow reason, mere popular opinion is a distraction. While freedom of speech is guaranteed, the fact that the constitution is rational, the government is stable, and debates in the Councils of State are publicised, is taken to guarantee that the state pursues the public interest and therefore what the citizens say is of no great importance (see *Philosophy of Right*, para 319).

How can the average citizen gain reassurance that the state is indeed rational, and that by consenting to the legal order he is 'willing the universal in the light of the universal', instead of being tricked into assenting to laws which are only promoting selfish interests? Although he can follow the political debates, his confidence that the whole system is rational rests on non-rational grounds. Religion and patriotism serve as the real foundations.

> The guarantee of the constitution ... lies in the spirit of the whole people, namely in the determinate way (differentiated and structured) in which it has the self-consciousness of its reason. Religion is this consciousness in its absolute substantiality (*Encyclopedia*, para 540).

> The political sentiment, patriotism pure and simple, is assured conviction with truth as its basis ... and a volition, which has become habitual ... in general, trust ... or the consciousness that my interest is contained and preserved [in] the state's interest and end (*Philosophy of Right*, para 268).

But how can we be sure that this deeper consciousness – this protection from mere popular opinion – is common, rational and capable of providing a real foundation? What prevents it from being just another particular interest masquerading as universal? What prevents the populace giving their allegiance to the law from an irrational, merely habitual, state of (un)consciousness? Ultimately Hegel's scheme offers no guarantees against false consciousness. The citizen cannot know that the state is actually rational, he can only trust that the state is rational.[36]

---

35 Since all that is real is rational, all that exists is natural, thus all that exists is good inasmuch as it exists. All action must of its nature upset what currently exists; thus it must contradict the good of the present. Thus all action is, in that sense, bad, or sinful (to use the Christian phraseology).

36 Liberals claim that the philosophy of Hegel leads to a state which is a single, organic whole, which aims to behave rationally and order everything rationally, but which cannot permit individual enterprise, initiative, eccentricity or dissent, to operate, since these would constantly go against rational planning. It becomes intolerant of individual initiative and thereby totalitarian in character – the opposite of (individual) freedom. Hegel was not opposed to individual freedom, but his vision of freedom was different to that of the liberal. Take the idea of freedom in the economic sphere, in the ...

CONCLUDING SUMMARY: HEGEL AND THE DREAM OF A FULL MODERNITY

Hegel offers a philosophical dream where the goal of modern freedom is to attain a state of total knowledge and reconciliation of human tensions. Law is both the medium of social construction – structuring the resolution of conflicts – and the artefact wherein the humanity of modern rationality is expressed. By implication, Hegel warns that if law were to lose its expressiveness and become viewed merely as an empty instrument, the modern age would lose its spirit. Modernity needs to consider not only its goals, but also its means. If law is the instrument of power – as in the legacy of Hobbes – what will power will? What is the contract for? Mere survival is not enough, and we need to transcend the possibility of rampant individuality.

In this narrative, history is the struggle of intersubjective human rationality, acts of human willing, to create a social whole – the totality of *Geist*, mind. History is the progress of man's consciousness as it moves through the dialectical struggles of time. The modern constitution – is both legal and non-legal. The constitution of the modern social entity rests upon the framework of law, but law is the mediation, the setting into relationship of the subjectivities of concrete human beings. And, as modernity develops, it loses any transcendental guarantor – God disappears to be replaced by human desire. There can be nothing absolutely to found 'natural law' except human rationality. The effects are dramatic – what for example, guarantees that a just state can be achieved? How could we be sure that we could recognise it? The modern loses the capacity to transcend the immanent in search of the purity of the pure or naturally 'just', by reference to which he wishes to cleanse the law of the unjust. It comes as little surprise that legal positivism was to dominate the jurisprudential imagination from the middle of the 19th century, since, with modernity, all law that is posited as law becomes real, becomes proper law. As the legal consciousness – in its critique of natural law – becomes an early form of legal positivism, then the ability to distinguish the just from the unjust law is not something which inheres in the capacity to recognise law, but moves itself into the capacity to say what law ought to be(come). But this may mean that, with

---

36...market. The Liberal view holds freedom as people being able to do as they prefer, to follow their preferences. The choice of programmes to view or concepts of obscenity, for example are questions of preference. The individual is free when he or she is not prevented from viewing the material they prefer. That is all the liberal economist needs to know to decide if one is free. But to followers of the Hegelian legacy this is a simplistic view of freedom, they want to know why I prefer to view x over y, why I wish to purchase certain goods rather than others. It may appear to them that I'm being manipulated, that my preferences, rather than being 'my own' are a result of advertising campaigns, of others forming my opinions for me. I become a slave to fashion. And if I have been manipulated then I am not free. To know that I am free, from this perspective, one needs to know not only that I can do what I prefer, but why it is I prefer what I do. Are my preferences rational?

For Hegel freedom would be more than the ability to follow my desires, my caprice, to follow desires that others have induced in me so that they can sell me something. Freedom will consist in fulfilling myself as a rational individual.

But who can know what real needs are, and when desire is truly known? Can the gap between reason and desire, or between morality and self-interest, really be overcome? Can we build a social synthesis to create a harmonious society in which the divisions of human nature are reconciled? The Liberal prefers to say no, that the entire image is suspect.

modernity, law is only an instrument of power – or put in language that Nietzsche was to give us – as God disappears, as we lose all teleological imagination, the question of justice becomes a battle between different wills to power. The will to inscribe into the positivity of law the 'oughts' which the intellectuals – those who create and control the jurisprudential imagination – present us with. Does then law become the instrument of dreams? In the dreams of the philosophical prophet, are we – the subjects of the intellectuals of modernity – presented with images of potentiality and asked to create?

As natural law disappears, law can no longer be read as a declaration which nature makes as to what ought to be; it can only arrange what nature ought to be. Law may shape our nature, our social world, our socially constructed being, but the modern becomes a contingency.

The classical questions: who am I? what am I? are asked again. But, if nature does not trap us in her laws, those questions transform into 'who should I become?' 'What shall I make myself into?' In the classical conception of Plato and Aristotle, law was to enable us to live out our natural roles and purposes and, ultimately, to die honourably. In turn, Hobbes tied law to fear; fear of destruction. Now Hegel asks us to throw away the fear that underlies liberalism and become; we are to join ourselves to the spiritual movement of world history. We are to dream of the greatness of our own reason, and, by living it, make ourselves great. Or put in more Hegelian terms, we must dialectically oppose the individualist nightmare with the dream of total unity. We must believe that the only reason the fear of social chaos is in us, is that we may dream of the totality of an expressive modernity in which we become what we dream we will be, and then come to know what we have become. We then will live a way of life that expresses the truth of our free, but communal, nature, in that city made possible by *Law's Ethical Life*.

CHAPTER 8

ADAM SMITH, JEREMY BENTHAM AND JOHN STUART MILL: the early development of a utilitarian foundation for law

PART ONE
INDUSTRY, CAPITALISM AND THE JUSTICE OF THE HIDDEN HAND OF THE MARKET: THE WORK OF ADAM SMITH

The coarse clay of which the bulk of mankind are formed, cannot be wrought up to ... perfection. There is scarce a man, however, by discipline, education, and example, may not be so impressed with regard to general rules, as to act upon almost every occasion with tolerable decency, and through the whole of his life to avoid any considerable degree of blame (Smith: *The Theory of Moral Sentiments*, 1976, III 5.1).

As every individual ... endeavours as much as he can both to employ his capital in the support of domestic industry, and so direct that industry that its produce may be of the greatest value; every individual necessarily labours to render the annual revenue of the society as great as he can. He generally, indeed, neither intends to promote the publick interest, nor knows how much he is promoting it ... he intends only his own gain, and he is in this, as in many other cases, led by an invisible hand to promote an end which was no part of his intention (Smith, *An Inquiry into the Nature and Causes of the Wealth of Nations*, 1970: 456).

UNDERSTANDING THE MORAL FOUNDATION FOR ADAM SMITH'S PROPOSAL OF THE HIDDEN HAND OF THE MARKET

The Scotsman Adam Smith[1] has often been parodied as the father figure of *laissez-faire* capitalism. Held out as espousing selfishness as the guiding motive for human action, Smith is taken to argue social relations should in large part be left to the hidden hand of

---

1   Adam Smith (1723-1790) has been acclaimed as one of the most influential political economists of Western society but his officially paid post was as a moral philosopher and lecturer in jurisprudence. Born in Kirkcaldy, Scotland, Smith entered the University of Glasgow in 1737, where he attended Francis Hutcheson's lectures. He studied and worked at Balliol College, Oxford, for seven years from 1740 and then returned to Kirkcaldy. In 1748, he moved to Edinburgh, where he became a good friend of David Hume and Lord Kames. He was elected Professor of Logic at the University of Glasgow in 1751, but he exchanged Logic for the Chair of Moral Philosophy the next year holding this for 10 years. Smith was expected to deal with natural theology, ethics, law and government. *The Theory of Moral Sentiments* was developed from his lecture course and published in 1759 going through six editions until 1790. The work was well received in Britain (see the comments David Hume made in a letter to Smith; quoted in Raphael, 1985: 16-17) and caused the stepfather of the young Duke of Buccleuch to invite Smith to become the Duke's tutor, promising a pension for life. Smith resigned his professorship at Glasgow to take up this post which involved two years' travelling on the Continent and after his tutoring duties ended he returned again to Kirkcaldy, where he spent the next 10 years in retirement at work on *The Wealth of Nations*, published in 1776, which provides the basis for his enduring reputation.

the free market, to the outcomes of countless interactions of egoistical, self-serving individuals – the true ontological entities of (non-)society. This is a gross oversimplification. While he is far from being a social perfectionist, Smith tries to develop a theory empirically based on his understanding of the human condition, which unites individual interest with social interest in such a way that a policy-orientated perspective for progress is developed.

Smith is famous for two works: *The Theory of Moral Sentiments* ([1759] 1976) and *An Inquiry into the Nature and Causes of the Wealth of Nations* ([1776] 1970). In *The Theory of Moral Sentiments*, which was founded upon the concept of sympathy as a general human faculty, the idea of the 'impartial spectator' offers a mechanism to judge the justice of transactions. While that work seemed to offer an account of what enabled social bonds, the *Wealth of Nations*, with its key ideas of the division of labour and the self-interested nature of the individual human, seemed to stress a contrasting concern; namely, how can a society become wealthy in terms of consumer goods.[2]

Economic growth is only possible when some people in a society possess a supply of either raw materials or manufactured goods greater than is required to fulfil their own immediate needs; this surplus stock provides the opportunity for trade among people with varying needs. A person will begin to specialise in the production of a certain item when demand for it is great enough to assure a producer that his other wants may be supplied in exchange for producing this item. A division of labour is begun which will develop until some labourers are producing only a very small part of a manufactured product. Such minute specialisation increases productivity and begins mass-production.

Self-interest is the dominant motive behind economic activity: 'Every individual is continually exerting himself to find out the most advantageous employment for whatever capital he can command'. Capital is most advantageously employed in producing and selling the goods which satisfy the greatest needs of a people. The capitalist is led unwittingly to work in satisfying those social needs for although he seeks only his own gain, he contributes nonetheless to the general welfare: 'led by an invisible hand to promote an end which was no part of his intention'. The general welfare – measured as the increase in consumer goods and thereby enjoyment in their use – will be best served by permitting each person to pursue his own interest.

Smith's image of the hidden hand of the market is not some asocial phenomenon. Smith assumes a theory of human interaction, and a role for law, which lays out the conditions for the economics of *The Wealth of Nations* to work. These factors he had specified earlier in the *Theory of Moral Sentiments*. The relentless pursuit of self-interest (or self-love as Smith actually called it) is constrained by the same factors which give us social solidarity; in particular Smith refines the notion of sympathy which David Hume

---

2   *An Inquiry into the Nature and Causes of the Wealth of Nations* intermingles a description of the actual conditions of manufacture and trade in Smith's own time, a history of European economics, with policy recommendations. Smith is sharply critical of mercantilism with its belief that money is wealth and that the best economic policy for a country is the retention within its borders of as much gold and silver as possible. Instead, he defines wealth in terms of consumable goods and the wealthiest country as one that either produces itself, or can command from others, the greatest quantity of consumable goods.

had indicated formed the basis of moral psychology.[3] We all share a 'general fellow feeling which we have with every man merely because he is our fellow creature' (1976: 90). Selfish desire is not the dominant motive for action: what we may call selfishness is in fact distinguished by Smith as that form of self-love which results in harm or neglect to other people. Humans are self-regarding creatures; as Smith makes clear in *The Theory of Moral Sentiments* (VII ii 3.16, 1976: 304), all virtue involves a 'laudable' regard for our 'own private happiness and interest', but this self-regard is tempered by sympathy.[4] This is the key concept for Smith: how does it work?

DEVELOPING THE IDEA OF SYMPATHY

Sympathy is neither an absolute intuitive grasp of the right (as if proposed by a God's eye view of the essence of human nature), nor is it subjective emotivism; rather it is a concept which refers to Smith's rational reconstruction of our intelligent and reflexive concern for understanding the feelings we experience when we engage in social intercourse. Sympathy is the natural capacity of a person to participate (in his imagination) in the sentiments of another. For example, we often share in the joy or sorrow of competitors in a sporting achievement, or are upset by the suffering of another person; in doing so we experience similar pain or pleasure to the person(s) actually engaged. The emotion(s) which we feel, as spectators, is not the same as the original feeling(s) of the person(s) directly involved, but we spectators can compare our own (sympathetic) reactions to a given situation with the sentiments of those principally involved. We may find there is 'perfect coincidence' between our sympathetic reaction and the original feeling of the person principally concerned; if so, then, Smith suggests, we accept with approbation the feelings of the participant.[5] We judge them right and proper:

---

3   Many critics have claimed that the two books lead us in different directions: the jurisprudence of *The Theory of Moral Sentiments* emphasises the role of sympathy as if it were the binding force of social solidarity, while the *Wealth of Nations* appears to stress self-interested individualist action as the motor of social interaction and social growth. Some critics, such as H T Buckle, in the 19th century, reconciled the two in claiming Smith was dealing with two aspects of human nature: the sympathetic and the selfish. Others have said the Adam Smith of the *Theory of Moral Sentiments* was an idealist; while the *Wealth of Nations* displays a more realist tendency. Critics have overstated the difference between the two texts. Both provide a sociological or empiricist account of features Smith felt structured the human condition. In *The Theory of Moral Sentiments*, our imagination and sympathy are the operative mechanisms of socialisation, while in the *Wealth of Nations*, the developing division of labour leads to mutual dependence.

4   Most of *The Theory of Moral Sentiments* is an account of moral psychology. Smith places his account of moral philosophy upon the bedrock of a discussion of human nature or empirical psychology. The key concept of Smith's moral psychology is sympathy. Sympathy is our fellow feeling with the passions or affections of another person: 'Whatever is the passion which arises from any object in the person principally concerned, an *analogous* emotion springs up at the thought of his situation, in the breast of every attentive spectator'.

5   'The man whose sympathy keeps time to my grief, cannot but admit the reasonableness of my sorrow. He who admires the same poem, or the same picture, and admires them exactly as I do, must surely allow the justness of my admiration. He who laughs at the same joke, and laughs along with me, cannot well deny the propriety of my laughter ... If the same arguments which convince you convince me likewise, I necessarily approve of your conviction' (*Theory of Moral Sentiments*, 1976: 16-17).

... in the sentiment of approbation there are two things to be taken notice of, first, the sympathetic passion of the spectator, and, secondly, the emotion which arises from his observing the perfect coincidence between this sympathetic passion in himself, and the original passion in the person principally concerned. This last emotion, in which the sentiment of approbation properly consists, is always agreeable and delightful. The other may either be agreeable or disagreeable, according to the nature of the original passion.

This is no mere emotivism. Of course we may occasionally be moved by the simple apprehension of great joy or sorrow on the part of some stranger(s) in conditions we know little about. But Smith is actually referring to the arousal of emotions in an interpretative field of everyday experiences. Sympathetic feelings do not come about from the simple observation of a certain emotion in another person, rather the grief or joy we witness arouses similar feelings in us, since these feelings suggest to us the general idea of some good or evil that has befallen the person we observe. We cheer the individual who has won the Olympic 100 metres and share in their joy, or are disappointed with our representative's obvious distress at coming in well down the field, because we share some knowledge as to the nature of the feat attempted and the emotion experienced. Moreover, we may be mistaken as to the cause of some passions and be disgusted until we understand their cause and background, at which point we may change our attitude completely. Smith argues that sympathy does not arise so much from viewing the passion or emotion, as from our considered view of the situation which excites it, and he reinforces this claim by noting that we sometimes feel for another a passion which they seem to be altogether incapable of experiencing, as when we feel embarrassed at someone's behaving rudely although they have no sense of the impropriety of their behaviour. Thus, while Smith claims that sympathy is the basis for our judgments of both the propriety and the merit of other people's feelings and the actions which follow from them, this is a complex process. It is only when the original passions of the principal person are in perfect accord with the sympathetic emotions of the spectator that the passions of the principal appear to the spectator as just and proper.

Smith, like Hume, believed that people should be constantly asking themselves questions about their life and the nature of their actions. How can we gain a fair impression of our own conduct? Smith thought that we could only be impartial if we looked at our own behaviour as though it were someone else's. Thus, we may judge ourselves from the same point of view that we judge others, and our approval or disapproval of our own conduct will depend on whether we can sympathise with the sentiments from which our actions flow. Conscience, 'the judge within us', enables us to make a proper comparison between our own interests and the interests of others. By its aid we may approach the ideal of the man of perfect virtue, who is possessed of both a command of his own feelings and a sensibility for the feelings of others.

The general rules for what is appropriate in human conduct provide us with guidelines. Properly based, that is, operating on the foundations of a natural jurisprudence, these rules have their basis in the sentiments which certain kinds of behaviour evoke, and our own respect for the rules should follow from the correspondence between them and our own feelings as we observe the conduct of others. Smith stresses that the rules are generalisations, stemming from particular instances in which conduct has excited the sense of propriety and merit in mankind. In turn we adopt a sense of duty, or a just regard for these general rules. The sense of duty provides us with a motive for action, even where we lack the appropriate sentiment to follow the rule naturally on a given occasion. There are various sets of rules operating within society, of which the rules of justice have been developed with the greatest exactness. Those rules, embedded in the legal order, require a strict sense of justice to be developed, for there will be many times when we do not see their utility as obvious.

IS THERE ANY ABSOLUTE GUARANTEE FOR SMITH'S IDEA OF SYMPATHY AND THE IMPARTIAL SPECTATOR?[6]

Taken together, the concept of sympathy and the regulative idea of the impartial spectator give us both an idea as to the basis of social solidarity, and an operative mechanism for judging the common or everyday sense of the rightness and wrongness of our actions. The idea of the impartial spectator enables us to be rationally impartial; it is not a perfect vantage point. It is a mechanism of rational adjustment rather than a metaphysical guarantee. Using the language of our earlier discussion of David Hume, it operates when we are embedded in the narratives and traditions of everyday life; in the language of the later liberal theorist John Rawls (discussed in Chapter 14 of this text), we seek by this idea to gain a 'reflective equilibrium'. Such a pragmatic outcome did not appeal to those who wished (or needed) metaphysical security. David Hume was turned down for the chair of Moral Philosophy at Edinburgh University in favour of James Balfour of Pilrig. Balfour's moral philosophy included the idea of a perfect judge, an 'ideal spectator', or 'angel from heaven', who could take a total 'view of human affairs', and see all events that would 'weaken the common tye, and disturb the peace and tranquillity of the public' (1753: 73-4). Smith's impartial spectator does not have such superhuman qualities:

> ... the present inquiry is not concerning a matter of right, if I may say so, but concerning a matter of fact. We are not at present examining upon what principles a perfect being would approve of the punishment of bad actions; but upon what principles so weak and imperfect a creature as man actually and in fact approves of it (1976: 77).

How is man to be guided? Smith continued the argument Hume had laid out:

> Though man ... be naturally endowed with a desire of the welfare and preservation of society, yet the Author of Nature has not entrusted it to his reason to find out that a certain application of punishments is the proper means of attaining this end; but he has endowed him with an immediate and instinctive approbation of that very application which is most proper to attain it (*ibid*).

If there is a metaphysical guarantee, it is the idea of some natural order underlying human interaction. Smith's theoretical foundation lies 'in the unalterable principles of

---

6   On Smith's impartial spectator theory generally, see A L Macfie, The Individual in Society (London, 1967), Ch 5; TD Campbell, Adam Smith's *Science of Morality* (London, 1971), Ch 6; DD Raphael, 'The Impartial Spectator', in *Essays on Adam Smith*, A S Skinner and T Wilson eds, (Oxford, 1975) essay IV.

human nature', observable by the empiricist imagination, and in our acceptance of an 'all-wise Author of Nature'. Sympathy is the gift of the all-wise Author of Nature.[7]

What of eschatology? What takes the place of the final judgment? The idea of the impartial spectator ensures that while sympathy works to ensure fellow feeling and our desire for praise and avoidance of blame, it is not a simple mechanism. Smith distinguishes between the 'man without' who is moved by the unreflective state of his desires – to avoid blame and pursue praise – and the 'man within', operating under a deeper set of qualities 'in the desire of praise-worthiness and in aversion to blame-worthiness'. The impartial spectator, the man within, may stand confused by the force and violence of the actions and words of the man without; the existential crisis lies in the rupture and conflict thus ensuing. The existential tension can only be resolved for Smith by recourse to our belief in an underlying universality to the human condition; but, if we were to reduce this to faith in a God that would adjust all things, who would provide perfect justice in the world to come, we hand a powerful ideological weapon to those who claim to know God's will. It should be our understanding of the empirical condition of mankind, rather than an appeal to the power of an ultimate judge, and a system of right and wrong beyond our interpretation of the empirical acts and fate of man, with which we should be concerned.[8]

THE ROLE OF POSITIVE LAW AND PUNISHMENT IN GUARANTEEING MODERN 'COMMERCIAL' SOCIETY

In *The Theory of Moral Sentiments* Adam Smith adopted the idea of a game, or a race, to serve as his metaphor for social life. Life is a competitive game in which the participants strive for success, while resenting those who break the rules in pursuit of gain.

> In the race for wealth and honours and preferments he may run as hard as he can, and strain every nerve and every muscle, in order to outstrip all his competitors. But if he should jostle or throw down any of them, the indulgence of the spectators is entirely at an end. It is a violation of fair play, which they cannot admit of (1976: 83).

The population 'readily ... sympathise with the natural resentment of the injured, and the offender becomes the object of their hatred and indignation'. Thus the test is the critical reaction of the spectator, which is a device rationalising the natural empirical reactions of everyday individuals to the person's breach of the rules and seizure of unfair advantage. However, such knowledge and fear of the critical reactions of others will not, in itself, suffice to constrain behaviour. Sanctions are required to reinforce this process.

---

7   'The all-wise Author of Nature has, in this manner, taught man to respect the sentiments and judgments of his brethren; to be more or less pleased when they approve of his conduct, and to be more or less hurt when they disapprove of it. He has made man ... the immediate judge of mankind; and has, in this respect, as in many others, created him after his own image, and appointed him his vice-regent upon earth, to supervise the behaviour of his brethren. They are taught by nature to acknowledge that power and jurisdiction' (1976: 128–130).

8   In a rich passage (1976: 131–132) Smith recounts the image of the just God who will remedy the sufferings of this world in the next. While acknowledging the rhetorical appeal of such a figure, Smith is thankful that it has often been 'exposed to the derision of the scoffer', since it is often at odds with the pattern of rewards our natural moral sentiments accept.

There are three types of sanctions:

(i) unjust actions normally create remorse on the part of the offender: this 'most dreadful' sentiment is 'made up of shame from the sense of impropriety of past conduct; of grief for the effects of it; of pity for those who suffer by it; and of the dread and terror of punishment from the consciousness of the justly provoked resentment of all rational creatures' (1976: 85);

(ii) Smith believes that all men have a natural tendency to 'abhor fraud, perfidy, and injustice, and delight to see them punished';

(iii) the offender will fear the judgment to come in the afterlife. He understands he will face a final judgment where the wicked receive punishment and the just reward (1976: 91);

(iv) sanctions are provided by an operational system of positive law with agencies of government and magistracy enforcing it. Ultimately, whatever discourse we may have on the social sources of solidarity and the fellow feeling of mankind, realistically, in conditions of 'commercial' society there is no escape from the Hobbesian imperative:

> As the violation of justice is what men will never submit to from one another, the public magistrate is under a necessity of employing the power of the commonwealth to enforce the practice of this virtue. Without this precaution, civil society would become a scene of bloodshed and disorder, every man revenging himself at his own hand whenever he fancied he was injured (1976: 340).

But Smith does not believe that the state should merely lay a set of rules of the game and treat justice as the matter of their impartial enforcement; he is acutely aware of the unjust nature of social organisation. While it is necessary to protect property – which serves as the foundation point for security – *the reality of social administration is usually social injustice.*

> Civil government, so far as it is instituted for the security of property, is in reality instituted for the defence of the rich against the poor, or of those who have some property against those who have none at all (*Wealth of Nations*: 715).

The system of positive law – with an administration itself governed by other rules – should strive to be in accordance with the 'rules of natural justice'. Positive law can all too easily become 'the interest of particular orders of men who tyrannise the government, [and] warp the positive laws of the country from what natural justice would prescribe'. But how can we be sure – particularly if we give up the notions of the expressive tradition (for example, those of Rousseau and Hegel) – that positive law reflects 'natural justice'?

PART TWO
JEREMY BENTHAM (1748-1832) AND THE
ORIGINS OF MODERN UTILITARIAN
JURISPRUDENCE

UTILITY PROPOSED AS THE FUNDAMENTAL PRINCIPLE
FOR A NEW SCIENCE OF MORALITY

Bentham[9] accepts that enlightened progress is to be found by developing a strictly empirical, as opposed to hypothetical or expressive, mode of thought. Hume and Smith provide the central ideas of self-interest, sympathy and natural history. The search is for the key to natural history that can account for changes in law, moral opinion, and government, both descriptively and prescriptively. One must read behind the surface phenomena of historically particular motives and interactions, of the bonds of human connection, to see the reality of imperatives of interest, industry and individualism. The point to social progress was the search for justice; but where could the standard on which to rest the technology of justice be found? The solution Bentham found was utilitarianism.

Bentham's utilitarianism is an attempt to found an objective science of society and politics, as free from human subjectivity as he hoped our destiny is to become free from

---

9   The eldest son of a prosperous lawyer and property dealer, Jeremy Bentham was born in London in 1748, and lived through the death of five brothers and sisters in their early childhood and of his mother when he was 11 years old. A child prodigy, Bentham entered Queen's College, Oxford at the age of 12, taking a BA degree in 1763. His father wanted him to become a lawyer and Bentham entered Lincoln's Inn, but returned to Oxford to hear the lectures on law given by Sir William Blackstone. Bentham relates that while listening he 'immediately detected Blackstone's fallacy respecting natural rights.' Bentham believed there could not be any basis for a theory of 'natural rights' which was in reality 'rhetorical nonsense – nonsense on stilts'. He took his MA degree in 1766 and again returned to London, but was shocked by the unprofessional nature of much of the legal profession and decided against being a lawyer. He dedicated his life to writing and proposing social change along the lines of utilitarian philosophy.

Although Bentham was chiefly a social and political reformer, he was also concerned to preserve British society from the ravages of the revolutionary fervour which had swept France which such dramatic consequences. Bentham was in the tradition of the empiricists John Locke and David Hume (whose *Treatise on Human Nature* Bentham read with such profit that he said it was 'as if scales fell' from his eyes regarding moral philosophy). His first book, *Fragment on Government* (1776) was an attack upon Blackstone, and provided an opposing view to the American *Declaration of Independence*, which also appeared that year. Bentham had argued that this document was a confused and absurd jumble of words wherein the authors assumed the very 'natural rights' of man, that they purported to prove. *The Fragment* was well received while it was thought that a well-known lawyer had written it but once it became known that the author was a young man of no considerable experience it was ignored. The sense of reason being ignored by the British establishment was to be a constant feature of Bentham's life (along with his love of cats! He once offered cats a general apology for demeaning them when he compared English politicians to them.). His life-long practical project was to build a new series of prisons based upon a revolutionary design – the Panopticon – which he thought would both make him rich and provide the institutional support for a new society. Among his later writings were *A Defence of Usury* (1787), his famous *Introduction to the Principles of Morals and Legislation* (1789), *A Plea for the Constitution* (1803), and *Catechism of Parliamentary Reform* (1809). Bentham became an influential public figure and his group founded the University of London; he died in 1832 at the age of 84.

the contingencies of religion and historical accident.[10] The principle of utility is a gift of nature; nature herself provides the Archimedean point where interest and reason are combined. In *The Introduction to the Principles of Morals and Legislation*, privately printed in 1780 and published in 1789, Bentham united psychology, ethics, and jurisprudence upon the classical lines the French philosopher Helvetius had suggested,[11] that of the governance of the human being by the dictates of pleasure and pain. While other scholars were to argue this reduced the complexity of human beings to an 'inhuman' behavioural complex,[12] Bentham thought these two features provided not only the standard needed for a 'censorial' (ie a critical) jurisprudence but also a model of the causes of human behaviour which the skilful legislator could control and use to direct social behaviour.[13]

> Nature has placed mankind under the governance of two sovereign masters, pain and pleasure. It is for them alone to point out what we ought to do, as well as to determine what we shall do. On the one hand the standard of right and wrong, on the other the chain of causes and effects, are fastened to their throne (Bentham, from *An Introduction to the Principles of Morals and Legislation*, Ch 1, Sect 1; text used Penguin Classics, 1987: 65).

---

10 It is a moot point to what extent utilitarianism takes its life from the emerging middle classes of 18th century capitalism. For the later Marxist writer Trotsky, utilitarianism arose as part of the ideological factors which give an image of social cohesion when conflict is the reality. 'Bourgeois evolutionism halts impotently at the threshold of historical society because it does not wish to acknowledge the driving force in the evolution of social forms: the class struggle. Morality is one of the ideological functions of this struggle. The ruling class forces its ends upon society and habituates it into considering all those ends which contradict its ends as immoral. That is the chief function of official morality. It pursues the idea of the 'greatest possible happiness' not for the majority but for a small and ever-diminishing minority. Such a regime could not have endured for even a week through force alone. It needs the cement of morality. The production of this cement constitutes the profession of the petty-bourgeois theoreticians and moralists. They radiate all the colours of the rainbow but in the final analysis remain apostles of slavery and submission' (Leon Trotsky, *Their Morals and Ours: The Moralists and Sycophants against Marxism*, Union Books [1939] 1994: 8).

11 Helvetius is widely credited as setting out the psychology Bentham was to develop in *De l'Esprit* (1758). With Helvetius salvation becomes fully secularised. He constructs a perfectionist image of society upon an anthropology which strips humans of a basic moral ontology: humans are neither good nor bad, they are simply a collection of drives, instincts and motivations. The most powerful drive is the desire for power, which Helvetius understood as the product of a more basic desire for pleasure. Thus laid bare, human nature provides the scientist with the material to create a well-ordered society. By influencing the operation of the desires and appetites the legislator can create harmony, order, happiness and well-balanced social interaction. The jurist becomes an 'analyst-legislator'. Since man does not have a natural ontological state of 'grace' or natural morality, social and individual order, and thus social and individual happiness, become a matter of rationally arranging the pieces, drives and influences, in the correct or most socially effective way.

12 To quote the Jewish social theorist Voegelin (1975: 69-70), order is now seen as 'intimately connected with the ... instrumentalisation of man. Man is no longer an entity that has its existential centre within itself; he has become a mechanism of pleasure, pain and passions which can be harnessed by another man, the 'legislator', for purposes of his own ... Only when the spiritual centre of man, through which man is open to the transcendental *realissimum*, is destroyed, can the disorderly aggregate of passions be used as an instrument by the legislator'.

13 Bentham did not discover the principle of utility and although we need not go as far as Marx's assessment (for whom Bentham was a 'homespun commonplace' who 'strutted about in so self-satisfied a way' and concluded that 'the principle of utility was no discovery of Bentham. He simply reproduced in his dull way what Helvetius and other Frenchmen had said with *esprit* in the 18th century'), the view of his importance currently held in some quarters of England may be an overestimation.

Utility cuts through the fictions and theories of natural rights, those claims of Blackstone which Bentham thought were 'nonsense on stilts'.[14] Properly understood, Hume's *Treatise on Human Nature* allows us to read in the natural history of law, a story of nature's working out of the costs and benefits of moral and legal duties. Morality is not an abstract categorical imperative, its real basis is natural necessity. However, we cannot assume that the structure of our social institutions actually corresponds to the basic principles; many will not.

CAN THE PRINCIPLE OF UTILITY BE PROVED? OR HAS BENTHAM ASSUMED ITS VALIDITY?

What is the status of this natural necessity and how does it give us a morality? In a few sentences, without indicating just how he does it, Bentham moves from the fact that we desire pleasure to the judgment that we ought to pursue pleasure, or from a psychological fact to the moral principle of utility. Utility, or 'that principle which approves or disapproves of every action whatsoever, according to the tendency which it appears to have to augment or diminish the happiness of the party whose interest is in question' *(ibid*: 65), provides us with the master criterion based upon the reality of self-interest. *Bentham does not explain how the gap between stating that men desire pleasure and claiming that they ought to, or that it is right that they should, is to be crossed.* However, he is confident that he has discovered a master principle which can judge the aptness of actions: '[When an action] is conformable to the principle of utility one always says either that it is one that ought to be done ... [or] it is a right action' *(ibid*: 67). Linking ought to pleasure is the only way 'the words ought, and right and wrong, and others of that stamp have a meaning: when, otherwise, they have none.' Bentham was aware that he had not proved that happiness is the basis of 'good' and 'right', the very nature of the principle of utility, he says, is that one cannot demonstrate its validity:

> Is it susceptible to any proof? It should seem not: for that which is used to prove every thing else, cannot itself be proved: a chain of proofs must have their commencement somewhere. To give such proof is as impossible as it is needless *(ibid*: 67).

Although the validity of the principle of utility could not be proved, Bentham argued that he could demonstrate that so-called 'higher' theories of morality were either

---

14 The principle of the greatest happiness of the greatest number was held out as the only rational guide both to private morals and public policy. A comment on methodology. Bentham did include a lengthy discussion of pleasure and pain as motivating forces and tried to show how a calculation of their amounts and influence is possible. He assumed that pleasure and pain were commensurable, with a given amount of the one offsetting a given amount of the other, and that they could be added so that a sum of pleasures could be calculated. This calculation would define the greatest happiness of an individual and a group of individuals. Occasionally, he acknowledged that the basic structure of adding pleasures and, in particular, the pleasures of other individuals, was fictitious, but he considered this fiction to be 'a postulatum without the allowance of which all political reasoning is at a stand'. Bentham aspired to be the 'Newton of the moral sciences', and thought his psychological fictions to be no more fanciful than those that had proved so effective in the developing science of mechanics.

Moreover, Bentham believed that by using his theory he could cut down the dangerous fictions he saw throughout contemporary jurisprudence and political reasoning. Thus, terms such as rights, property, the crown, the general welfare, were all liable to fictitious usage, and defended specific vested interests. Conversely, the fictions Bentham used were ideals that 'dissolved' harmful fictions.

reducible to the principle of utility, or else were inferior to this principle because they had no clear meaning, or could not be consistently followed. Take the social contract theory as an explanation for our obligation to obey the law; apart from the difficulty of determining whether there ever was such a contract or agreement, Bentham argues that the obligation to obey, even in the contract theory itself, rests upon the principle of utility, for it really says that the greatest happiness of the greatest number can be achieved only if we obey the law. If this is the case, he expands, why develop an involved and scientifically dubious theory when the whole problem can be swiftly solved by saying that obedience is better because disobedience does more harm than good? Similarly, competing propositions that goodness and right in an act are determined by our moral sense or understanding or right reason or the theological principle of the will of God, are reducible to the principle of utility. Since we cannot know God's pleasure, we must observe 'what is our own pleasure and pronouncing it to be his'. Only pains and pleasures, therefore, give us the real value of actions, and in the last analysis, we are all concerned with maximising happiness whether in private or public life.

LAW AS THE INSTRUMENT OF UTILITARIAN REFORM

The optimistic structure of 'classical legal positivism' is thereby visible. Its key belief is simple; a new science of law and reform could create the conditions for a modern orderly society. Bentham's interest in law predated his later concerns with political and constitutional reform, and his theory of utility provided both a methodology for guiding reform and a support and justification for the reform. While reform may appear philosophically radical, it was also conservative, intended to save British institutions from the effects of worse things which may occur; Bentham held a life-long fear of the revolutions which he witnessed sweeping continental Europe and the Americas. Good order and security were overriding concerns; to achieve this predictability of interaction and certainty of outcome are crucial. Good commerce requires a legal system that enforces promises and guarantees legitimate expectations.[15]

Bentham's definition of law

Our concern is positive law, which is, most typically, the product of the legislator's will.

A law may be defined as an assemblage of signs declarative of a volition conceived or adopted by the sovereign in a state, concerning the conduct to be observed in a certain case by a certain class of persons, who in the case in question are or are supposed to be subject to his power: such volition trusting for its accomplishment to the expectation of certain events which it is intended such declaration should upon occasion be a means of bringing to pass, and the prospect of which it is intended should act as a motive upon those whose conduct is in question (1970: 1).

15 'In order to form a clear idea of the whole extent which ought to be given to the principle of security, it is necessary to consider, that man is not like brutes, limited to the present time, whether in enjoyment or suffering, but that he is susceptible of pleasure and pain by anticipation, and that it is not enough to guard him against an actual loss, but also to guarantee to him, as much as possible, his possessions against future losses.'

There are four elements: namely (i) law is the product of the sovereign's will; (ii) such a product is made known to the citizens and officials in the state; (iii) law lays down certain courses of action or demands restraints from action; (iv) it relies upon the use of sanctions.

Bentham appears to have rejected the simple idea of 'command'; his is a complex imperative theory·in which he preferred the term 'mandate'. The course of action mandated by law may take one of four forms, specifically: (a) a command – 'wear seat belts'; (b) a prohibition – 'do not wear seat belts'; (c) a permission to forbear – 'you may refrain from wearing seat belts'; (d) a permission to act – 'you may wear seat belts'. Behind these forms, however, are the twin features of (i) the sovereign, and (ii) coercion structured by sanctions.

Law need not originate directly with the sovereign, since a law may be regarded as the produce of the sovereign's will by way of conception or adoption, namely:

> when it was he [the sovereign] who issued it and who first issued it, in the words or other signs in which it stands expressed; it may be said to belong to him by adoption when the person from whom it immediately emanates is not the sovereign himself ... such will should be observed and looked upon as his (1970: 21).

The sovereign

The supreme legislature is omnipotent. Although there may be 'checks' and guides there cannot logically be any legal limitation upon this power.[16] Utility itself, however, presents a guiding principle for legislation:

> Of the constitutive authority, the constant will (for such it cannot but be presumed to be) is – that the national felicity, the happiness of the greatest number – be maximised: to this will, on each occasion, it is the duty of the supreme legislature, according to its ability, to give execution and effect (in Parekh, 1973: 218).

However, if the legislature passes laws against the principle of utility they are 'not on that account to be, by any judge, treated or spoken of, as being null and void' (ibid: 218).

How exactly does the sovereign make his will known and effective? There are actually two sets of laws, one – called *principal laws* – addressed to the citizens, another – called *subsidiary laws* – addressed to officials to enforce the first.[17] If the officials fail to enforce the principal law, they will themselves be subjected to scrutiny by other officials acting in accordance with further subsidiary laws. And while some laws may be invitations to citizens to act in a way in accordance with their own wishes – to make

---

16 '... the authority of the supreme body cannot, unless where limited by express convention, be said to have any assignable, any certain bounds – That to say there is any act they cannot do – to speak of any thing of theirs as being illegal – as being void – to speak of their exceeding their authority (whatever be the phrase) – their power – their right – is, however common, an abuse of language' (Bentham, 1977: 485-6).

17 'The will of the legislator concerning the matter in question has indeed been declared: and punishment has been threatened in the case of non-compliance with such will: but as to the means of carrying such threats into execution nothing of the sort hath as yet been made appear. What course then can the legislator take? There is but one which is to go on commanding as before ... All he can do ... is to issue a second law, requiring some person to verify the prediction that accompanied the first' (Bentham, 1970: 137-9).

wills and so forth – Bentham stresses that punishment and sanctions are essential features of a legal system (1970: 134).

THE ROLE OF SANCTIONS

The primacy of sanctions stems from Bentham's view of the operation of utility underlying social interaction. Just as pleasure and pain give the real values to acts, so do they also constitute the efficient causes for behaviour. In *An Introduction to the Principles of Morals and Legislation* (Chapter III), Bentham distinguishes four sources of pain and pleasure which he describes as causes of behaviour, calling them sanctions. A sanction is what gives binding force to a rule of conduct or to a law, and these four sanctions are termed the physical, the political, the moral, and the religious.[18] In all these areas, the sanction, or the efficient cause of behaviour, is the threat of pain. In public life, the legislator understands that men feel bound to do certain acts only when such acts have some clear sanction connected with them, and this sanction consists of some form of pain if the mode of conduct prescribed by the legislator is violated by the citizen. The legislator's chief concern is, therefore, to decide what forms of behaviour will tend to increase the happiness of society and what sanctions will be most likely to bring about such increased happiness. The word obligation was given concrete meaning by Bentham's concept of sanction, for obligation now meant not some undefined duty but the prospect of pain if one did not obey the moral or legal rule. Unlike Kant, who argued that the morality of an act depends upon having the right motive and not upon the consequences of the act, utilitarianism leads to the opposite position – morality depends directly upon the consequences. While Bentham admits that some motives are more likely than others to lead to more useful conduct, that is, conduct which increases happiness, it is still pleasure, and not the motive, that confers the quality of morality upon the act. Moreover, Bentham took the position that, especially in the social arena where the law is at work, the law can punish only those who have actually inflicted pain, whatever their motive may be, though some exceptions were admitted.[19]

THE PLEASURE-PAIN CALCULUS

Each individual and each legislator is concerned with avoiding pain and achieving pleasure. But pleasures and pains differ from each other and therefore have different

18 For example, if 'A man's goods, or his person, are consumed by fire. If this happened to him by what is called accident, it was a calamity: if by reason of his own imprudence (for instance, from his neglecting to put his candle out), it may be styled a punishment of the physical sanction: if it happened to him by the sentence of the political magistrate, a punishment belonging to the political sanction; that is, what is commonly called a punishment: if for want of any assistance which his neighbour withheld from him out of some dislike to his moral character, a punishment of the moral sanction: if by an immediate act of God's displeasure, manifested on account of some sin committed by him ... a punishment of the religious sanction' (1987: 85).

19 While it may be true that the legislator cannot always take account of motives, the question of motive is vital in morality. Bentham, however, seemed to regard both the moral and legal obligations as being similar in that in both cases the external consequences of the action were considered more important than the motives behind them.

values. With an attempt at mathematical precision, Bentham speaks of units, or what he called lots, of pleasure or pain, suggesting that before we act, we should, and really do, calculate the values of these lots (Chapter IV). Their value, taken by themselves, will be greater or lesser depending, says Bentham, upon (i) a pleasure's intensity, (ii) duration, (iii) certainty, and (iv) propinquity (or nearness). When we consider not only the pleasure by itself but what consequences it can lead to, other circumstances must also be calculated, such as (v) a pleasure's fecundity, or its chances of being followed by more of the same sensations, that is, by more pleasure, and (vi) its purity, or the chances that pleasure will not be followed by pleasure but by pain. The seventh circumstance is of pleasure's extent, that is, the number of persons to whom it extends or who are affected by it.

As this calculus indicates, Bentham was interested chiefly in the quantitative aspects of pleasure, so that all actions are equally good if they produce the same amount of pleasure. Therefore, we 'sum up all the values of all the pleasures on the one side, and those of all the pains on the other. The balance, if it be on the side of pleasure, will give the good tendency of the act ... if on the side of pain, the bad tendency' (1987: 88).

As it is the function of the legislator to discourage some acts and encourage others, how shall he classify those that should be discouraged as against those that should be encouraged?

THE OBJECT OR PURPOSE OF LAW

Bentham's method of legislation was first to measure the 'mischief of an act,' and this mischief consisted in the consequences, the pain or evil inflicted by the act; acts that produce evil must be discouraged. There are, says Bentham, both primary and secondary evils that concern the legislator. A robber inflicts an evil upon his victim, who loses his money, and this is a case of primary evil. But robbery also creates secondary evil because successful robbery suggests that theft is easy; thus weakening respect for the sanctity of property, with the consequence that property becomes insecure. These secondary evils are often more important than the primary evils since – using the example of robbery – the actual loss to the victim may very well be considerably less than the harm in terms of lessening in stability and security (for example, fear of crime) in the community as a whole.

Law aims to augment the total happiness of the society by discouraging those acts that would produce evil consequences. A criminal act or offence is, by definition, one that is clearly detrimental to the happiness of the society; only an act that in some specific way inflicts in practice some sort of pain – thereby diminishing the pleasure of some specific individual or group – ought to be the concern of the law. For the most part, the government accomplishes its business of promoting the happiness of society by punishing men who commit offences that the principle of utility has clearly measured as evil. It was Bentham's confirmed belief that if the legislator used only the principle of utility in deciding which acts should be considered 'offences,' many acts that the laws of his day controlled would have to be considered a matter of private morals to be subject only to the sanction of opinion. Utilitarianism had the effect, then, of requiring a reclassification of behaviour to determine what actions or activities were appropriate for the government to regulate. The principle of utility provided a new and simple theory of punishment, a theory Bentham thought could not only be justified more readily than the older theories, but also could achieve the purposes of punishment far more effectively.

THE CENTRALITY OF PUNISHMENT

Given that 'all punishment in itself is evil' (since it inflicts suffering and pain) it follows 'upon the principle of utility, if it ought at all to be admitted, it ought only to be admitted in as far as it promises to exclude some greater evil' (1987: 97). At the same time, the 'object which all laws have in common, is to augment the total happiness of the community'. Punishment must therefore be 'useful' in achieving a greater aggregate of pleasure and happiness, and has no justification if its effect is simply to add still more units, or lots, of pain to the community. The principle of utility would clearly call for the elimination of pure 'retribution', where someone is made to suffer only because his act caused his victim pain, since no useful purpose is served by adding still more pain to the sum total society suffers. It is not that the institution of punishment is rejected, rather, accepting the principle of utility indicates a reappraisal of the question of why society should punish offenders, and a reclassification of cases that are 'meet' and 'unmeet' for punishment. Punishment should not be inflicted (i) where it is groundless, where, for example, the offence could be simply compensated and there is virtual certainty that compensation is forthcoming; (ii) where it is inefficacious, in that it cannot prevent a mischievous act, for example, when a law made after the act is retroactive, or ex post facto, or where a law already exists but has not been announced. Punishment also would be inefficacious where an infant, an insane person, or a drunkard was involved, though Bentham admitted that neither infancy nor intoxication were sufficient grounds for 'absolute impunity'. Nor should punishment be inflicted (iii) where it is unprofitable or too expensive, 'where the mischief it would produce would be greater than what it prevented'; or (iv) where it is needless, 'where the mischief may be prevented, or cease of itself, without it: that is at a cheaper rate', particularly in cases, 'which consist in the disseminating pernicious principles in matters of duty,' since in these cases persuasion is more efficacious than force (quotes, 1987: 97-102).

Whether a given kind of behaviour should be left to private ethics instead of becoming the object of legislation was a question Bentham answered by simply applying the principle of utility. If to involve the whole legislative process and the apparatus of punishment does more harm than good, the matter should be left to private ethics. He was convinced that attempts to regulate sexual immorality would be particularly unprofitable, since this would require intricate supervision, as would 'such offences as ingratitude or rudeness, where the definition is so vague that the judge could not safely be entrusted with the power to punish'. Duties that we owe to ourselves could hardly be the concern of law and punishment, nor must we be 'coerced' to be 'benevolent,' though we can be liable on certain occasions for failing to help. But the main concern of law must be to encourage those acts that would lead to the greatest happiness of the community. There is, then, a justification for punishment, in that through punishment the greatest good for the greatest number is most effectively secured.

Besides providing a rationale for punishment, the principle of utility also provides a clue as to the nature of the appropriate punishment. Bentham describes the desirable properties of each unit, or lot, of punishment by considering 'the proportion between punishments and offences' (title of Chapter XIV), and he gives the following rules: the punishment must be great enough to outweigh the profit that the offender might get from the offence; the greater the offence, the greater the punishment: if there is a situation where a potential offender is determined to commit an offence but could choose between several, the punishment for the greater offence must be sufficient to induce a man to prefer the less serious; punishments should be variable and adaptable to fit the particular circumstances, although each offender should get the same punishment for the same offence; the amount of punishment should never be greater than the minimum required to make it effective; the greater the uncertainty that an offender will be caught, the greater should be the potential punishment; and if an offence is habitual, the punishment must outweigh not only the profit from the immediate offence but also that from the undiscovered offences. This thinking led Bentham to argue for rules ensuring that punishment would be variable, to fit the particular case; equable, so as to inflict equal pain for similar offences; commensurable, in order that punishments for different classes of crimes be proportional; characteristic, so as to impress itself upon the imagination of potential offenders; frugal, so as not to be excessive; reformatory, in order to correct faulty behaviour; disabling, to deter future offenders; compensatory to the sufferer; and, to prevent new problems, punishment should have popular acceptance and be capable of remittance for sufficient cause.

After an extensive (and tedious) cataloguing of the basis of law and punishment Bentham closed by noting the objection that some offenders simply do not act as rational calculators. His reply is categorical:

> There are some, perhaps, who ... may look upon the nicety employed in the adjustment of such rules as so much labour lost: for gross ignorance, they will say, never troubles itself about laws, and passion does not calculate. But the evil of ignorance admits of cure: and ... when matters of such importance as pain and pleasure are at stake, and these in the highest degree ... who is there that does not calculate? Men calculate, some with less exactness, indeed, and some with more: but all men calculate (1987: 111).

BENTHAM'S LIMITED RADICALISM IS SHOWN IN HIS IDEAS OF REFORM WHICH WERE IN THE INTERESTS OF GOOD ORDER AND THE PROTECTION OF PROPERTY

It was clear to Bentham that many elements in the law and the general social structure of England did not fit the requirements set out by the principle of utility. Wherever he found a discrepancy between the actual legal and social order on the one hand, and the principle of utility on the other, he wanted reform. He traced most of the evils of the legal system to the judges who, he charged, 'made the common law. Do you know how they make it? Just as a man makes laws for his dog. When your dog does anything you want to break him of, you wait till he does it and then beat him ... this is the way judges make laws for you and me.'

Bentham found the chief obstacle to reform in the structure of the aristocratic society. Why should social evils and evils of the legal system persist even after he had demonstrated that different modes of behaviour would produce the 'greatest happiness of the greatest number'? The answer, he thought, was that those in power did not want the 'greatest happiness of the greatest number'. The rulers were more concerned with their own interests. Bentham was acutely aware that men seek their own happiness. The object of government, however, is to help achieve the greatest happiness of the greatest number. Whenever those in power represent only a class or small group, their self-interest will be in conflict with the proper end of government. The way to overcome this conflict or contradiction is to combine rulers and ruled, or to put the government into the hands of the people. If the rulers and the ruled become one identity, their interests will be the same, and the greatest happiness of the greatest number will be assured. This identity of interest cannot, by definition, be achieved under a monarchy, for the monarch acts in his own interests, or at best aims at the happiness of a special class grouped around him. For much of his life Bentham set faith in an enlightened elite, but, realising that his reforms were not likely ever to be accepted, changed his views to argue for radical democracy. Therein, he believed, his ideas would gain acceptance since the rulers are the people, and the representatives of the people are chosen precisely because they promise to serve the greatest good. The application of the principle of utility clearly required, as Bentham saw it, the rejection of monarchy with all its corollaries, and so he would abolish the king, house of peers, and the established church.

THE TRAP OF THE PANOPTICON

There is a duality to Bentham's conception of law: at first sight, the civil law and the criminal law appear two separate realms. The civil law protects the contractual acquisition of goods, and appears to operate according to natural conceptions of utility which players of the games of commercial life understand. The pain of the obligation to abstain from another's goods is incomparably less than the benefits conferred by the corresponding rights acquired in property, while the criminal law penalises different sorts of attack upon social life. However, civil law is not self-contained; it needs criminal law to give it ultimate sanction. Thus, criminal law defends the social artefacts that civil law uses – property, contracts, obligations, goods.

Perhaps Bentham pushed the connection between natural history, industry, protection of property, the benefits to be gained from playing the rules of the commercial game, and reinforcement of civil law by criminal law as far as it would go. Behind the hoped-for normality of civil society, behind security and social peace, lurked the inevitability of coercion. An absolute confidence in utility justified this coercion. Moreover, although Bentham's various writings on the use of punishments to replace the death penalty often verge upon implying – even occasionally outrightly stipulating – penal torture and terror, the panopticon (a sort of prison or inspection house) encodes the close ties between the utilitarian state and the galago society. For over 20 years Bentham was obsessed with a project for building and running at a profit a series of ideal institutions of surveillance, which was to provide a multi-purposive technology of rule.

> Morals reformed, health preserved, industry invigorated, instruction diffused, public burdens lightened, economy seated as it were upon a rock, the Gordian knot of the poor-laws not cut but untied – all by the simple idea of architecture ('Panopticon, or the Inspection House' (1838-43) vol IV in Bentham's *Collected Works*, Edinburgh: Bowring Edition).

A rigorous system of total and continuous surveillance and control. Even exercise was to be a 'marching parade'. The result?

> Whether the liberal spirit and energy of a free citizen would not be exchanged for the mechanical discipline of a soldier, or the austerity of a monk? – and whether the result of this high-wrought contrivance might not be constructing a set of machines under the similitude of men? Call them soldiers, call them monks, call them machines: so they were but happy ones, I should not care (*ibid*).

It is an understatement to say that the panopticon – which an elderly Bentham summed up as 'a magnificent instrument with which I then dreamed of revolutionising the world' (quoted, Semple, 1993: 288) – has been neglected in jurisprudential literature;[20] it is a remarkable absence.[21] For some it is the proof that Bentham's utilitarianism leads on to totalitarianism; for others, it demonstrates the weakness of the visions of social progressives in which we all should be governed by the new knowledges which modernity is producing; since the great check on both the power of the panopticon, and on the exercise of power under the legitimation of knowledge, was visibility, but what sort of check is visibility if those who observe are in awe of the claims of the knowledge? To yet others it stands as the final result of the naturalist reductionism inherent in utilitarianism – human beings are simply reduced to pleasure-pain complexes; where then is the dignity that the 'rights-orientated' Kantian tradition sees as fundamental to humanity?

---

20 As Janet Semple (1993:1) begins her recent study of the panopticon: 'Bentham's panopticon penitentiary is a project full of contradictions and ambiguity; a prison that is at the centre of philosophical disquisition, managed by a gaoler who has been depicted both as a ruthless entrepreneur and as a personification of the utilitarian state. It is an individualist enterprise that seems to presage totalitarianism. Scholars have accorded it little interest or respect, yet for 20 years it obsessed the superlative mind of one of our greatest philosophers; it was the tragedy in the life of a man who seemed to his friends happy and successful.'

21 The panopticon has not, however, been ignored in criminology where it was picked up by the modern French writer Michel Foucault (1977) who saw it as the 'slip of penal reason'. Although very few were actually built, Foucault interprets the panopticon as the prime example of trends in the conditioning and production of modern subjectivity. It was an 'omni-disciplinary' institution, having no particular focus other than the production of an austere discipline and conforming behaviour. Although the panopticon did not come into wide use, prisons have become deeply inscribed in the hidden structures of modern society. Interestingly Bentham wanted the panopticon to be open for the public to come and go witnessing the sights and keeping the institution under control, whereas prisons are closed institutions. Prisons are penal failures which are expanding in number – how can these failures be such a success? Foucault argues prisons work through, rather than in spite of, failure – prisons produce a particular form of delinquency, the pathology of crime. The experience of imprisonment creates a set of social problems for inmates which ensures that they continue to commit crime on release, but this, instead of pointing to the need to abolish prisons, appears rather to necessitate that offenders be returned to prison, and that greater rates of imprisonment are needed. This is linked to power relations: power allows knowledge to be produced, knowledge is a form of power, concretised this power allows more forms of knowledge. Social change becomes a continuous spiral of power and knowledge. The idea of the prison as a reformatory requires that a social knowledge is created that visualises the perpetrator of crime in such a way that he/she can be viewed as being in need of reform. A new form of domination is ensured.

THE DUAL IMAGES OF VISIBILITY AND CONTROL INHERENT IN UTILITARIANISM

The panopticon was the end point of the various processes of reductionism, calculation and desire for control inherent in Benthamite utilitarianism. Utilitarianism is closely linked to the idea of control; it purports to offer us a mode of calculation through which we can gauge the superior policy or distribution outcome. It offers us a mechanism by which we can view the scene and calculate outcomes, and by the use of which we imagine we can take control. In recent writings on justice, the American philosopher John Rawls (1971) reminded us of how central to utilitarian thought was an hypothetical decision-making model – the independent spectator – which presumed total vision and total understanding.

The image of an independent spectator uses some of the ideas employed in the 'impartial spectator' created by Adam Smith – particularly the concept of moral sentiments being part of the natural operation of human interaction – but builds upon this to offer us a mechanism for judging the totality of social happiness.[22] In outline, the idea of the perfect independent spectator runs as follows. The moral capacity of individuals is contained in the notion of sympathy. People, however, vary in the degree of sympathy or empathy they can experience. Some people are very capable of experiencing sympathy while others are not. Now imagine someone who is perfectly capable of sympathy – he or she would be almost saintly. This person would reflect and accept your own pain and pleasure completely; there would exist a complete symmetry of sympathy. Imagine if we add a second condition. The fact that this spectator is also omniscient. No one's pains escape him/her. He/she knows all the pleasure and pain and re-creates them in his/her own experience. Since this person experiences all the pain and all the pleasure existing in the world, surely this entity would act in such a way as to maximise the totality of pleasure s/he experiences. And, since everything is aggregated, the actual distribution of pain and pleasure would not matter, it would be the sum total of the patterns of distribution that counted. The figure would always prefer the pattern of distribution that resulted in the higher aggregate of pleasure; no matter the pattern. In other words, such an ideal being would prefer a world which conformed to the principle of utility. The well-organised utilitarian world must be the ideal state for the impartial perfect spectator.[23]

The model appears to structure – scientifically – the exercise of power and provide the appropriate vantage point (or hypothetical decision-making model) for judging human relations and actions and determining concrete courses of action to follow. The

---

22 The leading late 19th century utilitarian liberal philosopher, John Stuart Mill, said utilitarianism was concerned with the general social happiness and that the power holder – the sovereign/governor – if operating in the utilitarian fashion is required by utility to be an impartial and disinterested observer – an independent spectator. But utilitarianism seems to presuppose perfect vision and perfect power.

23 This ideal figure is, of course, a God-substitute, for in the Christian tradition God is personified as exactly an all-seeing and all-knowing and all-powerful figure who towers above the lived-in world. No wonder that a confirmed utilitarian like John Austin – who still believed in God – could refer to utility as 'the index of God's commands'.

argument looks persuasive, but things are rather more complicated. The model amounts to an unjustified claim to an image of totality which no human institution can actually rightly lay claim to.[24] Adam Smith was much more modest; the idea of totality was replaced by a hidden hand, and no human institution or body of rulers should presume that they can perform that task. Two different constitutional imaginations and sets of reformist desires are at work. Utilitarianism looks to ideals of control and reform, while the idea of the hidden hand limits our self-conceptions of ourselves as powerful. John Stuart Mill was to attempt reconciliation.

---

24 What if our person did not experience the problems peculiar to certain groups, for example, he was incapable of feeling sympathy for certain groups according to sex or race. That person's capacity for sympathy is defective. Correspondingly if our ideal spectator is less than all-knowing a similar problem exists, since the defect in knowledge makes the capacity for sympathy thereby imperfect. This ideal image of the spectator is impossible. It is simply impossible to ascertain complete knowledge or complete symmetrical understanding of all others' positions.

PART THREE
JOHN STUART MILL: THE REFORM OF UTILI-TARIANISM AND THE DEVELOPMENT OF THE PRINCIPLE OF LIBERTY

The change which is thus in progress, and to a great extent consummated is the greatest ever recorder in human affairs ... Whosoever can meditate upon it, and not see that so great a revolution vitiates all existing rules of government and policy, and renders all practice and predictions grounded only upon prior experience worthless, is wanting in the very first and most elementary principle of statesmanship in these times (John Stuart Mill, 'Civilisation').

If it were felt that the free development of individuality is one of the leading essentials of well-being; that it is not only a co-ordinate element with all that is designated by the terms civilisation, instruction, education, culture, but is itself a necessary part and condition of all these things; there would be no danger that liberty should be undervalued. (John Stuart Mill, *On Liberty*, [1859])

UNDERSTANDING THE CONTEXT OF JOHN STUART MILL'S HUMANISING OF CLASSICAL BENTHAMITE UTILITARIANISM

While not perhaps as severe as legend has it, John Stuart Mill's childhood was an experiment in utilitarian socialisation. The son of James Mill, a close friend of Jeremy Bentham, Mill said of his father that it was his opinions 'which gave the distinguishing character to the Benthamite or utilitarian propagandism', and of the channels through which his father's utilitarianism was to influence the reform of England, 'one was through me, the only mind directly formed by his instructions, and through which considerable influence was exercised over various young men'.[25] In his *Autobiography* Mill relates the impact of reading Bentham's writings on punishment and prisons (since they were not published in English at the time, Mill read the French edition by Etienne Dumont): 'When I laid down the last volume of the *Traite*, I had become a different being ... It gave a unity to my conceptions of things. I now had opinions; a creed, a doctrine, a philosophy; in one among the best sense of the word, a religion' (1966: 256). But he also describes a devastating 'mental crisis' which he suffered in his early twenties, and blamed this upon the incompleteness of his early education. His teachers had been so confident of the doctrine of utility that they had neglected the emotional side of life, thus he had found it impossible to merge his personal feelings with this social doctrine. Specifically, as a result of the emphasis placed upon learning the skills of analysis he had not been able to grasp an overall picture of social life. Utilitarian education had 'failed to create ... feelings in sufficient strength to resist the dissolving influence of analysis'. Moreover, although utilitarianism appeared a remarkable technique of decision-making,

---

25 We are, of course, treating John Stuart Mill out of historical order. Jurisprudentially he was perhaps the favourite student of John Austin: in developing the text of the full lectures, it was Mill's notes of Austin's lectures that Sarah Austin used to supplement the scripts her husband had left.

it offered no images of social progress which stirred the imagination. The 'old familiar instruments, praise and blame, reward and punishment' created an 'artificial and casual' adherence to utilitarianism, rather than deeper natural ties of feeling. Thus was set up a duality which, in various forms, was to be at the centre of all his writings: the difference between, and yet interconnectedness of, the personal and the social. The relationship took several forms: the impossibility of scientifically creating the foundations for the new society, since the foundations of human society were, in the final analysis, ultimately beyond science;[26] a scientific approach to law and social ordering could not create the conditions for obedience; instead, the individual needed to find his own realm of belief and feeling at the same time as he recognised the role of the legal order in laying out the space within which this personal pursuit was performed. After his personal crisis Mill was to develop utilitarian thought – which had so nearly caused him a total mental collapse – in ways that ultimately undercut the purity of its conceptual strength and its reach.[27]

In his famous essay on *Utilitarianism*, Mill sought to defend the principle of utility, and began with a definition of utility that was consistent with Bentham: 'The creed which accepts as the foundation of morals Utility, or the greatest Happiness Principle, holds that actions are right in proportion as they tend to promote happiness, wrong as they tend to produce the reverse of happiness. By 'happiness' is intended pleasure, and the absence of pain; by 'unhappiness', pain, and the privation of pleasure' (1987: 278). But – in expanding on the theory – Mill argued for a qualitative as opposed to a quantitative approach to the issue of pleasure. Bentham's system had run together forms of pleasure differing only in their amount, ie different ways of behaving produce different quantities of pleasure. Bentham stated it confidently: 'pushpin is as good as poetry', implying the only criterion for goodness is the amount of pleasure an act can produce. Bentham even talked of producing a moral thermometer which could measure the different degrees of happiness or unhappiness – goodness for Bentham was not connected to particular *kinds* of behaviour. Mill could not agree: 'it is better to be a human being dissatisfied than a pig satisfied', and Mill reiterated he would 'rather be Socrates dissatisfied than a fool satisfied'. The assumption that all pleasures were commensurable was false: 'Human beings have faculties more elevated than the animal appetites, and when once conscious of them, do not regard anything as happiness which does not include their gratification' (*ibid*: 279). It was absurd to calculate happiness as a function of the quantity of pleasures alone.

---

26 Mill describes the early belief in the power of positive knowledge as naive: 'we did not expect the regeneration of mankind from any direct action on .. unselfish benevolence and love of justice ... but from the effect of educated intellect, enlightening the selfish feelings.' But this failed and the elitist strand in Mill now caused him to argue that only 'those who are themselves impelled by nobler principles of action' were so affected; the majority were not.

27 Mill's education left him aware of divisions which he could never reconcile, and his legacy for modernity was to create a social mechanism which actually survived in that it did not attempt to reconcile them. When Mill strained towards reconciliation he appeared to be heading towards socialism; when he refrained he was the classic liberal of our times espousing the open society, women's rights and tolerance. Mill has sometimes been described as 'two Mills', *cf* John Rees, (1977); while another writer has claimed that in Mill's writings one can detect 'traces of every wind that blew in the early 19th century' (Anschutz, 1953: 5).

This ruptured the intellectual edifice of utilitarianism. If pleasures have to be graded for their quality and not for their quantity, then not only is a mathematically based calculation impossible, but pleasure is no longer a coherent standard for morality, since morality becomes more linked with the classical (Aristotelian) question of occasioning situations which bring out the potentiality to be truly human. Mill was, moreover, a modern. Whatever the 'natural' mode of life for the modern person was to be, it was a life created by man's technological power to construct social orders.[28] This took Mill into a different search for first principles by which to govern modern society and thereby create conditions which would allow human flourishing and true human happiness.

ON LIBERTY, AND THE SEARCH FOR THE FIRST PRINCIPLE TO GUIDE POLICY

Mill's most famous work is his essay *On Liberty*, published in 1859 when he was 53 and the well-respected author of leading texts on logic and political economy. Mill boldly states that his subject is not a philosophical topic, but 'the nature and limits of the power which can be legitimately exercised by society over the individual' (edition used is the Penguin Classics, 1974: 59, the above quote being from the opening sentence of the essay). However, at least on the surface, there is a certain amount of ambiguity in his construction of guiding principles, which brings to mind the 'two Mills' thesis; there appear to be two central principles to the essay, each claimed as supreme.

Mill first announces that he is going to assert one principle as the touchstone for the relationship of liberty (autonomy) and authority:

> The object of this essay is to assert one very simple principle, as entitled to govern absolutely the dealings of society with the individual in the way of compulsion and control, whether the means used be physical force in the form of legal penalties or the moral coercion of public opinion.

His actual principle has come to be known as the *harm principle* (or the principle of liberty).

> That principle is that the sole end for which mankind are warranted, individually or collectively, in interfering with the liberty of action of any of their number is self-protection. That the only purpose for which power can be rightfully exercised over any member of a civilised community, against his will, is to prevent harm to others. His own good, either physical or moral, is not a sufficient warrant (*ibid*: 68).

Adherence to this principle makes possible a form of social life which maximises liberty; conversely if individuals or the collective (the government), continually interfere with others, a liberal form of social life is impossible. An individual is to be given a private 'social' space, in which the individual can do as he/she pleases, and what the individual does is not the government's business or anyone else's, so long as the individual does not

---

28 'On the other hand if, as is my own belief, the moral feelings are not innate, but acquired, they are not for that reason the less natural. It is natural to man to speak, to reason, to build cities, to cultivate the ground, though these are acquired faculties. The moral feelings are not indeed a part of our nature, in the sense of being in any perceptible degree present in all of us; but this, unhappily, is a fact admitted by those who believe the most (1987: 303).

harm other people in the relevant sense to be defined. Over time, this has come to mean so long as the individual does not interfere with the rights of others.

Mill draws a crucial distinction between *harm* and *offence*. Interference with the activities of an individual is not warranted by other persons not liking what the individual is doing, there must actually be harm in the sense that they are physically interfered with, or their property rights or other entitlements are interfered with. Apart from these instances the activities of an individual are no one else's business.

This is a vital principle which has become one of the fundamental principles of modern liberal states.[29] To justify state regulation and state coercion over individual conduct, we require that the conduct we seek to deter must produce harm to other citizens. Society can only regulate that part of the conduct of individuals which affects others. The parts which merely concern himself and his indulgences are part of the individual's dominion over himself, over his own body and mind – the individual is sovereign over his private domain. Mill goes on to define an entire sphere of action carved out by this principle. The principle allows a reflexive, or self-regarding, sphere of activity which society has distinguished for the individual and in which the state only has an indirect interest. This self-regarding sphere comprises:

> First, the inward domain of consciousness, demanding liberty of conscience in the most comprehensive sense, liberty of thought and feeling, absolute freedom of opinion and sentiments in all subjects, practical or speculative, scientific, moral and theological.

At first sight, Mill claims, 'the liberty of expressing and publishing opinions may be seen to fall under a different principle, since it belongs to that part of the conduct of an individual which concerns other people'. However, the freedom to publish is as important, or almost as much, as the liberty of conscience. The same reasoning is, in practice, inescapable.

> Second, the principle requires liberty of tastes and pursuits, of framing the plan of our life to suit our own character, of doing as we like, subject to such consequences as may follow, without impediment from our fellow creatures, so long as what we do does not harm them, even though they should think our conduct foolish, perverse, or wrong.

---

29 The principle takes social plausibility from its 'fit' within the social progress of developing differentiation in Western modernity – an image of social development which the first 'official' sociologist, the Frenchman Emile Durkheim – read as the result of a growing division of labour and splitting of social existence into a plurality of social spheres. Increasing differentiation demands a morality encompass the great deal of diversity resulting from people having very different occupations and different moralities, which come about either because they have professional moralities, or developed moral views which are relevant for people in their particular social roles or sections of life. There is no single or simple overriding set of moral beliefs which constitute a simple or uniform *collective conscience* laying down comprehensive guidance for the entire population. Instead the substance of what people morally ought to do is ambiguous. Mill's principle fits Durkheim's image of what Durkheim called the *collective conscience* (*cf* Cotterrell, 1995: Ch 9) which the latter foresaw as becoming a more problematical entity in the conditions of advanced modernity (organic solidarity). There is a need for guidance and limits on what people are to do; but people are living in diverse conditions, forming different lifestyles, and coming from different social backgrounds. They pursue different activities (different projects), and this is to be allowed so long as they do not in any relevant way harm other people. Without this harm being occasioned, the state should not either interfere with them, or otherwise determine their lifestyles.

We must be free to see our lives as projects, and each of us 'ought' to have the social space to develop and follow our individual life projects free from interference, so long as we do not harm others.

> Third, from this liberty of each individual follows the liberty, within the same limits, of combination among individuals; freedom to unite for any purpose not involving harm to others: the persons combining being supposed to be of full age and not forced or deceived.

Thus individuals should also enjoy freedom of interaction, the coming together of people acting consensually among themselves, again so long as they are not harming other individuals. Mill summarises his doctrine:

> The only freedom which deserves that name is that of pursuing our own good in our own way, so long as we do not attempt to deprive others of theirs or impede their efforts to obtain it. Each is the proper guardian of his own health, whether bodily or mental and spiritual. Mankind are greater gainers by suffering each other to live as seems good to themselves than by compelling each to live as seems good to the rest. (All quotes, 1974: 71–72.)

Mill is certain that his 'doctrine stands directly opposed to the general tendency of existing opinion and practice'. It also stands opposed to the tendency in Benthamite utilitarianism towards 'discipline'. Mill concedes that the interest of the ancient republics in the 'whole bodily and mental discipline of each one of its citizens' may have been admissible in a small city-state surrounded by enemies; however the state of modern world development, in particular the greater size and the separation of temporal and spiritual authorities (and the rise of individual consciences), offered the potentiality for new freedoms, as well as techniques and desires which might extinguish individuality.[30]

So what of the governing power of the principle of utility? Has Mill destroyed it as the principle that was meant to provide the guiding standard for modernity? *On Liberty* at first seems a puzzle in this respect. Mill first claimed there must be one ultimate principle to guide modern social interaction and he proposed the liberty or harm principles as ultimate principle – and presented this without qualifications or compromise – but then on the next page he offered another candidate. There he stated:

> I regard utility as the ultimate appeal of all ethical questions, but it must be utility in the larger sense grounded on the interest of man as a progressive being (*ibid*: 70).

At first sight we are offered two possible ultimate principles. Why the contrast? Is this proof of the 'two Mills' thesis?

THE COMPLEX INTERACTION BETWEEN THE LIBERTY PRINCIPLE AND GENERAL UTILITARIANISM

In *On Liberty* there are all kinds of apparent conflicts between the principle of liberty and utility. Mill himself describes a number of potential situations where the majority can be

---

30 In the same section Mill is at pains to criticise the new 'Religion of humanity' proposed by August Comte (1973; 1974), whose writings had been among those Mill turned to in his early personal crisis. While favourably inclined to Comte's understanding that we needed a new basis for social solidarity, he came to see as totalitarian the moral pressure that Comte proposed.

seen to interfere; some seemingly rather trivial, others dramatic. He describes the case of Muslim countries banning the eating of pork even on the part of Christians who happen to live there, or Catholic countries objecting to clergy marrying. Eating pork, or clergy marrying, are items Mill places within the self-regarding sphere. That is, provided what is eaten does not harm the others, even if they are offended, as long as no harm occurs, there is no right to interfere. Harm, and no offence, however, legitimates interference.

The acceptability of utilitarianism was greatly helped by the publication of *Utilitarianism* in 1861, only two years after *On Liberty* was published. Many of the most important and dramatic applications of *On Liberty* have stressed the conflict between individualism and utilitarianism, or between the harm principle and utilitarianism. Mill's principle has been a constant reference point in debates on the criminalisation or decriminalisation of certain activities such as drug taking or homosexuality (in the famous HLA Hart versus Lord Devlin debate which ensued after the publication of the Wolfenden Report (*Report of the Committee on Homosexual Offences and Prostitution*, 1957) Hart explicitly took the Millsean position,[31] while Devlin argued that we must be prepared to use the legal system to defend a core morality:

> ... society means a community of ideas; without shared ideas on politics, morals and ethics no society can exist ... they cannot be kept private from the society in which we live (Devlin, *The Enforcement of Morals*, 1965: 10).

Devlin was a refined moral essentialist; he appeared to assume moral principles never change, what changes is public toleration of departure from them.[32] The Millsean liberal may be more sceptical towards a thesis of a timeless foundation or existence of such moral standards. This 'epistemological' difference may help us understand many of the other conflicts between liberty and utility apparent in late-modernity; for example, debates over state paternalism or health and safety legislation. The harm principle appears to specify that rulers cannot authorise coercive intervention for the person's own

---

31 The debate between Hart *(Law, Liberty and Morality*, 1963: this full defence of jurisprudential liberalism and critique of 'judicial moralism' is perhaps HLA Hart's finest writing, certainly superior to *The Concept of Law*) and Lord Devlin about the decriminalisation of homosexuality saw Devlin offer a criterion for what should, or should not, be decriminalised in terms of *what would deeply offend the reasonable man*. In part this is close in spirit to Durkheim's analysis that things are criminal if they shock the collective conscience. Devlin uses a broad utilitarian argument citing cases (for example *Bowman v The Secular Society*, [1917] AC 406) to show previous judicial opinion that the law must intervene and enforce morality to safeguard areas 'essential to its existence'. Devlin was therefore happy to argue for state interference and to expect the state to criminalise certain acts, irrelevant of harm actually occasioned. In Devlin's argument it is better for the communal good to ban certain practices. Although the debate was occasioned by homosexuality, which Devlin seemed to suggest deeply offended the public, Devlin actually swallowed his apparent dislike of homosexuality to accept that the law should be relaxed.

32 Perhaps Devlin's basic concern was actually nihilism, or the prospect of the consequences if the contingency and potential arbitrariness of social life was revealed. The experience of nihilism comes with the perception that there is no one obligatory way to perceive things. One's former beliefs, goals, purposes seem to be demeaned and the unity of purpose to social life dissolves. Devlin appeared to suggest that if the basic moral principles of a society were shown as contingencies then society would collapse. He provided three principles to balance the Millsean impulse with his own desire for stability: (i) maximum freedom compatible with social integrity; (ii) the law should be slow to change its morality since it must preserve the moral social base; (iii) privacy should be respected to the greatest possible extent.

good; however, at least from certain political points of view, much of the administration of the modern welfare state interferes with people's choices for their own good.[33] To what extent are these kinds of laws an invasion of lifestyle choices, and what are the limits? How far should this line of thinking go? Should, for example, fatty foods be banned? Should smoking be banned?

Is the fact of two competing principles within *On Liberty* a real contradiction or does it show differing aspects of a complex whole? To answer this question the respective roles of the liberty principle and utility need to be positioned in Mill's image of the development of modernity. Mill offers an account of liberty where liberty – in the sense defined by the harm principle – and the creation of a self-regarding sphere, will lead to increased diversity of lifestyles, opinions and knowledge. This is not a neutral image; there is a specific connection between the issue of why it is desirable to have this kind of liberty, and what is the good of diversity.

The argument takes place first at the level of freedom of thought and opinion, and moves to a level which Mill calls experiments in living. At the level of freedom of thought and opinion, Mill argues there really are four reasons why one should tolerate other kinds of opinion than those you agree with.

First, if any opinion is compelled to silence, that opinion may, for aught we can certainly know, be true. To deny this is to assume our own infallibility.

Second, though the silenced opinion be in error, it may, and very commonly does, contain a portion of truth; and since the general or prevailing opinion on any subject is rarely or never the whole truth, it is only by the collision of adverse opinions that the remainder of the truth has any chance of being supplied.

Third, even if the received opinion be not only true, but the whole truth; unless it is suffered to be, and actually is, vigorously and earnestly contested, it will, by most of those who receive it, be held in the manner of a prejudice, with little comprehension or feeling of its rational grounds. And not only this, but

Fourth, the meaning of the doctrine itself will be in danger of being lost or enfeebled, and deprived of its vital effect on the character and conduct: the dogma becoming a merely formal profession, inefficacious for good, but cumbering the ground and preventing the growth of any real and heartfelt conviction from reason or personal experience (1974: 115-6).

Life in a society that allows diversity in opinion is a different existential phenomenon than life in a closed society. Mill is concerned to create the conditions where free-thinking people can develop, and where thought can be freed from the despotism of custom.

Among the works of man which human life is rightly employed in perfecting and beautifying, the first in importance surely is man himself (*ibid*: 123).

---

33 For example, the laws relating to the wearing of seat belts. We could argue that this is an interference with our liberty to drive free from having to use the seat belt. Of course there is a utilitarian justification. Namely, that if people do not wear seat belts, there would be many more people dying in traffic accidents, and a greatly increased cost on the National Health Service in treating the higher incidence of accidents. The same argument holds for motorcycle helmets. Utilitarian calculations of the lives saved if helmets are worn, or if seat belts are worn, are thought to justify the creation and enforcement of this legislation.

> Truth gains more even by the errors of one who, with due study and preparation, thinks for himself than by the true opinions of those who only hold them because they do not suffer themselves to think (*ibid*: 95).

People should create their own views by thinking for themselves, by contesting the alternatives. Something of value surfaces from this diversity of arguments, even if many of the views are wrong. If a person argues through ideas and positions for themselves, the person becomes free from the despotism of custom, and achieves rational individuality.[34] We can become more fully human in the future only if we are not programmed into some machine-like form, but are allowed to flourish in a variety of diverse ways. Mankind should have different opinions and different modes of living, different life projects and competing sets of ideas as to the meaning of life. Diversity, in both thoughts and ways of living, will yield individuality. Reflexivity is crucial:

> If the cultivation of the understanding consists in one thing more than another, it is surely in learning the grounds of one's own opinions (*ibid*: 97).

Nor should we accept our beliefs as sensible merely because they are of long standing:

> The fatal tendency of mankind to leave off thinking about a thing when it is no longer doubtful is the cause of half of their errors (ibid: 105).

The two principles come into union and work together for social progress. Having separated his position from Bentham by arguing that we needed to distinguish the quality as well as the quantity of utility, Mill further argues that there are higher and lower forms of utility. The higher forms of utility are the kind that flow to an individual from self-questioning, from the experience of arguing and considering carefully alternative viewpoints and alternative lifestyles. It is a utility which arises out of the experience of diversity and complexity. Mill implicitly argues that certain social conditions are necessary so that individuals in the long term will yield utility in this higher sense. Over the long term liberty is instrumental to utility in the highest sense; liberty produces the sorts of diversity that free us to create diverse forms of living and new technologies.

THE END PRODUCT OF THE INTERACTION OF LIBERTY AND UTILITY IS SOCIAL PROGRESS

Liberty and reflexivity raise society to a higher level. The life experience of the individual should therefore become an issue of considered alternatives.[35] Mill's image of life is that it should be self-creative and self-chosen out of the conflicting demands of all

---

34 Mill (*ibid*: 123) implicitly argues against the Benthamite combination of utility and discipline inferring what is the value if we have achieved technical superiority but produced people who were 'automatons in human form'. 'Human nature is not a machine to be built after a model, and set to do exactly the work prescribed for it, but a tree, which requires to grow and develop itself on all sides, according to the tendency of the inward forces which make it a living thing.'

35 So the position is that liberty produces diversity, which produces modern individuality, which produces utility in the higher sense. This is an argument based inside a society in which people are constantly asking and arguing: 'Why are we here?' 'Why are we living this way?' 'Why are we law students desperate to become lawyers' 'What is going on in my life?' 'What sort of person am I?' 'What do I stand for?'

the alternative possibilities on offer. We choose our life course, develop our life projects, from the awareness of these alternatives, and, just as from freedom of thought we learn from the mistakes of others, in experiencing diversity we learn from contrasting our thoughts and experiences against those of others. We learn by witnessing the mistakes and gains in living that others make in the same way that we learn from the wrong, and the right, arguments of others. Individuality is served by treading this Socratic self-chosen, self-questioning, self-directing path. Moreover, in the long term, utility in the higher sense may be served.

This requires careful delineation of the areas wherein people face diversity. Mill's harm principle tries to shape the law in such a way that legality delineates a social space where individuals can develop as they freely choose, within boundaries defined by avoidance of harmful interference with others. The jurisprudential imagination Mill offers to law thus enables law to constitute the space for individuality; but we should also be aware of how limited a role the written or state law plays in social regulation. Mill was keenly aware of what he called unwritten law – social convention – and if we were to forget the role of social opinion or the impact of the mass media, we would be ignoring a vital source of social oppression.

THE RESPECTIVE ROLES OF WRITTEN OR STATE LAW AND UNWRITTEN LAW AND THE NEED FOR TOLERANCE

The use of sanctions was mandated to enforce official or state law, but social sanctions – for example, ostracism – attended unwritten laws. Mill argued that people could be repressed by unwritten laws and social sanctions even more than by official laws. It is clear that Mill felt a deep repugnance for the narrow-mindedness of Victorian society and argued for tolerance because he felt liberty, individuality and plurality were of a higher ethical value than conformity and standardisation; they made man 'nobler to contemplate'.

James Fitzjames Stephen's defence of intolerance

Mill's *On Liberty* was extensively attacked by the Victorian judge James Fitzjames Stephen (*Liberty, Equality, Fraternity*, 1861). Stephen defended intolerance by arguing it preserved society from law-breaking. His choice of the label intolerance was, perhaps, a mistake, and Stephen is usually dismissed as a reactionary (later followers have preferred to use the language of social order, discipline, authority, or the need for social control to counter Mill's liberty principle). However, Stephen highlights a vital sociological insight: the operation of the state or official laws depends on their fitting with the unwritten or unofficial laws operating in the society. For Stephen, the Victorian liberal state was only possible because of the social discipline unwritten laws enforced. Stephen felt the wisdom of the ages was encoded in these laws and social intolerance was therefore a natural protective mechanism. Moreover, Stephen disagreed with Mill's claim for a class of self-regarding actions which were to be tolerated since they did not harm anyone else. He argued this was too atomistic; almost everything a person did affected others. Suicide, debauchery, drug taking did not injure the agent alone; thus society had a right to interfere to protect those others and itself. Additionally, Mill appeared to be too optimistic in his opinion of the common person; Stephen thought the mass of men were too ill-educated to be able to think out moral codes of their own, nor did they have the strength of character to obey the codes that they had so created. Therefore external social sanctions were needed to uphold morality. Finally, Stephen rejected Mill's view that plurality and diversity were good in themselves. The fact that goodness took varied forms did not mean that variety was goodness. A nation of deviants would demonstrate more variety; but it would also be more criminal and could not be a better nation. Thus Stephen branded dissent and variation for its own sake as frivolous and weak-minded.

CAN THE BOUNDARIES OF HARM AND OFFENCE BE EASILY DRAWN?

Are we able to draw easily a distinction between harm and offence? The American Professor Joel Fienburg, in his book *Harm to Others* (1984), laid out a list of examples in which we face the issue of where offence becomes harm. For instance, he relates a whole series of possible disgusting things that people do on a bus. From merely reading a newspaper the other passengers do not agree with, through playing loud music, to masturbation and full sexual intercourse and on to sex with animals. These examples are designed to probe differences between being simply offended and experiencing hurt. This is the crux of Mill's harm or liberty principle dressed in a different mode. Yet the metaphor of these disgusting things done on a bus, to some extent de-centres and challenges the proponents of individualistic modern society. For one wonders whether society could really cohere without some control over disagreeable public conduct? The experience of institutions such as the Living Theatre movement, or in its different way, the surrealism of the *Theatre de Complicité* is to challenge, and through transgressing, demonstrate the strength of conventional role playing and expectations of everyday behaviour.

The question is complex and fluid: the dividing line between harm and offence is a gradient where the crucial point of distinction is obviously very subtle. Today many people fear this process has gone too far – throughout the western world there are conservative arguments which state the West has lost a sense of authority, and, as a result, the West has lost social cohesion. On the other side, people ask whether, in fact, there is a cohesive society that has achieved great diversity and people engaged in experiments of living? Individuals argue that we are not tolerant enough.[36]

MILL'S OPTIMISM CONCERNING MODERNITY

Mill was an optimist: he believed that real experiments in living could become synthesised by a vibrant society which experiences both a wide level of diversity and yet

---

36 Currently there is great rhetorical use made of the so-called permissive Sixties; it is argued that therein lay a period of experimentation and social diversity – but the Sixties may well have produced the reaction of the moral majority, the demands for a kind of oppressive, coercive conformity and resentment to those labelled as deviant we are currently witnessing.

coheres, and this produces utility in the higher sense. But if liberty and utility are not to conflict, we need tolerance and a narrative notion of social progress. The question is: will diversity and liberty produce tolerance or resentment? If they produce resentment, then resentment may lead to coercive forms of social control; the form of social dynamic that comes out of diversity can be unpredictable. Many may seek to turn away from the experiments of diversity and liberty. Mill calculated that over the long term mutual understanding and tolerance will operate; people will learn from each other's experiments in living. From allowing different lifestyles, no matter how much you might disagree with them initially, society will experience a growth in the quality of moral and political argument over the longer period. Through freedom of thought and expression we will learn from the 'other'; by tolerating them, by allowing difference and diversity we set up a kind of basic web which creates a new form of social solidarity.

How does this reflect upon the question of justice? Perhaps we are stating that the solution to the question of justice is a function of the picture of human nature and social existence. Mill appears optimistic that if there really were societies of liberty and diversity, of experiments in living and individuality, people would get along with minimal resentment. However, the nightmare scenario is that the society would fall apart; it would not serve utility in the higher sense but instead produce dramatic divisions between liberty and utility. There is no easy answer. Which way one leans on this issue may be a question of one's optimism or pessimism concerning the development of modern societies.

WHAT OF THE IDEA OF A SCIENCE OF SOCIETY? DOES THE LIBERTY PRINCIPLE MEAN THAT NO SECURE SCIENCE IS POSSIBLE? THE SEARCH FOR TRUTH PROVIDES THE MODEL FOR THE OPEN SOCIETY

If all mankind minus one were of one opinion, mankind would be no more justified in silencing that one person than he, if he had the power, would be justified in silencing mankind ...

The peculiar evil of silencing the expression of an opinion is that it is robbing the human race, posterity as well as the existing generation – those who dissent from the opinion, still more than those who hold it. If the opinion is right, they are deprived of the opportunity of exchanging error for truth; if wrong, they lose, what is almost as great a benefit, the clearer perception and livelier impression of truth produced by its collision with error (*ibid:* [1859] 1974: 76).

There is the greatest difference between presuming an opinion to be true because, with every opportunity for contesting it, it has not been refuted, and assuming its truth for the purpose of not permitting its refutation. Complete liberty of contradicting and disproving our opinion is the very condition which justifies us in assuming its truth for purposes of action; and on no other terms can a being with human faculties have any rational assurance of being right (*ibid:* 79).

The panopticon may have held such an allure for Bentham's utilitarianism since Bentham appeared to have few doubts as to the 'truth' of his position.[37] Coming half a

---

37   The same holds true for John Austin's jurisprudence, *cf* Chapter 9 of the present text.

century later, Mill's social philosophy was a reflection of a more 'liberal' epistemology; humans cannot know absolute truth for certain. His reconciliation of the harm principle and utilitarianism allows a diversity of living practices to develop. It was hoped that effective and worthwhile forms of social life would thereby come to flourish. At stake is who can tell the 'truth' of social life? And what is truth? What social-structural conditions are necessary for allowing future possibilities for human existence to come about? Hume's dictum that humans are only as good as their institutions holds the key – a progressive society requires a legal order, and a set of social and political institutions which allow tolerance, diversity, and pluralism to grow – at any time those who seek in the name of some superior knowledge to close off pluralism for the sake of purity and certainty are liberalism's enemies. But what will found liberalism? Must liberalism be founded on scepticism? Surely that offers no defence against those who would point to the weakness of pluralism in decision-making?

When Mill experienced his personal crisis and questioned his utilitarianism he turned, among others, to the writings of Comte and Coleridge. From them he drew several conclusions:

> That the human mind has a certain order of possible progress in which some things must precede others, an order which government and public instructors can modify to some, but not to an unlimited extent: that all questions of political institutions are relative, not absolute, and that the different stages of human progress not only will have, but ought to have different institutions: that government is always either in the hands, or passing into the hands, of whatever is the strongest power in society, and that what this power is, does not depend on institutions, but institutions on it: that any general theory or philosophy of politics supposes a previous theory of human progress, and that this is the same thing with a philosophy of history (*Autobiography*, 1873: 162, quoted Sabine and Thorson, 1973: 649)).

We return to Hume: philosophical understanding needs both an historical awareness and to be complemented by an empirical knowledge of the human situation – a sociology – to be realistic. The individualist psychology that late-19th century liberalism relied in large part upon, needed to be married with a historical analysis of the development of social institutions and the rationality that was inherent in these institutions.[38]

---

38 Sympathetic critics of Mill have suggested Mill took three lessons from the reading he conducted in his crises: (i) it is not enough to merely criticise institutions, laws and political policies, criticism should be accompanied by proposals for something better; (ii) Bentham's tactic of dismissing those who defended outmoded institutions as lying in defence of vested interests was wrong; since what was now outmoded once served a social purpose, and those who defend it are still seeing a good in the practices or institutions, thus the reformer must work through the good that is in their opinions and demonstrate how better things will follow from reform; (iii) the tactics of the reformer must be adapted to the times and the place where s/he lives. The English had a distrust for speculative or systematic thinking; hence the reformer would have a greater chance of success by concentrating on particular issues, and only slowly insinuating more general principles.

These were probably Mill's own tactic and the fact that he may have quite deliberately have refrained from writing a statement of his general political and social principles – preferring instead to write essays on particular topics – may have both helped his reception among the English, and given rise to the impression that he could hold contradictory points of view.

LIBERAL PHILOSOPHY NEEDS TO BE COMPLEMENTED WITH HISTORICAL AND SOCIOLOGICAL UNDERSTANDING

The notion of evolution was firmly in the air of mid-Victorian society, and many turned for their idea of progress to a crude evolutionary idea of inevitable stages of human development, but while Mill believed that British institutions should be spread around the world, crude evolutionary determinism was alien to Mill's work. Instead 'he had grasped two ideas that were both sound and important. The first was the dependence of political upon social institutions and the second was the psychological nature of society' (Sabine and Thorson, 1973: 650). When one understands this, Austin's idea of 'habits of obedience' (see Chapter 9 of this text), used to characterise one aspect of sovereignty, becomes a mode of behaviour induced by a social institution. Similarly, the arguments assumed by Austin and Mill's own father concerning psychological attitudes towards work and consumption, are not natural or unchangeable, but rather the effects of the capitalist order. Moreover, *On Liberty* presents the thesis that liberal government is dependent upon a social and moral respect for individuality and for freedom.

Let us be sure of what this combination of individuality and freedom entails. It is not a freedom in the sense of playing one's part in the well-oiled machine of Benthamite utilitarianism, or of the *eudaemonia* of the classical Aristotelian tradition, or the expressive communitarianism of Rousseau and Hegel. Instead this 'liberal' freedom is the practical possibility for each individual to pursue happiness as he/she sees fit, to turn one's life into a set of personal projects, and to seek to attain them. Liberal pluralism thus appears to turn away from the thesis that there is a substantive and unique conception of the common good which society must express and embody. This can all too easily be stated in negative form: a form in which liberal freedom appears an empty, rootless freedom 'enjoyed' within legal rules of an essentially predatory commercial game – a society of atomistic, egoistical monads. But it can be expressed in positive fashion; liberal society does stand for certain values: it is not neutral since the very avoidance of working for one image of human perfection amounts to espousing a different image of human social development. It may become the mistake of liberal jurisprudence – particularly in the legal positivist tradition – to neglect positive representations (leaving them to the realm of mythological, unstated presuppositions, *cf* Fitzpatrick, 1992). Contemporary work in jurisprudence, for example that of Ronald Dworkin, clearly argues that legal positivism failed in that respect,[39] but in doing so in an expressly normative orientation, Dworkin fails to follow through the implication that the normative can only claim to be legitimate

---

39 Ronald Dworkin is the subject of a separate chapter, suffice here to say that he feels liberalism must state itself in positive fashion. Thus, he can describe the Millsean position: 'Since the citizens of a society differ in their conceptions, the government does not treat them as equals if it prefers one conception to another, either because the officials believe that one is intrinsically superior, or because one is held by the more numerous or more powerful groups' (1978: 127). But this is not to make liberalism a compromise position, agreed to only in the absence of truth, instead Dworkin (turning to a rather Kantian position) states: 'Liberalism cannot be based on scepticism. Its constitutive morality provides that human beings must be treated as equals by their government, not because there is no right or wrong in political morality, but because that is what is right' (*ibid*: 142).

if the social institutions are present to make it so (as this text will later argue, see Chapter 15, the absence of an historical and sociological account, or even the need for such an account to complement and critically interact with the normative, is a basic weakness of his project). But the message is there: a liberal-democratic regime, agnostic in terms of the specificity of religion and morality, cannot be agnostic in terms of the very political values that constitute liberalism, since, by definition, it asserts the principles that constitute its specificity qua political association. That is, the political principles of plurality, liberty, and the need to be recognised as a human worthy of equal respect. For, although 20th century liberalism may find that faith in utilitarianism fades, it will need a vigorous debate as to its political principles; without confidence in its institutions, a healthy 'modified scepticism' may threaten to turn to nihilism.[40]

---

40 The enemies may be different: while the Nazis may have ambushed the pluralist democracy of the Weimar Republic, indifference, apathy and populism may be the enemies of liberalism at the end of the 20th century.

CHAPTER 9

JOHN AUSTIN AND THE MISUNDERSTOOD BIRTH OF LEGAL POSITIVISM

Never accept criticism of any author before satisfying yourself of its relevance ... 'reconstruct the problem'; or 'never think you understand any statement made by a philosopher until you have decided, with the utmost possible accuracy, what the question is to which he means it for an answer' (RC Collingwood, *An Autobiography*, 1939: 33).

[In his discussion of] the office or duty of the sovereign Hobbes insists on the following propositions: *That good and stable government is simply or nearly impossible, unless the fundamentals of political science be known by the bulk of the people*: that the bulk of the people are as capable of receiving such science as the loftiest and proudest of their superior in station, wealth, or learning: that to provide for the diffusion of such science throughout the bulk of the people, may be classed with the weightiest of the duties which the Deity lays upon the sovereign: that he is bound to hear their complaints, and even to seek their advice, in order that he may better understand the nature of their wants, and may better adapt his institutions to the advancement of the general good: that he is bound to render his laws as compendious and clear as possible, and also to promulge a knowledge of their more important provisions through every possible channel: that if the bulk of his people know their duties imperfectly, for want of the instruction which he is able and bound to impart, he is responsible religiously for all their breaches of the duties whereof he hath left them in ignorance (Austin, 1873: 289).

An enlightened people are a better auxiliary to the judge than an army of policemen (Austin, 1873: 134).

INTRODUCTION: THE MODERNITY OF JOHN AUSTIN'S JURISPRUDENCE

John Austin (1790–1859) founded the professional enterprise of educational jurisprudence at London;[1] in turn his jurisprudence took its foundations from the work

---

1 The University of London was founded in 1826 by a group loosely associated with Jeremy Bentham with the express aim of reforming the range and substance of university education in England.. John Austin accepted the offer of the Chair in Jurisprudence with enthusiasm and prepared himself by moving with his wife Sarah to Bonn where he taught himself German and studied the historical work of German scholars on the Roman Codes and read the most recent works of Hugo, Thibaut and Savigny. He returned to lecture in 1828 and 1829 where amongst those attending his lectures were John Stuart Mill, George Cornewell Lewis (who went on to become a Commissioner in Malta with Austin), Sir John Romilly and Sir William Erle, all of whom were to become prominent reformers in the years to come. Austin did not receive a salary for his position but was expected to earn his fee from subscriptions which the students themselves paid. Although offered a stipend for his position in the early 1830s, he gave up the Chair in 1832 for financial reasons publishing in the same year *The Province of Jurisprudence Determined*, an expanded version of the first part of his lectures. According to Sarah, John Austin was acutely depressed at the failure of the Chair in Jurisprudence. She describes this as 'the real and irredeemable calamity of his life – the blow from which he never recovered'. The second edition of *The Province* was published in 1861, two years after his death, and the first complete edition of *The Lectures on Jurisprudence* or *The Philosophy of Positive Law*, which had been reconstructed from his notes by Sarah, was published in 1863.

of Hobbes and Bentham.[2] While Bentham provides the immediate influence, Austin acknowledges his debt to the clarity by which Hobbes laid out the necessity for strong and rational government; government which uses positive law – the commands of the sovereign – as the instrument shaping and reforming the body of duties and obligations which provide the framework for civil society to progress.[3] To concentrate upon power and command is, however, to miss the second point of how Austin understood Hobbe's legacy: the need for knowledge of the human condition and the conditions of government and the necessity to build a modern social order.[4]

The young Austin displayed a 'dogmatically held ... belief that the aristocracy used Parliament and other institutions such as the courts, the church and the army to promote its own interests, which because they were the interests of a class, were sinister. Consequently, while the aristocracy pursued its own interests, those of the entire population were sacrificed, and the people were exploited' (L and J Hamburger, 1985: 31). Both the political system and the legal system were in dire need of radical reform. The reformed nation-state envisaged would have an extended suffrage and be an enlightened and rational political association which would not hesitate to use authorised coercion – commands backed by the powers of punishment and the prison – according to the guidance of the developing positive knowledges. In turn, Austin's jurisprudence laid bare the structure of a new constitution – a socio-political constitution – comprising the essential elements of knowledge, power, command and obedience – held together and given guidance by a new social faith: utilitarianism. The foundation of this constitution – this new social order – is not the subjective will, or desires of those elites who physically make up the sovereign, nor is it simply a matter of power relations. Austin holds an objective faith; as he states clearly in his Lecture III, he believes in the ability of positive knowledge(s) to reveal the underlying truths of the socio-political structure,[5] and the role of education is to spread at least the fundamentals of these

---

2   The relationship of Austin to Bentham is more complicated than the assessment that Austin merely applied Bentham's ideas. While the young Austin once declared to Bentham that 'I am truly your disciple', his early wholehearted support for Bentham's constitutional radicalism appears to have waned by the time he came to prepare his lectures. His subsequent conservative position took him further away from Bentham, who remained a constitutional radical to his death.

3   While lauding the lesson in the passage quoted in our opening section, specifically 'that good and stable government is simply or nearly impossible unless the fundamentals of political science be known by the bulk of the population', Austin believed Hobbes's work suffers from two 'capital errors: 1. He inculcates too absolutely the religious obligation to obedience [and does not allow for those cases where utility demands disobedience] ... 2. He ascribes the origin of sovereignty, and of independent political society, to a fictitious agreement or covenant' (1873: 278).

4   In *Legislators and Interpreters*, Bauman asks us to free our ideas of education from the later idea of schooling and try to recreate a feeling for the enlightenment ambitions education stood for. Bauman (1987: 69) suggests that education was rather the idea of the whole society and total human environment being 'moulded in a way which makes human individuals learn, appropriate and practise the art of rational social life. In no way was education seen as a separate area in the social division of labour; it was on the contrary, a function of all social institutions, an aspect of daily life, a total effect of designing society according to the voice of Reason ... "education" stood for a project to make the formation of the human being the full and sole responsibility of society as a whole, and especially of its lawgivers'. Bauman views education as part of the growing right of the state to form its citizens and guide their conduct, the practice of a managed society.

214

knowledges throughout the society. In the combination of rational government and educated populace lies the key to social progress. The aim is modernity and this modernity is to become a knowledge-bound social space with a self-consciousness provided by a thoroughly rational and realistic grasp of its composition.

Austin's first published writing, which appeared in *The Westminster Review* – a journal established by Bentham in 1824 – was a critical analysis of the law of primogeniture and the role of the aristocracy in social administration. Austin even commented favourably on the French Revolution, calling it a 'grand and necessary reform', unfortunately 'not accomplished with greater discrimination and forbearance'.[6] Austin's criticism of the regressive role the aristocracy were playing in social institutions was part of general intellectual movement or awareness that a new style of social administration was required. In the age of feudalism, rule by the aristocracy, or landed nobility, operated through being tied to locality and an ideology whereby the nobility administered order and watched over the interests of all. The nobility were born into privilege *and* a functional role. However, aristocratic administration could only secure social order and supervise the continuation of custom and privilege by the twin factors of tradition (including religion which allowed for the administration of Christendom) and a political geography which consisted of the social fragmentation of loosely federated localities. By the late eighteenth century the canons of the landed nobility were dysfunctional to the demands of a new social order. Bauman (1987:29) suggests that the governing horizons and administrative zeal of the landed aristocracy were tightly interwoven with their property rights and circumscribed by the boundaries of the latter: 'They had no foundation of their own and not enough flexibility to be easily redeployed in the service of a centralised government and a centralised legal system which cut across the boundaries of noble estates'. Austin's article was followed in 1826 by his appointment as Professor of *Jurisprudence and the Law of Nations* in the new University of London. Austin moved with his wife Sarah to Bonn for a time to prepare for the lectures, a period in which he was not only impressed by the rational structure of Roman law, but also by the reasonableness of the Prussian ruling elites and the social deference the populace held them in. This period – perhaps the happiest of Austin's life – proved important in changing his political views to favour rule by enlightened elites. The bankrupt rule of the will of the aristocracy was to be replaced by rational

---

5   This is not to suggest that nature has this objectivity. Austin, however, appears to have thought so (although I do not go as far as Morison (1982), who attempts to tie together Austin and James Mill, whose *Elements of Political Economy* was specifically a rigid conceptualisation of 'natural laws' made visible by the 'science of political economy'). Austin was a passionate believer in the emerging sciences of man and economics. He believed that the truths of the human condition were being made visible.

6   Quoted in Lotte and Joseph Hamburger (1985: 32), who summarise Austin's article as follows: 'Austin first criticised primogeniture on economic grounds, but in the end it was "aristocratical ascendancy and aristocratical misgovernment" that was condemned. Not only did primogeniture lead to the concentration of landed wealth in a small class, but it also led to exploitation of the people, for the younger sons and other relations, excluded from their fathers' estates, would have to be provided with incomes at public expense: "To maintain the custom of primogeniture amongst the governing class, the people could be taxed and pillaged with little moderation ... Offices which had survived the ends for which they were created, would be kept alive at the public charge, because the emoluments of such useless offices would yield a convenient provision for the younger children of the aristocracy"' (1985: 31–2).

government according to the dictates of positive knowledge; a formula which also served to keep at bay ideas of rule by popular majority that the Benthamite circle had come to favour after despairing at the prospect of changing the views of the ruling elites.

Jurisprudence can play a unique role in social education; it can provide an analysis of a key tool of modernity – positive law – and it can highlight the responsibility that goes along with the power associated with that tool. The exercise of political power is primary to Austin's jurisprudential imagination, as he makes clear in his opening definition (following quotes from Lecture I): 'The matter of jurisprudence is positive law: law, simply or strictly so called: or law set by political superiors to political inferiors'. Laws are rules 'laid down for the guidance of an intelligent being by an intelligent being have power over him'; they are 'the aggregate of the rules, established by political superiors'. The science of jurisprudence should distinguish positive law, the rules created by political 'will', or what Austin identifies as 'reason'. The key to this science Austin calls understanding the nature of the specific kind of 'command' that is positive law. A command is an expression of a wish, a signification of a desire, which is distinguished 'by the power and the purpose of the party commanding to inflict an evil or pain in case the desire be disregarded'. Being liable to evil, the party commanded is '*bound* or *obliged*' by the command and placed 'under a duty to obey it'.

Austin specifies that 'a law is a command which obliges a person or persons to a course of conduct' and proceeds by way of a relationship of 'superiority'. Austin denies any traditional justification to the term superiority. Although, the term has often been 'synonymous with precedence or excellence', Austin turns to Hobbes' clear identification of power as the key to command.[7] But while the power of God is absolute and simple, human power is embedded in reciprocal relationships; viewed from one perspective, a party is superior, but from another is inferior; governments can be toppled by the people's resistance. This duality of imagery – of political power and weakness – runs through Austin's work and is moderated by his faith in education, in the role of the advance of knowledge to provide a template for rational government.

But while Austin believes that secure knowledge(s) will be provided to serve as the foundations and structures of the new social order, it was not specifically the role of the jurist to delve into such knowledge, instead the task was to concentrate upon clarifying the nature of the key technique or technology of guidance – positive law. A new jurisprudence is necessary to lay out the domain of law, while other developing positive knowledges, specifically the science of ethics – largely reducible to utility – provide the direction and social justice for the power to command. The modern science of government is to be a governmentality of law and knowledge not of arbitrary desire; while society is a relationship of men dominating other men and women, the

---

7   '... the term superiority signifies might: the power of affecting others with evil or pain, and of forcing them, through fear of the evil, to fashion their conduct to one's wishes ... The might or superiority of God, is simple or absolute ..:.'

domination structuring modern society was to operate according to law, guided by knowledge, and confident in its justice (utility).[8]

---

8   The basic issue which linked together Bentham, Austin and John Stuart Mill politically can be phrased as 'how to get more intelligence into government?' Bentham favoured making the interests of the rulers and the ruled the same – ie radical democracy; but that only works if one is convinced that utilitarianism is both a realist political doctrine and that it will be accepted by the people. If the people are ill-educated then they will not follow the principle of the greatest happiness of the greatest number; an enlightened elite will be better if they have reason to associate their happiness with that of the society. John Stuart Mill favoured representative democracy with plural voting – the educated and responsible person would have more influence than the uneducated by being given several votes – and a well educated populace would not only select the best people to represent them but understand the rationality of the policies proposed.

PART ONE
RESCUING AUSTIN FROM THE COMMENTATORS

WHO IS THE JOHN AUSTIN OF JURISPRUDENCE TEXTS?

John Austin has the dubious distinction of being the father figure of modern English jurisprudence; in particular he is regarded as the originator of legal positivism[9] and as putting forward a command or imperative theory of law (Hobbes has been rather neglected as a jurisprudential figure).[10] To many commentators Austin is a lesser jurisprudential figure than Bentham, and his historical role is partly due to the accident that while all of Austin's major work was in print in the 1860s, Bentham's lay largely unpublished until much later.[11] Austin appears readily understandable and easily dismissible; moreover as legal positivism has come under attack in recent years, Austin can be blamed for unduly reducing the field of study for jurisprudence by giving us a narrow conceptual definition of law and a methodology which separates moral and political concerns from the study of law.[12] Thus Austin can be seen as responsible for

---

9   A central claim of legal positivism is the analytical separation of law and morality, specifically that while the empirical legal order of a society may well be founded upon moral arguments, there is no necessary or conceptual linkage between law and morality. In other words, while natural law or expressive positions, may argue that law is 'morally justified power', or 'the expression of truly human concerns', legal positivism argues that law can have any sort of content. Two central ideas of positivism are: (i) we can identify what existing law is without making any moral judgments. Whether some rule is a legal rule depends upon whether it has been laid down in some source such as a statute or a case. If it is found in some valid source it is a valid legal rule whether it is good or bad, just or unjust. Equally, the mere fact that a rule is just and reasonable does not make it part of the law if it is not found in any recognised source of law; (ii) propositions of law, in which we state the existence of legal rights and duties, are not of their nature moral judgments.

10 'Within a few years of his death it was clear that his work had established the study of jurisprudence in England. And it is now clear that Austin's influence on the development in England of the subject has been greater than that of any other writer' (HLA Hart, Introduction to *The Province of Jurisprudence Determined*, 1954).

11 As Cotterrell (1989: 53) explains, however, Austin's work had a distinct appeal to the legal profession which makes the argument of publication only a partial explanation. 'The form of Austin's legal theory and the ordering of its concerns enable it to offer a normative legal theory which was particularly appropriate to the political and legal professional concerns of its time. Further, it exemplifies a certain general conception of law in an extremely concise and straightforward manner. In fact, Austin's "failure" in so many worldly things may have been the condition of his success in this. He pursued with apparently total singlemindedness a distinct image of how a 'science' of law might be possible. Lacking Bentham's restless intellectual curiosity – which diverted the greater thinker into an immense diversity of projects – Austin meticulously worked on the theory of law which had been merely part of Bentham's concerns. Where his ideas differ from Bentham's, it is often because he prefers a stubborn logic (for example, on the nature of sovereignty) or a hard-headed realism (for example, in discussing judicial law-making), where Bentham equivocates or tries to develop more radical analyses in the cause of legal or political reform.'

12 Some of the criticisms of legal positivism have been little short of polemical. For sympathetic accounts see Guest (1992), while Simmonds (1986) defends the positivist scholar by considering various erroneous perceptions relating to positivist theory. First, positivists do not necessarily deny the importance of morality. They need not be moral sceptics of any sort, but may be keenly interested in moral criticism of the law with a view to its reform. Second, positivists do not deny that morality   ...

professionalising and rationalising the potential tradition of legal positivism, rendering it into the form where it became suitable to found a science of law. In this interpretation Austin, in the name of analytical and conceptual rigour, divorced the study of law from the task of identifying the social context of law in and its constitute effects on social reality. Such an impression is, however, the result of oversimplification in the usual teaching material. Simply put, while the *Lectures on Jurisprudence* involve a complex argument constructed as a synthesis around a design for modern government, jurisprudential scholars have abstracted the outline of an analytical jurisprudence, ignoring the political and ethical structures which give it life. Austin has been the victim of a particular form of analytical philosophy, an analytical approach which he himself is often regarded as epitomising,[13] but one which has given the impression that Austin can be reduced – without loss of intellectual integrity – into a few basic propositions which can easily be comprehended, shown up as simplifications, and dismissed as one-sided. This result, however, is more the effect of the dominant tradition of interpretation than of the original material.[14]

ASPECTS OF THE USUAL TREATMENT OF AUSTIN

Three features are apparent in the usual treatment of Austin. First, Austin is seen as striving to create a methodology for studying law which, although unduly limiting the concept of law to a structure of command, habitual obedience and sanction, is of value in arguing that legal studies must become scientific.[15] Second, the legacy of Austin is

---

12. ...influences the content of law. Obviously legislators often enact particular laws because of their moral convictions and the law is influenced in its content by the moral view prevailing in society generally. But a rule does not become law until it has been laid down in a source such as a statute or a decided case. Nor do positivist legal scholars deny that judges sometimes decide cases by reference to moral values or consideration of social policy. What they deny is that judges have to make moral or social judgments in working out what the existing law is. Having established what the relevant rules are, however, a judge may discover that the relevant legal rules do not give an answer in the case he is dealing with. Since the pre-existing law does not give an answer, the judge must decide the case on the basis of extra-legal considerations. In doing so he will establish a new legal rule. But what makes the rule a legal rule is that it has been laid down by the judge, not the fact that it was based on moral considerations. Third, positivists do not deny that there may be a moral obligation to obey the law. They simply argue that the question of what the law is, and the question of whether or not it ought to be obeyed are two separate questions.

13. As Hart continued in the section quoted above: 'For English jurisprudence has been and still is predominantly analytical in character ...' (1954: xvi)

14. The first moves to a proper, contextual and integrated approach came with the work of WL Morison (1982). The detailed texts of Rumble (1985) and the Hamburgers (1985), which give an overall picture of Austin's life and arguments, have been largely ignored in jurisprudential writings. An exception to this is Cotterrell's (1989) Weberian text *The Politics of Jurisprudence*.

15. Thus Davies and Holdcroft (1991: 16) begin their chapter on Austin: 'John Austin (1790-1859) is probably the most influential English legal positivist ... His aim is to distinguish law from other phenomena, in particular from rules of morality. For him clarity of thought about the nature of law requires a strict, watertight demarcation of the subject matter of jurisprudence'.

   Similarly Lloyd: 'As a positivist Austin sought to show what law really is, as opposed to moral or natural law notions of what it ought to be ... To the Benthamites positivism seemed to require some simple empirical explanation of law devoid of metaphysics or mysticism ... What was rationally needed was merely some prior command, so that law was really no more than a series of orders given to   ...

seen as his laying down the ground rules of the analytical form of jurisprudence that came to characterise legal positivism (namely, clear and precise discussion of 'concepts' and setting out a doctrinal analysis of the basic legal materials), and thereby the methodology which Austin gives to jurisprudence seems to indicate that law can be understood as if no contextual account need be considered.[16] Third, to read Austin in the light of the criticisms of HLA Hart (1961), and to accept Hart's account as demonstrating the deficiencies of Austin.[17] As a result Austin is viewed as Hart's inferior, and, while very much a figure to be studied because reference to him is required to see the birth of modern legal positivism, he is seen as too simplistic and crude to be relevant to our contemporary concerns.

These three features can be repositioned as problems for a self-conscious jurisprudence. First, we can raise the issue of the use to be made of Austin and the values of analytical jurisprudence as a methodology of understanding; second, by placing Austin's work within the context of the development of modernity we can see an important chapter in the social constitutive imagination jurisprudence offers; third, by raising the problem of the use made of Austin by HLA Hart we can address questions both about the proper way or the politics of reading other writers and the (de)construction of theory. This last issue will be reserved for the later discussion of HLA Hart's work. The degree to which Austin separated his science of law from broader social concerns, the value of analytical jurisprudence, and the institutional imagination Austin offers will serve as guiding threads in this chapter, complementing the presentation of the meaning of Austin's theory of law.

Most commentators have not contextualised Austin's work. Instead, a limited number of uses have been suggested for studying Austin's basic scheme. First, it has been claimed that there is an experiential justification for studying Austin's theory: a purpose of 'clearing the head' as Sir Henry Maine claimed. In reading Austin, it is suggested, we encounter 'the difficult art of precise thought'. As Rumble puts it: 'In particular, careful study of his work encourages students of it to clarify if not develop their own ideas on a number of the most basic questions of jurisprudence. This experience is beneficial no matter how different these ideas may be from Austin's own conceptions' (1985: 2). Second, it has been claimed that studying Austin we can see mistakes in defining the key to jurisprudence, which stimulated intellectual development but which we now realise were wrong conceptions of law. As Hart put it in the preface to his 1954 edition of *The Province of Jurisprudence Determined*: 'the demonstration of precisely where and why he is wrong has proved to be a constant source of illumination' (1954: xviii). This second use

---

15. ...human beings, with penalties or sanctions attached for disobedience. Whether this was an oversimplification, or in what sense the word 'command' was here used, were questions not fully explored by those to whom this approach seemed so obvious an explanation of the essence of law: to Austin the problem was merely to link this logically with the universally recognised and esteemed doctrine of legal sovereignty' (Lloyd's *Introduction to Jurisprudence*, 5th edn 1985: 255-6).

16. 'Nevertheless, Austin's thought still remains worthy of examination not only on account of his widespread influence, especially in common law countries, but also by reason of his penetrating powers of applying analysis to jurisprudence' (Lloyd's, 5th edn 1985: 255).

17. Davies and Holdcroft (1991), for example, devote nearly eight pages of an 18-page chapter on Austin to 'Hart on Austin'. Moreover, Hart's criticisms do not receive any critical response.

of Austin's work combines with a third, specifically, to understand and to teach the meaning of the dominant tradition in English jurisprudence, the combination of *legal positivism and analytical jurisprudence*. Viewed as an analytical philosopher Austin is seen not to be interested in an empirical enquiry about actual societies, but to be concerned with clarification of concepts, not historical or sociological questions.[18] It is certainly true that a great deal of the work of Austin is devoted to the clarification and exposition of the relations between legal concepts. Moreover, Austin sincerely wished to provide a framework or theory for 'general jurisprudence', which enables us to position the essential features of any legal system without describing the details of any particular system, a task reserved for 'particular jurisprudence'. Austin appears to begin his lectures by setting out a clear answer to the question of 'what is law?', an answer which appears reductionist and simple – the standard criticisms are that he has reduced the idea of law to those of sovereignty, command, habitual obedience and sanction, and neglected the various meanings that the legal enterprise of subjecting human behaviour to the governance of *rules* may have. While Austin used the terms rules and principles, he is said to have been blind to their subtle meanings for legal studies. In the dominant reading, Austin is viewed as a methodologist whose substantive contributions are mistakes. Thus it is valuable to study his theory in that we can read the mistakes of the past, since we move forward as much by establishing falsehoods as by through accepting correct positions.

Additionally Austin is taught as the key figure in the development of the tradition of legal positivism and the powerful stimulator of techniques of analytical jurisprudence. While it is not conceptually necessary to be both a legal positivist and an analytical jurisprudent, Austin epitomised both. Thus his *Lectures on Jurisprudence* are 'the best single expression of these strands of thought in the Anglo-American jurisprudence of the 19th century ... [moreover] contemporary forms of legal positivism may be interpreted as a continuation of the Austinian tradition' (Rumble, 1985: 3).

---

18 Such, for example, is the opinion of Herbert Morris in *The Encyclopedia of Philosophy* published in 1967, which was a prime example of the orthodox view on Austin (particularly after the publication of HLA Hart's *The Concept of Law* (1961). Morris argues that 'the key to the science of jurisprudence for Austin' is found in a rigorous conceptual analysis using certain key, clearly defined terms – sanctions, superiority, obligation, sovereignty.

'The inadequacies of Austin's theory result mainly from his selecting as basic tools of analysis the concepts of a command and habitual obedience ... [Morris outlines several of the usual criticisms]. In addition to these criticisms, Austin has been charged with lack of originality, even in his fundamental mistakes, for identical views may be found in Hobbes and Bentham ... It is understandable that we should wonder at Austin's great influence, and his reputation as a great legal philosopher.

First Austin's positivism, his insistence on separating questions of fact and value, has made legal philosophers sensitive to how easily these questions may be confused and how we may, as a result, delude ourselves into thinking we have answered one of these questions when we have, in fact, answered the other. Even more important, Austin's failures, all associated in some way with his imperativism, have been helpful. He was not alone in feeling the grip of a certain idea, the idea that law is simply the impressing of the will of the stronger upon the weaker. Austin's chief virtue was that he systematically developed, defended, and refined this idea, stripping it of excess focus with greater precision on those features of law that connect it with coercion. More than this, his model presses viewing law as coercion obscures its complicated role in our lives. After Austin, we understand better what there is in law that does not. This is his principal legacy. He provides one more instance in philosophy of our gaining something from a false statement that we might not have gained from a true one.'

REREADING AUSTIN AS AN ANALYTICAL POSITIVIST: DO WE NEED TO CONSIDER AUSTIN'S OVERALL PROJECT TO APPRECIATE HIS ANALYTICAL DISTINCTIONS?

So-called 'critical' writers in legal theory and positivists dispute the consequences of the legal positivist tradition. Analytical jurisprudence, however, narrowly defined the range of theoretical questions that could be raised about law and sealed into a tight circle the confines of the discipline of jurisprudence. In this tradition, jurisprudence ruled out of its sphere of interest questions requiring the exposition of the actual contents of the particular jurisdiction, questions of legal or intellectual history, both particular and general, and questions calling for ethical judgments of the content or effectiveness of particular laws. These, it is said, Austin delegated to the 'science of legislation'.[19] Analytical jurisprudence concerned itself with questions of conceptual analysis in four main areas. First, the analysis of the concept of law itself; second, the definitions of basic terms; third, the interrelationships of basic legal terms – the so-called jural relations; fourth, the analysis of other non-legal concepts and the distinctions between these concepts and legal concepts.

In Lecture II Austin stated: 'It really is important that men should think distinctly, and speak with a meaning'. Subsequent analytical jurisprudence has valued intellectual rigour, and lucidity of writing, at the expense of any wider concern with social and political reality. As a result, in recent decades legal positivism came under attack for being a self-sustaining, acontextual enterprise. Divorced from any necessity to find in law social rationality, according to more sociologically informed critics, analytical jurisprudence loses any claim to be other than a partial perspective on the reality of law.[20]

Against this backdrop, actually to read Austin's lectures is an experience of encountering something 'other' than the commentators' image (Austin's *Jurisprudence*, text of the full Lectures first published 1863: the edition used in this chapter is the 1873 fourth edition). Austin's writings are a strange mixture of dryness, abstract reflection, claims to knowledge of political and ethical truths, and passionate rhetoric. For example, immediately after the dictum demanding clarity of thought and speech quoted above,

---

19 Interestingly Cotterrell (1989: 81) suggests that it is this very fact of formal rationality that Austin brings to his emerging science of law (as opposed to a substantive discussion of the content of particular laws) which made his jurisprudence so acceptable to the legal profession of the late 19th century. '[Austin] is primarily concerned with the form of law and the structure of legal authority. Perhaps, it can be suggested, professional knowledge of law in an era of continuous legal change promoted by the directive, legislative activity of the state, could only be unified around ideas about the form and structure of law, and not around ideas about law's substantive content. The content of law was not only potentially in constant flux, but was beyond lawyers' control (unlike the situation in earlier eras when judges both explained and controlled legal development). It was the result of political considerations which could not themselves easily be brought within the professional knowledge field of lawyers.'

20 For Cotterrell (1989: 227), 'the essential systematic rationality of law can be reduced to a capacity to identify the formal origins of each rule or regulation in some specific, unambiguous and accepted governmental source. As regards the substance of legal doctrine, law's rationality appears merely 'piecemeal' or localised ... The effect of this positivisation of law is that the 'obvious utility' of legal practice tends to appear as one of atheoretical technique, rather than theoretically justified reason.'

Austin argues that concentrating upon concepts can cause us to lose sight of social and political reality. (His criticism of David Hume sums up his own underlying enterprise: Hume is criticised for 'handling detached topics with signal dexterity, but evincing an utter inability to grasp his subject as a whole' (1873: 153).) Austin is clear that the war with the American colonies, and the state of ongoing tension which existed between America and England, flew in the face of sensible utilitarian calculations and was engendered by apolitical assertions of 'sovereignty' and 'rights': 'The stupid and infuriate majority who rushed into that odious war, could perceive and discourse of nothing but the *sovereignty* of the mother country, and her so called *right* to tax her colonial subjects'. By contrast, the dominant question should have been what it was in England's best interests to do. Governments have 'projects', and if the project of the English government was changing, so talk of rights should lessen in importance. The term sovereignty denotes a living, changing social phenomenon; we are not dealing with some abstract linguistic concept. Similarly, people who talked of rights as if they existed outside the process which created them and gave them meaning were deluded: 'As if a right were worth a rush of itself, or of something to be cherished and asserted independently of the good that it might bring' (1873: 123-4). For Austin concepts are embedded in social processes. It makes no sense to talk of rights as if they were standing on their own foundations – rights are not free-standing, but take their foundations from the reality of corresponding duties; duties which must be enforceable for rights to exist in reality.[21]

AUSTIN'S CONCEPTS ARE PART OF AN OVERALL SYNTHESIS

Austin constructs his lectures with reference to an overriding intellectual synthesis of analysis and social progress; he presents a view of the human condition which depicts a master principle – that of utility – which will serve as the signifier of social justice. Austin's discussion of the principle of utility in Lecture III, and of the common good in Lecture IV, demonstrate the underlying synthesis which sets the meaning for the analytical object of his lectures, ie 'to evolve and expound the principles and distinctions involved in the idea of law'. Lecture III provides the context of Austin's analytical approach; it is above all an indication of his comprehensive grasp of the socio-legal enterprise for building modernity. But to consider Lecture III as of great importance in understanding Austin's jurisprudence we need to consider the nature and meaning of Austin's 'positive' jurisprudential thought itself.

---

21 Austin is so certain of this that he argues duties precede rights. Rights are a derivative of a set of duties. In his review of Austin's *Lectures on Jurisprudence*, John Stuart Mill doubted this dependent relationship giving the example of the respective roles of jailor and inmate in prisons. 'It is [the jailor's] duty to keep [inmates] in confinement, perhaps in bodily fetters', but how can we say that a prisoner's right is created? Similarly, 'it is the duty of the hangman to inflict capital punishment upon all persons lawfully delivered to him for the purpose: but would the culprit himself be spoken of as having a right to be hanged?' ('Austin on Jurisprudence', in *Dissertations and Discussions*, in four vols, Boston, 1868, 4: 236, and 234.)

WHAT IS THE EPISTEMOLOGICAL BASIS OF AUSTIN'S ANALYSIS: IS HE A SIMPLE CONCEPTUAL POSITIVIST, AN EMPIRICIST, OR A SOCIOLOGIST?

A famous criticism of Austin made by HLA Hart is that Austin began his theorising by proposing a conceptual definition of law rather than coming to an understanding of law after observing the nature of legal phenomena. By defining law in terms of commands, habitual obedience and sanctions, Austin can be charged by Hart (1961: Chapters 2, 3 and 4) with failing to see the richness of legality; specifically, the role of law in the political constitution of the modern state, the normative element to legal rules, and the power-conferring aspect of many legal rules. While agreeing that legal positivism was the correct methodology, Hart then felt able to offer a new start, a beginning based on teasing out various linguistic traps and returning our concern to the reality (supposedly at any rate) of law's everyday operations. In Hart's view, Austin began with a definition and then built a framework upon this, rather than looking at the variation in law's effects and roles. Hart's point (although his criticisms of Austin are misplaced for various reasons) had been made better in the 19th century by Nietzsche, who once complained that the positivist approach to philosophy detached concepts from life by subjecting them to a conceptual analysis without any concern for the circumstances which gave them life and provided the context from which they take their real meaning.[22] Austin is partly a conceptualist; he begins with a definition of law, but there is a very serious point to this definition. Austin's definition fits his reformist agenda; it makes clear that law is an instrument of government But Austin is not usually contextualised; instead whatever else is said of Austin the ascription to him of a positivist epistemology and an analytical methodology predominates. HLA Hart claims the lasting legacy is that of separating law from morality.[23] The strength of Austin is thus to have abstracted the core meaning of concepts from their social embeddedness and to give them independent and autonomous life.[24] In putting into place this autonomous structure, this independence, 'it was Austin who first demonstrated to English lawyers in their own idiom how the understanding even of unsystematised English law, with its forest of details, could be increased and its exposition improved by the use of a theoretical structure and precise analysis' (Hart, 1954: xvii).

But what is the status of Austin's analysis of law? In other words what is the nature of Austin's claim to 'know' the law? This issue is not normally regarded as a problem in teaching texts: Austin can be labelled a arch-positivist, or a naive empiricist.

---

22 'Philosophy reduced to 'theory of knowledge', [is] in fact no more than a timid epochism and doctrine of abstinence – a philosophy that never gets beyond the threshold and takes pains to deny itself the right to enter – that is philosophy in its last thrones, an end, an agony, something inspiring pity. How could such a philosophy – dominate!' (*Beyond Good and Evil*, A 204)

23 'The main doctrines of *The Province of Jurisprudence Determined* can be easily identified in Austin's predecessors ... Austin's achievement was to segregate these doctrines from the political and philosophical discussions in which they were embedded and to restate them with a new firmness, grasp of detail and precision so that lawyers and political thinkers could not only understand them but use them to dispel the haze ...' (Hart, 1954: xvi).

24 By 1881 Amos could claim that Austin 'delivered the law from the dead body of morality that still clung to it' (Amos, *The Science of Law*, 5th edn, 1881: 4).

Alternatively, critics claim he takes one type of law, the criminal law with its centrality of coercion, and unquestioningly expands from this. Certainly Austin's analytical concern puts much effort into the exposition of the law as he finds it. As he is quick to point out:

> The existence of law is one thing, its merit or demerit another. Whether it be or be not is one inquiry; whether it be or be not comfortable to an assumed standard is a different inquiry (1873: 220).

Thus Austin places the questions of legal reform, the questions of what law ought to be, into the province of the science of legislation, while analysis of law becomes confined to a positivist study of the laws posited under the central authority of the state.[25] He bequeaths a methodology to the legal positivist tradition of answering the question 'what is law?' by engaging in a root-of-title search, since so long as we can demonstrate that the laws have been validly passed we rest our analysis of the nature of law; we turn to mere clarification of the law. Austin's definition, however, is actually wider; it is a political conception of law. To Cotterrell (1989: 61), this 'governmental view of law' entails that 'in a sense, law is, for him, effective government'. If this is the case then to know the meaning of law is to know the meaning of government. In other words law cannot exist outside the *process of government.*

For Austin, law is essentially a matter of process: a law/rule is a species of command given inside a political society by political superiors to political inferiors, wherein the political superior has the power, if he wishes, to inflict an evil or pain in the case of the command being disregarded. If a series of commands is not obeyed and no evil is inflicted, and hence no ensuing obedience is brought about, there simply is no sense in saying that a system of law is in operation.

Austin uses the terms sovereign, commands, sanction, habitual obedience to grapple with a complex social phenomenon.[26] Thus for Sir Henry Maine, writing in the latter part of the 19th century, Austin was responding to a social transformation.[27] The German social theorist Max Weber (1978), writing at the end of the 19th century, cited Austin as the writer who carried out the necessary process of rationalisation (within English legal studies) that the Anglo-American legal system required for the

---

25 Although certain writers, for example in Lloyd's 5th edn, claim that 'Austin avoids the word "state"', Austin claims that while the 'state' has a variety of meanings 'the "state" is usually synonymous with "the sovereign". It denotes the individual person, or the body of individual persons, which bears the supreme powers in an independent political society. This is the meaning which I annex to the term.' (1873: 249, note (p))

26 For Cotterrell (1989: 79), 'they are conceptual reflections of a particular time and place, transformed in a way that gives them the potential to speak to other generations in other legal conditions. In Austin's case, however, these concepts were formulated with a clear awareness of the sociological questions they entail.' A dimension of his thought 'almost totally ignored by his critics in the field of normative legal thought'.

27 'But if the Analytical Jurists failed to see a great deal which can only be explained by the help of history, they saw a great deal which even in our day is imperfectly seen by those who, so to speak, let themselves drift with history. Sovereignty and law, regarded as facts, had only gradually assumed a shape in which they answered to the conception of them formed by Hobbes, Bentham, and Austin but the correspondence really did exist by their time and was tending constantly to become more perfect' (Sir Henry Maine, 'Sovereignty and Empire', in *Early History of Institutions*, 396-7).

development of a new form of government administration. Cotterrell, writing in 1989, depicts Austin as providing concepts and descriptions of law suitable for the rise of the centralised state. How Weber defined this process of rationalisation is the subject of Chapter 11 of our text, but it is tempting to say that the distance between Austin and Hart is that Austin witnessed the development of the rationalisation process (and was a keen devotee of it) while Hart (1961) lived amidst its result.[28]

There is more at issue than simply saying that Austin is acutely aware of sociological realities; this is an easy point to establish.[29] All Austin's discussions of his concepts are subjected to tests of social reality whatever one thinks of their actual effectiveness. Three examples: (i) Austin draws a distinction between societies natural and political, and the test is a sociological one: 'The positive mark of sovereignty and independent political society is a fallible test of specific or particular cases' (1873: 233). (ii) In revolutionary situations, the acceptance over time of the commands of new rulers is the test of whether a new set of laws is in place. (iii) Austin is clear that all the individuals of a society could theoretically be part of the sovereign (or, more correctly 'exercise sovereign powers') but as a matter of social reality no society allows more than a minority access to political power.

There is no doubt that Austin is keenly aware of the complexity and ambiguity of the social and political world. Moreover, Austin appears conscious of the ever-present contingency of human affairs. Although, ideally, utility 'ought' to win out if left unorganised[30] (left, that is, without the strength of will to organise human society rationally or the political instruments to do it), human affairs can – at any time – plunge into fanaticism and chaos. Modern human society is an advancement upon what has gone before (Austin often remarks about the remnants of a barbaric past), while the past has also much of greatness which was somehow lost (for example, Austin has great reverence for the clarity and logic of the structures of thought which flourished in Roman times although they were imperfect[31]); in short, human life is precarious. In a

---

28 Indeed, Hart's (1961) theory of law as a self-regulating system of rules where legal and political officials are themselves constituted in their roles by rules, is an almost text-book rendition in the idiom of analytical jurisprudence of a Weberian system of legal regulation; complete, as we shall see with the pre-rule normative disciplining of the late-modern subject.

29 Austin always has a keen eye to social reality. His message to those who would argue with the positive power of the state to command that a certain law was immoral and therefore not valid law was sociologically realistic. As he put it when stating that positive law may have any moral content: 'A law, which actually exists, is a law, though we happen to dislike it, or though it vary from the text, by which we regulate our approbation and disapprobation ...

   To say that human laws which conflict with the divine law are not binding, that is to say, are not laws, is to talk stark nonsense. The most pernicious laws, and therefore those which are most imposed to the will of God, have been and are continually enforced by judicial tribunals. Suppose an act ... be prohibited by the sovereign under the penalty of death; if I commit this act, I shall be tried and condemned, and if I object to the sentence, that it is contrary to the law of God ... the Court of Justice will demonstrate the inconclusiveness of my reasoning by hanging me up, in pursuance of the law of which I impugned the validity ...' (1873: 220-223) Pleas of civil disobedience were not discussed in depth by Austin, who was a committed act utilitarian.

30 See Austin's discussion at the beginning of Lecture III, (1873: 127).

31 For example, although the notion of the common good was rightly put as the goal of politics, ancient republics sacrificed the individual to the 'barren abstraction' of the common weal (1873: 161).

very real sense the quality of human life in society depends upon the will of political superiors to impose and enforce rational order. It depends on their will to be moderns.

Here jurisprudence has a role to play. The jurisprudence of pre-modernity makes sense when the meaning of concepts is read as part of a larger synthesis. Against this, Austin's creation of an 'abstract science of law' has both a destructive and constructive role. It breaks the grip of past opinion and allows a new rationality.[32] His knowledge claims are part of, and not antecedent to, his overall project. Austin is not a simple positivist in the sense that his knowledge claim has no pretence to anything other than the 'thing-in-itself', for his image of positive law is one element of an overall framework. The essential positive message is to clarify the extent to which one can make claims which make sense about law, but this does not mean that an overall grasp is, by necessity, lost. Austin's claims for jurisprudence are pragmatic in the sense that the demand for a clear jurisprudence arises to get something done, and that something was to create an image of law suitable for law to become a powerful and rational instrument of modernity. It may, however, be suggested that Austin's early confidence in this as a practical and achievable social phenomenon was compromised by later doubts. It may be that in the ultimate dilemma of Austin's thought we can see prefigured the fate of our present (post-modern?) times: the non-directedness of law.

EXCURSUS UPON THE RELATIONSHIP OF POSITIVISM AND AUSTINIAN LEGAL POSITIVISM

... In physical science a single experiment conducted with accuracy is deemed a good basis for a universal or general conclusion, and is properly called induction (Austin, 1873: 679).

Thus Austin defended the use of induction as the method by which the *ratio* – or the true rule or principle of law – could be produced even from a single case cited to a judge. His model for positivism, as elsewhere in his jurisprudence, was the progress made in the physical or natural sciences. Austin's legal positivism was expressed with the growing confidence in the progressive power of knowledge developing in the early 19th century. Although the term positive law was used by Hobbes, for example, for whom it denotes man-made law as distinct from divine or natural law, the 19th century witnessed the development of a more encompassing body of thought which called itself 'positivism'. This positivism really takes its full flavour from Auguste Comte (1798-1857), a 19th-century social thinker (and founder of the term 'sociologist') who juxtaposed the investigation of positive facts, the observation of phenomena and the inductive development of law, with metaphysical speculation and theological dogma;

---

32 As Austin continues his discussion of disobedience of the law: 'To incite the public to resistance by determinate views of utility may be useful, for resistance, grounded on clear and definite prospects of good, is sometimes beneficial. But to preach generally that all laws which are pernicious or contrary to the will of God are void and not to be tolerated, is to preach anarchy, hostile and perilous as much to wise and benign rule as to stupid and galling tyranny' (1873: 221).

the positivist methodology was believed to have vital social consequences, it made a new world order possible.[33] Positivism has come to be associated with empirical methods of investigation and, in particular, with a unified approach to research that claims universality for the methods of the natural sciences.

Austin is clear, the reason to become a positivist is that this is the route to truth, and it is only truth that can be a secure guide for social progress in modernity. In Austin's analysis of law, once we have agreed upon the positive methodology we must accept the truth of the analysis (hence we must accept the truth of political economy as telling us the truth of economic policy) and in conducting our analysis we ought to strip ourselves of our subjective desires (Lecture III). But what is the status of Austin's desire to follow truth? This argument can be clarified by examining Karl Popper's critique of the purity of positivism.

Objections to positivism: the example of Karl Popper

In a series of writings dating from the mid-1930s, Karl Popper, perhaps the best known philosopher of science writing in English this century, criticised positivism for its tendency to project the scientific process as a mechanical or value-free enterprise. Popper saw that positivism, or naturalism or scientism, as he preferred to call it, fitted the common sense view of how scientists worked but failed to accord with the reality of scientific practice.

First, the common sense view. In this image, scientists begin with observations and measurements, collecting data carefully and compiling statistics; perceiving patterns and regularities, they then advance by induction to general conclusions or laws that describe their data. This approach secures objectivity, since the scientist endeavours to eliminate all subjective prejudices. When applied to the social sciences such a procedure may then be termed 'value-free', meaning that the researcher brackets to the largest extent his/her own values and opinions. A descriptive methodology provides the starting point for the process (we may note that the criticisms advanced by HLA Hart in *The Concept of Law* (1961) of Austin are made in the context of Hart's methodological claim that he is

---

33 The tone of Austin's Lectures on Jurisprudence, particularly Lecture III, closely parallels the confidence in the development of knowledge which Comte displayed. Auguste Comte perceived the 19th century as the emerging age of 'positive science' constructing a world view and a social imagination which was replacing the earlier eras of the theological or fictive and the metaphysical. Comte believed that 'mankind is now on the threshold of the fully positive life, the elements of which are all prepared, and only awaiting their co-ordination to form a new social system, more homogeneous and more stable than mankind has hitherto had any experience of' (*Cours de philosophie positive* VI: 436). This new knowledge, a positive sociology, would provide a body of scientifically verifiable beliefs (a 'positive religion') which would provide a new foundation for European societies disrupted by revolution and the breakdown of religious unity. In the *System of Positive Polity* (particularly Book IV) Comte argues that while unity of belief is essential for both domestic and international society it will be possible to fashion this out of new knowledges and real insights into the social and international condition. For example, a new common interest among nations could be based on 'the establishment of a social doctrine, common to the various nations, and, consequently, of a spiritual sovereignty fitted to uphold this doctrine ... Until this takes place European order will always stand on the verge of disturbance, notwithstanding the action, alike despotic and inadequate (although provisionally indispensable) exerted by the imperfect coalition of the ancient temporal powers, but which can present no solid guarantee for security' (1973: 642-643).

engaging in mere descriptive analysis of legality – a claim repeated in the postscript to *The Concept of Law* published in 1994).

Popper believes this description is an unfortunate myth. Arguing that naturalism or scientism is not only an inaccurate depiction of the way scientists actually go about their business, but also no guarantee for objectivity or value-freedom, Popper indicates another version of the scientific procedure. Rather than starting by collecting data or making observations, scientists have sets of problems in their mind to which they formulate tentative solutions. For Popper the true test of good science is whether these solutions are framed in such a way as they are open to criticism and enable the scientific community to pick up on the ideas and experimental data and subject them to testing – rather than being dogmatic assertions of the 'truth' – which may be based on observation and the collection of data. If a solution is refuted, the scientist tries another solution until one solution is found that withstands criticism temporarily. This solution is then accepted until further criticism refutes it. Science thus proceeds not inductively from observation to generalised laws, but deductively. By the word 'deduction' Popper is not so much concerned with the transmission of truth from premises to conclusions, that is, the notion that if the premises are true, then the inferences from these true premises are also true. Rather, he is concerned with the reverse transmission of falsity from the conclusions to the premises. If we find that conclusions are false, then one or more of the initial assumptions must also be false. The procedure of the scientist therefore depends not on theories derived inductively from positive facts, but on the falsification of tentative solutions proposed to problems. The science of nature as well as the social sciences are conducted as never-ending trial-and-error experiments.

Popper also calls into question the purported objectivity of scientific procedures. The mythical schema he attacks sets out the objectivity of science as depending on the objectivity of the scientist. Thus we are led into a position where the scientist must purify him/herself of human concerns and personal subjectivities. Only when the scientist as a person eliminates all subjective presuppositions is an objective result secured. But for Popper objectivity is a factor not of the person but a product or quality of the critical method itself; Popper claims objectivity comes about through the mutual criticism of scientists – objectivity is a social product. According to this view the natural scientist is neither more nor less partisan or 'subjective' than his social science counterpart. All science derives its objectivity from a critical tradition that allows and fosters the criticism of dominant theories. Objectivity in science is related directly to social and political circumstances, not to prejudices of the individual investigator. Ultimately it is explicable:

> ... in terms of social ideas such as competition (both of individual scientists and of various schools); tradition (mainly the critical tradition); social institutions (for instance, publication in various competing journals and through various competing publishers; discussion at congresses); the power of the state (its tolerance of free discussion) (1976: 96).

It is not that there is some perfect realm of true reality that we can use to correct our theories and our linguistic assertions; instead we can keep the idea of reality existing independent of the human mind as a regulative ideal while realising that our conceptions and scientific experiments concern themselves with a level of 'knowledge' which falls far short of that true 'reality'. We do not need to rely upon the idea of our knowledges reflecting absolute reality; instead we can cope with a functional notion of objectivity, and we should strive to create the conditions within which scientists can apply the critical-rationalist method and relate to the claims and real results of others.

PART TWO
UNDERSTANDING THE STRUCTURE OF
AUSTIN'S JURISPRUDENCE

To recap the earlier argument: many of the commentaries on Austin's work have singled out certain definitions or extracts for critical analysis and have downplayed the essential interconnectedness of the whole. The guiding theme of Austin's lectures is the role of law in the creation of good government; utility provides the key. Utility provides a bedrock conception: 'in a chain of systematic lectures concerned with the rationale of jurisprudence, such an exposition is a necessary link' (1873: 84). Utility is not only a measuring rod of what the law ought to be it is the key to uncovering how social interaction actually creates the law as it is. Austin was a fully fledged utilitarian, a fact that recent commentators feel made him move beyond any mere empiricism into a committed normative explanation of law: law is the mechanism of utilitarian government.[34]

THE DEFINITION OF LAW

As already noted, Austin begins his lectures with a clear definition of law; the intellectual question is not to remember how Austin begins Lecture I but to understand the full meaning behind the words:

> The matter of jurisprudence is positive law; law, simply and strictly so called, or law set by political superiors to political inferiors ...

> A law, in the most general and comprehensive acceptance in which the term, in its literal meaning, is employed, may be said to be a rule laid down for the guidance of an intelligent being by an intelligent being having power over him ...

> Of the laws or rules set by men to men, some are established by political superiors, sovereign and subject; by persons exercising supreme and subordinate government, in independent nations or independent political societies [this is the subject matter of the positive science of law].

Austin has not denied a role for natural law, but has sidetracked it. In some senses Austin is a legal pluralist: his *positive theory of law is a theory of only one sort of law: the commands of political superiors set to political inferiors in an independent political society.* Austin's theory of positive law is a state-centred image of law. Austin does not deny that a large part of

---

34 'Austin's discussion of the principle [of utility] is much more, however, than an explanation of what it is. He not only elucidated the meaning of the principle, he also defended it as the index to the tacit commands of God. He criticised the theory of the moral sense. He explained how the rules which ought to guide human conduct can be discovered. He justified the need for rules and an ethical authority. He emphasised both the "importance" and the "truth" of the principle of utility, which he ardently wished to commend to others. His discourse on ethics crosses the line, which divides "meta-ethical" explication from "normative" prescriptions ... [moreover] the purpose of the discourse is not [just] to facilitate evaluations of positive law as good or bad, which is the business of the science of legislation. Rather, the aim is to provide a basis for evaluating concepts of jurisprudence' (Rumble, 1985: 80).

everyday life is lived by people under the domination of status, custom and moral prescriptions, he simply states that the proper subject matter for a positive science of positive law are those laws which are set in independent political societies (nation-states) by political superiors over political inferiors, and which have the authority of the coercive powers of the state behind them.

LAW IS BOTH A CREATION OF AND CONSTITUTIVE ELEMENT IN CIVILISATION

The nation-state provides the life for positive law, and utility provides the measuring rod by which progressive policies can be achieved. Without the fact of obedience by the general public to laws no secure government is possible; without secure government there is no property, no enjoyment of possessions, no culture. Law, properly so called, comes into existence only with the rise of independent political societies and the creation of a sovereign, but law also enables such organisations to exist (see the discussion of sovereignty).

THE RELATIONSHIP OF POWER AND SUPERIORITY

Only God enjoys a relationship (with man) of absolute power. Social relationships are reciprocal and fluid: 'the party who is the superior as viewed from one aspect, is the inferior as viewed from another' (1873: 99). In normal times a monarch may be 'the superior of the governed: his power being commonly sufficient to enforce compliance with his will. But the governed, collectively or in mass, are also the superior of the monarch: who is checked in the abuse of his might by fear of exciting their anger; and of rousing to active resistance the might which slumbers in the multitude' (1873: 99). Individuals have a variety of roles and functions: an individual may be a 'member of a sovereign assembly' and thus superior to a judge in that he is one of the members responsible for creating the laws which bind that judge, but that same individual is also a 'citizen or subject' answerable to that judge for his law-abiding life.

UTILITY IS THE KEY PRINCIPLE OF SOCIAL JUSTICE

Lectures III and IV set out a defence of the principle of utility (the proximate test of law, and the technique for policy making in social administration) and an understanding of the goal of political organisation, namely the common good.

Austin's first claim is that men are fallible, human beings simply cannot alone master the truth of the human condition, authority, testimony, and trust are inescapable. Even in an ideal system of law and morality, exactly attuned to the principle of morality, the rules may be known but the rationale behind them could not be known in its entirety. All science requires some faith in authority for while the role of experts is to investigate, analyse and disseminate their findings, the public must 'commonly trust the conclusions which we take upon authority'. While this trust, this deference to authority, is 'perfectly rational', no such structure presently existed in relation to ethics. Thus the sciences related to ethics (legislation, politics, and political economy) are in a state of confusion in large part because those who have investigated ethics have not adopted the scientific attitude of impartiality, and 'therefore have differed in their results'. This dooms the majority of the population, who have neither the time nor the resources to adopt a fully critical and enquiring attitude to the evidence, to be at the mercy of opinion. Concomitantly, much of the legal and moral structures currently in place 'rest upon brute custom and not manly reason', and there are many obstacles to the diffusion and advancement of ethical truth. At the time of his jurisprudential writings Austin was, however, optimistic that a proper science of ethics could establish itself and overcome its obstacles. In time, while profound knowledge would be confined to the few who were experts, the populace could grasp the leading principles, and 'if imbued with these principles, and were practised in the art of applying them, they would be docile to the voice of reason, and armed against sophistry and error' (1873: 131). Such a diffusion of ethical truth would drastically reduce social strife and lay bare a proper understanding of the nature of social co-operation.[35] Austin gives the example of the institution of private property, demanded by utility but about which many 'pernicious prejudices' exist. 'To the ignorant poor, the inequality which inevitably follows the beneficent institution of property is necessarily invidious. That they who toil and produce should fare scantily, whilst others, who "delve not nor spin," batten on the fruits of labour, seems, to the jaundiced eyes of the poor and the ignorant, a monstrous state of things: an arrangement upheld by the few at the cost of the many, and flatly inconsistent with the benevolent purposes of Providence.' This prejudice has many effects. It causes many of the crimes which have poverty as their immediate cause but which really come out of a misunderstanding of what is socially possible. Crucially, it blinds the people to the real cause of their sufferings and the only real remedies available. 'Want and labour spring from the niggardliness of nature, and not from the inequality which is consequent on the institution of property.' Austin then claims the condition of man on earth demands the institution of private property, and the crucial mechanism of capital is a direct consequence of property. Although the poor are used by capital, necessarily parting with their labour and are presently 'condemned' to 'incessant drudgery', Austin recognises the co-dependency which the process engenders: 'In effect, though not in law, the labourers are co-proprietors with the capitalists who hire their labour'.

Austin then makes a remarkable claim: in effect he states that if the poor come to understand the principles of political economy they can change the nature of their position and bargaining strength and thereby force a dramatic betterment of their condition. Again it is Austin's absolute certainty in the force of a 'truth' which allows this: 'In the true principle of population, detected by the sagacity of Mr Malthus, they must look for the cause and the remedy of their penury and excessive toil' (1873: 133). Using their knowledge they would break their 'sordid subjection to the arbitrary rule of a few', they would understand that attacks on property are actually attacks on the

---

35   For both Sarah and John Austin knowledge guaranteed rational authority. Their arguments for
     universal primary education was that 'it allowed for the creation of intelligent, informed loyalty to
     authority' (Lotte and Joseph Hamburger, 1985: 38). A new rational foundation for authority was
     required because of moral and social disintegration and the fact that the traditional sources of authority
     had been undermined.

institutions which create accumulation, they would see they are actually deeply interested in the security of property and 'if they adjusted their numbers to the demand for their labour, they would share abundantly, with their employers, in the blessings of that useful institution.'

As noted in the third of the quotations at the beginning of this chapter, Austin asserted that an enlightened people were a better auxiliary to the judge than an army of policemen. Chisick (quoted Bauman, 1987: 80) has claimed that 'not even during the high enlightenment were the people deemed capable of independent thought or political choice', while Bauman (ibid: 80) states that 'the intrinsic flaws of the "multitude" set unencroachable limits to enlightenment, understood as the development of a capacity for clear, rational thinking and informed decision-making. Enlightenment was something the rulers needed; their subjects were in need of training, orientated towards discipline'. Bentham had written with the most clarity, displaying confidence in a social division wherein many were to be keyed into the market and utilitarianism, while the panopticon and discipline awaited the 'uncivilised' (Moarrison, 1996). If the panopticon was Bentham's Gordian knot which tied together the social order, the belief in the attainment and clarity of positive knowledge was Austin's. The world was the subject of analysis and various sciences could render it transparent; the language of these sciences could picture an underlying reality. Austin is certain 'that there is no particular uncertainty in the subject or matter of those sciences'; the difficulties are external, in the attitudes of those who have studied them. Progress is assured if they would pursue truth 'with obstinate application and with due indifference'.[36]

Austin's confidence in the truth of *An Essay on the Principle of Population*, which the Reverend Thomas Malthus placed as the foundation of political economy, is instructive. Partly as a response to optimistic readings of the necessity for human progress (put forward by Condorcet and Godwin among others), Malthus interjected the pessimistic contention that population, if unchecked, increases geometrically while food supplies increase arithmetically, with predictably disastrous consequences. Malthus's 'scientific' achievement in uncovering one of the basic laws that govern human society was not seen as theory, but a truth which necessarily ought to guide policy. As he put it: 'I see no way by which man can escape from the weight of this law which pervades all animated nature'. With this principle Malthus attacked all utopian, radical and grand social engineering projects; limited and piecemeal reform was the only realistic course. Furthermore, the law must align itself with the underlying law of social development; nothing must take place which would encourage the poor to breed. If the legal structure contained any provisions which improved the conditions of the poor it would simply result in their producing more children and a corresponding reduction in wealth creation. Legal enactments were not to be prohibitive of choice but designed to make

---

36   What of today? It is a banality to state simply that things have not worked out as Austin expected or hoped. The disinterested pursuit of knowledge has not resulted in a structure of coherent and settled truths. Instead perspectivism, relativism, and subjectivism reign. The confidence in underlying natural laws of social and human development has long vanished. Law cannot claim a legitimacy simply to bring out the underlying functionalities and structures of social interaction.

clear the negative consequences of certain choices. To discourage the poor from producing children in conditions where their support could not be guaranteed, a law should be made declaring that no child born from future marriages would be eligible for poor relief. Thus: 'if any man choose to marry, without a prospect of being able to support a family, he should have the most perfect liberty to do so'. To the consequences they must, however, be left. 'To the punishment therefore of nature he should be left, the punishment of want ... He should be taught that the laws of nature, which are the laws of God, had doomed him and his family to suffer for disobeying their repeated admonitions.' This is not the punishment of the politically powerful, but of the operation of natural social laws; the positive law is only the mediatory instrument. Moreover, no provision can be made for abandoned or illegitimate children: 'If the parents desert their child, they ought to be made answerable for the crime. The infant is, comparatively speaking, of little value to society, as others will immediately supply its place.' Malthus is equally hostile to any notion of inherent rights, even, as the following passage suggests, any talk of a right to social existence:

> A man who is born into a world already possessed, if he cannot get subsistence from his parents on whom he has a just demand, and if the society do not want his labour, has no claim of right to the smallest portion of food, and, in fact, has no business to be where he is. At nature's mighty feast there is no vacant cover for him. She tells him to be gone, and will execute her own orders (Quotes, Arblaster, 1984: 246).

Strict adherence to the principles of political economy soon led to British liberalism's greatest 'massacre', the condemning of one and a half million of the Irish population to starvation in the mid to late 1840s, and the cruelty of the new poor law (See Arblaster, 1984: 254-259).

THE CONCEPT OF SOVEREIGNTY

For Austin, 'every supreme government is legally despotic'. Given the overall framework of Austin it would be illogical for the sovereign to be limited by law, since the sovereign is the highest body, or site of concentration of power in the nation.

> ... It follows ... the power of the sovereign is incapable of *legal* limitation [Austin's emphasis] ... Supreme power limited by positive law, is a flat contradiction in terms ...

> The laws which sovereigns affect to impose upon themselves, or the laws which sovereigns affect to impose upon their followers, are merely principles or maxims which they adopt as guides, or which they commend as guides to their successors in sovereign power (1873: 270-1).

In Lecture VI Austin explains 'the marks which distinguish positive laws' by analysing the expressions:

> Sovereignty, the correlative expression subjection, and the inseparably connected expression independent political society ... Every positive law, or every law simply and strictly so called, is set by a sovereign person, or a sovereign body of persons, to a member or members of the independent political society wherein that person or body is sovereign or supreme (1873: 225-6).

Law, as the instrument of political command, is depicted as a key element in ensuring social progress. Austin makes a central distinction between a natural (a primitive, simplistic society) and a political society (a society where law can operate).

> A natural society, a society in a state of nature, or a society independent but natural, is composed of persons who are connected by mutual intercourse, but are not members, sovereign or subject, of any society political (1873: 231).

> A given society is not a society political, unless the generality of its members be in a habit of obedience to a determinate and common superior (1873: 228).

Such a society must be independent, the political elites owing habitual obedience to the commands of no other.

> The generality or bulk of its members must be in a habit of obedience to a certain and common superior: whilst that certain person, or certain body of persons, must not be habitually obedient to a certain and common superior: whilst that certain person, or certain body of persons, must not be habitually obedient to a certain person or body.

This test is not simply a matter of definition but a question of sociology: 'the positive mark of sovereignty and independent political society is a fallible test of specific or particular cases' (1873: 233). It will be an easy matter to identify core examples and Austin states that such is the ordinary state of England and of every independent society somewhat advanced in civilisation, but in others obedience to the same superior is rendered by so few of the members, or general obedience is so infrequent and broken, that they are simply natural societies.

Austin also calls an independent political society a 'political community' (1873: 234). Austin's questions of command and obedience are notions which reflect his concern with the power of political government to achieve its wishes. At times of civil war or the revolt of colonies (Austin refers to the English war between Charles I and Parliament; and the revolt of Mexico against Spain), the questions asked are of the socio-political situation as it empirically exists:

> When did the revolted colony, which is now the Mexican nation, ascend from the condition of an insurgent province to that of a independent community? When did the body of colonists, who affected sovereignty in Mexico, change the character of rebel leaders for that of a supreme government? Or when did the body of colonists, who affected sovereignty in Mexico, become sovereign in fact? (1873: 235)

While the numbers involved in a political society are considerable, 'an independent political society is divisible into the portion of its members which is sovereign or supreme and the portion of its members which is merely subject'. The composition is a matter of historical fact.

> In most actual societies, the sovereign powers are engrossed by a single member of the whole, or are shared exclusively by a very few of its members: and even in the actual societies whose governments are esteemed popular, the sovereign number is a slender portion of the entire political community. An independent political society governed by itself, or governed by a sovereign body consisting of the whole community, is not impossible: but the existence of such societies is so extremely improbable (1873: 243).

Austin explains further in a footnote:

> If every member of an independent political society were adult and of sound mind, every member would be naturally competent to exercise sovereign powers: and if we suppose a society so constituted, we may also suppose a society which strictly is governed by itself, or in which the supreme government is strictly a government of all. But in every actual society, many of the members are naturally incompetent to exercise sovereign powers: and even in an actual society whose government is the most popular, the members naturally incompetent to exercise sovereign powers are not the only members excluded from the sovereign body. If we add to the members excluded by reason of natural incompetency, the numbers (women, for example) excluded without that necessity, we shall find that a great majority even in such a society is merely in a state of subjection. Consequently, though a government of all is not impossible, every actual society is governed by one of its members or by a number of its members which lies between one and all (1873: 243-244).

Austin's concept of sovereignty is often misunderstood. Sometimes bizarre statements are made, such as, that Austin could not have coped with the creation of the European Community (EC, now EU). This is nonsense. Austin gives an example of the allied armies occupying France in 1815 after the defeat of Napoleon. During the occupation, 'the commands of the allied sovereigns were obeyed by the French governments, and through the government by the French people generally. But since the commands and the obedience were comparatively rare and transient, they were not sufficient to constitute the relation of sovereignty and subjection between the allied sovereigns and the members of the invaded nation ... in spite of those commands, and in spite of that obedience, the French government and its subjects were an independent political society whereof the allied sovereigns were not the sovereign portion' (1973: 228). The implication is clear, if a political structure had been created by which commands were regularly issued and obeyed, a change in the nature of the sovereignty of France would have occurred. Perhaps if a council of ministers were set up, with a representative from each of the nations concerned, a new structure of subordination but also independence could have been created; but the critic may argue, these structures are themselves made up of laws. The EC (EU) is created by law. Austin's answer would be that of Hobbes; the law which constitutes the sovereign as an institution is itself the expression of a pre-legal seizure of power. What creates the EC is not a legal constitution. The constitution – the Treaty of Rome – may represent its 'founding text' and reflect its 'founding moment', but this is to concentrate into one document, or into one historical moment, a political process involving a complex set of wishes, or volitions, to become. The real foundation of the European Union is 'Europe', and Europe does not exist except as a complex phenomenon of desires, volitions and projects.

WHILE THE SOVEREIGN IS NOT LEGALLY LIMITABLE, IT IS ANSWERABLE TO POSITIVE AND CRITICAL MORALITY (PARTICULARLY THE PRINCIPLE OF UTILITY)

The sovereign is not legally limitable but is answerable to the dictates of positive morality, and the laws of God, as known through the principle of utility. The fundamental concern Austin expressed was common in what we now call the politically liberalist thinkers of early 19th-century England: namely fear of society dissolving and necessity for strong government. While for both Bentham and Austin a reformist government should not be thought of as a weak government, whereas Bentham argued for the existence of constitutional limitations, for Austin devices for legal limitations on sovereignty, such as bills of rights, and the separation of powers were problematic, sometimes self-defeating in practice and logically indefensible. It was not that there were no effective constitutional limitations, but that in reality these were complex sets of beliefs and practices; they were not law strictly so called but a form of critical morality. That is to say, enlightened public opinion and the dictates of the principle of utility in reality ensure responsible government.[37] Late in his life Bentham argued that political sovereignty should reside with the people, since in this way the interest of the people, the general interest, and the governmental interest become one and the same. While the young Austin may have agreed, the older Austin came to despair at the rational basis for such a move; how could mere opinion guarantee rational government?

  '*Herein lies the difference between governments of law and governments of men*' (1873: 519).

Opinion, however, is central. Underpinning the sovereign is a pre-legal void. The sovereign – the state – comes out of a set of social arrangements which are pre-justice; it has neither the possession of rights nor the absence of rights.

> Now since it is not restrained by positive law from dealing at its own pleasure with all things within its territory, we may say ... that the state has a right to all things within its territory, or is absolutely or without restriction the proprietor ... thereof. Strictly speaking, it has no legal right to any thing, or is not the legal owner or proprietor of any thing (1873: 871).

The state is subject to a radical legal non-determinacy. On the one hand, Austin's sovereign appears the all-powerful personification of the hopes and desires of the elites who make up the state, while on the other, it dissolves into networks of procedures and conventions. Public law – what we otherwise call constitutional law – is either aspects of 'the general law of procedure', or 'miscellaneous and supplemental' forms of the law of persons. Nor is the public-private distinction an absolute: 'every part of the law is in a certain sense public, and every part of it is in a certain sense private also' (1873: 776). Civil law requires tracing to a sanction; all law, from the creation of contracts to the enforcement of wills is 'designed among other purposes, for the prevention of crime'

---

37 The Hamburgers suggest another consideration that led Austin to depreciate the idea of constitutional limitations. 'Since science could discover how to maximise general happiness ... sovereign authority guided by such a science ought not to be limited by constitutional checks. Such checks Austin called positive morality. They originated in opinion, moral beliefs, and tradition; they did not have legal status and they were binding only to the extent that morality and opinion were felt to be compelling. The constitutional limitations and norms of constitutionality that were known to Austin originated in a pre-scientific age, and he argued that it would be undesirable to allow such norms to check the laws made in the light of the science of legislation. He would have opposed constitutional limitations, however, even if they originated in scientific positive morality. If they were justified by the same science of ethics that was also the source of positive law, it would be pointless to have them serve as checks on positive law, for constitutionalism had meaning only when it invoked standards that were independent from and "higher" than the laws that it judged. Thus his lack of sympathy for the very idea of constitutional limits reflected an understanding of sovereignty and the state both as they existed and as they could exist ideally' (1985: 41).

(1873: 774). The civil law rests, ultimately, upon a dialectic between the power of criminal law and normative acceptance of the rights and duties the civil law lays out. The sovereign is ultimately constituted by sets of understandings, within a nebulous realm of 'general opinion' and 'ethical maxims which the sovereign observes' (1873: 771).

> Although, in logical rigour, much of the so-called law which relates to the sovereign, ought to be banished from the *corpus juris*, it ought to be inserted in the *corpus juris* for reasons of convenience which are paramount to logical symmetry. For though, in strictness, it belongs to positive morality or ethics, a knowledge of it is absolutely necessary in order for a knowledge of the positive law with which the *corpus juris* is properly concerned (1873: 771-772).

The use of sovereign power rests upon opinion and acceptance of authority. Opinion rests upon the state of knowledge of the public and the reasonableness of the sovereign. Although prison provides the apex of criminal law as the ultimate external sanction, reasoned opinion is the internal sanction; an educated population is of more benefit to an enlightened legislator than an army of police. Furthermore, 'the difference between governments of law and that of men' lies in the elites rescinding their power to make arbitrary decisions in favour of their ethical agreement to act according to the law.[38] Modern government requires a form of practical wisdom in the exercise of its discretion. Jurisprudence cannot exist outside a partnership with the positive knowledges; to do so is to forsake the meaning of law in favour of its pale positivity, it is to strip out understanding of law as a living social phenomenon to a conceptual shell.

THE ISSUE OF INTERNATIONAL LAW

It follows from the logical structure of Austin's theory of law and his grasp of sociological reality that the term 'the laws of nations' (or what we now call 'international law'[39]) was a misnomer, referring to what was actually a form of 'positive international morality'. Without an international sovereign there could be no determinate body to lay

---

38 Austin's discussion is worthy of quoting in full, if only to dispel the idea that he was unconcerned with the image of 'government of law and not of men'. 'When I speak of the discretion of the sovereign or state, I mean the discretion of the sovereign or state as exercised according to law. For, by a special and arbitrary command, the sovereign may deprive the injured of the right arising from the injury, or may exempt the wrong-doer from his civil liability. [Herein lies the difference between governments of law and governments of *men*.] *In one or two of the bad governments still existing in Europe, this foolish and mischievous proceeding is not uncommon. For example, letters of protection are granted by the government to debtors, and by these the debtors are secured from the pursuit of their creditors. But in cases of this kind the sovereign partially abrogates his own law to answer some special purpose. This is never practised by wise governments, whether monarchical or other. The Great Frederick, in spite of his imperious temper and love of power, always conformed his own conduct to his own laws.*

Letters of protection were granted in this country by the king, so late as the reign of William III. These must have been illegal. For though the king is empowered by the constitution to pursue and pardon criminals at his own discretion, he is not sovereign. It is not competent to him to disregard the law by depriving the injured party of a right of civil action' (1873: 519).

39 It appears that the term international law was first coined by Bentham in *The Introduction to the Principles of Morals and Legislation*.

out what exactly the law was, or to ensure sanctions were imposed when it was breached. Austin asked for clarity of language:

> Grotius, Puffendorf, and other writers on the so-called law of nations, have fallen into a confusion of ideas: they have confounded positive international morality, or the rules which actually obtain among civilised nations, in their mutual intercourse, with their own vague conceptions of international morality as it ought to be, with that indeterminate something which they conceived it would be, if it conformed to that indeterminate something which they call the law of nature (1873: 222).

Austin was following a long line of sceptics, originating with Hobbes and including Kant and Rousseau.

In the absence of a supreme power to declare and enforce it, Hobbes stated, no positive law could be said to be in existence. Certainly, the different sovereigns of individual nations would find themselves subjected to the law of nature – if they rationally analysed their position and their goals as a totality – but in the absence of a common superior, who could interpret what the actual conventions individual sovereigns had agreed to, confusion and uncertainty reigned. In Hobbes's analysis, epistemological uncertainty as to the customs and agreements went hand in hand with the absence of a power to enforce rules. Similarly, Kant declared it was pointless to claim a law of nations could be discerned in international customs and agreements so long as states were 'not subject to a common external constraint' (Kant, *Political Writings*, 1970: 103).

Rousseau continued the theme that current international relations were riven by contradictions and uncertainty which rendered all examples of the laws of nations hopelessly ineffective and therefore not real law. The so-called public law of Europe was 'full of contradictory rules which nothing but the right of the strongest can reduce to order: so that, in the absence of any sure guide, in case of doubt reason will always incline in the direction of self-interest ...' (*Complete Works*, 3: 568–569). Nations engaged in international intercourse and co-operation on the basis of self-interest, there was no condition resembling a civil society, and no possibility of discerning an international general will. What was needed to create a law of nations? Both the ethical desire for a common association and a superior coercive power which could 'give their common interests and mutual obligations that stability and strength which they could never acquire by themselves' (*ibid*: 569).

Defenders of international law argue that if the definition of law is taken to mean only those rules made and enforced by a sovereign power, then the rules of customary practice and those voluntarily agreed to with no sanction attached cannot fit into such a scheme, but that it does not follow that there are no rules governing the conduct of states. Austin would agree: the rules, however, are for him simply 'positive morality'. A state may experience a range of costs and criticisms when it breaches such a rule, but these are in practice unpredictable and vague; in the absence of some international common power there is no realistic point to calling the rules law.

THE ROLE OF JUDICIAL LAW-MAKING

Given that Austin depicted law as a rational instrument of governance, it was impossible for him to perceive of law as some closed system of legality. The law as law should strive for certainty, at any one time the legal analyst should bring out the interrelationships and meanings of legal concepts, but law was both a 'living' phenomenon[40] and a dynamic one; development came from outside of the law. Governmental power led the law, and governmental power was to be guided by utility and the developing positive knowledge.

While, however, 'either directly or remotely, the sovereign, or supreme legislator, is the author of all law; and all laws are derived from the same source; but immediately and directly laws have different authors' (1873: 526). The most direct source of law was legislation, the judiciary were another source (operating with delegated power) when they adopted custom or when they created '*judge-made* law'; Austin recognises '*judicial* legislation' as a '*subordinate* source' of law (emphasis in original, 1873: 549).

Although Austin cannot accept Bentham's 'sweeping dislike of law made by judges' (1873: 549), he describes how the judiciary often conceal the fact of their own activism. Judicial law-making occurs within the practical task of the courts dealing with disputes. A case must be decided and a point of law established even where it appears that no written law can be found that covers the situation under dispute. The aim of the court is to do justice; to resolve the dispute, but in so doing a new rule is created. The judges, however, hide their creativity behind a discourse of interpretation and construction, of finding or declaring law.

> Although this specific case is decided by a new rule, the proper purpose of the judge is not the introduction of that rule, but the decision of the specific case to which the rule is applied, and so, speaking generally, the shew of legislation is avoided. Generally the new rule is not introduced professedly, but the existing law is professedly ascertained by interpretation or construction ... and is then professedly applied to the case or question that awaits decision. If the new rule obtains as law thereafter, it does not obtain directly, but because the decision passes into a precedent: that is to say, is considered as evidence of the previous state of the law; and the new rule, thus disguised under the garb of an old one, is applied as law to new cases (1873: 548).

Austin has little time for the separation of powers. This flows from his belief in the unity of community interests, utility, and knowledge (of political economy etc). This is most apparent in his quick dismissal of an objection to judicial law-making that 'when subordinate judges have the power of making laws, the community has little or no control over those who make the laws by which its conduct must be governed'. Austin reads this as a question of responsibility; judges must be made responsible 'to the mass or bulk of the community'. One way is that they must apply the 'positive law' when it is clear, another is to ensure that their appointment be such as to free them from being at

---

40 For the sociologically inclined Austin one must distinguish 'living from dead law' (1873: 1040, also 1048), and understand the role of legal officials. After all, when Austin looked back at Roman law, he saw beyond the *Digests* to 'the living Roman law or the Roman law administered and enforced by the tribunals' (1873: 604).

the beck of the king alone, so that they serve the sovereign or state proper: 'let their appointment be vested in some party or another whose interests do not conflict with those of the community at large' (1873: 665).

Austin moves to combat the idea 'that judicial legislators legislate arbitrarily'. That would result in law becoming variable, uncertain, and incoherent. Arbitrary decision-making must be controlled by (i) the hierarchical nature of a legal system in which Courts of Appeal rationalise the decisions of inferior courts; (ii) judges being guided by their conception of what the sovereign legislature would do directly, 'if it cared sufficiently for the general interests'; and (iii) the censuring of professional bodies (ie the Bar), and the opinions of other lawyers who preserve 'the interests of the craft'. The 'backwardness of judges to innovate', rather than judicial law-making, has been the great evil; 'too great a respect for established rules, and too great a regard for consequence and analogy, has generally been shown by the authors of judicial law' (1873: 668); equity was forced into existence.

Judges must not be given a free discretion; various steps in the path of decision-making must be imposed. Step one: the judge must endeavour to identify what the law is. If the law is certain, the judge must apply it. But in the case of a statute where the words may be clear but appear at odds with the clear purpose of the statute, the judge 'may depart from the manifest sense of the statute in order the he may carry into effect its ratio or scope. But in these cases, he is not a judge properly interpreting the law, but a subordinate legislator correcting its errors or defects ...' This is a dangerous process in which the court runs the risk of becoming an arbitrary tribunal. Above all what runs through Austin's lectures is a plea for professionalism; the judicial task is important and elusive. Progress will be ensured by undertaking a reflective and scientific analysis of the nature of the undertaking. This will help the judge scientifically conduct his craft. Note the atmosphere of Austin's phrases:

> The terms or expressions employed by the judicial legislator, are rather faint traces from which the principle may be conjectured, than a guide to be followed inflexibly in case their obvious meaning be perfectly certain. (1873: 651)

Nor is the legal system a coherent universe when much of it is necessarily judge-made:

> The entire legal system, or the entire *corpus juris*, is necessarily a monstrous chaos: partly consisting of judiciary law, introduced bit by bit, and imbedded in a measureless heap of particular judicial decisions, and partly of legislative law stuck by patches on the judiciary law, and imbedded in a measureless heap of occasional and supplemental statutes (1873: 682).

Austin then concludes his lectures on the sources of law with an argument for codification. He was aware of the weakness of a poorly constructed statute, stating that case law could be both richer in detail and more flexible than a badly expressed statute, but thought that codification, albeit a delicate and difficult task, afforded the opportunity for a principled and scientific statement of the law. Codes must be drawn up carefully with both an historical grasp of the law and a clear idea of the aims to be achieved. His final argument is a rhetorical flourish critical of the existing legal profession yet hopeful of an improvement in the character of the profession if a more scientific approach to law could be achieved:

If the law were more simple and scientific, minds of a higher kind would enter into the profession, and men in independent circumstances would embrace it, who are now deterred by its disgusting character; for disgusting it really is. What man of literary education and cultivated intellect can bear the absurdity of the books of practice, for example: and many other parts of the law? Nothing but a strong necessity, or a strong determination to get at the rationale of law through the crust which covers it, could carry any such person through the labour. But if the law were properly codified, such minds would study it; and we might then look for incomparably better legislation, and a better administration of justice, than now. The profession would not be merely venal and fee-gathering as at present, but, as in ancient Rome, would be the road to honours and political importance. Much, no doubt, of the drudgery of the profession would still be performed by persons aiming only at pecuniary reward, but the morality prevailing in the entire profession would be set, in a great degree, by this high part of it, which would also comprise the practical legislators of the community (1873: 703-4).

PART THREE
CONCLUSION

THE SUFFOCATING NATURE OF THE TRADITIONAL INTERPRETATION OF AUSTINIAN POSITIVE JURISPRUDENCE

In a sense it is easy to forget the synthesis and take out of Austin only the dry analysis; the result is to create a prison for the intelligence. In the vast bulk of his lectures Austin codifies interests and psychology into a self-contained whole. In detailed language, across the terrain of civil and criminal law, Austin combines psychology and legal terminology into a unified and supposedly consistent form. Law can control and direct our chaotic subjective desires. Law sets out conditions where a person can use his will to control his desires. While man 'cannot be obliged not to desire ... the desire of avoiding the sanction may master or control, but cannot extinguish a desire which urges to a breach of duty' (1873: 462). Similarly, 'a change in the mind may be wrought or prevented, whether we desire the change or whether we do not desire it' (1873: 469). Government by utility brooks no hesitation; it governs by necessity. Political power and prison walls, Austin writes, are both general contexts of suffering within which we involuntarily find ourselves. Utility is 'an absolute standard of what is good and true' (Campbell's editorial comment at 1873: 466); we can no easier avoid its commands than we can the order of imprisonment. But this very confidence alerts us to a *failure of the Austinian position*. Benthamite thinking appeared to deal with the tension between political democracy, with its reliance on popular opinion, and the idea of a rationally knowledge-based government, through a theory of utility which gave the common good as the sum total of desires. Austin's utility was more of a qualitative kind; in time a creeping conservatism overcame him. After 1848 Austin's politics – although dominated with the concern with security from Hobbes and the centrality of property from Locke – espoused invisible ties of tradition, custom and the 'unthinking feelings' – Hume and Burke came to be his intellectual forebears rather than the rationality of Hobbes and Locke. When implored to republish his *Province of Jurisprudence Determined*, which had sold out and was fetching good prices on the second hand market, Austin refused. Instead, he stated his intention was to rewrite radically and extend the lectures to produce a book to be entitled *The Principles and Relations of Jurisprudence and Ethics*. This never moved beyond the stage of vague ruminations.

THE PROBLEM OF AUSTIN'S INABILITY TO REWRITE HIS LECTURES

Why did Austin not revise and extend his lectures as he had constantly promised to do? Two answers suggest themselves: (i) that it was a personal failure of character; (ii) that he had changed many of his original views or lost confidence in the linkage between the various knowledges. This second consideration reflects upon the whole enterprise of tying together positive law and ethics.

The first answer undoubtedly has support and the combination of a depressive personality and lack of personal drive explains to some extent the failure to rewrite.[41] However, there is the further possibility that the answer may be found in a growing intellectual self-doubt as to the whole edifice of confident utilitarianism. Austin's rule of the enlightened, scientifically based knowledge-bound elite demanded a belief in the attainment of ethical clarity and consistency, but it is this very goal which has remained elusive, perhaps unattainable, for modernity. What if furthering the analysis of the foundations for law succeeded only in a destructive project, and was not able to offer a scientifically defensible alternative?[42] Positive knowledge may demonstrate our social need for feelings of unity and images which stimulate collective activity – and it may indicate that such feelings have a real history as well as any hypothetical one – but it cannot rationally create a true concept of unity which escapes any critique of its mythological nature.

If Austin's rewrite did not proceed further than embryonic thoughts and a longing, those who have taken up the challenge with fervour have reached no settled answer. Austin's synthesis of his lectures depended upon a particular combination: accepting the principles of science as capable of reflecting the indisputable truths of the social condition, and accepting that disputes about value and policy can be resolved according to the (perceived) standards of rational truth; but his subsequent doubts may have anticipated the path that modernity has followed. Namely, that while many hold that adherence to the scientific enterprise is the only path for enquiry, we cannot accept that disputes about value and desires can be resolved according to the standards of rational truth. The liberal compromise has been to leave open the question – it has favoured the conclusion that John Stuart Mill was to give; specifically to leave open the issue of the good life to tolerance and experimentation. This has not satisfied all, indeed we need not even use the Marxist experience as an example, we are surrounded by living reminders that millions find an ethical void underlying the structure of liberalism. Phrasing the issue somewhat differently, by separating law from morality Austin also separated 'consciousness of freedom' from the positive law; it became all too easy for law to rest solely upon the image of its own (mere) positivity. Then what? The law may well set out the contours of a very late-modern game: lacking a commitment to the ends of life, we mindlessly act out that motive Hobbes told of in Leviathan, that 'desire for power after power until death'. Only we may now do it without any faith that there is something other than this game, and us, to call it all to account.

---

41 For Rumble 'Austin was the example *par excellence* of a person who lacked strength of will ... If Austin had been more energetic, persistent, and steadier in the pursuit of his great ends, he might have achieved more than he in fact did' (1985: 59).

42 A parallel with John Stuart Mill who, in the *Logic*, argued that for a permanent political society to function there needs to be a feeling 'that there be in the constitution of the state *something* which is settled, something permanent, and not to be called into question ... some fixed point: something which people agreed in holding sacred' (Quoted in Lotte and Joseph Hamburger, 1985: 181).

CHAPTER 10

KARL MARX[1] AND THE MARXIST HERITAGE FOR UNDERSTANDING LAW AND SOCIETY

The political constitution as such is brought into being only where the private spheres have won an independent existence. Where trade and landed property are not free and have not yet become independent, the political constitution too does not yet exist ... The abstraction of the state as such belongs only to modern times, because the abstraction of private life belongs only to modern times. The abstraction of the political state is a modern product (Marx, *Contribution to a Critique of Hegel's Philosophy of Right*, 1843: 31-2).

All fixed, fast-frozen relations, with their train of ancient and venerable prejudices and opinions, are swept away, all new-formed ones become antiquated before they can ossify. All that is solid melts into air, all that is holy is profaned, and men at last are forced to face ... the real conditions of their lives and their relations with their fellow men (Marx and Engels, *The Communist Manifesto*, 1848, in the *Marx-Engels Reader*, 1978: 476).

MARXISM AS HOPE AND TRANSCENDENCE

To write a solitary chapter on Marxist approaches to law is a daunting task. The first issue appears simple but is elusive: what is Marxism? Is it a philosophy, a sociology, a religion ... or a mystification? Does it comprise the dangerous ramblings of a power crazy group of outsiders, or a set of writings based on the deeply concerned humanist reflections of one of the world's greatest scholars? It has been called all of these things. Marxism represents, perhaps, the greatest attempt to analyse the spatial-temporal contingency of the empirical world, while still retaining the desire for a thoroughgoing transcendence. Fundamental to its methodology lies the recognition and elucidation of oppositions – the dialectics – while deeply embedded in its core lies the dream of reconciliation.[2] Whatever else it is, Marxism is a radical product of the Enlightenment quest for answers to problems of the human condition by a thoroughgoing analysis of human society, history, human failings and power, within the confines of this world. *For Marxism we are of this world and the world is a unity.* Hence, whatever divisions, whatever conflicts we witness, they can be reconciled, since ultimately we and the world are of the same kind. It is mankind, not some transcendent God, that is the secret to religion; thus we must transform the narratives of religion into secular messages. The Marxist

---

1   Marx (1818-1883) was born in Trier, in what is now Germany. He was the oldest son of a Jewish lawyer and the descendent of a long line of rabbis. His father converted to Protestantism in order not to harm his legal business and Marx was educated as a Protestant. Rationalism, humanitarianism and a pragmatic view of the world were the messages of his upbringing, rather than religious fundamentalism.

2   'Communism as a fully developed naturalism is humanism and as a fully developed humanism is naturalism. It is definite resolution of the antagonism between man and nature, and between man and man. It is the true solution of the conflict between existence and essence, between freedom and necessity, between individual and species. It is the solution of the riddle of history and knows itself to be this solution.' (Marx, *Early Writings*, 1964: 155).

reconciliation draws upon the eschatological desire given promise in the Bible: the Old Testament had referred to a future time when God would establish his everlasting reign of righteousness and peace (for example, Isaiah 11: 1-9); the New Testament affirms that Christ represents the overcoming of death and believers join in the promise of eternal life. Whilst experiencing the pain of this life they have a foretaste of the age to come (John 3: 36 – 5: 24). While the Marxist philosophy of history owes its form to Hegel's dialectic, its content owes much to a secularisation of Christian eschatology.[3] The fully developed Marxist philosophy of history, called in technical terms 'materialist determinism', or 'historical materialism', provides a form of personal providence; the chosen people are replaced by the proletariat, and the justice of the kingdom of God by the classless society of communism.[4]

INTRODUCTION TO MARXIST THEORISING: THE DIALECTIC OF THE UNIVERSAL AND THE PARTICULAR

Marxism is a rich body of writings and doctrine[5]: there is no, one Marxist interpretation of the role of specific social phenomena such as law(s) or the role of state and supra-state organisations in individual societies or world politics. Marxism is based on the writings of Karl Marx (1818-83) in co-operation with Friedrich Engels (1820-95), with perhaps the greatest later contribution being made by V I Lenin, leader of the 1917 Bolshevik revolution in Russia.[6] In this century, Marxism, however, has been a political doctrine in which interpreting the meaning of Marx's work has often been subordinated to political necessities, rather than providing the route to a deeper understanding of modernity.

Central to Marxism is the methodological injunction of paying attention to empirical data; but the data is viewed as reflections, or examples, of universal social structures and processes. The central focus is on the totality of human existence, rather

---

3   Marxism claimed to be the high point of empirical science, while castigating the moral backwardness of capitalist society. It promised a new world order to come that would be totally free, yet fulfilling – wherein man would realise his destiny as a species as he realised his absolute, yet concrete, freedom – an uncorrupted and uncorrupting, harmonious society.

4   Marx takes the place of the prophets, and affirms that the end of history is an actual human state of affairs. While the earlier actors and the bourgeois do not understand the significance of their acts, the proletariat have been provided by Marxism with a scientific view of things which makes clear the significance of their innovative acts.

5   Not to mention the effectiveness of Marxism in providing a political stimulant. At one stage – quite recently – about half of the world's population lived in societies whose official political creed was Marxist. Marxism has also provided a substantial body of writings and concepts serving as the major intellectual opposition to the liberal-capitalist axis the West has relied upon.

6   Lenin was a Russian political leader, Marxist theoretician and the most explicit Marxist philosopher after Marx. Expelled form the university of Kazan for student disturbances (1887) he graduated in law (by correspondence) from the university of St Petersburg (1891). He was imprisoned in 1895 and exiled to Siberia in 1897; except for a brief period, he lived abroad from 1900 until the revolution in 1917, when he returned to lead the Communist Party and headed the Soviet Union until his death. He was succeeded by Joseph Stalin.

than particular social institutions. For example, neither Marx nor subsequent Marxist theoreticians have taken the state as a self-contained unit of analysis.[7] As a result, not only was nationalism one of the weak spots in the Marxist analysis and one reason for its failure in predictive ability, but the forces shaping law were not seen through the spectacles of the nation-state; rather the state was afforded little autonomy as a site of activity. Moreover, unlike functionalist accounts of social order, which have stressed the developing multiplicity of operations and division of labour in modernity, Marxists have emphasised class relationships, both within societies and internationally. Class, however, is not a self-explanatory tool of analysis but a concept which makes sense only within a larger structure of theoretical analysis.[8] Marxism does not begin with the concept of the individual as its basic unit – by contrast with philosophical liberalism – but takes the idea, vaguely expressed, of social totality as its starting point. Marxism is often considered an opposite form of social analysis to the methodological individualism Hobbes bequeathed, and is commonly labelled holistic.[9] The significance of any particular entity of study lies in how it fits within and influences the development of the whole. With law, as for other social phenomena, it is difficult to separate out a Marxist view of the particular entity and create a free-standing theoretical model, since this separates one particular aspect of human behaviour, divorcing it from the underlying tenets of Marxist social analysis. Marxism provides a framework of understanding by which, it is claimed, society past and present can be explained and the future development of mankind predicted. Marxism has claimed to be the final 'overcoming' or 'going beyond' of philosophy. For Marx philosophy, particularly critical philosophy, was essential, but his critique of philosophy, part of a general critique of ideology, demonstrated philosophy's

---

7   'Capital drives beyond national barriers and prejudices as much as beyond nature worship, as well as traditional, confined, complacent, encrusted satisfactions, of present needs, and reproductions of old ways of life. It is destructive towards all of this, and constantly revolutionises it, tearing down all the barriers which hem in the development of the forces of production, the expansion of needs, the all-sided development of production, and the exploitation and exchange of natural and mental forces' (Marx, *Grundrisse*: 410; quoted in Seidman, 1983: 98).

8   The concept of class is fundamental to Marx's mature writings although he did not lay out a clear definition. All societies other than Communist society (which has never existed in the form Marx envisaged and was not to be confused with the regimes experienced in the USSR, China, Eastern Europe etc) are class societies. When men 'fight out' the contradictions of economic structure – which Marx refers to in the 1859 *Preface* – they do so within classes and in terms of class interests.

   Marx appears to have accepted that class conflict was so obvious as not to need a full theoretical justification. Only when he focuses upon the classes in capitalist society – where two, the bourgeoisie (middle class) and proletariat (working class), are in direct conflict, did they receive an adequate treatment. He defined these in terms of their situation in relations of production characteristic of capitalism. The bourgeoisie is the capitalist class which owns the means of production. The proletariat is defined by its lack of such ownership and by the fact that it sells its labour power to the capitalist for wages, working on means of production it does not own and producing profit (surplus value) to which the capitalist is legally entitled by virtue of his ownership of the materials and tools by which it has been produced. Other classes – eg peasantry – were discussed as peripheral categories in relation to the basic class division between capitalist and proletarian who stand at opposite ends of the basic relations of production of capitalism.

9   As Seidman (1983: 94–100) makes clear, however, while Marx repudiated methodological individualism he did not become a fully fledged holist. Society was not to be thought of as an independent collective 'personality'. But while 'men are the actors and authors of their own story', they are at the mercy of the forces and resources that are provided for them by the social structure and social processes.

incomplete grasp of the human condition. Reality can only be made visible by a fully fledged social analysis, and concrete action can only be successful when based on that analysis.

ONE APPEAL OF MARX'S THEORY WAS HIS NARRATIVE OF HISTORY

Creating an adequate history, or narrative, of their past, present and future, is central to the self-understanding and confidence of modern western societies, and much of the focus of Marx lies in providing a philosophy of history. This is a necessary task for Marx, since without a knowledge of the earlier modes of productive activity, capitalism and the bourgeois structure of life, its forms of individual freedom and social interaction, would appear our natural way of life and their inhuman reality remain a mystery. We need to use critical reason to destroy the ability of capitalist political economy to represent itself as the natural forms of immutable, eternal truths; if it can be shown that the obstacle to existential satisfaction is a particular historical form of social interaction, then our limitations are not inescapable. Moreover, if these knowledges are embedded in a progressive narrative, namely a philosophy of history, then we ourselves have an ability to act with confidence. Marx devotes huge amounts of intellectual energy to the task of uncovering the nature and causes of specific limitations on modern man and society. These studies emphasise the historicity of our limitations and provide hope that these limitations can be overcome; the hope for the future is thus defined by negation of the limitations of the present and not by specific utopian blueprints. Marx never constructed a blueprint for the organisation of the 'pure' Communist society.

MARXISM AS PRAXIS

Marx's writings were not intended as speculative theorising, they were meant to lead to practical changes – they sought to offer a combination of 'theory and practice', or *praxis*. The radical 'sociology' of the later Marx, for example, epistemologically claims to be fully scientific while simultaneously offering predictions of social development; it expresses a desire to provide both an intellectual analysis of our separation from the true destiny of the human race, and a picture of the unification of our position in nature and the meaning of our struggles. The mature Marx combines analysis with a call to radical action, specifically a longing for total revolution; we are asked to complete modernity. Marx believes the obstacle to human satisfaction and happiness is the 'dehumanising' spirit of modern society. This is particularly, but not entirely, expressed in the (non-) social relations of capitalism.

CAVEATS FOR UNDERSTANDING THE ROLE OF A MARXIST JURISPRUDENCE

Before looking at Marxist themes on law and society it is necessary to sound certain warnings, or qualifications to any analysis.

Marx did not construct a specific body of work on law

Marx's understanding of law is a subset of the general intellectual approaches to society which he held at different times in his life. Many writers are responsible for providing Marxist accounts; whether or not they correspond to the complexity and subtlety of Marx's original analyses, is a different question.

Marx's writings and concerns span many years of intensive study and scholarly production

The full body of his early writings was not widely available until relatively recently; as a result the mainstream interpretation of Marx was based on his later, dryly scientific writings – of which *Capital* is best known. With the full corpus of his work available we have a more developmental picture of Marx and several different stages of intellectual concerns are apparent. Some writers talk of an epistemological break between the early and the later Marx, others talk of a distinction between the humanist and the scientist (or the expressive and the analyst). We can distinguish several themes in his writing or 'kinds of Marx',[10] namely:

(i) the *humanist*, who writes against exploitation, who argues that the conditions of modern society do not go far enough to liberate man, to serve 'real' human interests;[11]

(ii) the *social scientist*, who proclaims that his final theories embody 'laws of social change' and are a 'true' depiction of the human condition, who further claims to have discovered the 'essence' of capitalism and social history;

(iii) the *rhetorician*, who sometimes writes quickly and freely, striving to stir the reader into action and revolution – 'workers of the world unite'! We may note the speed with which certain key texts were constructed, for example *The Communist Manifesto* (Marx and Engels, 1848) was written in a matter of a few days.

---

10 This does not mean to say that these are separate and distinctive. Marx often writes in a strongly rhetorical way condemning dehumanising conditions, while allowing us to see the problem in a novel way. For example in the following quote on commodity fetishism: 'Private property has made us so stupid and partial that an object is only ours when we have it, when it exists for us as capital, or when it is … utilised in some way' (Marx, *Early Writings*, 1964: 159).

11 'The young Marx is heir of the radical Enlightenment, first, in his notion that man comes to shape nature and eventually society to his purposes. He is its heir, secondly, in his critique of the inhumanity of the present order. The Enlightenment gave rise to a new kind of indignant protest against the injustices of the world. Having demolished the older visions of cosmic order and exposed them as, at best, illusions, and, perhaps, even sham, it left all the differentiations of the old society, all its special burdens and disciplines, without justification. It is one thing to bear one's lot as a peasant if it is one's appointed place in the hierarchy of things as ordered by God and nature. But if the very idea of society as the embodiment of such a cosmic order is swept aside, if society is rather the common instrument of men who must live under the same political roof to pursue happiness, then the burdens and deprivations of this station are a savage imposition, against reason and justice, maintained only by knavery and lies. They would cry to heaven – if heaven still existed – for redress and even vengeance. The Enlightenment thus provoked a new consciousness of inhumanity, of gratuitous and unnecessary suffering, and an urgent determination to combat it. For, if man is then only a subject of desires who aims at their fulfilment (ie happiness), then nothing in heaven or earth compensates for the loss of this happiness. Unrequited deprivation is inconsolable, absolute loss' (Charles Taylor, 1979: 141-2).

Two preliminary points: law must be viewed in relation to the forces constructing modernity (ie the forms and cultural supports of modern western societies). The procedures which are allowed in this search for the actual and real forces and structures of modernity are those which are special to modernity. An important issue for interpretation is how active or constitutive, as opposed to merely passive or reflective, vis-à-vis social relations, did Marx perceive law to be? In answering this question, the narrative of this chapter shall be as follows: (i) the young Marx believed in law as a progressive vehicle for change; but (ii) the writings of the later Marx are much more complex and open to various readings. Perhaps the dominant reading has tended to focus upon his determinist, materialist, theoretical structure which has the consequence of relegating law to a minor role as part of an *ideological superstructure,* where it has the task of assisting to maintain social relations which have been determined by the economic foundations of society (called the base in many accounts). Is this reading correct? Or is it a partly correct, but incomplete, interpretation of Marx's scheme? Certainly Marx came to believe that law and jurisprudence were a central part of the ideological fabric of any society; they not only partially sustained aspects of the living social body, but they helped present an unnatural (in the sense of being against the 'true nature' of man) and dehumanising social order as natural or necessary.[12] Additionally, however, (iii) in

---

12   The French philosopher Destutt de Tracy first used the concept of ideology in *Elements of Ideology,* published at the beginning of the 19th century, where it indicated a science of ideas. The term came to mean a total system of ideas, attitude and emotion – a comprehensive outlook or orientation to the world – but developed a specific political usage which blended its descriptive capabilities with an emotive aspect capable of stimulating social action. Marxists usually claim that ideology expresses ideas and beliefs which represent or cloak material interests, especially class interests. Consequently, the concept embodies the assertion that systems of ideas and beliefs are formed through the pressure of material (ie economic) interests.

Broadly two kinds of analysis are represented in Marx's and Engels' work:

(a)   In one kind of analysis ideology is seen as determined structurally, that is, it is an outcome of the logic of the socio-economic system which, at the same time, hides that logic from most of those who live under the system. Thus in his most important work Capital (1867, plus two posthumous volumes) Marx describes the way social relations under capitalism become relations between things. People relate to each other primarily as property owners selling commodities in the market place. Even the propertyless sell commodities! Workers without capital have to sell their own labour power to employers in return for wages. Most relationships outside the family sphere become instrumental 'business' relationships in one form or another. 'Commodities' and 'capital' take on an existence of their own, determining the relationships of human beings. Yet, in reality, these 'things' are only the product of human labour. In a strange way everything has been turned around. The product has come to dominate the producer. This ideological view of reality which people have under capitalism is not, strictly speaking, false. It is the way things really are; the way they are actually experienced. At the same time reality is presented to both capitalist and worker alike in a manner which obscures the real nature of the socio-economic system.

(b)   The other type of analysis is one which sees ideology as directly expressing class interests. Thus the ideas which dominate in a society tend to be the ideas of the ruling classes: ideas which justify and present as natural the social order under which the rulers rule. Ideology thus serves class interests. This line of approach to analysis of ideology naturally sees the conflict of ideologies as a part of class struggle. Modern Marxists have paid considerable attention to ideological struggle. The Italian writer Antonio Gramsci (writing in prison between 1929 and 1935) developed the concept of 'hegemony' which refers to the domination of thought and political practice in a society by a system of beliefs and attitudes which maintain a general consensus in support of the established order. Marxism does not therefore necessarily deny the existence of an actual consensus of beliefs among members of a class-divided society. But the origins and nature of this consensus have to be explored. Ideological struggle is seen as part of the means by which the   ...

moving beyond reductionist accounts of Marx, we can develop ideas for a *Marxist constitutive theory of law*, or, put in another form, a Marxist theory of law as one of the vital social techniques constituting modern social relations and social identities. In developing this narrative we should consider additional points:

Marx always views law as an expressive phenomenon

The early Marx believes that law is a great progressive force. Under the influence of Hegel, the early writings of Marx identify law as a symbol of a society's thinking, and imply that law can be an expressive instrument, enabling a society to lay out central values. In this period Marx adopts a natural law approach; the test of real law is that it enables freedom to enter into man's social existence. By contrast:

While the later Marx appears to downgrade the role of law, law continues to be presented in expressive terms

Throughout his work Marx implies that by reading the social reality of law we can see the hidden play of the real social forces. The 'real' operation of law becomes a crucial site where the contradictions which are fundamentally part of capitalist social life can be exposed.

Dominant traditions of interpretation: class instrumentalism versus economic determinism

Collins (1982) distinguishes two ways of regarding the views on law of the later Marx:

(a) class instrumentalism – here the law is seen as a weapon in the class struggle. Law is an instrument in oppressing the lower social classes, and a conflict model of social development is most appropriate to explain change;

(b) economic determinism – this is a more complex vision, which sees law as not simply an instrument of class domination, a tool of the ruling class, but as a phenomenon produced and reproduced by the most important driving forces for socio-political-cultural changes in a society (for Marx the economic mode of production). The issue we shall return to is the relative freedom of law in this relationship.

Each tradition is open to serious doubts. First, the repressive class instrumentalist accounts may have seemed to observers in the early 19th century to be simply reflecting the practices whereby a privileged class maintained its position, by force if necessary, (and there is a range of both theoretical argument and empirical support (see, for

---

12...   ruling class seeks to guarantee its power and position. What Marxists find it harder to agree on is the nature of the beliefs and outlook of a revolutionary working class or a revolutionary party. Are these equally ideological – hence justifiable only in terms of class interests – or do they somehow transcend ideology and become objectively 'true' or scientific? Unsurprisingly many Marxists have sought to argue the latter but no satisfactory way of clearly distinguishing scientific and ideological thought in this context has yet been found.

example, Hay, 1975): both Bentham and Austin at times indicated that they saw the legal order as a weapon of domination, a theme developed in the sociology of Max Weber (see Chapter 11 of this text); clear statements supporting this reading are made in the Marxist tradition, see Lenin 1976, Pashukanis 1978 – particularly concerning public law – and critical criminologists such as Quinney, 1973), but the subsequent course of social development makes it extremely hard to identify this as the essence of law. It has proved hard either to identify a coherent class which controls the law, or to illustrate the mechanisms by which such a class fashions its will successfully into a legal regime which serves its interests (Cotterrell, 1984: 16 ff). However, while force is not the secret of modern domination, it has not disappeared, and force is an essential aspect of the power to govern. Moreover, it is true that the force of law is unequally spread; if post-modern societies are developing a socially neglected or 'lost' underclass, this will bear the brunt of coercive policing. The coercive side of modern law may be focused on particular parts of the population (Bauman, 1994, Morrison, 1995; 1996).

Second, the accounts which saw law as a passive reflection of the economic base either reduce social development to a one-sided account of 'progress', or reduce the variation in both the forms and the concerns of law. Some law, especially the core concerns of the criminal law, for example the prohibitions on deliberate taking of human life, appear transcultural, while other aspects of its content are highly culturally specific. The Soviet writer Pashukanis (1978) sought to get around this by arguing that, in developed countries, the form of law reflects the 'commodity form' of economic relations (the subject of the legal relation is the individualistic social bearer of rights in the same way as the market treats the individual as the economic possessor of units of labour or market exchange).

These two distinctions are not enough to cover the wide range of Marxist views on law and modern accounts have paid a greater attention to the ideological effect of law and legal thought (see our footnote 12). Hunt (1991, 1993: 249-50) offers a summary containing six themes:

  (i) Law is inescapably political or law is one form of politics.
  (ii) Law and state are closely connected; law exhibits a relative autonomy from the state.
  (iii) Law gives effect to, mirrors, or is otherwise expressive of the prevailing economic relations; the legal form replicates the forms of economic relations.
  (iv) Law is always potentially coercive or repressive and manifests the state's monopoly of the means of coercion.
  (v) The content and procedures of law manifest, directly or indirectly, the interests of the dominant class(es) or the power bloc.
  (vi) Law is ideological; it both exemplifies and provides legitimation for the embedded values of the dominant class(es).

Hunt stresses that these themes are present in Marxist writings in a variety of forms, with different degrees of sophistication and complexity. Some of the themes conflict, some reinforce each other. No one theme provides the 'correct' interpretation of Marxism. While accepting that these themes reflect tendencies in the vast array of Marxist writings, we will not develop a description of other writers' ideas, but rather outline a concept of law's role in modernity which we shall call a 'constitutive' role.

Towards a constitutive Marxist theory of law's role in modernity

Earlier chapters, drawing upon writers as diverse as Augustine, Hobbes, Hume, Kant and Austin, have highlighted the duality in perspectives of law's foundationalism and capacity to act as an element of social foundation. In one view, law appears as if it can be brought in from outside the operative relationships in society's social forms and imposed upon society to shape social interaction coercively. But this image is opposed by another, in which law seeps up and takes its life as an expression and reflection of underlying daily small-scale social interactions. A constitutive theory of law involves law in a complex set of processes where it is both a reflection and an imposer, both a productive force enabling social forms, and a product of social forms.

AN OUTLINE OF THE DEVELOPMENT OF MARX'S LEGAL THOUGHT

At no time in his life did Marx construct a specific body of work called his sociology of law, but law (and jurisprudence), was his first focal concern. After leaving school in 1835, Marx enrolled to study law at Bonn University (where John Austin had moved to prepare his lectures only eight years earlier). As well as studying law, Marx was expected to undertake theological studies and he enrolled upon a course in classical mythology and the history of art. But it was poetry, and his youthful excesses, that moved him. The next year he transferred to Berlin where he immersed himself in the study of law, science and art, and developed a love for the young woman he was later to marry. He wrote to his father that a 'frontier post' of his life had arrived: he had learnt from Hegel's work (see Chapter 7 of this text) the task 'of seeking the idea [the totality of existence] in reality itself. If previously the gods had dwelt above the earth, now they became its centre' (letter of 10 November 1837). Art, science, poetry, speculative philosophy, romantic passion, religion ... were all now seen by the student Marx as different ways of approaching the complex unity of man's historical existence in this world. The intensity with which Marx now approached the task of understanding 'the totality of reality' caused him to collapse with physical and nervous exhaustion; while he took a period of leave from the university to recover from his nervous collapse he read the entirety of Hegel's work. Hegel presented a problem; although he had succeeded in bringing divinity down to earth, did his *thesis of idealism* really answer the questions as to the driving force(s) of historical development? Was law really the instrument wherein the moral beliefs of a society were expressed and human freedom realised?

Some years later in 1859, Marx summarised the pattern of his intellectual development in the famous preface to *A Contribution to the Critique of Political Economy*. Allowing for the fact that reflections by a writer of his own intellectual development can be self-serving, we can, nevertheless, follow the structure of this preface for the purpose of constructing our own template for Marx's development.

Marx begins by stating: 'Although I studied jurisprudence, I perused it as a subject subordinated to philosophy and history' (all references to the preface from the text translated in *Karl Marx: Early Writings*, Penguin Classics (1992)). His student desire to become a legal academic was frustrated when, after completion of his doctoral thesis, several progressive academics were forced from their posts in 1841. The most important intellectual influence upon him was the impact of reading Feuerbach's *Essence of Christianity*, which argued that religion was a response to the material conditions of life. Feuerbach argued that history was really the story of man struggling to realise his possibilities in the actual, material condition he found himself in, and, while man may appeal to God, this was an exercise of man separating his existential desires from their worldly domain and it amounted to an exercise in alienation. In reality, it was man and not God that was the focal point of existence and history (with the consequence, seemingly, that man's attentions ought to be directed to the study of mankind's entire situation and the betterment of it).[13] This was a revelation to Marx, for it espoused the importance of the material conditions of life in contrast to the stress Hegel placed upon the creation of ideas. Marx began to write for a newspaper – the *Rheinische Zeitung* – which represented industrial and liberal interests. He became its editor, was introduced to the young industrialist Engels, whilst on a trip to Cologne, and soon became embroiled in disputes as to the nature of legal change that were to result in him becoming depressed as to the ability of law to serve as the instrument of progressive change.

First, however, what were Marx's views on law as editor of the *Rheinische Zeitung*? Writing in 1842, Marx defined man's humanity in terms of a capacity for self-rule that distinguishes truly human from naturally conditioned ends: 'Freedom is so much the essence of man that even its opponents actualise it even when combating its reality'. Modernity's great achievement lies in the discovery of man's true humanity: 'Antiquity was rooted in nature, in the substantive. Its degradation and profanation means a fundamental break with the solid substantive life. The modern world is rooted in spirit and can be free.' In this Hegelian idealist frame, Marx in *The Debates on the Freedom of the Press* sees that 'laws are the positive clear general norms in which freedom has gained an impersonal theoretical existence, independent of the arbitrary will of individuals. The law book is the people's Bible of freedom'.[14] Surely there have been few more optimistic and romantic statements made about law!

---

13   This is crucial point for the development of Marxism. Marx has earlier taken from Hegel the idea of the unity of the world – there is no Platonic division of the life of the cave and its transcendence. From Hegelianism the student Marx understood that (i) there is only one reality and this can be understood as the expression of the rationality of the world; (ii) history is a teleological process of development and change from less to more perfect forms of all reality, including social and political life, and human thought; (iii) the thoughts and behaviour of men at any given time are the reflection of some identical process, specifically the operation of *Geist*, or spirit, or mind.

14   The early Marx retained the distinctions which natural lawyers use – giving hints of a conception of a true, natural form of right, and thus a true natural form of law in the cosmos able to be used to criticise what we loosely call positive law. Marx's writing at this time was full of hope for progressive change arising from the production of ideas and debates from within the existing social conditions. His articles concerning the press law for instance can, without much theoretical abuse, be characterised as 'natural law' writings – as by Paul Phillips for example (Paul Phillips, *Marx and Engels on Law and Laws*, 1980: 6-23).

The key aspect to this period is his allegiance to Hegelian idealism. Idealism, briefly stated, holds that the most important element to the constitution of the world is ideas or thought – through thought the world constitutes itself and the reason of thought becomes the reason of the world. [cont'd] ...

Thus Marx could contrast a law with which he agreed, the press law (which gave rise to possible prosecution of the authors of written material after publication if it offended certain categories) with a law with which he disagreed, the censorship law (which forced writers to submit material in advance of publication) explicitly in the Hegelian terms of a re-vamped natural law.

> The press law punishes the abuse of freedom. The censorship law punishes freedom as an abuse. It treats freedom as criminal, or is it not regarded in every sphere as a degrading punishment to be under police supervision? The censorship law has only the form of a law. The press law is a real law.
>
> The press law is a real law because it is the positive existence of freedom. It regards freedom as the normal state of the press, the press as a mode of existence of freedom, and hence only comes into conflict with a press offence as an exception that contravenes its own rules and therefore annuls itself.
>
> [Thus] censorship cannot, any more than slavery, ever become lawful, even if it exists a thousand times as a law. [Since] where law is real law ... it is the real existence of human freedom (all quotes in Phillips, 1980: 7).

Here, in the cradle of Marxism, we observe in the spirit of natural law a partiality for the humiliated and degraded, a partiality which expresses itself in the fight for human dignity and does not allow any recently expressed authority, as here the positive law, to become an answer in itself.

When Marx came to enter into the realm of socio-economic criticism, in his article on *The Debates on the Law on Wood Thefts in the Rhineland Assembly*, his explanation of what was wrong or unjust with laws that legitimise the economic deprivation of the poor and reinforce the customary privileges of the rich, was phrased in these same Hegelian terms:

> By the so-called customs of the privileged are understood to mean customs contrary to the law. The date of their origin falls in the period in which human history still formed a part of natural history, and in which, according to Egyptian legend, all gods concealed themselves in animal forms. Mankind appeared to fall into definite species of animals which were connected not by equality, but by inequality, an inequality fixed by laws. The world condition of unfreedom required laws expressing this unfreedom, for while human law is the mode of existence of freedom, animal law is the mode of existence of unfreedom. Feudalism in the broadest sense is the spiritual animal kingdom, the world of divided mankind ... The customary rights of the aristocracy conflict by their content with the form of universal law. They cannot form law because they are formations of lawlessness.

14...But the natural law/positive law distinction depends on the freedom of thought, of philosophic imagination, whether rooted in the intuition of individual man or in the systematic formulations of the teacher, to express and recognise truth. One can only realise that there is an 'other' legal formulation which contains the 'true' essence of 'right' by an experience of thought or the appreciation of thought. But even if this could be achieved, the fear then grows that all that one has done is recognise the incomplete or the non-right only in 'thought', and that one but reconciles, by the act of opposing the positive non-right with the actual essence of right in thought, only in thought, as in the philosophy of law, whilst it had still to be brought about practically.

For Marx the notion of an abstract realm of natural law was reversed in time into the economic foundations which his 'true science' gave him.

In this situation 'private interest seeks to degrade' the reason of the state and its laws. The state, as the realisation of human freedom, should recognise:

> ... only spiritual forces. The state interlaces all of nature with spiritual nerves, and at every point it must appear that it is the form, not the material, that dominates, the nature of the state, not nature without the state, the free human being, not the unfree object. (Quotes from Phillips, 1980: 00)

The reason of the state must cry out at attempts to disguise private interest in the form of law stating loudly: 'Your ways are not my ways, your thoughts are not my thoughts!'

In these works, Marx argues that the goal of modernity is to achieve the task of human freedom and happiness, and that obstacles to this aim can be overcome through the progressive force of social reason and the communication of ideas. But while Hegel's philosophy seemed to provide the tools to reconcile the diversity of the empirical world into a narrative of totality and social progress, over time the gap between the 'theoretical reconciliation' and the 'practical disharmony' of the world becomes pressing, both as a theoretical problem to be analysed and understood, and as a practical socio-political project to be overcome.

With the newspaper forced to close, and the owners seeking a new editor – in the hope that following the government's line might succeed in getting permission to reopen – Marx was forced to turn to private study. As Marx puts it: The first work which I undertook to dispel the doubts assailing me was a critical re-examination of the Hegelian philosophy of law' (Preface, 1992: 425). As a result of this work – the *Contribution to the Critique of Hegel's Philosophy of Right (Law)* (1843) – Marx changed his opinions as to the driving force of social change. In the standard accounts, Marx claimed to have discovered the proper 'scientific' knowledge of the nature of modernity by inverting the 'abstract' idealist philosophical system of Hegel. Hegel's system held that society moved towards completion of the human task and the creation of true human peace by a progressive unfolding of the 'spirit', or 'Geist', of being (or existence) through the conflicts or dialectic between opposing strands of reality or ideas. This dialectical progression leads in the end to the discovery of that perfect state of man's being, glimpses of which were always immanent in the present. As a result of his studies, by 1859 Marx felt able to 'invert' Hegel replacing 'spirit' by the 'material' basis of social existence – the mode of economic production in the social system.[15] If man were to

---

15 This answer also appears to give us a theory of the foundation of human existence. Specifically, while another key notion from Hegel is that there exists some foundational presence outside all the conflicting aspects of everyday life which gives meaning and unity to existence – and in Hegel we see this in *Geist*, in the development of *Geist* in the progress of history – for Marx the social foundation to existence is ultimately the changing structures of economic formations. This answer thereby allows us a glimpse of a post-modernity which will overcome the tensions and dehumanising forces of the modern. Namely, once we overcame the economic structures which lead us to compete in the market place, the divisions between my interest and your interest, or between our individual interests and the social interest, would vanish. This idea underpinned the call to action in the name of a Communist utopia, and lately fell victim to the bitter disappointments Marxists felt in the face of terrible history their systems occasioned in this century. Many now feel that history appears to show us that although you may change a variety of social conditions, you can never get rid of the basic divisions between reason and desire, between my interest and yours, or between the individual position and society. It is therefore little surprise that the events of 1989 encouraged writers, such as Francis Fukayama (1989), to announce that history was over, but that capitalist liberalism and not socialism was the victor.

realise his possibilities in history he would have to change the actual, material conditions of his existence.

Thus Marx now sees the relationship between freedom and law in complex and dialectical fashion. He reinterprets Hegel's problem, not as the progressive unfolding of the spirit of freedom, but as the need to make freedom actual and social. As a famous passage from the Contribution to the *Critique of Hegel's Philosophy of Right* explains:

> The critique of religion ended with the doctrine that man is the highest being for man, and thus with the categorical imperative to overthrow all relations in which man is a degraded, enslaved, abandoned, or despised being ([1844] 1992: 251).

Practically, this replaces his previous distinction between genuine and non-genuine laws, with a vision of the contradiction between the formal universality of legal and political institutions, and the actual particularity of human interests and behaviour. The continual reforming of the laws of the state will not overcome the obstacles to human happiness without a transformation of the 'practical' foundations of the state. 'Political emancipation' is to be distinguished from 'human emancipation'; left to itself political emancipation creates only the isolated, egotistical individual in the sphere of a modernity devoid of the practice of liberated general interests. The failure of the French Revolution (its degeneration into Jacobin terror and the dictatorship of Napoleon), owed much to a mistaken concentration upon the idea of the social will, and the notion of using force and law to design a new social order. Thus the Jacobins had mistakenly thought that:

> ... the principle of politics is the will. The more one-sided and therefore, the more perfected the political mind is, the more does it believe in the omnipotence of the will, the more it is blind to the natural and spiritual limits of the will, and the more incapable it is therefore of discovering the source of social ills (Collected Works, Vol 3: 199).

Marx's point was simple but deadly. Political power can only realise possibilities allowed by the tendencies in existing social and cultural conditions. By itself, political emancipation cannot make humanity free – modernity will have to change into a form which will allow the freedom of the 'species-being' of mankind to be realised. Not only in the images of philosophy, but 'in his empirical life, in his work, and in his relationships'. All conditions which fall short of this fully human condition enslave man and render him contemptible. The task is to locate and analyse the actual conditions which produced the gap between man's humanity and his world. In time, Marx appears to have found this in the theory of *historical materialism*.

THE STATEMENT OF THE SCIENTIFIC FOUNDATION OF THE LATER MARX

Marx (1859) continues the narrative of his intellectual transformation by stating his final guiding idea:

> The general result at which I arrived and which, once won, served as a guiding thread for my studies, can be briefly formulated as follows: In the social production of their life, men enter into definite relations that are indispensable and independent of their will,

relations of production which correspond to a definite stage of development of their material productive forces. The sum total of these relations of production constitute the economic structure of society, the real foundation, on which rises a legal and political superstructure and to which correspond definite forms of social consciousness. The mode of production of material life conditions the social, political and intellectual life processes in general. It is not the consciousness of men that determines their being, but, on the contrary, their social being that determines their consciousness. At a certain stage of their development, the material forces of society come into conflict with the existing relations of production, or – what is but a legal expression for the same thing – with the property relations within which they have been at work hitherto. From forms of development of the productive forces these relations turn into their fetters. Then begins an epoch of social revolution. With the change of the economic foundation the entire immense superstructure is more or less rapidly transformed. In considering such transformations a distinction should always be made between the material transformation of the economic conditions of production, which can be determined with the precision of natural science, and the legal, political, religious, aesthetic or philosophic – in short, ideological forms in which men become conscious of this conflict and fight it out. Just as our opinion of an individual is not based on what he thinks of himself, so we cannot judge of such a period of transformation by its own consciousness; on the contrary this consciousness must be explained rather from the contradictions of material life, from the existing conflict between the social productive forces and the relations of production. No social order ever perishes before all the productive forces for which there is room in it have developed; and new, higher relations of production never appear before the material conditions of their existence have matured in the womb of the old society itself (from the 1859 Preface to *A Contribution to the Critique of Political Economy*, 1992: 425).

Writing with Engels, he had earlier laid out the conditions for a real analysis of the human condition:

We set out from real, active men, and on the basis of their real life-process we demonstrate the development of the ideological reflexes and echoes of the life-process. The phantoms formed in the human brain are also, necessarily, sublimates of their material life-process, which is empirically verifiable and bound to material premises. Morality, religion, metaphysics, all the rest of ideology and their corresponding forms of consciousness, then no longer retain the semblance of independence. They have no history, no development; but men, developing their material production and their material intercourse, alter, along with this their real existence, their thinking and the products of their thinking. Life is not determined by consciousness, but consciousness by life (Marx and Engels, 1846, *The German Ideology: in the Marx-Engels Reader,* 1978: 154-5).

Law, and jurisprudence, do not develop responding to demands of internal coherence or by virtue of their own development: instead they are objects determinate upon the development of the productive forces which men find themselves in. Marx can turn his full polemic against the liberal jurisprudence of the time:

Your very ideas are but the outgrowth of the conditions of your bourgeois production and bourgeois property, just as your jurisprudence is but the will of your class made into a law for all, a will, whose essential character and direction are determined by the economical conditions of existence of your class (Marx and Engels, *The Manifesto of the Communist Party*, 1848, in the Marx-Engels Reader, 1978: 487).[16]

The analytical mistake which liberal political economy and jurisprudence (for example, in the work of Hume, Smith, Bentham, and Austin) had made was to accept the operation of capitalism as somehow a surface reflection of underlying natural laws of form, utility and function. In philosophy 'alone rule freedom, property, equality and Bentham' (1867: 176), but these were mere superficialities; the real 'laws of motion' transcended capitalism. The liberals were crass empiricists, accepting the operation of private property and contract as naturally given, rather than something itself to be explained.[17]

> Political economy proceeds from the fact of private property. It does not explain it. It grasps the material process of private property, the process through which it actually passes, in general and abstract formulae which it then takes as laws. It does not comprehend these laws, ie it does not show how they arise from the nature of private property. Political economy fails to explain the reason for the division between labour and capital, between capital and land ... it assumes what it is supposed to explain (*Collected Works*, Vol 3: 271).

The Marxist analysis was aimed at the deeper structural processes and seeking out the developmental logic of social change. Bourgeois jurisprudence obscured the reality of class conflict and strove to create an image of the legal realm as self-contained, an image of the legal order as the expression and continual search for justice. While Austin may have argued that law was the instrument of the power of the state to create the socially just conditions for life, for Marx and Engels writing in *The German Ideology*:

> Right, law, etc are merely the symptom, the expression of other relations upon which state power rests ... These actual relations are in no way created by the state power; on the contrary they are the power creating it. The individuals who rule in these conditions, besides having to constitute their power in the form of the state, have to give their will, which is determined by these definite conditions, a universal expression as the will of the state, as law ([1846] 1968: 366).

But this connection is, and must be, obscured by liberal jurisprudence. Under capitalism, law reflects the economic structure of unequal and exploitative economic relations, it

---

16   The reflexive sting in the tail of this analysis is that so too must his own theory!

17   Marx reads liberalism as linked to capitalism and founded upon selfishness and was scathing towards Bentham, whose work appears not to warrant a detailed critique: 'This sphere that we are deserting, within whose boundaries the sale and purchase of labour-power goes on, is in fact a very Eden of the innate rights of man. There alone rule freedom, equality, property and Bentham. Freedom, because both buyer and seller of a commodity, say of labour-power, are constrained only by their own free will. They contract as free agents, and the agreement they come to is but the form in which they give legal expression to their common will. Equality, because each enters into relation with the other, as with a simple owner of commodities, and they exchange equivalent for equivalent. Property because each disposes only of what is his own. And Bentham because each looks only to himself. The only force that brings them together and puts them in relations with each other, is the selfishness, the gains and the private interests of each.'

'Classical economy always loved to conceive social capital as a fixed magnitude of a fixed degree of efficiency. But this prejudice was first established as a dogma by the arch-Philistine, Jeremy Bentham, *that insipid, pedantic, leather-tongued oracle of the ordinary bourgeois intelligence* of the 19th century' (*Capital*: The World's Classics, Oxford University Press, 1995: 335).

contains the inscription of the interests of the dominant class, an inscription legitimated as representing the need for law to reflect political economy or the quest for socially just relations. As Engels stated in a letter to C Schmidt after Marx's death, if the law were too obviously a reflection of the economic structure it would lose its capacity to be seen as something worthy of respect. This may mean that some law is, indeed, not a direct, but an indirect, reflection of economic conditions, or an adjustment to the need to display an ideology of justice.

> In a modern state, law must not only correspond to the general economic condition and be its expression, but must also be an internally coherent expression which does not owing to its inner contradictions, reduce itself to nought. And in order to achieve this, the faithful reflection of economic conditions suffers increasingly. All the more so the more rarely it happens that a code of law is the blunt, unmitigated, unadulterated expression of the domination of a class – this in itself would offend the 'conception of right' ([1890] 1960: 504).

Law must dress itself up in an ideology of right, of progress, of social interest, to hide the reality of domination. In a remarkable passage (which Kelsen – see Chapter 12 of this text – could have placed as the dedication to *The Pure Theory*) Engels relates how 'juristic motive' came to be understood as the driving force of law, rather than domination.

> But once the state has become an independent power vis-à-vis society, it produces forthwith a further ideology. It is indeed among professional politicians, theorists of public law and jurists of private law that the connection with economic facts gets lost for fair. Since in each particular case the economic facts must assume the form of juristic motives in order to receive legal sanction; and since, in so doing, consideration of course has to be given to the whole legal system already in operation, the juristic form is, in consequence, made everything and the economic content nothing (Marx-Engels, *Selected Writings*, 1958: 396–397).

The secret of domination through law is to hide the domination. As the Italian Communist Gramsci was later to observe, *hegemony*[18] – or the situation where the dominated perceive the instruments of domination as in their best interests – is the most effective form of ensuring that the dominated follow the wishes of the dominating.

ASPECTS OF MARXIST METHODOLOGY

Marx sought to construct a method of analysis to explain the essence of social formations and historical change. In other words, Marxism was a total social theory of which the primary target for study was capitalism. Marx was intrigued by the search for the key elements in the structure of capitalist society, the way in which it developed, its ability to reproduce itself as an economic and social system, and its destiny. According to Marx, relationships between people, and the forms that institutionalised those relationships, depend on the 'economic structure of society'; the way that production is organised. Mankind has moved through five historical stages – primitive Communism, Asiatic,

---

18 Hegemony denoted the process creating 'the spontaneous consent given by the great mass of the population to the general direction imposed on social life by the dominant fundamental group (ie the ruling class)' (Gramsci, 1971: 12, quoted Hunt, 1993: 20).

slavery, ancient feudal, and the capitalist – with a socially developed socialist structure to come. Each has different dominant methods of production leading to 'a complicated arrangement of society into various orders, a manifold graduation of social rank' (Marx and Engels 1965: 40). Each form of society contains conflictual divisions which helped transform the nature of that society: contradictions in the mode of production place strain on the existing social order, sharpening the divide between the base, or economic foundation of society, and its superstructure, or its legal, political and religious institutions.[19] These contradictions are the source of social change and find their most potent site in class confrontations. By the confrontation of class contradictions, one historical form of society is transformed into a higher stage of social development: 'the history of all hitherto existing society is the history of class struggles' (ibid: 39).

THE STATE

The state is both a political organisation, something functionally determined by social processes, and illusionary. The state depends upon law and ideology to operate; to take its form. States have not always existed (nor, believed Marx, will they exist in the future); they are an historically specific organisation of power. What social arrangement existed before the state? Engels argued that a gentile constitution, a community where free, equal individuals communally owned and controlled their products, preceded the political constitution of the state. The state was brought about by the development of the division of labour and the corresponding rise of class relations. Conflict arose and individuals developed the notion of private property to mediate the conflict between themselves and group life. As individuals and families formed larger groupings a state arose through a process whereby individual freedom was exchanged for social protection. The state was born out of these exchange operations.

> In order that these antagonisms, classes with conflicting economic interests, shall not consume themselves and society in a fruitless struggle, a power apparently standing above society, has become necessary to moderate the conflict and keep it within the bounds of 'order'; this power, arisen out of society but placing itself above it and increasingly alienating itself from it, is the state (Engels, [1884] 1973: 229).

---

19 Commentators refer to the relationship of *base and superstructure* as a metaphor. The image is of law, politics, religion, art, etc, all resting on a foundation of economic activity and relationships (the ground which supports the building). The structure of the building is thus determined by what lies underneath. While appealing in its simplicity, there are numerous problems with the metaphor. For example, critics note that economic relations are themselves defined by law (which is part of the superstructure). Does this mean that actually the base is partly built on the superstructure!? Contemporary Marxists argue that what is essential is to recognise that in some way the economy determines the fate of society 'in the last instance'. For example, Louis Althusser, an influential French Marxist philosopher in the 1970s, argued that in fact the political, ideological and economic levels of society all influence each other and all have considerable independence of each other. Only ultimately does the economy determine the general movement of society. Many Marxists use the concept of the 'relative autonomy' of the estate, law, ideology etc from the economy. In this way they indicate a great deal of room for independence by or action in 'levels' of society other than the economic level. Economic determinism – the idea that the economic aspects of society ultimately determine all the other aspects – is thus fundamental to Marxist thought, but at the same time is a complex notion which can be interpreted in many different ways.

What is the essence of those power relations underlying the modern state? In *The Communist Manifesto* Marx and Engels displayed a succinct flourish: 'Political power, properly so called, is merely the organised power of one class for the oppression of another' (*Communist Manifesto*: 490). Thus Engels was clear:

> The ancient state was ... the state of the slave owners for holding down the slaves, just as the feudal state was the organ of the nobility for holding down the peasant serfs and bondsmen, and the modern representative state is an instrument for exploiting wage labour by capital (1973: 231).

For Marx and Engels, class location formed a central unit of analysis. From the 18th century onwards, the class struggle has been primarily between the capitalist class (the bourgeoisie) and the labouring class (the proletariat). In the transformation which they predicted from capitalist society through socialism and on to Communism, the superstructure of bourgeois society – religion, the laws and jurisprudence, national divisions, bourgeois political institutions, the state – would be swept away and, in Engels' famous phrase, the government of 'persons' would be replaced by the administration of 'things'. The state was to be relegated to be the museum of history, together with the spinning wheel and the bronze axe.

For Marx, it was clear that the European states of his own time allowed the ruling class to oppress the working class by using the agents of state such as the judiciary, the police, the army and the Church. What does this imply for the style and content of legislation, of the new modern law? Marx is an expressionist. Modern law expresses desire, law involves will, it involves the transformation of human volition into a statute laying out a structure of rules and regulatory mechanisms, or an authoritarian announcement by a judge of the position in case law, but we move into ideological mystification if we believe that the aim of this volition is merely an instrument of progress, or an expression of the progressive social consciousness. We should not blind ourselves to the reality of domination inherent in law. Class interest must be a powerful element of legal power. The external activities of the state are also clearly influenced by its class nature. In the Marxist analysis, the national bourgeoisie of Britain, France, Germany and other European states undertook imperialist expansion in pursuit of greater profits. Against this, Marxists argued that transnational relations of a more meaningful kind could be created by trade, the movement of capital, and increased contact and solidarity between the proletariat of various nations. Marx understood capitalism to be a global phenomenon and, therefore, transnational class relations, as well as interstate class tensions, were possible vehicles of change.[20]

---

20   In this context it is worth noting that the international organisations of which Marx and Engels had direct experience were the First International and, for Engels, the Second International, both of which attempted to organise the representatives of working people across frontiers.

MARX ON THE EMPIRICAL LEGAL ORDER AND (SOCIAL) JUSTICE

According to Marx, the character of the means of production unambiguously indicates the level reached by a particular phase of history.[21] Man must slowly rise to becoming authentically man through his productive labour. For this reason the various phases of history show also different phases of authenticity and these phases, says Marx, are determined by the man's situation in the material reality of the means of production.

The character of the means of production also determines the character of the *relationships* of production. The fact that a society uses a particular type of productive means, has as its consequence the fact that the productive men enter into relations with one another in a particular way. Where wool is produced on a spinning wheel people do not relate in the same way as in modern textile mills. In juridical terms the relationships of production are called ownership relations.

Marx appeared to suggest that early forms of social life were communistic in the relationship of means of production and labour: 'Property ... means belonging to a tribe (community)' (1858: 416); but in a subsequent phase of economic development, the modern means of production make all primitive productive forms economically valueless. These modern means of production will, at least at first, be privately owned. This contains an inherent contradiction since, says Marx, these modern means of production are, by their very nature, social. Because the primitive means have become economically valueless, those who earned their living through them have now to depend on working for hire in the service of owners of modern productive means. In this way the private ownership of these means gives the possessor absolute power over those without possessions; the owner becomes an exploiter and those without possessions are his victims.

The legal order, says Marx, is to be understood on the basis of the actually existing ownership relations. The coercive expression of a state constituted by this order – commands, rules, dictates, administrative decrees – cannot be other than the will of the ruling class elevated to law even if their content is to preserve the actual operative conditions of the economic system. The content of this will is implied in the material

---

21 The ideas of the relations of production and productive forces were central concepts:

(i) *Relations of Production* – these are the specifications of employment in a dual way – they serve as descriptions of what a person does in the performance of his activity, but they are also quasi-legal since they indicate a person's due, or the degree to which he/she is able to participate in the consumption and productive aspects of the economic structure.

(ii) *Productive forces* – technology plus resources (human and material) necessary to production. Marx uses the term 'means of production' to refer specifically to the tools and materials with which people work in order to produce.

The difference between costs of production and the value in the marketplace of what is produced constitutes *surplus value*. This is the key element producing exploitation. Who owns this surplus value depends upon who owns the means of production. Under capitalism it is the capitalist factory owner (the industrialist, etc) who owns the means of production and takes the profit. The worker sells his labour power – ie his capacity to work – to the capitalist. In return he gets wages. This situation constitutes the basic relations of production characteristic of capitalism (though not of other socio-economic systems).

living conditions of the ruling class, who cannot help but interpret the common good in terms of the preservation of the social structure which places them in an elite position, and enables them to see what the laws of political economy require.

But law is not a simple weapon of the ruling class, nor an open-ended phenomenon to be used and abused at the will of the elite. It arises out of social conditions and structures, and makes possible other social conditions and particular interactions. Historically, when society reaches a certain level of development, there arises a need to establish a common regulation for the daily recurrent actions of production, distribution and exchange, in order to prevent each individual from going his own way within this system. Such a regulation is called a 'law'. As the development of society progresses, the law becomes more or less elaborate and slowly man forgets that these laws are an expression of the economic living conditions. Law comes to seem autonomous; as if it can be read as originating solely in the expression of the will of the sovereign. In philosophical discussion the discourse of law bespeaks ideas of universality and necessity, but contrasting this universality to social effectivity demonstrates that the idea of law is imprisoned in philosophy; for example, the social reality of the operation of the prohibition on stealing and the laws of property means that the owners – who are exploiters of those without property – must be allowed to have their way. But legal discourse closes its range of concerns and avoids awareness of this contrast; the legal order, then, begins to take on a kind of independent existence. This independence gives rise to professional jurists and, at the same time, to the science of law which tends to forget the social reality of law as it captures and visualises it in terms of its own ideological self-reflexivity. The professional jurists compare the legal systems of the various peoples, not as expressions of economic conditions with quite particular effects, but as independent and self-sufficient systems. This comparison shows that there are certain similarities, and these similarities the jurists call the 'natural law', or 'the object of justice', or, as with John Austin, the phenomenon of a 'general jurisprudence' as opposed to 'specific jurisprudence'. Although, personally, they may be motivated by desires for progressive change or for achieving the just society, once the jurists have reached this point they cannot escape the confines of ideology; even if the development of the law consists for them in the effort to bring the relationship between men closer to 'eternal justice', this so-called 'eternal justice' is in reality nothing but the ideological, 'heavenly' expression of economic relationships. In vain they may construct theories which purport to be founded on 'a priori theses' which transcend their contemporary conditions, but in reality they are working with discursive and ideological reflexes of economic conditions. Thus, a true theory of natural law or natural right which will be embodied in a 'just' state cannot be found, since all the modern jurist's thought patterns are structured in terms of property, exchange and contract. The jurist is, thereby, simply reproducing the exchange relations expressive of certain powers lurking within and behind the juridical forms of the capitalist structure. In reality:

> ... the justice of the transactions between agents of production rests on the fact that these arise as natural consequences out of the productive relationships. The juristic forms in which these economic transactions appear as wilful acts of the parties concerned cannot, being mere forms, determine this content. They merely express it. This content is just

wherever it corresponds ... to the mode of production. It is unjust whenever it contradicts that mode (*Capital*, Vol 3: 339-340).

The state and its power maintain the law. Whereas, from a class analysis, the state is in large part the organised power of the possessing class – the major landowners and capitalists – over the exploited class – farmers and labourers – the state as an organisational formation needs to create an illusionary bond of self-interest between the dominating and the dominated. But any theory of organic harmony, such as Hegel's inclusive idealism, is an 'external, forced, specious identity' (Marx, *Critique of Hegel's Doctrine of the State*, 1992: 60). As long as society is composed of classes, politics will be a relationship of domination, and the ruling class will use every means to oppress the exploited class to preserve its domination. The state considers itself the official representative of the entire society, but when subjected to class analysis, it represents most clearly the economic interests of the ruling class.

Class and domination structure the underlying reality of the state's guidance of the social body. The state establishes public power, but this power is not the armed power of the organised people, for the people are divided into classes. State power must represent itself as public power although failing to become a true instrument of the whole of society. Now, contrasted with previous social systems based on slavery, the modern society appears as progressive and offering freedom; in reality, exploitation is merely more hidden. Slavery was both a personal and state phenomenon; slaves belonged to the people of a state, but they were kept in submission by the state's public power. Under capitalism, the (in)justice of slavery is now apparent, but justice remains always class justice. Bourgeois justice hides its class effect, yet, for all its ideological mystification, the state and public power are reflexes of economic interests.

DOES THE LEGACY OF MARXISM DOOM US TO PESSIMISTIC ACCOUNTS OF THE LEGAL ORDER IN WHICH ENTITIES SUCH AS RIGHTS ARE MERE POWER EXPRESSIONS?

In capitalist liberal society individuals are possessed of rights granted them by the legal order. These rights enable them to achieve their ends, to fashion the social space around them to their personal projects. As a consequence, the very idea of public space becomes problematic; it becomes merely that space where individuals interact and intervene as their own, private, interests dictate. In effect public space is transformed into a (non-)public space; it is commodified into spheres of production (factories, work-places), exchange (shopping complexes, entertainment centres) and consumption (homes, clubs). Further, these rights are, in essence, negative liberties – freedom from the interference of others – rather than freedom to achieve real social purposes. While the regime of law appears to guarantee everyone the right to dispose of what they own at freely contracted market prices, this freedom to dispose of person and property is of little positive use to the masses who have little or nothing except their meagre bodies. The regime of the rule of law, the liberal talk of rights, thus obscures this social reality; beneath lies the cold reality of class positions and class relations.

If power is taken as the basis of right, as Hobbes, etc do, then right, law, etc are merely the symptom, the expression of the other relations upon which state power rests. The material life of individuals, which by no means depends merely upon their 'will' ... this is the real basis of the state and remains so at all the stages at which the division of labour and private property are still necessary, quite independently of the will of individuals (Marx and Engels, *The German Ideology* 1846:106).

What is liberal freedom? 'By freedom is meant free trade, free selling and buying' (CM: 486). The formal freedom cannot disguise the social domination. The violent expulsion of peasants from the land into the cities has created the horrible freedom of the 'free labourer'. He is indeed 'free from the old relation of clientship, villeinage or service, but also free from all goods and chattels, from every real and objective form of existence, free from property' (Pre-capitalist 00:111). Since he is free from all means of support, the labourer is forced to sell his labour power in order to survive; the capitalist is free to exploit the labourer's labour power by extracting surplus value. The so-called free contract of employment cannot hide the reality whereby 'capital obtains this surplus labour without an equivalent, and in essence it always remains forced labour – no matter how much it may seem to result from free contractual agreement' (*Capital*, Vol 3: 819). 'The whole system of capitalist production is based on the fact that the workman sells his labour power as a commodity' (1867: 571).

LAW AS CONSTITUTIVE REGULATION

Modern capitalism is based on 'the fact that the workman sells his labour power as a commodity' (1967: 571); this relationship 'has no natural basis, nor is its historical basis one that is common to all historical periods' (*ibid*: 169). Thus, while capitalism rests upon specific forms of class relations, it requires the contract, and requires a subjectivity in which the person is seen as an individual rather than as a unit of the social whole. Law constitutes this subjectivity and enables this economic structure. It is juridical imagination which sets out the pre-contractual norms within which the contract is to operate, and the whole structure of individual subjectivity.

Law constitutes the modern subject. It does so in two ways, one destructive, and one constructive.

1   *The destructive.* The pre-modern social harmony and integration into a social unit must be broken down. Bourgeois historians have described this as the history of the individual becoming free; of the progressive overcoming of social ties and bonds which constrained the person in social ignorance.[22] But this involves the tearing apart of the human from ties with the soil and the conditions of primitive harmony: a form of alienation occurs – force is central. In Capital Marx relates how law is the weapon, the means used in the disbanding of feudal retinues, the eviction of

---

22   Marx agreed with the assessment of lack of freedom in pre-modern social relations. Writing an article for the *New York Daily Tribune* in 1853 he displays a fervent disgust at the conditions of British rule as well as disgust at the conditions of Indian village life. He argues that 'sickening as it must be to human feeling' the exploitation of the British contained elements of social progress.

customary tenants to turn arable land into sheep-walks, the spoliation of church properties, enclosure Acts and the clearance of estates. Legal violence lies at the heart of the historical birth of capital. Capitalism is born 'dripping from head to toe, from every pore, with blood and dirt' (ibid: 760); capital accumulation occurs by 'conquest, enslavement, robbery, murder, briefly force' (ibid: 714); all of which are achieved and legitimated through the prevailing legal enactments. As a consequence a new human is created; a new formation consisting of 'those physical and mental capabilities existing in a human being, which he exercises whenever he produces a use value' (ibid: 167).

In England the law was 'the instrument of the theft of the peoples' land'; 'bloody legislation against the expropriated' had penalised vagrancy, forcing the dispossessed 'onto the narrow path of the labour market' (ibid: 724, Ch 28). Laws extended the working day, regulated the conditions of work and laid out the appropriate wages, structured labour mobility and criminalised workers' combinations. On the world stage, state power claimed to civilise the non-modern world. Colonial administration, along with the structures of the law, the contractual regulation and franchising of operations, enabled raw material to be taken by 'undisguised looting, enslavement and murder' back to Europe.[23] The power of the state was utilised to transform the feudal mode of production into the capitalist one. So-called international law is the result of treaties imposed by the powerful; international capitalism is the result.

The law drove humans into the market and then laid out the conditions for them to operate; it destroyed the old social space and human constitution, but in so doing it provided the tools for building a new one.

2   *The constructive.* The decomposition of traditional social structures created the 'isolated individual'; both worker and consumer. The human units of capitalism are 'new-fangled men ... as much the invention of modern time as machinery itself' (1856: 656). The solitary individual is visualised through the lenses of bourgeois philosophy and immortalised in the rights of man. The human being is a 'juridical person'. This is a necessary transformation for the very 'act of exchange' to take place; exchange requires 'subjects as exchangers'. For Marx, the attributes of the juridical person are precisely those of the individual engaged in exchange. The subjectivity of the basic unit required by capitalism is created by the laws which both reflect capitalist relations and make them possible.

We do not need to be Marxist to appreciate the force of Marx's sociological analysis of the development of modern subjectivity. Our narrative has been arguing that modern subjectivity is, in large part, a legal subjectivity. Whereas the subjectivity of the classical Greek is that of his/her natural relationship to the context of the polis, and that of the medieval that of his/her relationship to God and the created cosmos, the subjectivity of

---

23   'The rosy dawn of capitalist production [involved] the discovery of gold and silver in America, the extirpation, enslavement and entombment in mines of the aboriginal population, the beginning of the conquest and looting of the East Indies, the turning of Africa into a warren for the hunting of black-skins.'

the modern is the relationship of the self to the self and the selves of others, mediated through law. We may call the modern a distinctly 'privileged' creation (privilege from priva and lege, meaning the private law). Legality, the developing rule of law, the creation of a delineated social space of rights and duties, the creation of regulatory regimes which make possible bureaucracy, creates an epistemological space within which the ontology of modernness takes substance.

THE MARXIST SEARCH FOR JUSTICE IS A STRUGGLE AGAINST INHUMANITY AND EXPLOITATION

In the Marxist reading, human suffering in capitalist society is embodied in the dehumanised existence of the proletariat; an existence made possible by the relationship of property law to contract law, underpinned by the jurisprudence of liberalism, and further obscured by the illusory equality which the legal system announces. Bourgeois law and jurisprudence join with political economy to deal in concepts abstracted from social reality; reification results. The free sovereign individual of capitalism is an ideal creation; in society persons differ in the class location, in the amount of capital(s) they possess. The legal rights, which look so fine in philosophy, which are announced as proof of emancipation, are largely chimerical because they are formal-legal and not social rights. Real social rights would concern the 'production of life'. The abstract individual who claims political and judicial rights is a representation, a subject whose existence is ideal, and hence illusionary, and yet forms the 'ideal' subject of all bourgeois political, legal and ethical discourses. Further, the empirical manifestation of these subjects, the real living people of capitalism, are blinded by the illusory satisfactions of the bourgeois order. How can Marx break this illusion? Only by a 'positivist' faith in the emancipatory role of 'true' knowledge. The knowledges made possible by the developing 'hard' sciences of mankind, not romantic ideas, will make humanity's destiny visible. As early as his critique of Feuerbach, Marx, for example, expressed his conviction that love is unimportant. He berated Feuerbach for, on the one hand, abolishing religion, while on the other hand, introducing a new religion, namely that of men's love for one another. Marx argues that if Feuerbach had been sensitive to the importance of praxis, he would have noticed that not love but *work*, with its socio-economic structures, brings men together and unites them. But, for this unity, Feuerbach substituted the unity of the human species, 'the internal and dumb universality that connects the many individuals in a natural way'. This unity is an 'abstraction'. Real unity among men comes about through the truth of social life and participation in work; the continuity of history is secured by the continuity of the means of production, not by all kinds of political and religious 'nonsense.'

Marx claims the mantle of a pure, positivist science for his ideas, but this is undercut; ultimately, he offers a critical interpretation of the human condition. As in our discussion of positivism in the previous chapter, Marx needs a criterion of justice to motivate his theory. On what grounds, however, can Marx call the capitalistic legal order unjust and the Communist order just? If a legal order is nothing but the mirror image of actual conditions and relationships, one can never say of any *order* whatsoever that it is just or unjust. In *reality*, Marx calls the liberalistic-capitalistic legal order unjust only because he sees this order as a violation of his fellow man's ideal human subjectivity.

WHAT RELEVANCE IS THERE FOR THE LEGACY OF MARX AFTER THE COLLAPSE OF MARXISM?

This text is written in the mid-1990s. Communism collapsed in Europe after the Berlin Wall was breached. 1989 and 1990 saw a revolution against Communism and the historical period which began in 1917 has now come to an end. The combination of Marxism-Leninism[24] is a failed political project, its history rewritten as a horrific failure – as inhuman and extracting a terrible price from the environment. It is a classic understatement to say 'things have not worked out the way Marx predicted'! Not only did a Communist revolution occur in countries least likely, according to the Marxist narrative of history, to experience such revolutions (since they were too underdeveloped – that is, capitalism had not worked itself out and the class divide had not developed into an uncontainable tension) but capitalism has changed and strengthened itself in countries where Marx predicted revolution. This is not a text telling the historical story of the struggles of this century; suffice to say, however, that in the era of liberalistic laissez-faire capitalism it was almost impossible to offer a theoretical defence against the Marxist identification of the legal order and injustice, nor argue against the definition of progressive social justice as the willingness to overthrow that legal order and that state in the name of creating a more humane social order. Possibly, the strength of the socialist critique helped the countries of the West to make fundamental revisions to their legal order. Marx's *Communist Manifesto* enumerated 10 points of the programme for social reform to be realised at once after the revolution. But they had a great effect in the West without the revolution desired by Marx. While Lenin could characterise these reforms as bribes to the working class of capitalist countries which needed to be fought against on an international level,[25] in time little could hide the fact that as the Soviet experience

---

24 It is best to call the philosophy which underpinned the USSR as Marxism-Leninism due to the great influence of V I Lenin (1870-1924). Lenin gave Marxism its political praxis by his advocacy of the leading role to be played by the Communist Party as the vanguard of the proletariat in its struggle against the forces of capitalism. His early writings concentrated on the need to develop a successful party (stressing partiinost, or party spirit). He expounded on the ideas of dialectical materialism, the materialist conception of history, and the need to combine revolutionary activity with theoretical understanding. Lenin opposed the fatalism which the determinist image of history gave many theoretical Marxists, and argued it was necessary to seize the historical moment through deliberate revolutionary organisation.

Lenin developed the idea of dialectic into an internal characteristic of the matter of all phenomena. The principle of opposition was not merely a clash of opposing forces or entities in the world, but rather a feature inside the composition of all entities. Each and every entity is composed of oppositions and countervailing forces.

25 In *Imperialism: The Highest Stage of Capitalism* (Petrograd, [1916] 1966), Lenin argued that capitalism had reached a stage of development at which the dominance of monopolies and finance capital was established, in which the export of capital had acquired pronounced importance; in which the division of all territories of the globe among the biggest capitalist powers had been completed (Lenin 1966: 82-3). Lenin thought that the gains enjoyed by the imperialists would be used as bribes for sections of the European working class – 'opportunists'. However, the damage would be done: the extension of capitalism to the rest of the world in order to prolong its life would forge links between the oppressed peoples of the exploited areas and the proletariat of the developed countries. Due to the unequal development of capitalism, socialism would not triumph simultaneously, but gradually.

under Lenin and then Stalin[26] became more and more a pale mockery of Marx's hopes, western countries humanised themselves. Marxist-Leninist writings developed arguments designed to sustain the legitimacy of the Soviet state in the face of Marx's predictions of the state withering away,[27] but purges and vast inhumane systems of administration were required to modernise the society. One theoretical justification Marxist writers defending the USSR adopted was to move the issue of capitalist exploitation onto the international level and stress the need for the USSR to counter capitalist imperialism.[28] One result was that the state acquired a meaning that differed radically from that existing in Marx's time. Does this mean that reading Marx has no purpose? Far from it. Marx is both an essential commentator on modernity, and responsible for providing an enormous body of social thought which encompasses many of the hopes and fears of modern humanity. As well as understanding his writings, appreciating what happened in the application of his ideas provides a sobering case study on the fate of the scientific approach to explaining humanity and the historical human condition.

It has become clear that, generally speaking, the capitalist West enabled a range of economic, social and political liberties to occur in a more effective and more comprehensive way than the countries in which Marxism was given a chance to do so. Communist states became burdened with stifling bureaucracy and regulation; the banner of equality meant standardisation rather than equal dignity, to enjoy freedom meant being a member of the party. While work was a social right, its rewards were

---

26 Stalin, as leader of the Soviet Communist Party (and in effect the Soviet Union) from 1924 to 1953, contributed little directly to Marxist thinking. However, as Soviet leader he had to respond to the failure of the rest of the world to follow the Russian example of moving towards communism. Faced with 'capitalist encirclement', he adopted a ruthless policy of 'socialism in one country' (the building up of a socialist state in the Soviet Union) and modernisation. The details do not make nice reading.

27 In *State and Revolution*, (Petrograd, 1918) Lenin developed the Marxist idea of the state as an instrument of class domination, and argued that the instruments of class dominance were nowhere near 'withering away'. The dictatorship of the proletariat existing in the USSR after 1917, was threatened by the bourgeoisie within and imperialists without. He stressed the need to shatter the bourgeois state machinery, and distinguished between a lower stage of communism, in which reward is proportionate to work and where the state is still needed, and a higher phase, in which reward is proportionate to need and the state will wither away. The Soviet state was seen by Lenin as a proletariat class state acting to repress the Russian bourgeoisie, to repel foreign invaders, as well as taking on administrative and proselytising functions. The Bolsheviks also had a duty to encourage socialist revolution in countries outside Russia – this was the task of the Communist International established in 1919 when Lenin considered world revolution imminent. Over the following two years, as fervour in Europe cooled or was suppressed, Lenin wrote about the delay of the revolution outside Russia and turned his mind to the question of relations with capitalist states: 'we have entered a new period, in which we have, in the main, won the right to our international existence in the network of capitalist states' (Lenin 1970: 264).

28 In his writings on imperialism, Lenin, like Engels and Marx, stressed the exploitative class nature of imperialism rather than any formal colonising policy of the European states. Exploitation was not tied to a simple formula which could open up the potential for diverse theorising by later neo-Marxist students of the relations between industrial and developing nations and the institutions involved. Lenin stressed the potential for solidarity among those oppressed by capitalist world domination. The emphasis was placed on transnational relations in international affairs – relations between the proletariat of all countries. On jurisprudence, Soviet writers largely were forced to keep to the line dictated by the Communist Party of the Soviet Union. Of course there were some disagreements. After the death of Lenin, Soviet commentators stressed the isolation of the Soviet Union within a capitalist-dominated world.

limited. The West simply outperformed the socialist/Communist countries and the huge spending on arms which the cold war required finally could not be economically sustained by the USSR. But, if rewards for work were higher in the West, as post-industrialism has surfaced, a basic tension regarding work has become ever more apparent. In the Marxist scheme work is central: man would simply disappear if he did not work, but what happens in a post-industrial world in which there is simply not enough work for all? Is a new form of alienation and exploitation inevitable? What concepts and tools of intellectual analysis do we need in the new conditions?

Many of the insights of Marx which made an impact beyond his immediate political following have been absorbed into the critical conversations which have energised social democratic and liberal thought. Among these was a uniquely powerful image of the global energy and unrelenting expansiveness of capitalism, an unforgettable focus upon the authority relations of modern industry, and a dramatisation of the structural antagonism generated by its productive process. The imaginative power with which Marx highlighted the dizzying volatility of modern economic and social life provided some of the basic premises of modernism in both literature and the arts as well as politics. At the most general level, Marx's work has entered our language, transforming our questions about the world. But the organisation of Marx's ideas into what came to be called 'Marxism' was quite another matter. Marx was far more successful in evoking the latent power of capitalism than in demonstrating in any conclusive fashion why it had to come to an end. His conviction of a future society based upon a higher notion of freedom amounted to a desire to transcend the dehumanising aspects of modernity but his science of predictions was a false historicism.

THE POST-CAPITALIST ORDER?

Some current commentators (for example Peter Drucker, 1993) ask what would Marx write today and their answer is not *On Capital* but *On Knowledge*. For Drucker, we live in *post-capitalist society*, where the basic economic resource – the 'means of production' – is no longer capital, nor natural resources, nor labour; it is, and will be, knowledge. Along with the development of the information or knowledge society comes *The End Of Work* (Rifkin, 1995). A post-capitalist society may be a society where the highly educated person reigns supreme over a new era of labour saving devices and enjoys freedom from exploitation; or it may be a hell wherein the vast majority of the population – who had previously been the 'workers' – are no longer needed. What happens to the 'worker' in post-modernity? The changes in social class seem dramatic in recent decades. Marx's exploited and alienated 'proletarian' has moved either into a member of the 'affluent working class', or into the new middle class (as a result of the productivity revolution of this century, along with the legal structure of the welfare state), or become surplus, creating a new underclass. But even the middle class has experienced new problems with the development of the management and information revolutions of the late 1960s (when the numbers of 'blue-collar' workers began to decline in numbers and in status, until it is predicted that soon after the year 2000 there will be no developed country where traditional workers, making and moving goods, account for more than a small proportion of the workforce). Globalisation and the speed of technological change threatens to dramatically change the life chances of vast sections of the population world-wide.

If this is the case we are indeed in a radically different situation from that which has characterised much of modernity. How will social order and a humane social life be maintained? Moreover, on a world scale, the gulf between the world's rich and poor is as great as ever; inhuman forms of labour exploitation, indebtedness and intimidation are still to be combated.[29] New conflicts have emerged while old ones persist. The need for critical theory and analysis remains, the subject of analysis is increasingly the dialectics of a global environment and local situation.

---

29 An example is the Bhopal incident in India in the early 1980s where a large multi-national company clearly ignored safety requirements in the egoistic pursuit of profit which resulted in the poisoning of thousands of working class people (Pearce and Tombs, 1989, 'Realism and Corporate Crime', in *Issues in Realist Criminology*).

CHAPTER 11

WEBER, NIETZSCHE AND THE HOLOCAUST:
towards the disenchantment of modernity

PART ONE
MAX WEBER (1864–1920): LEGAL DOMINATION AND THE DIALECTIC OF RATIONALISATION – DISENCHANTMENT

Like the political institutions historically preceding it, the state is a relation of men dominating men. A relation supported by means of legitimate (considered to be legitimate) violence. If the state is to exist, the dominated must obey the authority claim by the powers that be (Weber, 1984: 33).

For civilised man death has no meaning. It has none because the individual life of civilised man, placed into an infinite 'progress', according to its own immanent meaning should never come to an end; for there is always a further step ahead of one who stands in the march of progress. And no man who comes to die stands upon the peak which lies in infinity. Abraham, or some peasant of the past, died 'old and satiated with life' because he stood in the organic cycle of life; because his life, in terms of its meaning and on the eve of his days, had given to him what life had to offer, because for him there remained no puzzles he might wish to solve; and therefore he could have had enough of life. Whereas civilised man, placed in the midst of the continuous enrichment of culture by ideas, knowledge, and problems, may become 'tired of life' but not 'satiated with life'. He catches only the most minute part of what the life of the spirit brings forth ever anew, and what he seizes is always something provisional and not definitive, and therefore death for him is a meaningless occurrence. And because death is meaningless, civilised life as such is meaningless; by its very 'progressiveness' it gives death the imprint of meaninglessness (Weber, 1970: 139–40).

THE RATIONALISATION OF THE WORLD

Of the founding fathers of modern sociology – Karl Marx, Emile Durkheim and Max Weber[1] – Weber's influence is the most understated yet widespread. In critically analysing capitalism Marx looked forward to a future of mankind's emancipation: 'the free association of free human beings'. Weber, conversely, seemed to see no way out of the deep contradictions of modern life. His writings depict modernity as a social epoch of immense complexity producing vast advances in power, but also making it ever more

---

1   The German social theorist, Max Weber, witnessed the unification of Germany under Bismarck and the emergence of the modern German state founded in part at least upon the strength of Prussian hegemony. In his later life he saw the phenomenal growth of industrialisation in Germany, the failed attempt to create a German empire and the culmination of great power rivalry in the catastrophe of the First World War.

difficult to live as a fully rounded human being. Perhaps we can see in Weber the forerunner to the self-doubting that has come to characterise the post-modern era. Certainly while analysing modernity, Max Weber already talked the language of the post-modern. It was not just his implicit battle with nihilism, nor his use of the imagery of *le transitoire, le fugitif,* and *le contingent,* but also the sense of irreplaceable loss which imbued his work.

Weber theorised as a reflexive modern; writing in the late 19th century it had become time to take stock, to analyse the processes and structures which had transformed past societies and constituted the present position of mankind and ask what sort of situation did the new subject of history – the civilised modern – find himself in. Rationality provided the key for Weber. In the narrative of enlightenment, modernity waged war on tradition and custom in favour of reason, progress and freedom. Its creation – the civilised, rational man – was to be provided with the keys of knowledge, and as a consequence of knowing the structure of things be free from the domination of ideology, of the falsehoods of tradition and custom;[2] Weber, however, saw another twist. The rational man would be committed to the task of visualising the true structure of the cosmos, but, as the price of using reason, he would be condemned to perform only the rational task and obey the outcome of formal calculation. As a consequence, the magic of life disappears into the irrational. Knowing the strength of the social structure, man would not fight against the insurmountable, he would instead surrender to the destiny reason outlined for him.

What was the essence of modernity? Against Marx, Weber argued that a growing rationalisation of the social world, rather than capitalism *per se,* constituted the driving force of modernity. Capitalism is but one theatre among others where rationalism wins out; but rationalisation was immanent in emerging ideas of administration which were both challenging and coexisting with the ideology of the *rule of law* as well as outlining the conditions under which discretion in the rule of men was exercised.

> This whole process of rationalisation, in the factory as elsewhere, and especially in the bureaucratic state machine, parallels the centralisation of the material implements of organisation in the discretionary power of the overlord (1968: 39).

Nor was politics exempt. Rationalisation imbued politics, providing a mode of constitution and development for the modern state, creating a style of governmentality in which reason, rather than arbitrary discretion, was held out as the engine for decision-making.

Rationalisation was becoming all-pervasive; while rationalisation links with the development of capitalism it is not a subsection of capitalism.[3] It empowered technology

---

2   For once the gender specification is deliberate – modernity was, in large part, an order imagined and designed by men for men ... and women, in appropriate roles.

3   The modern state rises out of 'the expropriation of the autonomous and private bearers of executive power ... who in their own right possess the means of administration, warfare, and financial organisation ... The whole process is a complete parallel to the development of the capitalist enterprise through gradual expropriation of the independent producers' (1968: 29).

and weakened the human spirit, it dissociates mankind from the flows and natural rhythms of the pre-modern life. The process was hinted at in Hegel's and Marx's fear of alienation as the consequence of modernisation. Torn from settled existence in the routines of pre-industrial life, the modern person was in danger of becoming dissociated from the mystery of life, reconstituted as a rationalised machine. If rationalism succeeded, no faith in an other realm would be able to sustain our encounter with the structures of this life; they would need to become self-sustaining – capable of creating their own internal structures of meaning – or appear meaningless.

THE ELEMENTS OF RATIONALISATION

Rationalisation would dominate through three procedures:

(i) the *control of the world through calculation* and the collection and recording of information (through the growth of the technological attitude the world becomes the site of problems to be solved with the correct technology);[4]

(ii) the *systematisation of meaning and value* into an overall consistent scheme;

(iii) the methodological living of daily life according to *rules*. Rationality means following a rule, or an abstract moral principle, rather than acting on impulse, randomness or emotionality. Rationality means building up a logically consistent pattern linking our thoughts and actions and following this pattern to its conclusion. It means commitment to consistency in linking our words and actions, our aims and like activities; it entails creating an efficient ordering of means to ends.

As a consequence we faced an inevitable systematisation of belief, the elimination of logical inconsistencies, the disarming of the magical and mystical, and a movement away from particular or local patterns of thinking to more abstract or universal forms. This entailed the reduction of all individual instances of experience and of thought, whatever their diversity, to the status of general classes. Moreover, rationalisation demanded that we purge our ways of thinking and acting of forms that could not be justified on the basis of their anticipated consequences, themselves rationally justified by more universally defined ends and rendered predictable by generally valid empirical laws. Rationalisation denoted the systematisation of belief and action, but it also entailed the destruction and stifling of a great deal of the richness of human life. Our lives become radically divided into public and private spheres: 'The bureau is in principle separate from the private domicile of the official, and, in general, bureaucracy segregates official activity as something distinct from the sphere of private life'. The personal is distinct from the official: 'Public monies and equipment are divorced from the private property of the official', and 'the executive office is separated from the household, business from private correspondence, and business assets from private fortunes' (1970: 197). This

---

4   'The management of the modern office is based upon written documents (the 'files'), which are preserved ... [read and noted by] a staff of subaltern officials and scribes of all sorts' (1970: 197).

separation is a key feature, without which, along with the development of rational bookkeeping,[5] modern capitalism would not have been possible.[6]

In this 'complete de-personalisation of administrative management by bureaucracy', it is as if a commitment to pure methodology takes on an independent existence irrespective of any specific view of the world – Weber calls this commitment to calculability and technical administration, formal rationality. Calculative rationality emphasises the rationality of thought itself, and downplays the nature of the conduct or morality of the ends to be achieved – all that matters is that the appropriate 'logical train of reasoning' has been complied with. By contrast the pre-modern was embedded into ways of life and world-views that did not allow him/her to achieve the degree of independent distance necessary for formal rationality to take over. The tribal person who believed in demons and gods, who followed customs and traditions, may have been consistent in his/her thoughts, actions and beliefs. Subjectively positioned inside the pattern and structures of his/her beliefs, s/he is behaving in a rationally consistent fashion; this rationality Weber calls substantive. Under substantive rationality there are certain ideological positions, things and values which are simply accepted as true and fit a picture of the cosmos (world) so accepted. But we 'moderns', as a result of the processes of sceptical critique conducted by Hume and Kant, among others, argue that everything has to be subjected to the test of sceptical reason, and if something cannot survive rational testing then we reject those beliefs while committing ourselves to the methodology of reason itself. Rationality becomes something that dominates life; we must calculate, analyse, reduce.

THE NATION-STATE, LEGALITY AND THE RISE OF CAPITALISM

The emergence of modern rationality is closely linked to the development of capitalism as a mode of economic and social life and to the growth of the nation-state. 'It is the closed national state which afforded to capitalism its chance for development ... as long as the national state does not give place to a world empire capitalism will also endure' (Weber, 1966: 249). In his famous lecture *Politics as a Vocation* – in which Weber demands we look at the world in strictly realist terms and take responsibility for all the effects of our actions – he asks the question: 'but what is a political association from a sociological point of view?' His answer:

> Ultimately one can define the modern state sociologically only in terms of the specific means peculiar to it as to every political association, namely, the use of physical force. Every state is founded on force, said Trotsky. That is indeed right. If no social institution

---

5   Weber traces this to the device for striking a balance, invented by the Dutchman Simon Stevin in 1698 (Weber, 1966: 207).

6   Capitalism is a form of rationalisation: Not only does it provide a total social system but one in which calculable rules become known to all. 'The capitalist economy of the present day is an immense cosmos into which the individual is born ... It forces the individual, insofar as he is involved in the system of market relationships, to conform to capitalistic rules of action. The manufacturer who in the long run acts counter to these norms, will just as inevitably be eliminated from the economic scene as the worker who cannot or will not adapt himself to them will be thrown into the streets without a job' (1974: 54-5).

existed which knew the use of violence, then the concept of state would be eliminated, and a condition would emerge that could be described as anarchy in the specific sense of this word. Of course, force is certainly not the normal or the only means of the state – nobody says that – but force is a means specific to the state. Today the relation between the state and violence is an especially intimate one. In the past the most varied institutions have known the use of physical force as quite normal. Today, however, we have to say that a state is a human community that (successfully) claims the monopoly of the legitimate use of physical force within a given territory. Note that 'territory' is one of the characteristics of the state. Specifically, at the present time, the right to use physical force is ascribed to other institutions or to individuals only to the extent to which the state permits it. The state is considered the sole source of the 'right' to use violence. Hence, 'politics' for us means striving to share power or striving to influence the distribution of power, either among states or among groups within a state (1984: 32-33).

The modern state relies upon a specific form of domination, but when and why do men obey, and upon what inner justifications and upon what external means does this domination rest?[7]

FORMS OF LEGITIMATE DOMINATION

For Weber, coercion is fundamental to the power of the state, but there is no guarantee that power will be stable or effective if it is based on coercion alone. Weber coined the concept of *Herrschaft*, sometimes translated as 'imperative control', or 'leadership', but for which 'domination' seems the apt term, and Weber's particular idea of *legitime Herrschaft* implies legitimate command or authority. To maintain political authority, power based purely on physical force is both unstable and ineffective. It is important to achieve *legitimate* domination 'ie the probability that a command with a given specific content will be obeyed by a given group of persons'. Weber stresses the fact that the mere compliance with a command may be due to (i) habit;[8] or (ii) a belief in the legitimacy of the command; or (iii) considerations of expediency. In the modern state, the commands of the political elite rely not just on the readiness of the subjects to comply with the commands, but on reinforcement by a staff which ensures conformity to the commands, and which themselves may act on the basis of (i) habit; (ii) legitimacy; or (iii) self-interest. Thus, sociologically speaking, 'a *Herrschaft* is a structure of superordination and subordination, of leaders and led, rulers and ruled; it is based on a variety of motives and means of enforcement' (Editors' Notes, ES, I: 62). *Even legitimate domination is double-sided: it involves both legitimacy (authority) and force (coercion).* Weber proposes a model of three 'ideal types' of authority:

---

7   The 'inner justification' of the modern state is 'the belief in the validity of legal statute and functional competence based on rationally created rules' (Weber, 1970: 78-9). But the modern state is still 'a compulsory association which organises domination' (Weber, 1970: 82).

8   An important consideration for Weber's analysis of domination was discipline. Discipline was 'the probability that by virtue of habituation a command will receive prompt and automatic obedience in stereotyped forms, on the part of a given group of persons'. Weber specifies it 'includes the habituation characteristic of uncritical and unresisting mass obedience' (Weber, *Economy and Society*, 1978, I: 53). Further references to this text annotated as (ES, vol number: page number.)

(i) *Traditional authority* – which rests on an established belief in the sanctity of immemorial traditions and the legitimacy of the status of those exercising authority under them. This form of authority has been most widespread in the history of the world;

(ii) *Charismatic authority* – which rests on devotion to the specific and exceptional sanctity, heroism or exemplary character of an individual person, and of the normative patterns or order revealed or ordained by him.[9] This form was unstable and unpredictable; and

(iii) *Rational-legal authority* – which rests upon a claim to rational grounds, a belief in the 'legality' of patterns of normative rules, and the right of those elevated to authority under such rules to issue commands. This form was coming to predominate among modern western societies.[10]

Modernity saw the growth of rational-legal authority. Whereas for most of human existence the legitimacy of social systems had rested on traditional, magical or religious elements, modern society appeared to be founded on an authority which had itself become rational; that is, it was understood as a calculated form of social structuring, enabling the functional integrity of a society or social organisation. This in turn, Weber thought, depends upon:

1   A legal code that consists of legal norms which are established by agreement or by imposition, but which are accepted on grounds of expediency, or rational values, or both. This has a claim to the obedience of at least the crucial members of the corporate body, and usually claims the obedience of all members of the society or organisation.

2   A logically consistent system of abstract rules which are applied to particular cases. Thus social order exists within the limits laid down by legal precepts and follows principles which are capable of generalised formulation.

3   The typical person in authority occupies an 'office', which defines his or her responsibilities. This person, who is an official, even the elected president of the state, is also subject to the impersonal regulation of the law.

4   The person obeying authority does so only by virtue of his or her membership of the corporate group (that is, not on any personal basis) and what is obeyed is the law (rather than the person in authority).

5   Obedience is given to officials not as individuals, but to the impersonal order they represent. An administrative staff (that is, a bureaucracy) is formally charged with

---

9   'The term "charisma" will be applied to a certain quality of an individual personality by virtue of which he is considered extraordinary and treated as endowed with supernatural, superhuman, or at least specifically exceptional powers or qualities. These are such as are not accessible to the ordinary person, but are regarded as of divine origin or as exemplary, and on the basis of them the individual concerned is treated as a "leader"' (ES, I: 241).

10 Weber contrasted 'rational law' to 'Kadi-justice', or that justice which worked on the *ad hoc* basis of the perceived merits of an individual case. 'All non-bureaucratic forms of domination' involved elements of 'strict traditionalism' with a 'sphere of free arbitrariness and lordly grace' (1970: 217). Rationalised law is characterised by 'the rule of general and abstract norms' (*ibid*: 219).

looking after the interests of the corporate body within the limits of the law. The power of the state officials does not reside in them personally, but in their legal office.[11]

Law provides a formal framework which makes quite precise demands and if administered rationally ensures we can predict the outcome of our compliance and non-compliance with its demands. Hence this rational-legal framework enables the element of calculation in rational-legal authority.[12] Consistency in decision-making is crucial. As contrasted to a substantive law based on 'material principles', and a justice which would be substantial and thereby ad hoc, 'formalistic law is calculable' (Weber, 1966: 252). Law in turn requires the modern bureaucratic state to ensure the 'reliable formal guarantee of all contracts by the political authority' (1966: 249).[13]

Weber considered that the emergence of western forms of capitalism had given an immense stimulus to rational-legal authority and the calculative attitude. The predictability of relationships and outcomes required for capitalist interaction was enabled by the formally rational structure of legal domination in which 'specifically modern' discourses of rational calculation of the interests of the state surfaces. This is not to say that class interests were not both specific and differentially positioned *vis-à-vis* law. 'Ideas such as "state", "Church", "community", "party", or "enterprise"', which are claimed to be realised 'in a community', in reality provided 'an ideological halo for the master', being '*ersatz*' (1970: 199). In particular, 'the property-less masses especially are not served by a formal "equality before the law" and a "calculable" adjudication and administration, as demanded by "bourgeois" interests'. The lower classes demand 'substantive justice orientated toward some concrete instance and person' (1970: 220-1), while the bureaucratic mode of regulation creates an interest on behalf of the bureaucracy itself for the maintenance of its power via 'the canonisation of the abstract and "objective" idea of "reasons of state"' (1970: 220). A similar process overtook the general discourse of law which became subordinated to the demands of legal professionals.

THE PROBLEM OF LEGITIMACY IN MODERNITY – THE REASON FOR JURISPRUDENCE?

All social orders need legitimacy. Modernity is an historical epoch which emphasises rationality and knowledge and thus exhibits a greater demand for legitimacy than traditional action and authority.

---

11 'It is decisive for the specific nature of modern loyalty to an office that ... it does not establish loyalty to a person, like the vassal's or disciple's faith in feudal or in patrimonial relations of authority. Modern loyalty is devoted to impersonal and functional purposes' (Weber, 1970: 199).

12 'The characteristic principle of bureaucracy is the abstract regularity of the execution of authority, which is a result of the demand for "equality before the law" in the personal and functional sense – hence, the horror of "privilege" and the principled rejection of doing business "from case to case"' (Weber, 1970: 224).

13 Although Weber argued that bureaucracy was the most effective form of administration yet devised ('from a purely technical point of view ... the most rational known means of exercising authority'), he also saw it as 'a house of bondage'.

> The fates of human beings are not equal. Men differ in their states of wealth or social status or what not ... he who is more favoured feels the never-ceasing need to look upon his position as in some way 'legitimate', upon his advantage as 'deserved', and the other's disadvantage as being brought about by the latter's 'fault'. That the purely accidental causes of the difference may be ever so obvious makes no difference (ES, II: 953).

What can justify the rampant inequality apparent in modernity? The historical recourse to 'nature', and the customary position embedded in life flowing uninterrupted from the past, now becomes all too obviously contingent, fortuitous. Sociologically, social inequality in modernity is clearly related to class position[14] and access to political power and social status,[15] while *reason* – for example, philosophy and jurisprudence – undercuts and strives to replace the legitimacy of the past. Legitimacy is both an intellectual and practical issue: (i) it is the underlying structure of the analysis of the presently existing ways in which domination and obedience are created in actual historical situations – the sociological analysis of social order; and (ii) the need for legitimacy requires the production of discourses of legitimacy which take as their mandate the justification of the existing social order, or the reform of that order in specified ways.

While modern rational-formal law needs to be understood in its historical context, it is also crucial to recognise the uniqueness of modern legality. Legality enables a special kind of domination, one where domination comes to be exercised as if the dominated willed the conduct themselves. When 'the command is accepted as a "valid" norm', there is a special form of domination in play, specifically 'the situation in which the manifested will (command) of the ruler or rulers is meant to influence the conduct of one or more others (the ruled) and actually does influence it in such a way that their conduct to a socially relevant degree occurs as if the ruled had made the content of the command the maxim of their conduct for its very own sake' (ES, II: 946). Legitimate domination (*legitime Herrschaft*) requires two things: (i) a factual state and (ii) grounds of validity. Thus *the basis of legitimacy or 'validity' of any given order is both a matter of social fact: 'the probability that to a relevant degree the appropriate attitudes will exist' (ES, I: 214), and the obligatory and expressive character of the order itself.* The latter constitute the 'ultimate grounds of the validity of a domination' (ES, II: 953). The claim to legitimacy for an order is denoted by the obligatoriness of certain social activities. While custom, convention and general usage, as well as motives of self-interest, may generate regular patterns of behaviour, these are to be distinguished from the obligatory nature of actions in accordance with the norms of an established order.

> The validity of a given order means more than the mere existence of a uniformity of social action determined by custom or self-interest. If furniture movers regularly advertise at the same time many leases expire, this uniformity is determined by self-interest ... However, when a civil servant appears in his office daily at a fixed time, he does not act

---

14 Class denoted 'the typical probability of enjoying material and social benefits as a result of control over goods and skills and hence benefiting from the fact that these things can be used to produce an income within a given economic order' (ES, I: 312). Class was a matter of 'market situation' which determines what is now commonly referred to as 'life-chances'.

15 For Weber as well as the economic determination of life-chances there is determination by status. Status refers to the social determination of life-chances based upon the use and distribution of social prestige ('status honour').

only on the basis of custom or self-interest which he could disregard if he wanted to; as a rule, his action is also determined by the validity of an order (viz, the civil service rules), which he fulfils partly because disobedience would be disadvantageous to him but also because its violation would be abhorrent to his sense of duty ... The content of a social relationship [may] be called an order if the conduct is, approximately or on the average, orientated towards determinable 'maxims'. An order may be called 'valid' only when the orientation towards these maxims occurs, among other reasons, because it is in some appreciable way regarded by the actor as in some way obligatory or exemplary for him (ES, I: 31).

To understand law sociologically, Weber argues, we need to observe a pattern of action and appreciate the subjective meaning of the actors involved in the action. We need both an external and an internal perspective. Weber thus picks up Hegel's understanding that the social relations of a given era provide internal criteria for the moral imperatives in force in it, as well as the argument that the 'content' of any moral judgment is fully revealed only in understanding the context of the social network and determinations of the actual social-historical situation. Our knowledge will therefore need to consider a duality: the internality of action and the situation of that action within the vast picture of social development.

THE METHODOLOGY OF SOCIOLOGICAL UNDERSTANDING

The aim of intellectual enquiry is to understand the world, but we are of this world and there is no way of escaping to some neutral point to view the world. A sociology is needed, therefore, that will be a 'science concerning itself with the *interpretative understanding of social action* and thereby with a causal explanation of its course and consequences'. What makes human action social? A human action involves 'the acting individual attaching a subjective meaning to his behaviour', and the action is social 'insofar as its subjective meaning takes account of the behaviour of others and is thereby orientated in its course' (ES, I: 4).

The subject matter of sociology is human action and Weber stresses two features addressed in the above quotation: namely, social action (i) involves relating, dealing with and taking account of others; and (ii) the behaviour is orientated in its course, ie it is meaningful. How are we to understand this? Weber stressed an anti-positivist message: the meaning of action is never self-evident – there are no plain facts available for us solely to describe. All actions require interpretation. Much of the time we do the interpretation without realising it, relying upon our place in a tradition of interpretation. However, human sciences are inescapably interpretative and rely upon humans understanding the subjective position of (other) human actors. All actions have the particularity of the actor – which we can use our capacity of empathy to comprehend – and the universality of the context. All human actions are particular events; they can, however, also be placed in models which allow us to probe for the probability of regular occurrence. In science we are looking for predictable chains of events and, as an aid, we use three types of meaning: (i) the actually intended meaning of that concrete individual action; (ii) in looking at sociological mass phenomena we can construct the average of the meanings, or an approximation of the intended meaning; (iii) the meaning appropriate to a scientifically formulated pure type (an ideal type) of a common phenomenon. But would this knowledge be able to guide us into a richer world? Weber's answer was perplexing: modernity was to become disenchanted through this very pursuit of knowledge.

DISENCHANTMENT IS THE FATE OF A MODERNITY COMMITTED TO FREEDOM GUIDED THROUGH KNOWLEDGE

In the Enlightenment the appeal to reason – to rationality – was on behalf of the desire to be free. Freed from the bondage of false belief and the hierarchies of feudal society, humanity would enter into a new age of enlightened reason. Modernity should bring freedom – the liberation from the restraints of substantive rationality, freedom from the necessity to believe X because that is what your social group or society socialised you into believing. Freed from illusion we can choose our values, and develop new ones in the interaction with other individuals, cultures, and ways of life. This freedom of culture could mean the potentiality for a more varied and exciting world than any previously existing in history, but Weber was pessimistic; while wage labourers – who, together with their dependents, comprised the mass of the working class – would, in principle, be free to dispose of their labour on the open market, they are in fact situated in a network of compulsion and cannot escape the bars of a social structure which situates their life-experiences in spaces between the various factory sites making them puppets of the industrial mode of production. The Protestant's desires, whose patterns of subjectivity, Weber believed, had given a tremendous stimulus to the growth of capitalist modernity, were to live a life of meaning, but the modern industrial worker finds his work and life routines determined by the machines that constitute so much of the industrial complex.[16]

In one of the most memorable phrases coined to describe modern life, Weber claimed modern man would become trapped in a cage surrounded by iron bars of rationality. There were three crucial factors: (i) it is impossible to demonstrate any substantive meaning to the discourse of natural law; (ii) a disciplinary force was increasingly exerted upon mankind's everyday life creating routines determined by the structural demands of role and function; and (iii) our pursuit of knowledge cannot save us, instead we will move ever more into a spiral of activity-reflection-knowledge-technology-reaction-reflection. Man will be condemned to become a victim of

---

16 'The puritan wanted to work in a calling; we are forced to do so ... when asceticism was carried out of monastic cells into everyday life, and began to dominate worldly morality, it did its part in building the tremendous cosmos of the modern economic order. This order is now bound to the technical and economic conditions of machine production which today determine the lives of all the individuals who are born into this mechanism, not only those directly concerned with economic acquisition with irresistible force. Perhaps it will so determine them until the last ton of fossilised coal is burnt' (*The Protestant Ethic*, 1958: 181).

calculation upon calculation, trapped by rational necessity.[17] We sought reason to make us free, but we became its servants, condemned to its visions and to the outcomes it deems logical.[18]

WEBER ON THE FATE OF NATURAL LAW IDEOLOGY

'Nature' and 'reason' are the substantive criteria of what is legitimate from the standpoint of natural law. Both are regarded as the same, and so are the rules that are derived from them, so that general propositions about regularities of factual occurrences and general norms of conduct are held to coincide. The knowledge gained by human 'reason' is regarded as identical with the 'nature of things' or, as one would say nowadays, the 'logic of things'. The 'ought' is identical with the 'is', ie that which exists in the universal average (ES, II: 869).

It was clear to Weber that the separation of types of knowledge – a process illuminated by Hume and Kant among others – made it rationally impossible to believe in some necessary coincidence between 'a course of history' and a set of normative values. We can learn from history, but the stories history presents of the 'is' of our past are no proof of any 'ought'. Thus, Weber argued, there was no meaning, no goal or 'telos', that could objectively be 'found' in history. This was the 'fate' of 'an epoch which has eaten of the tree of knowledge' (Weber: [1904] 1949: 57). Similarly, nothing could be said by scientists about the foundation of value-judgments (1904; 1917).[19] Value (meaning) was

---

17 Contemporary scholars of the post-modern condition claim that 'the modern idea of a global rationality of social and personal life ended up disintegrating into a multiple of mini-rationalities at the service of a global, uncontrollable, and unaccountable irrationality' (Boaventura de Sousa Santos, 1991: 94). Thus Gellner (1987: 153) claims that Weber's idea of the trap of a cage of iron bars refers only to a particular stage of industrial capitalism, today, with a shrinking working week, the expansion of leisure, and with emphasis upon Cartesian thought diminishing, we are inhabiting a rubber cage. Santos replies: 'the rubber cage is still a cage' (1991: 102). Claus Offe (1987: 8) defines an important aspect of the post-modern condition as the simultaneous awareness of contingency and choice (thrust upon all) whilst the structural conditions of the macro-scale seem even further removed from being within human control: 'on the one hand nearly all factors of social, economic, and political life are contingent, elective, and gripped by change, while, on the other hand, the institutional and structural premises over which that contingency runs are simultaneously removed from the horizon of political, indeed, of intellectual choice'.

18 The pessimistic strand in Weber's analysis is taken up by the French writer Michel Foucault who blends Nietzsche and Weber to give us an image of our humanity being stripped away from us in the guise of knowledge and the rule of 'expertise'. The contemporary American philosopher Richard Rorty (1983: 164) comments: 'Foucault is doubtless right that the social sciences have coarsened the moral fibre of our rulers. Something happens to politicians who are exposed to endless tabulations of income levels, rates of recidivism, cost-effectiveness of artillery fire, and the like – something like what happens to concentration camp guards ... The rulers of the liberal democracies come to think that nothing matters but what shows up in the experts predictions. They cease to think of their fellow citizens as fellow citizens.'

19 Of course, Weber accepts that scientists could say that the reason (they proposed) why X thought in such a way was Y; social scientists can and must record what individuals and groups value; but they cannot state that this or that is intrinsically valuable, and, therefore, ought to be (universally) valued. Note: this does not mean Weber argues that values were unimportant. Far from it. In his classic paper, *The Meaning of Value Freedom in Sociology and Economics* (1917: 1-47), Weber demanded that the difference between reporting what one has observed (the 'facts' or interpretations), and evaluation should be clearly maintained. When someone expresses a value-judgment, they cannot argue that this is mere science: it is not. It is a policy recommendation and so on, it is a human assertion.

something we imposed on the world; it could not be scientifically verified. In the face of this relativism and subjectivity, we see more clearly that law is a specific technique of human domination:

> Legal positivism has, at least for the time being, advanced irresistibly. The disappearance of the old natural law conceptions has destroyed all possibility of providing the law with a metaphysical dignity by virtue of its immanent qualities. In the great majority of its most important provisions, it has been unmasked all too visibly, indeed, as the product or the technical means of a compromise between conflicting interests. (ES, II: 875)

Through legality we can create a particular configuration of reason – legal doctrine – with its own truth. Through its ability to manufacture rights and duties, liabilities and remedies, legality is the most suitable technique for modern rule. Law can create its own universe of sense and necessity. Thus law offers great liberating and enabling potential, but in its linkage with rational administration it can provide a dangerous combination: it encourages obedience. Weber goes on to warn:

> But this extinction of the metajuristic implications of the law is one of those ideological developments which, while they have increased scepticism towards the dignity of the particular rules of a concrete legal order, have also effectively promoted the actual obedience to the power, now viewed solely from an instrumental standpoint, of the authorities who claim legitimacy at the moment. Among the practitioners of the law this attitude has been particularly pronounced (ES, II: 875).

MODERN DISCIPLINE AND THE ROUTINES OF EVERYDAY LIFE

In the absence of any legitimate telos or overriding expressionist meaning to social life what would provide individuals with meaningful existence? Weber thought that everyday life would be dominated by the functional roles in the structures of the economic system. A person's daily routines would be shaped by the freedoms which their role allowed, and their hopes and dreams would be a reflection of their education and the specific cultural pressures to which their class was subjected. For those whose structural position allowed them freedom from the drudgery of industrial production, there is the trap of the dominant social rationality – a constant search for effectiveness in task completion, and the pursuit of momentary success[20] – and the only non-structural happiness Weber foresaw lay in the anti-rational spaces. The individual would find solace in personal relationships, romantic love and escapist music, experience of art, and cultivation of a limited private sphere, as this-worldly escapes from institutional routines. The overall picture Weber drew of the future of the human condition was pessimistic: the only hope was that we could sustain a will not to be ruled like sheep – but this was doubtful.

Nowhere was Weber's gloom more evident than in his concept of *disciplinisation*. For Weber the control of individuals in modern society was increasingly a matter of

---

20 ' ... man is dominated by the making of money, by acquisition as the ultimate purpose of his life. Economic acquisition is no longer subordinated to man as the means for the satisfaction of his material means. The reversal of what we should call the natural relationship, so irrational from a naive point of view, is evidently as definitely a leading principle of capitalism as it is foreign to all peoples not under capitalistic influence' (PE, 53).

discipline – an adherence to the norm and an internal attitude of restraint and foresight. Two institutional orders, the monastery and the army, had provided the original sites for the development of techniques of discipline which had spread throughout the social order with the rise in the industrial complex. The monastic orders of medieval Europe had provided a life lived under normative structures of rigorous diets and timetabled regularities which subordinated passion to will, and which separated desires of the soul from those of the flesh. For Weber the Protestant ethic (spirit) transferred this culture to the wider society. The army was the original focus of secular social discipline, whereby large bodies of men were moulded into a disciplined unit by personal habituation and bureaucratic demand systems.[21] Weber warned that our individuality was becoming increasingly stripped from us as we were disciplined into a society of mass conformity.

MODERNITY INVOLVES A COMMITMENT TO RATIONAL KNOWLEDGE BUT WE CAN HAVE NO KNOWLEDGE OF THE DEEPEST FOUNDATIONS OR OF VALUES; HENCE THE PARADOX OF MODERNITY IS THAT IT IS COMMITMENT TO KNOWLEDGE, BUT KNOWLEDGE CANNOT TELL US THE MEANING OF LIFE, NOR, ULTIMATELY, WHAT IT IS MEANINGFUL TO DO

The fate of an epoch which has eaten of the tree of knowledge is that it must know that we cannot learn the meaning of the world from the results of its analysis, be it ever so perfect; it must rather be in a position to create the meaning itself. It must recognise that general views of life and the universe can never be the products of increasing empirical knowledge, and that the highest ideas, which move us most forcefully, are always formed only in the struggle with other ideas which are just as sacred to others as ours are to us (*Methodology of the Social Sciences*, 1949: 57).

The pursuit of true knowledge which the Enlightenment unleashed in a truly critical way undercuts all forms of foundationalism. When we engage in reflexivity we realise the impossibility of coming to an empirical knowledge of the totality of the world or gauge its meaning, yet we are committed to the calculative outlook as if we could know

---

21 'Military discipline gives birth to all discipline. The large-scale economic organisation is the second great agency which trains men for discipline ...

... military discipline is the ideal model for the modern capitalist factory, as it was for the ancient plantation. However, organisational discipline in the factory has a completely rational basis. With the help of suitable methods of measurement, the optimum profitability of the individual worker is calculated like that of any material means of production ...

... The psycho-physical apparatus of man incompletely adjusted to the demands of the outer world, the tools, the machines – in short, it is functionalised, and the individual is shorn of his natural rhythm as determined by his organism; in line with the demands of the work procedure, he is attuned to a new rhythm through the functional specialisation of muscles and through the creation of an optimal economy of physical effort. The whole process of rationalisation, in the factory as elsewhere, and especially in the bureaucratic state machine, parallels the centralisation of the material implement of organisation in the hands of the master. Thus discipline inexorably takes over ever larger areas as the satisfaction of political and economic needs is increasingly rationalised. This universal phenomenon more and more restricts the importance of charisma and of individually differentiated conduct' (ES, II: 1156).

everything.[22] Mystery ensues; but we cannot call it that. Life is, instead, simply a series of problems to be solved.

THE PARADOX OF RATIONALISM

Modernity is thereby subject to a strange over-determination; it dreams a greater rationality than it can achieve. Life in the iron cage is dangerously irrational.

The survival of the irrational

To put Weber's point in more post-modern terms, the grand narrative of enlightenment (for example in Hegel) was that a fully rational society would result in social order and peace. But while the search for a full societal rationality gave us procedure and rational calculation, it was founded upon a myth. The myth was the idea that everything was in principle knowable, while in 'truth' we could never know it all. Weber is ambiguously celebrating the creation of a modernity structured by 'modernised' – ie rationalised – social practices, occupied by disciplined social selves who will carry out the demands of the social structure and the commands of the rulers. Weber is ambiguous in that he both describes a process and indicates there is very little we can do about it, while the whole edifice is based on weak foundations. Specifically – and as others have subsequently put it – the whole looks like a gigantic machine, but the machine has a ghost in it: the ghost is the subjectivity of humanity. If the metaphysics of life could not be understood, a whole set of desires and concerns of the individual agent could not be contained in this model: 'Increasing intellectualisation and rationalisation do not, therefore, indicate an increasing general knowledge of the conditions under which one lives'. On the one hand, we become pawns of the process of 'knowability' and 'mastery through calculation'; and in giving us this message Weber presaged a tendency of his times which we can now see – looking back from our current position with the 'benefit' of having seen the Holocaust and the camps of Stalin – reflected fear of the fate of individuality in a society dominated by calculation, mass consumption and mass standardisation. But, on the other hand, Weber left just enough space for unpredictable, or irrational forces, to ensure that an element of instability was built into his idea of this developing rational machine so that some 'hope' could be preserved. A key element was charisma.

The appeal of the charismatic

Since it is 'extra-ordinary', charismatic authority is sharply opposed to rational, and particularly bureaucratic authority, and to traditional authority, whether in its patriarchal,

---

22 Weber is specific: 'increasing intellectualism and rationalism do not ... indicate an increased and general knowledge of the conditions under which one lives. It means something else, namely, the knowledge or belief that if one wished one could learn it at any time.' As a result the sense of wonderment inherent in the magical and religious outlooks is lost in favour of the dryly calculative. 'It means there are no mysterious incalculable forces that come into play but rather that one can, in principle, master all things by calculation' (1949: 139). But while this is the case in principle, in reality calculation is always occurring with the knowledge at hand. It must remain incomplete and pragmatic. The totality is a mystery.

patrimonial, or estate variants, all of which are everyday forms of domination; while the charismatic type is the direct antithesis of this (ES, I: 244).

In radical contrast to bureaucratic organisation, charisma knows no formal and regulated appointment or dismissal, no career, advancement or salary, no supervisory or appeals body, no local or purely technical jurisdiction, and no permanent institutions in the manner of bureaucratic agencies, which are independent of the incumbents and their personal charisma. Charisma is self-determined and sets its own limits. Its bearer seizes the task for which he is destined and demands that others obey and follow him by virtue of his mission. If those to whom he feels sent do not recognise him, his claim collapses; it they recognise him, he is their master as long as he 'proves' himself. However, he does not derive his claims from the will of his followers, in the manner of an election; rather, it is their duty to recognise his charisma ... Charismatic authority is naturally unstable (ES, II: 1112-14).

Modern society produces radically new dangers; while rationalisation and formalisation bespeak mastery and control, there is a dialectic of irrationality. Specifically, Weber hints at images of (i) the mass of citizens whose disciplined subjectivity fits into the demands of rational administration; buttressed by (ii) a system of all-embracing law, which, however, is a formal structure without any need for substantive content (modern law can have any content); but this rational edifice (iii) contains an underbelly of irrationality, with the ever-present potentiality of charisma to break the routines of the structure. Weber is ambiguous concerning charisma. Charisma is unpredictable; it is a disruptive force leading to unascertainable consequences.

FOUNDING A SCIENCE OF LAW

Modern law – ie legal positivism – is a particular technique of domination involving rationalisation and formalisation. At the basis of modern law is human willing.[23] Perhaps the best interpretation of Weber's sociology of law has been provided by Kronman (1983). As Kronman reads him, Weber's analysis is prefaced by two assumptions: (i) human actions are informed by the purposes and intentions of the actors; (ii) the ends pursued by the agents are not in any way dictated to them by nature – rather they are chosen or willed by the agents. They are in essence 'irrational' products of the will. As a consequence legal analysis concerns itself with material which has legal meaning identifiable via 'the logical analysis of meaning', or 'the abstract interpretation of meaning'. Only the analysis of a primitive legal system – which, by definition, involves only a limited range of social possibilities – could use an 'external test' based upon 'extrinsic elements' or 'sense-data characteristics'. With an advanced legal system the analysis would require one to consider all the circumstances that surround the (legally relevant) act, as well as the consequences that flow from it and which determine its legal relevancy; in short the modern legal analysis considers the agent's purposes and intentions. Of course the agent is situated in a structure. The nature and structure of modern legal thought tends towards formalisation; that is, it displays a concern with classification and representation, with the drawing of boundaries, and the reduction of

---

23   In the German tradition, from Schopenhauer onwards, the creation of goodness is an act of willing.

social phenomena to legal concepts in a process which aims to make a (legal) reality which is both intelligible and manageable.[24]

And what of the fate of law? There will be 'a continuous growth of the technical elements in the law and hence of its character as a specialists' domain'. It will become more and more apparent that 'law is a highly technical apparatus, which is continually transformable in the light of expediential considerations and devoid of all sacredness of content' (ES, II: 895). Law, also, and rather conversely, becomes flexible. Nothing is, in principle, beyond its structures and procedures. Cast adrift from any ideological need to link it to an ascertainable natural reality, law can create its own reality, or invest a new status of reality upon previously accepted notions of natural reality (such as conferring participatory rights to women and members of ethnic minorities).

THE OPENNESS OF LAW'S TRUTH AND LAW'S CREATIVITY

Modern law is paradoxical because it allows openness[25] – and is thereby enabling – while it is definitely a technique of restraint. The paradigm of the criminal law – in that all and any behaviour could be criminalised or decriminalised, penalised or de-penalised – merely expresses, albeit in clear cut terms, the idea of boundary drawing and transgression at the root of legality. The processes of formalisation and rationalisation inherent in modern law render it entirely suitable for ordering procedures of representation and classification, boundary drawing and social valuation. The technique of classification orders certain phenomena – possibly at the bequest of political orders – by the construction of legal concepts that represent certain aspects of the world. The process of classification does not merely reflect and name entities of the world, it (re)presents them for (new) rationality, it presents something which is not naturally like that to our sensibilities in some or other form where now have to accept that this is the way it is. The process of classification may, for example, involve selecting out a specific group from the community and subjecting them to a particular regime of legal and social meaning. Classification constitutes boundaries, it renders (some) phenomena of the world as different, others similar (of the same class), enabling difference and equality. At the same time the process of formalisation can be reductive; it makes the openness of social reality intelligible and manageable by reducing reality to one or a few decisive qualities. Through these techniques modern law can constitute its own truth, and help create a new social 'truth'.

---

24 'A collection of concrete rules and decisions, no matter how numerous, can never produce a comprehensive legal system. To achieve comprehensiveness, principles having a high degree of generality must be employed: only in this way can a legal order acquire the scope needed to cover all imaginable situations in a gapless fashion. These general principles are themselves the products of a process of abstract or 'reduction', as Weber calls it: they are arrived at by reducing 'the reasons relevant in the decision of concrete individual cases to one or more "principles", ie legal propositions'. Consequently, if a type of legal thought discourages abstraction, it must also impede the formulation of those general principles that a true legal system requires for its construction' (Kronman, 1983: 90).

25 A central focus is the critique of tradition in that the idea of repealability, ie legal contingency, is fundamental to the operation of legal positivism. The law-making process is such that so long as the 'law' has gone through the correct process of creation it can have any content; thus the content can be changed tomorrow. There is no sacredness to the substance of (legal positivist) law.

PART TWO
FRIEDRICH NIETZSCHE (1844–1900): RADICAL MODERN OR THE PROPHET OF THE POST-MODERN?

And do you know what 'the world' is to me? Shall I show it to you in my mirror? This world: a monster of energy, without beginning, without end; an immovable, brazen enormity of energy, which does not grow bigger or smaller, which does not expend itself but only transforms itself ... enclosed by 'nothingness' as by a boundary ... as energy throughout, as a play of energies and waves of energy at the same time one and many, increasing here and at the same time decreasing there; a sea of energies flowing and rushing together, eternally moving, eternally flooding back, with tremendous years of recurrence, with an ebb and a flood of its forms; out of the simplest form striving towards the most complex, out of the stillest, most rigid, coldest form towards the hottest, most turbulent, most self-contradictory, and then out of this abundance returning home to the simple, out of the play of contradiction back to the joy of unison, still affirming itself in this uniformity of its courses and its years, blessing itself as that which must return eternally, as a becoming that knows no repletion, no satiety, no weariness – this my Dionysian world of the eternally self-creative, the eternally self-destructive, this mystery world of the two-fold delight, this my 'beyond good and evil', without aim, without will, unless a ring feels goodwill towards itself – do you want a name for this world? A solution for all your riddles? A light for you too, you best concealed, strongest, least dismayed, most midnight men? – This world is the will to power – and nothing beside! And you yourself are also this will to power – and nothing beside! (from *The Will to Power* notebooks of 1884–1886.)

INTRODUCTION TO FRIEDRICH NIETZSCHE: PHILOSOPHER OF THE POST-MODERN CONDITION

Friedrich Nietzsche has become the most controversial writer/philosopher read in this century.[26] Until relatively recently, in the Anglo-American world his writings were

---

26 Friedrich Nietzsche was born in Saxony in 1844 and had a short academic career of extreme brilliance as a classical scholar, becoming a full professor in his mid-twenties. He gave up his university career suffering from ill-health and the reception of colleagues to his writings and became a lonely writer, often residing in cheap lodging houses in the Swiss mountains. He turned out an amazing stream of writing over the next 16 years, mostly either short books or books of essays and aphorisms, for example, *The Birth of Tragedy; Human All Too Human; The Gay Science; Beyond Good and Evil; The Genealogy of Morals;* and his most popular, *Thus Spoke Zarathustra.* He was for a time a friend of the German composer Richard Wagner but came to dislike him and to believe the powerful romanticism of Wagner's music was a dangerous incitement to anti-human values.

Nietzsche became convinced of the need to destroy previous value systems and is most famous for his 'death of God' writings, by which he meant that the foundations of our previous intellectual and moral systems had been destroyed, while we were still living as if the world made sense. He was desperately working on a 'transvaluation of all previous values' but was plagued by ill-health and in 1899 collapsed in mental illness, probably caused by tertiary syphilis, perhaps caught on the few occasions he visited prostitutes when on a brief spell of military service in his youth. He remained insane until his death in 1900. Nietzsche warned of nihilism overtaking Europe and has become the philosopher of the post-modern condition.

treated as abstract literature and he was regarded as the champion of those who declared the 'death of God' or the advent of nihilism, as well as accepted as the adopted philosopher of Nazi Germany: 'a raving, ranting anti-Semitic, pro-Aryan irrationalist'.[27]

However, whilst prophesying that nihilism could overtake modernity, Nietzsche demanded that we reconsider the basis of our values and develop a new social imagination. In his early writings, Nietzsche looked to the depths of Greek tragedy and the ideas of Schopenhauer (a pessimistic scholar who emphasised the power of human will and argued that a universality of will underlay the diverse phenomena we observed) and the composer Richard Wagner. Against their tragic visions, Nietzsche came to advocate that life should be affirmed; men had to have the courage to face things as they truly were and not deny or reject aspects of reality. His injunction can be misinterpreted, and it is true that Nietzsche transformed the central idea of the German philosophical tradition – that of will – into a demand to harness what he came to call *the will to power* towards a constant striving for greatness, which the Nazis adopted as a guiding principle. Nietzsche, however, was a bitter opponent of the mass psychology used by the Nazis and of the utilitarian structure which underpinned their 'final solution' to 'the Jewish problem'; he would have castigated the entire movement as 'herd-mentality/morality'. This is not to argue that Nietzsche could sit easily in some liberalist, humanist tradition. Far from it. Nietzsche favoured a radical modernisation; there are many frightening sections in his writings. Nietzsche himself argued that all entities in the world required interpretation – there were no such things as *plain facts* – and his own ideas are disquieting, disturbing, obscure, open to multiple interpretations and often contradictory.[28] Among his ideas which have provoked extreme reactions are those of the will to power as the basic drive of humanity; the impossibility of reaching truth; the statement that there are no plain facts, or non-interpretative statements or entities, in the world; that God is dead; that religion is a means by which some individuals dominate others and an ideological lens through which people avoid subjecting the real world to radical interrogation; the idea of the superman or overman (a radical individual who subjects himself to exacting self-analysis and self-control); the need to breed a new individual for modern conditions; ambiguous writings concerning war; that morality is a means by which the oppressed generalise their resentment ... there are numerous others.

Nietzsche's writings evoke a variety of moods and impressions. Weber had read Nietzsche and breathed much the same intellectual air; but while Weber foresaw a

---

27　To quote Alexander Nehamas (1985: vii) on his image of Nietzsche before he began to read him seriously.

28　Nietzsche often penned aphorisms which appeared to propose differing positions. Nietzsche understood that his writings often argued for contradictory positions, claiming that a man as 'big' as himself could live with his own contradictions! Other commentators have taken this as proof of incoherence or, as in the case of Walter Kaufmann as evidence of an experimental style of writing: 'Nietzsche is ... not a system-thinker, but a problem-thinker ... [Nietzsche espouses] experimentalism ... the goodwill to accept new evidence and to abandon previous positions, if necessary' (Kaufmann, 1974: 86). Kaufmann, who was the first to 'rehabilitate' Nietzsche for the Anglo-American world, unduly tames Nietzsche, trying to find in this principle of 'experimentalism' a unifying theme which we can use to understand him. Nietzsche believed the world could not be subjected to any one interpretation, hence there is no one interpretation of his own writings.

disenchantment of the world as it secularised, and saw individuals as trapped in the iron cage of rationality, Nietzsche emphasised the need to go beyond such reflections and re-create. Modernity had yet to become truly modern; social philosophy and ethics had not yet became fully reflexive. Modernity had 'killed God', but humanity had not fully secularised; Europeans still lived amidst the products of previous systems of thought – systems which were founded upon religious traditions containing ideas of some transcendental authority – at the same time as modern rationality undercut the beliefs underlying those values. Nietzsche portrayed the cosmos not as ultimately a coherent rational structure but as an enormous flux of power(s) where we were lonely souls. All we had was our will to power; we were our will to power.

In describing modernity as a tumultuous mixture of a multitude of forces in which deconstruction and construction, liberty and discipline, freedom and constraint, were intertwined, Nietzsche celebrated the open possibilities. Nature did not contain sets of values to be imposed upon us, hence the entire world – including human projects – was but a play of forces. Life was recast in terms of a vast cosmic adventure; the script was not written, but to be made and re-made as we journey.

Nietzsche has become a fashionable philosopher as modernity has moved into the period of late-modernity or post-modernity. Two features of his relevance to jurisprudence are obvious: (i) his perspectivism and insistence on interpretation is a fertile source of ideas for contemporary interpretative arguments in critical legal theory – as an enterprise law relies upon a range of texts;[29] (ii) his radicalising of the institutional imagination of modernity throws up a host of questions and issues.

Nietzsche is not an easy writer to summarise, and there are many themes contained in his writings. In large part it is best to let his unique style of writing tell the story.

PROBLEMATISING TRUTH

> What then is truth? A movable host of metaphors, metonymies, and anthropomorphisms: in short, a sum of human relations which have been poetically and rhetorically intensified, transferred, and embellished, and which, after long usage, seem to a people to be fixed, canonical, and binding. Truths are illusions which we have forgotten are illusions; they are metaphors that have become worn out and have been drained of sensuous force, coins which have lost their embossing and are now considered as metal and no longer as coins (*On Truth and Lies in a Non-moral Sense*, 1873).

Perhaps one of the most disturbing of Nietzsche's arguments has been his open pragmatism concerning truth. 'Truth' is a function of the processes by which an answer is arrived at, it is a unit of representation of a world which consists of many different and conflicting flows of energy, always escaping our attempts to gain an 'accurate vision'. All 'truths' are partial, a product of a methodology, but they have pragmatic effects; they may be useful for some or other purpose, have some or other effect. We must pursue truth, yet there are unsettling consequences – truth is dangerous. The truth of today

---

29 Thus we can learn from treating law as literature; indeed one commentator (Dworkin, 1986) goes as far as suggesting that the development of the common law is to be seen as writing a chain-novel.

proves the truth of yesterday wrong – similarly, the truth we will produce or find tomorrow will 'prove' our current 'truth' wrong. A society may only have as much truth as it can stand. If the 'masses' knew the truth of 'truth', would they be able to stand it?

ON PERSPECTIVISM

In prison – my eyes, however strong or weak they may be, can see only a certain distance, and it is within the space encompassed by this distance that I live and move, the line of this horizon constitutes my immediate fate, in great things and small, from which I cannot escape. Around every being there is described a similar concentric circle, which has a mid-point and is peculiar to him. Our ears enclose us within a comparable circle, and so does our sense of touch. Now, it is by these horizons, within which each of us encloses his senses as if behind prison walls, that we measure the world, we say that this is near and that far, this is big and that small, this is hard and that soft: this measuring we call sensation – and that is all of it an error! According to the average quantity of experiences and excitations possible to us at any particular point of time one measures one's life as being short or long, poor or rich, full or empty: and according to the average human life one measures that of all other creatures – all of it an error! If our eyes were a hundred-fold sharper, man would appear to us tremendously tall; it is possible, indeed, to imagine organs by virtue of which he would be felt as immeasurable. On the other hand, organs could be so constituted that whole solar systems were viewed contracted and packed together like a single cell: and to beings of an opposite constitution a cell of the human body could present itself, in motion, construction and harmony, as a solar system. The habits of our senses have woven us into lies and deception of sensation: these again are the basis of all our judgments and 'knowledge' – there is absolutely no escape, no backway or bypath into the real world! We sit within our net, we spiders, and whatever we may catch in it, we can catch nothing at all except that which allows itself to be caught in precisely our net (*Daybreak*, 1881).

Our image of reality is the consequence of the material we use to see it. *Perspectivism* is Nietzsche's argument that each and every view is one among many possible interpretations. Of course this is a subject to the paradox of reflexivity: specifically it is an interpretation, therefore the view that each and every view is only one among many possible interpretations is itself only one among many possible interpretations. That difficulty is more logical than real, in that perspectivism is both an interpretation and an understanding of the nature of the general context. To his opponents this looks like the path to meaninglessness, or nihilism. But Nietzscheanism denotes, rather, self-conscious interpretation and creativity. Perspectivism has consequences for all accounts of knowledge but there are obvious applications to the understanding of legal texts and legal material (decisions, professional relations). Perspectivism holds there are no independent facts (in the sense of facts that do not need themselves to be interpreted) against which the various interpretations can be compared so that we can agree on which interpretation is 'correct'. In this case, the task of making sense of processes or sets of institutions, such as the legal system, or reading texts, such as legal texts, may be a question of obeying certain methodological rules and/or imposing order among many possible interpretations and purposes.

COMBINING ONTOLOGICAL FLUX WITH PERSPECTIVISM ENABLES US TO SEE THAT KNOWLEDGE WORKS AS A TOOL OF POWER

If Nietzsche's views on truth, and the make-up of the cosmos, are combined with perspectivism, we get an important thesis of radical pragmatism which announces that we can shape reality, we can form ourselves and our social structures in a continual process of destruction and reconstruction. This means knowledge is a distinct tool of power. We have 'in us a power to order, simplify, falsify, artificially distinguish' (*Will to Power*, n 517); 'knowledge works as a tool of power' (*ibid*: n 614). Our knowledge is not the result of the world revealing itself to us; rather it is a mode of power in which we impose order on the multiplicity of the self and the world, rendering the self and the world manageable and comprehensible. Knowledge is a tool of life.

ON THE UNCONSCIOUS, AND THE NEED TO CONDUCT A GENEALOGY OF MORALITY[30]

At least among us immoralists today there is arising a suspicion that the decisive value of an action is precisely in what is not intentional in it; that all its intentionality, everything that can be seen, known, made conscious in it belongs only to its surface, its skin which, like any skin, reveals something but conceals even more! In short, we believe that intent is only a symbol and symptom, requiring interpretation; furthermore that it is a symbol which signifies too much and consequently means little if nothing by itself; that morality in the old sense, ie morality of intent, was a prejudice, a premature, perhaps a preliminary thing; something in the order of astrology or alchemy, but in any event something which must be surpassed ... this may be taken to be the name for that long secret labour which is in store for the subtlest, most candid, also most malicious consciences of today. They are the living touchstones of the soul! (Beyond Good and Evil, 1886, sec 32)

It is sometimes thought that Freud discovered the unconscious; however, the idea was relatively common among intellectuals in the 19th century and Freud was almost certainly more in debt to Nietzsche than he ever admitted. Nietzsche implies we must not be fooled by claims to rationality; beneath apparent rationality lies irrationality. Behind the reason of the law lies unreason. Dig beneath the surface of civilisation and one finds a mass of conflicting emotions and desires. Reason imposes order; but the specificity of reason is actually adherence to a tradition.

Nietzsche argued that there were four moral traditions of western civilisation: Christian morality, secular morality (constituted in the work of moral philosophers such as Kant), the ordinary everyday morality of the mass of mankind (which Nietzsche dismissed as 'herd' values), and the pre-Socratic values. Each tradition had been compromised. The Christian tradition by its softness – through its injunctions to turn the other cheek, to demonstrate compassion for the weak[31] – which lowers life.

---

30 Genealogy is a form of historical or psychological explanation of moral practices in which we search for their origins and practical effects.

31 To show honest compassion is a virtue of the superman, but compassion is only valuable when it is real; not the product of socialisation or community practice.

Nietzsche argued that Christ may have been a powerful figure, willing to espouse his own values even in the face of death, but the established Churches were institutions which furthered the interests of those who could not stand on their own feet. Compassion and sympathy are not wrong in themselves; rather they are dangerous when they are institutionalised to protect and support weak people, thus denying the person the need creatively to affirm his being for himself. Secular moralities unjustly universalise from particular cases. All appeals to general values are ruled out of court by Nietzsche as appeals to common values, that is reducing the question of values to the lowest common denominator. Instead society should be geared to bring out the greatness of the individual. One could look back to pre-classical Greece. There, Nietzsche discerned a golden age of vitality, strength, tragedy and beauty, a world of spontaneity and goodwill, which became compromised by the Socratic demand to use reason and communication. Since that time we have been told that our institutions ought to be legitimated by their ability to embody reason; Nietzsche believed their only real defence ought to be an ability to affirm life. He believed that if we subjected our institutions to a genealogy of interests we would see the real processes at work underlying 'moral' claims. In chilling terms Nietzsche related that a great deal of moral discourse had been influenced by the resentment of the weak, it had been created by the losers in life in order to place restraints upon the strong, upon the victors, who ought to reject traditional morality in favour of creating new values for themselves.

ON THE DIFFICULTY OF GIVING A SIMPLE DEFINITION OR EXPLANATION OF SOCIAL INSTITUTIONS

Yet a word on the origin and the purpose of punishment – two problems that are separate, or ought to be separate; unfortunately, they are usually confounded. How have previous genealogists of morals set about solving these problems? Naively, as has always been their way; they seek out some 'purpose' in punishment, for example, revenge or deterrence, then guilelessly place this purpose at the beginning as *causa fiendi* of punishment, and – have done. The 'purpose of law' however, is absolutely the last thing to employ in the history of the origin of law; on the contrary, there is for historiography of any kind no more important proposition than the one it took such effort to establish but which really ought to be established now, the cause of the origin of a thing and its eventual utility, its actual employment and place in a system of purposes, lie worlds apart; whatever exists, having somehow come into being, is again and again reinterpreted to new ends, taken over, transformed, and redirected by some power superior to it; all events in the organic world are subduing, and becoming master, and all subduing and becoming master involves a fresh interpretation, an adaptation through which previous 'meaning' and 'purpose' are necessarily obscured or even obliterated. However well one has understood the utility of any physiological organ (or of a legal institution, a social custom, a political usage, a form in art or in a religious cult), this means nothing regarding its origin; however uncomfortable and disagreeable this may sound to older ears – for one had always believed that to understand the demonstrable purpose, the utility of a thing, a form, or an institution, was also to understand the reason why it originated – the eye being made for seeing, the hand being made for grasping.

Thus one also imagined that punishment was devised for punishing. But purposes and utilities are only signs that a will to power has become master of something less powerful and imposed upon it the character of a function; and the entire history of a 'thing', an organ, a custom can in this way be a continuous sign-chain of ever new interpretations and adaptations whose causes do not even have to be related to one another but, on the contrary, in some cases succeed and alternate with one another in a purely chance fashion. The 'evolution' of a thing, a custom, an organ is thus by no means its progress toward a goal, even less a logical progress by the shortest route and with the smallest expenditure of force – but a succession of more or less profound, more or less mutually independent processes of subduing, plus the resistances they encounter, the attempts at transformation for the purpose of defence and reaction, and the results of successful counteractions. The form is fluid, but the 'meaning' is even more so (*On the Genealogy of Morals*, 1887, sec 12).

Social institutions are over-determined sites; there are multiple processes at work.

ON THE NEED TO CHANGE THE DESTINY AND THE TYPE OF HUMAN

The problem I thus pose is not what shall succeed mankind in the sequence of living beings (man is an end), but what type of man shall be bred, shall be willed, for being higher in value, worthier of life, more certain of a future. Even in the past this higher type has appeared often – but as a fortunate accident, as an exception, never as something willed (*The Antichrist*, 1888).

It is only as an aesthetic phenomenon that the being of man and the world are eternally justified (*The Birth of Tragedy*, 1872).

What is the significance of this? Consider a statement from Hart (1961) in *The Concept of Law* criticising Austin: ' ... the operation of a *promise* ... in many ways is a far better model than that of coercive orders for understanding ... features of law.' Nietzsche would simply ask: 'How does the capacity to make promises come about?'

To breed an animal with the right to make promises – is not this the paradoxical task that nature has set itself in the case of man? Is not it the real problem regarding man?

But how many things this presupposes! To ordain the future in advance in this way, man must first have learned to distinguish necessary events from chance ones, to think causally, to see and anticipate distant eventualities as if they belong to the present, to decide with certainty what is the goal and what the means to it, and in general be able to calculate and compute. Man must first of all have become *calculable, regular, necessary*, even in his own image of himself, if he is to be able to stand security for *his own future*, which is what one who promises does!

This precisely is the long story of how responsibility originated. The task of breeding an animal with the right to make promises evidently embraces and presupposes as a preparatory task that one first makes men to a certain degree necessary, uniform, like among like, regular, and consequently calculable (both quotes from *On the Genealogy of Morals*, 1887, 'Second Essay: Guilt, Bad Conscience and the Like').

While the finest men were those who gave themselves commands for themselves to obey, the mass of men were being turned into controlled and disciplined selves for a society of mass consumption and mass standardisation. What was the context for this process?

ON THE HOMELESSNESS OF MODERN MAN

We who are homeless – among Europeans today there is no lack of those who are
entitled to call themselves homeless in a distinct and honourable sense: it is to them that I
especially commend my secret wisdom and gay science ... We children of the future
how could we be at home in this today? We feel disfavour for all ideas that might lead
one to feel at home even in this fragile, broken time of transition ... The ice that still
supports people today has become very thin; the wind that brings the thaw is blowing;
we ourselves who are homeless constitute a force that breaks open ice and other all too
thin 'realities' (*The Gay Science*, 1887, n 377).

Modernity is not a stable Kantian ship with a pilot certain of his bearings. We are on an
unknown sea and many of us are seasick. The masses long for simplicity and certainties;
the true intellectual finds himself alone. All around is mediocrity and short-termism.[32]
The masses long for romantic escapism, as provided by the music of Wagner.[33] But,
Nietzsche warns, there will be a terrible price to pay if we fail to confront the reality of
the world of blood and will to power, or if we do not develop self-control, self-
direction, and attain values which derive not from personal weakness but personal
strength. If we fail to adopt the ethics of radical self-determination, we will become
mere units of the herd. Nietzsche demanded a society of radical individualism, as he
foresaw a society of herd obedience. If the Nazis appropriated him as their official
philosopher, Nietzsche actually warned of their coming.

---

32 Nietzsche coined his own categorical imperative – that of the eternal recurrence – to counter this. We
    ought to live and make decisions that we could live with forever, as if we were doomed to repeat
    exactly the same course of action and decision again, and again, and again ...

33 Wagner came to exemplify the longing for romantic belonging, for losing one's individual spirit in the
    structure of a totality which carried one away with its forms and rhythms. 'One pays heavily for being
    one of Wagner's disciples. Let us take the measure of this discipleship by considering its cultural effects
    ...

    Do you understand this: health, brightness having the effect of a shadow? Almost of an objection? To
    such an extent have we become pure fools – never was there a greater master in dim, hieratic aromas –
    never was there a man equally expert in all small infinities, all that trembles and is effusive, all the
    feminisms from the idioticon of happiness ... Nowhere will you find a more agreeable way of
    enervating your spirit, of forgetting your manhood under a rosebush ... he thus wages war against us,
    us the free spirits! How he indulges every cowardice of the modern soul with the tones of magic
    maidens! – Never before has there been such a deadly hatred of the search for knowledge! – One has
    to be a cynic in order not to be seduced here; one has to be able to bite in order not to worship here'
    (*The Case of Wagner*, 1880).

PART THREE
THE HOLOCAUST: AN EXAMPLE OF MODERNITY TAKEN TO THE EXTREME, AND OF THE EXTREME DISENCHANTMENT WITH MODERNITY

... Consider if this is a man
Who works in the mud
Who does not know peace
Who fights for a scrap of bread
Who dies because of a yes or a no.
Consider if this is a woman,
Without hair and without name
With no more strength to remember,
Her eyes empty and her womb cold
Like a frog in winter.
Meditate that this came about;
I commend these words to you ... (Primo Levi, *If This Be a Man*, 1947).

Transport from Berlin: Arrived 5.3.43. Total load – 1,128 Jews. Registered for work – 389 men and 96 women. Special treatment [that is to say, sent to the gas chambers] – 151 men and 492 women and children. Transport from Breslau: Arrived 5.3.43. Total load – 1,405 Jews. Registered for work – 406 men and 190 women. Special treatment – 125 men and 684 women and children. Transport from Berlin: Arrived 7.3.43. Total load – including 25 preventive detainees – 690. Registered for work – 153 men, 25 preventive detainees and 65 women. Special treatment – 30 men and 417 women and children.[34]

INTRODUCTION

Within three years of Max Weber's death the German Jewish social theorist Husserl could describe Germany as being in 'political, national, religious, artistic, and philosophical chaos' (*Hua XXVII*, 1923: 95). The pluralist democracy of the Weimar Republic proved incapable of withstanding the multiple pressures a weakened Germany was subjected to; the ruling elites failed to grasp the need for modernisation and were locked into traditional conceptions, while they were increasingly faced with a diffuse mass of people aware of new challenges but lacking in the intellectual resources to articulate their concerns within modern discourses. Several of the political parties recalled the programmes and ideological propositions of the pre-war period, and various

---

34 These extracts offer two contrasting aspects of Auschwitz, perhaps the most famous of the death camps. Primo Levi was a young Italian Jewish chemist arrested for resistance activities and deported to Auschwitz in February 1944. Levi describes the dehumanising process and asks us to remember the inhumanity of the events. The second is an extract from camp records (reported in Krausnick et al, 1968) detailing the mundane normality of Auschwitz (the reception of slave labour and performance of human destruction) and therein providing an example of 'the machine-like, bureaucratic, regulated character as well as the Promethean ambition ... of the Nazi Holocaust' (Marrus, 1987: 22), that ensured the trains always ran to Auschwitz, even to the detriment of other war aims.

loose groupings developed which were to provide sympathetic soil when the Nazis invoked Reich romanticism and a statist mentality against the Weimar Constitution. As a result National Socialism under Adolf Hitler came to power in the early 1930s proclaiming the commencement of 'The Thousand Year Reich', which was to mirror their ideological portrayal of the 'thousand years' of 'pure' German history that had been destroyed with the First World War; their rule provoked the Second World War which ultimately saw their defeat.[35] One legacy is the Holocaust, an event which for many marks the end of confidence in the civilising process.[36] Was it possible to believe in inevitable progress, or remain committed to increasing rationality, if the Holocaust lay at the end of these processes?

How are we to understand this event? The uniqueness of the Holocaust lies not so much in the actual numbers killed (which must be put in the context of the war – in which 55 million died in total, including 20 million Soviet citizens, 15 million Chinese, 5 million Germans, and 3 million non-Jewish Poles – and this blood-soaked century) but in the wholesale aim of extinction which it embodied and the single-minded efficiency with which the task was pursued.[37] Isaac Deutsche defines the Holocaust as an event of 'absolute uniqueness'; whilst other massacres contain some 'human logic' the holocaust can 'baffle and terrify mankind ... a huge and ominous mystery of the degeneration of the human spirit' (quotes, Marrus, 1989: 8-9). However, while the Holocaust was unique, the argument that it is a mystery is wrong; the Holocaust is the prime case of the disenchantment of modernity not because it denotes the survival of pre-modern passions and emotions in the midst of modernity, but, rather, because the Holocaust is a reflection of the grand narratives of calculation, mastery and hygiene. While some commentators have tried to contain the Holocaust by locating it solely within the discourse of authoritarianism, or defining it as the result of pathology – of the specific evilness of Hitler or the Nazis – sophisticated commentators, such as Bauman (1989, *Modernity and the Holocaust*), have come to see it as a central part of the process of

---

35 The grip the Nazis developed is remarkable (given that their political breakthrough was the Reichstag elections in September 1930 where the Nazis won only 6.4 million votes – 18.3% of the electorate) and owes much to the system of representation and the radical pluralism of the German electorate at the time. Another structural weakness of the Weimar Party system (apart from the Communist Party and the National Socialist German Workers' Party) was the remoteness of their policies to the concerns of young people. The 'established' parties could not bind politically the ascendant generation whose members had not fought the First World War. The National Socialist (Nazi) Youth movement thus could incorporate a vital group into anti-republican sentiments, whilst playing on generational conflict. Party leaders resorted to disciplinary techniques of organisational variety encouraging antagonistic attitudes to the forces which were presented as behind the present crisis (including the Jews and the lack of firm leadership from established power positions).

36 The Holocaust or the Nazis' 'final solution to the question of European Jewry', refers to the systematic and bureaucratically administered policy of liquidation of European Jews during the period of Nazi domination of Europe. It claimed the lives of between 5 million and 6 million Jews – about two-thirds of the European Jews and one-third of the world's Jewish population. It is usually calculated that 4 million died in camps and 2 million perished elsewhere – mainly by shooting in the Soviet Union or by starvation and disease in the ghettos of eastern Europe.

37 The 20th century has seen many massacres (in recent decades the death of 3 million Bengalis with the creation of Bangladesh; 2 million dead out of a total population of 7 million in Cambodia; at the end of the 19th century and during the First World War the mass killings of Armenian populations by the Turkish administration; and the Croatian dictator Ante Pavelic is deemed to have ordered the massacres which killed some 700,000 orthodox Christian Serbs).

modernity.[38] The Holocaust was not a retreat to a Hobbesian state of nature, it was an example of the Weberian rational cage of modern civilisation.

AN OUTLINE OF THE MAIN WAYS OF VIEWING THE HOLOCAUST

The Holocaust has been seen: as a product of German ideologies, particularly a tradition of anti-Semitism joined with authoritarianism; as a product of pathological individuals who ascended to power in unique circumstances (the Nazis and particularly Hitler); more recently as a problem of modernity, as a result of the structures of thought inherent in modernity itself.

As a problem of German ideologies, particularly the tradition of anti-Semitism

The latest in this line of argument is Daniel Goldhagen's (1996) controversial, *Hitler's Willing Executioners: Ordinary Germans and the Holocaust*. Using a variety of primary material – including extensive testimony from the actual perpetrators themselves – Goldhagen argues that those involved in providing Jews for the concentration camps and those who staffed the death squads and who killed by shooting were not primarily SS men or Nazi Party members, but perfectly ordinary Germans from all walks of life; men (and women) who brutalised and murdered Jews both willingly and zealously. In his narrative they carried out their orders not because they were coerced (for many were informed by their own commanders that they could refuse without fear of retribution), nor because they slavishly followed orders (a view supported by Stanley Milgram's famous Yale 'obedience experiment'; see Bauman 1989, Ch 6), nor because of any tremendous social, psychological or peer pressure to conform to the behaviour of their comrades. Instead, they acted under the influence of widespread, profound, accepted, and virulent anti-Semitism which led them to believe that the Jews were a demonic enemy, whose extermination was not only necessary, but also just. Goldhagen draws upon the accounts of the participants wherein the banality and thoroughness of operations in the killing fields is recorded, including everything from sports and entertainment to the hobby of taking snapshots of the events and victims, photographs later exchanged for collection among themselves.

To what extent did the tradition of anti-Semitic writings presage the Holocaust? Note the words of Klemens Felden, who carried out a content analysis of 51 prominent anti-Semitic writers and publications that appeared between 1861 and 1895 in Germany:

> Some [writings] advocated the simplest solution, to kill the Jews; since the duty to defend … 'morals, humanity and culture' demanded a pitiless struggle against the evil … The annihilation of the Jews meant for most anti-Semites the salvation of Germany. They were apparently convinced that the elimination of a minority would bring an end to all the miseries and make the German people again the master in its own house (quoted, Goldhagen, 1996: 71).

---

38 The Holocaust is premised in both a naturalist foundation and techniques of calculation, the constant denial of the subjectivity of both the self (the German) and the other (the Jew, the gypsy, the sick and elderly), but it is also premised in ideas of progress and rational administration.

Twenty-eight of Felden's sample proposed 'solutions' to the Jewish problem. Of those, 19 called for the physical extermination of the Jews. In the late-19th century period of relative calm and civilisation two-thirds of these prominent anti-Semites pursued their beliefs to extreme logical consequences and indicated a genocidal outcome. Of the 40 who wrote about and explicated their understanding of the corporate basis of the Jews' unity, only one considered the Jews to be purely a religious community, and just six others mentioned religion along with other attributes as a unifying feature of Jewishness. In contrast, 32 conceptualised the nature of Jews as unchanging, and 23 of these presented the Jews as a race. Having understood the Jews as unchanging and unchangeable in nature, it is not illogical for the solution to 'the Jewish problem' to become physical annihilation: 'The eliminationist mind-set tended towards an exterminationist one. And it did so already in the 19th century, prior to the political birth of Hitler' (Goldhagen, 1996: 139).[39]

As a Nazi problem, or the product of Hitler's charisma

The charismatic leadership of Hitler, however, certainly played a large role in creating the actual mechanism of destruction. Accounts of 'ordinary Germans' as well as committed Nazis refer often to their belief that the Führer possessed magic-like qualities, and this was aided by the jurisprudence of the Führer-principle.

> Anti-Semitism in Germany may have been a necessary condition for the Holocaust, but it was not a sufficient one. In the end it was Hitler, and his own determination to realise his anti-Semitic fantasies, that made the difference (Marrus, 1989: 18).

Hitler often sounded like an extreme Nietzschean: 'In the search for self-preservation so-called humanitarian ideals melt away like snow in the March sunshine'.[40]

In *Mein Kampf*, Hitler (English translation, 1943) wrote:

> If, at the beginning and during the war, someone had only subjected about twelve or fifteen thousand of these Hebrew enemies of the people to poison gas – as was suffered

---

39 The argument is possibly overstated. By way of contrast, David Levy (1975), in *The Downfall of the Anti-Semitic Political Parties in Imperial Germany*, demonstrates that between 1887 and 1912 representatives of such parties constituted only 2% of deputies elected. Peter Pulzer (1964: 219; quoted, Marrus, 1989: 10), however, noted: 'the decline in the virulence of organised party anti-Semitism was matched by its increasing pervasion of social life, semi-political bodies, and ideological and economic pressure groups'.

40 Or to quote from an unpublished speech to a group of officer cadets on 22 June 1944: 'Nature is always teaching us ... that she is governed by the principle of selection; that victory is to the strong and that the weak must go to the wall. She teaches us that what may seem cruel to us, because it affects us personally or because we have been brought up in ignorance of her laws, is nevertheless often essential if a higher way of life is to be attained. Nature knows nothing of the notion of humanitarianism which signifies that the weak must at all costs be surrounded and preserved even at the expense of the strong.

Nature does not see in weakness any extenuating reasons – on the contrary, weakness calls for condemnation. War is therefore an unalterable law of the whole life – the prerequisite for the natural selection of the strong and the precedent for the elimination of the weak. What seems cruel to us is from nature's point of view entirely obvious. A people that cannot assert itself must disappear and another must take its place. All creation is subject to this law; no one can avoid it. Since life on earth began, struggle has been the very essence of existence' (quoted in Krausnick et al, 1968:13).

by hundreds of thousands of our best workers from all walks of life and callings on the battlefield – then the sacrifice of millions at the front would not have been in vain.

But Hitler's charisma could not have operated had it not been for a whole set of social narratives and structural conditions. Bauman (1989: 12) argues the Holocaust was 'a rare, yet significant and reliable text of the hidden possibilities of modern society'. He suggests:

> The Holocaust was an outcome of a unique encounter between factors by themselves quite ordinary and common; and that the possibility of such an encounter could be blamed to a very large extent on the emancipation of the political state, with its monopoly of means of violence and its audacious engineering ambitions, from social control – following the step-by-step dismantling of all non-political power resources and institutions of social self-management (*ibid*: xiii).

The Holocaust is both a reflection of tendencies in modernity, and a unique event. As a unique phenomenon it could not have occurred without quite specific sociological conditions in which modern technologies and techniques of rational administration were aided by a specific political and jurisprudential institutional imagination. This institutional imagination was provided, in part, by narratives of social construction, aided by specific jurisprudential theses on leadership, democracy and the crisis of liberalism.

Narratives of construction and the societal rationality of 'gardening' and social engineering

In the background lay problems of ambivalence, identity and social construction. Nietzsche had mockingly stated that 'what characterises the Germans is that with them the question, 'what is German?' never dies out.' After the wars of liberation Ernst Moritz Arndt had offered an ambiguous definition: 'Wherever the German tongue is heard, wherever God in heaven sings songs [in German], this, brave German, is what you shall call your own'. This was, already – in the light of the political development of Switzerland and the Netherlands – anachronistic by 1913, but the image of liberating the fatherland was fundamental to the Nazi appeal.[41] Although Nietzsche's favourite writer, Goethe (along with Schiller), had asked for nationalism to be replaced by universal humanism – 'you hope in vain, German, to form yourselves into a nation; develop yourselves instead, as certainly you can, more freely into human beings' – nationalism was the historical victor. To quote Grillparzer, the actual path was 'from humanity through nationality to bestiality'. It was not a coincidence that after 1933 National Socialism was publicised as 'the biological will of the German people', or as 'political biology'. In the words of the German historian Hans Buchheim:

---

41 Members of the Hitler Youth movement were disciplined via the wearing of uniforms, the hoisting of flags, participating in memorials commemorating heroes and the singing of songs. A typical one contains the following passage:

Holy fatherland in peril,
Your sons rally round you.
Before strangers rob you of your glories,
Germany, we shall fall, one and all.

The National Socialists considered that their own people, and during the Second World War the people of Europe, had squandered their substance; they looked on them as a plantation overgrown with weeds, which must at all costs be cleared by isolating the 'incorrigible', cutting out the 'cancer of decay', propagating the worthwhile elements and letting the less valuable wither away, sterilising the sick, and either transplanting or suppressing the unstable varieties. The end product of this policy would be a new, biologically sensible, well-ordered European community ... This programme would be carried through by means of euthanasia, deportation, Germanisation and, last but not least, the 'extirpation of all those classes of people considered to be worthless or dangerous'. (Quoted Krausnick et al, 1968: 15).

In furtherance of Social Darwinist theories the concept of usefulness to society (ultimately to the state) served as a yardstick in determining human worth; for the sake of progress people must be placed unreservedly at the disposal of the state which should be accorded full powers of control.[42] Nazi population policy was dominated by a so-called euthanasia campaign which involved many doctors in a scheme of racially engineering a new race. The Nazi biomedical vision drew upon eugenic ideas common in much of the western world in the 1920s, and depicted the entire German nation as a biological organism threatened by a kind of collective illness, a potentially fatal threat to a formerly healthy society. The Nazi task was to strengthen the German Volk by eliminating all sources of corruption – carried mainly by the Jews, but evidently also in the feeble-minded, the incurably ill, and the insane. Nazi theorists coined the term 'biocracy' to denote a model similar to theocracy, a state committed to purification and revitalisation, secure as if divinely commanded to perform the task.

Beginning with children, the Nazis encouraged and directed a programme of systematic killing of the physically and mentally impaired, eventually using gas chambers, to rid the Reich of those deemed 'unworthy of life'. Estimates of the death toll are uncertain – in part due to the fact that many doctors were allowed to continue with the scheme after the campaign was officially stopped – but it is generally accepted that the total killed was between 80,000 and 100,000 people. This technique served as a precursor to 'the final solution'; it set out the organised killing of people as part of its operation, focused, in particular, upon Jews, and it developed killing methods and trained personnel who would eventually organise many of the death camps of eastern Europe.

---

42 As a training manual for SS soldiers put it: 'It is an untenable position when the relationship between the efficient and the ineffective in a state assumes an unhealthy form. The nation has to spend a great deal of energy and money in dealing with the feeble-minded, the criminal and the anti-social. If these examples of poor heredity were eliminated, large sums of money would be saved and could be diverted to other, more productive ends. A responsible state leadership should devote all its attention to plans for maintaining and increasing those of sound stock. In primitive societies, the community rids itself of its weaklings. In so-called civilised nations, a false attitude of brotherly love, which the Church has been especially assiduous in fostering among the broad masses, operates in direct opposition to the selective process.'

Another extract makes clear the practical application of the accepted theories.

'Two things are essential for the building up and maintenance of a healthy race. Not only must the hereditary factor be unremittingly sustained, but an environment favourable to this "race" must be established. This can be achieved only if the whole community of the people consciously aligns itself behind this principle (the principle of sound breeding) and if each member of the community conducts his life accordingly.' (Quoted from Krausnick et al 1968).

Although Social Darwinist ideas served to intensify anti-Semitic views, it should be remembered that organised anti-Semitism actually showed signs of decreasing in the period preceding the First World War. From 1916 onwards as the military and economic situation deteriorated anti-Semitism intensified, particularly after the military collapse of 1918. Large sections of the German population mistakenly believed that all was well with the war effort until the final collapse, which led to a search for some hidden factor as its cause. The military defeat, the break-up of the monarchy, the economic depression, the trials of domestic and foreign policy in an 'imported' democracy, the reluctance of a great many people to try to understand the latest developments and to accept them, provided fertile soil for Hitler's message.

Hitler's rhetoric stressed collective danger and the necessity to distinguish friend from foe.[43] Hitler had already explained the 'rational intellectual basis' of his anti-Semitism and how he intended to reach his objective, in a letter dated 16 September 1919:

> Anti-Semitism as a political movement neither can nor should be based on fleeting emotions, but on the acceptance of fact – and the fact is that Judaism is a matter of race and not of religion … Reasonable anti-Semitism … must lead to a systematic and lawful campaign for the removal of those privileges which the Jew enjoys – unlike other foreigners living in our midst, who are subject to the law applying to aliens. The final aim of such anti-Semitism must be, unquestionably, the expulsion of the Jews.

In the Nazi Party manifesto of 24 February 1920 Hitler's above-mentioned objective became the official position as set out under points 4 and 5:

> Point 4: State citizenship can only be claimed by nationals and only those of German blood, regardless of religious persuasion, can be nationals. No Jew can therefore be national.

> Point 5: Those who do not possess state citizenship can live in Germany only as guests and are subject to the laws applying to aliens. (Quoted Krausnick et al, 1968: 21).

Both positive law and governmental regulation came to be instruments of this policy.

THE USE OF LAW TO TRANSFORM THE JEWS INTO SUBHUMAN MATERIAL

The use of law was part of what Goldhagen calls a three-pronged sustained attack upon the social existence of the Jews involving anti-Semitic propaganda, physical abuse and legal separation. The aim was to transform Jews into 'socially dead beings, beings who were seen to be owed few if any moral obligations by Germans and who were conceived of as being thoroughly dishonourable, indeed incapable of bearing honour' (Goldhagen, 1996: discussion 137ff).

---

43 As he openly declared in a speech of 13 August 1920 dominated by the 'Jewish question': 'We are convinced that scientific anti-Semitism, which clearly recognises the frightful danger that race represents to our people, can only be our guide; the broad masses, who will always react emotionally, must first be made aware of the Jew as the person, who in daily life, is always and everywhere thrusting himself forward – our task must be to arouse the mass instinct against the Jew, to stir it up and keep it on the boil until it decides to support the movement which is prepared to take the consequences' (quoted, Krausnick et al, 1968).

One strand was a barrage of propaganda concerning the Jews containing the theme of the Jews as subhuman creatures who were the source of evil. This 'verbal violence upon the Jews' helped to render the Jews of lesser social importance, preparing Germans for still more drastic eliminationist measures and, by inducing Jews to emigrate, reducing their influence.

A second strand was actual physical assaults on Jews. The regime perpetrated, encouraged, or tolerated violence against Jews (from impromptu physical attacks and ritualistic degradation by local officials to sometimes centrally organised campaigns of violence and terror, and finally incarceration in concentration camps). These displays indicated that the Jews were not members of the moral community and that normal feelings of sympathy and compassion were not appropriate. The assaults also suggested the dire fate that might await the Jews.

Against this backdrop, an ever-increasing, legally and administratively promulgated social separation of Jews from Germans developed. Goldhagen refers to this as:

> ... the most closely related non-verbal analogue to the verbal violence; unlike most of the anti-Jewish measures that they eventually adopted, Germans put this into effect almost from the moment of the Nazis' assumption of power and never relented from this programme, which they intensified as the 1930s and 1940s wore on. The progress of the gradual, systematic exclusion of Jews from all spheres of society – the political, social, economic, and cultural – was as grinding as the hardship that it created for Jews was punishing (*ibid*: 139).

Goldhagen reports that the Germans began to exclude Jews from governmental service one week after the boycott on 1 April 1933, by means of the Law for the Restoration of the Professional Civil Service of 7 April, and from many professions in the ensuing weeks. The Germans' exclusion of Jews from the economy proceeded throughout the first years of the regime as the economic health of the country permitted, and with increased vigour in 1938. On 22 September 1933, the Germans removed Jews from the cultural spheres and the press, which many deemed to be especially poisoned by Jews. The Nazi administration eventually came to proscribe virtually all aspects of general Jewish intercourse with Germans, as well important Jewish religious practices, publishing a deluge of restrictive laws regulating what Jews might or might not do. They prohibited Jewish ritual slaughter soon after the Nazi era began on 21 April 1933, which, because it was a defining practice of Jewry, could be understood only as a declaration that Jewishness itself was a violation of the order and moral norms of society. Almost 2,000 laws and administrative regulations were created that degraded and immiserated German Jews.

The historian Michael Marrus (1989: 27) argues that the legal response mediated contrasting tendencies towards the Jews by the Nazis after their ascent to power. On the one hand, brown-shirted storm troopers and party activists engaged in physical assaults on Jews; on the other hand, while wishing to see the Jews excluded from German society, more conservative elements in the Nazi movement were worried about possible harm to the economy and the international reputation of Germany. Law provided the mechanism for directing persecution 'from the centre', with the Nuremberg Laws of September 1935 setting the legal framework for a campaign of 'Aryanisation' organising the confiscation of Jewish property. The 'legality' of the measures ensured that those sectors of the population in opposition to the Nazis were able to feel comfortable with the campaigns. The German historian Christof Dipper concludes that among most of the conservative opponents of the Nazis 'the bureaucratic, pseudo-legal deprivation of the Jews practised until 1938 was still considered acceptable' (quoted, Marrus, 1989: 91). How would civil servants, including legal officials, react? The Nazis passed a law for civil servants which specifically prescribed the political loyalty of all civil servants.

Together with subsequent decrees the Nuremberg Laws defined who was a Jew, and provided a clear national understanding of which people were to be subject to the laws and decrees regulating Jews. The definitional criteria relied essentially upon bloodlines and not religious identity. German (Nazi) legality deemed to be Jews those people who (owing to their or their parents' conversions) were Christians if a requisite portion of their ancestry was Jewish – no matter that they might have no psychological or other social identification with things Jewish. The Nuremberg Laws also stripped Jews of citizenship and proscribed new marriages and extramarital sexual relations between Jews and non-Jews. The law was both instrumental and expressive; the classifications of the law symbolised and expressed the thesis of difference and inferiority. The laws, regulations, and measures of the 1930s robbed Jews of their livelihoods, impoverished and demoralised them, and isolated them from the larger society in which they had moved freely only a few years earlier. They made Jews socially dead, transforming them into subhuman material, weeds to be cleansed from the garden.

THE ROLE OF JURISPRUDENCE IN CREATING THE INSTITUTIONAL IMAGINATION OF THE NAZI ERA: THE EXAMPLE OF CARL SCHMITT

The legality of the rule of the Third Reich flowed from the constitutional arrangements of the preceding Weimar Republic. Hitler was elected *Reichskanzler* in 1933 in accordance with the Weimar constitution, and after a series of dramatic incidents (probably instigated by the Nazis and culminating with the burning of the *Reichstag* building in February 1933) the elderly President von Hindenburg – having been placed under extreme pressure – agreed that there was a national emergency, and granted Hitler, as *Reichskanzler*, powers of government by emergency decree. These powers were confirmed and consolidated by a *Reichstag* vote on 24 March and were thereafter renewed every four years by the Nazi *Reichstag*.

German National Socialism had a strong ideological core which emphasised historical destiny and the need for strong leadership. Let us be clear: the Nazi state was directly opposed to the tradition of liberalism as an organising theme of the discourses constituting modernity. Liberalism appears to deny the need for expressive unity and identification of people and state (legal constitution);[44] rather, the social body is increasingly portrayed as a number of relatively autonomous economic, political,

---

44 Although, as discussed with regard to John Stuart Mill and in later chapters, liberalism relies on an unstated identification between the populace and can be recast in positive terms, ie as a thesis of the good life.

scientific, ethical, religious, and cultural spheres, differentiating themselves from each other and capable of self-steering if left to the 'free' interaction of their participating individuals. For the liberalist narrative of modernity, (social) freedom lies in the very differentiation of these spheres and the state ought not to attempt to subject them to forms of domination or corporate steering (such as in Fascism and Marxism). Nazism, conversely, conceived of the state as a corporate body with a hierarchy of authoritarian structures staffed by members of the party with a strong leader at its head. The idea was for a 'rational mastery' of the destiny of the nation and people, the key political principle was that of leadership, and onus was placed upon the leader to provide direction to the nation. In essence, while liberalism implied the very question was dangerously misconceived, National Socialism purports to answer the question: 'How is a collective determination of the objectives of human striving to be made?' by embodying and reducing the general will of the people to the will of the party and ultimately to that of the leader. The leader's will is thereby the ultimate source of legitimacy for ordering (for law). This leadership principle, or *Führerprinzip*, determined that each level in the hierarchy was subservient to the next above, with Hitler at the apex. The leader's will can not be subject to any institutional constraint, since it ultimately is the foundation for such practical forms, and rule by positive law (as decreed by the full state legislature) was only one amongst several regulation-making devices which could express the will of the leader and the party.

Carl Schmitt's critique of the parliamentary democracy of the 1920s republic

The Catholic, and later Nazi, legal theorist Carl Schmitt[45] was a devastating critic of the early modern attempt to create liberal democracy. His famous *The Crisis of Parliamentary Democracy* (1923), which took up themes from his *Political Romanticism* (1919), was based on his theory of an opposition between liberalism and democracy. The contradictory nature of modern mass democracy was due to the opposition between certain implications inherent in the practical nature of democracy and those of liberalism.

Schmitt defines democracy as the principle that equals are to be treated equally, which he claims necessarily implies that unequals should not be treated equally. How, then, can a society which is composed of a plurality of groupings and interests cohere? The answer Schmitt offers is chilling: democracy requires homogeneity, which only exists on the basis of eliminating heterogeneity. His claim is simple: for democracies to exist they must exclude whatever threatens their homogeneity. Liberalism, by contrast, offers the idea of the equality of all persons as persons, but Schmitt believes this principle is only an individualistic humanitarian ethic and is not of sufficient strength to serve as the foundation of political organisation. Once democracy is defined in this manner, it follows that to seek a democracy of humankind would be to impose an absolute equality on people – a standardisation – which would strip them of variation and individuality,

---

45 Carl Schmitt was a year older than Hitler but outlived him to die in 1986 at the age of 97. His provocative writings marked out a basic intellectual divide in German intellectual opinions.

and destroy creativity. Universal and equal suffrage is only possible within a society of equals, since it is only when such natural homogeneity provides the foundation that equal rights make sense. Schmitt thus rationalises the inclusion/exclusion opposition so central to the 'democracies' of early modernity. Schmitt explained that a philosophy of legalist universal human equality along with its jurisprudence of equal rights, in practice relied upon the exclusion of those who did not belong to the state.

Schmitt thus conceives of democracy as a means of answering issues of legitimation and governance. Modernity involves the process whereby humanity takes control of the world, subjects the world to analysis, and constructively builds the new world order. To what extent does the new order(ing) need justification? Is it only those aspects of social order directly attributable to construction and constitution via deliberately set norms?[46] In which case do we deny that the outcomes of 'hidden orderings', such as the market, need legitimation (being seen, somehow, as 'natural'), while the law is exposed to an overburdened demand for legitimation? How much control is desirable? Or feasible? Schmitt – reaching into his Catholic metaphysics with its inbuilt ideology of a cosmos ultimately subjected to the control of God and man in their respective domains – cannot offer the openness of liberalism as an answer. Instead, democracy is deemed to be the movement that asserts that control of the social body is to be exerted by the people and that control is to be encompassing. But how can that control be operative, how can democracy be possible, if there is no common set of political values underlying it? By giving a narrow reading to this issue, Schmitt argues that modern mass democracy confuses the liberal desire for human equality, and the core requirement of the democratic political form for the governed and governing to be identified together. Thus, he claimed, he had found the reason why liberal democracy in Germany was in crisis; it was partly because of a confusion between political and jurisprudential analysis, and social desires and human pathos. While liberal individualism is essentially a moral desire, the task of governing society – including a democracy – requires sentiments dictated essentially by political ideals and guided by strict philosophical analysis.

Schmitt argues that the 19th-century struggle against royal absolutism and the goal of creating a national identity had kept the contradiction between liberalism and democracy from revealing itself openly. But the crisis that the German Republic was facing was, at base, the inescapable contradiction of the desires for liberal individualism and the need for democratic homogeneity.

Parliamentary democracy contained unrealisable aims and the regimes that were established in its name were unstable unions between two completely heterogeneous political principles. One such principle was the identity between people and state inherent in the democratic form of government, while another was the absolutist mode of representation proper to monarchy. Schmitt lambasted the Weimar Republic as a weak hybrid system brought about by the compromise that the liberal bourgeoisie managed to establish between the historical tradition of absolute monarchy and the struggle for proletarian democracy by way of combining two opposite principles of

---

46 The positive law, defined as orders of the political centre in the eyes of Austin; more clearly legal norms in the eyes of Weber and Kelsen.

government into an impotent edifice.[47] As democracy, early 20th century mass democracy attempts to realise an identity of governed and governing, and thus it labels the institution of representative parliament as outmoded. If democratic identity is taken seriously, then in an emergency, no other constitutional institution can withstand the sole criterion of the people's will, however it is expressed. Particularly, at times of crisis, the state must be able to act quickly and decisively; power must be embodied in the person of the leader.[48] Only thereby could the friend of the nation be clearly distinguished from the enemy and appropriate action taken.

THE HOLOCAUST AS A PART OF THE GENERAL RATIONALISATION OF MODERNITY

Socially and politically, therefore, the Holocaust was part of a process wherein a corporate body (the Nazi state) addressed the problem of constructing a new society in the face of the multiple pressures of middle modernity. With the old certainties gone, the ship was to be built anew by organisation, but this was not to be the liberal (ideal) motif of self-determining practices joined up only by functional interaction and free communication; rather it was a process of central decision-making and communication from the centre (propaganda). To use the words of Wagner (1994: 69), this form of organisation meant hierarchisation, and it meant exclusion. Those who found themselves at the bottom or outside the realm of organised practices suffered often more than before. To effect this process the resources of technology lay at hand.

> [Auschwitz] was also a mundane extension of the modern factory system. Rather than producing goods, the raw material was human beings and the end product was death, so many units per day marked carefully on the manager's production charts. The chimneys, the very symbol of the modern factory system, poured forth acrid smoke produced by burning human flesh. The brilliantly organised railroad grid of modern Europe carried a new kind of raw material to the factories. It did so in the same manner as with other cargo. In the gas chambers the victims inhaled noxious gas, generally by prussic acid pellets, which were produced by the advanced chemical industry of Germany. Engineers designed the crematoria; managers designed the system of bureaucracy that worked with a zest and efficiency more backward nations would envy. Even the overall plan itself was a reflection of the modern scientific spirit gone awry. What we witnessed was nothing less than a massive scheme of social engineering ... (Feingold, quoted in Bauman, 1989:8)

---

47 Among the industrialised countries Germany had a unique political constitution. In England, France and the United States a politically and economically powerful (and, in the main, liberal) middle class had occasioned that national unity be combined with civil liberties, but Germany was founded on the remnants which the Thirty Years War and the peace of Westphalia had left behind of the 'Holy Roman Empire of the German Nation'. It was little wonder that Hegel had celebrated the advent of Napoleon since he enabled the first redevelopment of the medieval empire to the orientation of state sovereignty. But the German state was driven by a multiplicity of small and medium-sized states and cohesive action was difficult.

48 If the historical prejudices of the German middle classes (the *Burgertum*) were shaped by any one experience it was the tradition in the 19th century to fashion German nationalism from 'above', particularly through the principle of 'the primacy of foreign policy', which took the form ultimately of war, or 'blood and iron'.

Bauman makes the telling point:

> The truth is that every ingredient of the Holocaust – all those many things that rendered it possible – was normal; normal not in the sense of the familiar, of one more specimen in a large class of phenomena long ago described in full, explained and accommodated (on the contrary, the experience of the Holocaust was new and unfamiliar), but in the sense of being fully in keeping with everything we know about our civilisation, its guiding spirit, its priorities, its immanent vision of the world – and of the proper ways to pursue human happiness together with a perfect society (1989:8).

THE DISCIPLINING OF CAMP GUARDS AND SS MEN

The Holocaust could not have occurred without the destruction of the sympathetic and empathetic qualities Hume and others have placed as the foundations of the moral life. Propaganda, law, and practices of dehumanisation, all played their part. At the cutting edge – in the persons (ie in the minds and bodies) of those who staffed the death camps and partook in the shootings – discipline prevailed, provided, as Weber indicated, from the army to the social body. Staffing the camps, so instrumental in the 'final solution', was the prize of the SS. And the SS man was not a pathological misfit; he was a disciplined subject of a partial modernity. To achieve this disciplined self, on the military side training in 'hardness' degenerated into an inhuman system for humiliating a man.[49] The humiliations to which an SS recruit was subject were similar to those meted out to an inmate of a concentration camp (examples given and discussed, Krausnick et al 1968: 340–41). Discipline led into obedience through brutality. The final solution allowed of little individual initiative or passion.[50] The successful operation of the final solution required the disciplining of its operatives; in case of indiscipline, of breaches of the norms so created, lay Nazi law.[51]

---

49 The concentration camps and the treatment accorded to their inmates began as a form of militarism – at least until 1942 when the camps became definite forced labour institutions. Before that, the ostensible purpose of the concentration camps was re-education of the Nazi's political opponents and the SA and SS men who ran them practised military training with the inmates.

50 Another example of the centrality of rational discipline is an order by Himmler of 16 August 1935 forbidding independent individual action against the Jews: '1. Any independent individual action against the Jews by any member of the SS is most strictly forbidden. 2. The solution of the Jewish question, as of all other questions, is the business of the Führer and not of individuals. 3. Any, even the most minor, contravention of this order will be punished by dismissal from the SS.'

51 On 9 June 1943 the Supreme SS and Police Court gave judgment upon an SS-Untersturmführer who, with his own hand, had killed hundreds of Jews in atrocious circumstances. The judgment reads as follows: 'The accused should not be punished for his actions against the Jews as such. The Jews must be annihilated and no tears need be shed over any of the Jews whom the accused has killed. Although the accused must have known that the annihilation of the Jews is the business of commandos specially formed for the purpose, it is a point in his favour that he felt himself competent to take part in the annihilation of the Jews. Genuine hatred of the Jews was the accused's primary motive. Nevertheless in Alexandria he succumbed to the temptation to commit atrocities unworthy of a German or an SS commander. These excesses cannot be justified by saying, as does the accused, that they are a just recompense for the damage done by the Jews to the German people. Necessary though the annihilation of our people's worst enemy may be, it is not the in the German manner to use Bolshevist methods to do so. And the methods adopted by the accused border upon those of Bolshevism. The accused allowed his men to become so brutalised that, following his example, they acted like a barbarian horde. The behaviour of the accused constitutes the most serious danger to discipline imaginable. Although in other ways the accused may have taken care of his men, his behaviour ...

Over the years there developed in the SS an inextricable hotchpotch of 'normal' or 'official' and 'non-normal' or 'non-official' rules and regulations, both frequently being applied to one and the same case; normal and apparently official regulations were issued for technical, organisational or disciplinary reasons or to lend substance to the *order of chivalry* dream; on the other hand political objectives compatible with no normal rules were set and achieved, carrying with them the necessity to ride roughshod over all normal regulations as required. In many cases, however, an attempt was made to give extra-constitutional measures some form of legal camouflage cover; finally it became standard practice to give individual SS authorities the rights and prerogatives of official state institutions in order to assist them to fulfil some non-official purpose. In 1937, for instance, in his capacity as Inspector of Concentration Camps, Eicke forbade maltreatment of prisoners by the guards, saying:

> Although as a National Socialist I naturally sympathise with such action, I cannot and must not tolerate such behaviour; otherwise we shall run the risk of being reported by the Reich Ministry of the Interior as unfit to deal with prisoners. (Quoted Krausnick et al, 1968: 353).

Every three months members of the guard units had to sign a declaration that they understood that they must not maltreat prisoners; yet arbitrary action and cruelty were rampant. The concentration camps provided a terrain where *regulated* and *unregulated* action and behaviour overlapped. The camps belonged to a sphere of the Special Executive; nevertheless all sorts of apparently normal rules built themselves up around them without, however, providing any real safeguards for the inmates. The more prominent prisoners were to some degree protected against arbitrary action on the part of the guards, but at any time a man might find that he had been demoted into the general faceless mass of prisoners who had no protection of any sort (see Primo Levi's [1987] account in *If This is a Man*, and *The Truce*).

JURISPRUDENCE AND THE RESPONSE TO THE NAZI REGIME AND THE HOLOCAUST

It is difficult to grasp the existential shock that the defeat of the *Thousand Year Reich* and the discovery of the terrible deeds committed in its name occasioned. As Wallershoff (1985: 340) describes it, for the youth of Germany, who had flocked to fight believing they were being offered their historical chance of greatness and purity, there was only shock and mourning: 'All the sacrifices and sufferings of this war had been not only in vain but meaningless and false as well. Not only had we lost; we had fought for a vile cause'.

Jurisprudentially, the shock concerned the relativity of law and jurisprudential concepts. Positive law was exposed as only too easily the instrument of a legislative

---

51...constitutes a gross dereliction of his duty as a leader, part of which in the view of the SS is to preserve the moral standards of his men. To this extent therefore the accused has rendered himself liable to punishment under para 147 of the Military Code of Law. The maximum sentence under this paragraph, however, is 15 years' imprisonment or fortress arrest; since so serious an undermining of discipline calls for a more severe sentence, para 5A of the Special Wartime Punishment Code should be applied.' (Extract from Bachheim, 'Command and Compliance' in Krausnick et al, 1968: 251–2.)

reason which attained ideological power. It was difficult to hide from the fact that from a legal positive perspective the decrees promulgated by the Nazis were valid law. Even the Holocaust was possibly legal, buttressed by the fact that it was carried out in the name of the (Nazi) good. Reviewing the experience of the Holocaust, the Jewish writer Hannah Arendt (1963) coined the phrase 'the banality of evil', by which she meant that the Nazi regime was a product of modern political structures and constellations which – using all the resources of the modern state – proved capable of justifying slavery and oppression in the name of what is purportedly a common good. Had the jurisprudential imagination of legal positivism helped make the evil of the Nazi regime a slowly acceptable banality? In an exercise of personal soul searching, the German theorist Gustav Radbruch apparently thought so (*cf* discussion in Pock, 1962).

Radbruch had been a legal positivist in large part because he believed – along with most German theorists, such as Kelsen (see discussion in Chapter 12 and Chapter 14) – in the relativity of values claimed in the name of justice. In an article published after the war, Radbruch explained his position as follows. Law is the set of general rules for the common life of man and has as its overall goal the pursuit of *justice*; but justice is a indeterminate concept. Justice demands that equals be treated equally, and those that are different be treated differently, but this in turn (i) requires a standard by which equality and inequality are measured; and (ii) says nothing of the type of practical treatment to be accorded to individuals. Hence justice needs to be complemented by other essential concepts, and Radbruch proposed two: *expediency* and *legal certainty*.

In legitimating a flexible legal system, we need to consider expediency (or the promotion of a concrete goal). What sort of goals did he envisage? Radbruch proposes the aim of creating conditions which maximise the possibility of the development of the individual human personality (individualism), the pursuit of national power and glory (supraindividualism), or the promotion of civilisation and works of culture (transpersonalisation). The choice was a matter of preference. However, to prevent the legal order being rendered ineffective by conflicting social and political opinions, what is right and what is wrong needs to be authoritatively settled, and therefore justice and expediency needs to be supplemented by the idea of legal certainty. Legal certainty requires the promulgation and maintenance of a positive binding legal order by the state: 'if what is just cannot be settled, then what ought to be right must be laid down; and this must be done by an agency able to carry through what it lays down' (1950: 108).

Each element is required by the legal order, but each pulls in different directions. Legal certainty, for instance, requires fixed and stable laws, while justice and expediency require the system to adapt easily to new social and economic circumstances. There is no absolute formula by which the correct balance can be arrived at. Before the Second World War Radbruch favoured legal certainty: 'It is more important that the strife of legal views be ended than that it be determined justly and expediently' (*ibid*: 108). After the collapse of the Third Reich, Radbruch argued that legal positivism had left the German jurists defenceless against the Nazis and that law must satisfy certain absolute postulates in order to be truly law. In particular, law requires some recognition of individual freedom, and a legal order which completely denied individual rights would be 'absolutely false law' (1947: 27). Radbruch's new formula for balancing justice, expediency and legal certainty, however, merely amounted to a moderate revision.[52] Natural law was only a resource for emergencies.

Legitimating the Nuremberg trials

What responses were the victorious Allies to make? What politics were they to pursue? Although the measures taken to prosecute German leaders for war crimes after the First World War had been ineffective or counter-productive,[53] it was decided to set up a legalistic forum to deal with those Nazis who had been apprehended. Whereas, however, the dominant discourse for public consumption concerned the rule of law ideology, the objectives of the Nuremberg trials, were not merely to punish the Nazi leadership, but also:

(i)   The establishment of a precedent establishing 'aggressive war' as an international crime;

(ii) The creation of a comprehensive record of Nazi Germany's atrocities;

(iii) A means of re-establishing the rule of law in Germany, by the use of judicial process. (Memorandum of Justice Jackson, in Harris, 1988: 867)

There was, however, no unanimous agreement among the Allies.

There were two major jurisprudential questions: the foundation of the Tribunal and the legality of the Nazi actions. Had the Nazis breached existing law? What of Nazis who committed terrible atrocities under orders? Did the need to respond to the events override the considerations of legality only to punish if an ascertainable law had been breached? What was the law?

Moreover, at first it appeared difficult to avoid charges that the Tribunal amounted to the justice of the victorious being imposed upon the powerless vanquished, or refute the charge that the trials were ex post facto in that they allegedly punished individuals for actions that had not been criminal when committed. The charges of crimes against peace and some of the charges covered by the term 'crimes against humanity' could hardly be legitimated by positive law. The Tribunal was founded on a charter which offered legitimation, but to the cynic the whole structure amounted to making new law

---

52 'Preference should be given to the rule of positive law, supported as it is by due enactment and state power, even when the rule is unjust and contrary to the general welfare, unless the violation of justice reaches so intolerable a degree that the rules becomes in effect 'lawless law' and must therefore yield to justice' (*Rechtsphilosophie*, 4th edn 1950: 353).

53 Under the terms of the Versailles peace treaty of 1919 it was agreed both that the Kaiser, Wilhelm II, would be tried by a specially constituted international tribunal, and that Germany accepted the right of the Allies to bring to trial before national or international military tribunals persons accused of having committed acts in violation of the laws or customs of war as well as an undertaking by the German government to hand such persons over for trial. The former Kaiser had fled to the Netherlands which would not agree to extradition. After the German government blocked the giving out of individuals accused of war crimes, the Allies consequently agreed to allow the cases to be heard by the supreme court of Leipzig but the trials were ineffective. There were many acquittals in the face of evidence of guilt, and the sentences of those found guilty were light. Moreover the media and public appeared to consider the convicted as heroes and several were helped to escape from prison.

in various areas and then retrospectively enforcing it.[54] The Austinian would have recognised that for a brief time a form of international sovereignty was at work – the Allies had the power and the political will to provide a backdrop to the creative rereading of international customary law so that a new form of international positive law was created. But did that not imply that the Tribunal was therefore making law as it sat? Against this viewpoint, if one accepted the basic legality of the enterprise, then the jurisdiction of the tribunal was easily defended.[55] The legitimacy of the procedures involved the fact that the application of the 'laws' which gave substantive structure to the Tribunal's activities depended on the a fortiori validity of the actual laws applied.

What sort of view should one take of the situation and the proceedings? What are the contours of the jurisprudential imagination that we should utilise? Could the victory mean that the jurisprudence of the victors could appeal to God? Had the defeat of the Reich proved that God had walked not with the Reich – as the expression 'God with us' engraved on the German belt buckles had indicated – but with the Allies? John R Roth put the point of historical might succinctly:

> Had Nazi power prevailed, authority to determine what ought to be would have found that no natural laws were broken and no crimes against God and humanity were committed in the Holocaust. It would have been a question, though, whether the slave labour operations should continue, expand, or go out of business. Those decisions would have been made on rational grounds (quoted, Bauman, 1989: 7).

The question was both a practical one of responding to specific actions, and attempting to fill the void of *meaning* the advent of the rise and fall of the *Thousand Year Reich* occasioned. For Wellershoff, Germans found themselves without any of the supports that the Nazis had made sound so reasonable, so intoxicating ... so enticing:

> [Now we realised that] we were certainly the biggest idiots – from a foolishly trusting need for community and for a meaning to life that transcended everyday existence and assigned everyone a place in the greater totality. What other possibilities were there for self-definition? Petit bourgeois families, schools, offices, factories – was this life, was this one's identity? This was no model, no plan, all this was far too limited. The language of drums and banners carried us away from the tedium – into a bloody transcendence. Meaning is the greatest opiate; millions died from it (1986: 341-2).

Germany had no intellectual capacity to provide meaning, to provide a jurisprudential imagination to fill the void of Nazism: 'by contrast, the capacities of the victorious powers to provide meaning were not exhausted'. One could be a Englishman, or American, 'without shame or guilt'.

It was not, however, as a social and political exercise of the power granted by victory to shape the meaning and destiny of the constitutional imagination of the post-

---

54 The Tribunal was set up under the *Agreement for the Prosecution and Punishment of the Major War Criminals of the European Axis, Charter of the International Military Tribunal*, 8 August 1945, Art 3, 82 UNTS 280, reprinted in 39 *AJIL* 257 (1945). This convention 'recognised' certain laws, and thus crimes, which were said to be part of customary law. For example the tribunal went on to recognise that war crimes as defined in article 6(b) of the Nuremberg Charter were already recognised as war crimes under international law (covered by the Hague Regulations).

55 For example by Lord Wright, 'War Crimes Under International Law', 62 *LQR* 1946, at 141.

war society that the Nuremberg Tribunal publicly legitimised their foundations. Instead, the picture offered was as if legalism were self-reproducing, or simply the recognition of international customary law.[56]

The post-war situation is often said to have occasioned a revival of natural law thinking but this did not provide the basis for the Nuremberg trials (it was to play a part in the trials of Japanese war criminals in Tokyo and provoked the leading dissent of Justice R Pal of India who charged natural law with cultural specificity [see Shklar, 1964: 179-190]). The acts of the Nazi regime had certainly offended against ethical values but natural law ideology appeared to many – as Judge Pal specifically argued – too subjective to provide the foundation for an international tribunal. The sense of injustice and horror had been aroused:[57] perhaps it was not time for philosophical reflection but for action; a political structure had been 'liberated' from Nazi domination, it was time to insert the western understanding of freedom, responsibility and self-determination.

Although natural law seemed too vague a basis, few espoused a foundation based on the realism of Austinian legal positivism. Several of the defence lawyers attempted to argue, *inter alia*, that their clients were being tried on an '*ex post facto* law of murder' (Gluek, 1946), but this was not accepted. Few wished the audience to understand that the Tribunal was set up under new authority and effectively made new law as it 'recognised' customary law. The legality was rather legitimated in terms of pre-existing legal principles inherent in the customs of war which were merely being better articulated. However, not only was the actual statue of the Tribunal mostly the work of one man – Justice Jackson – who went on to be the Chief Prosecutor for the US, but the whole operation of the London Agreement amounted to judicial legislation.

The politics and imagination of legality

In her book *Legalism*, Judith Shklar (1964, 2nd edn, 1986) argues that the trials demonstrate the political nature of liberal legalism. Shklar distinguishes two kinds of legalism. The first is an attitude of mind by members of the legal profession and writers of jurisprudence which separates off legality from social processes and has resulted in a

---

56 The official story was that before the Nazis carried out their various actions a series of international declarations, acts and treaties, culminating in the Paris pact of 1928 (ratified by Germany and almost all other states) had established a rule of customary international law making aggressive war illegal and the initiation or waging of such a war, with knowledge of its character and freedom of choice, an individual crime. Of course, there were precedents for the enforcement of such customary law; The Hague Convention of 1907 provided a basic international document. But the charges of crimes against humanity, which included genocide, inhumane acts committed against civilian populations, deportation and enslavement, and crimes against peace, lacked historical grounding. The foundation for holding many of events/actions as 'crimes against humanity' was that they were recognised as offences under the criminal law of every civilised nation.

57 For Lord Wright (1946) the challenge of the Nuremberg Tribunal was to respond to the horror the victors found: 'This has been called for many ages "natural law"; perhaps in modern days it is simpler to refer to it as flowing from the instinctive sense of right and wrong possessed by all decent men, or to describe it as deriving from the principles common to all civilised nations. This is or ought to be, the ultimate basis of all law.' Wright was engaging in rhetoric rather than specifying the exact basis for these 'instinctive' senses of right and wrong.

mind-set where the prevalence of law and legalism is taken for granted and defined and analysed as if this could be done on its own terms.

> This procedure has served to isolate law completely from the social context within which it exists. Law is endowed with its own discrete, integral history, its own 'science', and its own values, which are treated as a single 'block' sealed off from general social history, from politics, and from morality ... This habit of mind ... aims at preserving law from irrelevant considerations, but it has ended by fencing legal thinking off from all contact with the rest of historical thought and experience (1964: 2-3).

The second is a social technique, 'the ethical attitude that holds moral conduct to be about rule following' (*ibid*: 1).

Legalism, Shklar argues, is a political choice; furthermore the question, 'what is law?' is not a question lawyers can answer, precisely because the question is profoundly political.

The two definitions of legalism pull in opposing directions. If legalism is only one among a range of possible social techniques of ordering society what gives law the 'right' to dominate alternative methods of ordering? Moreover, the ideology of legality seemed to offer us a moral certainty complete in itself. When Shklar says that legalism is a political choice, she seems to imply that it can be sacrificed to the competing political objectives of prosecuting or not prosecuting defendants as the political desires of the powerful nations so decree.

The logical consequence of Shklar's analysis – that since legalism is a political choice, it can be sacrificed for more important ends – is not the message Shklar is offering. Shklar asserts there is good and bad politics, and there are good and bad political trials; Nuremberg was a good trial offering full legal protection to the defendants.[58] Few would argue that Nuremberg was not a good trial, but what are the criteria to distinguish good political trials from bad ones? Does Shklar argue that legality has no self-referential criteria and that legalism must be reduced in total to politics? The whole basis of the Nazi overthrow of democracy and (liberal) legalism in pre-war Germany, as explained by Goering (see Neave, 1982), was that legality was no longer necessary, that the policies of liberal democracy were less important than the ultra-nationalistic objectives of National Socialism. For Shklar, if the Allies had not utilised classic principles of legalism then the Allies would have lost central features of the culture that distinguished them from the Nazis. Moreover, key players looked – Kantian-like – towards a further extension of the criminal law to an international jurisdiction. Beyond question, Jackson saw the deeper importance of the 'crime of aggressive war' as creating a concept and category of law which would be capable of making a great contribution to the future development of international relations and law. Shklar demands that we understand the political situation and the political aims to be achieved as inherently part of the legality of the process. There was a need to reassert the rule of law after the blows

---

58 One attack directed against the Nuremberg trials was that they were exercises in partial justice, if at all, in that the vanquished were being tried in the courts of the victors, where it was thought they would not receive fair and objective treatment. However, as the trials progressed, the procedures and the quality of arguments and deliberations demonstrated their objectivity and fairness.

the idea had received by the Nazis; additionally the trial would serve as a communicative mechanism and history lesson for the American public demonstrating that there was a need for America to intervene in international affairs. The proceedings and testimony of the trials could not only serve as a forum of truth and principle but counteract tendencies in the traditionally isolationist American political culture; non-intervention could then be cast as condoning the atrocities.

Shklar's argument is at odds with the apparent legalist reasoning of the Tribunal itself, and that of many post-war commentators. It rings with a similar line of realism to Austin and serves as a counter-discourse to the legal positivism then entrenched at the time she wrote.

The questioning of legal positivism and debating obedience to Nazi law: the grudge informer case

The West German courts in 1945 and 1950 had to consider certain grudge informer cases, and a rather brief and misleading account of their decision ((1950 1) 64 *Harv L Rev* 1005) provoked a debate between the positivist HLA Hart and the procedural natural lawyer Lon Fuller (see Chapter 14). An account of the case is given in HO Pappe, 'On the validity of judicial decisions in the Nazi era' (1960) 23 *MLR* 60. The grudge informer cases concerned persons living under Nazi jurisdiction who had made use of oppressive laws and procedures for the settlement of personal grudges or ambitions.

In one case, the defendant had decided to be rid of her husband – then a German soldier – and in 1944 reported to the authorities critical remarks which he had made about Hitler whilst on leave from the army. He was charged under laws of 20 December 1934 and 17 August 1938 with making statements critical of the Reich and potentially impairing its defence. Originally convicted and condemned to death, his death sentence was rescinded to service on the eastern front. He survived the war and in time his wife and the judge who had tried his case were brought to trial upon charges under the 1871 German Criminal Code, para 239, relating to unlawful deprivation of liberty. The West German court found the judge not guilty, reasoning that his judgment had been rendered under a then-existing law, whatever one might think of its moral status. The situation of the man's wife was distinguished in that her actions were motivated by personal malice contrary to conscience, and she acted in a way that was thought immoral at the time. The court expressly denied that the question of the moral status of the laws under which the victim had in 1944 been convicted was relevant, their decision was based on their reading of the actuality of the existing law and they would not accept any argument to find Nazi law invalid on moral grounds.[59]

---

59 In another post-war decision upon very similar facts (reported in HO Pappe, 'On the validity of judicial decisions in the Nazi era' (1960) 23 *MLR* 260), the defendant was charged with unlawful deprivation of liberty and attempted homicide. Initially acquitted, the West German Federal Supreme Court quashed the decision on appeal referring the case back to the lower court. The Supreme Court made three fundamentally significant points. First, if the proceedings were improper then the presiding judge was as guilty as the informer who had initiated them. Second, there was no need to consider the validity of the Nazi laws in question since even upon their face they had not been correctly applied. The law concerned public statements and if this meant anything at all it must imply a distinction from ...

The points of dispute between Hart and Fuller was based upon a brief report which mistakenly implied that the post-war court decided the laws in question were formally invalidated by their immoral substance. Hart's argument (1958) was relatively simple: each society has a particular sociological practice whereby it 'recognises law' and the laws made in Nazi Germany, no matter that they were oppressive or immoral, were created methodologically in line with what he later came to call the operative *rule of recognition*, therefore we must recognise them as valid law. This did not resolve the issue of punishment and Hart implies that this question was an existential one for the courts: 'Are we to punish those who did evil things when they were permitted by evil rules then in force?' (1961: 211). However, for Hart it was a question of 'choice between [two] evils, which, in extreme circumstance, may have to be made', namely: (i) to decide not to punish would be to condone evil and was therefore an evil in itself; (ii) yet the principle of *nulla poena sine lege* demanded that the courts could not punish for something that was not subject to law at the time the act was brought about. To make inroads into this principle was an evil. However, Hart concluded that it would be better in the particular circumstances to enact straightforwardly retrospective penal legislation, than to rely upon an invalidating effect of immorality; however, 'a case of retroactive punishment should not be made to look like an ordinary case of punishment for an act illegal at the time' (CL: 212). Fuller (1958), on the other hand, argued that the formalistic conception of the duty to obey law embodied in positivist attempts to isolate legal obligation from all other forms of obligation was unsustainable. In the post-Nazi context, judges, according to Fuller, had no choice but to consider moral questions in their attempt to rebuild a viable legal order and must make considered statements regarding the validity and moral coherence of the Nazi mode of regulation. Fuller introduces the concept of 'fidelity to law' which is dependant upon the legal system's 'ability to command'. A legal system requires a 'minimum quantity of morality to survive'; if the 'level' of morality falls below a certain point, then the legal system can be said to cease to function since it is unable to have a claim to its citizens' obedience. Thus without a minimum moral content, a legal system ceases to be a legal system.

Let us paraphrase Fuller on the positivist enterprise. The basic aim of positivism is to demarcate legality from other forms of social ordering. The separation thesis and the rise of utilitarian thought was part of the ambitious task of distinguishing 'order' from 'good order'. However, while that is a laudable aim, by insisting on the separation thesis the positivists have not achieved their aim of promoting and protecting fidelity to law. Hart's rule of recognition leads him to conclude 'under the Nazis there was law, even if

---

59...private statements which would surely include the conversation between spouses here in question. Third, even if this point were not well taken, the court had a broad sentencing discretion and to apply the death penalty (later commuted) in a case of this type amounted to a culpable abdication of responsibility.

Thus, the wartime proceedings had been procedurally improper and both the defendant and the judge had a case to answer. The defendant had, through malicious misuse of process to encompass injury, the mens rea of crime which found its actus res in the improper proceedings to which she was an accessory. This line of argument has surely much to commend it in that it relies upon procedural abuses for the resolution of the formal question and these are far from hard to find in Nazi jurisprudence.

it was bad law'. Hart's position on moral obligation is simple (and, perhaps, dangerously optimistic, see later comments): such obviously immoral law creates an obligation to resist. Since morality is separated from the analytical definition of law, it becomes a major component in the criticism of law, and a tool to advocate for reform. Upon what grounds Hart expects the subject of an ideologically dominant system – such as Nazism – to make the claims of moral inequity, we are not told.

A central tenet of legal positivism is the separation of law and morality. This involves two distinguishable ideas: (i) positivists claim we can identify what existing law is without making any moral judgments. Whether some rule is a legal rule depends upon whether it has been laid down in some source such as a statute or a case. If it is found in some valid source, it is a valid legal rule whether it is good or bad, just or unjust. Equally, the mere fact that a rule is just and reasonable does not make it part of the law if it is not found in any recognised source of law; (ii) positivists claim that propositions of law, in which we state the existence of legal rights and duties, are not moral judgments. Opponents of positivism might argue that we cannot speak of a law as imposing duties and conferring rights unless we regard the law as morally binding. Positivists reply that such an argument plays upon two different senses of the words 'right' and 'duty'. Perhaps a law cannot confer moral rights and impose legal rights and impose moral duties unless it is morally binding, but we can treat it as conferring legal rights and imposing legal duties whether or not we regard it as morally binding. Thus positivists hold that legal rights are not a variety of moral right or duty, but are quite different. Hart's argument (developed in Chapter 9 of *The Concept of Law*) can be called a 'moral citizenship test'.[60]

In responding to Hart's earlier formulation, Fuller dismissed such a view as 'unrealistic and dangerous'. It is unrealistic in that legal positivism assumes that there can be order in a legal system without any moral content in it, it is unrealistic in that it places too heavy a burden upon the common man. While legal positivism assumes that morality can be divorced from the task of identifying the law, in actual societies the common process of identifying law – the rule of recognition, to use Hart's phraseology – is imbued with moral considerations. To recognise something as law without picturing a 'halo' around it, or feeling the pull of obligation, is perhaps a course of action

---

60   The positivist does not deny that judges sometimes decide cases by reference to moral values or consideration of social policy. What they deny is that judges have to make moral or social judgments in working out what the existing law is. Having established what the relevant rules are, however, a judge may discover that the relevant legal rules do not give an answer in the case he is dealing with. Since the pre-existing law does not give an answer, the judge must decide the case on the basic of extra-legal considerations. In doing so he will establish a new legal rule. But what makes the rule a legal rule is that it has been laid down by the judge, not the fact that it was based on moral considerations. Positivists do not deny that there may be a moral obligation to obey the law. They simply argue that the question of what the law is, and the question of whether or not it ought to be obeyed, are two separate questions. Indeed, positivists such as Bentham, Kelsen and Hart argue that our moral reflections on the scope of the obligation to obey the law are clarified by adopting a positivist conception of law. For Austin – as a thoroughgoing rule utilitarian – it would usually be in the greater good to follow a rule that one disagreed with, since the consequences of setting in train a practice of rule breaking would be worse than the inconvenience or evil caused by following a rule requiring you to perform a disagreeable task.

only open to the cynical.[61] The Nazis played on the fact that there was a great deal of cynicism in the Weimar Republic; the cynic is often searching for (lost) meaning. What is problematic about Hart's assertion is that the reality of action in the heavily mediated and bureaucratic conditions of modern life is that structural conditions of decision-making make moral reflexivity and the questions of expediency extremely difficult. Many played the games of which the Nazis were making the rules. To repeat features of the argument; would Hart wish all the members of those Jewish councils which co-operated in the production of Jews for the camps to stand trial for murder if they had lived? How was it possible to have so many Jews co-operate in the destruction of the Jews? In his analysis of the Holocaust, Bauman (1989: 26) argues that the technical-administrative success of the Holocaust was due in part to the skilful utilisation of 'moral sleeping pills' made available by modern bureaucracy and modern technology. Most action is sequential, that is, the full implications are not apparent at the beginning and once in motion a chain of involvement is hard to stop – the subject has usually more to lose by stopping than in taking that next step. Additionally, not only is it usually impossible to grasp the totality of the enterprise, but the person can close his or her eyes to anything other than the small scene they are observing/participating in.

To complement and make a realistic assessment of Hart's critical citizenship test, we need research on obedience and resistance in the conditions of modern societies. The research that we currently have does not make optimistic reading; citizens obey too easily figures in authority. The evidence of the Milgram experiments on obedience (1963; 1974) appears devastating. In conditions where a person who is regarded as in authority orders subjects to perform acts that are morally questionable, many of the subjects obey readily. Milgram is specific that a plurality of sources of power and ethical values helps avoid unquestioning obedience. 'Its only when you have ... an authority who ... operates in a free field without countervailing pressures other than the victim's protests that you get the purest (obedient) response to authority' (quoted, Bauman, 1989: 165; for general discussion on the problem of obedience and modern society see Mixon, 1989).

The response of legal positivism may be to argue that the anxieties about arbitrary power (expressed by legal theorists such as Fuller or Dworkin) cannot be controlled by changing the internality of some recognition criteria for law but by separate means, namely by close attention to understanding the relationship of law, authority and obedience, that is, to social processes. Such a response can only be sustained if the legal positivist positions his/her image of legal science as part of an interdisciplinary enterprise. While some scholars – for example Kelsen (see Chapter 12) – specifically endorse this, many appeared blind to such an implication. But the implication of this area is clear: modernity needs to be understood through a variety of lenses, and only by a critical interdisciplinary conversation can any one discipline escape its own limitations.

---

61 Even in contemporary 'unreal' accounts of law such as *LA Law*, which depict the reality of law as a glamourous bureaucracy, to be a lawyer is also to enter into a heavily morally charged field where the essence of law is the morally right.

CHAPTER 12

THE *PURE THEORY* OF HANS KELSEN

When we have grasped the unity of State and law, when we have seen that the law, the positive law (not justice), is precisely that compulsive order which is the State, we shall have acquired a realistic, non-personificative, non-anthropomorphous view, which will demonstrate clearly the impossibility of justifying the state by the law, just as it is impossible to justify the law by the law unless that term is used now in its positive sense, now in the sense of right law, justice. The attempt to justify the State by law is vain, since every State is necessarily a legal State. Law, says positivism, is nothing but an order of human compulsion. As to the justice or morality of that order positivism itself has nothing to say. The State is neither more nor less than the law, an object of normative, juristic knowledge in its ideal aspect, that is, as a system of ideas, the subject-matter of social psychology or sociology in its material aspect, that is, as a motivated and motivating, physical act (force) (Kelsen, 1935: 535).

In social and especially in legal science, there is still no influence to counteract the overwhelming interest that those residing in power have in a theory pleasing to their wishes, that is, in a political ideology ... If the author, nevertheless, ventures to publish this general theory of law and state, it is with the belief that in the Anglo-American world, where freedom of science continues to be respected and where political power is better stabilised than elsewhere, ideas are in greater esteem than power; and also with the hope that even on the European continent, after its liberation from political tyranny, the younger generation will be won over to the ideal of an independent science of law; for the fruit of such a science can never be lost (Kelsen, 1945: Preface to *General Theory of Law and State*).

APPROACHING THE *PURE THEORY*

The Austrian Hans Kelsen (1881–1973)[1] is widely regarded as having created the most extreme version of legal positivism in his self-proclaimed 'pure' theory of law. Kelsen's theory is *'pure'* in two senses:

(i) it is claimed to be free from any ideological considerations, no value-judgments are made concerning any legal system, and the analysis of 'legal norm' is unaffected by any conception of what just law is;

---

1 Hans Kelsen was born to middle-class Jewish Viennese parents who moved back to Vienna shortly after his birth in Prague in 1881. He was to become the most prominent continental legal theorist of the century. Professor of Constitutional Law at the University of Vienna from 1911 to 1930, he witnessed the collapse of the Austrian-Hungarian Empire and the troubled birth of new nations in the wake of the First World War. He set up the Austrian 'Constitutional Court' – modelled on the Supreme Court of the United States – which operated from 1921 to 1930, and Kelsen was the central framer of the 1919 constitution of the Austrian Republic. He advocated democracy and pluralism in the face of totalitarianism and had to flee to the United States from Nazism, where he became Professor of Political Science at the University of California, Berkeley.

(ii) the sociological study of law observance and the study of political, economic, or historical influences on the development of law are beyond the purview of the pure theory.

Kelsen argued that such studies presuppose a prior investigation of the nature of law, in the manner of pure theory. In other words, Kelsen claims the pure theory is antecedent to any other investigation of law; for those scholars who adopt an 'external' perspective on law actually to claim to investigate the reality of law and legal systems, must presuppose that the entity to be observed is actually law. Kelsen's work first appeared in English in 1934 with the claim that:

> The pure theory of law is a theory of positive law. As a theory it is exclusively concerned with the accurate definition of its subject matter. It endeavours to answer the question, 'what is the law?' but not the question, 'what ought it to be?' It is a science and not a politics of law (1934: 477).

Critics have marvelled at the theory's rigour but found its purity an example of formalism run wild. As a result, the theory is often studied as illustrating a continental fetish with conceptual rigour. This treats law solely in terms of formal structure leaving all issues of purpose or content beyond the interests of legal scientists, its 'purity' labelled as narrowing the role for legal theory in theorising about the social world. Thus Kelsen's theory can be charged with weakening the jurisprudential imagination in the face of social power; it turns the jurisprudent or lawyer into the meek servant of whatever political ideology is dominant (Schmitt, [1922] 1985: 45; Bloch, 1985: 146-9). Paradoxically, it was exactly those concerns which inspired Kelsen, and Kelsen regarded the charge of formalism as the most stupid criticism advanced against his theory. How then are we to approach Kelsen's theory? The *Pure Theory* can only be fully understood against the backdrop of Kelsen's concern with political and social ideology, and with his pluralist conception of knowledge; his quest for purity arose from both methodological and political concerns. Understanding this context will, hopefully, advance our appreciation of the meaning of The *Pure Theory*, and better position it within the trends of modernity.

KELSEN'S SOCIAL AND POLITICAL AGENDA

Kelsen wrote to defend a humanist conception of man against both the reductionist tendency of the scientific imagination and the encroaching power of bureaucracy. In order to save a realm of freedom for humanism, Kelsen turned to the insights of Kant, Weber and Nietzsche. To save us from the scientific reductionism by the simple application of positivism in the model of the natural sciences effected upon our ideas of human agency, Kelsen turned to the epistemology of Kant.[2] To save us from being trapped in iron bars of bureaucratic rationality, dressed up in a mystification of the state and history, he turned to the debunking ethos reminiscent of Nietzsche. Ultimately, following Weber, Kelsen argues bureaucracy is essential to the modern state, but we

---

2 'The pure theory of law rests not on Kant's philosophy of law but on his theory of knowledge' (Kelsen, 1945: 444).

should see it for what it is, an empty structure of necessity, and strip the organisational form of the state of any mystical significance or claims to historical destiny. In Kelsen's hands the state becomes a legal order, but this is neither a legal order which automatically fulfils some functionality determined by the natural order of things, nor is it assumed to embody our hopes and yearnings. To understand law in its pure structure we must strip law of its expressive dressings; law is a simple structure of coercion, a hierarchically organised system of (non-moral) norms laying out the conditions by which agents of the state are entitled (authorised) to enforce sanctions. And let us be clear: Kelsen builds this system, not to remove humanity from the legal enterprise – which is the way his work is most commonly read – but so that we understand that law has nothing to drive it forward except human projects.[3] How does Kelsen attempt to save humanism in the face of the pressures of the early 20th century?

Step one: to recognise the essential freedom of man. Man must be recognised as something more than that to which the positivist empirical sciences appear to reduce him. Kelsen argues that the social sciences once took as their subject matter a juristic or free image of man, but a rather deterministic and reductionist methodology was imported from the natural sciences as positivism developed. The result was a weakening in our ability to understand the human condition.[4] Kelsen strives to preserve the special status of human existence by arguing we must rigorously demarcate nature and society. Nor can we escape from society – social experience is inescapable in that an individual's life is bound up with other beings; the individual feels both entrapped, entangled in networks of ties which restrict him even as they offer him comrades in life's perils. We dream of transcendence in search for a full self-consciousness, but are always deluded. We want to look at reality, to look into and at ourselves in our full location; but we cannot see the totality. Thus we face mystery and relativism; we have not, historically, been able to bear

---

3   Kelsen is at pains to stress that the norms of the legal system are not pressed upon us by some 'mirror' of natural design, nor is the legal scientist when he/she attempts to analyse the objective structure of a legal order investigating some naturally produced structure, as if formed by some non-human machine. Instead, he asserts (1957: 179–80), 'from the statement that a norm 'exists' does not follow that it exists like a fact and hence must be embedded in [some non-human] reality. The statement means only that a norm is valid, that it has been created by a human act, and that means that a norm is the specific significance of a human act.'

4   'The problem of society as an object of scientific knowledge was originally the problem of determining a just order of human relationships. Sociology made its appearance as ethics, politics, jurisprudence, whether independently or as a systematic part of theology. In each case it was a normative science, a doctrine of values. Only with the beginning of the 19th century does the tendency emerge to employ a causal method in the treatment of problems of social theory. It no longer promotes an enquiry into justice, but into the causal necessity in the actual conduct of men; it is not a study which seeks to determine how men ought to act, but how they actually do act and must act according to the laws of cause and effect.

The whole turn of social theory from a normative to a causal inquiry signified a denaturation of its object of knowledge. That the natural sciences should thus push the social sciences into something not unlike an act of self-destruction, cannot be explained entirely by the fact that the successes of natural science in the 19th and 20th centuries commended its method as a model. This transformation of the science of social relationships from an ethical science into a causal sociology, explaining the reality of actual conduct and therefore indifferent to values, is largely accomplished today. It is, fundamentally, a withdrawal of social theory before an object which it has lost all hope of mastering, an involuntary admission on the part of a thousand-year-old science that, at least temporarily, it abandons its essential problem as insoluble' (Kelsen, 1945: 391).

it. We have, instead, believed in 'moral absolutivism' and in the truth of some objective reality which, existing independently of human cognition, we can use our knowledge of to correct mistakes and enable the experts (those who have looked into the 'mirror of nature') to tell us what to do.[5] Kelsen suggests that the mystery of social existence has traditionally been expressed through the framework of religious encounter; what was the basis of this experience? Primitive men faced a mysterious world, a world in which they were relatively powerless; to make the world understandable they conjured up false idols which they invested with the powers of the cosmos. To sustain community, mankind created idols of significance; and in so doing constituted centres of authority. The need to experience unity helped conjure up a supreme body which represents underlying unity while offering an incontestable source of authority. Social experience revolves around these poles of authority and community, but, Kelsen argues, authority and community 'are not two distinct objects, but merely different stages in the mind's progression, which are not successive in only one way' ([1922] 1973: 62).

Society is an object distinct from nature. It is humanity not nature that is its real subject matter; hence we cannot merely apply the same procedures to study man as we do in the natural sciences. The distinctiveness of humanity lies in mankind's special ability to issue and live by norms; the normative element confers upon humanity its ability to transcend nature. Law is a specific technique of normative structuring of human relations; it is the constitutive device for advanced human society. Law – legality – provides the mechanism by which human society can create webs of social structuring the study of jurisprudence, the study of what earlier writers have called the 'civil science', provides a route into the unique constitutive technique human society possesses: 'only insofar as consideration directed to the social maintains itself as an ethically (or juristically) normative standpoint, can society be constituted as an object distinct from nature' (ibid: 64). Thus Kelsen's analysis begins with a description, but this is a particular description; it is a phenomenological description which purports to bring out what is so essentially human about the legal order – the internal or normative aspect.

Step two: to strip law of the dangers of the expressive tradition. We have already dealt with the birth of the expressive tradition in Rousseau and Hegel; but for Kelsen the expressive reading was being co-joined to an ideology of historical destiny and historical expressionism. Legal positivism, in that it gave us the idea of law as the product of human deliberation or power, was open to being read as if it implied that right must be identified with the legal order, that is, with the rules laid down by laws, customs and jurisprudence, and with the institutions established in the course of history. Kelsen is

---

5   Kelsen contrasts 'moral absolutism', which he believes leads on to anti-democratic and authoritarian government, to 'philosophical relativism' which, while leading to sceptical arguments, links to pluralist and democratic politics. Philosophical relativism leaves the totality of existence a mystery. 'Philosophical absolutism is the metaphysical view that there is an absolute reality, that is, a reality that exists independently of human knowledge. Hence its existence is objective and unlimited in, or beyond, space and time, to which human cognition is restricted. Philosophical relativism, on the other hand, advocates the empirical doctrine that reality exists only within human knowledge, and that, as the object of cognition, reality is relative to the knowing subject. The absolute, the thing in itself, is beyond human experience; it is inaccessible to human knowledge and therefore unknowable' (1957: 198–99).

clear: we must make a choice; while it is existentially comforting to accept that our particular legal order expresses our social and political beliefs and principles, and that these are the result of the movements of historical destiny, this weakens our critical subjectivity. We become immersed in a web of ideological configurations; only a rigorous scientific approach will break this chain.[6]

Kelsen believes we must strive to create a human order worthy of respect; one that has a claim to legitimation and authority. But while we must appreciate the deed of establishing worthwhile social life, and the role of the legal order in humanising social relationships, it remains essential to maintain a critical distance from that process. Put another way: the historical search for social justice is impossible without the establishment of a concrete structure of legal ordering that makes possible more complex human interaction, which allows it to take particular forms. That legal order, however, should not be explicated either as the *essential* nor the sufficient aspect and embodiment of right and justice in human society. There were many in Kelsen's immediate context who fell into this trap. After World War II, many scholars believed that in Germany and Austria the institutional imagination sustained by legal positivism had lowered the ethics of law and mirrored uncritically a belief in the power of the state to create justice (*Recht*). The regime of legal regulation – the distribution of legal rights and obligations – was read as the concrete embodiment of the process whereby rights came into existence, as reflecting an underlying semi-mysterious historical process wherein 'rights wish to become', wish to express themselves in the historical progress of material things, to 'realise themselves', to 'embody themselves in time'. The law (*Recht*) is there, has a reality (*Wirklichkeit*), through the necessity of natural process – an objectivity of natural 'praxis' wherein nature has worked out for us the true path to the 'regime of human peace'. In this line of thought, legal rules are not so much made contingently by humans, but discovered in a progressive historical development. Legal order becomes confused with the order of justice; legal power with right. It is worth repeating the position of the German jurist Radbruch, who as late as 1932 in the third edition of *Rechtsphilosophie*, seemed in the grip of the German romantic image of historical destiny when he argued that those who had attained the power to impose legal regulations thereby showed that they were called upon by historical mandate to do so. The ideology underlying the work appeared to be a belief that history brings forth the true and the right, and the right belongs to those who win the battle of history. The judge has the professional duty to make the law's will to validity become *de facto* validity. The judge need only ask himself what legally ought to be done, and leave aside any subjective considerations of what morally ought to be done, or what is just or unjust. The judge is to recognise the objectivity of the law's command, trusting to the working out of the historical destiny of *right*, rather than his own sense of justice. A judge must not be

---

6   'The Pure Theory desires to present the law as it is, not as it ought to be ... that is, [it is] a theory of legal positivism. The pure theory regards itself as obligated to do no more than to grasp the essence of positive law, and by an analysis of its structure, to understand it. Specifically, the pure theory refuses to serve any political interests by supplying them with an 'ideology' by which the existing social order is justified or disqualified ... Thereby the pure theory places itself in sharp contrast to traditional jurisprudence which, consciously or unconsciously, sometimes more, sometimes less, has an 'ideological' character' (Kelsen, in Weinberger, 1973: 246–7).

influenced by his subjective, non-legal, sense of justice. Thus legal positivism appeared to instruct judges that they could not resist commands of the legal order provided the commanding authority had the valid power to execute its orders. When the Third Reich was defeated, Radbruch claimed the very attitude he had earlier advocated demonstrated the ethical powerlessness of legal positivism, and indicated the necessity to return to some form of natural law thinking. Thus he wrote in 1947 that the legal scientist should again return to the classical wisdom that there is a higher *right* than the law, a natural *right*, a divine *right*, a *right* of reason, and that injustice remains injustice as measured by that yardstick, even if that injustice is given the form of law. One who identifies *right* with the legal order makes a mistake; just as does he who identifies *right* with power. Legal positivism was held out as an impoverished form of legal imagination. In the 1920s the Catholic (later Nazi) jurist, Carl Schmitt, even went as far as claiming that Kelsen's *Pure Theory* supported this identification of power and rightful legality; it was, claimed Schmitt, the thesis of the pure bureaucrat ([1922] 1985: 45).[7]

But it was exactly this connection between law and the ideology of historical blessing that Kelsen had sought to sever. For Kelsen the pure theory was a radically realistic theory of law. It, above all, asserted that legal rules have been made by humans; they are made, not discovered by some structure of reason founded upon historical destiny. Mankind makes these laws, these structures of coercive power, these allocations of rights and duties, for social purposes, for there to be justice in the world; but their existence is no guarantee that any legal order is just. We must sharply distinguish the procedure, and the necessity for the structural form the procedure takes, from the arguments about the purposes of social life; to analyse the structure of coercive power is different from discussing the question of justice and social progress. To understand the one we analyse as legal scientists; to understand the other we analyse as philosophers, as sociologists, as concerned humans, but they are different projects. We restrict our intellectual capacities not to lessen our humanity; but to understand the limits of our knowledge and save ourselves from the enthusiasm of the petty dictators who would convince us that they have the justice of history, or of God, on their side.

We cannot fail constantly to ask: 'Who are we?' 'What is the meaning of life?' Kelsen consciously recalls the answer of the Stoics: life is a vast cosmic drama with a plot and a script. But while the Stoics argued that we must accept our ignorance of the script, in turn organised religion gave the script an author, gave variation a designer, gave cause and effect a first causer ... and ended up presenting us with a God who was the site of all power before whom we must bend down in prayer. We trembled in awe ... and then Hobbes wrestled some of that power, took the mana and gave it to the state, invested *Leviathan* with the hopes and fears of our progress. For what? Writing in the early 20th century, Kelsen saw the increasing hold of an authoritative state as buttressed by ideologies of secular historical destiny which took over the awe once given to God and

---

7 '[We can] view Kelsen's jurisprudence as the ideology of the lawyer-bureaucrat practising in changing political circumstances, who, under the most diverse forms of authority and with a relativist superiority over the momentary political authority, seeks to order systematically the positive decrees and regulations that are handed down to him.'

trapped the legal subject within the political party machinery and the bureaucratic discipline of the state apparatus. Individuality, once thought to be the emerging theme of modernity, was being reduced to nothing. Nietzsche had told of the mob psychology underlying such institutionalised awe; why, Kelsen asked, had modernity not had the courage to live without God?

> If we take the actors who play out the religious or social drama on the political stage, and strip the masks from their faces, then we no longer have God rewarding and punishing, or the state condemning and making war, but men putting coercion on other men, whether it be Mr X triumphant over Mr Y, or a wild animal slaking its reawakened thirst for blood ([1922] 1973: 67).

Once the masks have fallen, the play loses its capacity to hold us in the spell of a preordained meaning; we open ourselves up to a different set of meanings. But how are we to see the 'true' reality? Will we not simply have to adopt some new perspective to replace the illusions of the old? If we adopt, for example, a strictly naturalist scientific perspective, we discount the masks but look through 'to the naked, naturally necessary, causally determined motions of souls and bodies'. Using, thus, the tools of a strictly reductionist, empirically focused psychology or biology, we deconstruct the power of religion, the nation, the state, into ideological fictions, but then we see life only in terms of 'physical and mental acts', and asking 'for their cause and effects, will see only nature and nothing else' ([1922] 1973: 67). Man, as a human creature, a moral and political agent, dissolves into a mere complex of cause and effect. How can man be saved from extinction at the hands of naturalist science, and yet a science of law be made possible?

KELSEN'S *PURE THEORY* IS A FORMALIST ANSWER TO THE PROBLEM OF CONSTRUCTING SOCIAL STRUCTURE IN A PLURALIST REALITY

Kelsen's solution to the dilemmas he exposes is to adopt a neo-Kantian pragmatic epistemology. We can never reach absolutely 'true' reality but will always work through some conceptual scheme; the question becomes what conceptual scheme is appropriate for the material to be examined?

This issue is of vital importance for the study of law in two ways: (i) if we are to understand the uniqueness of the phenomenon of law we need a science which is faithful to the phenomenon; (ii) law itself needs to cope with the epistemological relativism that characterises the world if we face up to the absence of God, which means, epistemologically, that there is no one master script to be found to reconcile all the variation we experience. This impacts upon the political use of law; for if epistemological relativism characterises the world then we cannot accept one master script for the purposes of legal regulation. The image of Austin, wherein law is to be the rational instrument of utilitarian rule guided by the truth of the sciences of political economy and ethics, must only appear as a suggestion. How then can we establish a legitimacy for law, which ensures that our jurisprudential imagination does not overstep its capabilities, and create new illusions?

Kelsen's solution to these questions is to adopt a formalist procedure.[8] To resolve epistemological uncertainty, to confront the issue 'of error in the system of truth', the answer is procedure. In politics democracy, discussion and voting offer a method for agreeing policy, while the legal system can create a truth internal to legality.

> According to the content of a statement of law, a coercive act is to be imposed under specific conditions, and only under these conditions; and yet in a concrete case in which the coercive act, eg punishment, was imposed, it may be doubtful whether the condition foreseen in the statement of law, eg crime, was actually present, whether an innocent person has not been wrongly convicted by the state. The legal order provides for a series of checks on the judgments by superior courts, yet it understandably sets a limit to this series. The final judgment terminates in legal validity, and can no longer be altered. And hence properly speaking, the statement of law should not be held to run: if anyone steals, murders, etc, he is to be punished – for how is the absolute truth about whether anyone has done a thing to be established? It should be: if, under a specific procedure, it is presumed in the last resort of any one that he has stolen, murdered, etc, then he is to be punished. And in regard to this statement, there is no judicial error, no illegality on the part of the state (*ibid*: 79).

Truth, therefore, is internal to the set of procedures for determining it. Legal guilt or innocence, the validity of the ascription of guilt or innocence, lies in the correct procedure having been complied with. The aim of the procedure is to establish truth, but absolute truth can never be reached. There is always the possibility of some other perspective, some further step being made. But enquiry must stop somewhere.

What is the subject matter of jurisprudence? Law, and law is a human creation. What is the 'presence' specific to law? The human 'person', not reduced to an object of the empirical sciences, but viewed similar to the person possessed of a soul which provides the material for theology, a person of legal capacity; the legal subject.[9] As belief in the existence of a soul is necessary for traditional religion, so is belief in the existence of the free legal subject necessary for jurisprudence; but belief in the soul is captured by theology to establish the existence of God, and a relationship of God and subject is set up, the goal of which is to establish a unity. The believing subject is swallowed up in his love of God, and God's love of the subject. When this 'unity' is transferred to the legal subject, the state swallows up the subject in an organic unity. But when we analyse the history of man's thought we realise that God cannot exist other than as the embodiment of man's psychological crystallisation of his awe at the mystery of existence. God and

---

8　'The "purity" of a theory of law which aims at the structural analysis of positive legal orders consists in nothing else but in eliminating from its sphere problems which require a method different from that appropriate to its own specific problem. The postulate of purity is the indispensable requirement of avoiding syncretism of methods ... Elimination of a problem from the sphere of the Pure Theory of law, of course, does not imply the denial of the legitimacy of this problem or of the science dealing with it. The law may be the object of different sciences; the *Pure Theory* has never claimed to be the only possible or legitimate science of law. Sociology of law and history of law, are necessary for a complete understanding of the complex phenomenon of law' ([1948] 1957: 294).

9　'Just as man, made in the image of God, a spiritual being, appears within the system of theology not really as a physical, ie, animal organism, but as a soul, so jurisprudence must stress emphatically that man enters its consideration, not as a biologic-psychological unit, but as a "person", a specifically legal entity; and hence it creates its man likewise after the image of the state, the legal person' (Kelsen, [1922] 1973: 79–80).

state exist only if and insofar as they are believed in, and all their enormous power, which fills the history of the world, collapses if the human soul is able to rid itself of this belief (*ibid*: 80). We must destroy God in order to become fully human, but in removing our belief in God we risk losing the capacity to give ourselves a soul. Similarly, if we were to strip all expressive connotations from the idea of the state, would we lose important intellectual capacities as legal subjects? Possibly, but we would retain our freedom as humanity.

What of legal positivism?

THE INCOMPLETE RATIONALISATION OF LEGAL POSITIVISM

Legal positivism had not succeeded in freeing itself from the tendency of natural law to offer justifications to the contingent order of society. Austin's legal positivism, while purporting to separate the science of law from all moral content, actually amounted to a defence of political economy; a defence of private property. A pure legal science should not justify anything:

> In rejecting a justification of the state by the law, the Pure Theory of law does not imply that no such justification is possible. It only denies that legal science can perform that office. Indeed, it denies that it can ever be the task of legal science to justify anything. Justification implies judgment of value, and judgment of value is an affair of ethics and of politics, not, however, of pure knowledge, to the service of that knowledge legal science is dedicated (Kelsen, 1935: 535).

THE STRUCTURE OF THE PURE THEORY

Kelsen appeared to accept the Weberian picture of legal authority and analyses its formal structure. Kelsen makes certain assumptions concerning the nature of the legal system to build his *Pure Theory*, specifically he presumes that a legal system is autonomous, completely self-contained and is logically and systematically interconnected. Legal systems are hierarchical in structure (*Stufenbau*). The bulk of his writing on the *Pure Theory* is concerned with detailing the relationships of norms within a system, the possibility of conflicts or contradictions between norms, and the nature of interpretation and legislation.

The starting point is the distinction Kelsen draws between the 'is' and the 'ought' of law; Kelsen claims to provide a 'pure' theory which is descriptive of existing legal structure. But the subject matter of the legal science is the normative material of the legal order; the 'is' of Kelsen's conception of legal science consists of a description of (legal, not moral) 'oughts'. The legal order consists of a system of ought-propositions.

Kelsen reads Austin as being a relatively simple empiricist, that is to say that Austin left his analysis at a general descriptive level without making the necessary acts of interpretation required to see the specifically legal nature of the social activity observed. In essence Kelsen charges Austin with not understanding the normative structure of legality, and argues that Austin's theory in the end purported to derive 'legal oughts' from 'is's' (Kelsen, 1973: 271–287). The basic building blocks of Austin's theory were observations of social facts and the reduction of the idea of rules and obligations to the commands of a sovereign and the enforcement of these; looking for empirical data to build a science of law, the observer noted the regularities of a sovereign who was habitually obeyed and who obeyed no one else, and who commanded subjects who habitually obeyed. But Kelsen asked 'how does this describe the process wherein someone "ought" to obey the law?'

For Kelsen rules were the observable (in writing etc) features of a normative system. Rules were thus the surface features of law, norms its internal essence; while these may have originated as acts of 'will', of a Parliament, or a judge adopting custom, once accepted as 'law', they take on an independent existence; they do not depend upon the will of some commander to retain their validity: 'A norm is a rule stating that an individual ought to behave in a certain way, but not asserting that such behaviour is the actual will of anyone' (1973: 273). In an actual legal system there are things we can empirically observe – rules and behaviour – and things we cannot observe but which we impute – norms – in order to make sense of the empirical events. Norms are the non-observable intelligible aspect, the essence, of the legal order. And our analysis has to remain faithful to the nature of norms. As the legal order imposes obligations upon us, these obligations – these 'ought propositions' – cannot come from some natural order, they can only originate from an act of human willing.[10] Humans create norms by an act of human will that something ought to be done or refrained from. But once established, norms can take on an independent existence in the continuing legal order.[11] But what is this kind of ought? Is it a moral ought? Does the very existence of a legal system imply that we morally ought to obey it? No. This is a legal ought not a moral ought. The description of the legal order as a set of ought-propositions is quite different from saying what the law ought to be (prescribing a substantive content), or saying that it is worthy of moral respect.

> Legal norms may have any kind of content. There is no kind of human behaviour that, because of its nature, could not be made into a legal duty corresponding to a legal right (1945: 113).

---

10 'Nature as a system of facts, connected with one another according to the law of causality, has no will and hence cannot prescribe a definite behaviour of man. From facts, that is to say, from that which is, or actually is done, no inference is possible to that which ought to be or ought to be done. So far as the natural law doctrine tries to deduce from nature norms of human behaviour, it is based on a logical fallacy.

The same holds true with respect to human reason. Norms prescribing human behaviour can emanate only from human will, not from human reason; hence the statement that man ought to behave in a certain way can be reached by human reason only under the condition that by human will a norm has been established prescribing that behaviour; human reason can understand and describe such behaviour but cannot prescribe it. To detect norms of human behaviour in human reason is the same illusion as to deduce them from nature' (Kelsen, from *What is Justice*, 1957: 20–21).

11 I can see no reason to hold that Kelsen was committed to any version of some Platonic ideal or essences to norms. His theory of justice is not our human search for the ideal structure of norms or any such thing; humans create norms, but once created they take on an existence of their own. I see more similarities to Karl Popper's 'three worlds' idea than to any Platonic realm.

Legal norms are a specific subset of norms. Their specificality flows from the fact that (i) a norm is in essence action-directing – it may impose a duty, but may also amount to a permission; and (ii) while moral norms are mere propositions describing our subjective preferences for behaviour – thus it is impossible to prove natural law objectively – legal norms are institutionalised, and hence have a subjective and an objective character.

Note: for Kelsen moral judgments are essentially irrational in that they originate as expressions of our feelings or intuitions. Moral relativism, or the situation where no absolutely valid moral truths can be demonstrated, is the fate of modernity. It is the procedural aspect of the legal order which gives legal norms their objective validity. We have the opposite conclusion to that which motivated Austin's undeveloped final project. Austin's hope was for the coming together of law and ethics – a science of law and ethics combined – but Kelsen, far from implying that the reason Austin never took up his imagined final project was his inability to perform that task, instead argues that value irrationalism (the impossibility of scientifically proving a coherent structure which will tie in all value positions) implies that the law cannot be a natural extension of the truth of ethics since ethics is condemned to pluralism.[12] In its purity the legal system is a structure of order; its purpose is non-legal; the subject of other social sciences.

THE SPECIFIC NATURE OF THE LEGAL NORM

'Law is an order of human behaviour' (1945: 3) created by the legal method, which 'designates a specific technique of social organisation' (*ibid*: 5). This technique is essentially: (i) a coercive methodology operating through the systematic use of sanctions; and (ii) applied by agents, or officials, authorised by the legal order to apply sanctions. These two conditions mark out what is unique about the law, and what is common to all uses of the word 'law' allowing us to apply 'the word "law" to appear as the expression of a concept with a socially highly significant meaning' (*ibid*: 19). This concept it, however, true to historical reality; historically law has been about coercion.[13]

---

12 Thus Lee (1990: 188) argues that Kelsen gives us 'a conception of legal positivism as a philosophy of order but not of reform. Conceptually, the notion of good order has been rendered empty, trivial and insignificant. If this were so, the law can really only enforce order.' This is only partly correct since Kelsen believes that law as a specific social technique can be used for a variety of aims. Moreover, Lee goes on to argue that Kelsen cannot have a theory of justice and that his legal positivism amounts to the preservation of the legal order. This is wrong. Kelsen strips legal science of the responsibility for constructing 'good' order, but then leaves us to argue as economists, as political scientists, as people in search of justice.

13 'If the pure theory of law assumes that coercion is an essential element of law, it does so because a careful examination of the social orders termed "law" in the history of mankind, presents one common element, an element of great importance in social life: they all prescribe coercive acts as sanctions. In defining the concept of law as a coercive order, that is to say as an order prescribing coercive acts as sanctions, the *Pure Theory of Law* simply accepts the meaning that the term "law" has assumed in the history of mankind. In defining the law as a coercive order the Pure Theory of law conceives of the law as a specific social technique. This technique is characterised by the fact that the social order, termed "law", tries to bring about a certain behaviour of men, considered by the law-maker as desirable, by providing coercive acts as sanctions in cases of opposite behaviour' (Kelsen, 1957: 289).

While developing, or constructively reading, a normative element to 'rules', Kelsen builds upon Austin's realism, he stresses the reality of coercion and the role of officials: a legal norm is an ought-proposition directed at officials to apply a sanction in certain circumstances. In general, law consists of directions to officials to apply sanctions in the case of behaviour occurring contrary to that which the legal order demands. Law is, however, not simply prohibitory, it may enable people to create sound relations and reshape transactions, say in the creation of a will. The law is a form of social control that proceeds by way of either imposing duties or conferring powers upon officials to apply sanctions. Legal science observes the subjectivity of norms behind legal norms, such as 'thieves ought to be punished', into an objectivity of the legal order, such as 'if anyone were to steal then the legal officials ought to apply the appropriate sanction'.

A citizen, strictly speaking, does not have a legal norm directed at him at all. If a citizen does something which gives rise to the circumstances under which an official ought to apply a sanction, that citizen has not done anything contrary to the legal norm, the citizen has, rather, committed what Kelsen calls a 'delict'. If we, as legal scientists, seek to understand how the policy of protecting property or preventing theft operates through law, we note the legal system does not say 'one shall not steal', it has instead a Theft Act, which lays out the conditions which constitute the crime of theft, and then lays down certain sanctions to which a person judged guilty of theft will be liable. Nowhere does the legal system actually say 'one shall not steal', instead, and objectively, it says 'if somebody steals, he shall be punished'.

Kelsen argues that particular social norms, such as 'one ought not to steal', are subjective norms which may or may not be shared by more than the sovereign body which is constructing the legal order. The subjective will, or prescriptive proposition, which the particular legal or coercive norm relates to, only lies behind the objectivity of the legal order. The legal order, however, can impose a legal objectivity over moral relativism; that is its great advantage. In a democracy the social moral norm underpinning the legal or coercive norm may be widely shared; in a totalitarian regime only a small group may share it; the legal order contains an objective legal norm in both circumstances. Kelsen terms the first social or moral norm a 'secondary norm', and the genuine legal norm as a 'primary norm'. Note: only the primary norm is regarded as a proper legal norm. Within Kelsen's scheme to argue that both norms are part of a legal system would be to fall into the trap of natural law thought, wherein an ultimately subjective (no matter how widely shared) world view is deemed as the natural order of things, requiring the law to take a certain substantive form.[14] Law is pure, and can fit on

14 'The common view has it that there are two legal duties, or norms, specifically connected with each other: (1) you are to behave in a certain way; (2) If you ... violate the duty or norm designated in (1), a coercive act is to be directed against you. But this will not do, for it does not correspond to the structure of the positive law, which essentially presents itself as an order of coercion. This whole distinction between a primary norm and a secondary statement of law, which in case of violation of the first-mentioned norm decrees an act of coercion, is not only superfluous but misleading, for the function of obligating to a ... coercion-ordaining statement of law introduced under (2), and, in the system of positive law, qua essentially coercive order, by this alone ... this whole dualism of a first norm and second, which threatens violation of the first with an act of coercion, is manifestly derived from natural law thinking' (Kelsen, in Weinberger, 1973: 53–4).

top of whatever social or moral structure you wish; even the event which constitutes a crime is not, strictly speaking, a contradiction of the legal order, rather it is the event (what Kelsen calls the delict) which calls into action the legal norm and the application of the sanction.

> Law is the primary norm, which stipulates the sanction, and this norm is not contradicted by the delict of the subject, which, on the contrary, is the specific condition of the sanction (1945: 61).

In his search for the essence of the legal system Kelsen combines a positivist observation of the role of officials and the legal institutions. The institutions apply the procedure of law's truth within evidential techniques of applying ascertaining procedures to disputed facts to see if a delict has occurred: this is a legal process, and then the legal norm is applied; sometimes the legal truth contradicts the legal norm – as in the case of a false conviction – but this is still the operation of law.[15] Kelsen is searching for the structure underlying the appearance of law by combining an analysis of law's rules and law's action. In doing so Kelsen believes it is necessary to assume that a uniform deep structure underlies all law, and he depicts this as a set of norms that takes the form of (various) directions to officials to apply sanctions in certain circumstances. In distinguishing between what he calls 'rules of law in the descriptive sense' and legal norms, Kelsen asks that legal science refrain from mere doctrinal analysis. A doctrinal approach would identify law as 'rules of law in the descriptive sense', such as, for example, the various sections of the Law of Property Act 1925, or the various rules that are obtained from case law. But these, he says, only partially describe what are the real laws, which are the legal norms, or ought-propositions, directed at officials. It is, instead, the task of legal science to transcribe all the raw material for our science produced by legal authorities into the form of statements describing what the legal norms are. In other words, a proper description of the law requires everything that we identify as law to be converted into statements of the form: 'if a person does X, then an official Y ought to apply a sanction Z'. One task of legal scientists is to bring forth the legal norms inherent in the laid-out rules of the system.

THE INTERPRETATIVE FACULTIES OF THE LEGAL SCIENTIST

In neo-Kantian terms we split our observational faculties. If we simply observe events occurring in the spatial-temporal world – the world – of simple factual events – we have no way of identifying what is significant concerning those events; isolated events or 'facts' cannot in themselves have significance. To make sense of the world we rely upon the narratives of everyday life, our memory, and in Kantian terms, our categories of understanding. Thus the legal meaning of an act is not something which is naively perceived by the senses; the legal significance of an act or event is ascertained by

---

15 As Kelsen put it in 1928: 'If somebody is validly convicted of a theft which in fact he never committed, the general norm of positive law, that 'whoever steals shall be punished' is certainly not realised, but yet "law" has been made' (Kelsen, in Weinberger, 1973: 48).

interpreting it through the materials provided to us by the memory, the narratives of social life, and, for the legal scientist, the specific tools of legal interpretation. Specifically, the existence of a legal set of statutes, for example, those concerning the killing of other human beings, determines that the act of killing is a murder.

[Identifying] an act as the execution of the death penalty rather than as a murder ... results from a thinking process: from the confrontation of this act with the criminal code and the code of criminal procedure (1967: 4).

THE MATERIAL FOR INTERPRETATION IS FOUND IN THE LEGAL SYSTEM'S NOTION OF LEGAL VALIDITY

In arguing that written reports of law, in statutes or cases, function as a scheme of interpretation, Kelsen positions legal norms within a theory of legal validity which is a hierarchical, or root of title, theory. Legal norms receive their validity from higher, more general norms, until a point is reached where we stop: at that point we come across what Kelsen calls a *basic norm*, or *Grundnorm*, which imparts validity to the whole legal order. Given the particular form of the legal norm – namely the systematic application of sanctions by officials, so that laws are in essence directions to officials to apply sanctions in certain circumstances – the hierarchy of norms should be thought of as a hierarchy of directions to officials to apply sanctions. These range from, as Kelsen says, the 'concretised sanction' which takes the form of a particular direction to a particular person to apply a particular sanction, such as a judge telling a bailiff to levy exemption on someone's goods after a warrant of execution has been issued, through to the most general form, in the form of the basic norm, which says: 'coercive acts ought to be applied in accordance with the historically first constitution'. Kelsen describes how this works in a famous example in which he contrasts the demands of a gangster for money to that of a tax official:

The command of a gangster to turn over to him a certain amount of money has the same subjective meaning as the command of an income tax official, namely that the individual at whom the command is directed, ought to pay something. But only the command of the official, not that of the gangster, has the meaning of a valid norm, binding upon the addressed individual. Only the one order, not the other, is a norm-positing act [which ought to be obeyed], because the official's act is authorised by a tax law, whereas the gangster's act is not based on such an authorising norm. The legislative act [ie creating or positing the tax law] which subjectively has the meaning of an ought, also has the objective meaning – that is, the meaning of a valid norm – because the constitution has conferred this objective meaning upon the legislative act [the constitution has laid down the methodology for the creation of valid laws]. The act whose meaning is in the constitution has not only the subjective but also the objective meaning of 'ought', that is to say, the character of a binding norm, if – in case it is the historically first constitution – we presuppose in our juristic thinking that we ought to behave as the constitution prescribes. (1970: 8)

We see here the chain of authorisation and the foundational function of the basic norm or *Grundnorm*. Since only norms can validate other norms, the validity of a norm is established by locating that norm within a hierarchy of norms. Once we accept this image, all questions of the operation of the legal order can be subsumed into this interpretative classification, for example, the legal validity of the official action of imposing a fine. As a factual event a person leaves his car in a particular place and, several weeks later, is fined a sum of money. Of themselves the factual events tell us nothing; they need interpretation through the applicable legal statutes for us to identify the legal significance of the factual acts. We look into the decision and find that he has been fined in accordance with a local byelaw that (say) requires him to park only in certain places. We examine the byelaw, and find that it has been made in accordance with a local government Act. We examine the local government Act, and find that it has been passed in accordance with the procedure that makes it an Act of Crown in Parliament. In each stage of this process, in searching for the root of title, we are looking for a more general norm that encompasses the more specific one. There is, therefore, a relationship of logical entailment between the more general norms and the more specific norms. All Acts of Parliament are valid. The Wills Act is an Act of Parliament. Therefore, the Wills Act is valid. All instruments effected in accordance with the Wills Act are valid. Therefore, this instrument effected in accordance with the Wills Act is valid, and so on, and so forth. Is there a necessary finishing point? Going up the chain of validity or hierarchy of law in order to find its root of title, must surely come to a finishing point which grounds the whole process?

Kelsen argues that we must make a logical system out of the material of the legal order. Furthermore, he appears to argue that it is only by assuming such a point that we are able to make sense of the actual activities of the legal officials and legal academics. If we were to continue the process on, then we would never be able to establish the validity of any norm, because we would have to go to infinity. But since we can establish the validity of legal norms, then we must be able to get back to some ultimate norm that confers validity upon all other norms.

THE *GRUNDNORM* OR BASIC NORM IS A PRESUPPOSITION OF THOUGHT RATHER THAN SOME EMPIRICAL EVENT OR BEING

We come across the basic norm when we cannot, in principle, trace our chain of validity back any further. Thus we find, in tracing the root of title of a byelaw, that we get back to the point beyond which we cannot go: namely to the fact that the byelaw was ultimately validated by Crown in Parliament. If we ask ourselves what the reason is for the validity of the enactments of Crown in Parliament, the answer is the set of understandings that constitute the constitution. If we ask why the constitution confers validity upon the process authorised by the constitution, the answer is that this is just what we presuppose.

> The norm which represents the reason for the validity of another norm is called the 'higher' norm. But the search for the reason of a norm's validity cannot go on indefinitely. It must end with a norm which ... is presupposed. It must be presupposed, because it cannot be 'posited', that is to say: created, by an authority whose competence would have to rest on a still higher norm ... Such a presupposed highest norm is ... the

basic norm. All norms whose validity can be traced back to one and the same basic norm constitute a system of norms, a normative order. The basic norm is the common source for the validity of all norms that belong to the same order – it is their reason of validity (1970: 194-5).

To make sense of a legal order we must presuppose that every legal order has a basic norm. In the case of some legal orders, we may trace our chain back to a constitution and find that it has been made in accordance with a previous constitution, and even there we might perhaps find that that constitution in its turn has been made in accordance with a yet earlier constitution. But ultimately there will be a point beyond which we cannot go:

> Ultimately we reach some constitution that is the first historically and that was laid down by an individual usurper or by some kind of assembly. The validity of his first constitution is the last presupposition, the final postulate, upon which the validity of all the norms of our legal order depends. It is postulated that one ought to behave as the individual, or the individuals, who laid down the first constitution have ordained (1945: 15).

It is not the first constitution which serves as the basis of validity but a more basic norm: 'The basic norm is that acts ought to be done in accordance with the historically first constitution and is not the fact of the first constitution'.

The constitution itself cannot be the basic norm, since it is a factual document or set of understandings, rather than a norm. Instead, the basic norm is: 'acts ought to be done in accordance with the constitution'. But there is no authority to lay this down or to enforce this; it is something we must presuppose.[16] In legal systems where there is no written constitution the constitution arises through custom. The basic norm of such legal systems takes the following form: 'Coercive acts ought to be applied in accordance with the customary ways of making law in that particular country'. Since the United Kingdom and New Zealand, for example, have no written constitution, we have to suppose that the basic norm of these societies is customary. A basic norm still structures the validation process, and it may be that one of the ultimate constitutional norms authorised or validated by that basic norm is: 'coercive acts ought to be applied in accordance with what Crown in Parliament enacts'. Another 'ultimate' constitutional norm would be, 'Coercive acts ought to be applied in accordance with what the common law courts decide'. How does this all fit together, and what is the exact function of the basic norm? Perhaps it is best to let Kelsen's words speak for themselves:

> This basic norm establishes the validity of positive law and expresses the hypothetical-relative character of a system of norms clothed only with the validity of positive law. It is

---

16 Kelsen was fond of illustrating this by giving the example of a father having a conversation with his son concerning the father's order to go to school (following example, 1986: 112). The son asks 'why should I go to school?', to which the father responds 'Because God has commanded that parents be obeyed – that is he has authorised parents to issue commands to children'. But the son can reply 'Why should one obey the commands of God?' The mere fact that God exists, and even the belief that he is the all powerful creator of the cosmos, does not provide an answer to the 'why should his commands be obeyed?' question. The ultimate grounding is simply 'because, as a believer, one presupposes that one ought to obey the commands of God. That is, the statement of the validity of a norm must be presupposed in a believer's thinking to ground the validity of the norms of a religious morality.'

not just the hypothesis of a special theory of law. It is merely the formulation of the assumption necessary for any positivistic grasp of legal materials. It merely raises to the level of consciousness what all jurists are, even unconsciously, doing when, in the comprehension of their subject, they reject natural law (ie, limit themselves to positive law) and yet consider the data of their cognition not as mere facts of power, but as laws, as norms. They ordinarily understand the legal relationships with which they are concerned not as the natural relation of cause and effect, but as the normative relations of obligations and rights. But why is a human act, occurring in time and space and perceptible by the senses, interpreted as a legal act (a legal transaction or a juridical decision) within the meaning of any positive (German, French, or English) law? Why should such an act be considered a norm and not simply a mere event in reality? Why should the subjective meaning of this act also be given an objective meaning? Why, in other words, does one not simply say that a certain human individual demands that another act in a specified way, but actually contends that the one is entitled to prescribe and the other obligated to act in accordance with the prescription? Why do we assume that what the act in question subjectively conveys must be done, objectively, by law? The answer of the positivist jurist is: because this individual act is based upon a norm, a general rule, a statute, because the statute prescribes that one is to act as the parties have agreed in their legal transaction, or as the judge has ordered in his decision. One may still enquire, why this 'statute' represents a norm, why it is objectively valid. *Prima facie*, the 'statute' is a mere factual matter, namely, the event of several people having expressed their will that other people should henceforth act in a certain way. But why should the will expressed by these people under these particular circumstances signify a 'statute' while, if it were done by others under other circumstances, it would by no means have the same significance? Here the answer will be: The event which we interpret as the making of a statute is in accordance with a still higher norm, the constitution, because these persons have been entrusted by the constitution with the power of making laws. This 'constitution' is, in turn, nothing else but a *prima facie* factual event whose normative meaning can only be found by recourse to the prior constitution according to whose rules it has been created. This recourse must ultimately end in the original constitution which can no longer be derived from a still earlier one. The positivistic jurist, who cannot go beyond the fundamental facts, assumes that this original historical fact has the meaning of 'constitution', that the resolution of an assembly of men or the order of a usurper has the normative significance of a fundamental law. Only by making this assumption can he demonstrate the normative meaning of all other acts which he comprehends as legal acts simply because he ultimately traces them all back to the original constitution. The hypothetical basic norm which establishes the original legislator expresses this assumption; it consciously formulates it, nothing more. This means that legal positivism does not go beyond this original constitution to produce a material and absolute justification of the legal order. It stops at that point. The basic norm is an indispensable assumption because, without it, the normative character of the basic historical event could not be established. This ultimate act, to which the positivistic jurist takes recourse and beyond which he does not proceed, is interpreted as an act of law-making as it is expressed in the basic norm, which in turn is not justified by a higher norm and therefore itself transmits only hypothetical validity (*The Basic Norm of Positive Law*, pp 395-396).

In outline this is a hierarchical root-of-title process, in which: (i) the legal norm is not an empirical phenomenon (it is not something written down, for example), rather it is an intelligible phenomenon imputed to the empirical structure of the legal order, which gives a direction, which includes a permission to an official to apply a sanction in certain circumstances; (ii) officials of the system are the main subject of legal norms; (iii) the empirical activities of citizens which call into play the legal system do not actually breach the legal norms, instead they commit delicts, factual events fulfilling the condition which gives rise to the official application of sanction; (iv) legal norms can only be validated by other norms, which are more general in scope. This process carries on, potentially to infinity; to stop the process we must postulate the existence of (v) a final basic norm, which does not depend upon another norm for its validity. This grounds the system and gives unity to the legal order.

Until 1963 Kelsen described the basic norm in terms of a postulate or theoretical presupposition. Since its function is only to make clear what we mean it has only a cognitive or an epistemological function.[17]

> The basic norm is not – as a positive legal norm is – valid because it is created in a certain way by a legal act, but … is valid because it is presupposed to be valid, because without this presupposition no human act could be interpreted as a legal act (1945: 116).

But who exactly assumes the basic norm? Kelsen appears sometimes to imply that it is anybody at all who exists as a citizen of a legal system and who talks of certain laws being valid, because it is the basic norm that gives meaning to such statements. Thus:

> The basic norm is only the necessary presupposition of any positivistic interpretation of the legal material. (1945: 116)

But he also talks of it being assumed by 'jurists':

> By formulating the basic norm … we merely make explicit what all jurists, usually unconsciously, assume when they consider positive law as a system of valid norms and not only as a complex of facts (1945: 116).

Elsewhere (in *The Pure Theory*, 1970: 204-5) he talks of it being assumed by what he calls the 'legal scientist'; it is the necessary postulate for the legal scientist to conduct the task of analysing the legal system. But we must note that two things are claimed: the first is that whoever interprets the laws as valid, and therefore, according to Kelsen, either consciously or unconsciously assumes a basic norm imputing validity to all the laws, does not thereby accept that the laws are morally valid: and, second, it is not necessary for

---

17 As Beyleveld and Brownsword bring out in their discussion of the basic norm (*Law as Moral Judgment* 1985: 239), the key to understanding Kelsen lies in understanding his epistemology:

    (i)   the basic norm performs only an epistemological function, not an ethical or political one;

    (ii) the presumption of the basic norm does not entail an attitude of approval towards the system of norms which it validates;

    (iii) neither the basic norm nor the norms validated by it have any required content. Inasmuch as they are moral norms, they are only formally moral. They are not substantially (materially) moral;

    (iv) a positive, effective, coercive order can never be described as legally invalid, though, by failing to refer to it in terms of a basic norm, it may be given a description in non-legal terms.

anyone to assume the validity of a legal order.[18] This second point is crucial: we might not want to treat the legal order as systematic, in which case we do not need to assume a Grundnorm. But, of course, as a consequence we will not be able to do positivist legal science.[19]

THE RELATIONSHIP OF VALIDITY AND EFFECTIVITY

It is a necessary condition of the presupposition or assumption of the basic norm that the system of norms to which it refers, and thereby validates, is effective over a particular territory, or as Kelsen says, is 'efficacious'. It is vital to note that this is a necessary condition only, and not a sufficient condition.

> The efficacy of the entire legal order is a necessary condition for the validity of every single norm of the order, a condition sine qua non, but not a condition per quam. The efficacy of the total legal order is a condition, not the reason for validity of its constituent norms (1945: 119).

What does this mean? First, the mere fact that there is an effective operating set of norms in a particular society – that is a set of directions to officials to apply sanctions in certain circumstances – does not guarantee that there is a set of valid laws in that society (and therefore it does not determine for the legal scientist that there is a legal system operating in that territory). The simple fact that we can observe effectiveness – cause/effect relationships between the application of sanctions by officials and non-delictual behaviour by citizens – does not provide us with the knowledge of a valid set of norms. In other words, facts of effectiveness do not mean validity; that requires a presupposition that the norms of the system are valid.

---

18 See Kelsen's 'Professor Stone and the Pure Theory of Law' (1965) 17 *Stan LR* 1128, 1143–4: 'An essential part of my theory of the basic norm is that it is not necessary to presuppose the basic norm ... A communist may indeed not admit that there is an essential difference between an organisation of gangsters and a capitalist legal order ... For he does not presuppose – as do those who interpret the coercive order as an objectively valid normative order – the basic norm'.

In explaining how the legal scientist finds values in the system, Kelsen argues (1971: 226–7): 'Taking the basic norm for granted, we may submit the juristic value judgements based on the presumed basic norm to an objective test. But there is no necessity to presuppose the basic norm. One may abstain from interpreting human behaviour according to legal norms, that is according to the meaning implicit in certain human acts. The system of norms that we call "legal order" is a possible but not a necessary scheme of interpretation. An anarchist will decline to speak of "lawful" and "unlawful" behaviour, of "legal duties" and "legal rights", or "delicts". He will understand social behaviour merely as a process whereby one forces the other to behave in conformity with his wishes or interests. The anarchist will reject the normative theory of value and accept only the interest theory. He will, in short, refuse to presume the basic norm which prescribes that ought to behave in accordance with the meaning implicit in certain human acts.'

19 The mistake many commentators make is to assume that Kelsen argues that such a system is thereby logically 'just'. For example Raz: 'For an individual to presuppose the basic norm is to interpret the legal system as normative, ie as just' (1979: 138). Raz's mistake may flow from his unconsciously reading an organist conception of the system into Kelsen. For example Raz states: 'For Kelsen all the values endorsed by one individual, all his moral opinions form necessarily one normative system based on one basic norm.' But Kelsen has a machine-like image of system, rather than any organist image as his comments aimed against Durkheim demonstrate. The organist image encourages one to think of the system as having a life, or as being more than its mere shell. Kelsen views the legal system as a mere structure which has no life of its own; life is breathed in by social and political processes.

Second, since Kelsen argues that effectiveness is a necessary condition of the validity of a legal order, it means that we can only assume effective orders of norms as valid, and it follows from this that as soon as a legal system loses its efficacy, then however much we want to assume that it is valid, we cannot.

In order for a legal norm to lose its validity, the whole legal order to which it belongs must lose its effectiveness. How can we judge? Kelsen offers an interesting proposition: when it no longer makes any sense for a legal academic to spend time analysing the laws of a previous regime.

In summary: you can't have validity without efficacy, but you can have efficacy without validity. Thus effectiveness is not a sufficient condition for the validity of a legal order, but it is a necessary condition.

THE UNIQUENESS OF THE BASIC NORM

There is only one, unique, basic norm for each legal system, and it is this basic norm that gives the system its unity:

> That a norm belongs to a certain system of norms, to a certain normative order, can be tested only by ascertaining that it derives its validity from the basic norm constituting the order (1945: 111).

The basic norm ensures that all the norms that it validates do not contradict each other. The basic norm unifies and gives 'meaning' to a set of non-contradictory norms.

> ... the principle of non-contradiction must be posited in the idea of law, since without it the notion of legality would be destroyed. This presupposition alone, which is contained in the basic norm, allows legal cognition to supply a meaningful interpretation of the legal material (1945: 406).

If two norms appear to contradict each other then one of the norms must be invalid, and we can adopt the principle that the later law in time is valid, whereby the first loses in validity. This happens according to the principle of derogation or *lex posterior derogat priori*. This principle also explains the operation of repealing laws.

> When the norms whose contents contradict one another are separated by the time of their origin ... the principle of *lex posterior derogat priori* applies. This principle, while it is not ordinarily stated as a positive rule of law, is taken for granted whenever a constitution provides for the possibility of legislative change (1945: 412).

In the case where there are contradictory legal norms referred to in the same statute, so they are not separated in time, he says that it is a matter of interpretation of the statute only; so that either one of them is valid, or perhaps neither of them is (1945: 404; see also Guest (1980))

DOES THE FICTIONAL OR PRESUPPOSED NATURE OF THE BASIC NORM DESTROY THE PURITY OF KELSEN'S THEORY?

For most of his writing the basic norm played only an epistemological role; it seemed like a Kantian category of thought. That is, it is essential to make sense of the material that the scientist wishes to analyse. But after 1963 Kelsen changes his position and the basic norm is no longer a presupposition of thought, but the fictitious product of a fictitious will. As the following extract makes clear, Kelsen seems to have realised that this depiction of the Grundnorm as a fictitious act of some fictitious will is a logical requirement if he is actually to be consistent with his idea of norms being human creations of human willing.

> To the assumption of a norm not posited by a real act of will but only presupposed in juristic thinking, one can validly object that a norm can be the meaning only of an act of will and not of an act of thinking, that there is an essential correlation between 'ought' and 'willing'. One can meet this objection only by conceding that, along with the basic norm, presupposed in thought, one must also think of an imaginary authority whose (figmentary) act of will has the basic norm as its meaning (1986: 116–7).

If the validity of a legal system is to be demonstrated by a root-of-title process then the Grundnorm must be a true norm, an act of willing, rather than a presupposition of thinking. But Kelsen admits this is not only a fiction, it is also contradictory: 'the basic norm becomes a genuine fiction in the sense of Vaihinger's philosophy of "as if". A fiction in this sense is characterised by its not only contradicting reality but also containing contradiction within itself.' The basic norm is meant to stop the possibility of infinite regress, but in that the only way of logically creating a unity to norms is by an authority, and the role of that authority is to be beyond all authority, we reach contradiction. It is therefore only by keeping in mind that we grounded our science upon a fiction, that we can keep the contradiction and the abyss at bay.

> The aim of one's thinking in presupposing the basic norm is: to ground the validity of the norms forming a positive moral or legal order; that is, to interpret the subjective meaning of the acts positing these norms as their objective meaning, ie as valid norms, and the acts in question as acts positing norms. This object can be attained only by way of a fiction. Therefore one has to keep in mind that the basic norm in the sense of Vaihinger's 'as if' philosophy is not a hypothesis – as I myself have occasionally characterised it – but a fiction, which is distinct from a hypothesis in that it is or should be accompanied by an awareness that reality does not correspond to it (*ibid*: 117).

To some critics, for example Lee (1990), recognising that the basic norm is a 'fiction' destroys any claim to being scientific. Lee argues that Kelsen's move draws his 'science' increasingly into the domain of legal realism. It then follows that the logical structure of validity and the entire defence of a legal system – as a closed hierarchy of norms able to be objectively established by the legal scientists – is compromised. What gives us a legal system after 1963? Behaviour and will … of the officials. In this reading, after 1963 the basic norm becomes a fictional act of a fictional will, which finds its empirical reality in the fact that what drives the system is the will of the officials to act as legal officials. This appears to turn Kelsen into some form of legal realist.

To other critics, for example Stewart (1981, 1986), this admission of contradiction in the basic norm means that we do not need to take Kelsen's theory seriously; it self-destructs. But there are two counter-claims to Stewart: (i) his position misunderstands the role of analytical methodologies, as will be explained in the conclusion to this chapter; and (ii) Stewart does not appear to believe that Kelsen can live with mystery. Stewart argues that Kelsen was forced to bring back in an 'assumption of an absolute subject' behind the legal order. Not only, however, can this not be demonstrated by any textual reading of Kelsen, but it goes against the entire thrust of Kelsen's critique of the metaphysics of presence which has traditionally provided justification for authority (as well as being entirely against the message of essays such as 'Absolutism and Relativism in Philosophy and Politics' [1948] 1957: 198–208). For Kelsen, we must come to live without the need of some transcendental guarantor behind the law. It also appears to tie Kelsen into believing that the legal order was 'naturally' a coherent structure; rather than, as must logically follow from Kelsen's structure, such a supposition being only the necessary presupposition for carrying out positivist analytical jurisprudence. The tension for Kelsen's work lies rather in the specificity of the Pure Theory and the open-endedness of the social field in which legal orders are embedded.

ADDITIONAL PROBLEMS

This does not mean to say that the construction of the *Pure Theory* is without its methodological problems.

1   Who identifies what the norms actually are? Take, for example, the problems of dealing with offenders: there is a variation of norms built into the system. The UK sentencing structure confers a large discretion to the sentencer – the official authorised to announce the sanction – in a mixed philosophy of sentencing (punishment). Possible norms include:

   (i)   the offender ought to be dealt with in such a way as to maximise social protection;

   (ii) the offender ought to be dealt with in such a way as to minimise his/her future offending;

   (iii) the offender ought to be dealt with in such a way as to minimise the future offending of others;

   (iv) the offender ought to be dealt with in such a way as to equate the level of the pain inflicted under punishment with the level of harm resulting from his offence;

   (v)   the offender ought to be dealt with in such a way that he is not being used as an end to achieve other purposes, such as crime reduction, rather than dealing with him as an end in himself.

   These norms are irreducibly in conflict. It is open to Kelsen to respond by asking how are we to understand this variation and conflict? Rather than being evidence of a logical defect in the idea of a legal system, is it not simply a pragmatic failure of the (empirical) system?

2   A real legal system contains both formal and informal norms. Is Kelsen's legal science only concerned with formal norms? If so, why is the range of informal norms outside the scope of the legal scientist? Kelsen's system requires an informal norm that the legal official ought to take his/her role seriously. The operation of a normative structure depends upon a range of norms; where is the boundary between norms to be considered as part of the system, and those which are the proper subject material of other analysis, of the sociologist, of the psychologist, to be drawn? Upon what grounds?

3   The diversity of functions of the system. Kelsen argues that we see the legal order as a specific social technique. In some places Kelsen writes as if there were only one technique identifying law,[20] while on other occasions he refers to penal, civil (compensatory), and administrative legal techniques (1941: 89–93, 96–97) and commentators who have been inspired by him have suggested various others. Summers (1971: 751), for example, suggests that regulatory and private arranging techniques be added. Legal study then appears from this neo-Kelsenian perspective as the study of law's methodology, explaining 'not what social functions law discharges, but how law may discharge social functions. They are descriptive of the basic legal methods that a society might possibly use, but are not necessarily descriptive of the methods any particular society actually uses'. However, when this is allowed for, the idea of a legal system itself is under pressure. The range of social functions law is called upon to perform soon undercuts the reductionist tendency to construct the one system, moreover, this awareness would necessarily lead us into an analysis of law's methodology which must be conducted empirically. That is, the idea of the legal order as a coherent normative system is under pressure, and the only way of gaining information would be through empirical research. The Pure Theory fails to close its structure against the (sociological) enquiries of legal realism, and it becomes one perspective which suggests important topics for empirical research.

HAVING STRIPPED THE STATE OF ALL MYSTICAL SIGNIFICANCE, CAN KELSEN OFFER ANYTHING TO PROVIDE SOCIAL UNITY? WHERE ARE METAPHYSICAL GUARANTEES TO BE LOCATED?

Having restricted his role as legal scientist to analysis of the structure of the legal order under the methodological principles of the *Pure Theory*, Kelsen speaks as a different person when he talks of justice. The legal scientist, the legal positivist, knows nothing of justice; he will have to enter into a conversation with others to discuss that issue. What can we look for as a firm guiding principle? Can we rely upon a thesis of the unity of

---

20   'The social technique we call "law" consists in inducing the individual, by a specific means to refrain from forcible interference in the spheres of interests of others: in case of such interference, the legal community itself reacts with a like interference in the spheres of interests of the individual responsible for the previous interference' (Kelsen, 1941: 81).

nature and its knowability? In contrast to many readings of Kelsen, it appears not.[21]
*Although Kelsen presents the Pure Theory as if the world has a rational coherence and uniformity
to it, this is only a methodological accomplishment and we must remember the conditions of its
creation.* Kelsen's Nietzschean perspectivism moves beyond the nihilism of sceptical
deconstruction. In a sense Kelsen is arguing that it is too easy simply to deny to the
world a unitary reality; we need self-conscious construction to move over the void. Is
Kelsen successful in this? Take the example of the state.

Kelsen is at pains to critique the 'mass psychology' of the state which allowed
domination.

> The assertion that the state is not merely a juristic but a sociological entity, a social reality
> existing independently of its legal order, can be substantiated only by showing that the
> individuals belonging to the same state form a unity, and that this unity is not constituted
> by the legal order but by an element which has nothing to do with law. However, such
> an element constituting the 'one in the many' cannot be found (1945: 183).

We cannot find a foundational unity. Neither, Kelsen argued in a comment directed
against the French sociologist Emile Durkheim, can sociology provide us with one.
Sociology merely presents us with 'society'; but this either refuses to recognise the
Kantian distinction between our souls and our sentience, reduces the complexity of
existence into a meaningless formula, or secularises the will of God into some 'group-
mind'. It is only the state that holds us together in the relationship of citizenship. But we
must not romanticise or mythologise the state; what then provides unity? In place of the
mysticism of the state Kelsen can offer nothing.[22] There is no 'God of the law'.
Ultimately, perhaps, Kelsen never went beyond an image of power: *thus behind the
positive law there is 'neither the absolute truth of metaphysics nor the absolute justice of natural
law. He who lifts the veil, if he close not his eyes, will find himself confronted by the Gorgon's
head of power'* (Kelsen: quoted by Tur, 1986: 177, himself citing a quote in Ebenstein).
We are drawn back to the intimate connection between legal positivism and power.

IN WHAT WAY DOES KELSEN'S *PURE THEORY* ILLUMINATE THE FATE OF LEGAL POSITIVISM?

Using labels tends to obscure detail, however Kelsen is renowned as the classic modern
legal positivist. Legal positivism has been earlier defined (in Chapter 1) by reference to
three features, namely: (i) the argument that law is a human artefact; and (ii) the dictum
that our analysis of law ought to follow the methodologies so successful in the natural
sciences, specifically that they ought to be value-free and the quest of jurisprudence is a
quest for 'realist' truth; and (iii) that the concept of law entails no substantive statement

---

21 Schmitt ([1922] 1985: 5) claimed 'at the foundation of [Kelsen's] identification of state and legal order
rests a metaphysics that identifies the lawfulness of nature and normative lawfulness. This pattern of
thinking is characteristic of the natural sciences. It is based on the rejection of all 'arbitrariness', and
attempts to banish from the realm of human mind every exception.'

22 'The purely legal theory of the state, which gets rid of the idea of the state distinct from law, is a
stateless theory of the state' (Kelsen, [1922] 1973: 81).

of morality, in other words that law empirically can (re)present any ideological or moral positioning. Legal positivism can be rephrased in terms of theoretical dreams; specifically (i) the ethos of distance; (ii) the ethos of transparency; (iii) the ethos of control. Kelsen's *Pure Theory* is a rather special case of the dreams of legal positivism.

First, the ethos of distance. Legal positivism – in Hobbes, Bentham, Austin and Kelsen – stresses the problematic of constructing common purpose and stabilising social interaction in the face of the (modern) society of (or, at least, facing the possibility of an increasing condition of) disembedded subjective desire. Legal positivism is a jurisprudence which agrees on the necessity of imposing a unifying point (and process) to our imaginative representation of the legal order, and, thus, to social constructionism in modernity. At the same time, legal positivism strives to maintain a distance between the subject and the legal order; it raises – as separate issues – questions of validity, legitimacy and obedience. Legal positivism creates and celebrates the distancing of law, morality, social purpose and legal subjectivity. One purpose is to enable the subject to be free of ideology and orientate him/herself 'rationally' toward the law and its demands.

Second, the ethos of transparency. Modernity follows the narrative of emancipation through knowledge. Linked to the ethos of distance this can be phrased as follows: the modern subject becomes free where he/she attains a state of lucid self-consciousness based on the knowledge of the nature of one's context and how things function. The idea is to know where one stands and how things operate; the subject can then relate to things and rationally calculate, to achieve ends that he/she posits for him/herself though his/her self-assertion. In the jurisprudential imagination this dictum demands a full transparency as to the nature of law; legal positivism will play its role in the task of emancipation through knowledge. However, in the traditional narratives – from Plato onwards – freedom is deeply connected with attaining perfect knowledge of the necessary structures of reality and conforming to it. This dictum flows as a connecting thread through Hobbes, Bentham, Austin and Kelsen; but Nietzsche showed how the image of reality as a well-ordered rational order was only a reassuring myth for a yet-to-be-modern humanity. A strange dialectic is thereby set up which reaches its culmination in Kelsen. Legal positivism identifies modern law with human power – law as a structure of power involves coercion, violence, but its imposition creates a (social) structure which has as its aim survival, the basic condition for social life. Moreover, that power is to be guided by the entity which founds the system. Hobbes – who starts the dialectic – gives power to the sovereign's will; Bentham offers power as the servant of utility (the truth of nature's processes); Austin gives power to the political superiors to use under the guidance of the emerging 'truths' (of utility, of political economy, etc); but Kelsen refuses to surrender the power of law to any (one) master.

Kelsen follows the tradition in legal positivism by seeking to understand its (legal) reality by using one master analysis depicting the first principle upon which the legal order is founded. We are thereby seemingly presented with the key to controlling it (our third ethos) – since the combination of critical distance and transparency is thought to render law a tool of our usage. Kelsen's analysis, however, demonstrates how this soon becomes an empty guarantee. Kelsen will not embody power in the person of the prince (Machiavelli), the sovereign (Hobbes, Bentham and Austin); the state, as the master of law, is given only a conceptual existence. In Kelsen's hands the site of power – the law – becomes only a formal container; it is an empty site.

The *Pure Theory* speaks to a modernity which is grappling with democracy, perspectivism, and indeterminacy of social purpose. Kelsen clearly identifies his *Pure Theory* as an anti-natural law project. If the overall purpose of both classical and traditional Christian ethics was to enable man to progress from his present state to his true ends, the elimination of the idea of an essential human nature and any idea of telos robs the moral framework of any substantive content. Modern society can know many masters, it is social-temporal place wherein law, power, and knowledge are open to indetermination; it is – as Nietzsche expressed it – an open sea where we are made homeless and enter into the vast adventure of creating a modern home. Because its foundations are not 'natural' its institutions are never fully established; the known is always about to be undermined by the unknown (or yet-to-be-known); and the contours of the present are defined by a multiplicity of narratives. Kelsen offers no final guarantee; he offers no empirical source of legitimation and thus gives society no definable and knowable foundational substance. Empirically, society is without clearly defined structures, no single determinations; it is a complex which escapes depiction from any single, or universal, point of view. Faced with this collapse of the traditional templates of certainty, Kelsen offers the distance, transparency and control of the *Pure Theory*.

The *Pure Theory* appears a paradox in that Kelsen builds it in the midst of diversity. In announcing its very emptiness he speaks to the disorientation of the modern social subject; this disorientation can only be countered by interdisciplinary conversation, by communication. The self-transparency of the jurisprudential imagination becomes possible from a purely technical or formal methodology. The nature of the material – the legal order – is shown to be an ideal of domination, and not in itself emancipation. Kelsen's rejection of the legal order as the expression of historical destiny, or the calling of the political party, also rejects law as the people's bible book of freedom. At best Kelsen's legal order is but a form of structure, critics demand that a proper jurisprudence ought to have given it content, but from Kelsen we learn of the mistake in equating a conceptual existence – say the rule of law or liberal democracy – with 'actually existing legal systems' or 'actually existing liberal democratic capitalism'. The critical distance Kelsen offers, is the ability to say what we empirically observe – the 'corrupt' practice – is not pure legality. The weakness of this distance lies in our forgetting the conceptual nature of this legality and treating it as the answer to our quest for wisdom.

CONCLUSION

This chapter has sought to do two things: (i) to present a picture of Kelsen's *Pure Theory*, and (ii) to present it alongside Kelsen's other writings to offer some idea of his view on the nature of social science and the role of jurisprudence vis-à-vis the dilemmas of modernity in the 20th century. The argument is that Kelsen has been treated in an unduly dismissive manner. His *Pure Theory* is reductionist towards law, however this is a reductionism which does not deny the complexity of the subject material, but arises because of the complexity of the subject material. In the eyes of most critics, the *Pure Theory* ultimately fails to deliver the truth of law – the fate of the basic norm (the *Grundnorm*) is said to bear this out – but this chapter has suggested a different route. The fate of the basic norm suggests instead, that law is not some hierarchically structured system. Kelsen's portrayal of it depended upon a fiction that it was such; perhaps this was the real meaning of Kelsen's insistence that he was only bringing out what positivist scholars were assuming! Kelsen (in 1911) began with power as the phenomenon which gives unity to a legal system, makes this the state, and then deconstructs the state. His admiration for Austin's refusal to treat the state separate from the law of persons who staff its roles means Kelsen finds that the state is simply a body of men dominating others – but he cannot include this in his neo-Kantian science of the oughts, since this is a factual understanding. What then can give unity? Only a presupposition in the sense of a Kantian category of thought. But ultimately Kelsen realises that this is a function of thinking and thus cannot ground a 'basic norm' that has to bear all the weight of founding an entire system of logically inferred relationships of ought propositions. Only an act of some all-embracing will can found a system of oughts. Kelsen calls this a necessary fiction – we are to use it while at the same time not forgetting it is not true to reality. Following Kant, Kelsen philosophises about law as if there were, for everything found within the broad compass of a 'legal system', a single necessary ground, for the sole purpose of giving legal knowledge a systematic unity.[23] Why must it be seen as a failure that the *Grundnorm* is empty and formal? Perhaps any other result would be to a claim a truth which Kelsen – in the 'true' liberal spirit – would not wish to offer. For Kelsen to have given the *Grundnorm* substance would have defeated not only his epistemology, but his image of the human enterprise. Law is not naturally a system; while the positivist legal scientist must act as if it were to construct coherent legal doctrine, in reality it can only be so through creating a community of human willing and human acts while avoiding the trap of creating a totalitarian authority.

And there are other lessons to be drawn from this encounter with Kelsen's theory which reflect upon the analytical procedure. As with Austin, the analytical methodology arises not out of some withdrawal from the complex social world, but within the conceiver's comprehensive understanding of the human enterprise. Any such understanding is both unique to the person as well as drawing upon common themes. The task of analysis is to transform parts of that 'dream-like' comprehension into a hard model which can be argued about and understood by others. But that task of analysis begins as part of a wider project and when the audience forgets that wider project the temptation is to deconstruct the conceptual scheme of the conceiver without resurrecting the problems *vis-à-vis* the human condition which gave rise to it.

---

23 The phrase from Kant is 'You should philosophise about nature as if there were, for everything which belongs to existence a single necessary ground, for the sole purpose of giving your knowledge a systematic unity' (Kant, *Critique of Pure Reason*, A 672). This, as Tur brings out (1986: 174-5) is a regulative idea. I agree with Tur that there is not any 'absolute subject' lurking behind Kelsen's Grundnorm. As Tur puts it: 'Any attempt to go beyond the formal, empty presupposition of the basic norm necessarily involves an attempt to substitute a categorical basis for the hypothetical basis of pure theory; it reverts to natural law thinking and invokes speculative and illusory metaphysics.'

There is a fallacy at the root of analytical jurisprudence, that is, the idea that analysis somehow disposes of the original wonder inherent in the question 'what is being [law]?' *Analysis is the search for the essence in being, the foundational structure which gives being unity.* When we analyse, we are drawn into the logic of analysis, ie, we aim systematically to reduce the question of ontology to a point where the structure of being is rendered visible. Analysis is Platonic in that sense. But Kelsen was anti-Platonic – there is no realm of the absolute where non-human truth and pure ideas reside that it is our destiny to find. It is our destiny only to construct, and deconstruct: our idols must be deconstructed as soon as those among us who have seized power have constructed them.

And let us remember that Kelsen's theory does not entitle a discipline to tell the 'truth' of law other than as an internal product of its methodologies; instead it leads to a division of labour. Each, however, should stick to its own methodological rules. We may wish to question whether such a sharp distinction of roles and methodologies can be achieved. Additionally, it is questionable whether the subject matter – law – really is capturable in the idea of norms. But norms do highlight a highly significant aspect. One thing is clear, jurisprudence needs a self-consciousness as to its methodologies and understandings concerning the contexts and features within which it claims to be telling the truth of law. Jurisprudence reduces itself when it seeks to be a positivist analysis of 'law', rather than seeking wisdom about law and the 'legal enterprise'. Law does not exist differently from human enterprise(s). While Kelsen saw this, his solution was a rigorous demarcation of subject matter and tasks.

Our criticism of the standard way of dealing with Kelsen is that it underplays the extent to which Kelsen believed in the complexity of the social world – and the mystery at the root of being human. We can offer a message: to understand the world is to see the structure of the world; but the world, and hence its structure, is more complex than any one perspective can capture. A perspective is true to the places where it leaves the original dream-like comprehension of the whole and logically builds or reduces, seeking purity and strength, but it cannot do more than add, it cannot capture the whole. It can, however, show us elements that we have not seen before; it can create new modes of articulation which, transcending mere description, help create the phenomena to which they relate. The failure of analytical methodology to capture the structure of the whole provides ammunition to those who wish to reject the attempt to understand the world altogether, or who believe themselves understanding it when they are actually only playing with the conventions with which they are presented with. It is part of the task of understanding to comprehend when one is playing within convention and when one is moving beyond it in search of the truth. In remembering this, we would respect Kelsen's desire to protect the language game of the jurisprudent from being sucked into ideology; this remains a crucial task. In the end social science is a human project. The *Pure Theory* is only understandable as a methodology to clarify aspects of the tool; the tool that is law in the task of living and creating fully human societies. In modernity there is no answer to that quest, there are no metaphysical guarantees; but the fact that we cannot come to a full self-consciousness in that task is no reason to abandon the rational pursuit of it.

CHAPTER 13

THE HIGH POINT OF LEGAL POSITIVISM:
HLA Hart[1] and the theory of law as a self-referring system of rules

At any given moment the life of any society which lives by rules, legal or not, is likely to consist in a tension between those who, on the one hand, accept and voluntarily co-operate in maintaining the rules, and those who, on the other hand, reject the rules and attend to them only from the external point of view as a sign of possible punishment. One of the difficulties facing any legal theory anxious to do justice to the complexity of the facts is to remember the presence of both these points of view and not to define one of them out of existence. Perhaps all our criticisms of the predictive theory of obligation may be best summarised as the accusation that this is what it does to the internal aspect of obligatory rules ...

... though such a society may exhibit the tension, already described, between those who accept the rules and those who reject the rules except where fear of social pressure induces them to conform, it is plain that the latter cannot be more than a minority, if so loosely organised a society of persons, approximately equal in physical strength, is to endure: for otherwise those who reject the rules would have too little social pressure to fear (*The Concept of Law*, 1961: 88–9).

THE CONCEPT OF LAW: THE JEWEL OF MODERN JURISPRUDENCE, OR A TESTAMENT TO ITS TIMES?

The work of HLA Hart is widely recognised as providing the zenith of legal positivism. This chapter will both describe the central theses of his classic text, *The Concept of Law* (1961, 2nd edn 1994; further references to this text annotated as CL: page no) and explain the extent to which that text is an expression of its historical location, a period we can refer to as the peak of organised modernity.[2]

---

1   HLA Hart practised at the Chancery Bar, became a lecturer in philosophy and was at first regarded as a somewhat unusual choice when appointed to the Chair in Jurisprudence at Oxford in the mid 1950s. From the time of his inaugural lecture (1954) it was clear that Hart sought to apply the style of philosophy current at Oxford at the time, ordinary language analysis or linguistic analysis, to the field of law. From the late 1950s until the 1980s, Hart was regarded as 'the outstanding contemporary representative of the tradition of English analytical jurisprudence and as one of the leading spokesmen of English liberalism' (Cohen, 1967: 418).

2   In a highly stimulating recent text Peter Wagner (*A Sociology of Modernity: Liberty and Discipline*, 1994) highlights the interconnection between social sciences as 'representations of modernity' and the particular historical period writing occurs within. Wagner (1994: 118–9) sees the period around 1960 in western Europe as the culmination of 'organised modernity' which 'developed a particular kind of reflective self-understanding as conveyed in its social science ... Organised modernity was characterised by the integration of all individuals inside certain boundaries into comprehensively organised practices. No definite places in society were ascribed to individual beings according to pre-given criteria. Social mobility existed and was part of the liberties this society offered. But it was the linkage of such liberties with the organisation of practices that provided this social configuration with ...

As the opening quotation indicates, Hart was well aware that conflict and coercion were part of the social universe of law, but the main strand of *The Concept of Law* downplayed the elements of coercion, command and habitual obedience in law, replacing the images of power and violence in the jurisprudential imagination by conceiving of law as a system of rules upon rules, of social practices informed by their own criteria of validity and normative obligation. Hart presented the benign and functionalist face of liberal legality, transforming the early positivist theme of an external coercion enforcing the law and making the subject feel 'obliged' by threat of violence to remain lawful – the threat of sanctions – into an image of the legal subject's normative obligation to abide by legal rules. Hart's argument was simple: early positivism had misunderstood law's obligatory nature viewing legality as something politically imposed on an otherwise chaotic social order to structure it, whereas legality was something which developed in evolutionary fashion through a growing complex system of different kinds of *rules*. Beginning with a fundamental recognition that law entails obligation,[3] Hart was to develop a theory of law that rendered the source of this obligation an internal effect of the structure of a modern municipal legal system, and rather than highlighting domination, Hart spoke of 'the shared acceptance of rules' (CL: 98). The law, it seemed, belonged to us all; legal rules were not to be seen as external forces upon us, but as our resources.

In short, Hart domesticated and subdued the violence that had always been a part of the institutional imagination of liberal legality. *The Concept of Law* is an elegant text which breathes reasonableness and common sense. It is easy to read without looking beyond the text to the wider stories of the hopes and fears for law in modernity. Hart provides few footnotes or references to the earlier traditions which inform his work, yet he offers an institutional imagination which both describes and justifies key elements of the period of organised modernity. A period of social history which is both near and yet far from our present location; his writing assumes the efficiency and progressive nature of social institutions, it reflects a period of time where social order and peace appeared guaranteed by modern institutions and where those institutions looked as if they were designed to enable us to achieve our personal and social desires; a period where law seemed to offer us possibilities of enablement rather than threatened coercion, and

---

2... the assets that may explain its relative stability and "success" in terms of the, at least tacit, consent of most of its members. Organisation meant that each individual was "offered" a materially secure place ... it also meant that human beings managed to structure the fields of their action in such a way – by means of formalisation, conventionalisation and routinisation, that is, by the assumption of pre-given "agreements" about the possible paths of action – that their reach could be widely extended ...

This configuration achieved a certain coherence, or closure, at about 1960 ... it appeared as a naturally "interlocking order"... '

3   'The most prominent feature of law at all times and places is that its existence means that certain kinds of human conduct are no longer optional, but in some sense obligatory' (Hart, CL: 6). Hart goes on to say that there are various senses of making conduct no longer optional, one of which is by the presence of external threats, another, however, is that moral and legal rules impose obligations. Following Schauer (1991), it is, perhaps, more apt to describe Hart's thesis as one which concerns prescriptive rules, as opposed to descriptive rules which simply state empirical regularities or generalisations (for example, 'as a rule it does not snow in London in November'). Prescriptive rules have *normative* content and are used to guide, control or change the behaviour of agents with decision-making powers.

where one could be forgiven for believing that the rule of law had replaced that rule of men so obvious to Austin, Marx and Weber.[4] This is not to say that Hart announces that his work is a defence of liberal legalism or of the rule of law ideology. Far from it. Hart offered no explicit discussion of the political morality and philosophy of the rule of law; instead we are treated to a critical destruction of a model of the imperative theory of law, ongoing discussions of social practices involving law, the relationship of law and morals, the development of international law, and a reasoned depiction of judicial adjudication as straddling the twin extremes of formalism (the image where everything is determined by the rules) and rule-scepticism (the image of nothing being determined by previously existing rules). Hart does not see any need to (openly) found his text in traditions of jurisprudential or political philosophy, rather he presents his work in the language of sociological description or the analysis of our contemporary, everyday use of legally related terms.[5] Hart, therein, denies his theory has any 'justificatory' aims (a claim repeated in the postscript to the 2nd edition 1994); but Hart justifies by implication. Without clearly locating his text, Hart joined legal positivism with wider currents of social writings – currents which presented our social institutions as comprising relatively durable sets of rules and social resources (such as the discretion of officials, or the skills of officials in interpreting written texts, for example law cases or legislation) which both constrain and enable social life. Far from limiting human choices and life projects, modern institutions were presented as if they were the key to the achievement of man's desires, the essential prerequisite to the good society. And, with the openness of the modern liberal imagination – an imagination concerning the aims of social life which refused to accept any specific conception of the good life as the final story – modern institutions were increasingly presented as if they were merely the result of functional development and could be talked about in terms of the their structural-functional

---

4   As a contemporary commentator (Cotterrell, 1989: 99) notes Hart's work has deep affinities with the idea of the rule of law: 'Hart's legal theory portrays law as a self-regulating system of rules. The rule of recognition and the other secondary rules are seen as governing the entire process of production, interpretation, enforcement, amendment and repeal of rules within the legal system. In contrast to Austin's picture of a legal order as the expression and instrument of all too human political power (the power of the sovereign and its delegates), Hart's image of law is that of a system in which rules govern power-holders; in which rules, rather than people, govern. What is, indeed, implied here is an aspect of the deeply resonant political symbol so obviously missing from Austin's jurisprudence – the symbol of the rule of law, a "government of laws and not of men".'

5   The idea of the rule of law has a long intellectual history denoting a commitment to governance through general rules, consistently and fairly applied. The rule of law requires (i) a structure of rules; (ii) officials who enforce them; and (iii) further norms or modes of operating concerning the pronouncement, recognition and adjudication of the meaning of those rules. The rule of law involves operative concepts of impartiality, neutrality, objectivity and universality all of which are crucial to liberal legalism. Attacks on the 'reality' of these concepts came from a range of sources which stress that law is involved with various social forces and effects which cannot be contained in the rule of law ideology. Hart's strategy is to postulate that such concerns have some validity and their specific criticisms are welcomed, such as that of the rule-sceptic, 'at the fringe'. But Hart constrains the sceptic by arguing that we recognise that the legal system is buttressed in large measure by 'the prestige gathered by courts from their unquestionably rule-governed operations over the vast, central areas of the law' (CL 2nd edn 154).

characteristics and capabilities, rather than in terms of their expressive or moral character.[6]

THE STRUCTURE OF *THE CONCEPT OF LAW*

An important feature of Hart's *The Concept of Law* and a reason for its attractiveness and influence is that it has an apparently simple framework with a particular structure of development and exposition. In the preface to *The Concept of Law* Hart claimed his aim was 'to further the understanding of law, coercion, and morality as different but related social phenomena' and that his work could be read in two ways: (i) as 'an essay in descriptive sociology' (CL: vii), in which we recognise from an analysis of the language of everyday life, the centrality of rules and better understand the nature of rule-bound practices.[7] This analysis of everyday linguistic usage is in turn positioned in an analytical account of the development of modern law from its pre-legal origins; (ii) as an essay in analytical jurisprudence directed at revealing or clarifying the central features of law. Achieving this aim involves working through the idea that law is a 'complex' social reality constituted of many elements or facets, some of which are more important than others, and distinguishing the contingent aspects of law's life from the central elements of the concept of law. Thus many of the concerns of the legal realist – who sought to observe law through a predictive lens seeing only the behaviour of people in social institutions – were questions of law's practice, not of law's essence, peripheral in the sense that the essence of law would not be significantly affected if they were altered.

THE CRITICISMS OF A MODEL OF THE IMPERATIVE THEORY BASED ON HART'S READING OF JOHN AUSTIN

Hart begins *The Concept of Law* with a sustained criticism of a model of the positive approach based on his reading of Austin's work, which he calls 'the clearest and the most

---

6   In the midst of these tendencies each text is a specific creation. In Hart's *The Concept of Law* one can almost smell the aroma of the post-war English countryside. Cricket, chess, conformity ... a reflection of a nation largely at peace with itself, where class conflict had been institutionalised in the legitimate and rule-bound struggles of party politics and trade union activity, where the emerging welfare state held out the possibility of pensions, education and medical provision for all; a nation confident of the value of its institutions and the discretion exercised by its officials, looking forward to a future of full employment and the continual success of both the nuclear family and its sporting teams. The dominant sociological problem appeared to be ascertaining the exact function of everything, analysing where particular parts fitted into the social whole as if within an enormous progressive machine. Of course there were problems ... sociologists wondered why did everybody conform so much? Why did they all seem to follow the rules? What were the processes of socialisation which made rule-bound behaviour seem so natural? But Hart appeared to have no such worries: he simply assumed the naturalness of rule-following behaviour – or, perhaps, more fairly, he assumed the success of socialisation practices.

7   As Hart elucidates in his discussion of the point of distinguishing between 'being obliged' and 'being under an obligation': 'until its difference is grasped, we cannot properly understand the whole distinctive style of human thought, speech and action which is involved in the existence of rules and which constitutes the normative structure of society' (CL: 86).

thorough attempt to analyse the concept of law in terms of the apparently simple elements of commands and habits'. Hart thereby expressly claims that Austin was engaged in the same project, namely of 'analysing the concept of law'; as we have seen Austin was involved in a far greater project and clarifying the nature of legal terminology was only part of it.[8] Hart states that he is building an analytical model based on Austin's theory 'which is in substance, the same as Austin's doctrine but probably diverges from it in certain points ... so we have not hesitated where Austin's meaning was doubtful or where his views seem inconsistent to ignore this and to state a clear and consistent position' (CL: 18). In fact, Hart takes only a simplified model of aspects of Austin's complex synthesis and ignores the connections Austin made between types of law (remember Austin was primarily concerned with positive law – defined as a form of political power) ethics, psychology, political economy, and ideas of social progress. Whatever one thinks of the assumptions Austin made about these various items, Austin believed in a jurisprudence which strove to understand certain aspects of an interconnected set of projects. Hart lowers his gaze to the specifics of our common sense acceptance of law; legal philosophy for Hart begins in and as the discourse of ordinary speech. It assumes the reasonableness of our contemporary language usage, and thence of our practices. What are the weaknesses Hart claims to discover in the imperative theory? Or, more correctly put, in his version of the imperative theory.

First, Hart claims that Austin failed to understand the complexity of legality because the Austinian image of law is an image of one person or group imposing their will on another (through commands and sanctions). To illustrate, Hart (CL: 18–22) develops a discussion based on Kelsen's famous distinction between the demands of a gangster to a bank clerk to hand over whatever money the bank clerk has ('hand over the money or I will shoot ... if the gunman succeeds, we would describe him as having coerced the clerk'), and the demands of a tax official addressed to a citizen of a country to pay the tax monies owing. What is wrong with seeing the order of the gangster backed by his threats of violence as similar to that of the commands of a government agency? Hart draws a vital distinction:

> To command is characteristically to exercise authority over men, not power to inflict harm, and though it may be combined with threats of harm a command is primarily an appeal not to fear but to respect for authority (CL: 20).

Hart's point concerns *authority* and generality;[9] the demands made to the bank clerk are addressed to him personally, while law is generally addressed to a class of people,[10] and although the bank clerk may well be coerced to hand over the money and feel *obliged* to do so, he is under no *obligation* to perform as ordered. The bank clerk experiences fear, but not respect. Hart draws a clear distinction between the meaning inherent in our

---

8   Which Austin believed most people, even lawyers were confused about – Austin would never have started from ordinary language analysis since that would have only made existing confusions worse.

9   'Though it may be combined with threats of harms, a command is primarily an appeal not to fear but to respect for authority' (CL: 20).

10 '... in this fact of general obedience lies a crucial distinction between laws and the original simple case of a gunman's order' (CL: 24).

linguistic expression 'being under an obligation', and that of 'being obliged'; the first links with authority while the second does not. Only by distinguishing clearly between the sets of social meanings involved in 'having an obligation' and 'being obliged', can we understand 'familiar features of municipal law in a modern state' (CL: 77).

Additionally, Hart specifies, Austin's model neglected 'the variety of laws' (Hart's title to Chapter 3 of *The Concept of Law*). Although it bears some similarities to the criminal law, the Imperative Theory cannot, according to Hart, analyse the range of laws which are enabling and not punishing: laws which entitle individuals to make wills, engage in transactions, create contracts, and develop a range of social projects which are supported by the law.[11] Austin said of contracts, that if they were not laid out in the correct form, then no contract would be created and that this nullity was, in reality, a sanction. For Hart, this is an unreal conception; instead we are asked to see the functionality of the law: contract law is a device to make agreements. In entering into a contract, ie in their appreciation and use of the law, the parties are not thinking about the sanction of nullity; rather the law is operating in a facilitative manner.

Moreover, Austin does not explain why in a modern democratic system we assume that everybody is subject to the same law. The officials of the state are still subjects, even judges. The Austinian theory of legally illimitable sovereignty suggests to Hart a total divide and that the sovereign cannot be bound by the same laws as the subjects.

In addition, Austin's theory does not explain the way in which laws originate. Hart correctly reads Austin as specifying a top-down idea of law and, while of lesser importance in the modern world, Hart argues that custom – the prime example of a bottom-up type of law, cannot be fitted into his theory. Some laws clearly look like the commands of a sovereign, for example, legislation, but judge-made law also is difficult to fit into the model. Whilst Austin says that judges are acting as delegates of the sovereign and that their decisions are tacit commands of the sovereign, Hart claims that in modern times we observe that law is created by a variety of agencies, not all of which are organised in a hierarchical structure. Just because Parliament can reverse the effect of decisions of the House of Lords does not mean that the House of Lords is a delegate of Parliament – this is simply not the way we think.

Nor, to Hart, can the Imperative Theory explain why laws continue to be valid after the sovereign which had created them has been abolished. Laws are persistent, which suggests that their origin is not simply a command at a certain time by a person or body which is later replaced by another body or person.[12] Hart introduces an idea which Austin did not talk about in any detail, that is, the notion that laws are rules and that a legal system is a complex set of rules. Hart claims that the key to modern jurisprudence is understanding what the notion of a rule involves and he goes on to identify the modern

---

11 'There are other varieties of law, notably those conferring legal powers to adjudicate or legislate or to create or vary legal relations which cannot, without absurdity, be construed as orders backed by threats' (CL: 77).

12 Hart mistakenly reads Austin's sovereign as necessarily one person or a group. Having denied the corporatist reading Austin intended, Hart charges that Austin 'failed to account for the continuity of legislative authority characteristic of a modern legal system' (CL: 77).

legal system as a union of what he terms *primary* and *secondary* rules. The idea of a rule replaces the concept of orders of the sovereign as the central focus of legal positivism and Hart claims it is necessary to understand the full character of rules and the nature of rule-bound behaviour to understand legality.[13] Namely: (i) we should distinguish a rule from a mere habit. While people do many things habitually, habits do not necessarily have sanctions behind them. Breach of a habit is not necessarily met by a hostile act, whilst for rules (particularly of certain kinds), breach causes criticism. (ii) In the case of deviation from rules, the deviation is itself usually a good reason for criticising the breach. People make judgments on rules and the following of rules; (iii) rules have an internal aspect. In Hart's view, Austin adopted the methodology of a disinterested observer in the name of being committed to a scientific approach. Austin looked for observable regularities with the result that he just saw people being told what to do and that this command was backed up by punishment. This seems like a military parade-ground image. For Hart, rules are not like this at all. The external observer will not be able to come to a full understanding of the practice of following rules by simply seeing the process in operation (CL: 55-6, 87–9). If we look at a game, for instance chess, understanding the game involves knowing the rules and becoming able to adopt an internal view. To understand the game involves more than just observing the moves. By reference to the rules and how the players operate, you are able to make judgments about the quality of the moves. It is only by achieving an internal view that one can make judgments about the skill levels of the players and as to whether the moves they make are right or wrong. Consider the example of moving the Queen:

> Chess players do not merely have similar habits of moving the Queen in the way which an external observer, who knew nothing about their attitude to the moves which they make, could record. In addition: they regard it as a standard for all who play the game. Each not only moves the Queen in a certain way himself but 'has views' about the propriety of all moving the Queen in that way. These views are manifested in the criticism of others and demands for conformity made upon others when deviation is actual or threatened, and in acknowledgment of the legitimacy of such criticism and demands when received from others. For the expression of such criticisms, demands, and acknowledgments a wide range of 'normative' language is used. 'I (you) ought not to have moved the Queen like that', 'I (you) must do that', 'That is right', 'That is wrong' (CL: 56-7).

---

13 *The idea of rule following.* Law is a special case of social rules. These are not private rules. Social rules consist of a pattern of regular behaviour where deviations are met by hostile criticism and where ideally the person who deviates comes to accept that the criticism is justified. There are three elements: (1) regular behaviour; (2) deviations are met by hostile criticism; (3) that hostile reaction is based on the norm of behaviour which gives rise to a regular pattern. The distinction between the internal point of view and external point of view is that in order to understand the rule properly one has got to understand it from its internal point of view as well as its external point of view. The internal point of view is the point of view of a person who accepts that law or standard of behaviour as justifying the hostile reaction or criticism when a breach of the rule occurs. When we talk about rule following we are not just describing regularity in behaviour, nor are talking about instinctive actions, for example of the animals. The idea of rule-following implies doing things regularly as measured against some standard which implies the idea that you can deviate from that standard by way of a choice, otherwise criticism would not have any point. Criticism is designed to make you conform.

This passage highlights Hart's methodology and functionalist account of legal development. Hart claims that in order to play the game, one must have an insider's view of what is going on. This is a critical reflective attitude which the player has as to his own conduct and that of the other parties. It involves a judgment about a certain standard of involvement of all those who play the game. The external view of the game is unrealistic and actually impossible to convey any idea of the meaning of the moves. If you had never seen chess before it would be impossible to understand what actually was going on in front of you. What sort of information could an observer get if he did not know the rules? He might see pieces move in certain ways and by observing the game over time he could possibly come to predict the way in which they were usually moved, but he would not be able to realise that the players were following the rules by a simple process of observation.

As with games, a specific form of rule-bound practice, so with legally regulated behaviour. Law makes social practices possible, and to understand law, one needs to adopt an internal view of law. The internal view of law is one of a citizen living in a system and understanding what the laws are about. At first sight, this is a comforting view of law since all citizens know enough to be able to make legal judgments of right or wrong based on an interpretation of the legal rules. Thus, Hart claims that Austin does not consider the thought processes of a citizen living inside a stable legal system. People do not merely think of orders and punishment, but they reason with rules, interpret them and make judgments about their own and other's actions.

We can pause here to ask if this is a sufficient methodology to give us any total or critical appreciation of what is going on in the name of the legal system. Hart's approach may serve to illuminate many aspects of a stable system, to bring out the meaning of concepts in everyday usage, but does it tell us anything about the meaning of the system? Moreover, is there any way in which Hart can introduce a criterion in which we can distinguish occasions when it would not be desirable to achieve the critical reflective attitude?

Was Hart's criticism of Austin an advance in theorising?

With the publication of *The Concept of Law* in 1961 came the tendency only to read Austin through the criticisms Hart offers in the first four chapters. As argued in Chapter 9 of this text, it is easy to slip into a depreciation of Austin and ignore his complex synthesis. Hart replaces the central idea of the sovereign, and the sovereign's legislative reasoning laying out a structure of legal rules imposing duties and indicating sanctions for non-performance of duties, with a vaguer idea of a system of rules themselves recognised, applied and understood by reference to other 'social' rules. At first sight the idea of rules with the related idea of obligation seems to fit with how we normally perceive what law imposes, namely, obligation. In contemporary conditions all citizens have an obligation to file a correct tax return and pay the tax owed. The gain in compatibility to our practices is purchased at the expense of critical distance; it accepts the system as it appears to operate. Hart's analysis, in part, reads as a relatively unsophisticated interpretation of Weber's idea of legal-rational authority. But Hart's analysis does not seem to require any acknowledgment of the vast range of social theory which would offer modes of interpretation of the practices Hart assumes. Not only does he refuse to reconstruct the historical position of Austin's writings – which can be referred to as an imagination of legislative rationality[14] – but it neglects Austin's fundamental point of the interconnectedness of all law. For Austin, behind the everyday operation of the civil law lay the (potential at least) threat of the criminal law. It was not just that nullity could be seen as a form of sanction, but that ultimately the criminal law guaranteed the basic rules of the game (with sanctions for fraud, intimidation, theft and so forth). The 'outer side' to civil legal theory has always been the criminal law and political sanctions.[15] As Henry Maine put it, when society moves from the pre-modern to the modern – a movement he terms a movement from status to contract – law (both civil and criminal) loses its embedment in social custom and becomes all too obviously tied to coercion as the backdrop.[16] Hart appears to overlook the fact that simply because coercion is not a common feature in terms of its use, does not mean it is not present as a psychological pressure, in fact, for Bentham, the success of sanctions would be when they were so present to the rational thoughts of a potential law-breaker that they never needed to be exercised in practice! Ignoring this, Hart's criticism of the role of sanctions behind Austin amounts to a disassociation of liberalism and coercion. It is a fundamental misrepresentation of the history of philosophical liberalism and its link with coercion. What can account for this misrepresentation?

Perhaps part of the answer lies in the methodology of analytical positivism, namely the separation of legality from politics: the creation of a model which is abstracted from intellectual tradition and social reality. But while this may be a factor in explaining the almost naive way in which Hart assumes the naturalness of everyday rule-bound activity, another explanation may lie in the changing patterns of socialisation which the legal subjects have experienced. Simply put, Hart is describing a period of modernity where successful patterns of socialisation prepare young people for their roles in a social structure largely constructed of rule-bound practices.[17] To explain this, however, would take us into the realms of social history and sociological discussions Hart either assumes

---

14 Hart does not discuss Austin's utilitarianism and pays no attention to Austin's frequent mention of the need for law to provide 'guidance' or 'intelligent' direction.

15 As Hume put it in the *Treatise* 'without the separate sanction of government [contractual promises] would have little efficacy in large and civilised societies' (*Treatise*).

16 In modernity civil law is without 'the assistance of superstition, probably that of opinion, certainly that of spontaneous impulse. The force at the back of law comes therefore to be a purely coercive force to a degree quite unknown to societies of the more primitive type' (*Early History of Institutions*, 392–93).

17 The best known writer of 1950s and 1960s American social theory, for example, Talcott Parsons, developed what came to be called a structural-functional idea of society. Parson's solution to the issue of social order was to postulate that social dynamics tended towards equilibrium and dismissed the traditional (Hobbesian and other) idea of the social contract legitimating the state to impose order (1970: 69). Instead he implied that socialisation created a sort of 'internalisation' of the norms of a living social contract. The social contract does not operate as some conscious motif, but as an internalised set of understandings instilled through socialisation into the societies' norms and sets of practices.

or ignores.[18] What is important to note, however, is that for patterns of rule-bound behaviour to continue there must exist an attitude on behalf of the participants – one may call this an ideology of rule observance, or socialisation into the norms of the practice – that renders it appropriate for them to play by the rules. The 'joy' with which Hart's finding of a shared normative organisation as the basis of everyday legality was received in the Anglo-American jurisprudential universe was not matched by any felt need to analyse the underlying historical set of processes. In his macro-social analysis, Elias placed the attainment of a monopoly on violence by the state as being the crucial prerequisite. The picture Elias (influenced by Weber) offers is one where the normality of everyday life for organised modernity is a result of two power monopolies the state attains over violence on the body (which becomes the threat of sanction on the citizens for non-compliance with legitimate laws, or the possibility of military action against enemies of the state), and violence to possessions (the ability to tax, or take land, etc by compulsory purchase). Because of such monopolies, legitimate violence no longer looks like a threat (as with Austin) but a reassuring feature – part of the security of the state.[19]

TO WHAT EXTENT DOES HART'S ESSAY IN DESCRIPTIVE SOCIOLOGY ACTUALLY OFFER A NARRATIVE OF LAW'S FUNCTIONALITY?

In *The Concept of Law* Hart faced irresolvable tensions in his analytical aims and methodologies. Hart explicitly denied any need to talk in terms of the purposes of the legal system, other than postulating a basic aim of survival. His primary methodology was to adopt the linguistic philosophy then common in the department of philosophy at Oxford which was derived from the work of JL Austin (not to be confused with John Austin, the 19th century jurist) and L Wittgenstein. The starting point of their use of linguistic philosophy (otherwise called ordinary language analysis) was that by analysing the distinctions in our common language usage (such as the distinction between 'being obliged' and 'being under an obligation') we could gain a deeper understanding of the social practices we inhabited and the meaning of the social rules we lived by. The problem of this methodology was that it quite clearly told us nothing of the big

---

18   A contemporary discussion would involve, as a start, the work of Norbert Elias (1982) on the civilising of human conduct, and Michel Foucault (1977) on the disciplining of the modern self. In a wide range of work Elias has analysed how violence came to retreat from ordinary experience in the civilising process. Elias refers to the 'courtisation' of society, or the process whereby the manners and self-restraint of the court society was imposed on the lower classes and the development of an ethical value to the taming of social aggression. Additionally 'untamed' or 'irrational' desires became sublimated into our subconscious or relegated to fantasy. 'In the midst of a large populated area which by and large is free of physical violence a 'good' society is formed. But even if the use of physical violence now recedes from human intercourse, if even duelling is now forbidden, people now exert pressure and force on each other in a wide variety of different ways' (Elias, *Power and Civility*, 1982: 270–71).

19   The threat of violence 'is no longer a perpetual insecurity that it brings into the life of the individual, but a peculiar form of security ... A continuous, uniform pressure is exerted on individual life by the physical violence stored behind the scenes of everyday life, a pressure totally familiar and hardly perceived, conduct and drive economy having been adjusted from earliest youth to this social structure' (Elias, *The Civilising Process: State Formation and Civilisation*, [1939] 1982: 328–9).

concerns of life. Ordinary language analysis is not 'grand theorising', and its practitioners have never claimed that it was. What could such a limited methodology offer for the institutional imagination of law?

Excursus on the work of Ludwig Wittgenstein

The later work of the Austrian philosopher Wittgenstein was a strong influence on Hart. In his early work Wittgenstein (1921) believed that the function of words was to point to something, to serve as a reference point to real things in the world. Thus words pictured reality. When we used a word like knife, for example, we had in mind an intuitive picture of an essential knife, and we applied the word knife to objects depending on whether or not they approximated to this notion of an ideal knife. In his later discussions and teaching Wittgenstein (published 1958, 1969), however, was to alter his conception of language radically – instead of language being controlled by reality, Wittgenstein came to realise that language actually constructed social reality. Thus it was important to look at the meaning-in-use of words.[20] How could we do this? We must investigate actual social practices and these show that words only have the meanings they display as they are embedded in these social practices. He used the phrase *language games* to describe this. In the methodology of ordinary language analysis, the analysis of the meaning of a concept, take 'knife' for example, proceeds from the commonplace to the surprising, from what we simply assume without ever questioning our usage to discovering new things about our concepts and our structures of thinking in general. To have a concept is – in part at least – to be able to use certain words correctly, to pick out instances of that to which that word refers, and to make certain appropriate kinds of judgments and discriminations. Although I may never have consciously perceived it, Wittgenstein believes that when someone asks me to bring him a knife to the table so that he can eat his meal, my ability to pick out such a knife is not due to any magical correspondence between the word knife and some essential form of 'knife' but to our common socialisation into linguistic practices. In the social practice of eating, for example, which varies somewhat over cultures, we have created an instrument called in English a knife – this instrument has certain characteristics. For example cutting ability (a rubber imitation used in filming which does not cut will

---

20 Wittgenstein begins his best known latter work, *Philosophical Investigations* (1958), with an attack upon the designative theory of language – he gives a paragraph from Augustine concerning the process of learning to speak a language as an example of learning dependent upon the picture theory of meaning. In the Augustine view 'the essence of human language ... the individual words in language name objects – sentences are combinations of such names – in this picture of language we find the roots of the following idea: Every word has a meaning. This meaning is correlated with the word. It is the object for which the word stands'. For the later Wittgenstein, this view, on which he had based the only book he actually published in his life, the *Tractatus* (1921), is seriously defective in ignoring the context of the activities in which words are embedded. He now holds that words do not have an independent meaning apart from activity, and the combination of activity and language he calls a 'language game'. It is the operation of the language game which actually provides the bedrock, or limits, of human thought. The notion of an essential meaning of 'words' is replaced by the notion of 'meaning-in-use'. It is this 'meaning-in-use' – or practice of recognising correct usage – which serves as the foundation of his theorising, as the social practice or the *rule of recognition* was for Hart.

normally be rejected). Will a plastic one or an old instrument which now hardly cuts at all still be a knife? Often there will be no absolute answer. In some contexts, for some uses, we may say one thing and in others another, and the answers will depend on how important cutting ability is in that situation. However, we would normally assume that cutting ability is part of the proper recognition of a knife. Knives are artefacts that serve purposes, thus cutting well is not simply a criterion of a knife in some circumstances but of knives in general.

The application to the study of law seems now obvious. Previous jurisprudence had been in the grip of a false view of language, instead of seeking that essence or pure entity that the word 'law' must refer to, the theory of the latter Wittgenstein argues we should look at our language usage. In his inaugural professorial lecture, *Definition and Theory in Jurisprudence*, Hart (1954) appeared to claim that previous attempts to define the meaning of law had been misplaced. They ignored the important ways in which the real meaning of law-related terms, or the way an expression of the law is actually used, is inherent in our daily use of language. By not paying attention to our actual language usage previous speculation on law was inadequate. For Hart, by examining the ways in which we use law-related terms: rights, obligations and so forth, we can gain insights as to their real meaning.

Wittgenstein moved the emphasis onto the rule-governed nature of our practices. We cannot understand human behaviour as the isolated actions of individuals, since all actions only mean something in the context of a wider framework. Words mean what they do because of the context in which they are used; an observer who knew nothing of the context would not be able to understand the words (he/she would have to learn the language first), and with practices the observer would have to learn the rules of the practice to understand what was the meaning of the practice. Nor can the meaning of social practices be privately conferred and the ascertaining the meaning of things is not to be equated with receiving some natural set of sense impressions. Wittgenstein made several famous arguments against the possibility of a 'private language'. We understand all our sensations – such as understanding our pain – through the use of the resources provided by a public language. The meaning of our 'private sensations' is located in a public language with public checks on its being used correctly. It is only through the reality of social usage that 'criteria of correct usage' is possible; one cannot have private criteria for using a word, since in that case there would be no distinction between my keeping to a rule and my only thinking I was keeping to the rule when I was not in fact doing so.

> Is what we call 'obeying a rule' something that it would be possible for only one man to do, and to do only once in his life? ... It is not possible that there should have been only one occasion on which a report was made, an order given or understood; and so on – to obey a rule, to make a report, to give an order, to play a game of chess, are customs (uses, institutions).
>
> To understand a sentence means to understand a language. To understand a language means to be master of a technique (*Philosophical Investigations*, sect 199).
>
> ... Obeying a rule is a practice. And to think one is obeying a rule is not to obey a rule.

> Hence it is not possible to obey a rule 'privately'; otherwise thinking one was obeying a
> rule would be the same thing as obeying it (*ibid*: 202).

Wittgenstein used analogies with commonly played games and coined the phrase 'language games' to refer to practices and ways of life. When cricket is played it is imperative that a set of public rules is adhered to; the game cannot be played if each participant begins to abide by his/her own private set of rules. Nor can the officials suddenly change the rules without consultation. The public rules of social practices enable the practices to continue in existence. As a consequence our search for understanding must consider the social origins of thought and experience; we are what we are largely as a result of the practices and institutions we are immersed in. Our knowledge of ourselves and our society cannot come from the atomistic experience of individuals but is itself the product of rule-governed activities which must be public and social. A game of cricket cannot be understood in terms of the private intentions of individual players; what they are doing gets its sense from the rules of the game in which they are participating.

Where, however, do the rules come from and what guides their change? Here we begin to enter into a very problematic area or what we can refer to as the limits of the methodology. The rules are embedded in a practice; indeed the rules constitute the practice or the institution. Thus we have a constitutive interaction between the rules and the society – rules help constitute the society, but the society makes the rules. Different rules and institutions will by definition produce a different society; different societies will by definition produce different rules of their social games. How can we tell which practices are better and how can we tell which are moral or immoral? How, in other words can we tell which are right and which are wrong?

Now for the tradition of deontological reasoning based on Kant (see Chapter 6 of this text) the *right* has a self-sustaining nature, things are right in and of themselves, the basis of this ascription transcends our messy this-world life practices. Kantian deontology depends upon splitting existence into the realms of the *empirical* and the *transcendentally ideal* and many cannot accept Kantian metaphysics. Against both Hume and Kant, Wittgenstein adopted epistemological pragmatism and did not expect there to be a rational justification for every level of knowledge – no absolute 'explanations' can be given for the bottom level features of our understanding, only 'descriptions'. Moreover, these descriptions are not drawn from outside of language games, but are themselves made from inside one or other such game. It is not possible to stand in some position outside of language games and judge the relationships between the words, sets, propositions, and an objective 'reality', and thus judge whether language is correctly picturing, or correlating with, or representing, reality. We are permanently within some or other language game, and there can be no transcendental appreciation of the adequacy of language games. For the later Wittgenstein, thought came out of life contexts; this was not an arbitrary irrationalism, or a void as Hume had feared, but the actual human rationality of our life forms themselves:

> All testing, all confirmation and disconfirmation of a hypothesis takes place already within
> a system. And this system is not a more or less arbitrary and doubtful point of departure
> for all our arguments: no, it belongs to the essence of what we call an argument. The

system is not so much the point of departure, as the element in which arguments have their life (*On Certainty*, No 204).

When we refer to objects in the world and suggest correlations, and so forth, we are operating within a language game, and how the world divides up to us is conditioned by the structure of that language game.

The task of the enquirer is to draw out the intricate workings of the various language games – of the rationality of our ways of life. By this procedure we consciously strive to avoid our desire for a transcendental standing point creating a 'false' reductionism by denying the necessity of 'explaining' the operation of 'foundationalism' – instead we attempt to demonstrate the processes wherein the limits of actual thought and experienced 'reality' become evident, or attested to, from within the living structures of language games.[21]

Philosophy was to be of practical use in the process of people's projects, purposes, and life forms, to say that we always operate within a language game is to accept a radical understanding of the contingency of social practices as defining what we are, and our human interrelations as constituting the social – to say, however, that these are contingent does not mean that they are arbitrary, if that means that we are entirely free to leap totally out of one historical situation and simply choose to create one's position in some other set of contingent social practices. We are, instead, to look at the substance of our language games as constituting the material expression of our lives, and seek to appreciate the rational traditions within them, while, alternatively, always posing the question of transformation: we seek to be concerned with our 'series of reminders' only because it is these which offer some real hope of solutions to cope with the concrete 'problems' of mankind in their various socio-economic-political positions.

The supposition that we can find some item absolutely independent of already operating language games upon which to base the construction of a new system is mistaken – instead of being concerned with the notion of some fundamental foundation to the bottom level features of language games we should get on with the business of identifying how we actually use and live inside our existing ones and what are the implications of their use in social life. Our general need to base our actions upon some foundation is neither embedded in a universal scheme of pure reason, nor in the constraints of a deep empirical framework conditioning existence, or in arbitrary desire, but in the operative forms of life we inhabit.

> How am I able to obey a rule? – if this is not a question about causes, then it is about the justification for my following the rule in the way I do. If I have exhausted the justifications I have reached bedrock, and my spade is turned. Then I am inclined to say: 'This is simply what I do' (PI: No 217).

What provides the guarantee of truth? Only the forms of human life:

---

21 Wittgenstein called his approach therapeutic, and claimed that he was proposing something quite different from the traditional approach to explanation. His version of philosophy was to be open-ended and non-authoritative: 'Philosophy simply puts everything before us, and neither explains nor deduces anything – Since everything lies open to view there is nothing to explain. For what is hidden, for example, is of no great interest to us.' But he went on to say in the same paragraph: 'The work of the philosopher consists in assembling reminders for a particular purpose.'

'So you are saying that human agreement decides what is true and what is false?' – It is what human beings say that is true and false; and they agree in the language they use. That is not agreement in opinions but in form of life (*ibid*: No 241).

Our attention is turned back by the pragmatic imagination to the conduct of life and the formations which human sociality develops. Specifically Wittgenstein calls us to investigate the operation of 'language games', the words and the actions in which they are woven, 'in the practice of use', as when 'one party calls out the words, the other acts upon them' (*ibid*). Learning our language means learning how to exist inside differing language games, in which words are used in differing ways.

As a consequence it looks as if the philosopher – and by implication the jurisprudential scholar who has read his Wittgenstein – must simply clarify the odd bit of language usage (concerning law, for example) and hand over further investigations to the sociologist. But how can the sociologist offer a superior language game?

The paradox is simple: if the activities of individuals only gain sense through participation in social practices then we have to look at the latter as the sources of our explanations and we have to continually contextualise both what we are investigating and our own position. But our methodology of understanding will itself be a practice, and will itself need understanding. Thus we will need to understand the social practice of sociology before we can accept its discourse – and that in turn will be another language game, another practice, which in turn ... and so on ...

Stating that rules such as law can only be understood by embedding them in society – as Hart, following Wittgenstein, claims – does not offer us an answer about their origins. This finding leaves Hart with terrible holes in his theory. He tries to plug this possibility of infinite regress by recourse to an ultimate social practice of recognising law which he calls the rule of recognition. He cannot, however, tell us how to find the rule of recognising the *rule of recognition*; instead it is left as a presumed social practice. Hart also wishes to keep to a legal positive definition of law to save our capacity for moral analysis. Thus, simply because we agree that those rules that are accepted by a particular society's rule of recognising law are to be accepted as valid law, this does not answer the question of whether or not they command our moral obedience. However, Hart (unlike confirmed Kantian liberals like Ronald Dworkin) can offer no criteria by which we could judge the moral worth of claims to legal obedience. Because Hart keeps insisting that he is engaged only in descriptive analysis with no justificatory aims he soon looks like he is – against all his best intentions – encouraging legal nihilism; we are offered no criteria by which to judge legality.

Some critics (for example, Rosen, 1969) consider that ordinary language analysis is, *per se*, nihilist. Certainly, the charge of relativism was often labelled against Wittgenstein. If rules can be justified only in the context of a particular society, how can we make any decisions as to whether whole societies – such as Nazi Germany or South Africa under apartheid – can be 'correctly' judged right or wrong, morally acceptable or indefensible? If everything is contextual, is not everything relative (to the context)?

Wittgenstein – and Hart – have two lines of response. The *first* is to deny that we need foundations. This anti-foundationalism has become the way out for certain post-modern writers,[22] and Wittgenstein simply asserts we must always be using some or other system of rules.[23] We cannot step outside, thus we simply stop somewhere, to repeat part of a previous quote:

> If I have exhausted the justifications, I have reached bedrock, and my spade is turned.
> Then I am inclined to say: 'This is simply what I do' (PI 217).

Thus it is open to Hart to say that his rule of recognition is simply what he will use as the basis of his description of the legal system; but he must then accept that this leaves open and unanswered what constitutes the actual nature of the rule of recognition. Thus different societies may have different rules of recognition; the problem then is that such an expression as the rule of recognition needs to have some limitations imposed upon it, otherwise it cannot serve the role it plays in Hart's theory.

> The second answer Wittgenstein offers is one fundamentally at odds with relativism.
>
> Following a rule is analogous to obeying an order. We are trained to do so; we react to an order in a particular way. But what if one person reacts in one way and another in another to the order and the training? Which one is right?
>
> Suppose you came as an explorer into an unknown country with a language quite strange to you. In what circumstances would you say that the people there gave orders, understood them, obeyed them, rebelled against them, and so on?
>
> The common behaviour of mankind is the system of reference by means of which we interpret an unknown language (PI: 206).

Wittgenstein seems to suggest that we could provide an ultimate context, namely the 'common behaviour of mankind'. In other sections he talks of 'the correspondence between concepts and very general facts of nature', which implies that we could trace underlying reasons for human ways of acting to the most general facts about human nature.

The problem is that each solution leads in opposing directions. When he says that what has to be accepted as simply given is the forms of life, he condemns us to relativism, or at least to a plurality of language games; when he talks of the 'natural history of human beings' (PI 415), he looks like he is resurrecting the natural history of Hume.

---

22 A famous one is Richard Rorty (1979).

23 This seems to doom Wittgenstein into the position that as a philosopher he can say nothing about the worth of certain ways of life. This implication seems to follow from dicta such as 'philosophy may in no way interfere with the actual use of language; it can in the end only describe it' (PI para 124). The dilemma is actually about foundations, for Wittgenstein continues the paragraph: 'for we cannot give it any foundation either'. Philosophy in the pragmatic mould cannot give it a foundation because there is no universal plane of sense, instead the practice must be understood on its own terms, thus non-foundational philosophy must 'leave everything as it is'.

HART'S UNSATISFACTORY RESOLUTION OF THE WITTGENSTEIN LEGACY

Hart resolved this dilemma by adding onto his quite legitimate use of ordinary language analysis – an analysis which shows us how much of the daily activity in the practices which we might use law to refer to are a matter of following rules – an outline narrative of law's development from a so-called 'pre-legal' state to that of a modern municipal legal system. Many critics (for example, Fitzpatrick, 1992) have found this to be the weakest area of Hart's work and see Hart's claim to be simply doing a descriptive analysis as actually amounting to presenting a theory which justifies the procedures of the contemporary legal system by an implicit assertion that they have come about as the functional evolution of a social structure to accommodate the increasing complexity of social life.[24]

What is Hart's narrative of law's existence? Hart's presumption is that all social life involves normative regulation (the existence of social norms, expectations, sanctions for violation and/or rewards). Hart calls upon us to 'imagine a society without a legislature, courts or officials of any kind'; this is a social structure 'of primary rules of obligation'. At this 'early' or 'simple' stage of social development these norms are of a simple character ('Human beings are required to do or abstain from certain actions' CL: 78), they impose duties and have the characteristics of rules.[25] At this early stage there are not necessarily any particular institutions that create or apply the norms (for example, there are no courts or judges), nor are different types of norms identical). Hart further explains that although there will be tremendous variety in the primary norms between different societies, there must be a common core of 'rules obviously required for social life' (CL: 167). These rules lie at the empirical basis of the common concern throughout the ages referred to in the discourse of 'natural law'. Natural law theorists have mistaken the need for a structure of regulation which stems from a few basic truisms of human nature for complex systems of morality.

Hart lists the following minimal rules: (1) rules restricting resort to violence; (2) rules requiring honesty and truthfulness; (3) rules restricting the destruction of tangible things; (4) rules forbidding seizure of objects from others. These rules are minimal conditions for the persistence of social groups, ie if certain rules did not exist the social group would not 'survive'. The 'survival principle' is the basic principle Hart proposes behind social interaction and 'survival' is the irreducible fact of individual life: 'Most men most of the time wish to continue existence' (CL: 187). Without restrictions on violence, some

---

24 It is clear that John Austin also relied heavily upon the distinction between the non-legal savage state of natural society and the legal regulation of a political society. As Peter Fitzpatrick points out (1992, Ch 6), Hart draws upon a particular tradition of telling stories or creating narratives about the foundations of law and implicitly using rhetoric to announce its necessity.

25 'If a society is to live by such primary rules alone ... the rules must contain in some form restrictions on the free use of violence, theft, and deception to which human beings are tempted but which they must in general, repress, if they are to coexist in close proximity to each other. Such rules are in fact always found in the primitive societies of which we have knowledge, together with a variety of others imposing on individuals various positive duties to perform services of make contributions to the common life' (CL: 88).

requirement of truthfulness in dealing with others, and so forth, social life would be impossible. Therefore, he concludes, all societies must have these minimum rules.

The particular 'minimum rules' can be derived from a number of 'simple truisms' about human nature. Hart lists these as: human vulnerability, approximate equality, limited altruism, limited resources, limited understanding (see CL: 189-194). Hart's view of human nature builds upon the ideas of Thomas Hobbes and David Hume (see Chapters 4 and 5 of this text). Hart civilises Hobbes when he insists that social rules which restrict pursuit of self-interest 'are at any rate less nasty, less brutish, and less short than unrestrained aggression' (CL: 191).[26]

In Hart's text the path of historical development moves to the stage when it becomes possible to identify the existence of a 'law' or 'legal system'.[27] Hart posits a critical stage or turning point. This involves the emergence of a second and different type of rule which he calls a secondary rule. Secondary rules are rules that:

> provide that human beings may, by doing or saying certain things, introduce new rules of the primary type, extinguish or modify old ones, or in various ways determine their incidence or control their operation ...They confer powers, public and private (CL: 79).

They mark 'a step from the pre-legal into the legal world' (CL: 91).

THE FORMAL EXISTENCE OF A LEGAL SYSTEM

The operation of the secondary rules provides the basis for the existence of a *legal* system as distinct from a mere collection of primary rules.[28] Hart is relatively unclear as to how these rules came about, or of their precise nature. He appears to link two rather different species of rules: (i) rules which confer powers on citizens/legal subjects to vary their legal relations. An important element of his criticism of Austin is the failure of the 'command theory' of rules to incorporate, for example, the capacity or power to make a

---

26 The foundational image of Hart's idea of 'human nature' is of the isolated individual, committed to personal survival, having albeit reluctantly to accept some restriction of the unrestrained pursuit of self-interest in order that survival (both individual and social) may be possible. Hart tries to lessen the dramatic harshness of Hobbes's view of human nature, but at no time does he present his theory as having political foundations. (For criticism of the Hobbes view see, in particular, CB Macpherson, *The Political Theory of Possessive Individualism*, 1962, Chapter 2). The basic objection to Hobbes and to Hart is that their model of isolated aggressive human beings is totally ahistorical; nothing can be gained by positing isolated human beings (motivated by self-interest and survival) coming together to form 'social life' and having to relinquish their egoism. Human life is inescapably 'social' at the outset. The evidence available about the earliest or simplest societies does not bear out the aggressive savage assumptions. Whilst we should avoid the opposite error of assuming some 'golden age', the assumptions Hobbes and Hart make are closer to the picture of life in Hobbes's time and the reality of human life in competitive capitalist societies. The assumptions about human nature are certainly not 'truisms' as Hart claims; they are highly disputable.

27 Hart is not very concerned about advancing evidence either about the first stage or the intermediate process. He does not draw on the considerable body of information that exists, for example, from the anthropological studies of law in simple societies.

28 As critics are quick to point out, Hart says very little about the conditions under which secondary rules come into being. What crucial or critical changes are involved? Are they directly linked to the emergence of specifically legal institutions? Are they dependent upon the development of a distinct role which we designate as 'judicial'?

will or to enter into a contract. These types of legal rules seem to be encompassed as *private* power conferring rules; (ii) rules directed to legal officials, in particular 'judges', about how they are to identify valid rules, change and interpret them. The great bulk of his discussion of secondary rules revolves around this type of rule (see below on the types of secondary rules). There are the 'public' power-conferring rules referred to in his initial definition of secondary rules. The problem is whether or not these two different types of secondary rules are sufficiently similar to be included within the same concept. The fact that the rules are directed to two distinct categories of persons, ie 'citizens' on the one hand and 'judges' on the other, suggests a negative answer.[29]

Having been led to consider law as a special form of rules we are now faced with a related concept, namely *obligation*. Not all rules impose obligations. Those that do, can normally be distinguished from the rest in three ways (CL: 84-5): (i) they have a seriousness of social pressure, that is they tend to be rules where the demand for conformity is strong and there is a strong social pressure to prevent deviation; (ii) they tend to be rules thought of as necessary for the maintenance of normal social life; (iii) they tend to be rules thought of as requiring some sacrifice in compliance.

The idea of rules highlights a particular need for a mental element to say that we are experiencing rule-bound activity and some rules are clearly more important than others. Rules with obligations attached we can recognise as legal rules. So the legal structure is a system following this approach. Society has a range of Austin-type rules, ie duty imposing rules which prevent violence, deceit, etc, and Hart calls these primary rules (duty-imposing). For a society to exist just with these types of rules would require a majority of the population to adopt the internal view of the primary rules. That does not mean to say that they would necessarily have to agree with them but they must use them as guides. In a developed society we need more than this approach for :hat structure of rules would not make a system; it would lack coherence and the reason would be that there would be no way of deciding the limits to the rule and the relation of rules to other rules. This would lead: (i) to the problem of social uncertainty as to the relative ranking of the rule and the strength of obligation imposed; (ii) it would mean that there are no means of changing the primary rules in such a society. All that you would have is a simple list of duty-imposing rules. The system would be static and therefore unable to cope with any change in its environment. (iii) There would be no way of finally ascertaining when a violation of the rules has occurred. Without some form of recognised adjudication process, disputes would continue as to whether rules had been actually broken or not. This would lead to a general inefficiency of the system.

Hart seeks to remedy these deficiencies by specifying three different types of *secondary rules*:

---

29 Some writers suggest that there is a simple solution to this problem. It is to treat private power-conferring rules within Hart's category of 'primary rules of obligation' and to leave secondary rules as exclusively directed toward officials. However there is some reason to think that Hart did not intend and would not welcome this solution. He takes strong exception to Kelsen's attempt to define all rules as directing officials (judges) to apply certain sanctions in specified circumstances (CL: 35ff). This solution is certainly at variance with Hart's own definition of secondary rules (CL: 79).

1   *The rule of recognition* – Hart holds this out for the remedy for uncertainty. This determines what is or is not a valid primary rule for the society. The rule of recognition actively serves or stands in the place of Austin's sovereign because we can see that it stands diagrammatically at the top of a legal system. It is a rule which determines what counts as law; it determines, for example, the procedural limitations for the creation of a rule by the statement of Parliament. It is the essence of a social practice which declares what will be recognised as a valid law.

2   *Rules of change* – indicating how the primary rules are to be created or existing ones altered.

3   *Rules of adjudication* – which specify the means by which decisions are to be taken as to whether a primary rule has been broken or not.

In a modern legal system, that is, under conditions of municipal life, the situation would normally be that the citizens generally obey the primary rules and officials running the legal system recognise the secondary rules from an internal point of view. They critically reflect as to their own conduct and the conduct of other officials as to the performance of their roles and their relationship to their task.

> What is necessary is that there should be a critical reflective attitude to certain patterns of behaviour as a common standard, and that this should display itself in criticism (including self-criticism), demands for conformity, and in acknowledgments that such criticisms and demands are justified, all of which find their characteristic expression in the normative terminology of ... 'right' and 'wrong' (CL: 56).

THE INTERNAL ASPECT OF RULES AND THE QUESTION OF OBEDIENCE

Although Hart claims to escape from Austin's notion of habitual obedience and command, the image of society that Hart suggests is one where most people obey. Hart relies heavily upon an idea of internalisation, whereby the agent has an internal point of view with respect to a rule and he treats a rule's existence as crucial to the issue of what to do. The existence of the rule is a reason for action. Hart engages in no discussion as to how this attitude is brought about. In fact, as his analysis proceeds, he concedes that the majority do not need to share fully an internal view of the laws; even if many simply obey the primary rules out of habit, we still have a fully operating legal system. The officials, however, must have a more complex view and they need to share an internal view of the secondary rules. As noted below, while Hart emphasises the states of mind of the population, in the end it is the view of the officials which really counts for the existence of a legal system. On the other hand, in a democratic system, Hart hopes that most citizens will take an internal view; they will be full participants in the system.

THE STRUCTURE OF HART'S ANALYTIC THEORY OF LAW

Part of the problem with Hart's work is that he offers a hybrid work, the narrative of law's development is actually just a set of analytical propositions. Specifically:

The idea of rules

The central or essential feature of the complex concept of law is to be found in the concept of 'rules', 'the idea ... without which we cannot hope to elucidate the most elementary forms of law' (CL: 78). John Austin often referred to rules but did not develop a specific conception of what sort of social activity is involved with rules; however, Hart draws upon Kelsen (Hart does not appear to have read Weber and a lot of the *Concept of Law* is the poorer for his neglect of Weber). Wittgenstein had argued that rules of their nature are social, the concept of 'rule' necessarily involves positing a relation between certain kinds of social agents: the maker/creator of rules, the addressee or subject of the rule and a notion of official who applies and adjudicates.

The idea of a legal system

Law only exists insofar as its rules constitute a system; hence the concept 'law' involves and requires the concept of 'legal system' to contain it.

Conditions for the existence of a legal system

There are two minimum conditions which are both analytical and empirical: (i) valid rules 'must be generally obeyed'; this condition involves the behaviour of citizens/legal subjects. (ii) The secondary rules of a system 'must be effectively accepted as common public standards of official behaviour by its officials' (CL: 113); this condition relates specifically to the behaviour of officials. Once we have clarified measurable criteria of 'generally obeyed' and 'effectively accepted' we could apply them to specific historical circumstances.[30]

The idea of law as the union of primary and secondary rules

This provides the most important and distinctive of Hart's propositions, namely that: 'law is the union of primary and secondary rules'. The operation of this 'union' reveals the essential or fundamental character of law; it distinguishes the pre-legal from the legal, the acts of simple coercion masquerading as law from real law. It is the central theme of Hart's critique of Austin and the command theory of law and clarifies what the concept law 'means'.

> Most of the features of law which have proved most perplexing ... can best be rendered clear, if these two types of rule and the interplay between them are understood (CL: 79).

The proposition is therefore intended to be explanatory, rather than just being a matter of definition.

---

30 Without considering the detail of Hart's remarks we can note that the *Concept of Law* exhibits a particular trend: in the end the 'citizen requirement' becomes fairly minimal and would be met by passive forms of acceptance, whereas the 'official requirement' becomes all important. He is aware that his dual requirement leads to problems (although his discussion is not very convincing; CL: 114ff).

Hart positions the transformation of primitive society to advanced municipal society in the creation of the secondary rules of change, adjudication and recognition – therein institutions of judgment appear. Now primitive law, which did not know itself as law, is judged: the *rule of recognition*. Now man's duties, which seem natural rather than socially imposed are judged: the *rule of adjudication*. Now the rules are stripped of our naivety and made to appear contingent: the *rule of change*. This change is the arrival of an existential demand: the world is to be ruled by (appeals to) justice. Justice denotes a concern for qualities of equality and the canons of judgement. Thus the state arrives, but so to do politics, the politics of judgment, and the constitutionality of the third institution: the judge who decides and recognises on my and the 'others' positions *vis-à-vis* the law. This judge must be distant from the parties; he/she must obtain an objectivity. The secondary rules themselves need 'objective criteria' of interests and advantages.

The 'external' and 'internal' aspect of law

Very closely linked to Hart's distinction between primary and secondary rules is the importance he attaches to the dual requirement for the existence of an external and an internal 'aspect' or attitude on the part of those subject to a rule.[31]

(i) *The external aspect.* For the rule to 'exist' it must have consequences for the behaviour of those subject to it; this involves some pattern of regular conduct by the majority, ie some degree of conformity between the requirement of a rule and the behaviour of people; this does not involve any reference to the attitude of those subject to the rule towards it.[32]

(ii) *The internal aspect.* What distinguishes 'legal rules' from customs, habits, conventions, etc (but not from morality) is that they involve some distinctive attitude or subjective response. This involves more than just 'the feeling of being bound' or of 'having an obligation': 'what is necessary is that there should be a critical reflective attitude to certain patterns of behaviour as a common standard' (CL: 56) This 'critical reflective attitude' expresses itself in the use of normative language, eg 'ought', 'should', 'right', 'wrong', etc.

It is clear that in his general discussion he suggests that this internal attitude must exist widely in the population (see our opening quotation (CL: 893). As he develops his distinction between primary and secondary rules he tends to effect a shift in emphasis;

---

31 In claiming that the idea of law is a matter of rules, Hart points us to the notion that law has to do with fundamental obligations. Law is a section of the social judging of peoples' behaviour. Rules are fundamentally, according to Hart, to do with standards of behaviour. We understand what standards we have by having hostile reactions. Thus rule-bound behaviour contrasts with habitual behaviour which consists of mere regularity. There is a fundamental difference between making a rule to do some actions and having a mere habit of doing so. Perhaps you can say that 'as a rule I go to the cinema on Monday nights', which describes your regular practice. No one will criticise you if you do not go on one Monday. But this is very different from there being a social rule which specifies that you must go to the cinema on Monday nights.

32 Hart is not much concerned to explore this 'external' aspect because his attention is focused on the 'internal'. But the rather vague formulation is full of problems: it does not clarify the degree of behavioural conformity required, or whether a rule that is unknown or systematically breached is still to be regarded as a legal rule.

increasingly he refers to the requirement that it is officials who must exhibit this special attitude which seems to amount to a conscious and explicit commitment towards rule-following as a central feature of their official activity as 'judge' etc.

> The assertion that a legal system exists is therefore a Janus-faced statement looking both towards obedience by ordinary citizens and the acceptance by officials of secondary rules as critical common standards of official behaviour.

The difference between Hart and Austin has narrowed to vanishing point: in an ideal society the people would be enlightened and accept the rationality of the rules (Austin); in a healthy society the people would accept the rules as common standards of behaviour and acknowledge an obligation to obey them (Hart). Moreover, Hart acknowledges that there is no reason to deny a society where a group of officials exercising power and internally coherent in their ideology the status of having an operative legal system.

> In an extreme case, the internal point of view with its characteristic normative use of legal language ('This is a valid rule') might be confined to the official world. In this more complex system, only officials might accept and use the system's criteria of legal validity. The society in this was so might be deplorably sheeplike; the sheep might end in the slaughter-house. But there is no reason for thinking that it could not exist or for denying it the title of a legal system (CL: 114).

Austinian realism cannot easily be killed off!

The validity of law

A common feature of legal positivism is the concern to identify what it is that makes a rule valid. The question of validity is important because once a rule is identified as being 'valid' it involves consequences. Inside an operative rule system, a valid rule is one which judges will apply and ought to apply in appropriate cases, and, with reference to the legal subject, creates a presumption that it should be obeyed. (A presumption in favour of obedience is not categorical or beyond dispute; thus moral criticism such as the inequity or injustice of a law, may provide grounds for disobeying the particular law (CL: Ch 9). For Hart a rule is valid if it satisfies the criteria specified by the rule of recognition. Of course, agreeing that a rule is valid within some system says nothing about the worth of the system itself. The question of validation appears in Hart's analysis as a question internal to a system.

If the rule of recognition provides that judges shall recognise statutes as law and the rule in question is contained within a statute then it is valid. In Hart's analysis the rule of recognition is more important than the other secondary rules. It is an 'ultimate rule' which has 'supremacy' over others, moreover, it is the foundational process for a legal system; there are no further rules determining the criteria of recognition.[33]

---

33 The rule of recognition 'provides criteria for the assessment of the validity of other rules; but it is also unlike them in that there is no rule providing criteria for the assessment of its own legal validity' (CL: 104).

The ultimate openness of Hart's chain of validity

Hart specifies the existence of a 'chain of validity'; a byelaw, for example, will be valid if it is in accordance with a statutory order, which in turn derives its validity from a statute. We can picture legal rules as forming a hierarchy. The critical question which has concerned all positivists, including Hart, is what happens, following our metaphor, at the 'top' or 'apex' of the hierarchy of rules: for example, if particular rules derive their validity from a statute, what makes a statute valid? There is no rule providing criteria for the legal validity of the statute. At the apex stands the 'ultimate rule', the rule of recognition.

This rule is different from all other rules, it does not derive its validity from any other rules. Up until this point the validity of a rule is internal, that is, it is provided for within the system of rules. But the rule of recognition 'can neither be valid nor invalid' (CL: 105). Rather the existence of the ultimate rule of recognition is a matter of fact ('an external statement of fact'); the crucial 'fact' lies in the 'practice of the courts, officials and private persons in identifying the law by reference to it'. The importance of the claim that the rule of recognition is a matter of fact or 'social practice' is that Hart thereby 'escapes' from the chain of validity being a merely analytical construction, rather it is founded upon a coherent social practice.

Hart further believes that his position on the chain of validity is more attractive than Kelsen's equivalent solution, which posits a *Grundnorm* or 'basic norm' as a theoretical construct, an 'assumption' or 'hypothesis'. Hart plumps for the apparently less problematic position of insisting on the factual or empirical existence of the 'ultimate rule of recognition' which is assumes overcomes the difficulty. Hart seeks to make the question 'What is the rule of recognition?' a factual or empirical question. On examination, however, we find that the solution is elusive. Hart immediately proceeds to talk about the officials' 'acceptance' as if it necessarily provides the factual foundations he desires. Again, we can question the methodology – it is necessary to caution that the rule that people say they accept and apply is not necessarily that which actually explains their conduct (ie what they say they accept may explain what they do, but it is no guarantee). The scepticism of the American legal realists led them to question the judges' own explanation of their conduct and to suggest that the judges may, albeit unconsciously, be motivated by a complex set of values and prejudices. It is not necessary to agree with the legal realist account of judicial behaviour to conclude that it is risky to allow ourselves to accept the judges' own account of what basic rule they apply as the sure and certain evidence of the 'social practice' that constitutes the ultimate rule of recognition. The best practical illustration of these difficulties expresses itself when we examine the judicial activity of statutory interpretation where, in claiming to adhere to the basic rule of parliamentary intention, the judges have time and again given effect to what can be more accurately accounted for as the principle of giving effect to what the judges think Parliament 'should' have intended.

The rule of recognition is a vital point of Hart's work, but it is also the place at which any idea of the existence of a self-sustaining legal system breaks down. Hart is clear that 'the foundations of a legal system consist ... in an ultimate rule of recognition providing authoritative criteria for the identification of valid rules of the system … The question whether a rule of recognition exists and what its content is, ie what the criteria of validity in any given legal system are, is … an empirical, though complex, question of fact … (CL: 245, fn 97).

But what is the ultimate rule of recognition. Hart gives the example of the simple 'formula "Whatever the Queen in parliament enacts is law" as an adequate expression of the rule as to the legal competence of Parliament, and if accepted as an ultimate criterion for the identification of law' is generally a rule which serves to identify 'the law'. But can Hart simply make reference to 'the law' when he has been at pains to reduce the law to various rules? He appears to be invoking some essential presence – the being of the law – which his theory sought to say should not be part of our legal imagination. Hart admits that it does not actually identify the actual rule, rather it points us to the practice of recognising a statute, after which another set of practices, those of statutory interpretation, identify the applicable rule. This simply makes the question return in a more specific form: is there one identifiable way of interpreting statutes which would provide 'authoritative criteria for the identification of valid rules of the system'? Hart dismisses this query as being 'merely a case of the uncertainty or open texture of a particular statute and raises no fundamental question' (CL: 144).

Interestingly Hart gives the game away in the following section (similar versions are reproduced at other parts of the book) occurring in a narrative whereby the courts are called upon to adjudicate where the core and the penumbra of the 'rule' wherein the English doctrine of parliamentary sovereignty is given meaning by the courts. Hart calls this process, wherein 'the courts will have made determine at this point the ultimate rule by which valid law is identified', at first sight paradoxical, however:

> … the paradox vanishes if we remember that though every rule may be doubtful at some points, it is indeed a necessary condition of a legal system existing, that not every rule is open to doubt on all points. The possibility of courts having authority at any given time to decide these limiting questions concerning the ultimate criteria of validity, depends on the fact that, at that time, the application of those criteria to a vast area of law, including the rules which confer that authority, raises no doubts, though their precise scope and ambit do (CL:148–9).

Thus the system works as long as the parts of it that are open to question at any one time comprise only a small part of the overall whole.

The legal system may then be a diverse set of practices, ideologies, rituals and myths. Its foundations involving power and routine: perhaps, as long as it works it does not need legitimation – performance downplays the need for legitimation.

As Hart ultimately states:

> The truth may be that, when courts settle previously unenvisaged questions concerning the most fundamental constitutional rules, they get their authority to decide them accepted after the questions have arisen and the decision has been given. Here all that succeeds is success (CL: 149).

HART'S MINIMUM CONTENT OF NATURAL LAW

In *The Concept of Law* Hart suggested that there is a 'core of indisputable truth' in the doctrines of natural law. Again his tactics look back to Hobbes and he claims to be merely using reason to identify what minimum sorts of rules are required by the basic elements of the human condition. Five 'truisms' about humanity give a reason for postulating a 'minimum content' of social rules; these are:

1   Human vulnerability
2   Approximate equality
3   Limited resources
4   Limited altruism
5   Limited understanding and strength of will.

1   *Human vulnerability.* By human vulnerability Hart wishes to draw attention to the fact that *vis-à-vis* the natural circumstances we find ourselves, we are exceedingly at risk. We are at risk from natural events; we are also at risk from those around us who may be minded to cause us harm. We are not, generally speaking, endowed with full protection against our environment, either socially or naturally. We need to protect ourselves and the legal system is one of those mechanisms which we use to protect ourselves.

2   *Approximate equality.* Human beings are approximately equal. That is, although some people are more gifted than others, although there is a spectrum as it were of human relations, it is relatively narrow and so broadly speaking we are equally at risk from each other. If this were not the case there would be a host of serious differences from the way we organise life. We would have to think otherwise of ourselves differently from the way we currently perceive ourselves. If there were much stronger differences between human beings, if very strong people were even stronger and very weak people even weaker, then we might have found it difficult to justify the sort of control elements that have been used in society in order to iron out our differences. At the end of the day we might find it difficult to persuade those who are exceedingly strong to accept the limitations which those legal systems would decide to place on their ability ... Nevertheless we need to be aware of the fact that they may be inadequate.

3   *Limited resources.* There are not resources enough to go round well. This is more a problem of absolute scarcity and of distribution; there are a limited number of resources of a particular sort and we are in competition for those; we therefore need mechanisms to ensure that competition does not trigger reactions which result in social chaos. Hart is really drawing our attention to the fact that we do need some mechanism specifically because of a natural fact about the natural world which is that we do not have ready access to everything we want because the resources are limited. It follows of course that in times and places where particular resources are not in short supply we might expect a different analysis to apply.

4   *Limited altruism.* This has two aspects: (i) human beings are indeed altruistic. That is they are at times and at places minded to act in the interests of others rather than in the interests of themselves. We need to allow for that in different schemes of

management; but (ii) we must also allow for the fact that although human beings are altruistic they are altruistic in very haphazard ways. We cannot rely upon people acting for the good of their neighbour all the time. More importantly we have to take account of the fact that the reason why they act altruistically at all is often out of some sense of expectation that if they act nicely then people will act nicely back. So, although we might have some expectations that human beings might behave quite nicely towards each other we need to allow for haphazard application.

5   *Limited understanding and strength of will.* This really means we do not always know what is good for us. That is, we do not always know what we should be doing in our own interests. Additionally, even when we do understand our best interests we may not be in a position to carry out what needs to be done.

On one level these five factors are simply ways of trying to outflank the traditional natural law demand for a moral criterion for the power of law[34] and transform this into our recognition of problems which give us a basic need for certain types of legal and/or moral rules and normative systems. A legal system which did not offer a minimal level of protection for both our physical and psychological needs would scarcely be recognisable as a legal system at all. For Hart, the matter seems to be a question of practical reality of effectiveness. None of the external features of the existence of a legal system which he talks about seem to be relevant to the internal operation of a legal system. One cannot, for Hart, utilise the systematic failure of a given legal system to protect a particularly vulnerable person, a class of persons or to maintain a particular scarce resource, as a criterion to judge the legality of that system. The most that can be done is to criticise such a legal system for failure to meet the agreed necessary standards. The legal system which fails to provide the most basic protection for human interests may not be a very good legal system and, therefore, may make one minded not to obey, but degrees of goodness or badness of legal systems cannot, for Hart, be relevant to the question of the analysis of validity. Read in the context of the traditional approaches to natural law, Hart's minimum content of natural law is a defensive structure. Hart, in true liberal fashion, does not feel able to tell us what the purpose of social life is, he can only rephrase Hobbes' injunction to avoid death. But, ask critics such as Lon Fuller, what sort of conclusion is it to say that all the talk of natural law amounts to is the realisation that if humans are to 'survive' (which is put forward as our ultimate aim), then the law must provide minimum protection to persons; property and promises? One immediate criticism here is that these truisms are merely what is apparent in certain images of man – there is no 'higher law' here. Hart of course was not seeking to establish one; he goes on to admit that even this minimum content will not ensure justice in any community. There is still no certain method of identifying 'like cases', and equality must always be a value-judgment, so that even impartiality is 'compatible with very great iniquity'.

In constructing his argument for a 'minimum content to natural law', Hart is following a common tactic for building modern theory, specifically to strip mankind of

---

34   As Hart summarises the traditional foundation of natural law: 'That there are certain principles of human conduct, awaiting discovery by human reason, with which man-made law must conform if it is to be valid' (CL: 186).

all 'particularistic' trappings, clothing and reduce him/her to the presumed basic-human core – the independent, autonomous and thus essentially non-social being. Stripped of all features of historical situation, or concrete embeddedness, that situate but confuse us as to his pure essence, it is hoped that what is common to man as such, common to all mankind, will be visible. From Hobbes and Locke social institutions emerge to preserve, protect, conserve, defend the basis self-interest of individuals. The 'other', as one's bond extension of self is relegated to the unsaid, the neighbour is presented as the stranger, the friend only as a threat. The essential elements are universality, purposive implications, and substantive outcomes.

First Hart offers universality:

> Reflection on some very obvious generalisations – indeed truisms – concerning human nature and the world in which men live, show that as long as these hold good, there are certain rules of conduct which any social organisation must contain if it to be viable ... such universally recognised principles of conduct which have a basis in elementary truths concerning human beings, their natural environment, and aims, may be considered the *minimum content* of natural law ... (CL 193).

Second, the structure of his argument is purposive in nature: the truisms 'afford a reason why, given survival as an aim, law and morals should include a specific content'. The creation of the minimum rules is therefore a rational creation with a purpose, and that purpose is self-preservation – survival of the individual and the collective. Thus, Hart returns to the foundation Hobbes offers Liberalism; but again Hart is at pains to distinguish his approach from the command tradition.

To reinforce the rule sanctions are 'required not as the normal motive for obedience, but as a guarantee that those who would voluntarily obey shall not be sacrificed to those who would not. To obey without this would be to risk going to the wall.' Sanctions protect the day-to-day operation of the legal order, or what Hart calls 'the system of mutual forbearances', only at the extremes; on a daily level it is as if we have an operational understanding of the rationality of rule-observance.

But morality is distinct from what Hart terms 'morals'. It is rather that which is left over and which can never be captured in a code of ethics. As Bauman (1993: 34) puts it:

> Only rules can be universal. One may legislate universal rule-dictated duties, but moral responsibility exists solely in interpolating the individual and being carried individually ... The morality of the moral subject does not ... therefore have the character of a rule. One may say that the moral is what resists codification, formalisation, socialisation, universalisation.

The ambiguity is not teased out by Hart, it is rather the gap between the minimum which he accounts for and the exceptional he demands (for example in the case of resistance to Nazi laws). Again Hart's discourse of rules implies standards of convention, not a social order peopled by persons with conviction. The minimum content of natural law is the image of social norms, conventions, rules which enable security – everybody must do this minimum. Yet Hart hints at something else; his six headings of the different domains of law and morality serve to distinguish the task of recognition of legal validity from the ambiguity of assigning moral worth to that valid law: 'that sense that there is something outside the official system by reference to which in the last resort the individual must solve the problems of obedience ...'.

But what is the nature of this 'other', this reference point or call to be moral? The traditions of natural law are torn between transcendence and rationalization; between mystery, and proposing a narrative wherein we see – at least in outline terms – the reasons why we must be moral. But to reduce morality to a matter of reasonable rules, the obedience of which is necessitated by human need – survival – ignores the existential void underlying the moral demand.

Thus, ultimately, Hart's thesis of the minimum content of natural law can only work as a narrative foundation for the legal order, not for morality. The foundation of morality is something *other*, it is not self-preservation in the sense of mere personal security; for to be moral, as Antigone showed, may mean to choose death. As Bartoszewski said of the moral responsibility of those who survived the horrors of the Holocaust: 'Only those who died bringing help can say that they have done enough' (quoted, Bauman, 1993: 80). No law can exhaust the moral duty, for morality cannot be a matter of convention. Or is it? To reduce morality to conventions may appear reductionist to some, while to others it is merely being realistic. At stake is transcendence; the demand to think of a core to human existence which defies being captured in dryly scientific terms. Fear is also involved: for if morality is merely conventional, it is relationistic and we appear to lose our hope in human uniqueness. Of course it is also easier. For if morality is conventional, then socialisation replaces moral responsibility with the obligation to obey procedural norms. Complex society is impossible without sustained and deep institutions of socialisation; yet over-socialisation into obedience can produce some of modernity's greatest excesses; crimes of obedience. The creation of a moral populace is an ambiguous process, for structure is sustained by socialisation, social structure is the repeated deeds of people; without social structure there can be neither daily life nor social history. But socialisation can also be the stripping of the self of the potential for moral individuality. Humanity requires both socialisation and counter-structural sociality – or critical distance. The humane society requires both but it is not a simple combination. Socialisation may disarm critical morality, whilst counter-structural sociality may overburden the subject with moral doubt and existential weight.

HART'S THEORY OF LEGAL REASONING: A MIDDLE WAY BETWEEN FORMALISM AND RULE SCEPTICISM?

Formalism and rule scepticism are the Scylla and Charybdis of juristic theory; they are great exaggerations, salutary where they correct each other, and the truth lies between them (CL: 144).

In Chapter 9 of *The Concept of Law* Hart attempts to produce an account of legal reasoning midway between the traditions of legal formalism and the strand of legal realism which postulated rule scepticism.

First, what is the tradition of formalism? Austin bequeathed the demand that the study and understanding of law be made into a science. There were two strands to Austin: (i) the logical analysis of legal concepts and their interrelationship; (ii) the direction of law by legislative reason – specifically, guidance by the principle of utility. Formalism is a name given to a tendency (a tradition) which seized upon the idea of law as science but subtracted the concern with legislative reason from the picture. Instead law was portrayed as if it were self-developing. The inherent gradualism of the metaphysics of the common law tradition – the underlying foundations of the Humean imagination – seemed to postulate a self-developing, relatively autonomous realm of law; legal reasoning and exposition could be contained by canons particular to the field of endeavour, and that endeavour was to develop law in a scientific manner according to its inherent rationality. In the United States the person most usually associated with developing legal formalism was Christopher Columbus Langdell – from 1870 the first Dean of the Harvard Law School. Langdell passionately believed that law was a science and that all

> the available materials of that science are contained in printed books [case reports, statutes, case commentaries] ... The library is ... to us all that the laboratories of the university are to the chemists and physicists, all that the museum of natural history is to the zoologists, all that the botanical garden is to the botanists (Langdell, 1886, address to Harvard Law School, quoted Gilmore, 1977: 42).

The aim of legal scholarship was to create a perfect unitary body of rules which would cover all situations. The methodology was to take from the vast array of cases those which 'got the law right' and discard those which did not.[35]

> The cases which are useful and necessary bear an exceedingly small proportion to all that have been reported. The vast majority are useless, worse than useless, for any purpose of systematic study. (Langdell, 1871, preface to *Cases on Contracts*, quoted Gilmore, 1977: 47).

The legal order consisted of a number of 'fundamental legal doctrines', and the legal scholar must rationally order and prune the variation so that the doctrine could be so classified and arranged that each should be found in its proper place'. The presupposition of this image of legal order was that a rational universe of legal doctrines existed which could be uncovered and which reduced the apparent (empirical) diversity of law to an underlying unity. In the – rather opinionated – analysis of Gilmore (1977) Holmes aided this process by proposing that

> it was possible, on a high level of intellectual discourse to reduce [varying principles in any particular field of law] to a single, philosophically continuous series and to construct a unitary theory which would explain all conceivable single instances and thus make it unnecessary to look with any particularity at what was actually going on in the real world (Gilmore, 1977: 56).

This tradition of law as science became the mainstream ideology of American law scholarship. In the 1920s onwards it was attacked by legal realists who wished to acknowledge the human element in legal development. Instead of emphasising doctrinal coherence and focusing upon the rules mentioned in decisions as the material for analysis, realists claimed the truth of legal decisions lay in the social philosophies, motivations and mind-sets of the judges. Judges, it appeared, could not be blind to the social reality of law – even if in their judgments they did not specifically refer to their consideration of the social effects of their decisions.

---

35 *Note*: the model of truth used in the 19th century for science was that of verification – one believed that scientific truth was final, absolute and that one's task was to discover and declare it. Popper (1959, 1969) dramatically reversed this verification criterion with his writings from 1934 onwards in which he argued that the criterion should be one of falsification. Post Popper, science proceeds by doing the best it can with the material and results at its disposal and seeks truth; these scientific statements, however, will not be the final story, it will always be possible to improve; thus scientific theories ought to be open to testing, to attempts to prove their weakness, to falsification.

Hart sees the issue as relatively simple: no matter how extensive the regime of rules, neither a body of social rules, the rules developed by case law, nor the statutes or other regulatory devices created from scratch are ever entirely clear and immune from indeterminacy and conflicting interpretations. Law cannot escape being somewhat open-textured.[36] Hart's particular use of open texture highlights our 'relative ignorance of fact' and 'relative indeterminacy of aim':

> If the world in which we live were characterised only by a finite number of features, and these together with all the modes in which they could combine were known to us, then provision could be made in advance for every possibility. We could make rules, the application of which to particular cases never called for further choice. Everything could be known, and for everything, since it could be known, something could be done and specified in advance by rule. This would be a world fit for 'mechanical' jurisprudence. (CL: 125).

For Hart, conversely, the open texture of laws means that the regulation of areas of conduct 'must be left to be developed by courts or officials striking a balance, in the light of circumstances, between competing interests which vary from case to case (CL: 132). However, this does not cause much difficulty. As Hart put it:

> At the fringe of ... very fundamental things, we should welcome the rule-sceptic, as long as he does not forget that it is at the fringe that he is welcome; and does not blind us to the fact that what makes possible ... striking developments by courts of the most fundamental rules is, in great measure, the prestige gathered by the courts from their unquestionably rule-governed operations over the vast, central areas of the law (CL; 150).

One difficulty is inherent to language: Hart insists that although most terms have a core of settled meaning that makes their average use clear and unproblematic, they have a penumbra or fuzzy region, where in many cases it is impossible to tell with certainty whether the term does or does not apply. At the periphery – but only there – discretion is required. His famous example was the rule 'no vehicles in the park' (1958: 607; CL: 123–27).

In formulating the problem, however, Hart appears to reduce the issue to one of language alone:

> There is a limit inherent in the nature of language, to the guidance which general language can provide. (CL: 123).

The words of the rule cannot cover all possible factual situations. As a result, policy must come into play in judicial decision-making:

> When the envisaged case does arise, we confront the issues at stake and can then settle the question by choosing between the competing interests in the way which best satisfies us. In doing so we shall have rendered more determinate our initial aim, and shall incidentally have settled a question as to the meaning, for the purposes of this rule, of a general word. (CL: 126).

---

36 Hart adapts the notion of open texture developed by Friedrich Waismann (1951). According to Weismann, open texture is the possibility that even the least vague, most precise, term might turn out to be vague as a consequence of our imperfect knowledge about the world and our inability to predict the future. Thus, no matter how precise the term seems when used, there is the possibility of unanticipated instances which render the term vague when one asks if it covers the situation.

In response, Lon Fuller (1958) contended that terms simply do not have core sets of meanings independent of the particular purposes for which those terms are employed (a position now widely supported, see James Boyle, 1985: 708–13; Drucilla Cornell, 1988: 1137–8; Robert Moles, 1987: 176–206). Fuller's example of a statue which included a vehicle, the exclusion of which from the park appears inconsistent with any sensible purpose behind the rule, was not particularly apt, for a statue is hardly a vehicle. Even adopting the necessity to interpret words of a statute in light of the purpose of the statute might not solve the question, since it is possible for there to be layers of purposes.

Hart's terminology and tone is comforting, the system works, on the whole, with minimum problems. Conversely, for Hart, the sceptic is a disappointed rationalist who has discovered 'that rules are not all they would be in a formalist's heaven' moves to the opposite extreme arguing that rules offer 'nothing to circumscribe the arena of open-texture'.

Moderation is required.[37] The fact that rules have 'exceptions that cannot be exhaustively stated' does not mean that they have no capacity to bind at all. Placing too much emphasis upon the 'penumbra' was itself an important source of 'confusion in the American tradition' (Hart, 1958: 593, 615).

The discourse of moderation and the hiding of coercion do not, however, close off the problem of law. For all his clarity, Hart constantly reopens classic dilemmas, or points, tantalising, to questions for sociological analysis. Here, in the heart of his analysis, where there is a gap, or when the rules run out, there is recourse to non-law. The very clarity of the positivist separation of law from morals implies that *sans* rules, non-law rules. In this gap what takes over? Hart has killed off Hobbes's and Austin's sovereign and his legislative reason. The discretion eats at the ideology of the rule of law and allows in politics, but this time it is a politics beyond the limits of the jurisprudential imagination. Thus the classic work of modern legal philosophy points, unmistakenly, beyond legal philosophy, for its 'truth'.

---

37 Hart is following a host of legal opinions. For example Benjamin Cardozo (1921: 164) 'Of the cases that come before the court in which I sit, a majority, I think, could not, with semblance of reason, be decided in any way but one.' Roscoe Pound: 'Every day practice shows that a great mass of rules are applied without serious question'. Ronald Dworkin was at first in agreement preferring to base his analysis upon 'hard cases'; but he came to argue that all easy cases must once have been hard cases. Put in terms of hermeneutics, a common sense or easy interpretation is only easy because it is deeply embedded in an interpretative community or tradition; there was once a first interpretation which was difficult.

CHAPTER 14

LIBERALISM AND THE IDEA OF THE JUST SOCIETY IN LATE MODERNITY: a reading of Kelsen, Fuller, Rawls, Nozick and communitarian critics

PART ONE
KELSEN AND THE TENSION BETWEEN DYNAMIC AND STATIC THEORIES OF JUSTICE

But what does it really mean to say that a social order is just? It means that this order regulates the behaviour of men in a way satisfactory to all men, that is to say, so that all men find their happiness in it. The longing for justice is men's eternal longing for happiness. It is happiness that man cannot find alone, as an isolated individual, and hence seeks in society. Justice is social happiness. It is happiness guaranteed by a social order (Kelsen, 1957: 2).

THE INTERACTION OF JUSTICE, HAPPINESS, AND AUTHENTICITY

Kelsen suggests the basis of our struggles to attain a just society is the desire to be happy. The just society would be that society in which humans would be happy.[1]

The formula is deceptively simple; yet it opens up still more questions which threaten to turn the issue into a morass of different perspectives. It gives rise to another question, namely, 'What is happiness?' (Kelsen, 1957: 2)

Kelsen presupposes a qualitative concept of social and human happiness; a just social order must imply 'happiness in an objective-collective sense, that is to say, by happiness we must understand the satisfaction of certain needs, recognised ... as needs worthy of being satisfied' (*ibid*: 3). Justice both structures and mediates a form of social existence in which the individual desire for happiness faces up to its inevitable social existence.

How can we rank human interests? Philosophers have not only disagreed about the essence of human nature but differed in their interpretation of virtue and vice, of the sources of morality, and of the respective roles of reason and emotion. From the time of Aristotle's attempt to distinguish the moral life from one of success in the techniques of production, we have seen – albeit in numerous variations – desires to resist reducing the question of the happy life to issues of utility, expediency, instrumentalism, or calculating self-interest. This – more existential – concern seeks justice as a means of dealing with fear and hope, desire and aversion, transcendence and faithfulness; above all, *it seeks*

---

1 Jurisprudence cannot escape considering justice since justice is – ideally – the master of law. But what if justice cannot be known? Justice appears an overburdened idea. Sometimes it is reduced to a question of technique: it is thereby posed as the problem of what will guide the techniques of constructing social order. At other times it appears as a problem of legitimacy, or put another way, as an answer to the question of what will provide a rational framework for judging the adequacy of the regulation of human relations.

justice in order to be able to live in the proper way. But, again, this is no answer to our question, for how can we moderns – we creatures of multiple perspectives and radical change – accept that any particular form of social structuring is *the proper way to organise social relations?*

The idea of attaining the just society is deeply problematic in modernity. On the one hand, we now realise our social existence is humanly created and, by implication, we ought to be able to construct a social structure which is responsive to our needs and desires. On the other hand, as moderns aware of the inevitability of contingency, we realise that any particular form of social structure could have been something else, and can become something more.

In Nietzschean terms, a settled conception of justice is difficult for the modern because the modern 'knows' too much and – as a result – finds pluralism and perspectivism, in short, pragmatism towards truth. We are an historical epoch that knows the inevitability of change over stability. *Whatever its theor(y)ies of justice, late-modernity is doomed to dynamic – as opposed to static – justice.*

KELSEN'S ESPOUSAL OF DYNAMIC JUSTICE OVER THE TRADITIONS OF STATIC JUSTICE

Kelsen (1957: Ch 1) felt his commitment to science meant he had to reject previous static conceptions of justice.

(1) The first has been the understanding that justice consists in living according to the true structure of the natural way of the world. With the advent of modernity we realised that there was no one way of life. What became of the idea of the perfectly just society? Kelsen was scathing:

> Absolute justice is an irrational ideal or, what amounts to the same, an illusion – one of the eternal illusions of mankind.

There is no natural consensus as to the goods of human life: we are left with human interests and hence conflicts of interest. The solution of these conflicts must involve either satisfying one at the expense of the other, or compromise. It is not possible to prove that only the one or the other solution to human ordering is just. The answer is relative; under certain conditions one solution is just, under others, another.

(2) The idea of living in a state of love with God provided a second conception of justice and true happiness. This appeals to our desire for transcendence, to our wish to escape from the dirt and pain of our empirical existence, from our loneliness. But this answer is founded on faith:

> God's wisdom – which implies his justice – is a mystery; and faith, nothing but faith, enables us to get hold of this justice (*ibid*: 80).

Christianity provides no answer to the modern pursuit of justice, since there is no this-worldly criterion for living which can be sustained without recourse to images of the other realm. Nor can the pursuit of love, as indicated by the teaching of Jesus, solve the issue, since the promise of love, as with the promise of Marxism, is that we may attain a state of being beyond justice, beyond any rational ideal.

Jesus' teaching is not the solution of the problem of justice as a problem of a social technique for the regulation of human relations; it is rather the dissolution of the problem. For it implies the request to abandon the desire for justice as conceived of by man (*ibid*: 45).

(3) A third conception is attainable but uninspiring; this is simply to live in accordance with the laws of the society. Kelsen suggests the principle 'behave in conformity with the general norms of the social order', and the similar Kantian categorical imperative (act only on the maxim whereby you can at the same time will that the principle of your action should become a universal law), are in the final analysis empty formulas. They have no real social content and therefore provide no answer to the question of the nature of the principles we would wish to be binding on all humanity. It is, however, precisely this emptiness which provides their ideological usefulness, and Kelsen suggests they will often – albeit wrongly – be accepted as satisfactory answers to the problem of justice.

Ultimately, Kelsen implies, we cannot ever agree upon a concept of justice let alone the structure of the just society. In his *Pure Theory of Law*, (Chapter 12 of this text) Kelsen develops a formal rational science of law in a neo-Weberian sense; however, the concept of justice cannot be dealt with in this way. There cannot be a formal science of justice, since even if a theory of justice were logically constructed it would be based on emotive premises.[2] It is not possible to identify in a scientific way the supreme values that a just order of social life should attempt to promote (1960: 5-6). One person may regard the advancement of individual autonomy as the foremost aim of legal ordering; another person may argue that law-makers should promote the goal of equality; yet another may claim that security is the overriding interest, and be willing to sacrifice equality and freedom for the fullest realisation of this value.

Thus we face an irresolvable pluralism of ideologies. If the structure of legalism embodies one dominant set of ideologies it will appear unjust from another perspective. To be just, the structure of legalism needs to accommodate perspectivism and accept that modern social existence entails the cohabitation of various emotive and narrative positions. Kelsen's particular resolution of this dilemma was to argue that legalism is a social technique which we need to understand and strip of its mysticism. If the world is unknowable – it is so in its final analysis – the methods by which we pragmatically construct our social existence ought not to be. But while Kelsen shared Weber's pessimism as to the rational defence of substantive issues, others have sought to develop a marriage of law and a relatively dynamic conception of justice.

---

2   Kelsen states that the content of justice is not amenable to rational determination. As an example he gives the following scenario. Certain ethical convictions hold that human life is the highest value, thus, according to this view, it is forbidden to kill a human being, even in war or as a measure of atonement for a grave offence. There is, however, an opposing view that claims that the highest value is the interest and honour of the nation and everybody is obliged to sacrifice his own life and to kill other human beings in time of war, and it is justified in the collective interest to inflict capital punishment as a sanction for certain kinds of criminal conduct.

Kelsen argues it is impossible to decide this conflict regarding the justice of killing other human beings in a scientific way. Ultimately, it is our feelings, our emotions and our will, that produces a decision.

PART TWO
LON FULLER (1902–1978) AND THE IDEA OF A
JUST METHODOLOGY OF LEGALISM

Law … is a purposeful enterprise, dependent for its successes on the energy, insight, intelligence, and conscientiousness of those who conduct it, and fated, because of this dependence, to fall always somewhat short of a full attainment of its goals (Lon Fuller, 1969: 145).

FULLER'S ATTEMPT TO CREATE A PURPOSIVE
ACCOUNT OF LEGALITY

Writing between 1940 (with the publication of *The Law in Quest of Itself*) and his posthumously published *The Principles of Social Order* in 1981, Lon Fuller developed a secular form of natural law which defined law as a purposive human activity. Fuller charged legal positivism with several faults: specifically, its adherents:

(i)   failed to include any account of how they framed important questions, and engaged in no reflexivity concerning their own positions;[3]

(ii) often attempted to give neat juristic answers to questions that were essentially questions of sociological facts;[4]

(iii) mistakenly perceived the study of law to involve first, the description of a 'manifested fact, to be studied for what it is and does, and not for what it is trying to do or become', and second, they lost themselves either in conceptual quibbles, increasingly removed from social reality, or raised to central focus a method of clarification of speech and writing (specifically, linguistic analysis, as per HLA Hart's *The Concept of Law*) which 'ought [only] to be viewed as a useful adjunct to philosophical thought'; and, above all;

(iv) refused to attribute to law any purpose, however modest or restricted. Being solely concerned to describe the law as it was, they felt they could say nothing scientifically about how law ought to be.[5]

---

3   In his postscript (1969: 242) Fuller asserted that the philosophy of science had seen a reorientation 'marked by a shift of interest away from the conceptualisation and logical analysis of scientific verification and toward a study of the actual process by which scientific discoveries are made. Perhaps in time legal philosophers will cease to be preoccupied with building "conceptual models" to represent legal phenomena, will give up their endless debates about definitions, and will turn instead to an analysis of the social processes that constitute the reality of law.'

4   As Fuller commented (1969: 141) concerning Hart's discussion of the rule of recognition in *The Concept of Law*: '[Hart] is throughout attempting with the aid of that rule to give neat juristic answers to questions that are essentially questions of sociological fact'.

5   In *The Law in Quest of Itself* (1940: 5) Fuller defined legal positivism as an extremely limited view of legalism: 'Its unavowed basis will usually be found to rest in a conviction that while one may significantly describe the law *that is*, nothing that transcends personal predilection can be said about the law *that ought to be*'. Fuller is partially overstating the case. As we have seen, for the early legal positivists Bentham and Austin, law was to be an instrument of rational government. However, legal positivism sees law itself as an empty container which is provided with substantive content from out-…

For Fuller, law is an ethical method of creating and guaranteeing form to social relations. Legal rules are expressive: each rule contains a purpose aimed at the realisation of some value of the legal order, and thus a rule is 'at once a fact and a standard for judging facts' (1954: 470). Can Fuller propose a conception of the overall purpose to social life? Fuller is a liberal, he cannot look back at natural law ideologies which give a settled telos to human life in the Platonic or Aristotelian tradition; how then can a standard be offered to guide us in the creation of our social life? In response, Fuller espouses a conception of dynamic potentiality while moving the idea of purpose to a high level of generality. The crucial distinction drawn in *The Morality of Law* (1969) is between the moralities of *duty* and *aspiration*. The morality of aspiration, or 'the morality of the good life, of excellence, of the fullest realisation of human powers', speaks to a society where human beings strive to function at their best. While, however, the morality of aspiration alerts us to the possibilities of human achievement, the morality of duty takes us at our most base.

> It lays down the basic rules without which an ordered society is impossible, or without which an ordered society directed toward certain specific goals must fail in its mark ... It does not condemn men for failing to embrace opportunities for the fullest realisation of their powers. Instead, it condemns them for failing to respect the basic requirements of social living (1969: 5-6).

Nature does not mould us into a particular destiny, it offers instead countless games of blind chance; the legal system is a complex of rules designed to rescue humans from contingency and put them safely on the road to purposeful and creative activity. However, we cannot compel a man to live a life of reason and value.

> We can only seek to exclude from his life the grosser and more obvious manifestations of chance and irrationality. We can create the conditions essential for a rational human existence. These are the necessary, but not the sufficient conditions for the achievement of that end (*ibid*: 9).

In pursuing excellence we strive to create conditions for social progress which will overcome mere adherence to duty and scale the heights of human aspiration. The law is a tool to help us but we do not, and cannot, have a perfectly defined statement of where our journey is taking us, or of the society that we are trying to achieve. While we can make judgments along the way, offer dreams and countless forms of articulation of our hopes and desires, we cannot have a settled idea of the final state. But, Fuller argues, accepting that we cannot have knowledge of the totality does not doom us to incoherence or mere emotive posturing: 'We can know what is plainly unjust without committing ourselves to declare with finality what perfect justice would be like' (*ibid*: 12).

There are, however, no simple answers. Is excellence instrumental, normative or expressive? Fuller appears to say that it can be all three, albeit with differing degrees of

---

5. ... side – by politics, morality – while having in its pure form no necessary political or moral substance. Fuller claimed Kelsen's theory presented law as 'utterly indifferent to ethics', and the legal scientist as forbidden from discussing the content of law (1940: 91). For Fuller, law is a moral social activity. He tries to redefine the actual origins of legal positivism; thus Hobbes used certain normative principles of 'natural law', and specified the preservation of a minimum of peace and order as the fundamental purpose of legal order. Fuller claimed that the tradition of legal positivism came to forget the purposive justification of law inherent in Hobbes's civil philosophy.

intensity. Moreover, part of striving for excellence is overcoming alienation, making our practices an expressive reflection of our humanity. As with social progress, so too with legality: Fuller conceptualises a 'procedural version of natural law' which he calls the 'inner morality of law' or a theory of *Eunomics* (Fuller, 1954: 477-8, had previously defined this term as 'the theory or study of good order and workable arrangements'). To understand legality we must 'discern and articulate the natural laws of a particular kind of human undertaking ... "the enterprise of subjecting human conduct to the governance of rules"'. Traditional natural law cannot be accepted by the modern, since instead of thinking in terms of ultimate ends or telos, to human life (which was conceived and then imposed via the proposed social ordering that law would create and maintain), jurisprudence/eunomics should examine and set out an understanding of the means that the legal order must use to allow a certain form of human flourishing to occur.[6] Our concern is with the internal operation and structure of the legal process, thus the natural laws of legality are not the old natural laws of God and man, but are more 'like the natural laws of carpentry, or at least those laws respected by a carpenter who wants the house he builds to remain standing and serve the purpose of those who live in it' (1969: 96).

In a series of articles (*The Forms and Limits of Adjudication*, 1961; *The Adversary System*, 1961; *Collective Bargaining and the Arbitrator*, 1963; *Mediation – Its forms and Functions*, 1971), Fuller distinguished legality from essentially managerial or bureaucratic forms of decision-making. Legality is a form of decision-making by reference to established rules and principles; moreover, looking back at classical common law, Fuller identifies the centrality of *integrity*. Legality is not a simple matter of technique; law is not a instrumental attainment of certain ends, but an expressive phenomenon. Integrity guarantees the processes which law uses in order to take form and character.[7]

THE SPECIFIC INTERNAL MORALITY OF LAW

In Chapter 2 of *The Morality of Law*, 'The morality that makes law possible', Fuller provides a narrative of an inept king who makes law in various ways, each with disastrous effect. The moral of the story is that a law-maker must abide by certain procedural 'excellences': each instance when he does not do so damages the effectiveness of law. This 'rule-morality' is an 'inner morality' by contrast to an 'outer morality' achieved in the substantive laws. It is a morality of 'aspiration' and not of duty.

---

6 In *The Problems of Jurisprudence* (1949), a collection of readings in legal philosophy Fuller published in a temporary edition, he argued that the legitimacy of the judicial adjudication stemmed from the specific moral force inhering to the decisions of an impartial tribunal. Certain conditions were required: for example, the judge should not act of his own initiative, but on the application of one or both of the disputants; the judge should decide the case solely on the basis of the evidence and arguments presented to him by the parties; each party to a dispute should be given ample opportunity to present his case. These requirements constitute an internal morality of adjudication.

7 Fuller specifies that by procedural 'we are concerned, not with the substantive aims of legal rules, but with the ways in which a system of rules for governing human conduct must be constructed and administered if it is to be efficacious and at the same time remain what it purports to be' (1969: 97).

Law-making is an interactional process, and failure of the law-maker to achieve procedural morality will result in the system ceasing to operate according to the precepts of legality. Fuller lists several 'excellences' designed to conform to this natural law of legality.[8] Laws must be:

1 sufficiently general;
2 publicly promulgated;
3 prospective;
4 understandable;
5 non-contradictory;
6 fairly constant;
7 possible of performance; and
8 administered by officials according to their content, and there must be congruence between official action and declared rule.

What do these requirements entail?

1 First there must be rules. An observer should be able to identify a certain regularity of behaviour within the legal process and be able to suppose that those regularities of behaviour are not mere matters of chance, but have to do with reflections by the participants of the process on what ought to be done.

2 Second these rules must not be retrospective in operation. They must always be available for the public to guide their actions by and people should not be caught out by the demands of a rule formulated after the event to be adjudicated.

3 Third, they must be made public. These rules need to be published in such manner and time as to enable people to discover what they are and adjust their conduct accordingly.

4 They must be comprehensible. That is, the rules must be presented in a way which enables those whom they are to direct to have a chance of understanding what it is they ought not to do.

5 They must not contradict one another.

6 It must be possible to comply with the rules. The rules ought not be formulated so that they contradict each other creating a situation where the subject cannot fail to break the rule, nor should they require people to do impossible things.

7 They must not be in constant flux. They should not change so rapidly that it is impossible to co-ordinate a course of conduct so that one acts in accordance with the legal rule.

8 They must be applied coherently and correctly. It is not enough to have a logical structure of rules if the actual processes of adjudication or interpretation are incomprehensible, or so difficult to follow, that there is no advantage gained by creating the rules; nor should the rules be ignored in practice. We must minimise the gap between the law as declared and the law as actually administered.

---

8 Fuller does not claim to get these eight interlocking principles from some secure point of reference, but rather states they are derived from established judicial practice, or the explicit provisions contained in conventional sources of law.

Since Fuller has defined law as the enterprise whereby human behaviour is subjected to the governance of rules, it is clear laws made in conformity with all these principles need have no specific substantive moral content. In his review of *The Morality of Law*, HLA Hart (*Harvard Law Review*, 1965) claimed that to refer to morality as part of this process was to confuse morality and purposive activity. While Hart accepted the eight principles as reflecting 'good craftsmanship', he saw them as having no intrinsic value; they were merely principles which enhanced the efficiency of law as a purposive enterprise rather than providing grounds ensuring final judgments could be arrived at concerning activities and purposes. Fuller's principles were neutral as between the 'good and evil substantive aims' of law, they provided no guarantee to advance the substantive ends of 'human justice and welfare'; they did not even establish 'any necessary incompatibility between government according to the principles of legality and wicked ends'. In a famous analogy, Hart claimed they would equally well apply to poisoning: 'Poisoning is a craft, it also has a purpose, but it cannot be called a morality'.

Fuller found Hart's comments virtually incomprehensible. In his opinion Hart was blind to the existential striving of legal professionals. Looking back over the development and operation of Anglo-American common law, Fuller claimed lawyers understood the need for integrity in law; in their work they give legality a moral meaning. Fuller acknowledges Hart was perhaps arguing that a legal system could exist quite effectively without the 'excellences';[9] and while conceding this point to some extent he countered by saying that although a legal system which disregarded all these 'excellences' might continue for a time, it could not continue indefinitely. Fuller actually believes that evil, and evil institutions, are intrinsically less coherent than goodness, and good institutions. His theory stresses the importance of institutionalisation; the coherent, principled, institutionalisation of legality.

> What is generally missing in these accounts [critical of Fuller's position] is any recognition of the role legal rules play in making possible an effective realisation of morality in the actual behaviour of human beings. Moral principles cannot function in a social vacuum or in a war of all against all. To live the good life requires something more than good intentions, even if they are generally shared; it requires the support of firm base lines for human interaction, something that – in modern society at least – only a sound legal system can supply (1969: 205).

For the Oxford legal philosopher Joseph Raz (1970), the value of the theory was limited to the negative task avoiding evils which could only have been caused by the laws anyway. But neither Raz nor Hart share Fuller's presuppositions. The critics want Fuller to build a clear and compelling statement of the relationship between law and the substantive ends of human morality and human flourishing.

---

9   A common criticism of Fuller's procedural natural law was posed in terms of a question: 'how many of the excellences did a legal system need to ignore for that 'system' to cease to be a system?

COMMUNICATION AS THE KEY PRINCIPLE TO BE SAFEGUARDED BY LIBERAL LEGALITY

Fuller actually developed a liberal synthesis of law and social progress which takes an agnostic approach to the question of what the ends of man are; while we take the journey of modernity we cannot know the final chapter. The goal is excellence, our enterprise endeavours to it, but what this comprises in total we cannot know. Instead we must keep open the channels of 'communication'. Our task is not to align law to some perceived natural uniformity of humanity, but rather to align it to the continual search for social betterment. Positivism is self-defeating since, while it may refuse to attribute to law as a whole any social purpose, in life we constantly ascribe meanings to law. If the jurisprudential imagination refuses to give purpose to law and legality, powerful ideologies and groups will provide purposes which are not in line with the proper aspirations of justice. Hart's criterion of the need for survival as providing the foundation around which to construct the minimum content of natural law (1961: Chapter ix), for example, is self-defeating for it raises the issue: why do anything? Why take any risk? Fuller decries such a limited image of social life, instead he turns to a modern liberal notion, that of communication itself:

> Communication is something more than a means of staying alive. It is a way of being alive. It is through communication that we inherit the achievements of past human effort. The possibility of communication can reconcile us to the thought of death by assuring us what we achieve will enrich the lives of those to come. How and when we accomplish communication with one another can expand or contract the boundaries of life itself. In the words of Wittgenstein: 'The limits of my language are the limits of my world'.

Fuller's proposal of a central core of substantive natural law amounts to an injunction:

> Open up, maintain, and preserve the integrity of the channels of communication by which men convey to one another what they perceive, feel, and desire (both quotes, 1969: 186).

Law was an expressive medium which did not have as its essential task ensuring stability, order and duty, but rather the creation of a social order in which communication and free social interaction could take place. Fuller remained convinced that a legal order which lived up to his inner morality of law would usually be essentially sound and just in its substantive contents. To his critics this was unduly optimistic, and, with the substantive ends of human flourishing left unstated, incomplete.[10] But if Fuller left open the substantive meaning of justice, quite practical political problems of late modernity – emphasised in the concrete demands of masses of people after two world wars for real social justice – were to draw jurisprudence closer to debates concerning a philosophy of (re)distributive policies.

---

10 To Finnis (1980) Fuller provides no non-procedural criteria for evaluating the purposive ends that could confer solid legitimacy upon the rule of law. Finnis agrees that law should be seen as a purposive activity, but goes on to assert that to understand these purposive aims we need to develop a naturalistic theory of morality which specifies the human goods and values which would be advanced through the rule of law. Thus, Finnis claims, the task that Fuller implicitly identifies but does not proceed with, is to bring the principles of the internal morality of law into some rationally coherent relationship with a fully developed ethical conception of human nature, and its essential goods and values.

PART THREE
JOHN RAWLS AND A THEORY OF JUSTICE[11]

Justice is the first virtue of social institutions, as truth is of systems of thought. A theory however elegant and economical must be rejected or revised if it is untrue; likewise laws and institutions no matter how efficient and well-arranged must be reformed or abolished if they are unjust ... The only thing that permits us to acquiesce in an erroneous theory is the lack of a better one; analogously, an injustice is tolerable only when it is necessary to avoid an even greater injustice. Being first virtues of human activities, truth and justice are uncompromising (1971: 3-4).

RAWLS PLACES THE QUESTION OF LEGITIMACY AT THE FOREFRONT OF MODERN SOCIAL LIFE

The American political theorist John Rawls begins his highly influential *A Theory of Justice* (1971) with the argument that social arrangements in modernity require legitimacy. Even if the arrangements of a society were efficient and perfectly logically arranged, that society does not satisfactorily express human aspirations unless we can defend its institutions as just. Moreover, 'only in the social union is the individual complete'. A fully satisfying existential life requires justice.[12] But an obvious problem arises: how are we to recognise whether the arrangements of any particular social ordering are just or unjust? Rawls's intellectual predecessors are Kant (who provides among other things the idea of the primacy of the right over the good, and the regulative idea of the social contract) and John Stuart Mill (who provides the spirit of tolerance).

Rawls's methodology is simple, he: (i) asserts the primacy of justice in social order;[13] (ii) asserts the facts of a degree of common self-interest among the people who make up a society (survival) as well as conflicts of interest; thus to enable a stable ordering to occur (iii) a set of principles is required for choosing among the various social

---

11 John Rawls was born in Baltimore, USA, in 1921, and taught philosophy at Harvard University for more then 30 years. He has latterly exerted a tremendous impact upon political and jurisprudential arguments through a series of articles and in particular *A Theory of Justice* (Rawls, 1971). This book was quickly seized upon as a magisterial work developing a 'new liberal paradigm'. This 'deontological' or 'rights-based' paradigm undercut the ascendancy of utilitarianism in Anglo-Saxon theories, and it is usually accepted that criticism of liberalism – both from the libertarian and anarchist right or the communitarians – must work through Rawls.

12 'It is a feature of human sociability that we are by ourselves but parts of what we might be. We must look to others to attain the excellences that we must leave aside, or lack altogether. The collective activity of society, the many associations and the public life of the largest community that regulates them, sustains our efforts and elicits our contribution. Yet the good attained from the common culture far exceeds our work in the sense that we cease to be mere fragments: that part of ourselves that we directly realise is joined to a wider and just arrangement the aims of which we affirm' (1971: 529).

13 Presuppositions cannot be avoided, and the major presupposition of Rawls is that only a rights-based theory of justice that respects our desires for equal respect and rational acknowledgment fits with our liberal conceptions. Moreover, Rawls accepts (1971: 563) that a view of 'the essential unity of the self is already given in the concept of right'. A presupposition of a rational and unified self is, therefore, the methodological foundation.

arrangements and underwriting any arrangement for the distribution of social goods; thus

> a society is well-ordered when it is not only designed to advance the good of its members but when it is also effectively regulated by a public conception of justice. That is, it is a society in which (1) everyone accepts and knows that the others accept the same principles of justice, and (2) the basic social institutions generally satisfy and are generally known to satisfy these principles. In this case while men may put forth excessive demands on one another, they nevertheless acknowledge a common point of view from which their claims may be adjudicated (*ibid*: 4-5).

While there is a multitude of perceptions and theories of justice, Rawls believes (following Hart's distinction in *The Concept of Law*, 1961: 155–9, between *particular concepts of justice* and *the concept of justice*[14]) the very fact of disagreements and arguments about justice indicates humankind's commitment to the pursuit of justice. Some 'political' – as Rawls (1992) was later to define it – choice must be made. *Rawls chooses the right over the good* – Kant wins over Bentham:

> Each person possesses an inviolability founded on justice that even the welfare of society as a whole cannot override. Justice denies that the loss of freedom for some is made right by a greater good shared by others ... in a just society the liberties of equal citizenship are taken as settled; the rights secured by justice are not subject to political bargaining or to the calculus of social interests (1971: 4).

Rawls is not a dogmatic neo-Kantian; his claim is to provide a reasonable theory giving a basic set of principles with which we might achieve consensus in the debate over justice.[15] These principles allow for some inequalities and innovations in the reasonable balancing of equality and efficiency. Rawls seeks impartiality, but his search is not for an intellectual Archimedean point which transcends the cave of our everyday life, rather it is one dependent upon its finding acceptance with our everyday intuitions.[16]

AS A FOUNDATION FOR AGREEING ON THE PRINCIPLES OF JUSTICE RAWLS REPLACES THE UTILITARIAN MODEL OF THE IDEAL SPECTATOR WITH THE IDEA OF AGREEING TO ABIDE BY DECISIONS MADE BEHIND A VEIL OF IGNORANCE

Rawls constructs a thought-experiment in which we are asked to imagine ourselves meeting together to form a social contract covering the principles which will bind us in real life. Rawls asks us to imagine choosing principles for determining the principle of

---

14 Another way of phrasing this is to say that *justice is an inherently contestable concept*. That inbuilt into the concept of justice is the impossibility of any one concept providing the end to the conversation as to what justice means.

15 We are to be persuaded that we would accept the principles underlying the operation of the Rawlsean just society 'by philosophical reflection', and the resulting well-designed society 'comes as close as a society can to being a voluntary scheme' (1971: 13).

16 Rawls is clear that 'we need a conception that enables us to envision our objective from afar' (1971: 22), but we cannot leave the cave of our traditions, our perspective is 'not a perspective from a certain place beyond the world, nor the point of view of a transcendent being; rather it is a certain form of thought and feeling that rational persons can adopt within this world' (*ibid*: 587).

justice of your society from an original position located behind a *veil of ignorance*. The aim of the original position is to 'nullify the effects of specific contingencies which put men at odds and tempt them to exploit social and natural circumstances to their own advantage'.[17] The parties know nothing either of themselves or their society; each does not his/her gender, race, intelligence, or class etc. The parties:

> do not know how the various alternatives will affect their own particular case and they are obliged to evaluate principles solely on the basis of general considerations.... nor does he know his fortune in the distribution of natural assets and abilities, his intelligence and strength and the like. Nor, again, does anyone know his conception of the good.

No one is in possession of the facts which could tell him/her how their life would be affected by the principles of justice and decision making procedures which they have chosen. If a person knew those things and if they knew their location, then they would probably devise principles which would bring them an advantage. However, Rawls' methodology allows only a general knowledge of humanity; each knows that social reality will contain specific contingencies but has no knowledge of what particular contingencies will affect them.[18] What then will motivate our choices behind the veil of ignorance? Rawls claims that one would obviously choose out of self-interest, but knowing nothing about oneself, self-interest becomes the interest of any one person. The consequence is that the resulting principles will be those that any one person would have voluntarily agreed upon.

THE PRINCIPLES OF JUSTICE

Rawls (1971: 302) believes that people in the original position would chose two principles. First, each person is to have an equal right to the most extensive total system of equal basic liberties compatible with a similar system of liberty for all. Second, social and economic inequalities are to be arranged so that they are both: (i) to the greatest benefit of the least advantaged, consistent with the just savings principle, and (ii) attached to offices and positions open to all under conditions of fair equality of opportunity.

The first principle is given operational precedent ensuring that liberty always has priority. 'Liberty can be restricted only for the sake of liberty'; in other words, it is not

---

17 'The aim of the original position is to set up a fair procedure so that any principles agreed to will be just. The aim is to use the notion of pure procedural justice as a basis of theory' (1971: 136). The epistemological aim is also to preserve the advantages of the Kantian idea of the separateness and autonomy of the rational person, but avoid the unworldliness of Kant's metaphysics. Rawls's theory is not meant to be proved in some formal rational manner, but appeal to us as a methodology and a principle of deliberation which respects our empirical desire to attain justice while treating each other as free and equal. Thus Rawls would be appealing to central values of our democratic traditions: liberty and equality – and provide a way for rationally inscribing them into a flexible account of justice.

18 'Thus there follows the very important consequence that the parties have no basis for bargaining in the usual sense. No one knows his situation in society nor his natural assets, and therefore no one is in a position to tailor principles to his advantage ...

The veil of ignorance makes possible a unanimous choice of a particular conception of justice. Without these limitation on knowledge the bargaining problem of the original position would be hopelessly complicated' (1971: 137-40).

acceptable to legitimise restricting liberty or equality of opportunity, with the argument that such restriction will improve the lot of the worst off. But holding firmly to that principle, a related proposition is that 'all social primary goods – liberty and opportunity, income and wealth, and the basis of self-respect – are to be distributed equally unless an unequal distribution of any or all of these goods is to the advantage of the least favoured' (*ibid*: 303-3).

Those behind the veil would chose liberty as their first principle since, not knowing the actual situation or their own conception of the good life, this would give them the greatest opportunity to pursue whatever ideal they favoured. They would choose the second principle because they would operate on the basis of a 'minimax principle', whereby they prefer the least worst option in case they turn out to be at the lowest level of society. Not knowing where they fit into the distribution of social goods, they will be rational pessimists.

Rawls draws an analogy with fair ways of cutting a cake. One cake is to be shared among several people with a person delegated to cut it. How will he do it? Let us suppose that the person cutting the cake knows he will get the last slice; if he is selfish, motivated by self-interest (we presume he loves cake) he will slice it so that – whilst the rest may get equal slices – the last is the biggest. If he knows, however, the last slice will not go to him, but that he will get one of the earlier slices, it is more than likely that the last slice will be the smallest. If our cake-cutter is either altruistic, or does not really like cake, and knows he will get the last piece, then he is likely to make the last slice the smallest. How are we able to guarantee that each slice will be exactly the same? Rawls suggests the answer lies in the cake-cutter not knowing which slice he himself will get; in that case both the totally altruistic cake-cutter, and the totally selfish cake-cutter, will ensure each slice is similar.

Let us consider for a moment what is going on here. Rawls provides a rational choice decision-making procedure in which the knowledge involved is crucial to the outcome of the decision. However, the example is of a static situation: there was but one cake and that of fixed size. There are clearly important differences between the distribution of a cake of fixed size, and justice in an on-going society. Moreover, the idea of cake lacks the degree of complexity which the goods of life involve; the goods of life involve questions of status, power, rights, money, property, and so forth. How are we to distribute this varied largesse? How are we to ascertain the worth of what is being distributed? Whereas, the consumption of the cake may provide a temporal pleasure, the consumption of many of life's goods (for example, access to university education) can lead to the consumption of a whole range of other of life's goods (ie made available by a higher class of job). Thus to concentrate only upon primary goods (such as cakes) provides a weak notion of equality for an ongoing society; flexibility must be built into the theory.

To illustrate, take two distribution patterns: 'A' comprising four equal shares of the following values 4, 4, 4, 4, and 'B' comprising four unequal shares with the values of 5, 6, 7, 8. What considerations of dynamic justice are acceptable for judging the legitimacy of these distribution patterns and how they came about? Rawls claims that a principle which serves to maximise the minimum share is preferable to absolute equality, since if we permit some inequality it may be the case that the worst-off person, albeit in an unequal distribution pattern, could in fact be better off than if all were in a situation of complete equality. In distribution pattern 'B' the person with the minimum share has five units, rather than four as in pattern 'A', while the overall unit for distribution is more than a third larger in pattern 'B' than in pattern 'A'. Some inequality is acceptable because the dogmatic pursuit of equality may prove to be restrictive of the interests of the least well off.

Rawls is trying to balance the need for growth in wealth, with respect for the least well-off in the society. Whilst the general aim of utilitarian justice is to maximise social wealth, Rawls holds his basic principles of justice based also upon a deontological respect for autonomy as checks upon such maximisation. Even if greater social wealth is created, a system of inequality may be too extreme to be defended as socially just. What if the distribution pattern was actually 5, 600, 700, 800? At what point do we say that we can no longer accept the position of the 5 in relation to the others' considerably greater goods? Is it in the 20s, 100s or 1000s? It may well be that one would prefer to live in the pattern where one only enjoyed the benefits of a 4 since there one enjoys equality, whereas in the other pattern, although one would benefit from a 5, the comparison with those who have greater shares could be too much to bear; we can be made unhappy with feelings of injustice.

RAWLS'S IDEA OF REASONABLE GROWTH: BALANCING DEVELOPMENT AND MORAL RESPECT

In Rawls's cake analogy those who help bake the cake can choose to enjoy free time (liberty) or to work on the cake. The cake will vary in size and quality according to how many ingredients are put into it, and the skill and hard work which goes into baking it. But people must have an incentive to provide ingredients and work hard and skilfully; the quality and size of the cake, therefore, will vary according to the level of incentives. So the degree of inequality allowed in a distribution pattern may affect the quantity and quality of the item(s) for distribution; but Rawls believes he provides principles for a dynamic, yet socially just, growth pattern by giving absolute priority to liberty. No rational person will risk his liberty for the sake of a prosperity that only others may enjoy.

On the other hand there may be room for some scepticism. While most of the communitarian critics have focused upon Rawls's views on the unity of the self, on the primacy of the right over the good, and the fact that this entails rejecting any thesis of the common good in the tradition of Aristotle, other, rights-orientated writers have charged that a latent utilitarianism creeps into Rawls's theory in his subtle movement towards maximisation; or pointed out that there is more than one possible decision procedure. Social realists have claimed that the only kind of agreements that we ought to be concerned with are the actual historical struggles that have been engaged in; although in an actual social agreement individuals may well be bound, Rawls takes us into hypothetical agreement. But what sort of hypothetical rights does society enforce?

There may be several.[19] Moreover, alternative thought experiments are imaginable which lead to radically different conceptions of the role of government in a 'just society'. Moreover, Rawls provides the principles of justice of the rational pessimist, but what of the gambler? Why should not someone behind the veil of ignorance simply say 'I'll vote for a society with great inequalities because I believe I stand a good chance of being one of the winners'?

---

19 For Ronald Dworkin (1977) the original position only gave rise to hypothetical decisions and it is illogical to make a theory of justice which is meant to legitimate real decisions based on such a procedure. Instead of asking what it is rational to do or refrain from doing in the hypothetical situation, we need to interpret the actual social contracts we are committed to – for example the American Constitution. Rawls would say that by considering rational examples, for instance of the cake cutter, we can understand the moral force of equal distribution. People can understand this decision without actually creating a cake and sharing it. The fact of the hypothetical nature of the argument does not destroy the force of the argument, and just as the cake example can work as a moral argument, so too can the notion of the hypothetical original position.

PART FOUR
THE RADICAL FREE-MARKET PHILOSOPHY OF
ROBERT NOZICK

NOZICK AS AN EXAMPLE OF PHILOSOPHICAL
LIBERTARIANISM

While Rawls's theory may justify social redistribution (it amounts to a defence of the modern liberal-democratic welfare state), for another group of liberals – whom we can call libertarians – big government is incompatible with liberty. Libertarians share a profound distaste for all theories which promote any idea of a social good which legitimates centralised social administration – even if this is the rather individualist conception of classical utilitarianism – and the aim is to abolish all governmental interference with the lives and 'rights' of the citizen. Libertarianism largely founds itself upon a reading of the classical social contract theorist John Locke, who is seen as holding a central thesis that in a state of nature mankind is possessed of inviolable individual rights and has supreme right to take possession of any goods which others do not own. Once seized of these goods, they become their property. The role of government is to protect those rights – particularly the rights to life and property – and social administration is only legitimated insofar as it reinforces and protects those rights and is never legitimated in overriding them. Society is conceived only as the space wherein individuals pursue their own projects, free from interference and respecting the rights of others. The political jurisprudence of Robert Nozick, characterised by his book *Anarchy State and Utopia* (1974), is the best known of the libertarian theories of justice.[20] Nozick begins from the dual premise that all persons are naturally individuals possessed of right,[21] and that all governments, and all social organisations, need justification:

> the fundamental question of political philosophy, one that precedes questions about how the state should be organised, is whether there should be any state at all. Why not have anarchy? (1974: 4)

To begin with this basic premise sounds strange to the European reader, but in the American context it represents an understandable, if extreme, beginning. While European writings are unable to look back to the existence of any actual history of their

---

20 His essay has been described as 'extolling the virtues of 18th-century individualism and 19th-century laissez-faire capitalism' (J Paul, ed, *Reading Nozick* 1981: 1), an 'original, remarkable and strikingly intelligent' piece of writing *(ibid*: 28), while Lloyd and Freeman called it one of the most 'provocative essays in political philosophy to have appeared in a long time' (6th edn, 1995: 367). More soberly it was regarded as 'highly theoretical in character, with the virtues of formal elegance as opposed to concrete realism' (Paul, ed, 1981: 35).

21 'Individuals have rights, and there are things no person or group may do to them (without violating their rights)' (1974: ix). Nozick offers no sociological or other explanation of how the emphasis upon individualism or rights has come about, instead his basis is merely to appeal to our intuitions about treating people as 'ends in themselves' and 'treating us with respect by respecting our rights' *(ibid*: 334).

own which resembles the Lockean narrative, the founding and development of the United States is often interpreted as the living embodiment of the Lockean narrative.[22]

Nozick's writings develop a theory of justice which reinforces a radical free-market approach and fits a so-called minimal or nightwatchman state. It is no surprise that he concludes:

> The minimal state is the most extensive state that can be justified. Any state more extensive violates people's rights (1974: 149).

WHAT IS NOZICK'S IDEA OF THE MINIMAL STATE, AND WHY DOES HE CLAIM THIS IS THE ONLY STATE THAT CAN BE JUSTIFIED?

Nozick defines his reference to the minimal state as 'the nightwatchman state of classical liberal theory, limited to the functions of protecting all its citizens against violence, theft, fraud and the enforcement of contracts and so on' (ibid: 26–7). How does he explain this as the only level of social organisation defensible?

Anarchy, State and Utopia is subdivided into three parts. Its structure is loaded in favour of minimalism. Part One purports to confront the anarchist who denies the legitimacy of any form of state, asserting that any state is 'intrinsically immoral' (ibid: 51). In response to this 'challenge', Nozick undertakes a thought experiment in which he traces the detailed evolution of the minimal state in which neither its emergence, nor its continued existence, infringes rights. Part Two examines the notion of the minimal state, and specifies that a more extensive state will violate rights and thus be unjustified. Nozick develops an 'entitlement theory of justice', whereby economic goods arise in society already encumbered with rightful claims to their ownership, which in turn discredits 'patterned' forms of distribution (ibid: 155–164). In Part Three Nozick presents his utopia, which enables him to argue that the minimal state is worth defending.

The opening chapter of Part One is entitled *Why State of Nature Theory*, and outlines a thought experiment which begins by imagining life without a state. Nozick does not, however, present us with a horrible state of nature such as Hobbes has done, since clearly if he were to make the state of nature as bad as Hobbes envisaged, then we would be likely to accept any state as providing a solution to the problem. Conversely, Nozick argues that we should imagine a benign state of nature; his father figure is Locke not Hobbes. However, in this situation, the question may arise whether we really need to

---

22 As Stephen Newman (1984:16) puts it in a book aptly entitled *Liberalism at Wits' End: the Libertarian Revolt against the Modern State*: 'the United States is the premier Lockean polity. Its founding was virtually an acting out of the principles of Locke's Second Treatise of Government, and for almost 100 years the nation seemed a near-perfect model of what Locke meant by civil society. Government was instituted to protect life and property. Authority was purposefully limited and made subject to multiple restraints in order to safeguard the liberty of the people. Fortunate material circumstances, notably an abundant supply of free land, allowed equal opportunity and virtual autonomy for (almost) all (not, of course, for blacks, Indians, or women). Free-market capitalism, nurtured by the state, served the interests of rich and poor alike by opening the avenue of success to ambition and talent.' At least that is the political narrative cherished by modern libertarians.

invent a state? We would need very good reasons to justify it. Nozick constructs a theoretical argument with several steps.

Step one: Individuals are placed in a state of nature, but – as with Locke's narrative – these individuals are possessed of rights. Nozick argues that there are two ways of thinking about rights. In one conception we accept that rights will conflict, or that we need to balance rights with other social goals. Ultimately, Nozick suggests, this leads into a utilitarianism concerning rights; we begin to wonder about either sacrificing or reducing rights or alternatively maximising the protection of rights. As Nozick puts it: '... suppose some conditions about minimising the total (weighted) amount of violations of rights are built in the desired end state to be achieved. We would then have something like a 'utilitarianism' of rights: violations of rights (to be minimised) merely would replace the total happiness as the relevant end state in the utilitarian structure.' Even if we are aiming at a minimum rights violation we would still in certain conditions be willing to sacrifice an individual for the common good. In the second conception of rights, a 'moral side constraints' view of rights prevails (*ibid*: 28–35). We are never to violate these rights.[23] For Nozick, it is never permissible to override the interest of the individual for the sake of the others in society.[24] In the thought experiment individuals possess these rights in a state of nature, but we are asked to imagine there was natural anarchy. This leads us to step two.

Step two: These individuals with rights form voluntary associations to defend their rights. These associations – 'mutual protection agencies' – are totally voluntary. Those who join receive protection and the others do not. As yet no state has been formed; there is no body that has legitimation for use of force over the whole area. Originally, therefore, the association has only those rights granted to it by other individuals. It is simply a collection of individuals in association.

Step three: The voluntary associations sort themselves out territorially. A 'dominant protection association' develops in each area. This is an inevitable consequence of the economics of protection and results in a logical requirement for protection services such as the courts and police, etc, to function within a certain territory.

Step four: In step three there are still some independents who have not joined any of the associations, thus the independents have the same rights to protect themselves as the

---

23 'Side constraints upon action reflect the underlying Kantian principle that individuals are ends and not merely means ... Side constraints express the inviolability of other persons.' (1974: 30) Again the foundation of this, Nozick claims, is our perception of our lives: 'The moral side constraints upon what we may do, I claim, reflect the fact of our separate existences. They reflect the fact that no moral balancing act can take place among us; there is no moral outweighing of one of our lives by other so as to lead to a greater overall social good. There is no justified sacrifice of some of us for others' (*ibid*: 33).

24 It has often been said that one of the possible problems with Rawls's veil of ignorance is that of gambling. (An individual may prefer to gamble on being one of those who have benefited rather than one of the losing few.) Rawls does not seem able to handle the fact that albeit, perhaps, to gamble is irrational, it is also part of the human condition. Perhaps in the example of the patient in room 306 (cf Chapter 6 of this text) we would choose the utilitarian solution, gambling that we would be far more likely to be among the five, not the one. Only a theory of the absoluteness of rights, such as that of Nozick, would be guaranteed to save the patient in room 306, even though the others could save the five others.

associations. Step Four consists of these independents joining or becoming incorporated; we thereby arrive at a minimal state, a body capable of exercising a monopoly in the use of force within a particular territory and extend protection to all its citizens *(ibid*: 113). The minimal state is limited in its legitimation of force to the protection of certain basic rights: it is the nightwatchman state of classic liberalism. Under utilitarianism, or the later theory of Rawls, we could have redistribution policies; but no redistribution is legitimate in the minimal state. All that is paid for would be a basic protection service. There is no welfare state etc in Nozick's theory. Some may call this classical capitalism. Nozick further claims the development of the minimal state is spontaneous, unplanned and unintended. It is portrayed as the result of natural history: 'an invisible hand process and by morally permissible means, without anyone's rights being violated' *(ibid*: 119).

How do we move from step three to four? It looks impossible[25] because the most basic assumption is that individual rights are so strong that they raise the question of what if anything a state could do; particularly if it never violates rights. Surely step four involves the violation of the rights of some members? Paying for protection must involve some redistribution of resources.[26] The step also seems to involve some violation of rights of the independents, since now there is an authority which has power over them to which they have not agreed. The crucial rights lost are those of self-help and to interpret and be the final arbiter of when one's rights are violated (the right to take the law into one's own hands and decide when justice is done). The state now becomes the final arbiter of when violence is to be used. The state alone sanctions the legitimate use of force.[27]

---

25 Many critics have simply felt it to be a 'hypothetical narrative ... a bizarre departure from any common sense account' (Bernard Williams, quoted in Paul, 1981: 5).

26 How can we judge? What criteria are possible? Nozick offers none. Robert Holmes turns Nozick's own arguments against him arguing that since no independent criterion is offered to assess the enforcement procedures of the dominant protective associations the 'usurpation of all the powers of adjudication and enforcement cannot be justified' (In Paul, 1981: 6).

27 It is for this reason that at first glance the move from protection associations to a minimal state appears too large. Hypothetically, since this is a thought experiment, Nozick might have solved the problem simply by saying that everybody would join the minimum state, but as this is an unlikely course he needed a more realistic narrative for his theory to gain credibility. Nozick proposes two problems for his own scheme: specifically, (i) it looks as though the members of the associations allow limited redistribution to the independents, and (ii) why do the independents join at all? Nozick replies it only looks like redistribution. For example if A owes B money and B steals goods from A's home this could be compensation rather than stealing. It could look like either; we have to look at the reasons, not just the appearance. Nozick argues that it is a matter of compensation. The minimal state incorporates the independents but owes them something because they have lost their self-help right. It owes them protection services and compensation. So we can get to step four. Nozick thinks that people can actively and voluntarily consent to anything provided that there is no violation of the rights of others. So we can consent to giving up rights. One could sell oneself into slavery; so we can consent to a state. But the compensation argument is not simple consent, and we must ask 'what is fair compensation?' He discusses compensation in various ways, one of which is by difference curves, but Nozick thinks we can use this argument to get to a minimal state. Again the critics are not convinced: Robert Paul Wolff (in Paul, 1981: 7) argues a rational calculation of the harm suffered in violating the rights is not possible owing to the 'fluidity and lack of structure' of the state of nature.

ARGUMENTS BASED ON FAIR ACQUISITION

In Part Two Nozick uses another set of arguments – which he terms an *Entitlement Theory of Justice* – to conclude that only the minimum state is justified. These are a set of arguments aimed specifically against redistribution of wealth. The entitlement theory promotes the idea that an individual has an intrinsic right to whatever he holds, provided that the way in which he came to hold each part of his property was justified. There are three ways in which a person is entitled to hold his possessions justly: *justice in acquisition* – this means that the property when acquired was not the property of someone else (eg a natural resource); *justice in transfer* – this is where the property is transferred to the present holder by valid means. These includes gift, sale, inheritance – the only stipulation being that there has been no fraud or theft involved. When there has been a failure to observe one of the above methods of entitlement by the present holder of the property, then the injustice should be rectified, and A should restore the property to B. This is termed *justice in rectification*.

Thus Nozick's argument is quasi-historical: 'A distribution is just if it arises from a prior just distribution by legitimate means' (*ibid*: 151). Nozick then launches into a series of arguments which attack rival proposals, such as those underlying distribution structures which are informed by arguments from the theories of utilitarianism (such as the maximisation of social welfare), or those which stress the desirability of equality. Nozick argues that underlying conceptions of (re)distributive justice are sets of principles which conflict with the primacy of liberty, and an absolute respect for rights.

A famous illustration Nozick provides is *the Wilt Chamberlain* argument. Nozick asks us to imagine a stable set of distributions we consider just. We are to call this distribution D1. Perhaps everyone has an equal share, perhaps people have a share in accordance with a particular distribution curve; the specifics do not matter, what matters is that we do not object to that particular distribution pattern. Imagine in that society there is a brilliant 7'1" basketball player, Wilt Chamberlain, extremely sought after by basketball teams, having tremendous draw power with the fans; people love to see him play and they are willing to pay more when he plays. Let us suppose his contract says for every home game, 25 cents from the price of each ticket goes directly to Wilt, or that during the season at home matches, each spectator drops 25 cents into a separate box with Chamberlain's name on it. They are all excited about seeing him play and consider they get value for money. Nozick asks us to suppose that in one year a million people pay to see him play; Wilt receives $250,000 more than other team players and naturally this sum is very much larger than the average income in the society. Is Wilt entitled to this income? At the end of the year we have a new distribution D2,, with Wilt having much more resources than anyone else. Is this distribution unjust? If so, why? By way of an answer, Nozick asks us to consider how D1 became D2. It was clearly achieved by people exercising their rights under D1. The individuals exercised their liberty and gave money to purchase what they wished; they freely chose to transfer a portion of their money to Wilt in order to enjoy watching him exercise his skills. Nozick does not claim that D2 is better than D1, merely that D2 is as just as D1. D2 is simply a position which arises as a result of individuals exercising the rights they possessed under D1, without harming anyone else. Therefore D2 is as 'just' as D1; but, if so, the accepted pattern of distribution which characterises D1 is broken. The operation of liberty has upset the settled pattern.

Nozick suggests that this will be the fate of all systems which are structured in terms of policies and patterns; such conceptions of justice are doomed to be unworkable. Instead we are asked to agree to a dynamic system which places primacy on rights which are not to be violated. For Nozick the fundamental principle of this 'historical entitlement theory' of justice is that 'whatever arises from a just situation by just steps is itself just' (1974: 151).

But what of coercion? Even the rightful exercise of rights by people can actually lead to very coercive outcomes and situations. Moreover, the Wilt Chamberlain argument is a very particular argument; in fact the market does not always work this way. Today the market is an all-embracing environment and in the main people experience the market in a different way to Nozick's arguments; they cannot simply take it or leave it when offered work, and there is a reliance upon certain goods. The market can be coercive, rather than freedom maximising.

Nozick (1974: 262–265) provides another example of what he considers freedom maximising to be. In this example he responds specifically to the idea of the coercive market, and the Marxist style argument that people are forced to work in order to survive. Nozick begins by agreeing that: 'other people's actions place limits on one's available opportunity'; but he goes on ' ... whether this makes one's resulting action non-voluntary depends on whether these others had a right to act as they did ... ' He proposes a sort of desert island example: there are 26 women (A-Z) and 26 men (A1-Z1) each wanting to be married. In this relatively simple society there is no disagreement as to the comparative attractiveness of each to each other. The order of attractiveness goes from A-Z in decreasing preferential order. A and A1 voluntarily choose to get married, each preferring the other to any other partner. Now although B would have preferred to marry A1, and B1 would prefer to marry A, the actions of A and A1 have destroyed this option. Since B and B1 also wish to marry, they therefore choose each other as representing the most preferable option out of what is left. Now although the options of B and B1 have been reduced, their rights have not been interfered with through the exercise by A and A1 of their liberty; thus B and B1 have not been coerced into their choice. Of course options become more and more limited down the line, but, Nozick says, even when one goes through X and Y, and accepts that by the time one comes to Z and Z1 and they are left with only each other or nothing, coercion is not involved. Both Z and Z1 admit that if they want to be married they must marry the least attractive person of the opposite group. The question is fundamental: have they been coerced if they marry each other rather than nobody?

Nozick claims that similar considerations apply to market exchanges between workers and the owners of capital. If one said that the employees were graded A-Z and the employers A1-Z1 can we consider the combination Z-Z1 as voluntary? Are there any legitimate grounds for Z or Z1 to complain? Perhaps Z is faced with the choice of working for Z1 or starving; and since the choice is a result of the actions of all the others which do not provide Z with any other option – does Z therefore choose to work voluntarily? For Nozick 'Z does choose voluntarily if the other individuals A-Y each acted voluntarily and within their rights'.

Both the marriage example and the entitlement of property fall, for Nozick, under the adage 'from each as they choose to each as they are chosen'; it is not something that redistribution policy should interfere with.

Whether, however, in the employment example, people voluntarily and freely choose, is surely a more complicated question; the marriage example is not an exactly analogous situation. Some might argue that people have a social right to a job although, perhaps, not a distinct social right to marry. Does that make the situation of Z coercive?

CONTRADICTORY PROBLEMS WITH THE PRINCIPLE OF RECTIFICATION

In Nozick's scheme the claim to just distribution depends on individuals having strong rights to ownership of their property, but how can we be sure of the historical validity of their claims? Nozick acknowledges that the issue of past injustices raises severe problems.

> If past injustice has shaped present holding in various ways, some identifiable and some not, what now, if anything, is to be done to rectify these injustices? How, if at all, do things change if the beneficiaries and those made worse off are not the direct parties in the act of injustice, but, for example, their descendants? How far back must one go in wiping clean the historical slate of injustices?

Having raised the issue Nozick can only conclude 'I do not know of a thorough or theoretically sophisticated treatment of such issues'. Ironically, as Bernard Williams points out, Nozick's theory may offer a substantial challenge to contemporary capitalism since

> Nozick's derivation theory does not imply that contemporary property holdings are just; on the contrary (though it is a matter of removable fact), it is 99% probable that almost all of them are not. (Mr Nozick may think that much of America rightfully belongs to the Indians) (In Paul, 1981: 27).

How can entitlement therefore be guaranteed historically? Given the infinite possibilities for injustices to have occurred historically, and the theoretical and practical impossibility of identifying and rectifying them, any attempt to put Nozick's theory into practice to justify present holdings as safe from interference is either historically arbitrary or self-contradictory.[28]

---

28 This conclusion follows from the honesty of Nozick's position. Nozick relies upon the Lockean principle of rightful initial acquisition, namely, that one must not make others worse off when acquiring a piece of unwanted material or natural resources, and claiming ownership. Kymlicka (1990) summarises Nozick as proposing a staged theory of property acquisition:

1 people own themselves;
2 the world is largely unowned;
3 you can acquire absolute property rights over a disproportionate share of the world, if you do not worsen the condition of others;
4 it is relatively easy to acquire absolute rights over a disproportionate share of the world; therefore
5 once private property has been appropriated, a free market in capital and labour is morally required. ...

Thus, while Nozick's argument that any state more extensive than a minimal state must – absolutely must – violate people's rights is, on the terms of Nozick's logical structure, true, it also follows that in Nozick's scheme it is impossible to establish what the rights of any one individual actually are in regard to property. The theory appeals to our individualist intuitions but cannot protect itself against its own attempts to be an historically or sociologically true account of the primacy of the minimal state or the free market.[29]

THE WEAKNESS OF THE LIBERTARIAN POSITION

The weakness of abstract philosophical argument that does not consider social history or social reality

Libertarians look back to the writings of Locke and follow him in constructing a hypothetical model of the state of nature to find a mechanism of judgment which will legitimate the justice of social arrangements while preserving the primacy of liberty. Locke's writings enable them to seize on a tradition of a narrative of natural history in which there exists a psychology positing economic motives as primary (the idea of possessive individualism). Thus the narrative history is viewed as timeless and the psychology as natural. But Locke wrote a 'narrative natural history' – in which individuals existed who were possessed of inviolable natural rights – to escape from a real history in which the majority did not possess rights. Locke espoused natural rights to repudiate the reality of feudalism; while he postulated the primacy of economic motives in order to fight all the other motives for human passion (in a sense to assert that economic motivation pacifies and rationalises the instability of human passion, expressed in religions and historical prejudice). Locke stands – with Hobbes, Hume and Adam Smith – at the beginnings of the modern period which has seen the spread of the market throughout the world. As libertarians are keen to point out, the market is the only

---

28...Kymlicka argues that point 3 is too weak to give rise to point 4. In appropriating a piece of land you inevitably make others worse off in some respects, by denying them a share or a say in the use of that land, or, in time, with the others dispossessed, by dictating the terms under which they must work on the land; moreover, since there are a variety of types of appropriation patterns, by choosing that particular one another may have made everybody better off.

Kymlicka argues that Nozick's theory cannot justify present property holdings, since historically force was used in almost all initial appropriation and thus all current titles are illegitimate. There is no moral ground why a government may not take and redistribute them, perhaps to make amends for past injustice. Nozick almost accepts this, even suggesting that a one-off redistribution according to Rawls's difference principle may wipe the slate clean before his entitlement theory comes into play.

29 Other libertarians, such as Rothbard (1982), are not as open as Nozick. Rothbard counters the unjust acquisition argument by stating that, if they are known, criminal owners should be dispossessed and their holdings returned to the just owners. If the just owners cannot be found, the goods simply become unowned and the first person to appropriate and utilise them acquires property rights. If the current owners are not actual criminals then there is no reason to dispossess them of the goods and even if the goods were originally acquired by theft or force – as in most colonial situations – the first owner is unlikely to exist, therefore the present owner can keep the property. Since virtually all original owners are long dead, nearly all current title owners are just possessors of the goods, except for property actually stolen by the present owners.

mechanism which does not consider the colour of your skin, religion, or aesthetic taste, in ways other than as selling opportunities. The social ironies of the measures they espouse – for example, that the state, in acting impartially to guarantee individual rights, ends up serving the interests of those particular classes with dominant market position – is lost because libertarians have an undeveloped feel for the reality of politics. Their political reality is rather a philosophical reality resembling one or other mythical state of nature. Philosophical liberals appear naive to critics who adopt a more sociologically informed perspective and who see both our contemporary intuitions and our social institutions as the result of a complicated set of historical, political and sociological processes. Ultimately, right-orientated philosophy is called upon to face one unanswerable problem: are not human rights and so-called 'natural rights' only natural to the extent that we use the word natural to describe the social processes which have allowed rights to be created and become entrenched in social structures? Rights are socially created, they were not discovered in history – as if they somehow existed in some timeless realm (of Platonic natural essences) – they were created in history. Similarly, the individual.[30]

5.2 Libertarian narratives avoid the political, and ignore alternative narratives of the actual traditions of our societies

The libertarian interpretation of the origin of the United States as an enactment of the Lockean rationalist defence of individualism and natural rights to property has been questioned by a range of recent studies which discerned a strong civic republican trend in the revolutionary period. Only with the advent of the federal constitution did the idea of public virtue and of the common good lose their central roles to a new concept of public opinion.[31] Government became a political compromise between interests whose existence was external to the political action itself.

Although this new 'liberal' conception became dominant during the 19th century, the republican conception never completely disappeared. Pocock asserts that it became somewhat subterranean, operating through upholding pre-modern and anti-industrial symbols in American culture. Many authors who criticise liberal individualism appeal to

---

30 As Charles Taylor (1985: 309) argues with respect to any theory which takes the atomistic view of the isolated individual as its basic unit: 'The basic error of atomism in all its forms is that it fails to take account of the degree to which the free individual with his own goals and aspirations, whose just rewards it is trying to protect, is himself only possible within a certain kind of civilisation; that it took a long development of certain institutions and practices, of the rule of law, of rules of equal respect, of habits of common deliberation, of common association, of cultural development, and so on, to produce the modern individual.'

31 Historians, such as Bailyn (1967) and Wood (1969), have shown that the American revolution had been profoundly influenced by the culture of neo-Harringtonian civic humanism. Bailyn's analysis of the pamphlets of the revolutionary period focuses in part upon the central place of the idea of 'corruption' in the political language of American patriots. The classical conception of politics, in which individuals actively participate in the republic, was only later displaced by a new paradigm of representative democracy. In Gordon Wood's (1969) analysis the end of classical politics came with the federal constitution of 1787, wherein the people were no longer conceived as connected by a common identity of interests, but seen rather as 'an agglomeration of hostile individuals coming together for their mutual benefit in the construction of a society'.

this tradition, affirming that this subtle influence of civic republicanism enabled Americans to retain a certain sense of community, and provided inherent resistance to the corrosive effects of individualism. They see the solution to the crisis that American society is going through today – a crisis that consists, according to them, in the destruction of social bonds due to the liberal promotion of self-interested individuals (who only know how to look after their own immediate concerns) and who reject obligations that shackle their freedom – in the revitalisation of this tradition of civic republicanism. Whereas the neo-conservatives see in the democratic idea the origin of the difficulties of liberal democracy – namely big government – 'communitarians' identify the real problem as a disappearance of civic virtue and denial of the need of the populace for identification with a political community which recognises that citizenship not only implies rights but also duties and social interdependency.

The ascendancy of rights over collective participation is further accentuated by recent processes of increasing privatisation of social life and disappearance of public space; for communitarians this can only be remedied by restoring political participation. In their eyes, the liberal illusion that harmony could be born out of the free play of private interests, and that modern society no longer needs civic virtue, has finally shown itself to be dangerous; it brings into question the very existence of the democratic process, and the meaning of society. From whence comes the necessity for a new political culture which reconnects with the tradition of civic republicanism and restores dignity to politics.

PART FIVE
EXAMPLES OF THE COMMUNITARIAN
CRITIQUE OF LIBERAL THEORIES OF JUSTICE[32]

THE CRITICAL ANALYSIS OF MICHAEL SANDEL

Michael Sandel (1982, *Liberalism and the Limits of Justice*) claims that Rawls posits an inconsistent treatment of the self. Although Rawls acknowledges the intersubjectivity of the self, he needs a conception of a rational and unified self to found his thesis of the priority of the right over the good. Moreover, Rawls's deontological liberalism requires a conception of justice which does not presuppose any particular conception of the good, to serve as the framework within which different conceptions of the good become possible. The primacy of justice is both a moral priority and a privileged form of justification. The right is seen as prior to the good not only because its demands have natural precedence, but also because its principles are produced in a non-consequential manner as rationally derived in the conditions of the original position. But for us actually to agree that we can accept the outcome, ie the principles of justice derived from the calculations of the original position, it is necessary to accept that the subject (the rational decision-making self) exists independently of his/her intentions and his/her ends. Rawls requires the acceptance of a subject who can have an identity defined prior to the values and objectives that he/she may choose. It is, in effect, the capacity to choose, not the choices made, that defines such a subject. This subject can never have ends which are constitutive of his identity, and is denied the possibility of participation in a community where it is the very definition of who he is that is in question.

According to Sandel, in Rawls's problematic a 'constitutive' or expressive type of community such as this is unthinkable; but this means that Rawls is limited to an ideology of 'community' as co-operation between individuals whose interests are already given, and who join together in order to defend and advance them. While, however, this unencumbered conception of the subject, incapable of constitutive and expressive engagements, seems within this context necessary so that the right can have priority over the good, it nonetheless appears in contradiction to the principles of justice which Rawls seeks to justify. Since the difference principle is in the nature of a principle of sharing, it presupposes both the existence of a moral bond between those who are going to distribute social goods, and therefore of a constitutive community whose recognition it requires. Moreover, Rawls accepts that an individual is hopelessly fragmented and only becomes human in social subjectivity, in the very type of community excluded by the Rawlsean conception of the subject without attachments, defined prior to the ends he chooses. Sandel argues that Rawls's theory has an internal contradiction: 'we cannot be persons for whom justice is primary and also be persons for

32   For a much greater analysis see Stephen Mulhall & Adam Smith (1992, 2nd edn, 1995) *Liberals & Communitarians* – essentially a 'Rawls and his critics' book on contrasting readings on justice.

whom the difference principle is a principle of justice.'

Sandel's analysis is directed against the original text of *The Theory of Justice* in which Rawls seemed to be searching for some absolutely secure point of reference; in other words that his original position should be rationally unassailable. In that case it appears Sandel is correct in arguing that Rawls has not succeeded in guaranteeing that his theory is rationally secure; but this does not mean that we ought to reject Rawls's theory as rationally appealing or the liberal politics which lie behind it.[33] Perhaps Sandel is calling for liberalism to lose its sociological weakness and remember both the fact of its historical creation and the necessity to fight for its advantages while attempts are made to improve it.[34]

CHARLES TAYLOR AND THE CHARGE OF ATOMISM

For Charles Taylor (1985: Vol 2, Ch 7) the liberal view of the subject is 'atomist' because it affirms the self-sufficient character of the individual. In contrast to the Aristotelian notion of man as fundamentally a political animal who can only realise his human nature within the bosom of a society, it impoverishes our ideas of ourselves and aids in the destruction of public life through the development of bureaucratic individualism. According to Taylor, only through participation in a community of language and mutual discourse concerning the just and unjust, the good and the bad, can a coherent rationality develop enabling man to operate as a moral subject capable of discovering the good; therefore there cannot be a priority of the right over the good. Referring particularly to Nozick, he shows the absurdity of starting from the priority of natural rights in order to deduce the entirety of the social context: Nozick 'does not recognise that asserting rights itself involves acknowledging an obligation to belong' (1985: Vol 2, 200). In effect, this modern individual, with his rights, is the result of a long and complex historical development and it is only in a certain type of society that the existence of such a free individual, capable of choosing his own objectives, is possible. For Taylor, we need to understand our communal existence, because the

---

33 Sandel wants to move from showing an internal contradiction in Rawls's theory – given the strongest rational reading – to concluding we must therefore accept the superiority of a politics of the common good over a politics of defending rights. The fact that Rawls's argument has internal contradictions, or antinomies, does not imply that his general objective must be rejected.

34 In his concluding paragraph Sandel (1982: 183) states that liberal justice is necessary for a society of 'strangers, sometimes benevolent', who 'cannot know each other, or our ends, well enough to govern by the common good alone'. The ultimate aim is to transform the conditions of social existence so that liberal justice is replaced by community, until then liberalism requires a greater political self-consciousness.

> Liberalism teaches respect for the distance of self and ends, and when this distance is lost, we are submerged in a circumstance that ceases to be ours. But by seeking to secure this distance too completely, liberalism undermines its own insight. By putting the self beyond the reach of politics, it makes human agency an article of faith rather than an object of continuing attention and concern, a premise of politics rather than its most precarious achievement. This misses the pathos of politics and also its most inspiring possibilities. It overlooks the danger that when politics goes badly, not only disappointments but also dislocation are likely to result. And it forgets the possibility that when politics goes well, we can know a good in common that we cannot know alone.

essence of the problem of being human is not the question of material survival, 'desire-fulfilment, and freedom and pain', but rather the struggle to become a fully developed human; something which our words may fail fully to articulate, but our dreams presage (*ibid*: 201–2). Again the core charge against liberal philosophy – exemplified by Nozick – is of ignorance of actual history and social achievement, the treating as natural that which in reality is a tenuous socio-human creation, and, as a consequence, weakening our political imperative to participate in the building of modernity:

> We owe our identity as free men to our civilisation …The crucial point is this: since the free individual can only maintain his identity within a society/culture of a certain kind, he has to be concerned about the shape of this society/culture as a whole. He cannot … be concerned purely with his individual choices and the associations formed from such choices to the neglect of the matrix in which such choices can be open or closed, rich or meagre. It is important to him that certain activities and institutions flourish in society. It is even of importance to him what the moral tone of the whole society is … because freedom and individual diversity can only flourish in a society where there is a general recognition of their worth (*ibid*: 207).

ALASDAIR MACINTYRE AND THE ATTEMPT TO REDISCOVER VIRTUE

For Alasdair MacIntyre (*After Virtue*, 1981, 2nd edn 1984; *Whose Justice, Which Rationality?*, 1988), Rawls and Nozick both ignore what should be fundamental to justice, namely the idea of virtue. MacIntyre argues that modernity has dislocated the language of morality; in effect we are surrounded by discourses of morality but all sense of coherence has vanished as the quest for the big picture has been abandoned in favour of analysis. MacIntyre plays off modernity, in the guise of individualism and subjectivity as espoused by Nietzsche, against his rereading of the classical tradition of Aristotle. For MacIntyre moral language only makes sense within a systematic exposition of the totality of human concerns. Our modern morality has become mere emotivism, expressions of subjective preferences. Moral theories have become apologies for individualism and subjective desire. This has occurred in part because modern theories can only conceive of society as if it were made up of individuals whose interests are defined prior to and independent of the construction of any moral or social bond between them. Conversely, the ancient Greeks placed great emphasis upon the notion of virtue and the character of the person, but virtue only makes sense in the context of a community whose original bond is a shared understanding of both the good of man and the good of the community and where the individuals recognise their fundamental interests with reference to these goods. However, the dominant philosophical tradition of modernity – liberalism – rejects all ideas of a common good other than the mere aggregation of the desires of those individuals who are deemed to comprise the (non-)society. This individualism – epitomised by Nietzsche's radical subjectivity – is to be regarded as the source of the nihilism that is slowly destroying our societies.

In *After Virtue*, MacIntyre (1984) identifies virtues by reference to their role in practices, rather than the historical scholastic method which looked for the correspondence of the act to substantive requirements of the nature of human beings.

MacIntyre attempts to return to the virtue-based ethics of Aristotle but without accepting Aristotle's 'metaphysical biology', or agreeing with any substantive theory of human nature (ontology). He neither accepts nor disagrees with the Aristotelian philosophy of nature. Instead, MacIntyre defines virtue in a relatively formal manner:

> A virtue is an acquired human quality the possession and exercise of which tends to enable us to achieve those goods which are internal to practices and the lack of which effectively prevents us from achieving any such goods (1984: 193–4).

Furthermore, he sees practices as relatively dynamic phenomena which do not have fixed goals for all time. Practices are sustained by relatively specific activities (methodologies), but the goals these activities strive for change over history, as may the criteria for judging the quality of the practice. Both technical skills and institutional settings may shape the historicity of practices. But does this mean that we can be virtuous simply by becoming good as expressed by the internal requirements for any practice? MacIntyre claims that before we can call an activity virtuous, it must also accord with a 'telos which transcends the limited goods of practices by constituting the good of a whole human life'. We need an overall grasp of the human condition, since as long as the excellences internal to practices are taken in isolation, an account of the virtues might of necessity be either socially arbitrary, or internal to a practice which we find abhorrent.

The problem of MacIntyre's communitarian account is that it appears circular. Moral qualities are defined by their ability to serve practices, practices in turn serve institutional goals, which in their turn may serve the needs of a society arbitrarily. We need a standard distinct from the social arrangements of the community which can assess the quality of needs. Is there any way of judging the specific value of different practices? MacIntyre resorts to the idea of *traditions*. Virtues must be integrated into the overall patterns of a tradition informed by a quest for the good and the best. Thus virtue is not just a problem for the individual; the conception of virtue requires a tradition that has accumulated some experience about goods internal to practices.

Which sorts of human dispositions, activities and, correlatively, institutions and skills, befit human nature? MacIntyre's answer is those which befit the telos or quest, and which are consonant with the tradition of the persons making such an enquiry. We save ourselves for the terrors of moral indeterminacy and nihilism by positioning ourselves within a tradition. The tradition gives us existential belonging and enables us to live the moral life of virtue.

Are all traditions equally worthwhile? The structure MacIntyre proposes offers coherence and a life of meaning; but it appears relativist. We can certainly engage in historical description and report what it meant to live in the Indian caste system and how this conferred a working sense of virtue and justice, but many of us would wish to say more. We would normatively state that a life of virtue within that structure was actually unjust. It did not agree with ideas we hold central to our ideas of human flourishing. Can the coherence of MacIntyre's system be retained, while at the same time we introduce or defend a normative account of what the telos of a whole life is? Critics of MacIntyre believe he has little chance of resolving this issue.

Alan Gewirth, writing as a neo-Kantian,[35] argues that MacIntyre's virtue theory is relativist. It cannot provide a rational foundation to judge which types of actions satisfy or violate a specifically moral rule.[36] MacIntyre's structure lacks substantive content, and thus we are unable to judge between traditions with mutually opposed substantive accounts of virtuous actions. Where can he find a secure place to stand if MacIntyre rejects the metaphysics of nature which supported Aristotle? Since judging virtue by its role in practices only give us ideas of internal coherence, MacIntyre must move to the second stage of the idea he proposes, namely that of the *telos* or quest of mankind, but again we could postulate any number of pictures of a unified end. What is the precise 'good' that anchors the quest such that we can judge the quality of Hitler or Stalin, for example? We can not accept defining 'quest' in terms of a virtue-like constancy or singleness of purpose, since all sorts of people in history that we usually consider evil displayed that quality. MacIntyre anchors his concepts in the idea of tradition, but there is no sure standard for adjudging whether the resources of a tradition lead to a genuine knowledge of the relevant goods. While MacIntyre asks *Whose Justice, Which Rationality?*, Gewirth asks:

> But which community? Aristotle's perfect community required the enslavement of farmers and mechanics; the Nazi community required the murder of Jews and others; the contemporary Afrikaner community requires the subjugation, economic and personal as well as political, of millions of blacks. For all his endorsement of a morality of laws, MacIntyre's specification of their 'point and purpose', together with his unclear evaluation of moral universalism, leaves available such violations of basic rights, and hence a drastic moral indeterminacy (1985: 758-9).

Writing from the Kantian perspective, Gewirth states that the 'conceptual resources [MacIntyre] deploys in making the virtues central to moral philosophy are inadequate substitutes for the more traditional view that derives the content of the virtues from moral rules about rights and duties'. If MacIntyre seems unable to convince the Kantian, neither does he seem to make much impression on the Nietzschean. MacIntyre sought to refute the emotive basis of moral claims, but appears to imply that belonging to a tradition gives greater weight to one's moral speech.

Behind MacIntyre's analysis is fear. Fear of existential loneliness and of Nietzsche's legacy. Although *After Virtue* was not a treatise on the substantive principles of morality – rather, it concerned historical and cultural contexts of arguments about such principles – one is left with the impression that it is Nietzsche, and not Aristotle, who wins. At the end of the text all MacIntyre can call upon us to do is retreat into communities while the social order collapses around us – *Blade Runner* foreseen?

---

35 Gewirth (1985) is eager to identify himself with a tradition more deontological than Aristotelian which strives to build a natural law of rights to be publicly avowed and deployed in the political and legal arena.

36 'When the criterion for a quality's being a virtue does not include the requirement that the virtue reflect or conform to moral rules, there is no assurance that the alleged virtue will be morally right or wrong' (Gewirth, 1985: 752).

THE COMMUNITARIAN DISPLACEMENT OF THE DEBATE OVER THE RESPECTIVE PRIORITY OF THE RIGHT AND THE GOOD

As Sandel has remarked, for liberals of the Kantian type such as Rawls, the priority of the right over the good means not only that one cannot sacrifice individual rights in the name of the general good, but also that principles of justice cannot be derived from a particular conception of the good life. This is a cardinal principle of liberalism, according to which there cannot be a sole conception of *eudaemonia*, of happiness, which is capable of being imposed on all, but that each person must have the possibility of discovering happiness as he understands it, to fix for himself his own proper objectives and to attempt to realise them in his own way.

The communitarians argue that one cannot define the right prior to the good, since it is only through our participation in a community which defines the good that we can have a sense of what the right is and attain a living conception of justice. Outside of community there is no good and no right. This is a highly persuasive argument which appears unanswerable from any perspective other than one which keeps an idea of a transcendental signifier (a God, or a metaphysics of the absolute essence of humanity). But accepting this argument does not entail that we must reject the priority of justice as the principal virtue of social institutions as well as the defence of individual rights, or return to a politics based on a common moral order. Our foundation can be more pragmatic, or political, and it is exactly to that position that Rawls has attempted to move.

CAN RAWLS RESPOND TO THE COMMUNITARIAN CRITIQUE?

Rawls is not quite as easy a target as the communitarians believe. Rawls (1985; 1993) has developed the foundations of his position rather substantially since the publication of *A Theory of Justice*. Originally his neo-Kantianism implied that Rawls was looking for an algorithm for rational choice, an Archimedean point guaranteeing the universal character of his theory of fairness. His problem was to determine which principles of justice free and rational persons would choose in order to define the fundamental terms of their association. Afterwards he declared that he only wanted to elaborate a conception of justice for modern democratic societies, by starting from the common intuitions of the members of these societies.[37] His objective was to articulate and to make explicit the ideas and principles latent within our common sense; he therefore would not claim to have formulated a conception of justice that was ahistorically true, but rather proposed the principles that were valid for us, as a function of our history, our traditions, our aspirations and the way we conceive our identity.

---

37 To 'settle a fundamental disagreement over the just form of social institutions within a democratic society under modern conditions' (Kantian Constructivism in Moral Theory', *Journal of Philosophy*, Vol 77, no 9, September 1985: 225)

Thus we need better modes of articulating the connections between the jurisprudential imagination concerning justice and political consequences. Rawls wants to defend the liberal pluralism that requires a conception of well-being and a particular plan of life not to be imposed upon individuals. Individual morality is for liberals a private question, and each person must be able to organise his life as he intends. This is a most valuable conception of aspects of the good life: the weakness of liberalism in this area stems from its apparent position that the importance of rights and the fact that the principles of justice should not be taken to privilege a particular conception of well-being. However, it is evident that this priority of the right over the good is only possible in a certain type of society with determinate institutions, and there cannot be an absolute priority of the right over the good since – as the communitarians reasonably assert – it is only within a specific community, defining itself by the good that it postulates, that an individual with his rights can exist. It appears necessary for liberals to specify that the search for justice is partly a question of actively working for, and intellectually defending, particular images of political community. As earlier argued (conclusion of our discussion of John Stuart Mill), although a liberal democratic regime must be agnostic in terms of personal morality and encourage pluralism and tolerance, this does not amount to being agnostic concerning the political good. Not only does this affirm the political principles of liberty and equality, but it is an argument for a certain form of existential survival. It is only within a political and social regime which values rights, diversity and personal fulfilment, that the priority of rights with respect to the different conceptions of the moral good is possible.[38] Justice is not a philosophical conception, it is an existential goal.

---

38 Thus while Sandel, for example, can criticise Rawls's specific formulation for the defence of liberal political principles, Sandel courts dangerous consequences in claiming that this requires abandoning liberal pluralism as well as a politics based on rights, since such a priority is precisely what characterises a liberal democratic regime and allows debate to occur.

CHAPTER 15

RONALD DWORKIN AND THE STRUGGLE AGAINST DISENCHANTMENT: or law within the interpretative ethics of liberal jurisprudence

A citizen's allegiance is to the law, not to any particular person's view of what the law is (Dworkin, *Taking Rights Seriously*, 1977: 214).

[Only] a community of principle, faithful to that promise, can claim the authority of a genuine associative community and can therefore claim moral legitimacy – that its collective decisions are matters of obligation and not bare power (Dworkin, *Law's Empire*, 1986: 214).

The courts are the capitals of law's empire, and judges are its princes (*ibid*: 273).

INTRODUCTION

Ronald Dworkin (born 1931 in Massachusetts, USA) is the leading contemporary exponent of liberal jurisprudence in the Anglo-American world.[1] His work explicitly picks up the questions and legacies of Fuller and Hart, and develops an interpretative methodology with a self-conscious political programme – to defend the ideas of fairness, due process and individual rights as fundamental to legality.

Dworkin's project is partly defensive – an attempt to revitalise liberal legality in the face of the challenges which overtook western societies from the 1970s – and partly inspirational – an attempt to provide a 'morality of aspiration'. The defensive nature flows from the background fact that Dworkin's writings from the 1970s onwards developed in the context of a crisis of confidence overtaking the western world as its meta-narratives and institutions became questioned. In the US, the Vietnam war and

---

1   Dworkin became Hart's successor to the Chair in Jurisprudence at Oxford which he combines with academic commitments in the United States. His views have highly sympathetic commentators (see for example, Guest, 1992), and critics. Commentating upon his early writings, HLA Hart (1977) described Dworkin as a 'noble dreamer', a theme picked up by many subsequent commentators. Fitzpatrick (1992) labels Dworkin's strategy to give systematic unity to the legal system and legal practice as myth-making: 'myth is a form which unifies without (apparently) totalising, a form which maintains unity in apparent inconsistency, and presence in apparent absence'. Dworkin's intellectual roots lie within the American political and legal tradition of liberalism and his rhetoric is an inspiration to continue that tradition in the face of the strong conservative tendencies which overtook America in the late 1970s onwards, as well as avoiding the temptations of radicalism. His work has consistently been concerned with the nature of judicial interpretation of law and the role of the judiciary and he writes directly against the sceptical approach, preferring to build a progressive self-image for the judiciary – a mind-set to shape their inevitable human contribution to legal development which is connected to a theory of political morality which constrains legal development at both a social and individual level. For Dworkin the legal system is a vast intellectual and practical structure – it is not necessarily logically consistent, it may contain many conflicting principles and implications of principles, of rules, principles and rights – which is an expression of the society's dominant political values. Legal principles express political and moral principles; thus a judge, in drawing out the principles involved in a line of precedents, is required to harness his own best understanding of the political and moral values of his community. Dworkin's contribution lies in developing a consistent theory which allows the judge to read his/her own moral and ethical responsibilities in a liberal fashion.

Watergate caused many to lose faith in the conduct of government; duplicity and double-dealing seemed all too clearly to be overtaking the 'principled democracies'.[2] For a variety of reasons politics turned popularist and the governments of Britain and the US turned conservative; while 'progressive' strands in academia became divided. Legal theory could no longer be thought of as simply 'legal philosophy' and diverse currents of thought implied that law ought be placed in social context to be properly understood, or that the underlying politics of law should be made visible; the Law and Economics Movement seemed to be proposing that traditional ideas of happiness, fairness, and justice be replaced by calculations of wealth maximisation; Critical Legal Studies was replacing the legal realist tradition, and feminism was beginning to gain in voice. The liberal idea of the rule of law needed clarification and redevelopment to retain intellectual credibility. A central methodological point concerned the issue of objectivity: how could the authority of jurisprudence be (re-)established in the face of the decline of the objectivism which positivism had appeared to offer? If Hart's jurisprudence led us unmistakably into an empirical project that he could not pursue, how could a methodology be constituted which could defend the idea of law as a system without falling into the conceptual relativity which, for example, Kelsen accepted, or survive the sceptical challenge of Critical Legal Studies? Could liberal jurisprudence be redeveloped, or would it only keep its coherence if it simply ignored all the challenges? Before addressing Dworkin's project it is as well to gain an idea of the problems and stakes involved.

EXCURSUS: THE FATE OF THE TRANSPARENT SOCIETY?

Modernity was founded by the Enlightenment; one aim of the Enlightenment was to make it possible for humans to see things as they truly are. Attaining a state of transparency enables us to have confidence in our social constructions; we become fully self-conscious.

The dominant epistemological stance for the jurisprudence of modernity has been positivism. As epistemology, positivism stressed a 'value-free' scrutiny or analysis; it presupposed an independent object of analysis which the appropriate methodology could uncover.

Legal positivism is, in a strong sense, a philosophy of transparency and social certainty. Whether in the attempt to make a pure science of law (Kelsen) or in the Austinian or Hartian versions, adherents of legal positivism stressed a distinction between identifying what the law is (sometimes specifically defined, as with Austin's careful delineation of the field of his analysis to 'positive law', but often thought of as simply law) and the further task of making moral evaluations of the law. This is a distinction between description – seen as an easy task – and evaluation – seen as a more difficult task and which is either subjective, or requires us to create a consensus

---

2 An impression which further information has only served to intensify. We now understand that the Vietnam war could have been settled in 1968 had it not been for the duplicity of Richard Nixon – the then Republican Party candidate for the Presidency – whose aids intimated to the South Vietnamese not to co-operate with President Johnson's moves to peace.

concerning a master principle of justice (as with utility or schemes such as Rawls's theory of justice).

To recap the narrative of this text, the writers of early modernity – for example Hegel, Marx, Bentham or John Austin – believed in the possibility of knowledge(s) telling man(kind) the truth(s) of the human condition. In John Austin's synthesis ethics, political economy, positive law and belief in social progress were intertwined. This dream of transparency is now compromised. The drive to knowledge has created a multitude of perspectives, of knowledge-claims, each with their presuppositions and techniques for viewing. The proliferation of images of reality entails that we lose, in part at least, our 'sense of reality'. The response of mature legal positivism – HLA Hart – was to retreat to ordinary language analysis and create a mythical (which he calls 'analytical') social history in order to position a discussion of our (then) contemporary sets of everyday language usage concerning normative obligation. Thus legal positivism needed to cut itself off from realist social analysis to retain its (internal) coherence; it assumed the unproblematic nature of the normal and the 'norm'. Reflecting on *The Concept of Law*, Hart claimed (postscript, 1994) that his foundations were epistemologically secure; after all, he was only observing and analysing the practices that he saw around him and bringing out the need to adopt an insider's perspective – a 'descriptive sociology'. But it was apparent to later commentators that Hart was fudging the issue; his work was in fact not real sociology, or as Harris (1980: 21) put it, it was 'a sociology fit for Martians'.

It has become obvious that social science is not a question of mere description; it is deeply interpretative. Perhaps the most fundamental change in the methodologies of the social sciences since the 1960s is the realisation that interpretation – hermeneutics – is inescapable. The world does not reveal its structures, its beingness, to us for our theories simply to reproduce or 'picture'; the truth of our theories was not a reflection of the objective entities of the reality of the world,[3] but the result of an interactive act of our interpretative faculties as we went about our practical business of living within and belonging to the world. Interpretation became the new methodology for late-modernity (a move deeply influenced by the work of Hans-Georg Gadamer, 1979); interpretation occurs within a community – a tradition – and moves in a circular process of seeking to understand the whole in terms of its parts, and the parts in terms of their contribution to the whole.[4]

---

3   For a highly influential critique of the reflective or mirror theory of social science as based on a description of the objective world, see Richard Rorty (1979), *Philosophy and the Mirror of Nature*.

4   Hermeneutics is a practical philosophy; it is a philosophy led by an inclination for ethics. 'The horizon is that of ethics, qua ethos, custom, the shared culture of an epoch and a society, and that which ultimately 'belies' scientism and its purported reduction of truth to single statements experimentally confirmed via the methodology of mathematical and natural science' (Vattimo, 1992: 106). One lives interpretatively. Interpretation understands that we cannot escape the cave of our everyday impressions to some pure site where we can see the objective entities of the world. Instead, with the interpretative understanding, we situate the truth of science within an historical-dialectical horizon orientated towards a mission. But how can we be sure of what the mission is if we become fully modern? That is, if we take completely on board the realisation that there is no goal inscribed into history? Are we therefore doomed to nihilism? Or, in a related discussion (Wagner, 1994: Ch 11), are we doomed to be bewildered selves in the midst of incoherent practices? Dworkin's project is, in part, a meta-narrative of legal practice(s), imposing order and (re)structuring their diversity.

What happens to the question of objectivity? Interpretation raises again the question of the moral and political stance of the interpreter. Positivism – or the naturalist paradigm – could suppose the surplus character of moral frameworks for pure legal science, as doing the science of law was more a question of stripping oneself bare of morality in order to attain objectivity. One must not allow impurities into the visualising process, or else the reflection is distorted. What was the place of politics in the positivistly-orientated space of organised modernity? Politics was made to 'appear as the mere administration of the social' (Wagner, 1994: 191). Positivism seemed to fit with the ideas of neutrality, objectivity and certainty that the ideology of the rule of law required, as well as with the ideas of a rational instrument of governance that the notion of legislative reason demanded. In the latter view, law was a technique of administration by the centralised power centres of a social body whose developing knowledges make itself visible to itself, or, in other words, made the exercise of power a rational process; administration was (at least it was presumed to be) by reason and knowledge rather than by political choice without secure guidance. Legal positivism seemed to make the instrument (positive law) seem clear cut; if knowledge is a reflection of an objective entity then it is either a true reflection of a false one and the claim that this is 'the law' is either simple and true, or false and hence the asserter is claiming for something the status of law when it is actually non-law.

Modern hermeneutics discards the metaphysics of a detached external observer seeking objectivity (so fundamental to the search for truth from the time of Plato's cave simile) in favour of the metaphysics of a committed scientist who *belongs* to a tradition and works with the intellectual resources of that tradition. What is the status of truth in the hermeneutical methodology? It is not the claim to self-transparency that the external observer is meant to bring back to the inhabitants of the cave of unreflective life, but rather the articulation – or interpretation – of action and meaning within a tradition to which that action and meaning belong.

WHAT IS THE AIM OF DWORKIN'S METHODOLOGY OF INTERPRETATIVE JURISPRUDENCE – IS IT TO BRING COHERENCE TO A SET OF INTENTIONAL PRACTICES, OR TO CREATE A NEW META-NARRATIVE FOR POST-MODERN TIMES?

The interpretative turn may appear to invite nihilism, to invite the response to the statements of the writer that 'after all your argument is just your interpretation and therefore I am secure in giving my own and you cannot claim that your interpretation is better than mine!'; does this mean that the concepts of neutrality, objectivity, universality and impartiality are redundant, or that they simply obscure the basic issue, specifically that knowledge is a question of power and politics?

The flipside of nihilism (Nietzscheanism) is disenchantment (Weber). As previously discussed (Chapter 11) disenchantment occurs when man realises that the world does not have an 'objective meaning', and he understands that it becomes man's task to create an 'objectivity for meaning'; furthermore, the interconnection of meaning and 'reality' is his responsibility. Disenchantment invites two outcomes: either we give up on science and come to accept that all claims that knowledge gives us the 'truth' are fraudulent and that life is in itself 'meaningless' (negative nihilism), or we take up the challenge and accept that social science becomes a human project. The first course encourages passivity, or decadence; the second, human responsibility. The second – although he does not use this terminology (in fact he appears to deny this interpretation of his methodology[5]) – is Dworkin's project; he seeks a new objectivity for legal discourse and a new meaning for legal practice. A practice which he enthuses with a particular ethical commitment; legal liberalism.

In recent years Dworkin has self-consciously defined his project as interpretative jurisprudence; in his own words he defines it as partly an answer to the question: 'what is the point of all these books which are called either textbooks of law or jurisprudence?' And 'what is the question to which these books (ie the history of jurisprudence or writing law) are addressed?'[6] For Dworkin the very act of interpreting (ie of making sense of an activity) presupposes that the activity to be interpreted has a point and purpose to it; one cannot engage in interpretation with this presupposition.[7]

The most easily ascertainable jurisprudential influence upon Dworkin is Lon Fuller who had earlier pointed to the fundamental difference between the social sciences (which deal with human behaviour and human institutions) and the natural sciences – social activity can only be understood through interpreting it in the light of the meanings it has for the participants.[8] Dworkin asks of legal practice in the widest sense: 'What is the point to all of this practice? What is the purpose? What is it we should understand law to be if we were to answer the question: what reason do we have for having law? Why do we want it and how should we bend and mould our practice to fit this aim?[9] His interpretative theory thereby supplies a purpose for the activity, but this purpose is held out as one which is already latent in the activities of the participants. Throughout his work Dworkin takes the interpretative turn over positivism, yet seems

---

5　To erase possible misunderstanding as to the tone or purpose of this chapter, Dworkin does not speak of his project in the pragmatic terms used here; in fact, he appears uncertain as to exactly what status of 'truth' to claim for his project. At times he claims an 'interpretative truth', while he also appears to claim a very rationalist truth for it, stating that his theory is 'true' to 'law's ambitions', or that it tells the story of the law beyond the law. In its defence of legal liberalism Dworkin's project is extremely worthwhile; his arguments that western law must be capable of political and critical justification follows in the Kantian tradition of seeing modernity as an epoch where social institutions must survive critical scrutiny. The aim of creating a principled jurisprudence and a principled practice is valuable. But his methodological insulation of his project from interdisciplinary conversation and interaction with other perspectives and his simplistic characterisations of other writers weakens his project and ensures that at times it verges on the banal. His closure of jurisprudence off from sociology is in danger of being socially irresponsible and politically naive.

6　Lecture, UCL London, 1995.

7　All the features and uplifting images Dworkin gives us, he claims, are 'already latent in the present law'.

8　'It is, then, precisely because law is a purposeful enterprise that it displays structural constancies which the legal theorist can discover and treat as uniformities in the factually given. If he realised on what he built his theory, he might be less inclined to conceive of himself as being like the scientist who discovers a uniformity of inanimate nature' (Fuller, 1969: 151).

9　Lecture, UCL London, 1995.

to keep some of the legacy of positivism. He has increasingly claimed that his theory is not only an interpretation, but it is faithful to the material – it tells the 'truth' of law. What sense can we make of this?

Dworkin is Kantian (see discussion in Chapter 6 of this text). He also appears Nietzschean (without realising it) in that he believes that the *force* of legal and political argument must be seen as separate from showing its *grounds* (*Law's Empire*, 1986: 100–112).[10] But his methodology – while sounding like modern interpretative analysis – is actually based on the Kantian acceptance that our current practices (or, more correctly, Dworkin's portrayal of our current practices) have an inherent rationality which his methodology will bring out. As Guest (1992: 1) says: 'Dworkin's theory of law is that the nature of legal argument lies in the best moral interpretation of existing social practices'. Is Dworkin's theory then simply his interpretation and thereby prescriptive? Is his entire project one of imposing his version of liberalism over the increasingly diverse field of legal theory?

Against such criticism, Dworkin claims he is bringing out a 'truth' inherent in the material. In his most developed work (*Law's Empire*, 1986, hereinafter referred to as LE) Dworkin states he is working with an insider's view of law and is concerned to retain 'fidelity' to the material; his interpretation will be faithful to the enterprise of law and not strip it of its latent meaning; refusing to discuss the nature of law with external observers, it will ignore sceptical comments and better articulate law's ambition for us so that we can conjoin our efforts. The question on the critic's lips is simple: is this law's ambition, or the ambition that Dworkin wishes the law to have? Moreover, can law be thought of as having a dominant purpose? In an era in which the terminology of legal pluralism has become commonplace (at least to those scholars who refuse to deal solely in normative jurisprudence) is there any way in which it is permissible to talk of a diverse set of practices such as comprise modern law (see Cotterrell, *The Sociology of Law*, (2nd edn, 1992) as if there were one distinct common thread? Again Nietzsche is stimulating. His argument was simple: modern institutions and practices have histories; there is no one dominant perspective. Conversely, the Kantian tradition implies that we must treat them as if there was a coherent underlying rationality. Kant – as Hegel (see Chapter 8) after him so succinctly put it in his claim that 'what is real is rational' – mandated the modern scholar to search for the rational underpinnings of everyday practice; to treat diversity as variations (and failures, mistakes, exceptions) on a theme; and treat the theme as rational. The rational structure of the social whole will be found within its operative structures of mutual recognition; individual actors attain self-consciousness only through a mutual recognition of each other and the rational worth of each other's practice, but this requires patterns and mechanisms of viewing through which such recognition can be mediated. Dworkin provides such an analysis and such a viewing frame for modern legality.

---

10 This distinction is the basis of the most sympathetic work on Dworkin, that of Stephen Guest (1992) who constantly uses the test of contrasting Dworkin's statements to our current moral intuitions concerning law. Guest's test is a matter of intuitive appeal, of 'fit' with our sensibilities.

There is epistemic validity in this project: human practices are intentional structures which express the ideas of the participants and consist of many people trying to realise various projects. Human practices do not need a philosopher to tell the players what they are about; the players have their own self-interpretations. Those who are committed to the practice/project – and Dworkin here distinguishes himself from Hart by stating he is primarily talking about players with integrity and conviction (who believe in the project), as opposed to players who only play out of habit or convention – try to intuit its point, to purify it of unessential elements, and to develop the practice further. Dworkin can seek the correct interpretation, therefore, in believing he is bringing out a point and purpose of the practice that the participants already understand, albeit somewhat dimly, and he can achieve a theoretical unification – a holistic account – that is already partly assumed by the various participants in the practice. Law seems to justify this confidence; or, put, perhaps, more correctly, there are ways of reading law which provide grounds for this assumption. The ideology of the rule of law is powerful and the imagery with which Dworkin begins his best-known work – *Law's Empire* (see the extract in Chapter 1 of this text) – is of the law speaking to us; he calls upon us to treat the law as written by the community personified. Legality is portrayed as not only one human project among many others, but the master project, furthermore as a project which has succeeded; in its rhetoric and structure *Law's Empire* is pure expressionism. Law embodies commitment, conviction, integrity and the pursuit of truth (we must believe in the possibility, if not the immediate attainability, of a right answer to legal and moral problems), nothing is irreconcilable, conflict not contradiction is inherent, lawyers take ethical oaths to be a servant of the law, an officer of the court. Law appears a complex human practice, in large part constituted by the interpretative actions of the players who orientate themselves – at least 'ideally' – by means of a self-conscious idea, the idea of the rule of law, or *Law's Empire*.

Furthermore, at least in its academic presentation, law is not a mass of disconnected rules and decisions but a structure organised under general categories such as property, contract, tort, and crime, and still further organised within these categories around concepts such as possession, consideration, the neighbour principle, negligence, *mens rea*, and the like. Legality appears, therefore, a terrain of ideas and concepts embodying intuitions concerning the scope of valid rights and legitimate coercion – intuitions that a valid strategy of interpretative coherence needs to clarify and develop into a substantive whole. The assumption that there is one master point and purpose to the practice seems justified when the interpreter constantly finds that the participants or players announce that they aspire to systematic unity and coherence.[11]

The practice of law involves reflection, reflexivity, theoretical clarification and criticism, the resolving of disputes and arguments, researching answers, 'finding the law',

---

11 Dworkin will make references to law's ambition and restate metaphors such as Hale's 'Argonauts Ship' that remains identical throughout successive change, Lord Mansfield's description of the common law as law 'that works itself pure', and such maxims as 'like cases must be treated alike' and 'where the reason of the law stops, there also stops the law'. Against this view, Charles Sampford (*The Disorder of Law*, 1989) argues that instead of law being a coherent system, it is a 'legal mêlée', given the appearance of a system only by the normative work of legal philosophers.

'arguing the case'; in short, items of interpretative practice – which are presented as already thoughtful, unifying, self-critical activity. Thus the interpretative project gains a confidence that it can produce a true understanding of law if it provides an integrated account of law's own ideas. Although the integration may alter the material originally presented to thought as a collocation of rules and principles, this altering is presented as no refraction or distortion, for it is just the fruition of law's own work.

THE CRITIQUE OF LEGAL POSITIVISM AND HART'S THEORY OF LEGAL REASONING

Dworkin's writings start in the late 1960s with his critique of Hart's *Concept of Law* (1967, 1975; reproduced in *Taking Rights Seriously*, 1977; further references to these articles are to the 1977 text). Hart had characterised his work as a response to that age-old question 'What is law?' (1961: 1) and emphasised that the question 'what is law?' was a question asking for an analysis of facts (*ibid*: 245). Dworkin defines the positivist thesis as a 'plain-fact' view of law (Ch 1 of LE) and argues that both legal positivism and natural law theories are actually searching for an answer to the question 'what is law?' by encountering some body of plain facts which give the answer ready-made and easily understood. Dworkin seductively asks if this is an adequate or realistic image of law?[12] Dworkin directs us towards another issue, a more professional question of understanding 'law', gained by asking 'how do lawyers in court argue to a judge, and how does a judge find 'the law'?' Dworkin argues that particularly in 'hard cases', judges and lawyers

> make use of standards that do not function as rules, but operate differently as principles, policies and other sorts of standards. (1977: 22)

Does the theory of rules cover the development of the common law through precedent? Does it adequately explain, for example, the creation of the neighbour principle in tort which came out of *Donoghue v Stevenson*?[13] Or was Lord Atkin's speech an exercise in judicial creativity? Certainly Lord Atkin presents his decision in terms of his constructively developing a principle which could be dimly recognised in earlier cases. If

---

12 Critics of Dworkin (for example, Moles, 1992) point out that his treatment of earlier positions is extremely superficial and makes no attempt to offer a constructive reading for either Austin or natural law theorists, whom he mentions only in passing.

13 [1932] AC 562. The case involved a conflict of precedents and the temptation which faced the judiciary was whether to adopt a policy decision to favour the manufacturers of a new product over the interests of the final consumer. In fact the leading judgment of Lord Atkin found the existence of a legal relation independent of contract between the manufacturer of a product and the final consumer. Lord Atkin noted the tendency of previous judges to write their judgments in a narrow way, thus making it difficult to read the line of principle, and he expressly stated he would present his decision in a fashion that would be of greater benefit to future judges. He commented on the relationship of law to moral beliefs and developed his decision in terms of translating the moral or political dilemma into a legal one (1932: 580): 'The [moral] rule that you are to love your neighbour becomes in law, you must not injure your neighbour; and the lawyer's question, "Who is my neighbour?" receives a restricted reply. You must take reasonable care to avoid acts or omissions which you can reasonably foresee would be likely to injure your neighbour. Who, then, in law is my neighbour? The answer seems to be – persons who are so closely and directly affected by my act that I ought reasonably to have them in contemplation as being so affected when I am directing my mind to the acts or omissions which are called into question.'

so then the creative role of Lord Atkin lay in his giving constructive interpretation to the earlier cases and better articulating and formulating the principles latent therein, thus creating a 'leading case' to be applied in later situations. For Dworkin, Hart's legal positivist analysis implies that beyond a certain point, where the rule runs out, no legal factors constrain the judge; when judges are working in a penumbral (as opposed to the core) area of law, they have a non-legal discretion. New law is made in 'hard cases'. Legal positivism presents us with a radically divergent set of expectations on the judicial function (See Guest, 1992, Chapters 7 and 8): (i) a static view, that is the plain-fact model of rules, which cover the situation, and which can be applied in 'mechanical jurisprudence'; or (ii) a dynamic view, where law is a process, and in understanding this process one must understand how the rules interact with non-legal influences. This positivist view can be expressed as an equation: *rules plus discretion equals new rules*. But this judicial discretion is outside the law and – apart from Austin – legal positivism says very little about this process.

For the legal positivist, legal change – whether in legislation or in the common law – is a political process.[14] Moreover, the claim of legal certainty is compromised in the situation where a rule has not been posited, or there is a gap in the realm of legal rules.[15]

IS THERE A RIGHT ANSWER INHERENT IN THE GRAMMAR OF LEGAL ARGUMENTATION?

Perhaps the most controversial assertion associated with Dworkin's early work was his claim that legal practice necessarily involves the acceptance of the idea of a right answer to legal and moral dilemmas. Dworkin presents two ways of reaching this conclusion: (i) involves the relatively weak assertion that since the nature of law involves handling and resolving disputes it is part of the practical reasoning of law that an answer must be sound for to the dispute – if we were constantly to say 'it's a tie', the practical dispute-resolution nature of legal practice would be a nonsense (see Dworkin, 1977; and 'A Reply by Ronald Dworkin', in Cohen, ed, 1984); (ii) is to look for the rational presuppositions involved in the very processes and practices of legal and political

---

14 As earlier discussed (Chapter 9), whilst Bentham opposed judicial law-making, Austin discussed it at length in two lectures. Austin's science of positive law was only part of a synthesis; the other part was the science of legislation governed by utility or legislating for the common interest. Austin appears to have little doubt that the quality of judicial decision-making needed to be improved and he intended to improve it by making clear that the judge could not ignore social benefit considerations (public opinion, the common good) in the name of being bound by some obscure non-rule legal standards (Austin's *Jurisprudence*, 1873: Lectures XXXVII and XXXVIII).

15 Taking, for example, the bye-law prohibiting vehicles from a park, when it comes to the court no decision has been made as yet as to whether the byelaw prohibits a skateboard. The actual legal question is likely to focus on language: 'is a skateboard a vehicle for the purpose of the byelaw which prohibits vehicles to be used in Hyde Park?' Since this issue has not been decided, the rule does not appear to extend to determine the question of skateboards. Thus there is a gap in the law. You can not simply say that because there is no mention of skateboards they are permitted. Both sides cannot refer to decided case law, but both sides may in all good conscience believe that they are right. The defendant might argue that since it has not been prohibited (after all no case tells us it is prohibited), therefore it is permitted. The prosecutor might say it is included in the mischief of the act and it is not posited anywhere in the law as an exception, therefore it is not permitted.

argument.[16] Dworkin wishes us to consider carefully what lawyers are actually doing as a matter of legal practice in hard cases and asks us to use their own discourse as a starting point. The law looks uncertain; there does not appear to be any obvious legal answer. But what is the rationality of the various aspects to the social practices involved? Take a usual case. The parties have instructed lawyers, and, perhaps, after various exchanges of letters, claims and counterclaims, the two sides decide to fight it out in court. If both sets of lawyers are acting as serious legal officers (that is, they are not engaging in unnecessary action), both sides believe that their arguments have greater weight than the other side's; in other words, both sides believe that they are correct in their interpretation and belief that the law is on their side. Both sides actually believe that there is an answer to be found, and that this is a legal answer. Why go to court if you do not believe that your side is correct? That is, that your arguments can correctly state the prevailing legal position – that your arguments can convince the judge to decide that the law is as you claim.[17]

Dworkin argues that the model of rules cannot cope with the argumentative nature of legal practice. Not only does it create gaps in the idea of the rule of law but – paraphrasing Dworkin – it is false to the social nature of legal argument in the wider sense of including others (academics, the public) as members of a 'legal interpretative community'. We can list a number of themes:

(i) the model of rules misunderstands the nature of discretion. Discretion is not free-standing but part of a process:

> Discretion, like the hole in the doughnut, does not exist except as an area left open by a surrounding belt of restriction. It is therefore a relative concept. It always makes sense to ask, 'Discretion under which standards?' or 'Discretion as to which authority?' (1977: 31)

(ii) if Hart was right a whole range of legal discussion would be irrelevant; a judge would not be subject to legal criticisms of legal discretion, but in fact they are. Lawyers talk of judicial decisions in hard cases and about good or bad judicial craftsmanship. We constantly make informed legal evaluations of whether the courts have developed a law in a legally acceptable manner, and Dworkin argues that judges should regard previous decisions that are 'widely regretted' by academic jurists as weak law and open to being declared bad law (1977: 122); moreover, we accept some decisions as 'mistakes' (ibid: 105). This indicates that we actually accept discretion as something which operates internally to law and as something which ought to be rendered understandable by a proper legal discourse;

---

16   Dworkin explicitly developed this theme in a 1995 (unpublished) lecture given at the IALS London entitled 'Are there right answers to legal and moral problems?'

17   The obvious counter is simply, what if the parties are gambling? What if they honestly believe there is no legal answer but take the opinion that the weight of 'judicial responsibility', and the practical structure of the courts, will mean that there will be a decision and that argued in a certain way they will win? There is an answer – an answer which might, from the legal realist perspective, be (reasonably) predictable. The prediction flows from their 'practical' understanding of the nature of legal practice. Dworkin's response is equally simple: that might well be practice, but it is not the sort of practice that makes law the best example of the type of practice that it is ideally.

(iii) if Hart were right we could not predict the outcome of hard cases, but we do. Although we may be surprised by Appeal Court rulings, we nonetheless can, and do, make informed predictions about decisions;

(iv) if judicial decision-making were unfettered discretion we would have to say that judges were merely political and administrative officials; yet we think of judges as different from politicians or administrators and as having a special role and special craft which does not require them to be democratically elected. Dworkin (1977: 140-3) argues that each particular country has evolved a constitutional practice, and theory, of the role of the judiciary. In the United States it is constitutionalism (the theory that the majority must be constrained to protect individual rights). Constitutionally, if judges were unfettered law-makers they would have to be democratically elected; judges are not elected and should therefore not engage in the production of new law, they should apply the standards inherent in the existing law;

(v) if we say that judges make law by exercising discretion, then we must say that each time they do so they commit a fraud on the litigants. Parties come to court and argue about the law, and the judge decides; yet if on appeal the judges exercised discretion and made new rules, they would be changing the rules of the game, which is hardly defensible. Judges typically speak and act in such a way that they present their decisions as if they were required by adherence to principles of the law, and they often refer to occasions where such principles are 'immanent in the law', or implied by 'the general fabric of the law'; judges convey the impression that they feel constrained by legal standards that can only be gauged by a holistic interpretation of settled law.

These points come from the interpretation of items of practice. We now have a choice. We can say that all of these observations may well be correct but they do not add up to a coherent practice; they are actually bits of coherence in an incoherent mêlée which defies attempts to totalise it. Or, we can say that properly understood we can read into the 'grammar' of these bits of practice evidence of the reality of a right answer, and of a closure of the legal universe; already law has the resources to enable it to answer all legal problems

DWORKIN'S EARLY THEORY OF JUDICIAL PRACTICE AS AIMING FOR PRINCIPLED CONSISTENCY

Dworkin's first step is to distinguish strong and weak discretion. Strong discretion is where the officials are not bound by pre-existing standards set by some authority. Weak discretion is when the standard cannot be applied in a mechanical way – there is a need for consideration and evaluation of what the standard means in a new case. By implication, in the second case, there are no gaps in the law; weak discretion is necessarily part of the judicial role and is acceptable. It is an internal discretion which is constrained by law and, in particular, by the reality that every hard case has a legally correct answer. *Donoghue v Stevenson* did have a correct answer to the case. The right answer was there to be found in the controversial arguments presented by the lawyers and in the principles contained in the precedents. Dworkin appears to distinguish rules and principles in two clear ways:

(i) rules operate in an all-or-nothing fashion. The rule either applies or does not; in deciding the judge looks at the factual situation, and then at the scope of the rule. Principles however do not operate in this yes or no way. Principles have a dimension of weight. They can apply to a varying extent;

(ii) rules can never conflict; if they do conflict, then one rule is either wrong or invalid. Principles can and do conflict; they point to different considerations, and the relationship between particular conflicting principles will depend on the circumstances of the particular case. Dworkin, for example, would recognise equitable maxims as principles of law which can conflict. The weighing up of principles is the task of legal craftsmanship working out the effect on the underlying system and the case in issue.

Resolving hard cases

In his classic article, *Hard Cases*, Dworkin argues that judges must apply a principle of 'articulate consistency' in determining the applicability of statutes and precedents to controversial cases. Dworkin posits an ideal judge, Hercules, 'a lawyer of superhuman skill, learning, patience and acumen' (1977: 105), who is fully conscious of his constitutional responsibilities. When faced with a difficult case, for example, a constitutional case, Hercules constructs a number of political theories which might serve as justifications for the body of constitutional rules that are directly relevant to the issue. If two or more theories appear to fit equally well – and thereby point to contrasting outcomes for the case – Hercules must turn to the remaining body of constitutional rules, practices and principles, to construct a political theory for the constitution as a whole. The successful theory will fit all, or most, of the rules of the constitution in a manner which represents them as a unified and coherent body of prescriptions and rules covering the civic behaviour.[18]

The same process is at work in the application of statutes and the common law. Hercules must 'construct a scheme of abstract and concrete principles that provide a coherent justification for all common law precedents, and so far as these are to be justified on principle, constitutional and statutory provisions as well' (1977: 116-7). Actual judges ought to emulate the behaviour of Hercules as far as possible; Hercules,

---

18 In effect Dworkin is seeking to find the background consideration which structures the actual operation of Hart's rule of recognition and rule of adjudication. Dworkin uses as an example a game of chess as a hard case: he asks is the tactic of one of the competitors to smile often at his opponent a valid tactic, or is it against the rules and thereby entitles his opponent to win by forfeiture of the game? The situation is not covered by the rules, so how does the official decide? Dworkin suggests that the game of chess has a character that the referee's decision must respect. But Dworkin asks: how does a referee know that chess is an intellectual game rather than a game of chance or an exhibition of digital ballet? The referee engages in various calculations, 'self-conscious' decisions which involve the judge continually interpreting his position and the meaning of the practices he is engaged in. 'His calculations, viewed in this way, oscillate between philosophy of mind and the facts of the institution which character he must elucidate ... The hard case puts ... a question of political theory. It asks what it is fair to suppose that the player has done in consenting to the forfeiture rule' (1977: 104–5).

moreover, is a reflection of the judge who accepts and exemplifies the doctrine of political responsibility that is inherent in the American system.[19] This doctrine demands that the judge (i) renders decisions that enforce the already existing law, but (ii) does so in a manner that represents the law as expressive of an internally consistent political theory. Do all judges observe this process? Dworkin is clear: not all judges attempt it, nor do those who try to necessarily obtain the theory of consistent constitutionalism arrived at by Hercules. Hercules' theory 'would be more or less different from the theory that a different judge would develop, because a constitutional theory requires judgments about the complex issues of institutional fit, as well as judgments about political and moral philosophy' (*ibid*: 117). In this complex matter, individual judges have different personal perceptions and follow differing constitutional theories, but Dworkin further suggests that some of these theories and preferences will be superior, will fit the overall coherence of the society's moral and political development better; yet how can we be sure? Dworkin makes a number of claims, although two crucial points are (i) the fundamental role that rights play in modern law, and (ii) the idea of legal development as an unfinished project of shaping social interaction into the form of a community of principle.

DWORKIN'S DEVELOPMENT OF THE IDEA OF RIGHTS

In contrast to classical legal positivism (see Bentham, Chapter 8, and Austin, Chapter 9), Dworkin makes the general claim that within legal practice the principled protection of *rights* is more fundamental than policy considerations, or a literal adherence to seemingly obvious rules. Legal rules and principles express and protect rights in the legal order, thus enabling individuals to have a secure social space, and minorities not be pawns of utilitarian calculations. Judges need a jurisprudence which enables them to distinguish clearly between arguments based on adherence to rules, weighing principles and uncovering rights, and following contrasting policy arguments.[20] Rights are trumps over assertions that the courts ought to make decisions based on the grounds of political policy (See *Taking Rights Seriously*, 1977, particularly Chs 6, 7, 12, and 13). This is a normative claim: in deciding cases judges ought to display moral integrity; they ought to

---

19 'Judges, like all political officials, are subject to the doctrine of political responsibility. This doctrine states, in its most general form, that political officials must make only such political decisions as they can justify within a political theory, that also justifies the other decisions they propose to make. The doctrine seems innocuous in this general form; but it does, even in this form, condemn a style of political administration that might be called, following Rawls, intuitionistic. It condemns the practice of making decisions that seem right in isolation, but cannot be brought within some comprehensive theory of general principles and policies that is consistent with other decisions also thought right' (1977: 87).

20 Dworkin (1977: 82) distinguishes these as follows: 'Arguments of policy justify a political decision by showing that the decision advances or protects some collective goal of the community as a whole. The argument in favour of a subsidy for aircraft manufacturers, that the subsidy will protect national defence, is an argument of policy. Arguments of principle justify a political decision by showing that the decision respects or secures some individual or group right. The argument in favour of anti-discrimination statutes, that a minority has a right to equal respect and concern, is an argument of principle.'

strive to be fair to the parties, and that means being faithful to the legal rights of the parties.

Legal reasoning is a specific form of decision-making in which principles[21] are more important than rules (as they surround the structure of rules), or policies (or the collective goals of society) which ought to be pursued by the legislature, democratically elected; principles[22] are internal to law and are developed by the judiciary. The law is to be treated as a seamless web – principles give the web structure with the protection of rights as its fundamental moral rationality.[23]

In summary, Dworkin's 'rights thesis' covers the following eight propositions:

1   Every stable legal system expresses a dominant political philosophy and it is this which gives coherence and unity to the legal system.

2   This philosophy is expressed in the values and traditions of the law and is worked out daily in the practice of developing law and deciding cases – it is not a purely academic philosophy, but a matter of professional commitment (or integrity).

3   The political system is also made up of legal principles, and these express the dominant political values of the system. Dworkin recognises that the development of the law is influenced by policy but policy is an external force at work through legislation.

4   Rules differ from principles in three ways:

   (i)   Whereas rules are created or destroyed by legislation or judicial creation, principles emerge slowly and sometimes imperceptibly and equally they decline imperceptibly (for example, *Donoghue v Stevenson* – Dworkin would say that the neighbour principle emerged gradually, it was not created there and then). Principles are extended, refined, developed, amended or reduced in later cases.

   (ii) Principles have a dimension of weight so that they can be more or less influential in any given case, whereas rules are applied in an all-or-nothing fashion.

   (iii) Rules cannot conflict: if there is an apparent conflict of rules then one is wrong and has to give way, or one rule is an exception and a new rule emerges. By contrast, principles can conflict and give opposite guidance. This problem is a matter of judicial craftsmanship; the judge must weigh up their relative significance, and balance which principle is more important in a given case.

---

21   'I call a "principle" a standard that is to be observed, not because it will advance or secure an economic, political, or social situation deemed desirable, but because it is a requirement of justice or fairness or some other dimension of morality' (1977: 22).

22   'Principles are propositions that describe rights; policies are propositions that describe goals' (1977: 90).

23   Rights are more important since they develop in the legal system through the working out of the political morality. In the US the rights derive from the constitution but the constitution says it is an expression of the rights which existed before the construction of the constitution. Dworkin says that the same is true in the UK even through there is no written constitution. If we had time in constructing any particular issue or case we would consider the whole political history underlying the legal system which has produced ideas about basic rights, eg political rights, property, etc. These are expressed in the form of rules and principles and when we argue about the law we give effect to them.

5   Judges do not, and cannot properly, exercise uncontrolled discretion in deciding any case, even where there are apparently no rules of law for the judge to apply. The task of a judge in a hard case is to decide the case in the light of the wider political morality of the legal system; in American law this will be to protect the fundamental legal values of the system.

6   In hard cases there is always a 'right' legal answer there to be found. However difficult legally this search is, the structure of the argumentative process implies that there will be an answer. The task of finding it is to consider rules and principle in interaction and by use of judicial craftsmanship. A right legal answer would be one that asserts and protects rights which are explicit or implicit in the fundamental values of the legal system. (Ask: did the rights occur before the legal system? If so then the rights trump and can override rules – does this take us back to some notion of original rights existing before the constitution?)[24]

7   Judging is not easy and ordinarily judges will not get it right. The only judge to get it right would be one with ultimate wisdom, who comprehended the entire history of decisions and possessed an omniscient understanding of the political values of a system: that is, Hercules. Hercules, however, is only a model: real judges do get it wrong, and Dworkin is adamant that Hercules is realistic in that he is the best interpretation of actual legal reasoning.

8   Although only Hercules can always get the right answer every judge has an obligation to aim for the right answer – lawyers are part of this same enterprise. Therefore, lawyers may criticise judges for misunderstanding the principles and values and traditions of the legal system. However, just judges and lawyers are involved: ordinary citizens also have a voice here as is particularly evident in Dworkin's discussion of the case of civil disobedience (see *Taking Rights Seriously*, Ch 8) and the right to disobey the law.

LAW AS THE OPEN-ENDED PRACTICE OF INTEGRITY: THE DREAMS OF *LAW'S EMPIRE*

In his major text, which he defines as a restatement of his overall work, Dworkin's methodological claim is to 'take up the internal, participants' point of view' (LE: 14). He grounds his developed legal theory upon a critique of legal positivism (with, or so he claims, its simplistic idea of plain facts) and its replacement by a theory of interpretation; but also announces dissatisfaction with social theoretical accounts of law which he terms 'external' accounts. His will be an internal account which works upon an interpretation of legal practice focused around the courts and the idea of law as argumentation.

In this work Dworkin conceives of law as a much more fluid and open-ended phenomenon than previously. His concern with the concept of a right answer is

---

24   Guest (1992: 7) resolves this search for foundation by relating how, as a student at Oxford, in the first set of seminars in which Dworkin participated, Dworkin simply asserted: 'as you will know, my view is that there are natural legal rights'.

transferred to a concern with the right methodology of decision-making. This strategy reflects broader moves within the methodology of the social sciences and is similar to the moves of so-called post-modern scholars such as Lyotard, who replaces the modernist search for justice with a post-modernist concern with 'acting justly' (see *Just Gaming*, 1985). Dworkin, however, does not abandon his Kantian foundations, his incorporation of pragmatic epistemological moves appears half-hearted. He focuses upon the nature of legal argument and legal practice by selectively choosing four favourite cases: three American – the famous 19th-century case of *Riggs v Palmer*, the 1973 *Snail Darter* case, and the segregation case of *Brown* – then the British case of *McLoughlin*. In all these cases Dworkin argues that the judges who were faithful to the 'truth' of law rejected any suggestions of policy considerations, and instead strove to resolve the issue by ascertaining what was the real law. Although there was disagreement in each case, for Dworkin the arguments concerned the search for the law; not only a search for a right answer, but a search for the right *legal answer*.

In *Riggs v Palmer* (discussed LE: 15-20) the New York Court of Appeals (1889) was asked to consider if the fact that Elmer Palmer had murdered his grandfather by poisoning meant he was not entitled to inherit under his grandfather's will.[25] The grandfather – who had made a will favourable to Elmer – had recently remarried, and Elmer was afraid that he would change his will in favour of his wife and leave him nothing. Elmer decided to prevent such an occurrence by poisoning his grandfather, as a result he was convicted and sentenced to ten years' imprisonment. Could Elmer be a legatee? There was nothing in the statute which explicitly prevented murderers from inheriting from those whom they murdered. The majority of the court thought that the ordinary rules, as they would operate on a 'literal' reading of the statute concerning wills, should not apply here – and the case is notable as much for the time spent discussing interpretation as for the actual outcome. Judge Earl, who provided the majority decision, was clear that 'literally construed, and if their force and effect can in no way and under no circumstances be controlled or modified' the statutes and rules concerning the effects of wills 'give the property to the murderer'. However, Judge Earl decided, under a theory of 'rational interpretation' or 'equitable construction', not the words but the intentions of the law-makers should be the important consideration: 'It could never have been their intention that a donee who murdered the testator to make the will operative should have any benefit under it'. Thus, Earl argued: 'we need not ... be much troubled by the general language contained in the laws'; instead judges should use 'fundamental maxims of the common law', which are maxims 'dictated by public policy, have their foundation in universal law administered in all civilised countries and have nowhere been superseded by statute'. The applicable maxim was clear: 'No one shall be permitted ... to take advantage of his own wrong'. Thus Elmer was prohibited from inheriting.

In dissenting, Judge Gray held a different conception of his constitutional position. The statute was clear: 'no will in writing, except in the cases hereinafter mentioned, nor

---

25 *Riggs v Palmer*, 115 NY 506, 22 NE 188 (1889); discussed Dworkin, LE 15–20; for an in-depth discussion see Kim Lane Schepple (1991: 42–77).

any part thereof, shall be revoked or altered otherwise' (quoted in Gray's judgment, 517). Thus he held that a judge could not interpret a meaning at odds with clearly stated rules:

> If I believed that the decision … could be affected by considerations of an equitable nature, I should not hesitate to assert the views which commend themselves to the conscience. But the matter does not lie within the domain of conscience. We are bound by rigid rules of law (*ibid*: 515).

Dworkin says simply: 'Judge Earl's views prevailed. They attracted four other judges to his side, while Judge Gray was able to find only one ally' (LE: 20). We should note, however, that while Dworkin does not see fit to mention it, a strong line of subsequent scholarly opinion argued that Judge Gray was correct, and that Judge Earl engaged in 'spurious interpretation' covering a case of unauthorised lawmaking.[26]

Was it judicial lawmaking? Dworkin is clear: the judges 'all agreed that their decision must be in accordance with the law. None denied that if the statute of wills, properly interpreted, gave the inheritance to Elmer, they must order the administrator to give it to him.' The judges disagreed about the meaning of the statute; they were concerned with a deep conception of law. They disagreed 'about what the law actually was, about what the statute required when properly read' (LE: 16). But surely it is easy to read the statute? Judge Gray had no problem. Dworkin makes a crucial distinction between the statute – as a piece of paper and ink denoting words – and the 'real statute'.[27] The real statute is an idealist construction, a conception of a deeper reality than the empirical statute of pages and words. Dworkin claims to get this distinction from the opinion of Judge Earl, who appeared to distinguish between the text, or 'letter' of the statute, and the 'statute' itself.

The case is a foundational text for Dworkin's vision of legal practice. Since the opinion that prevailed was 'that the law elsewhere respects the principle that no one should profit from his own wrong, so the statute of wills should be read to deny inheritance to someone who has murdered to obtain it' (*ibid*: 20), it appears that the majority in the court confronted the rules by positioning the rules within the context of wider principles of the common law which have greater 'weight', or are stronger law than the rules. However, we can also read into this situation the principle that ordinarily, compliance with the rules giving a valid disposition, means that the will ought to be enforced by the courts – in fact, one of the judges who dissented from the majority

---

26 Roscoe Pound (in 'Spurious Interpretation', 1907, quotes and discussion in Scheppele, 1991: 46–7) claims the majority opinion was 'judicial speculation' whereupon the judge 'puts a meaning into the text as a juggler puts coins, or what not, into a dummy's hair, to be pulled forth presently with an air of discovery. It is essentially a legislative, not a judicial process'. Pound argued that the court must read the statute as it is and wait for the legislature to change the law.

27 '… judges before whom a statute is laid need to construct the "real" statute – a statement of what difference the statute makes to the legal rights of various people – from the text in the statute book. Just as literary critics need a working theory, or at least a style of interpretation, in order to construct the poem behind the text, so judges need something like a theory of legislation to do this with statutes' (LE: 17). Dworkin's use of literary criticism is however, very limited; no Marxism or deconstruction is allowed to touch his poems.

decision did this, arguing that he was bound by this principle to enforce the will.[28] Dworkin only refers in passing to conflicting principles, but he could simply state that principles often conflict and that the majority of the court felt that one principle had greater weight than the other. Thus, we find a strongly embedded common law principle in conflict with the principle that the rules of statutes be given effect. Again the question is to be settled by the criteria of 'fit' and 'substance' or 'weight' within the broader conception of law which Hercules constructs.[29]

In the *Snail Darter* case the Supreme Court (1978) ordered work to stop on a nearly constructed dam costing 100 million dollars in favour of the legal protection given to the snail darter – 'a three-inch fish of no particular beauty or biological interest or general ecological importance' (LE: 21) – under the Endangered Species Act of 1973. Dworkin reads this as another example of 'fidelity' to law, as an example of judges endeavouring to 'decide what law is made by a particular text enacted ... when the [enactors] had the kinds of beliefs and intentions' the judges accepted. In this case, the majority took a theory of statutory interpretation, whereby the judges, in interpreting the statute must respect legislative intentions; the policy of protecting endangered species was the background consideration which structured the intention to protect the snail darter.[30]

The case of *Brown* concerned the substantive effect of the phrase 'equal protection': the question was whether it permitted equal but separate school facilities for black Americans? In Brown, the judges were called upon the consider the tradition of

28 When Benjamin Cardozo came to discuss the case he declared: 'There was the principle of the binding force of the will disposing of the estate of a testator in conformity with law. That principle, pushed to the limits of its logic, seemed to uphold the title of the murderer. There was the principle that civil courts may not add to the pains and penalties of crimes. That, pushed to the limits of its logic, seemed again to uphold his title. But over against these was another principle, of greater generality, its roots deeply fastened in universal sentiments of justice, the principle that no man should profit from his own iniquity or take advantage from his own wrong. The logic of this principle prevailed over the logic of the others' (*The Nature of the Judicial Process*, 1921: 41; quoted, Scheppele, 1991: 48). But what is the mechanism for deciding how it should prevail? For Cardozo it was 'because the social interest served by refusing to permit the criminal to profit by his crime is greater than that served by the preservation and enforcement of legal rights of ownership'. But this does not answer the question since we now need a standard to understand the ranking of social interests. This is why the continual movement outwards in the holistic account of Dworkin holds so much appeal. The Dworkinian judge, ideally, can explain the principled basis for his/her ranking.

29 On another reading the judiciary just do not want a person to profit from his/her own wrongdoing and will use whatever available tactic to prevent this. Before *Riggs v Palmer* the doctrine of civil death would have covered the issue. *Riggs v Palmer* was to be called into question only seven years after it was decided and this time the fiction of a constructive trust was used to prevent the murderer from inheriting. In time the statute was amended specifically to prevent the issue from arising. See discussion in Schepple (1991).

30 Later in the text Dworkin (LE: 338–9) gives his reading of what integrity demands in these situations: 'Integrity requires him to construct, for each statute he is asked to enforce, some justification that fits and flows through that statute and is, if possible, consistent with other legislation in force. This means he must ask himself which combination of which principles and policies, with which assignments of relative importance when they compete, provides the best case for what the plain words of the statute plainly require. Since Hercules is now justifying a statute rather than a set of common-law precedents, the particular constraint we identified [earlier discussing the common law] no longer holds: he must consider justifications of policy as well as principle, and in some cases it might be problematic which form of justification would be more appropriate.'

interpreting the Constitution and theories of racial equality. Dworkin poses the legal issue as a political question: which theory of racial equality did the Constitution endorse? the judges looked at the old case of *Plessy v Ferguson* in the light of actual sociological evidence relating to the equality of treatment in practice.

The case of *McLoughlin* provides an example of the possibilities of diverse interpretation, as well as an example of the House of Lords rejecting the strategy of the Court of Appeal which had specifically decided to distinguish between relevant precedents covering the issue on 'policy' grounds. While all the judges in the House of Lords agreed on a retrial, their judgments gave various reasons; but Dworkin points out that two Law Lords argued that the policy arguments of the Court of Appeal were the wrong kinds of reasons.[31] Dworkin states their argument as being:

> The precedents should be regarded as distinguishable only if the moral principles assumed in the earlier cases for some reason did not apply to the plaintiff in the same way (LE: 28).

Having determined that law is made up of various standards, policies, rules and principles, how are these related? This is a matter of the political values of a given society and a judge's differential positioning of these depends upon his particular political philosophy.

Dworkin is clear as to the political values to which he is committed. His philosophy stresses a rights approach over utilitarian calculations. Given that a society committed to utilitarianism (or the maximisation of welfare) may sacrifice minorities if the overall level of welfare was greater, or override individual interests in the name of community goals, Dworkin constrains utilitarianism by using the idea of rights as trumps (explained, for example at 1977: xv). The possession of rights enables people to be treated as equals.[32] The protection of individual rights is an essential role of the judiciary.

JURISPRUDENCE AND THE JUDICIAL ATTITUDE

Being a legal practitioner, a lawyer or a judge is a moral business. The argumentative nature of law, the unfinished nature of law and the legal enterprise, determines that lawyers and judges are part of an ongoing process; their approach to their task is crucial. For Dworkin:

> Judges normally recognise a duty to continue rather than discard the practice they have joined. So they develop, in response to their own convictions and instincts, working theories about the best interpretation of their responsibilities under that practice (LE: 87).

This means that their jurisprudence, their set of understandings of the nature of law and legal practice, is of crucial importance, for that is what will provide them with the necessary ideas and resources to carry out their task.

---

31 Again, the critic would say that Dworkin is selectively reading his case. Only Lord Scarman sounded like a Dworkinian.

32 *Note*: this is not the same as the communist adherence to the principle of treating people equally. Treating people equally may mean allocating to each a similar share from resources. Treating people as equals means that they have equal rights to self-respect, personal integrity, access to education and so forth. It is more a question of treating people as individuals. Individuals are possessed of rights, for Dworkin, and these rights should not be overridden in the name of serving social goals.

LAW AS AN UNFINISHED ENTERPRISE: THE JUDICIAL ROLE AND THE WRITING OF A CHAIN NOVEL

In *Law's Empire* Dworkin developed his views on interpretation, the judicial role, and the complex nature of the legal enterprise in modern society. He now argues that 'legal claims are interpretative judgments and therefore combine backward and forward-looking elements; they interpret contemporary legal practice as an unfolding narrative' (LE: 225). What is striking is the connection between Dworkin's enterprise and the implicit notion of modernity as a project.[33] Dworkin reinterprets the process as one of individuation, rights and the creation of a liberal 'community of principle'. Modern citizens of the state are not mere subjects but rights-bearing citizens; the legal system dresses them, mediates and constitutes their position in the social body. Without an image of integrity we are apt to lose our way – modernity will flounder.

Thus Dworkin can argue that his model judge, Hercules, can read the work of the Marxist or the CLS proponent (which traces particular pieces of law or legal doctrine back to the interests and ideologies that originally placed each in the law or moulded or retained it) to remind himself that there is nothing inherent in the empirical nature of the legal process which determines success. Perhaps Dworkin is sharing the post-modern realisation that there is no great underlying foundational flow which structures man's endeavours, no 'natural law' to find. Instead Hercules' task is different: he must impose order over doctrine – he must make sense of what has gone so that the project may be reinterpreted and given life for the future.

Legal development is understood only through narrative. To help understand legal or judicial interpretation we can use an analogy with the interpretation of literature. Several objects are involved in the criticism of a novel: its theme, its plot, its level of coherence, its characterisation. Dworkin says that legal critics need to employ similar criteria when considering what law is and how it is being developed. The difference is that legal critics are not presented with anything in its final state. Dworkin considers the doctrine of precedent is similar to the construction of a chain novel, that is a situation where several authors write one book but that it is never finished. What is the obligation on the second author? To write something that fits the first chapter and adds material which is new. Dworkin suggests that the judicial obligation is similar. Equally, however, we want judges today to carry on from what judges decided 100 years ago. There must be continuity. So the art is to make a fine balance between adding something that is new and providing continuity. We are telling the story of our society's development – a story of the growth of our society in modernity.

At any stage there are dilemmas – balance is required. One can give too much faith to the past, or rush too quickly into the pursuit of some community goal, thereby doing harm to what has been built up. There are two temptations:

---

33   Thus we can seen Dworkin as interpreting the current nature of the role of legality and modernity – essentially while legal positivism under Bentham and Austin had the effect of placing law as the instrument of social progress under the dictates of the political association to be guided for the pursuit of political goals and stabilised by the external principle of utility, we have lost faith in such a process.

(i) *Conventionalism* (LE: Ch 4). Law can be discovered by applying conventionally established texts (essentially the legal positivist approach of finding law through a rule of recognition). While conventionalism does justice to past political decisions and ensures predictability, it errs too much in favour of the continuity aspect; there is no movement forward.

(ii) *Pragmatism* (LE: Ch 5).[34] Law is discovered by finding what is just for the case in hand guided by community goals: 'People are never entitled to anything but the judicial decision that is, all things considered, best for the community as a whole, without regard to any past political decision'. The judge, while appreciative of policy, is made into a legislator. What is the 'just'? Justice seems arbitrary, the product of the latest fad in the social sciences. Again, Dworkin argues that pragmatism just does not fit the reality of legal practice.[35] Although pragmatism offers flexibility, it does not keep faith with the essential core of legality the protection of rights.

> Pragmatism does not rule out any theory about what makes a community better. But it does not take legal rights seriously. It rejects what other conceptions of law accept: that people can have distinctly legal rights as trumps over what would otherwise be the best future properly understood. According to pragmatism what we call legal rights are only servants of the best future: they are instruments we construct for that purpose and have no independent force or ground (LE: 160).

In a move which is similar to that of Lon Fuller,[36] Dworkin opts for a *law as integrity approach*: this is the approach that best fits a 'political community'. Thus:

> Law as integrity denies that statements of law are either the backward-looking factual instrumental reports of conventionalism or the forward-looking instrumental programs of legal pragmatism. It insists that legal claims are interpretative judgements and therefore combine backward and forward-looking elements; they interpret contemporary legal practice seen as an unfolding political narrative (LE: 225).

In contrast to the plain-fact theorist, Dworkin sees law as mediated by moral theory; in contrast to pragmatism, he views the relevant moral theory as one embedded in past decisions.

Ultimately Dworkin's morality of aspiration is the desire to become a community of principle, integrity is the inner morality of the law, and the image he constructs of the

---

34 The target for Dworkin is movements such as the law and economics movement and possibly legal realism with its emphasis upon social interests.

35 Dworkin argues that pragmatism is entitled to more respect than conventionalism because it is an interpretative theory of law; we could see legal realism as 'facts about legal practice better described in a less heated way'. He accepts that judges could be pursuing social goals under cover of using the rhetoric of rights – using *as-if rights* language – thus judges by and large decide cases as if they were upholding existing rights. Some 'pragmatists' argue that it may better serve community interests if some rights are treated as entrenched and difficult to dislodge (LE: 154–5).

36 Consider Lon Fuller's (1969) three themes: 1 A morality of aspiration which argues that human society and human institutions, including the law, should strive for excellence; 2 Legality must have an inner morality, that is, a number of processes and forms which make it truly legal; 3 It is impossible to tell the ultimate truth of the human condition, thus communication, the telling of stories, narratives, expressing things, is the process which the law must ultimately create and defend.

legal system is one of constant communication – of argumentation.[37] The key is integrity, a distinct political virtue which would not be needed in an utopian state but which:

> ... asks law-makers to try to make the total set of laws morally coherent, and an adjudicative principle, which instructs that law be seen as coherent in that way, so far as possible (LE: 176).

Integrity links together community aspirations and individual professional concerns. The judge is called upon to construe and interpret legal rights in a particular fashion:

> The adjudicative principle of integrity instructs judges to identify legal rights and duties, so far as possible, on the assumption that they were all created by a single author – the community personified – expressing a coherent conception of justice and fairness (LE: 225).

Integrity, the inner morality of law, specifies that:

> ... propositions of law are true if they figure in or follow from the principles of justice, fairness, and procedural due process that provide the best constructive interpretation of the community's legal practice.

Dworkin leads us away from the conception of law offered by the varieties of legal positivism (the plain-fact images). No longer are we being led towards a theory of law which attempts to describe the legal system in a drily scientific and objective way (Austin, Bentham, Kelsen, Hart). Dworkin demands 'constructive interpretation'. Does this mean that we get to a theoretical position where there is no difference between description and interpretation? Certainly you cannot be an impartial observer of what the law is – 'Law as integrity deplores the mechanism of the older "law is law" view', but neither are we to embrace the external view – for it also deplores 'the cynicism of the newer "realism"'. Law is continually worked out in the process of interpretation in which judges and lawyers are involved. You can't find pseudo-scientific texts for what law is. If law is always a matter of interpretation it follows that those determining the law are all of those within the legal order. Primarily this means judges but it also involves ordinary people. The image Dworkin offers of law is of a great conversation or debate where legally knowledgeable people argue as to whether rights exist. All can attempt to tell what are the right legal answers in a given situation. Dworkin says that we won't always get the right legal answer: judicial craftsmanship is not good enough, but the crux of the matter is to argue; law is an argumentative attitude. But in the structure of our decision to argue, it is implicit that there is law to discover.

OBJECTIONS AND CRITICISMS OF DWORKIN

(i) This is yet another internal view of law which strives to work out the meaning of law from the accounts of lawyers and judges with allowance made for positioning these accounts in social and historical processes; rather Dworkin adopts a deliberate

---

37 Although, within the structure of his interpretative sphere he has placed severe limits upon the types of discourses allowed. Thus he may be more limited than Fuller.

policy of silencing opposing, ie non-philosophical, viewpoints. This again ties jurisprudence to the ideology of the system – there is ultimately no 'objectivity' since we are trapped within the task of giving the 'best constructive reading';

(ii) it is actually prescriptive rather than descriptive. A theory of what the law and judicial decision-making ought to be like rather than what it actually is like. Dworkin responds by claiming his is an account of what is best in legal practice, a structural account of what is inherent in the nature of legal practice. What is the criterion for the 'best constructive reading'? This is answered by Dworkin's political morality – so is this theory not Dworkin's image of the law and society he wants us all to share?

(iii) Hercules is a myth, or worse, a hypocrite. While judges may sometimes sound like Hercules they are merely disguising their real motives. Dworkin responds by stressing that Hercules is a model of best practice. Moreover, it is clear that some prescription is bound in the practice of normative jurisprudence; part of the task of the philosophy of law is to ask and find standards for what is permissible and desirable in judging. We are concerned here with questions of justification and legitimacy of decision-making rather than purely describing it as an external observer may be attempting;

(iv) sceptical commentators argue that no coherent integrated account of political and moral values as underlying a society such as the US can be found. Instead of conflicting principles which can be reconciled under a best constructive interpretation the sceptics see incoherence and contradiction;

(v) what if the search for a coherent narrative of political morality results in a morality that the judge cannot accept – is the apartheid legislation really law, the expression of the community's political morality and hence should the judge extend it into new decisions?

(vi) the implication which follows from Dworkin's work is that actual empirical research is required to ascertain whether a sociological account of the reality of legal practice and the 'legal community', 'the structure and environment of the interpretative community', reveals whether collective professional interpretations of law actually occur and what, if anything, makes them possible? As Cotterrell puts it:

> Dworkin writes extensively about community as the basis of law and how it can be conceptualised, yet he can never offer any analysis of the actual social conditions under which a community can exist, or what the concept means when related to actual patterns of social life, or of the specific political and social circumstances in which it is useful to think of law as an expression of community values.

Cotterrell's (1989: 172–181) suspicion is that Dworkin's defence of the integrity of legal practice only works because of a rigorous demarcation of 'internal' perspectives, the accounts of legal practitioners, from 'external' perspectives, such as sociological knowledge. However, Dworkin's careful sealing off of his theory does not in fact work, as we shall now analyse.

INTERPRETATION REVISITED: OR IS DWORKIN AN INTERPRETATIVE IMPERIALIST?

[An Englishman,] having been told that the world rested on the back of an elephant which rested in turn on the back of a turtle, asked ...'What does that turtle rest on?' – 'Another turtle.' – 'And that turtle?' – 'Ah, Sahib, after that, it is turtles all the way down.' (Clifford Geertz, *The Interpretation of Cultures*, 1973: 29)

Officially, Dworkin is contemporary legal positivism's harshest (friendly) critic. His stated position is to have left positivism – defined as jurisprudence grounding or founding its knowledge of legal practice upon a 'plain-fact' view of law – behind in favour of 'constructive interpretation'; but what provides the foundation for his enterprise?

Dworkin's enterprise is founded on a crucial distinction: that which exists between the *grounds* of propositions and their *force*. His claim is simple: previous theories in jurisprudence have emphasised the grounds of law or propositions for which they claim the status of law – whilst they have neglected the force (moral, political) involved in making the claim that such and such a proposition is to be applied as a valid part of the legal universe.[38]

This is a highly interesting distinction. What is the basis for the appeal of this force? Or, put differently, what is the force that activates this force? Two readings come to mind: (i) the tradition of Kantian rationality, or (ii) the appeal of Nietzschean rhetoric.

The first beckons back to the tradition of intuition and the argument that those propositions which 'strike' you as being correct somehow gain from this fact. In the Kantian tradition we start with two assumptions, the first that there is rationality inherent in our social beliefs, or the belief patterns necessary to make a practice – such as mathematics – and the second that we accept the foundations of our rational selves. As a result of this combination we believe that our subjectivity can be controlled by our rational nature; or, put another way, that the core of our rationality imposes limits on our subjectivity. The universality of our rationality allows us to have confidence in our human ability to create universal institutions (such as the project of legality) out of (our social) difference, and recognise the universality beneath difference. In *Law's Empire* Dworkin repeats various combinations of this theme. The Kantian relies, however, upon a rationalist metaphysics, it relies upon our accepting that it is meaningful to talk of a law beyond law, of law working itself pure, because we need the 'noumenal metaphysical fact' of pure law as the object that we are striving to attain, an ideal phenomenon of which real practice represents only a dim image. Now Dworkin makes references to such a structure of belief, yet he denies his scheme needs it, for to do so would open him up to the challenges of the external sceptics.

Has Dworkin then joined with Nietzsche in the quest for the will to power? Has he created an interpretation of liberal legality to re-energise the system of liberal legality the basis of which actually accords with our (liberal) intuitions and subjective feelings? It is

---

38 'Philosophies of law are ... usually unbalanced theories of law: they are mainly about the grounds and almost silent about the force of law' (LE: 111).

easy to believe so ... to read *Law's Empire* is to engage with someone who writes like a Nietzschean – a committed liberal Nietzschean determined to combat nihilism and defeat legal disenchantment by creating an interpretative conception of liberal legality with great seductive power. As if to repeat Nietzsche's comment that 'the real world becomes a fable' Dworkin describes legal development in terms of a chain novel![39] Moreover, the acceptance of the theory makes the practice as the theory purported to develop! This is perfect pragmatism (the term is not used in any pejorative sense). Only Dworkin does not talk like this; he refuses to be a neo-Nietzschean. He claims to be bringing out what the law actually is like – is then Dworkin actually a positivist?

Many critics believe that Dworkin wants to have the best of both positivism and of interpretation; he wants the certainty that positivism sought, while he enjoys the constructive freedom that interpretation appears to offer. The problem for Dworkin is that the 'interpretative turn' is usually taken to imply that we must abandon acceptance of some universal conception of law (traditionally hankered after by those who stipulated an answer to the question 'what is law?'). As Gadamer puts it: 'In view of the finite nature of our historical experience there is, it would seem, something absurd about the whole idea of a uniquely correct interpretation' (1975: 107; also quoted in Douzinas et al, 1992, in their critical discussion of the weakness of Dworkin's ideas on interpretation).[40] Hermeneutics demands a deep sensitivity to the different ways of getting by in the lived-world, it invokes historical analysis and cultural relativity – thus 'the law' becomes a loose term which only has meaning in concrete situations knowable by historical analysis.

By contrast the idea that there is a right interpretation is deeply embedded in Dworkin's project. Moreover, Dworkin began by unpicking the positivist's *amoral*

---

39 In *The Twilight of the Idols*, Nietzsche relates how the 'real world' has become a 'fable'. The long journey from the world of Platonic ideas, to the created world of Christianity, to the Kantian a priori, through to the assumption of unknowability, the idea that beneath 'reality' there is a structure that is absolute, true, and which can serve as the source of certainty for epistemology, and of norms for morality, withers to the point of dissolution'. The real world becomes a matter of our stories, our interpretations, our perspectives; there is no one way of proving the structure. But with the disappearance of the real world, the apparent world must also be suspect. What right have we to take on trust the everyday stories, linguistic usages and accounts of their practice, which the participants give us? (Note: both Hart and Dworkin appear to do just that.) Either we are true to our presuppositions and announce that this is the pragmatic result of our methodology and this 'data', or we try to hide the problem hoping to win over the audience by the power of our stories.

40 The specialists may be questioning this all-too-brief comment on interpretation. Contemporary hermeneutics lives with the consequences of the interpretative turn, that is that interpretation moves in an inescapable circle. The authority ultimately resides in the tradition of interpreting and the ability to bring out the meaning of the interrelations of the practitioners of the tradition and their lived-world. As Gadamer – regarded as the founder of modern hermeneutics – consistently argues, 'traditional hermeneutics' tried to limit the horizon of interpretation. It was a theory of understanding which involved objectivist and psychological claims in which the aim was to apprehend objective intentions of meaning. It aimed to tell the truth of the intentions of the participants of a practice – such as interpreting the Bible – which would be the foundational activity for the Jewish or Christian tradition. Thus it needed an implicit or explicit idea of a pure 'pre-interpretative object' existing independently of interpretation. Augustine may have seen his role as interpreting the meaning of God's will and the relationship of man to that will; the meaning of law was, then, part of the larger interpretation of the meaning of God's creation. Contemporary hermeneutics loses the self-certainty of a comprehensive philosophical insight, its proponents can make no claims as to the absoluteness of their assertions and must recognise the finitude of all knowledge in the context of historical human

epistemology of law, offering a theory of law that sees legal practice as expressing an underlying public morality. Dworkin asks legal practitioners, such as lawyers and judges, to reason outwards and position their deliberation in a holistic conception of their society. He explicitly states that legal theory must fit the society which it interprets; a legal theory that attempted to fit all societies would have such a level of generality that it would be meaningless ('Legal Theory and the Problem of Sense', 1987: 14–15; LE: 102–3). The judge, in seeking guidance as to the right answer, constructs a theory grounded in the legal and political structures of that society. If so, then any particular country may well have a coherent political morality and social narrative – the Nazis certainly had. Does, then, against all his liberal intentions, his theory fit and defend whatever values inform a particular tradition, so that Nazi laws are not only recognised as valid laws but as laws with a particularly strong moral force? Laws that if one is within the Nazi interpretative community have an intense gravitational force, which cry out to be performed? As they were ... often with relish.

Furthermore, the foundation of traditional theories of law is usually found in the object of analysis – even if that object is made visible through an act of faith, as with Augustine, or a stipulative definition, such as John Austin's definition of positive law as the commands of the sovereign backed by sanctions and habitually obeyed. Conversely, *interpretation abandons the certainty of a fixed object towards which one's observations are either clearer or more obscure reflections, replacing this with the less secure interaction of a domain of activity and the interpreter's belonging to a tradition of interpretation.* The fact that one even recognises the tradition-bound nature of interpretation entails that one recognises that there may be other modes of interpretation. One's tradition cannot encompass the totality – the totality remains a mystery.

Interpretation necessarily involves a loss of certainty; this is part of the ethics of interpretation. Positivism stressed certainty and – favouring a descriptive analysis – presupposed that law was a settled object which was relatively easy to recognise. Dworkin argued (overly simplistically) that the same process occurred with natural law; he claimed both assumed that they could conceive of an essence of law, by which they could orientate their theoretical disagreements and legal practice could be fashioned. If there is thereby agreement as to the essence of law, this essence can be the touchstone by reference to which disagreements among lawyers about what the law is in particular cases can be resolved; there is a common standard to which they can appeal and that renders their disagreement meaningful.

If, however, there is no such abstract essence – if disagreement is over whether this or that theory of purpose best explains and unifies past decisions – then disputes about what law is seem inherently insoluble. They begin to look less like lawyers' disputes and more like the debates literary critics have when they argue about the most illuminating view of a novel (as Dworkin himself notes). Since there is apparently no right answer *concerning the totality*, what passes for a scholastic argument is really a political conflict among incommensurable perspectives.

Dworkin assures us, however, that the interpretative turn entails neither of these outcomes. The first consequence of relativism appears contrary to Dworkin's claim for the fundamentality of rights in legal practice – so which gives? The rights or the interpretative turn? Dworkin argues that interpretation does not entail the loss of a standard by which to evaluate opinions, because 'the competing interpretations are directed toward the same objects or events of interpretation' (LE: 46). Dworkin consistently claims an interpreter cannot make a practice, or work of art, anything he would have wanted it to be, since the 'history or shape of a practice or object constrains the available interpretations of it' (LE: 52). This is the ethics of interpretative fidelity, an interpretation must 'fit' the object. It need not fit every aspect thereof (for interpretation has a reformist potential), 'but it must fit enough for the interpreter to be able to see himself as interpreting that practice, not inventing a new one' (LE: 66). If this is the case then disagreements among interpreters are meaningful because they are disagreements about the best way of interpreting the same object. The object is the touchstone for the validity of theory.

But this raises the first set of concerns: either the 'object' has an independent validity and we acknowledge the possibility of finding its truth, or we must face up to the fact that the interpretative turn implies that there is no way of evaluating a practice except by standards internal to it. If so, then there is a danger that we become trapped in the circle of a community's expressed self-conceptions and have no transcendent essence, or other place to stand, whereby to escape from an uncritical accommodation to the given norms of a tradition. To return to Nazi law, unless we can be convinced that the Nazis had got the law wrong – that is, by finding principles and practices in that particular system that offer conflicting grounds to the Nazi ideology – the judge must actively work to make the Nazi code better, to bring its ambitions to a higher level. But having said that theory must be specific to a particular society to be meaningful, Dworkin then acts as if this is not the case by making the criterion of fit only one of the standards by which to assess the merits of an interpretation. He proposes another criterion as the extent to which interpretation makes the object 'the best possible example of the form or genre to which it is taken to belong' (LE: 52); additionally, 'all interpretation strives to make an object the best it can be, as an instance of some assumed enterprise' (LE: 53). Thus the best interpretation, the right answer to the question 'What is law?' is the one that makes the object – the specificality of this 'law' – the best it can be. But how can Dworkin invoke the security of this independent, ideal, object? Is it a Kantian *a priori*, or a Nietzschean rhetorical trope?

Dworkin uses these moves to constrain the freedom of the interpreter. First, the object's empirical character sets limits on the value that can be ascribed to it; a tyranny cannot be dressed up as an ideal political order, but it can be interpreted so as to approximate this order to the degree that its tyrannical character allows – say, by reading out as non-integral with the regime official acts lacking the elementary formal attributes (eg generality, prospectivity) of law. Thus interpretation renders a practice the best possible example of what it is. But second, the object's transcultural ideal nature sets limits on the kind of value ascribable to it, or it sets limits on the meaning of 'best'. The best is the object's own best, given that it is the kind of thing that it is. Thus, to return to Hegel, the ideal of the polity is different, presumably, from that of the family, so that the interpretation of a political despotism must be guided by the former ideal rather than by the latter. Accordingly, if the object as found is the touchstone of theory, this involves no mere accommodation to the given (to the historical vagaries of specific practice), because in turn the truth of the object is its ideal nature, in the light of which the interpreter construes the object as a more or less adequate approximation (In *Riggs v Palmer*, Judge Earl gave us a better form of legal practice than Judge Gray). Moreover, this construal is interpretative rather than arbitrarily constructionist, because it is constrained by the history and shape of the object. Thus interpretation, says Dworkin, 'is a matter of interaction between purpose and object' (LE: 52). But no sooner has Dworkin asserted the security of the object than the actual stages of his interpretative scheme undercuts it.

Dworkin's interpretative community

Let us return to the basic problem: Dworkin attempts to transform Hart's legacy by moving from a positivist framework to a hermeneutic or interpretative one. However, he wishes to avoid relativity by keeping an idea of an object or purpose to the practice that is independent of the rules and structures of the practice. He begins by assuming the existence of an 'interpretative attitude' which assumes that the practices to be interpreted have a value: 'That it serves some interest or purpose or enforces some principle – in short, that it has some point – that can be stated independently of just describing the rules that make up the practice'. This interpretative attitude appears a vital conception in Dworkin's later work and provides the grounds for his optimism that legal theory – making clearer the point and purpose of practice – can make a practical difference since the interpretative attitude involves the idea that the requirements of the practice will change insofar as they are 'sensitive to its point'. The meaning of the social practice is not self-evident but must be constantly interpreted, and is changing all the time in the light of those interpretations: 'people now try to impose meaning on the institution – to see it in its best light – and then to restructure it in the light of that meaning' (LE: 47).

Judges, lawyers and academic commentators on law are all involved in interpretative practice. The key requirement is that of constructive interpretation: 'a matter of imposing purpose on an object or practice in order to make it the best possible example of the form or genre to which it is taken to belong' (LE: 52). Interpretative practice is not free-standing but part of a tradition or community and has a reformist bent.

Dworkin posits three stages: (i) pre-interpretative, in which the practice is identified; (ii) interpretative, in which the person interpreting comes to a general justification as to why the practice is worth continuing; (iii) post-interpretative, characterised by reform, in which the practice is adjusted according to the demands of the justification established at the interpretative stage. This is reflexive or self-referential in that the justification comes out of (aspects of) the practice and in turn informs and shapes the development of that practice.

Dworkin thereby characterises law as an interpretative practice founded upon a general agreement as to what the law is about. Within such a general agreement, empirical and theoretical arguments may occur as to what parts of the practice are about without disrupting the overall functioning.

There is an obvious problem: in our contemporary times there is a diverse set of arguments as to what law is about and voices from the Marxist or critical perspectives are radically different from the liberals; therefore is there sufficient actual agreement about what the law is for a high degree of stability to exist within the system or will a meta-narrative like Dworkin's just be one interpretation? Albeit an interpretation highly pleasing to liberal sensibilities? Dworkin tries to maintain confidence in his interpretative scheme by arguing that it is true to the nature of our practice and by quietening the voice of the sceptics. To show that this does not fully succeed it is necessary to look in more detail at the first two of the stages of interpretation.

(1) The first stage is 'pre-interpretative' or the point at which 'the rules and standards taken to provide the tentative content of the practice are identified' (LE: note 1 at 65–66). The historical shape of the 'pre-interpretative' object – legal practice and the discourse of the practitioners – is to constrain interpretation and plays the role of validating the process as one of interpretation rather than invention. Here is where the paradox of interpretation comes into play,[41] for if the practice is to perform this function, then it must be capable of demarcation in a value-free (ie non-interpretative) manner, otherwise the definition of the object will itself be an interpretation in need of validation *ad infinitum*. But Dworkin acknowledges that value-free definition – the plain-fact view – is impossible. Identifying the law is implicitly theory-laden, hence subject to controversy, for 'social rules do not carry identifying labels' (LE: 66).

To take Hart's example of chess, the external observer not only would not be able to understand the meaning of the moves without knowing the rules, s/he would not be able to understand that the game was a game, or indeed was chess, without learning the tradition of playing games and being told this was chess. The categories under which rules are subsumed are not their own but are imposed on rules pursuant to some human interest and some human tradition of interpretation. The object has already been altered and shaped by interpretation and it is impossible to find the object (law) as it exists in itself. Thus, there is in reality no pre-interpretative phase (Dworkin acknowledges this by placing the phrase within inverted commas). This means that it is, after all, not the object that is to constrain interpretation but a 'consensus' within a tradition – or what Dworkin calls 'the interpretative community' – as to what the object is; a consensus that may, or may not, exist (LE: 66–68). Furthermore, the constraint posed by this consensus-defined object translates into a requirement of fit between the interpretation and the practice. The assessment of a good fit, however, requires the interpreter to have a 'pre-interpretative' sense of paradigmatic or essential features of the practice, those

---

41 The paradox of interpretation refers to the following problem which can be stated as a pair of opposing propositions:

  (i) one cannot begin an interpretation without having previously established the facts;

  (ii) there are no facts without an interpretation.

  The paradox was pointed out by Nietzsche: 'In opposition to positivism, which halts at phenomena and says: 'There are only *facts* and nothing more', I would say: no, facts is precisely what is lacking, and what exists consists of interpretation' (*Will to Power*, para 481).

features that 'any plausible interpretation must fit' (LE: 72). Again the practice does not autonomously announce its essential features, so these too will be a matter of intuition and conviction that – unless we take the Kantian path – are once again interpretative. Not only the definition of the object, but also the idea of a good fit, is implicitly theory-mediated. The problem here – at least for his critics – is that Dworkin refuses to analyse the conditions under which the supposed consensus he requires (as to the nature of the consensus of the interpretative community) is brought about; as with Hart, Dworkin ultimately assumes the unproblematic nature of the everyday.[42]

(2) In the second, or *interpretative*, stage the practice previously defined is integrated under a fully self-conscious theory of purpose. The aim of the interpretation is to make the object – for example, the development of the law in a particular area – the closest possible approximation to its own ideal nature, and the test appears simple: 'does the theory [of the judge, or the theorist] make the object the best it can be?' But since the differentiated object (the independent object which is meant to constrain interpretation) is actually only a set of interpretative practices, the value-laden interpretation is necessarily the imposition on the object of the interpreter's own opinion as to what reveals it in its best light (LE: 67, 87). Dworkin acknowledges that substantial differences in interpretation – internal disagreement within the community – are both possible, and indeed desirable (LE: 88), but an operative bind upon the interpreter is the requirement of a good fit between the valued purpose and the paradigmatic features of the practice. This only works, however, if both the identification of paradigmatic features and one's idea of a good fit are conceptually independent of the hypothesis as to the point of the practice (LE: 67-68). They must not presuppose or adjust to the hypothesis, for then they could not constrain. Yet since the selection of paradigmatic features, the assessment of fit, and the formulation of purpose are all interpretative – since they all fall within the same interpreting mind – no strong distinction between these operations is possible. Dworkin relies upon a 'psychological' constraint – a voice of intellectual conscience – urging the interpreter to keep separate his judgments about fit and his judgments about what purpose lends most value to the practice (LE: 234-235).

This conscience or moral bind only has a hope of success if one is a member of the interpretative community: (i) the interpreter is required to select paradigmatic features of the practice but such selection is interpretative and presupposes at some intuitive level a theory of the purpose that animates the practice. However, there is no clear or ontologically grounded distinction between the stages of interpretation which forces the moral choice to face 'reality' so that the moral disquiet against manipulating the precedents or other arguments – for example, techniques of reading statutes – loses its bite (LE: 235); (ii) the standard of fit one adopts, as much

---

42 As is apparent in Dworkin's description (LE: 66) of his idea of the 'interpretative community': 'But a very great deal of consensus is needed – perhaps an interpretative community is usefully defined as requiring consensus at this stage – if the interpretative attitude is to be fruitful, and we may therefore abstract from this stage in our analysis by presupposing that the classifications it yields are treated as given in day-to-day reflection and argument.'

as one's theory of purpose, reflects a judgment as to what lends value to a practice; and Dworkin admits that trade-offs will occur between one's aesthetic convictions about how much integration is required and one's substantive convictions about which ends most ennoble a practice.

As a result the distinction between the correct interpretation and an false interpretation or invention collapses: there are only inventions. To avoid this result Dworkin offers a defence of fidelity (and hence the possibility of a rational solution to interpretative disputes) by substituting the idea of interpretative consensus for the independent object. To avoid a relativism of interpretations Dworkin assumes that there must be a prior consensus about what the law is before an interpretative community can develop; and he further argues backwards from the fact of the current existence of an interpretative community to the proposition of some prior consensus upon which the community is able to develop.

To maintain this consensus the sceptic must be kept at bay. Too much information from diverse sources as to the nature of law would destroy the ability of the interpretative community to maintain its consensus. The enemy is 'external scepticism' (LE: 78). The external sceptic reads Dworkin's claims for value-oriented interpretation as necessarily perspectival because it lacks an independent object capable of validating it and thence the sceptic requires Dworkin to reduce the scope of his claims. The sceptic may hold and attempt to defend interpretative hypotheses as passionately as the interpretative realist; he will not, however, defend them as true understandings of the object but rather as projections that are pleasing to the aesthetic and moral sentiments of those he seeks to persuade. Since these sentiments are, however, equally ungrounded in an independent reality, they are as naturally manifold as the interpretative claims that appeal to them. Hence an interpretation may only be popular or unpopular; it can never be right, or even better than any other, except in terms of the explicit political purposes behind it and which serve as a criterion of acceptance.[43]

In opposing 'external scepticism' Dworkin appeals to our sense of his sincerity and rejects as 'silly', 'wasteful', 'confused', and 'to no point' (LE, 85-86) the discourse of the sceptic. The sceptic simply distracts us from the project; Dworkin would like to convert the external sceptic into an internal one, and transforms talk of scepticism into a discussion on the terrain of hermeneutics rather than the experience of law. We can read the sceptics in 'a calm philosophical moment'.[44]

---

43 Dworkin deals with the sceptic by almost accepting his epistemological assumptions but removing their bite. He argues that the sceptic has no force against his thesis because he does not claim for the hermeneutic concept of law the 'bizarre' kind of objectivity that the sceptic denies (LE: 81). Against the sceptics lost hope for absolute security, the kind of objectivity Dworkin claims is rather the subjective conviction of objectivity that accompanies moral statements as distinct from reports about taste. The difference, says Dworkin, between a statement like 'slavery is wrong' and one like 'rum and raisin ice cream is good' is that with the former the speaker intends a proposition he believes to be impersonally valid rather than valid only for individuals with certain kinds of needs or interests. The further claim of objectivity for the moral statement, he argues, adds nothing except emphasis to this belief. It is only objectivity in this philosophically redundant sense, Dworkin now tells us, that he is claiming for the best interpretative theory of law.

44 That is, into one whose denial of the truth of some moral claim (eg that slavery is wrong) is not an argument about the epistemological status of such claims but an interpretative hypothesis about the actual practice of morality (LE: 83-86).

Dworkin's interpretation itself must assume the existence of a right answer unquestioningly. Hence the only arguments Dworkin accepts as relevant to his thesis are those that cannot challenge the thesis because they take its truth for granted. Thus, the arbitrary silencing of opponents renders the thesis itself arbitrary and a mask for interest-based interpretation.

This critique of Dworkin can be summarised in the following way: in grounding law in the best interpretation of legal practice by use of the idea of the interpretative community, Dworkin keeps a 'truth' for his project only by fencing off this community from a greater interaction with perspectives other than those of liberalism. Dworkin consistently fails to appreciate the concerns of the 'others' – such as those of the Critical Legal Studies Movement, feminists or critical race scholars – since the terms of discussion that his interpretative community embraces are systematically organised to empower a particular tradition of interpretation. But, as a consequence, we are free to discuss with these others the nature of law, since law is still held out implicitly as something other than that which the interpretation has offered us. Because the interpretative turn holds that law is truly apprehended only through interpretation, it already implies an ideal of fidelity to the object or an intelligible distinction between interpretation and invention. To ensure that we do not notice the disappearance of this independent object (and thus notice the distinction between interpretation and invention) alternative talk of this independent object must be devalued, its demands ridiculed, its accusatory voice silenced. However, once the independent object – the criterion of fidelity – is declared to be of no significance for interpretation, there is nothing to distinguish the right answer thesis from the thesis that there are no right or wrong answers, only equally unprivileged perspectives. The project must be defended on alternative grounds; those of social constructionism. Dworkin's project is a political one of the use served by law and the meaning of law – a project which takes up the positivist message that law is an instrument of man and transforms this message through an expressionist idiom; ultimately with Dworkin, it is turtles all the way down, albeit, liberal turtles.

DWORKIN'S INSPIRATIONAL METAPHYSICS: THE POLITICS OF PRINCIPLED COMMUNITARIANISM

Dworkin may accept that this is the reality of his constructive interpretation. It is man trying to impose order over what has been thrown up in the contingencies of political and cultural human affairs rather than by a process which claims to find a rational order in the forces that have empirically created the conditions of contemporary society. But the order found is a circumscribed – liberalist – one. Accepting his narrative, we reject the narratives of empirical social theory which threaten to undercut our self-confidence. We can call this Dworkin's metaphysics; others may call this the structure of his dreams or the construction of his myths.

Modernity involves the notion that man can take control of the processes of the world to build up the conditions for a progressive and happy society on this planet. A question we have been playing with is 'what is to guide man in this project when the foundations that gave the medieval synthesis, namely, religion and custom, are discarded?' 'What positions the enterprise of individuals within the image of an overall enterprise?' We have noted that Weber was extremely pessimistic about this and we have seen the answer of legal positivism – namely, utilitarianism – we have also seen its problems. Briefly put, since this has been outside the ambit of this work, the search for a master principle of social justice to replace utilitarianism (pursued in varying ways in the works of Marx, John Stuart Mill, John Rawls, Robert Nozick, for example) has not resulted in a settled consensus. We do not have some master principle of justice – Bentham's fear of subjectivism, intuitivism and ongoing argument is instead the reality. But this does not mean that we are not committed to justice. Far from it, Dworkin would argue – the very fact of our arguments over justice indicate the extent to which we are acting as a political association intent on becoming a political community expressing justice.

Dworkin is revitalising Fuller's idea of the morality of aspiration. The whole structure of Dworkin's work is to convince us of 'law's optimism' and 'law's integrity'. Fuller was clear that we had to portray legality as having an ethic, and that a legality that was coherent and purposeful was somehow more sustainable and 'good', than an evil one. Dworkin gives integrity as law's ethic but his concept is wider – can we interpret Dworkin then as building up an ideal, an aspiration, for law?

If so then the desire to see coherence in law is itself to be seen as a guiding ideal rather than as a description of accomplished fact. This, reflexively, appears to be Dworkin's position. Consider the openness of the desire in the following section taken from his concluding chapter:

> We accept integrity as a distinct political ideal, and we accept the adjudicative principle of integrity as sovereign over law, because we want to treat ourselves as an association of principle, as a community governed by a single and coherent vision of justice and fairness and procedural due process in right relation ... our root ambition of treating ourselves as a community of principle ...

> Present law gropes toward pure law when modes appear that seem to satisfy fairness and process and bring law closer to its own ambition; lawyers declare optimism about this process when they say that law works itself pure. The optimism may be misplaced. A sceptical story seems better to some critics of law: they predict the triumph of entropy instead, of law losing its overall substantive coherence in the chaos produced by selfish and disparate concentrations of political power. Which attitude – pessimism or optimism – is wise and which foolish? That depends on energy and imagination as much as foresight, for each attitude, if popular enough, contributes to its own vindication (LE: 406-7).

Ultimately Dworkin calls upon lawyers to consider themselves as more than the servants of the state, they hold the keys to the development of their society. Modernity can be saved if we respect our own ambitions (as Dworkin interprets them for us!):

> What is law? ... Law's empire is defined by attitude, not territory or power or process ...
> it must be pervasive in our ordinary lives if it is to serve us well even in court. It is an interpretative, self-reflective attitude addressed to politics in the broadest sense. It is a Protestant attitude that makes each citizen responsible for imagining what his society's

public commitments to principle are, and what these commitments require in new circumstances ...

Law's attitude is constructive: it aims in the interpretative spirit, to lay principle over practice to show the best route to a better future, keeping the right faith with the past. It is finally, a fraternal attitude, an expression of how we are united in community though divided in project, interest and conviction. That is, anyway, what law is for us: for the people we want to be and the community we aim to have.

CHAPTER 16

SCEPTICISM, SUSPICION AND THE CRITICAL LEGAL STUDIES MOVEMENT

By demonstrating that social life is much less structured and much more complex, much less impartial and much more irrational, than the legal process suggests, the interests served by legal doctrine and theory will surface (Roberto Unger, *The Critical Legal Studies Movement*, 1984).

PROLOGUE: A MEDITATION UPON INNOCENCE AND SCHOLASTIC KNOWLEDGE

What an extraordinary episode in the economic progress of man, was that age which came to an end in August 1914! The greater part of the population, it is true, worked hard and lived at a low standard of comfort, yet were, to all appearances, reasonably contented with this lot. But escape was possible, for any man of capacity or character at all exceeding the average, into the middle and upper classes, for whom life offered, at a low cost and with the least trouble, convenience, comforts, and amenities beyond the compass of the richest and most powerful monarchs of other ages. The inhabitant of London could order by telephone, sipping his morning tea in bed, the various products of the whole earth, in such quantity as he might see fit, and reasonably expect their early delivery upon his doorstep; he could at the same moment and by the same means adventure his wealth in the natural resources and new enterprises of any quarter of the world, and share, without exertion or even trouble, in their prospective fruits and advantages; or he could decide to couple the security of his fortunes with the good faith of the townspeople of any substantial municipality in any continent that fancy or information might recommend. He could secure forthwith, if he wished it, cheap and comfortable means of transit to any country or climate without passport or other formality, could dispatch his servant to the neighbouring office of a bank for such supply of the precious metals as might seem convenient, and could then proceed abroad to foreign quarters, without knowledge of their religion, language, or customs, bearing coined wealth upon his person, and would consider himself greatly aggrieved and much surprised at the least interference. But, most important of all, he regarded this state of affairs as normal, certain, and permanent, except in the direction of further improvement, and any deviation from it as aberrant, scandalous, and avoidable. The projects and politics of militarism and imperialism, of racial and cultural rivalries, of monopolies, restrictions, and exclusion, which were to play the serpent to this paradise, were little more than the amusements of his daily newspaper, and appeared to exercise almost no influence at all on the ordinary course of social and economic life, the internationalisation of which was nearly complete in practice (J M Keynes, *The Economic Consequences of the Peace*, 1919: 6-7).

In 1919 Keynes – noted economist and senior British civil servant – was a disappointed man. The inability of the American President, Wilson, to shape the Allies' position in negotiations over the Treaty of Versailles, marked the victory of passion and desire for revenge over reasoned moderation.

Keynes believed an age had vanished; an age where everybody believed in a progressive civilising process led by the rule of law, property rights, proper behaviour and reasoned argument. The peace conference signalled the decline of rationality. In his own words, Keynes had grown up in a world in which 'the rules of the game' – whether in intellectual discussion or in personal behaviour, in the conduct of business or in industrial relations, in international diplomacy or in finance, in the rhetoric or in the actuality of politics – were widely known and largely accepted. His life had been a steady progression from school and university to the upper levels of the British Civil Service, marked by his powers of debate and rational discussion. His world was both pleasant and predictable, and he viewed the wider world, as he thought everybody else also perceived it, as still improving in the manner he thought it had done since the beginnings of the industrial revolution.

At the peace conference, however, Keynes witnessed the emasculation of rational argument in favour of political hatred. Keynes foresaw that the desire to make Germany pay for the terrible cost the war had wrought upon the Allies would result in disaster; choosing revenge over reasoned moderation would have extreme and counter-productive consequences. In reaction Keynes withdrew from public life to the colleges of Cambridge where he thought the old rules of argument still survived. There he was provided with the space to construct his polemical *The Economic Consequences of the Peace*. Later – as the economist widely credited with policies which helped save Western societies from the economic depression of the 1930s – Keynes admitted, with all the benefit of having observed the depression and political turmoil of the inter-war years and the great disaster of the Second World War which he had so accurately predicted, that he had always attributed 'an unreal rationality to the other people's feelings and behaviour (and doubtless to my own, too),' and that 'the attribution of rationality to human nature ... ignored certain powerful and valuable springs of feeling' (1949: 100–101). The war had tapped these springs, and unleashed emotions, most of which were inimical to civilisation, destructive of progress, rather than contributing to it.

So too is a common view of the Critical Legal Studies Movement (hereinafter referred to as CLS). Throughout the world, numerous lecturers and professors of law simply cannot understand the scepticism, the 'deconstructive urge', the 'unreasonableness', the polemical, the unsettling, the vague, the undisciplined, and the irreverent nature of the writings which fit under the loose label of CLS; many perceive CLS as dangerous or nihilist. But then the CLS writer would find Keynes's description of the lost age hopelessly naive; more than that, as dangerously simplistic. From the CLS perspective, Keynes ignored the foundations of a way of life that seemed so unproblematic and natural to him. In the account quoted above, not only did he seem to assume the naturalness of the British class system, but he somehow displaced the entire servant class from being one of 'the inhabitant(s) of London'. The whole globe served to provide resources for the civilised pastimes of the advanced world, whose inhabitants had no need of knowledge of the religions, language, or customs of the 'others'. Where in his conception was the rape of Africa, where was the conquering and stripping of India of its riches, where was the argument that Australia was unpopulated and no one owned any of its land, where was the destruction and enslavement of the native peoples throughout the lands that Western 'civilised' countries used as the source of their raw materials? What right had Western culture and Western ideologies to dominate? Did Keynes himself implicitly accept that the simple fact of Western domination made it progressive and right? Did he assume that might made right?

Was that pre-1919 age truly to be celebrated? Keynes had been, to our post-modern awareness, political in his interpretation of the state of pre-1919 Western societies. By contrast, writing in Germany, the communist Rosa Luxemburg (In *The Accumulation of Capital*, published in German 1913, English trans 1951) argued that Western capitalism required the continual subjection, absorption and assimilation of other parts of the globe and the expropriation of their resources to feed the ever-growing consumption of capitalist excess. Capitalism is compelled by its own inner dynamics to expand, but it can expand only by feeding off 'non-capitalist social strata and forms of social organisation'. Non-capitalist systems are stripped of their own dynamics and converted to extensions of the capitalist structure. Although Luxemburg was sounding a call for the reader to see the destructive side of capitalism, her own belief in socialism proved similarly afflicted. In that case, however, exploitation and domination achieved control without widespread creative excess.

Today, both capitalism and socialism appear as variants of modernity's drive to study, visualise, and subject to rational mastery our world and render its entities into commodities for our consumption. Perceptions differ: capitalism looked like civilisation to Keynes but a socially destructive system to Luxemburg, while she thought socialism would save our humanity. In its turn, CLS is a reflection of a contemporary loss of faith in all forms of thinking that make the social structures of the modern world appear natural, inevitable, inherently justifiable and unquestionably progressive.

For much of modernity the jurisprudential imagination has reinforced the desire for rational mastery of the social world. Whether in Kantian, Rousseauian, Hegelian, Benthamite, Austinian, or Kelsenian forms, to master the social world is to render it subject to the legal order. It is no coincidence that the key methodology of modern law is legislation, or that in the survival of the common law tradition an inherent idea of natural functionality provides a faith in universality and foundation. Jurisprudence cannot escape a concern with the final foundations for law since it is continually asked to ensure that law is 'well-founded', that is, that real law is reasonable and provides some answer to the question 'why should I, as a citizen, obey it?' and 'are my society's legal institutions justified?'

CLS upsets this confidence. What would the world look like if we broadened the jurisprudential gaze and allowed all sorts of other perspectives in? While Keynes played by the rules of the 'rational' game, what about all those types of (non-)knowledge excluded from the rules of the mainstream jurisprudential game?

DESTROYING INNOCENCE: THE TURN TO OTHER KNOWLEDGES

If my hypothesis is correct, the primary function of writing, as a means of communication, is to facilitate the enslavement of other human beings. The use of writing for disinterested ends, and with a view to satisfactions of the mind in the fields either of science or the arts, is a secondary result of its invention – and may even be no more than a way of reinforcing, justifying, or dissimilating its primary function (Claude Lévi-Strauss, *Tristes Tropiques*).

A key methodological principle of CLS is to open jurisprudence up to other disciplines and to refuse to accept that jurisprudence is merely a philosophical discussion of the idea of law; rather law is to be approached from a variety of perspectives and through the lenses of many disciplines. One such discipline is anthropology.

In the 19th century Western societies sent forth anthropologists to travel the conquered lands of the 'primitives'; to observe the 'savages' of Africa, Australia, New Guinea and so forth. Two underlying themes were apparent: the first was the task of uncovering what was the natural way of doing things, to strip bare the fundamental structures of human life. But if that could not be shown, a second mandate came into force; tell us stories of our superiority, of our natural power, of our right to dominate. And the anthropologists went forth and tried to find the natural laws of human order, but had difficulty; at least many of them obliged with images of the 'natural' inferiority of the other.

By the mid-20th century, however, the messages anthropologists delivered had upset the settled canons. Among the concepts the noted French anthropologist Lévi-Strauss bequeathed to our understanding of modernity was the idea of lost innocence; instead of an anthropology which celebrated the progressive glorious advancement of man, Lévi-Strauss spoke of deep structures and evolving forms which shaped and imprisoned us. Were we right to celebrate the achievements of modernity? The advances of modernity were achieved at the cost of exploiting others in their 'primitive' state and, realising the cost of modernity, we lose our innocence, our confidence as 'moderns' in progress.[1] Lévi-Strauss appears to take upon himself the burden of

---

1 Many commentators define post-modernism as a loss of confidence in the meta-narratives of progress which constitute modernity. For Harry Redner the essential faith of the modern person is in the idea of progress. Progress, like God for the pre-modern, is a concept that cannot be denied or seriously questioned. But in the 1980s scholars began telling other stories which undercut our confidence. Reflexively, we now understand that 'we Europeans launched ourselves on an unparalleled drive for power, which we called progress ... All other societies and cultures were crushed or exterminated or forced to engage with us in our race of progress; eventually perhaps, some of them will even outdistance us. All the natural and human resources were put at our disposal to be transformed in accordance with our sovereign will. This willed thrust of power was justified in the name of an unlimited future of man' (Redner, 1982: 13). In Weberian fashion Redner relates how the loss of innocence is occasioned. And how the acceptance of progress is diminished as we comprehend we become powerless to control the very forces that were meant to make us powerful. Modernity was a 'way of systematically dominating, controlling and disposing of things, which in the first place was directed against nature but which [humans] now find is also turning on themselves and depriving them of their human nature ... They can make themselves irrelevant, if not redundant, to their own schemes and so dispose of themselves' (*ibid*: 5).

recounting the guilt which lost innocence should occasion. Writing, for Lévi-Strauss, is an instrument of oppression, a means of colonising the primitive mind – but there is little escape, for once in place the new regime of truth and meaning enslaves also the user of the language. For Lévi-Strauss we can only remember our lost 'authenticity'. Similarly with CLS: the charge is simple, in giving us the imagery of jurisprudence as being the application of abstract reason and science, of social order being constructed through law and the power of rational administration underpinning such legal order, mainstream modern jurisprudence – the institutional imagination of foundations, universalism and legislative reason – has weakened our cultural and critical imagination. Modernity was meant to usher in societies of social justice and freedom and towards that aim individuals offered up authority to the state to construct the rational legal order. But for CLS that offering is misplaced and the people ought to develop a critical orientation and assume social responsibility for their lives.

What is CLS? Critical Legal Studies is a broad label encompassing a variety of subversive enterprises to what its members view as the mainstream traditions of scholarship in jurisprudence. CLS is a post-positivist enterprise involving: (i) a critique of the 'objective' scientific method which is seen to underlie traditional scholarship with the claim that 'interpretative understanding', or *hermeneutics*, must replace positivism; how we understand science is seen as a political choice. The hermeneutic approach is linked with and underpins a radical and sometimes expressly 'left-leaning' approach to legal phenomena; (ii) a change in the way law is viewed. Traditional legal scholarship is viewed as desperately making sense of the world, of holding out law as a coherent and rational body of rules and principles, and the aim of mainstream legal scholarship is to reconstruct rationally particular legal decisions to show how they fit, or do not fit, the proper and rational development of 'law'. Conversely, CLS uses a range of techniques to bring out underlying fissures, contradictions, and tensions. Where traditional scholarship – or so CLS claims – divorces the study of law from the study of society and finds the engine for legal development in the guidance of rules, principles and discretion, CLS tells us of the inescapably political nature of life.[2] Deeply embedded in the CLS movement are the motifs of suspicion and scepticism towards any claim for the purity of law; instead we must investigate how law as a field of action maintains its hold over us and contributes to sustaining the legitimacy of the system.

ORIGINS OF THE CLS MOVEMENT

The CLS movement began with a 'conference' held in the US in 1977 as a result of a circular to Faculties in US law schools.[3] The invitation to attend mentioned only a very

---

2   Additionally, however, law appears everywhere; almost every social practice is either a direct function of the application of legal rules and principles, or heavily influenced by the fact that law has held off. For example see the discussion of Duncan Kennedy (1991: 344–5) on the 'distributive conflict between men and women'.

3   For the background of the US movement see Mark Tushnet (1991) 'Critical Legal Studies: A Political History'; and Robert Gordon (1989) 'Critical Legal Studies as a Teaching Method, Against the Background of the Intellectual Politics of Modern Legal Education in the United States'. For the UK see Peter Goodrich (1992) 'Critical Legal Studies in England: Prospective Histories'.

vague idea: a gathering of people pursuing critical approaches to the study of law and society. The circular made no attempt to define in advance what should be the concerns of the meeting but indicated that several of the writers of the circular were trying to develop approaches emphasising the ideological character of legal doctrine and its internal structures. Most commentators classify CLS as radical scepticism (its critics go further, labelling it as nihilist, or simple negative critique) and portray it as a development out of American legal realism. This is only partly true. The American legal realists were sceptical of the traditional (largely legally positivist) image of law in modern Western societies, of legal scholarship's formalism and supposed conservatism. However, realists strove to make the legal system even more efficient in its role of an instrument of social change and social development than mainstream liberal political thought advocated. Realists were not sceptical of the outside or external knowledges they thought ought to complement traditional legal scholarship and influence legal development. The law and society movement which sought to subject legal practices, the operationality of legal enactments, and to observe *living law* or *law in action*, as opposed to law in the books, was broadly moderately socially reformist or liberal democratic in political orientation. And those who were turning to an interpretative methodology to replace positivism were not especially radical in their politics; Dworkin's (1977, 1982, 1986) depiction of the necessary narrative construction of political values underlying modern legal development was essentially liberalist. CLS adherents, conversely, were sceptical about the very basis of modern liberalism and saw much of legal practice as facilitating the forms of political domination which constituted the unequal and unjust social arrangements CLS scholars believe modern social arrangements to be. Legal scholarship justified modern social arrangements through investing them with some rational or natural justification instead of stating that they were simply the result of complex processes of political power.[4]

THE IMPORTANCE OF A MOOD OF SCEPTICISM AND FRUSTRATION WITH MAINSTREAM LEGAL EDUCATION

CLS appears wrapped up in some nostalgia for lost innocence, a memory of some lost presence which has been made problematic by the particular alienating conditions of modern social existence. This is the underlying current of Robert Gordon's (1982;

---

4   Hunt (in an article dating from the late 1980s, reproduced in 1993: 180) lays out the difference:

    'The realist disenchantment with legal formalism was pragmatic; orthodoxy did not provide satisfactory answers for the constituency that the realist sought to represent. Formalism provided no satisfactory guidance for legal practitioners concerned with improving the efficiency of their concern to predict the outcome of litigation nor an adequate framework for the policy concerns of legislators. Critical legal scholars are not preoccupied by such pragmatic preoccupations; they do not seek to articulate the concerns of legal practitioners or legislators or, in general, of 'insiders' within the legal process. Critical scholars are motivated by a much broader political objective within which it is "the law" itself that is "the problem"; law is not conceived as being capable of resolving the problems that it apparently addresses. Rather law is seen as a significant constituent in the complex set of processes that reproduces the experience and reality of human subordination and domination; thus the wider concern with the conditions and possibility of human emancipation forms the extended political perspective of the movement.'

revised 1990) description of the *mood of disillusionment* with legal studies that many academic and students felt in the late 60s, the 70s and the 80s and which provided fertile ground for the CLS movement to flourish. Gordon notes, in particular, dissatisfaction with approaches to teaching and studying law and legal practice which emphasised:

(i) the traditional or formalist picture of legal development which the American legal realists had argued against since the 1920s. This was an image of legal development occurring through doctrinal analysis – the argument of the legal realist had been that the mainstream view presupposed an image of the law as a complete and autonomous system of logically consistent rules, concepts and principles. To apply the law was no great task; it simply referred to the inescapable unfolding of implications which were inherent in the legal material presented. The judge's techniques were socially neutral and his/her private views were irrelevant. Judging was a matter of discovery; organising the discovery of the facts and declaring the law. Thus the actual final decision was presupposed as a matter of necessity rather than choice. American legal realists argued that the notion of legally-led development ought to be replaced with a model of development led by understanding socially desirable consequences. To the realists legal certainty was not only impossible to attain, it was actually undesirable. Modern society was in a state of flux; it needed understandings to guide, and institutions that accommodated, rapid social change. Both the traditional approach and the arguments of realists presupposed liberal consensus; reasonable people could agree upon the terms of discussion and a reasonably skilled lawyer could argue doctrinal issues out in an impassive, professional manner. The realists' demand for the addition of sociological and other perspectives was to usher in a more complex 'sociological jurisprudence' depicting the reality of social situations and the social interests to be served did not escape from the broad liberal framework.[5] However, in the context of the late 1960s and 70s America, a cultural atmosphere resonant with black/white, feminist, gay liberation, and generational conflict, in addition to increasing political polarisation, civil rights and anti-Vietnam war demonstrations, with numerous corruption scandals, such a view of liberal consensus appeared misguided;[6]

(ii) the view of lawyers playing their part in a policy science and operating with a social reform attitude to social change presupposed a disinterested, intelligent, governing elite that the lawyer could advise on legislation and policy. This had most clearly been the aim of Austin whose first target was to convince the ruling elites of the truth of the principle of utility and then place faith in education for the masses, but

---

5   As Horwitz (1992) puts it, realism was either a continuation of the reform agenda of pre-First World War progressivism responding to class inequalities in the name of attaining a real liberal society, or, as in the case of Karl Llewellyn, a new 'methodology' or technology of legality.

6   The critique (for example, Kennedy, 1976) would be even more severe of the European picture – exemplified by HLA Hart – of the legal system as dominated by rules (as opposed to standards), by individualist (as opposed to altruist) definitions of legal rights, and deductive (as opposed to policy-orientated) reasoning. Whilst the legal realist argument was that this picture was a misrepresentation of the reality of the legal process, CLS writers understand law as contradictory in all the areas where traditional scholarship presented it as coherent; hence an important task was to break the grip of this ideological misrepresentation.

this education consisted in large part of socialising them into the viewpoint of the governing class. To CLS scholars, Hart's work continued this bias with a view of the bulk of the population obeying out of habit and the critical reflective view being only really necessary for the legal professionals (the insiders of the system). But influences such as the Vietnam war, bilateral militarism and Watergate corruption disturbed this assumption. Instead, CLS pursue their writings not in the service of piecemeal social reform but radical politics.

As a result socially interested lecturers and students experienced:

(iii) the absence of real human concerns from the discussions in law schools. Duncan Kennedy (reproduced in Kairys, ed 1990), in a famous article entitled 'Legal education as training in hierarchy', talks of students coming to law school (in the US law school is postgraduate) thinking they will study the cutting issues of their times. Instead, much of the material is tedious, boring and refers to real, lived, social reality only through the abstract lenses of legal concepts. Real life is blood and guts, sex and vomit, hope and depression, oppression and profit – all outside the materials discussed in law schools.

(iv) when progressive students went out to practise they hoped to achieve real change. Arguing that they would make modern liberalism live up to its promises of individual rights, equality, independence of legality and social freedom, they soon realised that what looked like victories were often very ambiguous in their outcomes. As Gordon puts it:

Hard-won struggles to achieve new legal rights for the oppressed began to look like ambiguous victories. The official legal establishment had been compelled to recognise claims on its utopian promises. But these real gains may have deepened the legitimacy of the system as a whole; the labour movement secured the vitally important legal rights to organise and strike, at the cost of fitting into a framework of legal regulation that certified the legitimacy of management's making most of the important decisions about conditions of work (1982 :286).

Therefore, theoretical attention shifted to trying to understand how law served to legitimate the existing social order. One obvious target was legal theory; since

(v) the professional concern of prospective lawyers demanded a jurisprudence which fitted them for the demands of professional legal practice. Thus, much of legal theory, whether taught in a specialised course called legal theory or jurisprudence or as inherent part of core courses, appeared to work to justify the present arrangements. Traditional legal scholarship appeared to create an image of the present state of affairs and the legal system which buttressed and constituted the society as a functionally effective and progressive whole. CLS adherents cannot share this view.

THE PROBLEMATISING OF SOCIAL PROGRESS AND THE HUMANISING OF JURISPRUDENCE

The various problematics of CLS – which come to light when we escape positivism for interpretation or hermeneutics and critically interrogate the social phenomena of law – can actually be read as a major problematic of social progress and the constitutive role of law in building a thoroughly modern social order.[7] While this is the meta-problematic, various problematics running through CLS are those of

(i)   the person;

(ii) the text;

(iii) the liberal ascription of rights; and

(iv) the meaning of law's claims and effects (ideology and practice).

These problematics are intertwined; reflections on method implicate reflections on the social vision, the methodology of seeing, articulating and criticising social reality; a person's action is thus (hopefully) less under the grip of ideological mystification.

In part, CLS is an expression of the angst – the self-doubting – of legal academics at the end of the period of modernity. How to conceive of the relationship of law and person? To understand the meaning of contemporary legal subjectivity, it seems to the adherents of CLS that we must first understand and locate the (late-)modern person (conscious of his/her gender and race). Take the opening pages of the black, feminist law professor, Patricia J Williams (1991) *The Alchemy of Race and Rights: Diary of a Law Professor:*

> Since subject position is everything in my analysis of the law, you deserve to know that it's a bad morning. I am very depressed. It always takes a while to sort out what's wrong, but it usually starts with some kind of perfectly irrational thought such as: I hate being a lawyer. This particular morning I'm sitting up in bed reading about redhibitory vices. A

---

7   Contrast Dworkin: Dworkin asks us to consider what mood about law and legal development we would like to share – optimism or pessimism. He asks us to keep faith with optimism – to read the law as a progressive force and strive for an even better future. Dworkin is clear that legal theory should justify law and guide the system onwards:

> 'If a theory of law is to provide a basis for judicial duty, then the principles it sets out must try to justify the settled rules by identifying the political or moral concerns and traditions of the community which, in the opinion of the lawyer whose theory it is, do in fact support the rules'. (*Taking Rights Seriously:* 67)

For Dworkin, although 'this process of justification must carry the lawyer very deep into legal and political theory', we are only concerned with the best constructive reading of liberalism in order to carry on the tasks of liberalism. Dworkin asserts a narrative of law and legal practice to strengthen and critically reform legal liberalism from within, while, for Dworkin, CLS simply asserts a different narrative of legal practice. One which emphasises a flawed and contradictory account – of life as chaos. But for Dworkin such 'external scepticism' is of little aid, instead he will consider only 'internal scepticism'. Accounts which point out differing conceptions of what the law is. At stake is where one stands on the project of modernity and the development of liberalism. Does one read the history of social and legal/political development over the last 200 years as mostly progressive, as this would bring a greatly improved and 'better' place than before? Or does one see exploitation, misery, alienation, unfulfilled dreams, broken promises, a sham of liberal legality? CLS adherents, for example Roberto Unger, who is closely involved with trade union and human rights movements in his native Brazil, point out the downside of modernity and wish to include these images in the scope of items we consider as law and legal effects.

redhibitory vice is a defect in merchandise which, if existing at the time of purchase, gives rise to a claim allowing the buyer to return the thing and get back part or all of the purchase price. The case I'm reading is an 1835 decision from Louisiana, involving the redhibitory vice of craziness:

> The plaintiff alleged that he purchased of the defendant a slave named Kate, for which he paid $500, and two or three days after it was discovered the slave was crazy, and ran away, and that the vices were known to the defendant ... It was contended [by the seller] that Kate was not crazy but only stupid, and stupidity is not madness; but on the contrary, an apparent defect, against which the defendant did not warrant ... The code had declared that a sale may be avoided on account of any vice or defect, which renders the thing either absolutely useless, or its use so inconvenient and imperfect, that it must be supposed the buyer would not have been purchased with a knowledge of the vice. We are satisfied that the slave is question was wholly, and perhaps worse than, useless.

As I said, this is the sort of morning when I hate being a lawyer, a teacher, and just about everything else in my life. It's all I can do to feed the cats. I let my hair stream wildly and the eyes roll back in my head.

So you should know that this is one of those mornings when I refuse to compose myself properly; you should know you are dealing with someone who is writing this in an old terry bathrobe with little fringes of blue and white tassels dangling from the hem, trying to decide if she is stupid or crazy ...

Continuing this interaction of personal narrative and commentary on social reality Williams relates images from the television she turns on for inspiration; images which inform her that 'conditions are bad, very bad, all over the world ...' Williams seeks to upset the feeling that a major American economist John Kenneth Galbraith (1992) has called the 'culture of contentment', whereby those who are in the superclass, mostly those in work who share in the increase in prosperity of the economy, close their eyes to the suffering of the exploited and construct intellectual systems to avoid feeling socially responsible.

Her attack is also on what CLS call *reification*. What sort of process is it when courts can talk of a person only in the language of 'redhibitory' vices? How does this discussion of a woman, Kate, boil down to whether or not the buyer can get his money back – which in turn depends on whether the court finds her stupid or crazy? Williams plays on this, asking us to ponder if Williams herself is either stupid or crazy for getting upset.

Williams, and CLS writers generally, wish us to get concerned – to break down the comfortable structures of our thoughts. To see the poverty, irrationality, corruption, violence, closeness of death, and simply the weirdness of the world – their claim is that traditional legal scholarship is a barrier to such thoughts. Traditional legal scholarship implicitly tells us that everything is as it should be and that our role as lawyers, or thinkers about law, is assured. The law is the tool of modernity and modernity is sane, rational, functional, efficient (albeit sometimes writers of the right also claim current inefficiencies which more property rights, the rule of law and the free market would remedy) – CLS writings point out the underbelly of modernity's claims to universality, reason and coherence.

Another point: CLS writers, such as Williams, Kennedy, or Unger, move quickly from social analysis to individual concerns. This is not simply to make abstract propositions more accessible, nor to position the subject, but as Unger puts it:

> Every truth about people can be seen twice: as a truth about societies and their history and as a truth about the individual and his passions. (1987: 199)

Unger does not rely upon an underlying image of humanity corresponding to some essential human nature; for Unger one reason for the contradictions in the social order (which CLS brings out) is that they are an expression of 'the conflicting demands of self-assertion themselves'. While Unger believes that we have to self-consciously adopt a politics in our legality – and his is the politics of a super-liberal community (a somewhat contradictory position in usual terms) – his concept of 'community' is a regulative idea, rather than the belief in some actual (soon-to-be) existing state of affairs.

VALID TACTICS FOR CLS INCLUDE THE PERSONIFICATION OF THE REASON (OR RATIONALITY) OF THE TEXT, AND THE CREATION OF INSTABILITY AND AMBIGUITY IN THE TEXT

CLS writing is often complicated and difficult to read. Since they believe that traditional legal scholarship strives to keep the sadness, violence, and vomit of the real world at bay, they strive to break down the traditional way of writing and reading legal scholarship. The themes they introduce are also unconventional – feelings, personal identity, tragedy, the hidden violence of contemporary legal scholarship, the essential connectedness of things in the world. CLS writers disrupt the comfortable images of scientific value-freedom and objectivity of positivism – back come literary forms, a concern with rhetoric, an identification of the law as a text and so open to the same types of tactics that literary critics use to analyse the works of 'novelists'.[8] CLS writers strive to break clear of the narrow confines of modern scholarship to revitalise the interconnection of life, images of law and the concept of justice:

> That life is complicated is a fact of great analytic importance. Law too often seeks to avoid this truth by making up its own breed of narrower, simpler, but hypnotically powerful rhetorical truths. Acknowledging, challenging, playing with these as rhetorical gestures is, it seems to me, necessary for any conception of justice. Such acknowledgment complicates the supposed purity of gender, race, voice, boundary; it allows us to

---

8   Williams (1991: 6) on describing her book: 'It will be a book about the jurisprudence of rights. I will attempt to apply so-called critical thought to legal studies. I believe that critical theory has valuable insights to contribute to debates about the ethics of law and the meaning of rights; yet many of those insights have been buried in relatively arcane vocabulary and abstraction. My book will concern itself with the interplay of commercial and constitutional protection and will be organised around discussion of three basic jurisprudential forces: autonomy, community, and order. My chapters will address such issues as surrogate motherhood and ownership; neighbourhood and homelessness; racially motivated violence and disownedness. I will try to write, moreover, in a way that bridges the traditional gap between theory and praxis. It is not my goal merely to simplify; I hope that the result will be a text that is multilayered – that encompasses the straightforwardness of real life and reveals complexity of meaning.'

acknowledge the utility of such categorisations for certain purposes and the necessity of their breakdown on other occasions. It complicates definition in its shift, in its expansion and contraction according to circumstance, in its room for the possibility of creatively mated taxonomies and their wildly unpredictable offspring (Williams, 1991: 10).

Williams' desire to break free of what she perceives as the constraints of traditional writings verges on literary licence. As if expecting such a charge, Williams elucidates:

> I think that one of the most important results of reconceptualising from 'objective' truth to rhetorical event will be a more nuanced sense of legal and social responsibility. This will be so because much of what is spoken in so-called objective, unmediated voices is in fact mired in hidden subjectivities and unexamined claims that make property of other beyond the self, all the while denying connections (*ibid*: 11).

ESSENTIAL TARGETS FOR CLS

Liberalism is one target, so too is Marxism. All systems of thought that make the world seem unproblematic, that render some necessary connection between law and social formations are attacked. But there are difficulties with CLS – their criticisms sometimes appear so sweeping, so all-encompassing that they neglect the struggle to create modernity, the core of principles which, albeit very badly, serve to make liberalism a philosophy of individual creativity and freedom. The writing is often a message for the converted; which fails to reach out to the others in power and to make alliances for progressive praxis (sometimes the CLS writer is afraid of being co-opted by the system – but this falls into the romanticism of wishing some revolutionary situation).

Most CLS writings are expressly an assault on liberal legislation which is viewed as making several wrong assumptions.

(i) The assumption of law's neutrality. But, for CLS, this separation of law from politics is theoretically untrue and mystifies the populace. Liberalism is seen to mystify, in that it assumes that law can somehow be routinely invoked by individuals against the state even though law was created by the state.

(ii) The assumption that legal reasoning is somehow an unproblematic matter. CLS substitutes a criticism of the whole idea of a politically neutral 'legal logic' ie that there can be legal analysis that is not in some way politically charged or linked to political agendas.

(iii) The assumption that laws are positive data of social life, ie that they have fixed objective meanings which can't really be challenged; that their validity and significance are settled by objective unchallengeable methods. That laws and the legal system have some form of natural or functional relationship to underlying objectively knowable conditions of social existence (cf Austin and Hart's implicit functionalism, not to mention Hart's minimum conditions of natural law). By contrast CLS writers use a more post-modern form of writing which attempts to free legal analysis from the idea of neutral technicality and show that it is a political instrument. Hence lawyers need to make choices as to how they will use this instrument: what policies and politicians will they serve? Moreover, CLS writers, in particular Unger, have a radically contingent view of the foundations of social life. Contemporary society is no naturally evolving formation but 'frozen politics'.

(iv) the radical contingency and openness of modernity and hence the meaning of social progress. More shall be said on this when Unger is considered in outline.

LEGAL LIBERALISM IS SEEN AS REPRESENTING A SPECIFIC FORM OF POLITICS

Legal liberalism serves to preserve a status quo of social and economic inequalities. Liberal legal writings and decisions mask this inequality. Liberal legal philosophy talks of law in terms of underlining equality; especially equality before the law as in the notion of the rule of law. Contemporary legal scholars, such as Ronald Dworkin, are myth-makers in that they construct narratives of coherence and reason when law is actually political and contradictory.

CLS demand the substitution of legal liberalism with a *politics of transformation*. This outlook is dedicated to revealing the possibility of change in all forms of social relationships and institutional structures. Radical scholars are to act through legal practices and use deconstructive and debunking arguments to promote liberating change. By showing the falseness of any claims to social inevitability or absolutionism CLS writers hope to open up possibilities hidden by dominant existing ideas.

Most CLS writers distance themselves from Marxism and there is no attempt made to reach a settled view about what sort of legal structure or what sort of society CLS seeks. This refusal to specify the ultimate aim is dictated by the theoretical outlook CLS adopts. Specifically:

(i) An attack on all claims that there are some kinds of natural laws of history, uncontrollable by human beings. This is a rejection of the Marxist theory of historical materialism. Marxism is thus viewed as just another ideology, in that it claimed absolute truths for its picture of inevitable historical processes.

(ii) Equally this amounts to resistance to the idea that there are social forces or economic forces that control life in some irresistible or objective way. Rather social life is viewed as being continually created by people's individual choices and decisions as they coexist. So CLS demonstrates a lack of interest in social science which treats society and social phenomena as objects to be studied.

(iii) A distrust of all theories, and ideas that make the social world seem natural and inevitable.

(iv) The rejection of the idea of moral absolutes. Hence, we cannot lay down in advance what a perfect society or perfect law would be like. Unger on the radical project: 'There are no unique or predetermined practical forms it must assume in the course of its advance'. There is no point in trying to specify the forms of utopia or otherwise. The idea is only to resist all repressive claims that law and society cannot fundamentally be criticised; that their nature is settled and unchangeable: that it is impossible to open spaces for critiques and changes.

The approach to law reflects the overall approach to the social. Gordon speaks of CLS generally placing an interpretative or anti-positivist view of law in society. As Gordon puts it:

> one does not look only at the undeniably numerous specific ways in which the legal system functions to screw poor people ... but rather at all the ways in which the system seems at first glance basically uncontroversial, neutral, acceptable ...

What is law? The law is one among many systems of meaning that people construct in order to deal with necessary relationships with other people. But:

> Law, like religion and television images, is one of these clusters of belief – and it ties in with a lot of other non-legal but similar clusters – that convince people that all of the many hierarchical relations in which they live and work are natural and necessary (1982: 286–7).

Thus law is hegemonic. This is one of the two key ideas which are often used in CLS writings and which derive from the Marxist tradition; it stresses that domination in modern capitalist society is achieved mainly not through force or repression but through the dominance of belief systems shared by the ruling and subordinate classes alike. Ideas favourable to ruling classes come to be accepted by subordinate classes. In particular hegemony stresses that:

> ... the most effective form of domination takes place when both the dominant and dominated classes believe that the existing order, with perhaps some marginal changes, is satisfactory, or at least represents the most that anyone could expect, because things pretty much have to be the way they are (ibid: 286).

CLS adherents are very much concerned with how hegemony is constructed and maintained and in particular with the role that legal ideas have in doing this. They strive to *deconstruct the abstract stability of legal concepts*: legal concepts can only be seen in view of the relations of conflict and choice which underlay them.[9]

CLS claim that law is important ideologically. If social life is not an object, not something presented to us but something that is constructed by individuals, what is it that constrains people always to keep recreating it in the same way? It is that the hegemony of ideas prevent most people seeing possibilities beyond what has existed previously or is presented as familiar? Law contributes massively to the hegemony of ideas. Law provides a reservoir of ideas constituting the notion of private property, freedom of contract, authority and legitimate coercion, individual responsibility etc. Above all it creates the idea of rights which subsequently builds notional fences around individuals and sees the natural relation with others as one of confrontation and defence.

---

9 An important area for attack is the field of contract doctrine. In Britain, A Thompson, 'The Law of Contract' (in I Grigg-Spall and P Ireland eds 1992: 69–76) criticises the way in which contract law is usually taught in which 'questions of social and distributive justice, which relates to consequences and which threaten the orderly worlds and principles, are simply outlawed from the toytown world of the contract class ...' What is the effect? 'The law of contract creates a master-image of the well-ordered society; a society in which law appears as the 'haven of justice', divorced from the dirtiness of business, politics, power and the conflict of interests and values; a society which rises above the uncertainties and incoherences of political and moral argument ... it makes the contingent fact of capitalism, the appearance of social relations as market-exchange relations, look like the necessary facts of life ...' Contract law renders the social reality of real life as outside the reasoned discussion of the classroom.

Rights are weapons and the law makes sure that people feel they are well armed against each other.

But this is to fall into the trap of reification, or the process whereby ideas are treated almost as if they were things, objects in themselves. Although law is actually developed by battles over particular ideas and arrangements, over the manipulation of people, it is presented as if the doctrine were a fixed reality. Say there is an argument between A and B which is brought to trial. The court decides that the law favours A against B. We say that A has rights against B and B is under a duty to A. The right is now a possession of A. It has become a thing.

So we think of legal ideas as if they were things: 'property' is considered a thing; so is 'ownership'; a 'contract'; a 'tort'. These things populate our world of ideas. They seem solid and inevitable. They make the world seem unchangeable and remove the reality of human interaction,[10] but is it?

To combat hegemony and reification the CLS movement aims:

(i) to displace the idea that the social world is an objectively knowable scene of natural foundations by the political reality of interpretation. There is no one natural or objectively reasonable way of perceiving of the world; hence the interpretative or hermeneutic approach is intrinsically political. From this it follows that the social world is largely created by humans and, therefore, can be changed by humans if they change their ways of perceiving of it and use the power that is – in 'reality' – theirs. Legal change is thereby not to be a passive reflection of the truths of the human condition, but a weapon of progressive political struggle.[11] Against the determinacy of social conditions CLS writers such as Gordon (1982: 290) espouse social indeterminacy:

Things seem to change in history when people break out of their accustomed ways of responding to domination, by acting as if the constraints on their improving their lives were not real and that they could change things, and sometimes they can, though not always in the way they had hoped or intended ...

Against Gordon, however, the fact that the social world is created by people does not imply that it can be easily changed by people. The indeterminacy of the CLS movement is ambivalent; it is as if the very call to action is conducted in acknowledgment of the difficulty in combating the power and multiplicity of the social forces at work in late modernity. Moreover, we can ask: what will replace the reification of ideas? There is a subtle path to tread between plasticity and

---

10 Consider again the opening to Patricia Williams's book: how did Kate, an innocent black woman, come to be bought and sold, reduced to a discussion about the warranty of her commodification in terms of stupidity or craziness, talked of as the subject of a 'redhibitory vice'?

11 To continue quoting from Gordon (1982: 290) 'If we start to look at the world this way – no longer as some determined set of "economic conditions" or "social forces" that are pushing us around but rather as in the process of continual creation by human beings, who are continuously reproducing the world they know because they (falsely) believe they have no choice – we will obviously bring a very different approach to the debate over whether legal change can ever effect real ("social and economic") change, or whether law is wholly dependent on the real, "hard", world of production.'

incoherence, between interpretative perspectivism and nihilism; after all, the authority Hobbes imposes on the social order – an authority not desired by the CLS movement – arose partly because of the multiplicity of discourse as the coherence of the medieval synthesis was broken. However, this process of political interpretation is often decidedly critical or undercutting, openly deconstructive and playfully trashing towards legal texts and mainstream jurisprudential writings (see, for example Kelman, 1984). The other aims are:

(ii) to attack the reification of legal ideas. To show that these are just ideas and the result of particular arguments and conflicts, which are ultimately political arguments about how we should live. Hence the legal world is not a neutral, inevitable framework of regulation, but a political arena (and one in which, for example, the semiotic construction of legal arguments is of equal importance to the construction of facts and rules, see Duncan Kennedy, 1989, 'A Semiotics of Legal Argument').

(iii) to attack the hegemony of legal liberalism, particularly by showing the internal contradictions in legal ideas. If legal ideas are contradictory and riven by conflict then we can see their domination as a matter of choice, or imposition, rather than naturalness.[12] A good example is Duncan Kennedy's early essay on contract, 'Form and Substance in Private Law Adjudication'. Kennedy highlights the continual tension between form, 'for example the formal hallmarks of a valid contract – consideration, intention to create legal relation, offer/acceptance etc', and substance (or unreasonableness of terms, unconscionability, unequal bargaining power and public policy). He also refers to the tension between rule and principles or between strict law and justice or equity.

While the law aims for logic, precision etc in reasoning, it continually adopts pragmatic solutions in reality. Experience overrides any kind of rigorous legal logic. In the reality of contract law substance and formality contradict; for instance, the law appears to require the substance of consideration for a meaningful exchange to take place, but this consideration can be reduced to a peppercorn – something purely formal or nominal. Again substance demands that there must be an intention of both parties to agree. But there is an objective test of common intention – namely, would reasonable parties have understood the terms: thus we can see that the requirement of substance actually becomes merely formal. Such contradictions recur throughout law, and legal practice can be transformed (or so it is hoped) by our identification of them. Are these contradictions something that we can remove with a better science of law? Or are they irremovable? Kennedy suggests the latter, since the contradictions in law's reality reflect fundamental contradictions in the human condition in modernity. Specifically, liberal modernity creates a tension between concrete individualism under the idea of an abstract and certain rule of law and our communal feelings of empathy and altruism. The judge is pulled in opposing directions by these two contradictory desires:

---

12 Kelman's summary in *A Guide to Critical Legal Studies* (1987: 3) is instructive. He charges mainstream liberal legal thought with presenting an image of coherence and doctrinal logic when the reality is underlying contradiction and the hiding of contradiction. Legal thought is actually 'simultaneously beset by internal contradiction (not by "competing concerns" artfully balanced until a wise equilibrium is reached, but by irreducible, irremediable, irresolvable conflict) and by systematic repression of the presence of those contradictions.'

Altruism denies the judge the right to make rules without looking over his shoulder at the results. Altruism also denies that the only alternative to the passive stance is the claim of total discretion as creator of the legal universe. It asserts that we can gain an understanding of the values people have woven into their particular relationships, and of the moral tendency of their acts. These sometimes permit the judge to reach a decision, after the fact, on the basis of all the circumstances, as a person-in-society rather than as an individual (1976: 1773).

For CLS the law is a field of action, and how we reach legal decisions is a product of our 'legal consciousness' rather than our being determined by the material. Kennedy (1986) asks us to imagine what a hypothetical judge – a rather specific judge in that he is a liberal, activist judge committed to a role as one who uses the law to pursue social justice – experiences when he is faced with an individual case where he perceives the existence of a legal rule which is at odds with how he wishes the case to come out.

Faced with the demand to grant an injunction to stop picketing, our judge prefers to come out in favour of the worker, but how can he escape the apparent binding force of the 'law'? The law is only binding in the positivist view (Kennedy does not consider Dworkin's position in this paper). In the radical interpretative perspective we must consider purpose and role. Legal reasoning is a kind of work with a purpose – here the purpose is to make the case come out the way my sense of justice tells me it ought to, in spite of what appears at first sight like the existence or opposition of the law. But the legal materials do not bind – the constraint a medium imposes is relative to your chosen project or your choice of what you wish to make. There is no inevitable determination of the outcome in advance by the legal materials themselves. The chosen project is of course constrained by the material provided, but the contrast is not between some radically free, transcendental subject (the existentialist judge) who could do anything, or a robot conditioned by the law, rather it is a kind of work aiming at a purpose and working with particular materials.

DUNCAN KENNEDY AND THE IDEA OF THE FUNDAMENTAL CONTRADICTION

The liberal effort in law is to produce clear rules in all cases despite the contradiction of form and substance and between rule and principle – why? According to Kennedy's analysis in a 1976 article entitled 'Form and Substance in Private Adjudication', there is a set of contradictions at the heart of liberalism. Kennedy's (1979) article on 'The Structure of Blackstone's Commentaries', asks what are the social tensions, conflicts, and dichotomies which lie behind them.[13] With this knowledge, what then is the role of Blackstone's work? The basic tension is that between community and autonomy.

---

13   As Kelman (1987) summaries Kennedy's project in that analysis:

'Expanding on the realist insight that legal categorisation creates emphases that assume an appearance of "solidity, reality and inherent value," Kennedy anatomises the ways in which the commentaries legitimated existing social practices in Blackstone's England through the creation of artificial categories that gradually assumed an appearance of necessity. The structural analysis of the commentaries is, in effect, an indirect enquiry into the ways in which the boundaries and groupings of modern legal thought contribute to stabilisation of an existing social order.'

> Most participants in American legal culture believe that the goal of individual freedom is at the same time dependent on and incompatible with the communal coercive action that is necessary to achieve it. Others (family, friends, bureaucrats, the state) are necessary if we are to become persons at all ... But at the same time [that] it forms and protects us, the universe of others ... threatens us with annihilation ... Numberless conformities, large and small abandonments of self to others, are the price of what freedom we experience in society (1979: 211–2).

The contradiction is such that individual freedom depends on collective coercion. We need others at the same time as we define our freedom in opposition to them. For Kennedy:

> The fundamental contradiction – that relations with others are both necessary to and incompatible with freedom – is not only intense. It is also pervasive ... it is an aspect of our experience of every form of social life ... there are simply no legal issues that do not involve directly the problem of the legitimate content of collective coercion, since there is by definition no legal problem until someone has at least imagined that he might invoke the force of the state (*ibid*: 213).

In this article Kennedy claims that our awareness of the fundamental contradiction is not an inevitable aspect of human existence, rather it is the end point of a long process of historical change. *Rights* are the mechanism by which liberalism hides the contradiction. Rights are assertions of freedom in abstraction from social conditions without actually determining the nature of that freedom.[14]

Where does this lead? It is not clear! Ambiguity results: is the fundamental contradiction (i) a feature only of liberalism and thus will disappear when liberalism is overcome, or (ii) is it a fundamental feature of the human condition, which liberalism merely highlights?

If the first then CLS is tied to bringing out the contradictory features of liberalism in the hope of going beyond them – a traditional Marxist preoccupation; if the second, then bringing out the contradictions needs to be complemented by attempts to achieve some acceptable compromise (or social justice) while realising that we cannot overcome the contradiction. Certainly Kennedy's theme is that we need to re-emphasise the communal basis of freedom – liberty is a social rather than an individual matter. Rights discourse disguises the social conditions that need to be considered in defining areas of freedom and constraints in relations between people. For CLS rights divide people into individuals – rights downplay communitarian aspirations. They are the instruments of legal liberalism's mystification.

CONTRAST PATRICIA WILLIAMS ON RIGHTS TALK

> Another way of describing the dissonance between blacks and CLS is in terms of the degree of moral utopianism with which blacks regard rights. For blacks, the prospect of attaining full rights under law has been a fiercely motivational, almost religious, source of hope ever since arrival on these shores ... where one's experience is rooted not just in a

---

14 In general, CLS writers appear sceptical of rights (for example, Gordon, 1984) – seeing them as boundaries around us rather than humanising us, constituting us as separate individuals rather than as social beings.

sense of illegitimacy but in being illegitimate, in being raped, and in the fear of being murdered, then the black adherence to a scheme of both positive and negative rights – to the self, to the sanctity of one's own personal boundaries – makes sense (1991: 154).

While rights may divide one off, and create social distance, for many that distance is welcome. Williams recounts how the black experience is one of being too familiar, of being already known in the stereotypical imageries, while rights can create the boundaries of an abstract, but legal personhood. Rights create a person who can fit into the institutional structures which have traditionally excluded the real, human personality of the 'minority black'.

> I was raised to be acutely conscious of the likelihood that no matter what degree of professional I am, people will greet and dismiss my black femaleness as unreliable, untrustworthy, hostile, angry, powerless, irrational, and probably destitute. Futility and despair are very real parts of my response. So it helps me to clarify boundary; to show I can speak the language of [legal rights] is my way of enhancing trust of me in business affairs. As black, I have been given by this society a strong sense of myself as already too familiar, personal, subordinate to white people. I am still evolving from being treated as three-fifths of a human, a subpart of the white estate (*ibid*: 147).

From this experience, Williams's perspective on the utility and expressionism of rights is different from the mainstream CLS position. Rights are not to be downplayed but turned into a carnival of life, an aesthetics of legalism.

If CLS can claim that rights lead us away from community, then for those who have not enjoyed the fruits of modernity, for the excluded and the oppressed, being given rights is a way into being modern. Rights are both instrumental – they are instruments in gaining social power and enable an individual's or a group's life-projects to be attainable, and expressive – in enabling choice and creating a social space they express a social good, namely that kind of social life which allows individuals to construct life-projects and to constantly make choices. This is an institutional conception which embodies a richer notion of being human than one devoid of the idea of rights and the existential consequences.

REVISING THE FUNDAMENTAL CONTRADICTION: OR CAN CLS ESCAPE THE NEED TO BE RATIONAL?

In a famous dialogue with Peter Gabel (*Roll Over Beethoven*), Duncan Kennedy declared he renounced the idea of the fundamental contradiction. However, the renunciation was not meant to affect the substance of the charge – the fact of certain fundamental contradictions to social life – but amounted to recognising that they were in a sense beyond capturing in a rational and logical theory. The existential problems of the world could not be mirrored in theory. Kennedy was announcing the paradox which CLS faced in that it charged the enterprise of legal liberalism with claiming to capture the truths of the human condition in certain logical and formal axioms but CLS did this by writing terse and formal articles; hence CLS must allude to truths without claiming to produce true theories. To the critics of CLS this amounts to a retreat into silence, a renouncing of the tradition of critical engagement – but the CLS advocate would ask, in which language am I to speak? From Hobbes onwards the control of the dominant language-game has been a crucial part of the maintenance of social order and hence political domination. CLS wish to break the hold of legal language, but they must write sensibly to be heard – there is little escape from that criterion!

But there is a wider sense in pointing out the limits of sense – of course the limitations of formalism demonstrate that the whole cannot be captured axiomatically. The message is again that analysis and synthesis lie intertwined: *one cannot escape from the meta-narratives. It is necessary to have an image of the whole in order to grasp the difference between truth and theoremhood.* Perhaps this is most obvious in the work of Roberto Unger as the following discussion shall reveal.

KEEPING FAITH WITH THE META-NARRATIVES, OR WHAT DOES THE POLITICS OF TRANSFORMATION MEAN IN THE WORK OF ROBERTO UNGER?

Roberto Unger is extremely prolific. His work moves from his first application of epistemology and social theory to law in the mid 1970s (*Knowledge and Politics*, 1975), through a large-scale analysis of the development of Western law in the style of Weber (*Law in Modern Society*, 1976), to writing a manifesto of the CLS movement (*The Critical Legal Studies Movement*, 1986) to a gigantic work on social theory in the late 1980s, namely, *Politics, a work in Constructive Social Theory.*

The first influence upon Unger is the social theory of Max Weber, in particular the ideology of ideal types and the need to deal with the complex nature of modern administration. Unger begins his first jurisprudential work, *Law in Modern Society*, with an explicit recall of the narrative of emancipation; behind the development of the modern administrative state lie the concerns with liberty and the rule of law given political force by the experiencing of inequality.

> The basic issues of jurisprudential and political speculation arise from the two-fold experience of the unjustifiability of the existing rank order and of the corruption of moral agreements or traditions by the injustice of their origins. Insofar as people have this experience, they struggle to avoid or diminish enslavement to each other in the rank order and to establish the most far-reaching power, the power of government, upon a basis that overcomes the arbitrariness of ordinary social hierarchies. A major form of this struggle is the striving toward the rule of law (1976: 176).

The existential perception of social injustice that the modern person experiences in refusing to accept as natural a social order with inbuilt hierarchies, does not go away with the establishment of legal rights and the rule of law. Inequality persists, indeed the existence of social inequality provides the context for the legal order and stimulates the continual demand to transform society. Unger seems to indicate that we are doomed to experience a continual feeling of social injustice since we cannot invest the legal order (and the society constituted by it) with the status of some kind of natural order.

> Unless people regain the sense that the practices of society represent some sort of natural order instead of a set of arbitrary choices, they cannot hope to escape from the dilemma

of unjustified power. But how can this perception of immanent order be achieved in the circumstances of modern society? (1976: 240)

Unger suggests that a shared moral agreement would first have to presume some settled concept of 'a shared human nature or of the intrinsic demands of social order rather than as a product of the interests of dominant groups', and a 'universal consensus about the immanent order of social life'.

Only then would we be able to believe the pattern of distribution as a form of natural (in)equality. This would amount to a return to some form of customary law rather than the rule of law. But it would also have to be a specifically modern customary law: 'It would become less the stable normative order of a particular group than the developing moral language of mankind' (1976: 241).

We must inhabit an immanent order while we need transcendence. Unger's idea is not the movement to some platonic realm but an 'ideal of a universal community', where 'the sense of a latent or natural order in social life must be harmonised with the capacity to let the will remake social arrangements' (1976: 266). What will guide this will?

Unger refuses to espouse the cold rationality of the Weberian understanding that social inequality was the driving force behind individual work and thus economic development. For Weber we are doomed to the iron cage of the rational-legal state and its bureaucratic administration because we cannot surpass inequality. Unger seeks to return human thought back to a reconciliation with metaphysics.

> Much of social science has been built as a citadel against metaphysics and politics. Faithful to the outlook produced by the modern revolt against ancient philosophy, the classic social theorists were anxious to free themselves first from the illusions of metaphysics, then from the seeming arbitrariness of political judgments. They wanted to create a body of knowledge of society that would not be at the mercy of metaphysical speculation or political controversy, and up to a point, they succeeded.

> But now we see that to avoid its own dilemmas, social theory must once again become, in a sense, both metaphysical and political. It must take a stand on issues of human nature and human knowledge for which no 'scientific' elucidation is, or may ever be, available. And it must acknowledge that its own future is inseparable from the fate of society. The progress of theory depends upon political events. The doctrines theory embraces are ideals as well as descriptions: the choices theory embraces are ideals as well as descriptions: the choices theory must make are choices among views of what it is. These choices are neither arbitrary nor capable of logical or empirical proof. They build upon speculative conceptions of the requirements of social order and of the demands of human nature, conceptions that are informed by historical knowledge but which cannot pretend to follow necessarily from it.

Unger faces the same problematic as Kelsen but the methodological method and approach to social theory is the exact opposite. We cannot succeed in producing a pure theory, thus we must be clear as to the politics of our theoretical positions; we must combine the various aspects to our human longings in the name of a progressive and uplifting intellectual concern.

The richness of immediate concerns combines with the longing for universality in thought to give the mind an enthusiasm that prompts it to boldness, opens it up to the unusual and to the commonplace, and awakens it to the unity of things.

The great social theorists had this experience when they went from the speculative generalities of their predecessors to the narrower conjectures of a social science. Now it is for us to imitate our teachers by travelling in the opposite direction, back along the road by which they came (1976: 268).

By pursuing the intellectual rigour of 'narrower conjectures' rather than 'speculative generalities' we obey Popper's criterion of doing proper science (opening our theories, our conjectures, up to testing and refutation) but we are limited to a piecemeal social engineering which always overwhelms our hopes and energies. Instead we must engage in 'total criticism', the first step of which is a fundamental criticism of liberalism[15] and the binary opposition which comprise liberal society (for example, public|private, fact|value, reason|desire) in the task of transcending the liberalism which characterised advanced modernity. But while we have a vocation – the vocation of transformation – we have no natural law, nor can we be certain of God's grace.[16]

In the 1980s Unger appeared to change from wishing to go beyond modernity to espousing a radical political jurisprudence of modernism. Now it is the legacy of Nietzsche, in particular nihilism, which must be confronted. We must face and overcome nihilism,[17] by which Nietzsche meant we must destroy traditional values along with any God operating as the site of authority and understand our real position: *ultimately the fate of society lies in human willing, since the grounding of society is human willing.* Thus law as the mechanism for constituting social arrangements and jurisprudence – as the institutional imagination for that order – must create a social order and invest it with an institutional self-consciousness when all natural or transcendental justifications (and sanctions for human actions) have been abandoned. How can we take our bearings? How can the post-modern challenge be countered? Unger deliberately returns to the meta-narrative form of writing. In his introductory work to the major project of the late 1980s (*Social Theory: Its Situation and Its Task*) Unger begins by defining the social project of modernity:

---

15 Note Unger uses the term liberalism to denote the advanced countries of the West; his critique of liberalism is therefore nothing short of a critique of modernity. He is no Marxist.

16 In exposing the 'antinomies' of modern, that is to say, liberal thought, we seek to go beyond them. Only the regulative ideal of a universal community can achieve this allowing us the experience of 'the sense of immanent order ... brought into harmony with the capacity of criticism or transcendence', whereby 'the antagonism of the individual with the social aspect of personality', is dissolved through 'each person's recognition of the concrete individuality of his fellows'. But can this be guaranteed? Unger can only offer a cryptic prayer:

'When philosophy has gained the truth of which it is capable, it passes into politics and prayer, politics through which the world is changed, prayer through which men ask God to complete the change of the world by carrying them into His presence and giving them what, left to themselves, they would always lack ...

But our days pass, and still we do not know you fully. Why then do you remain silent? Speak, God' (Unger, 1975: 294–5).

17 Unger lays out a guiding principle in *Passion: An Essay on Personality* (1984: viii–ix): 'Thought speaks with authority about who we are and how we should live only when it puts our ideals and self-understandings through the sceptic's flame, risking nihilism for the sake of insight.'

Modern social thought was born proclaiming that society is made and imagined, that it is a human artefact rather than an expression of an underlying natural order. This insight inspired the great secular doctrines of emancipation: liberalism, socialism and communism. In one way or another, all these doctrines held out the promise of building a society in which we may be individually and collectively empowered to disengage our practical and passionate relations from rigid roles and hierarchies. If society is indeed ours to reinvent, we can carry forward the liberal and leftist aim of cleansing from our forms of practical collaboration or passionate attachment the taint of dependence and domination. We can advance the modernist goal of freeing subjective experience more fully from a pre-written and imposed script. We may even be able to draw the left-liberal and modernist goals together in a larger ambition to construct social worlds whose stability does not depend on the surrender of our society-making powers or on their confiscation by privileged elites. The practical point of the view of society as made and imagined is to discover what is realistic and what illusory in these objectives and to find guidance for their execution (1987: 1).

So, while modernity was begun with the break-out from custom, from religious and cosmological understandings of our social and individual identities, *we have not taken the transformative imagination far enough*. We have allowed a *weakened, institutionally conservative social imagination to rule us*. We have not 'taken the idea of society as artefact to the hilt'.

Unger identifies an important target as our understanding of context: in our everyday existence we cannot help but be creatures of routine. Unger here takes on board the pessimistic tradition of Weber in that he reads us as taking our routines and frameworks as somehow given, as more fixed than they actually are. Our routines exist inside frameworks. But we should not take this routine-framework distinction as fixed, as naturally given. We have to break out of the hold of rigid hierarchies and roles in our dealings with other people. The aim:

> ... is to break loose from a style of social understanding that allows us to explain ourselves and our societies only to the extent we imagine ourselves helpless puppets of the social worlds we build and inhabit or of the law-like forces that have supposedly brought these worlds into being.

Compare this to John Austin's belief that there were certain fundamental laws of political economy that we in society simply had to align our social institutions to. While for Austin we have to find the true knowledge of the natural and social world and make our legal institutions follow this, for Unger:

> History really is surprising; it does not just seem that way. And social invention, deliberate or unintended, is not just an acting out of pre-established and narrowly defined possibilities.

In our everyday lives we are misled when we believe that we are shaped and that society is structured by forces which cannot be swayed; that the contexts of life provide the natural determining junctures. But why do we persist in these beliefs? Because we are in the grip of an institutional imagination which invests our context with an illusion of fixture and structural inevitability. The present institutional structures have betrayed the hope of modernity. The project has been turned into a conservative benefit for elites. For the masses the reality is alienation, resentment and longing. Disenchantment works to the benefit of the elites since it creates apathy, and non-positive responses, such as crime, which only further strengthens the hold of the powerful imaginative forces.

Unger does not turn away from the language that modernity has relied upon. He constantly asks why certain concepts should be structured in the way that we have come to use them. For example rights. Why should rights be seen as individual things? Why not 'solidarity rights'? Market rights? Destabilisation rights?

Only a *super-liberalism* can take the transformative promise of liberalism further in radical directions. Empowered democracy with a decentralisation of powerful institutional structures, a destabilisation of institutional forms so that power flows from the foundations rather than from the top. We aim for new strategies of trust and dependence – to create a more defensible version of the communal ideal than currently available.[18]

What is the specific message for jurisprudence? Unger appears to suggest two master problematics: *the issue of contextuality*, and that of *social solidarity*. Jurisprudence must break free of the grip of restraining images of context and work for a more just form of social solidarity. How is this to be achieved?

First, the transformation of the linkage between jurisprudence and the idea of restraining context; second, the constant search for a fluidity to society and constant experimentation striving for more communitarian forms of solidarity which do not close themselves off to the otherness of each and every human person. But how can this reconciliation of community and liberality be possible? Perhaps it can never be other than a regulative ideal, certainly Unger refuses to state that some utopian society is possible. Instead, we must develop our jurisprudence into a fluid vehicle. In *Law in Modern Society* (1976) Unger linked legal thought and the creation of an image of social necessity in four ways which must be countered:

(i) Law as a system. This is the idea that Weber claimed was fundamental to the process of Western rationalisation – thus legality can be a structure which is enclosed and in which resides the answers to any legal problem. Instead of a determinant system why not accept a *principle of indeterminacy*?

(ii) Legal professionals come to understand the specific forms of legal rationality which enable them to find the answers to legal problems out of the resources of this system (thus they understand the techniques of precedent, statutory interpretation, legal argument).[19] In general CLS writers deny that there is such an autonomous and neutral mode of legal reasoning substituting a *principle of anti-formalism*.

(iii) The doctrines in the legal structure reflect a coherent view of the relations between people and the fundamental conditions and underlying nature of society. CLS

---

18 *Note*: Unger argues that the radical must escape from the utopian tone. If the radical is seen as utopian then it is all too easy for the conservative to say 'all very well in hope and theory, but I face up to the realistic and possible!' We have to imagine the not-as-yet-possible but that which is possible when we conceive it.

19 *Note* Cotterrell's (1989) argument in *The Politics of Jurisprudence* that most of normative jurisprudence reinforces this professional understanding and legal education equips individuals in the self-image and skills to enable this task to be accepted as the role of the lawyer.

advocates deny this arguing that the doctrines actually consist of competing, conflicting and contradictory views, none of which is a natural consequence of the fundamental condition of humanity: this is the *principle of contradiction*.

(iv) Legality shapes society and social development since social action comes to reflect norms generated by the legal system. Either through coercion or internalisation, individuals come to follow the legal prescriptions and thus society is steered by law. CLS gives the formal structure of law a lesser role in steering society: this is the *principle of marginality*. Rather it is the social consciousness which surrounds and provides the field of law which is important; perhaps Unger's early reliance upon Weber is instructive – legitimacy.

How does the system attain and preserve its legitimacy? The connection between the rigidity of the social system and the role of the legal system is clear in that certain key ideas prevent the transformative imagination functioning:

1   The idea that the social order is maintained by a system of beliefs which convince those in the system that it is the natural order of things;

2   The idea that the system is fixed and necessary, whereas it is transitory, arbitrary and reflects the interests of dominant classes and groups. The legal doctrines are presented as essential and rational whereas they are contingent, subjective and arbitrary;

3   Current legal thought hides the contradiction between the promise of equality and freedom and the reality of oppression and hierarchy.

WHAT CAN BE PUT IN PLACE OF THESE REJECTED IDEAS?

For Unger the thesis of empowerment, the notions of fluidity and flexibility of law, the politics of transformation ... the aim is to create a new institutional imagination in which a politics of social solidarity can develop. In this project Unger is actually not so far from the subterranean values of the legal enterprise since Hobbes; except that God, and his modern replacement, functionality, has been finally killed off. First, what is the programme of social transformation?

> The programme is neither just another variant of the mythic, anti-liberal republic nor much less some preposterous synthesis of the established democracies with their imaginary opposite. Instead it represents a super-liberalism. It pushes the liberal premises about the state and society, about freedom from dependence and governance of social relations by the will, to the point at which they merge into a larger ambition: the building of a social world less alien to a self that can always violate the generative rules of its own mental or social constructs and put other rules and other constructs in their place (*The Critical Legal Studies Movement*, 1986: 41).

This draws upon themes we have witnessed since Hobbes, and the statement that the central point to the social order is that it can be replaced is identical to the repealing procedure, to the idea that we try out law, that what is legal today can be gone tomorrow, so central to legal positivism. We have the proceduralism without now any guidance from a idea of human nature or human destiny. Having had the courage to 'risk nihilism' by 'putting our ideals and self-understandings through the sceptic's flame' (1984: ix), we have created the conditions for a social world which 'makes available the instruments of its own revision' (1986: 105).

What is our foundation? We reject any idea of a firm ontological foundation – our foundations are the recognition of contingency and our self-consciousness of their revisability. We refuse either to 'exalt a discrete value at the cost of others' (1987b: 354), or to choose 'one among several ideals of the same kind'.

Instead, the arrangements express our fundamental dialectic: that of inhabiting a context and transcending it. We are to turn context-transcendence into the great social political virtue. Unger speaks to the problems of the post-modern condition – his notion of plasticity is close to a radical version of the open society which Popper and Kelsen espouse as their vision of the just society – but no real substance can be given to the idea of super-liberalism. Thus, it appears to many to be in danger of becoming the best of liberalism plus Rousseau and Hegel, added to Nietzsche's dictum to confront scepticism.

CONCLUSION

From the vantage point of the late 1990s much of the heat has gone from the debate occasioned by the arrival of CLS. The fears of mainstream legal academics that CLS denoted an explosion of nihilism in the academy had passed by; many of their insights simply have been accommodated. As the political situation in the US turned more conservative and many sections of the population grew disillusioned with the political structures, law is now regarded as politics, at least in the 'widest conception'.[20] Has CLS contributed significantly to the standard of theoretical reflection, or the issue of the moral sensitivity of law? No neat answer, or satisfactory inventory of achievement can be offered. However:

(i) CLS appears successful in pointing out the insufficiency of a crude positivist position. But is the crude positivist position, that is to see law as a matter of determinate rules which either bind or run out leaving gaps which must be filled by discretion, actually held by anyone today? CLS, of course, goes further. CLS asks that we consider law not in terms of the liberal model of a system of positive laws as defined rules or a coherent body of rules and principles, but as a political process in which social relations are continually being negotiated, human hopes and ideas distorted and truncated. The American CLS movement emphasises that individuals need to seize opportunities to challenge established ideas and, especially, to challenge assumptions of their inevitability. This must be welcome, but is the CLS criticism of the ideology of legal liberalism apt? For:

20 Peller (1985: 1151) argues that 'the assertion that "law is politics" has ceased to threaten the legal world. This has happened not because the law side of the equation has been determinately reconstructed, but because the politics side has been impoverished'.

(ii) Legal liberalism is depicted not in terms of a moral position, either of the Hartian or Dworkin sense, but as mystification. Instead of 'integrity', cynicism, false-consciousness, inauthenticity, shallowness and cant are observed. But is this not to throw out the good with the mystification? Legality, has a morality to it; liberalism needs to be continually stated and restated in positive terms, rather than in its negative terms alone. Should not some linkages be built?

(iii) While correctly pointing to the complexity of life and the social situations that law must intervene in and partly constitute, CLS overstates the indeterminacy of law and fails to understand that law's closure may be a legitimate pragmatic stance in the face of the complexity of life.

(iv) CLS is a loose label. There are so many projects going on that it is hard to specify core positions.[21]

(v) CLS turns our attention to the hard side of late modernity. If liberalism sees law as a framework of regulations and rules embracing all citizens, CLS is concerned with how equal or unequal law actually is in its effects on different sections of society. But its concern is primarily with the way that the concepts and principles of law in themselves embody inequalities – for example, when corporations are treated like individual human persons for the purposes of making contracts but not for all purposes of criminal liability.

A concluding point on mood and hope. One way of typologising the themes presented in this chapter is to say that CLS is about closure and openness. It argues against all forms of closure of the legal, political and social universes – it argues for a radical openness of law, politics, and social formations. In this it reflects the changing social position of late-modernity (the onset of the post-modern). The contrast can be drawn with Weber. While Weber described the growing development of the bureaucratic way of life, in terms of a connection between government, a modern 'logic' of government with a special linkage with 'rationality', leading to the domination of formal rationality at the expense of humanity, CLS attempts to break the hold of this iron cage of rationality in the name of re-energised human forms of understanding. CLS advocates attempts to reintroduce forms of thought that are not so easily captured in the abstract rationality of modern legal discourse – namely, human wants, desires, passions, fears ...

We can also read CLS as a commentary on the fate of 'reason', of thinking itself in modern society. What does this mean? Take Weber's analysis again: in early modernity

---

21 This is to repeat an often heard point. In 'The Critique of Law: What is "Critical" about Critical Legal Theory?' (*Journal of Law and Society*, 14: 1987) the English writer Alan Hunt has argued that we need a far more explicit theory of CLS. Hunt sets out the kinds of tactics and aims of particular CLS works:

   –   examining internal consistency of legal doctrine and theory to show up its contradictions.

   –   identifying political and social assumptions made in legal doctrines and ideas.

   –   seeking social origin of particular legal ideas and doctrines.

   –   focusing on policies, principles and orderings of social life and political possibilities which are excluded by particular liberal theories or banished from legal doctrine.

   –   focusing on the location of power in legal practices.

'reason', ie intellectuals thinking, arguing, was a tool of freedom, of enlightenment, of sustained social criticism against the 'irrationalities' of false belief. Against the rigid social divisions and hierarchies of caste systems, feudalism, of the bowing down to religious beliefs, reason stood working for newness, for emancipation. As Kant put it, we can see the foundations of modern society in the motto that in modernity all things must stand subjected to the tribunal of reason. Thus before we accept any belief system it must be subjected to rigorous investigation; we must discard that which will not stand up and keep what is rationally accepted. We, ie individual humans, stand as the controllers of this process. But Weber points us to the trap that subsequently we must accept – ie that which appears rational is accepted simply because it is rational, but is it human? Instead of reason, of the rationally effective being our tool, being the weapon for humanity's freedom, reason becomes the new prison. Aligned with the institutions of state bureaucracy we, ie the individual subjects of modern society, lose control over reason and become the object of reason, the pawn of state bureaucracies. Instead of subject led or subject-centred reason (ie we being in charge of thinking for ourselves), individuals do not have much scope or grounds for thinking for themselves – instead they are surrounded by masses of stories, of advertisements, of images of the good, of the evil, of the beautiful, which it makes sense to join. And that which cannot be talked about in the language of rigorous reason becomes the castaway of modernity – the underbelly, the subject of games, of the pursuit of excitement, of love, of the extra.

For CLS as for Weber, the legal system is a representation of this process. Thus to break out the image of formalistic rationality of legality enables us to overthrow the iron cage of rationality, to see the human interests behind reason. In our opening quote from Unger, we see the narrative of a full self-consciousness which pervades modernity.

'Bring back humanity into reason!' is the cry. The scepticism of CLS is no nihilist project but a deeply concerned effort. At its deepest level CLS is full of rage. And hope. Hope that the human condition can be bettered – if only we learn to break free of the constraining thought processes which shackle us. But there is no utopia and there are no certainties – there is only struggle and the mystery of the human condition. And in that we are condemned to an endless struggle between our contexts, our powers, and our will to be human, jurisprudence is called upon to provide us with a self-questioning field for our 'agonism'; as the theoretical imagination of a key institutional site of political struggle and social constructivism. Ironically, while CLS scholars often sound like they want to reduce the pretensions of lawyers, they offer to law and legality – not to forget jurisprudence – the compliment of seeing in legitimacy the crucial arena of social and political struggle; one can doubt if the law is such a field and the system really needs legitimacy any more. But if we can suspect that our times are Hobbesian in that felicity is its own legitimacy, the CLS movement is counter-Hobbesian in its attempts to disrupt the strength of the dominant language-games. But we do well to remember that Hobbes constructed as he deconstructed and offered us a faith. The politics of textual deconstruction rather than rational reconstruction may seem like stripping the clothes from the emperor in the name of freedom to the committed and the initiated, but to the others it encourages a neo-Hobbesian authoritarian politics of law and order. Regulative ideals may not be enough to resist with, but there appears nothing else on offer which the fully self-conscious could accept. Thus the rage, and the lost innocence.[22] Perhaps also, the nostalgia;[23] for while CLS appears to accept that God is dead, the movement still seems to be searching for the 'will' to dispute.[24]

---

22 Unger seems fully aware of the weakness of the effectivity of the movement. Towards the end of his *The Critical Legal Studies Movement* he states:

    'Finally, there is the disparity between our intentions and the archaic social form that they assume: a joint endeavour undertaken by discontented, factious intellectuals in the high style of 19th-century bourgeois radicalism. For all who participate in such an undertaking, the disharmony between intent and presence must be a cause of rage.' (1986: 119)

23 As Peter Gabel opened his part of the *Roll Over Beethoven* dialogue with Duncan Kennedy: 'The project is to realise the unrelated relatedness that is immanent within our alienated situation' (1984: 19).

24 While at first sight this reading of CLS has stressed an image of law diametrically opposed to that of Kelsen, it is similar in that it demands that jurisprudence create a meta-grammar for the political. Whereas Kelsen's meta-grammar is of the fundamental separation of language games and the creation of a formal science of law, CLS creates a grammar of political hermeneutics. It is open to Kelsen to charge CLS with naivety and argue that law cannot be the site of redemptive politics.

CHAPTER 17

UNDERSTANDING FEMINIST JURISPRUDENCE

... God created woman. And then indeed there was an end to boredom – but also to something else! Woman was God's second blunder – 'woman is in her essence serpent, Heva' – every priest knows that: 'every evil comes into the world through woman' – every priest knows that likewise (Nietzsche, Parable 48 of *The Anti-Christ,* 1895, expressing the paradigm of misogyny).

The Queen is most anxious to enlist everyone who can speak or write to join in checking this mad, wicked folly of 'women's rights' ... It is a subject which makes the Queen so furious that she cannot contain herself. God created men and women different – then let them remain each in their own position (Queen Victoria, 1872, quoted in Kamm, 1977: 179).

I myself have never been able to find out precisely what feminism is: I only know that people call me a feminist whenever I express sentiments that differentiate me from a doormat (Rebecca West, 1988).

[Please] introduce me to a world where I don't have to miss myself (Leslie Reese, black feminist).

INTRODUCTION

Of all the cultural revolutions of the 20th century, feminism seems destined to have the greatest impact.[1] What is feminism? This is a loose category, and, although early movements which could be termed feminist can be seen as demands for emancipation, equality and liberation for women, later ideas stress the need for a social transformation of law, culture and social patterns which release women's potential. Feminist writers each have particular approaches, influenced by their own particular backgrounds, training, ideology and class.[2]

Perhaps a feminist is simply a person who is recognised by 'others' and recognises him/herself as a feminist.[3] As a working definition, however, feminism can be defined as

---

1 ' ... Feminism was, and has remained, the greatest and most decisive *social* revolution of modernity. Unlike a political revolution, a social revolution does not break out: it takes place. A social revolution is always a cultural revolution as well ... Female culture, hitherto marginalised and unacknowledged, is now on its way to articulating ... statement(s) on its own behalf, to claim its half of the traditional culture of mankind. The feminist revolution is not just a novel phenomenon of western culture, *it is a watershed in all hitherto existing cultures*' (Heller and Feher, 1988: 144-5).

2 Feminists writing from the Marxist and socialist traditions, for example, MacKinnon (1982, 1987, 1989), Mitchell and Oakley (1976), stress the interaction between the economic and political positions of women and class and focus upon the demands made of women by the social structure; Black feminists, for example, B Smith (1981) and Patricia Williams (1991), ask for a greater multi-layered analysis which seeks to uncover the variety of systems which position and oppress black women.

3 The gender is left open since it has been usual to refer to some men, for example, John Stuart Mill, as (liberal) feminists. The analysis of Engels (1978: 87-8, 96) in *The Origin of the Family* written in the ...

the self-conscious (sometimes 'unconscious') creation and vindication of representations of the feminine and the position of women in social reality by women themselves – in contrast to the accepted 'common sense' or 'everyday' notions which are taken as imbued with masculine conceptions – and which are aimed at the emancipation of women. Feminist scholarship is a varied set of discursive practices operating to resist and subvert the commonplace assumptions of the dominant masculine culture. Moreover, feminism is a form of praxis. Feminist writers acknowledge that they must struggle to live and write as women while existing inside a social world heavily structured and imbued with masculine practices; they claim the right to develop specifically critical perspectives to affirm and change for the better the position of women (and by implication to come to a fuller and deeper appreciation of the nature of 'humanity').

BASIC ISSUES INCLUDE THOSE OF DOMINATION, PATRIARCHY AND WOMEN'S SENSE OF JUSTICE

What are the problems that feminist jurisprudence is called to address? There are several, but three appear self-evident: (i) the first is the concrete reality of oppression repeatedly legitimated by legal regulations. It is undeniable that the position of women throughout history has been recurrently little better than that of slaves, the legal property of their masters (either fathers or husbands) who protect and control; (ii) the second is the issue of patriarchy, or the system of male authority which structures the institutions and organisational rationality which constitute the oppressive and exploitative relations which affect women; (iii) the third is the question of women's sense of justice, or what sort of 'truth' is involved in the traditional male argument that women are different from men and have an undeveloped sense of the abstract and impartial objectivity that justice requires.

In outline the feminist response involves:

(i) analysing, highlighting and politically fighting the structures of oppression[4] and violence;[5]

3... mid-19th century was provocative: '[Real freedom will be possible only] when a new generation has grown up ... a generation of men who never in their lives have known what it is to buy a women's surrender with money or any other social instrument of power ... a generation of women who have never known what it is to give themselves to a man from any other consideration than real love, or to refuse to give themselves to their lovers from fear of the economic consequences'.

4   Oppression and exploitation take various forms, but the economic statistics are startling. According to a UN report of 1980 (quoted Bryson, 1992): 'Women constitute one-half of the world's population, perform nearly two-thirds of its work hours, receive one-tenth of the world's income and own less than one-hundredth of the world's property.'

5   Feminist scholars point out that violence is both open and latent. For Kate Millett (1970), the violence of patriarchy is institutionalised and structurally inherent in the practice of legal systems, in the reality of the laws and social structures which result in illegal abortions and the constant possibility of rape. The ever-present background possibility of violence is the main mechanism by which unequal power relations are sustained. Other writers (Jessica Benjamin, 1980; Williams, 1991) point to the hidden violence of male rationality which defines the 'other' out of the calculations and thereby out of the decision-making mechanisms of mainstream organisation. The institutions of modern society – imbued with increasing formal rationality – thus objectify and control the 'other', while denying the 'other' a real existence. Commentators on the third world (for example, Brown et al, 1981) describe ...

(ii) analysing the pervasiveness of patriarchy and engaging in strategies to combat this. These range from consciousness-raising to arguing that *the personal is political* and that there are no spaces beyond the reach of patriarchal oppression.[6] The family is sometimes even castigated as 'patriarchy's chief institution' (Millett, 1985), while struggles over reproduction rights reflect the argument that reproduction is not an unchanging biological fact, but a process connecting the technological and ideological state of society (O'Brien, 1981). To gain in self-worth, women must explore new avenues for 'pleasure', counteracting a history where sexuality has been organised around the centrality of male significations;[7] they must allow themselves the need to experience, to feel new forms of subjectivity by taking the political decision to pursue styles of life that give them the freedom to experience and *feel*;[8]

5... how violence is used to ensure that women do not breach social rules. Women must move within the roles and behaviours allotted to them and violence is used to control women's sexuality and reproductive roles.

6   MacKinnon (1982) argues that only by following through the injunction to treat the personal as political can women make the connection between sociality and subjectivity so that the politics of women's structural position can be fought through the politics of women's (non-)'personal' lives.

7   The discourse of sexuality is the prime example of phallocentric logos. Women's sexuality is traditionally characterised by the absence, by a gap, by the void to be filled by the positive member of the male. Thus the phallus as original signifier (the organiser of symbols of meaning) is constructed on the foundation of the nothingness of women's sex. There is no such thing as the essence of women then, since all that women do in sex is to engulf, lead on power, excite and stimulate, accept and encourage desire and performance; women therein bring out truth, but cannot be truth (unless, as with Nietzsche, one holds that truth is a goal to be achieved, but always in reality a depth, destined to remain a mystery until death – then truth is that woman). By contrast recent feminist writing on identity strive to recast female genitalia not as absence, but as presence, and as the guardian of the mystery of creative birth. For the French psychoanalytical scholar Luce Irigaray (1984: 24), the feminine sex is an aporia, a mystery, harbinger of the miracle of (future) birth: 'A recasting of immanence and transcendence, notably through this threshold which is never considered as one: the female sex. Threshold of access to the mucous. Beyond classical oppositions of love and hate, of absolute fluid and ice – a threshold always half open. Threshold of lips, strangers to dichotomised oppositions ... Mystery of feminine identity?'

8   The transformation in views of female sexuality with the 'discovery' of the clitoris (in works such as Anna Koedt's *The Myth of the Vaginal Orgasm*, 1970) away from seeing the 'truth' of women's pleasure as experiencing penile penetration, and the recognition of a 'right to orgasm' led to demands for an 'equity of pleasure'. This is sometimes portrayed as part of a 'struggle for dignity and self-determination [which] is rooted in the struggle for actual control of one's body' (A Dworkin, 1981: 205). Freed from male perspectives and male desire, the meaning of women's pleasure is not self-evident. The strength of patriarchy colonises even fantasies, thus women must become reflexive concerning their pleasure. Historically pleasure for women was closely connected with danger, death and guilt. Sexual intercourse, for example, entailed a difficult-to-gauge probability of pregnancy, and – with the high mortality rates associated with childbirth – death (Giddens, 1992). Displaying too much pleasure during marriage through involvement in activities that were not supportive of the male risked moving outside of the expected marriage role, with the possibility of divorce or domestic violence. For black American women the situation was different: 'In the face of a dominant culture that characterised all black women as sexually promiscuous beings, public recognition of the self as a sexual being was seen as compromising the reputation of all black women and of the race in general' (Hazel Carby, reclamation historian, quoted, Jewell, 1993). Thus to take pleasure in their sexuality was a dangerous and ambivalent phenomenon. To find the space for a free and truthful discussion of need and pleasure a liberation; as the black activist Sabrina Sojourner put it: 'Each of us is entitled to define what our boundaries are and have them respected. Sex in and of itself is not wrong. What is done with sex can be very wrong' (quoted, Jewell, 1993). Early radical feminism argued that women need positive statements of their possibilities of pleasure – in areas of the body, sensuality, human connection, the infantile and the non-rational. Lesbian theorists question if a body of knowledge of women's lives can be created without placing central the question of sexual pleasure. Black feminism calls for the narratives of pleasure in black women's lives to be explored and celebrated; by accepting that black women can 'take pleasure in ourselves is subversive' (Shange, 1987: 178).

(iii) analysing the question of justice. Traditionally women have been portrayed as having an underdeveloped sense of justice (see Okin, 1980, 1989; Lloyd, 1984; Pateman, 1986, 1989; Coole, 1988; Nye, 1990). Even before classical Greece, mythology provided tales and images of women as irrational, unpredictable, emotional and earthy, as opposed to the qualities of balance, reason and distance which men (seemingly) brought to deliberations.[9] Throughout the history of western philosophy, male writers have moved in circles of complexity and ambiguity as a result of claiming that women are closer to nature than men and that women's proper realm was in the private space of the family, yet also portraying women as the guardians of morality and order which male excesses may endanger; women give the social body strength through endurance and stability, soothing men's rampant desires and will to power which may upset the balance of the cosmos. A dominant theme, however, is that women lack a sense of justice and cannot obtain the necessary objectivity to rule justly; they must be kept from the seat of political power in case they subvert the political structure. Put another way, the issue is that to create and maintain a just stable social order, individuals need to be educated and have a developed sense of justice so that they will fashion and abide by rules of civil association that command respect. Thus a sense of justice among the citizens is essential; but if women – as theorists from Rousseau (*The Social Contract*, 1971) to Freud[10] have maintained – are different in their psychological make-up and cannot attain the requisite sense of justice, then to give women full political and economic participation and responsibility threatens disorder. Civilisation is seen as the work of men, while women are essential to sustain it both through reproduction, childcare and softening and mending the rough edges of male creativity. What is the proper response to this ascription of difference? One response is to say (a) there is in essence no difference and any apparent difference is merely a result of the lack of opportunities that women have had to develop the life experiences that a sense of justice may be based upon, thus increasing opportunities will ensure that women's sense of justice is the same as males';[11] but another

---

9   This is usually presented (by men) as the claim that '*logos*', ie speech, reason, is male. Indeed logocentrism, or the primacy of the word, is connoted with a belief in a source of definite truth – a God, or transcendental signifier (transferred to the phallus in phallocentric discourse) – which provides a foundation for meaning. Feminist myth critics (Pagels, 1979) read Kali and Hecate as the female originators of languages and alphabets thus claiming that there has always been a (submerged) feminine language and theory.

10   For Freud, civilisation is the work of males since it requires the 'instinctual sublimations of which women are little capable' (*Civilisation and its Discontents*, 1961: 95).

11   Most theories of 'moral development' imply that there are stages of moral reasoning that individuals attain as a result of their life experience. Rawls argues 'our moral understanding increases as we move in the course of life through a sequence of positions' (1971: 468, following discussion based on secs 70–2). There are three main stages: (i) the child learns 'the morality of order' from its parents; then (ii) the 'morality of association' or a morality characterised by the co-operative virtues of justice and impartiality is developed when the individual occupies a range of roles in a variety of institutions; finally (iii) a 'morality of principles' is reached wherein we understand the fundamental role of abstract principles and the requirements of justice in the social order and we want to uphold it. This is the fully developed sense of justice. The most 'acceptable' form of feminism, 'liberal feminism', basically argues that the structural position of women – the pervasive denial to women of the right to move in the public space of jobs, political office and various associations – has prevented many from attaining the ...

approach is (b) perhaps there is a gain to be found in difference. What if women do have a different ethical and moral perception? Might this be as valid, or more valid, than the supposed objectivity of male justice?

HOW DOES FEMINIST JURISPRUDENCE SEEK TO ADDRESS THESE ISSUES?

(i) Feminist scholars highlight areas where the law either legitimates oppression or the operation of the law effectively treats men and women differently, perhaps by enforcing a separation in areas of life activities, or not taking the violence done to women seriously.

(ii) a common theme in feminist work is the critique of the epistemology of traditional jurisprudence and attempts are made to change the way areas of law are traditionally viewed;[12]

(iii) this work is joined to wider theorising which seeks to undercut the structure of abstract masculinity which is depicted as the organising force of a great deal of social, moral and political thought (theory).[13] At root this is at least two claims: (a) that western culture has structured its thinking in a sexual polarity in which the male principle was superior and central;[14] (b) that the issues which have most occupied the theorists of politics, of morality, of the legitimation of power, have surfaced through a process of masculine theorising from the masculine perception of the problems of life. Some feminists argue that a correspondence exists between the technological mode of relating to the world – that of analytically breaking it down, the better to dominate it rationally – and the masculine experience of life. The desire to separate and control formations corresponds to the masculine – the masculine response which is tied up with statements claiming that it is objective, logical, extroverted, realistic, mechanical and pragmatic. Many feminists argue that

---

11 ...experiences that the second and third stage requires. If follows from Rawls's scheme that only if men and women can move through the situations founding all three positions that such a moral development can occur. Feminist difference theorists assert, however, that this is a male dominated scheme of moral development and undervalues different types of reasoning.

12 For a review of the variable impact of feminist legal scholarship on the teaching of law, see the early article by K O'Donovan (1981) and for a collection concerning application to the core areas see A Bottomely (1995).

13 As O'Brien (1981: 5) presents the grounding of this wider project: 'What we need to do, to put it in the simplest way, is to be able to demonstrate that male-dominant culture and the male-stream thought that buttresses and justifies it are both, in some sense, prejudiced by the very fact that they are masculine.

One way of putting this, or at least of starting to do it, is to consider male philosophy as an ideology of male supremacy.'

14 Moreover, a privileging of abstract modes of reasoning as the only rational form of decision-making, an association of women with the irrational (as Mari Matsuda puts it, there is a dualism in operation opposing 'understanding of intuition, experience, and emotion as the inferior antitheses of logic, reason, and science, coupled with a tendency to equate women with the former grouping and men with the latter'. 'Liberal Jurisprudence and Abstracted Visions of Human Nature: A Feminist Critique of Rawls's Theory of Justice' (1986) 16 *New Mex LJ* 613 at 617.)

this means that the scientist, in order to become 'value-free', must split his personality and thus run the risk of becoming authoritarian or emotionally sterile;[15]

(iv) writers bring women's experiences directly into both theorising and the practice of understanding law in reality (showing the discriminatory effects of 'living law' or 'law in action');

(v) to move beyond mere critique, feminist scholarship tries to understand the dichotomies imposed by theory on the analysis of life and to reject as artificial those which claim a naturalness or universality which are based on masculine preconceptions; thus feminine modes of thought and relating can either be argued as superior, or alternatively, as necessary to complement the masculine mode which is no longer to be seen as superior but simply as one of the two analytical methods of relating cognition to the world;

(vi) scholars resist accepted or commonplace perceptions of the normality of standards, such as in the conception of equality, or the recognition of problems, such as domestic violence, since these may well be standards created under patriarchy – false to the 'reality' which we should aspire to;

(vii) feminist scholarship often makes problematic any simple reliance on law to resolve social disputes. For much of feminist jurisprudence the law (and the state) is male in its structure of rationality, decision-making and forms of resolution; thus law cannot be the answer to the problem of creating 'just' social relations (in the notions of the rule of law, equality, rights, justice). This raises the issue of going beyond law (thus the solution to rape is not anything the law can provide but an issue of structural inequalities);

(viii) feminist strategies seek to illuminate and define the wrongs done to women neglected by traditional perspectives. This can be done through letting in the range of voices, the experiences of women and others (particularly ethnic minority women), to redefine the wrongs of women.

Feminists have highlighted specific areas of women's victimisation that have been neglected by the traditional system. Within diverse areas, such as family law and victimology, concrete issues have been raised and many practical steps taken to alleviate problems. This chapter, however, will remain at a theoretical level and introduce the several schools of thought.

---

15 Robin Morgan (1989: 51) draws connections between patriarchy and the demarcating foundation of western philosophy: 'If I had to name one quality as the genius of patriarchy, it would be compartmentalisation, the capacity for institutionalising disconnection. Intellect severed from emotion. Thought separated from action. Science split from art. The earth itself divided; national borders. Human beings categorised: by sex, age, race, ethnicity, sexual preference, height, weight, class, religion, physical ability, *ad nauseam*. The personal isolated from the political. Sex divorced from love. The material ruptured from the spiritual. The past parted from the present disjoined from the future. Law detached from justice. Vision dissociated from reality.'

FEMINIST METHODOLOGY

Katharine Bartlett , 'Feminist Legal Methods' (1990) *Harv LR*, analyses three methods. Notably (i) *asking the woman question*, or identifying and challenging those elements of existing legal doctrine that leave out or disadvantage women and members of other excluded groups; (ii) *feminist practical reasoning*, or reasoning from an ideal in which legal resolutions are pragmatic responses to concrete dilemmas rather than static choices between opposing, often mismatched perspectives; (iii) *consciousness-raising, or seeking insights and enhanced perspectives through collaborative or interactive engagement with others based upon personal experience and narrative.*

Having argued that many of the projects and themes of traditional jurisprudence and moral and political theory essentially derive from the masculine experience of life, feminist writers offer counter-descriptions of life. Of course accounts vary, but a central theme is that women experience and thus come to perceive the world in a different way to men. The distinct form of feminist reasoning arises from this different experiential existence and the claims of feminist jurisprudence may be based on this foundation.

Narrative and poetic modes of writing create empathy and sympathy by presenting incidents and feelings which evoke a level of common human understanding transgressing demarcated identities. If the audience and the writer/speaker have common experience, the reader is more likely to appreciate the writer's basic assumptions. What the experience of white males may suggest is unproblematic and logical, female experience may suggest otherwise. A woman's experience of the world may lead her to conclude that the idea posited in mainstream political or social philosophy is illogical or irrational, or simply irrelevant. If she cannot reconcile the idea with her own experience of life, and the idea is the basis on which the main argument rests, the whole argument will seem flawed. Moreover, the narrative form 'humanises' theory, brings it down to the level of women's lived experiences; by crossing the divide in writing from the abstract to the personal, bridges can be created where a gulf would otherwise exist.

SCHOOLS AND PERIODS OF FEMINIST 'JURISPRUDENTIAL' WRITINGS

In outline (i) the first wave of feminist writing was of a *liberal* orientation calling for equality under the law; however, (ii) there was always a parallel strand of *radical feminism* which asserted the need to move beyond liberalism; and (iii) both became involved in a process of questioning aims and assumptions in the late 1970s when many of the measures proposed in the name of liberal equality having been achieved in the West raised the question: was it equality that should be sought if the criterion of equality was the male norm? Could not a difference be agreed that was valuable but still allowed both men and women to be treated as equals? A *cultural feminism* developed which looked for a positive orientation in women's experiences and modes of reasoning; this was complemented by (iv) ethnic, or critical race, feminism which looked at the particular experiences of black women; and latterly a (v) post-modern feminism has developed which tries to face up to the multiplicity of structural forces and sites of subjectivity that the post-modern condition occasions.

Liberal feminism

The first wave of feminism argued for equality of treatment for both men and women. Liberal feminists presented women as autonomous beings naturally endowed with the same basic rights and privileges as men and objected to the structural denial to women of the full array of rights and privileges of citizenship men experienced. *The Declaration of Sentiments* adopted at the 1848 Seneca Falls Convention[16] – perhaps the most famous document in 19th-century American feminism – was a feminist counterpart to the Declaration of Independence with 'man' substituted for 'King George': 'all men and women are created equal; they are endowed by their creator with certain inalienable rights; that among these are life, liberty, and the pursuit of happiness'. The legal liberal philosophy of the 18th and 19th centuries provided the intellectual foundational structure for the first wave of feminist writing, such as Mary Wollstonecraft ([1778, 1789] 1967),[17] William Thompson ([1825] 1983),[18] John Stuart Mill (1869),[19] and Mill writing with Harriet Taylor (1970).[20]

The jurisprudential aim was to attain equal legal subjectivity for women as with male citizens. John Stuart Mill, for example, was incensed that in marriage a woman became the sexual property of the man with no right to refuse sex:

> however brutal a tyrant she may be unfortunately chained to – though she may know that he hates her, though it may be his daily pleasure to torture her, and though she may feel it impossible not to loathe him – he may claim from her and enforce the lowest

---

16 A declaration drafted in the main by Elizabeth Cady Stanton, signed by 100 men and women and approved by the first women's rights convention in Seneca Falls. A comparison with the Declaration of Independence in presented in Davies (1994: 183-187).

17 In *A Vindication of the Rights of Woman* (1789) Mary Wollstonecraft depicts women as rational agents whose inferiority is largely due to inferior education which equality of opportunity would redress.

18 In his *Appeal of One Half of the Human Race, Women, Against the Pretensions of the Other Half, Men, To Retain Them in Political and Thence Civil and Domestic Slavery*, William Thompson replied to James Mill's article on government where James Mill had claimed women had no interests separate from that of their husband or father and had, therefore, no need for independent political representation. Thompson argued that women's intellectual capacities were at least as great as men's and that the biological differences ought never to be an argument against political rights. Thompson argued that by basing the distinction of the basis of some natural difference the law had 'erected the physical organisation into a crime' (1983: 171). Moreover he believed that women would not have created many of the laws that men had passed: 'Is it possible to conceive that legislative power lodged exclusively in the hands of women could have produced atrocities and wretchedness equal to those with which exclusive male legislation has desolated the globe?' (ibid: 131). Women required economic independence and discriminatory laws needed to be repealed. Historically: 'Whatever system of labour ... whatever system of government ... under every vicissitude of man's condition he has always retained woman his slave' (*ibid*: 196).

19 In *The Subjection of Women* (1869), John Stuart Mill argued the reason women appeared ill-suited for public life lay in their limited experience due to their traditional roles and the interest men had in maintaining those roles. However, Mill did not seriously question the division of roles in the family.

20 Harriet Taylor's views were incorporated in her husband John Stuart Mill's *The Subjection of Women*, but in 'The Enfranchisement of Women' (1851), and essays on marriage, Taylor proposed a complete civil and political equality for women to include opening public offices and occupations for women.

degradation of a human being, that of being made the instrument of an animal function contrary to her intentions (1869: 57).

Thompson argued that the legal enslavement of women prevented the enlightenment of men:

> As women's bondage has chained down man to the ignorance and vices of despotism, so will their liberation reward him with knowledge, with freedom and with happiness ([1825] 1983).

Under the banner of liberal feminism women won most of their legislative and judicial victories, including the suffrage, equal pay, benefits, access to employment and education, the right to serve on juries, and the limited right to choose to terminate a pregnancy. In the United States, recent leading adherents of this school included Wendy Williams, Herma Hill Kay, and Nadine Taub, although its most prominent representative is Justice Ruth Bader Ginsburg. Commencing in 1971, while a member of the Rutgers University law faculty, she, with the co-operation of the American Civil Liberties Union (ACLU), participated in a number of lawsuits that challenged gender-based discrimination in a variety of contexts and gained a considerable set of victories all based on legal liberalism.[21] Later critics, writing from a perspective sometimes termed *difference* theory, believed the victories were rather hollow, since, being based on the ideology of formal equality of the sexes, they amounted to equal treatment for women willing to be treated like men. Under liberal feminism women appeared to succeed only at a cost. On the one hand, women who espoused individualism often succeeded, but their success was on the condition that they acted as if there were no barriers for the success of women as a group.[22] On the other hand, was this success really a feminist success, or a partial transformation into the male standard? Nicola Lacey asserts:

> Liberal feminism's central ideal amounted to a strategy of assimilation of women to a standard set by and for men. The rights assigned to men as legal subjects had to be made available to women wherever a comparison between the treatment of the two revealed a disparity: the equalisation was almost invariably in one direction – towards a male norm. The radical potential inherent in the idea of 'treatment as an equal' was not realised, because the political debate issued in by liberal feminism was highly circumscribed. Far from engendering a substantial reconsideration of the way in which the world was

---

21 Many of the debates concern the American Supreme Court with its ability to declare laws unconstitutional. Prominent examples include *Reed v Reed* 404 US 71, 77 (1971), in which the court invalidated a statute that preferred men over women as administrators of estates; *Frontiero v Richardson* 411 US 677 (1973), where the court held that the families of female military officers were entitled to housing and benefits on the same basis as were the families of male officers; *Weinberger v Wiesenfeld* 420 US 636 (1975), is an example of the universal nature of the approach – for in that case it was males who were being represented – and the court struck down portions of the Social Security Act that awarded child care benefits only to mothers and not to fathers of deceased covered workers.

22 Cott (1987: 281) argues that many of the women who succeeded in the early years – particularly in the period 1920-1950 – could not offer guidance to their fellow women since they had to act as if their success was open to anyone who played the rules of the game: 'The resort to individualism took the feminist standpoint that women's freedoms and opportunities should be no less than men's, but individualism offered no way to achieve the goal except by acting as though it had already been obtained. Although it produced outstanding models of individual accomplishment, it could not engender a programme for change in the position of women as a group.'

organised, the public standards already in place were assumed to be valid, and the feminist conceptual tools of bias, discrimination, equal worth measured against them (1995: 7).

Given that key notions of legal liberalism are those of neutrality, impartiality and universality, arguments and legislative provisions had to be framed in such a way as not to contradict these ideals: for example, the 1975 Sex Discrimination Act in the UK prohibits discrimination on the basis of sex, rather than prohibiting discrimination against women. Given, however, that progressive strands in judicial and legislative culture have been dominated by legal liberalism, it is not surprising that most of the victories made for women's rights have been made by proponents of legal liberalism. Legal liberalism, however, offers little help in understanding the nature and causes of women's oppression, and may appear to downplay the real political struggles which daily take place. This does not mean to say that liberal legalism's emphasis upon rights and individualism provides no resources for critical work – Rawls's theory of justice, for example, has been recently applied to the justice of the family[23] – it is rather the case that concentrating upon such a principled approach is only one technique, only a partial remedy.

Radical feminism

Radical feminists view the existing cultural, social, economic, and legal differences between men and women as a product of male domination. The victories of liberal feminists are viewed as sometimes weakening the radical potentiality of feminism and allowing women success in professional occupations only if these women 'become as men'. Legal liberalism is charged with ignoring the reality of male power and domination in formulating the seemingly neutral principles of liberalism's agenda of sexual equality.

Catherine MacKinnon is a prolific writer from this perspective. Two issues may briefly introduce her style. In her view the liberal approach to abortion, which prevailed in *Roe v Wade*,[24] presents the issue of reproductive control in the context of a

---

23 Richards (*The Sceptical Feminist*, 1982) argues that liberal principles such as those contained in Rawls's work reflect a concern with justice, viewed as the individual's freedom to pursue his/her own destiny. Thus this principle would show up the systematic denial of these opportunities to women as unjust. Richards argues that Rawls's original position and veil of ignorance ought specifically to include ignorance of one's sex (in Rawls's original theory the parties were to assume they were male and heads of households) and the structure of households should be open to question. What would family arrangements look like if we agreed principles of justice for the family from behind a Rawlsean veil of ignorance?

Similarly, Okin (1990) presents an analysis which starts by proposing such a thought-experiment and argues for a society in which child-rearing and domestic work are shared equally, and includes state-subsidised nurseries and greater flexibility in employment patterns so that paid work and nurturing could be easily combined for both men and women. She also argues that those who choose the traditional pattern of family should not be discriminated against, and that both partners should have equal entitlement to all earnings coming into the household, sharing equally in the event of divorce.

24 In *Roe v Wade* 410 US 113 (1973), the US Supreme Court recognised a woman's qualified right to terminate her pregnancy. Radical feminists argue that pregnancy must be seen in the context of the social structure of the society, cultural feminists that pregnancy is a uniquely female experience; as a consequence liberal feminism is unable to understand the existential and political issues involved. *Roe* was decided in the context of liberal feminism and was based on conventional liberal concepts of privacy.

framework of privacy, personal liberty, and autonomy of the individual. Liberal thought obscures the fact that a multitude of factors including social pressure, learning, economic disadvantage, sexual force, inadequate contraception, and weak laws against sexual assault impact so that women do not control the circumstances under which they become pregnant. This structurally forced maternity is a perpetuation of economic, domestic and sexual inequality; abortion is needed to redress a woman's basic lack of control over the process of reproduction. Similarly, pornography is positioned and discussed by legal liberalism in the context of freedom of speech and individual autonomy, whereas MacKinnon sees pornography as dehumanising traffic in women that sets the standard for the mistreatment of women, engendering rape, sexual abuse of children, battery, forced prostitution, and sexual murder. The very nature of pornography contributes to, and defines, women's social and legal inequality. The attempts of radical feminists to restrict pornography, however, have been frustrated by the dominant forces of legal liberalism that pervade the American legal system's approach to speech issues; liberal feminists have joined with male interests to squash radical feminists' proposals.[25] For radical feminists, pornography is not speech, it is the induced silence of women.

Themes of the work of Catherine MacKinnon

Catherine MacKinnon works through a neo-Marxist perspective with its themes of power, domination, alienation and the pursuit of an emancipated future state of social relations. She suffers, in turn, from many of the same faults that have befallen earlier Marxist analysis, namely, she assumes a truth for her theory that transcends those of the other perspectives and is hostile to reconciliation, she claims the possibility of a true essence of women which will become apparent in conditions of freedom and insists on the totality of male domination throughout the social order.

In an early article MacKinnon (1982: 515) replaced the category of work in the traditional Marxist scheme with sexuality: 'Sexuality is to feminism what work is to Marxism: that which is most one's own, yet most taken away'.[26] The first site of domination lies in the male appropriation of women's pre-social natural sexuality, an appropriation which constitutes woman as the object of male desire. Thus women's sexuality in society is structured into an objectification of the male gaze rather than a

---

25 As Strossen (1994: 151) put her opposition to the proposals of MacKinnon and A Dworkin: 'First they contravene free speech principles. Second they undermine women's equality rights by giving government officials a powerful tool for suppressing works by and about feminists and lesbians; by perpetuating demeaning stereotypes about women as victims; by distracting us from constructive approaches to reducing discrimination and violence against women; and by undermining free speech, thereby depriving feminists of a powerful tool for advancing women's equality.'

26 In her later book *Toward a Feminist Theory of the State*, she is even more direct: 'Man fucks women; subject verb object' (1989: 124). It is the role of women to be the one who gets fucked (what MacKinnon calls the 'fuckee') and the role of man to be the one who does the fucking (the 'fuckor'). Out of this difference, out of the structure of interaction in the mode of activity of sexuality, comes a domination through difference: 'Difference is the velvet glove on the iron fist of domination. The problem then is not that differences are not valued; the problem is that they are defined by power. This is as true when difference is affirmed as when it is denied, when its substance is applauded or disparaged, when women are punished or protected in its name' (*ibid*:219).

consequence of natural or true forms. Gender formations are structured on the basis of this; ultimately the power which constitutes the structure of gender relations and the domination of women by men is the power of visualising and defining the nature of women's sexuality and thus gender.

As with Marx, we cannot look at the behaviour of the oppressed, of the hungry, as the behaviour of natural man, with MacKinnon we cannot look at the behaviour of women under contemporary conditions as the truth of their gender. Women's subordinate set of gender roles does not correspond to any extra-social natural division but has its 'truth' only as a creation of social processes.

> Gender is what gender means. It has no basis in anything other than the social reality its hegemony constructs. The process that gives sexuality its male supremacist meaning is therefore the process through which gender inequality becomes socially real (1987: 149).

What are the consequences of this pervasive male domination?

Women cannot trust the state

Even the supposed neutral liberal rule-of-law state is the embodiment of the male gaze:

> The state is male in the feminist sense: the law sees and treats women the way men see and treat women. The liberal state coercively and authoritatively constitutes the social order in the interest of men as a gender – through its legitimating norms, forms, relation to society, and substantive policies. The state's formal norms recapitulate the male point of view on the level of design (MacKinnon 1989: 161-2).

The secret of this domination, the key to its success, is the hegemonic belief that the structure of the liberal rule-of-law state actually prevents domination. For MacKinnon, liberal jurisprudence presents an image of the rule of law in which law is divorced from morality and adjudication is separate from government:

> In Anglo-American jurisprudence, morals (value-judgments) are deemed separable and separated from politics (power contests), and both from adjudication (interpretation). Neutrality, including judicial decision-making that is dispassionate, disinterested, and precedential, is considered desirable and descriptive. Courts, forums without predisposition among parties and with no interest of their own, reflect society back to itself resolved. Government of laws, not of men, limits partiality with written constraints and tempers force with reasonable rule-following (*ibid*: 162).

By creating such an image of impartiality the rule of law is blind to the fact that it operates to reinforce structural inequalities which pre-exist the appeal to law and which inhere also in the jurisprudence of the law. For if the subjects of the law come to the law as citizens, as the rights-bearing creatures of modernity, the subject of the woman as rights-bearer is male-identified and male-constructed. To claim the protection of the law is to claim the protection of something already established in the male point of view – to enforce the abstract law is to enforce that which has been constructed in the male view. The liberal rule-of-law state is the rule of men under the guise of the rule of law – its power intensified through the hegemony of subterfuge.

The very notion of equality is suspect

Not only is the state not to be trusted but the *very notion of equality is suspect* – instead one must ask *'equality as what?'* If women want to claim equal rights are they not claiming only the right to be viewed as men under the gaze of the male state?

> The state is male jurisprudentially, meaning that it adopts the standpoint of male power on the relation between law and society. This stance is especially vivid in constitutional adjudication, though legitimate to the degree it is neutral on the policy of legislation. The foundation for its neutrality is the pervasive assumption that conditions that pertain among men on the basis of gender apply to women as well – that is, the assumption that sex inequality does not really exist in society. The constitution – the constituting document of this state society – with its interpretation assumes that society, absent government, is free and equal; that its laws, in general, reflect that; and that government need and should right only what government has previously wronged. This posture is structural to a constitution of abstinence: for example, 'Congress shall make no law abridging the freedom of ... speech.' Those who have freedoms like equality, liberty, privacy, and speech socially keep them legally, free of government intrusion. No one who does not have them socially is granted them legally (*ibid*: 163).

We have seen this critique before. Under the liberal rule of law it is said that all are prohibited from sleeping under the main bridges of the capital; the law applies equally to both the poor man and the rich man. The fact is only the poor man would feel the need to sleep under the bridge; thus the law, applying equally in jurisprudence, only applies in action to the poor. MacKinnon's argument is at the level of hegemonic understandings, the social inequality which existed in the traditional patriarchical social order has not been destroyed by the legal rights offered by liberalism; such inequality is harder to see and to fight because it is the role of the state not to intervene in the reformulation of the social order. This compromise – the liberty principle of John Stuart Mill – is legitimate if it were true that the genders were actually equal before the law, if the liberties of the social body were evenly distributed; but they are not. MacKinnon gives a reading of the famous dictum that modernity has proceeded from 'status to contract' (from pre-modern identities based on the status of cast, gender, and family, to that of the equal abstracted individual):

> Once gender is grasped as a means of social stratification, the status categories basic to medieval law, thought to have been superseded by liberal regimes in aspirational non-hierarchical constructs of abstract personhood, are revealed deeply unchanged. Gender as a status category was simply assumed out of legal existence, suppressed into a presumptively pre-constitutional social order through a constitutional order designed not to reach it. Speaking descriptively rather than functionally or motivationally, the strategy is first to constitute society unequally prior to law; then to design the constitution, including the law of equality, so that its guarantees apply only to those values that are taken away by law; then to construct legitimating norms so that the state legitimates itself through non-interference with the *status quo*. Then, so long as male domination is so effective in society that it is unnecessary to impose sex inequality through law, such that only the most superficial sex inequalities become *de jure*, not even a legal guarantee of sex inequality will produce social equality (*ibid*: 163-4).

The real harm of various assaults on women is the depiction of subordination and objectification

A great deal of the 'success' of feminism in the legal arena has been in the highlighting of women's injuries, for so long hidden either behind a refusal to intervene (as in a refusal to believe in the prevalence of incest or rape) or as occurring within the private sphere (domestic violence). American legal feminists have made concerted interventions into the practical realm of policing and the creation of criminal norms through theorising women's gender-specific injuries – such as sexual harassment – as group-based social injuries. MacKinnon herself became recognised by the legal establishment through successfully defining sexual harassment so that it became an accepted category of harm suitable for legal redress. She has also joined with Andrea Dworkin to campaign against pornography. Her position on pornography has little to do with sexuality as such, indeed it denies that pornography has any natural or free sexuality in it. Instead the truth of pornography lies in its depiction of women as objects, objects to be dominated, abused, to have coercion imposed upon – pornography presents sexuality only through domination.

> We define pornography as the graphic sexually explicit subordination of women through pictures or words that also includes women dehumanised as sexual objects, things, or commodities; enjoying pain or humiliation or rape; being tied up, cut up, mutilated, bruised, or physically hurt; in postures of sexual submission or servility or display; reduced to body parts, penetrated by objects or animals, or presented in scenarios of degradation, injury, torture; shown as filthy or inferior; bleeding, bruised, or hurt in a context that makes these conditions sexual (*ibid*: 176).

Andrea Dworkin and MacKinnon imply that the representation of a free sexuality is possible: 'Erotica, defined by distinction not [pornography], might be sexually explicit material premised on equality'. Having spent so much energy on campaigning to have women's wrongs recognised by the law, MacKinnon is ambivalent:

> In point of fact, I would prefer not to have to spend all this energy getting the law to recognise wrongs to women as wrong. But it seems to be necessary to legitimise our injuries as injuries in order to delegitimise our victimisation by them, without which it is difficult to move in more positive ways (1987: 104).

Here feminism can join with radical criminologists in seeking to redefine 'harm'. In the criminological arena of victimology recent attempts have focused upon defining certain types of 'harms' beyond those normally recognised. Similarly feminist writers have focused on the maleness of legal proceedings, specifically the trial of sexual crimes such as rape. Simply put, in the rape trial the procedure is designed to break down the story of the woman complainant both by subjecting it to vigorous doubt and by implicitly sexualising it. The victim becomes an object of the male gaze and forced to relive her ordeal. As the English criminologist Carol Smart puts it:

> The woman telling the story of her rape, even in her own words and not those of the defence counsel, runs the risk of being sexually arousing.

> The process of the rape trial can be described as a specific sexualisation of a women's body which has already been sexualised within the confines of a phallocentric culture.

Her body becomes literally saturated with sex. Some women may be able to resist this to some extent, for example the very old, but the majority cannot ...

The rape trial is a process of disqualification and celebration. It disqualifies women's experience of sexual abuse. This is more than saying that law takes women's no to be yes, or that law is sexist. It is both of these; but the point is that the very spectacle she must relate draws the rape trial firmly into the realms of uncertainty and doubt. The law exaggerates a common sense understanding of women's sexuality. It allows it free rein and it constructs the story of the rape in a sexualised form. The sexualised women can then be disqualified. But at the same time it celebrates so-called natural heterosexuality. Because it is concerned with consent and non-consent, the sexual pursuit of women which may lead to submission is defined as outside the law. Being a sexual predator is regarded as normal, even desirable, for men. Sexualising all women is equally regarded as natural; pressing a woman until she submits is regarded as a natural, pleasurable phallocentric pastime. The rape trial will not allow for any critique of this 'natural' activity.

Women's experience therefore has no place in this process ... (Carol Smart, 'Law's Truth/Women's Experience', in *Dissenting Opinions: Feminist Explorations in Law and Society*, 1990: 18)

Much of the complexity of the victim's experience is ruled as unsuitable for the proceedings of the trial – she is forced to address only the stated legal notions and any concerns which cannot be put into the narrow legal discourse are reduced to silence (see Estrich, 1987).[27]

In Smart's analysis women can understand their own experiences on their own terms and use this as is a counter-truth to that of legal discourse. MacKinnon, conversely, argued that the domination of maleness places severe handicaps on women understanding the 'truth' of their own lives; feminist theory is an agent of liberation.

How can women trust their own experiences and self-conceptions?

If MacKinnon is correct on the power of ideology and hegemony then there is no secure way for women to think out their positions and strategy. MacKinnon solves this by granting men some privileged status as 'reality'. 'The feminist point is simple. Men are women's material conditions. If it happens to women, it happens.' Not only, however, does this deny that maleness must also be socially constructed, but this dooms

---

27 In *Real Rape*, 1987, Susan Estrich begins with a description of her own rape and moves into an analysis of the reporting, investigation, prosecution and disposition of rape cases. She proposes specific changes in the legal rules but focuses upon the way that the American criminal law has constructed sexual coercion as consent. She uses various case studies and discussion of legislation to develop a narrative of the exclusion of the victim's perspective; consent and coercion are defined from the male point of view with the expectation that force be used by the woman in response to the male aggression and the due process concerns reflect the concern that woman will cry rape against innocent men. Other studies which use MacKinnon's arguments on the way 'consent' is structurally coerced include Olsen's analysis of statutory rape ('Statutory Rape: A Feminist Critique of Rights Analysis', 1984). Olsen's analysis of arguments made by the members of the Supreme Court, by lawyers, by feminist lawyers and others, brings out how each argument leaves out particular interests and by cutting off insights may blind the advocate from seeing what has actually happened to the real woman in the actual case.

women to know only by resistance, to know only that they ought to assert the non-male, rather than the (fe)male.

Excursus on feminism and the technology of liberation: the example of birth control and abortion

A central myth of modernity is the 'technological fix'. Many feminists have looked to technological advances to transform employment opportunities and free them from the dangers of reproduction. Certainly changes in the structure of production may have done more to transform the actual economic opportunities for educated, middle-class women, while the technology of sexuality (better birth control mechanisms, the pill) have distanced sexuality from its close connection with death (Giddens, 1992). In the late 1960s radical feminists such as Shulamith Firestone, located the main handicap to women's emancipation as their biological reproductive roles and went so far as to denounce the very facts of natural processes as oppressing women:

> pregnancy itself, independent of male contempt, is invasive, dangerous and oppressive; it is an assault on the physical integrity and privacy of the body (Firestone, *The Dialectic of Sex*, 1970).

The biological trap created a 'sexual caste system'; it was impossible for women to know true love, since love ought to be an emotion which arises out of equality and the reality of relationships was of women's economic and social dependency. Thus 'love perhaps even more than childbearing, is the pivot of women's oppression today' (1970: 121). Women must seize the means of reproduction and use technology to create a technical separation of reproduction from women's bodies; this was to be a precondition for women's liberation. But women had to be careful since the male interest would still be in maintaining supremacy and thus women must change the social technologies of childbearing and child-rearing as well as controlling the decision to have a baby.

Firestone's analysis has attained mythical proportions; quoted for its overstatements as much as it is used as an example of feminist realism. Imagining the possibilities that the new technologies of reproduction could result in was common. In the earlier book that served as the main text of feminism for a generation or more – Simone de Beauvoir's *The Second Sex* (1953) – we find both an existentialist celebration of man's freedom from nature and a painful appeal for women to take control of their reproductive capabilities.

De Beauvoir celebrates men's transcendence of nature; men have given their existence worth by conquering nature and remodelling instinctual attitudes via human ordering (the law). Man has created instruments which invent possibilities, which shape the future; women conversely have been trapped by the body. Man seeks to control his environment and prevail over the forces of nature; women are linked with nature with the result that man 'has subdued nature and women' (1953: 91).

Women are in a state of bondage to the biological facts of pregnancy, birth and suckling-child, which cannot give their existence meaning since 'no project is involved'; a woman cannot locate in them 'a lofty affirmation of her existence' (*ibid*: 88). Reproduction is a central issue; it is the area where – in that they have no choice vis-à-vis their reproductive outcomes – women display their impotence, their passivity, and their inability to control and direct the conditions of their existence. Thus – whereas the technology of tools gave men the ability to transcend natural dependency – control over reproduction through abortion and contraception offers the potentiality of transcendence from nature for women.[28]

Abortion must be a crucial issue for the feminist struggle; even though there is no one feminist position on abortion, it is a contested site including arguments over women's power over their bodies and their right to self-determination, while, on the other side, some recognise 'foetal rights' and the denial of a (future) 'personhood' if the foetus is terminated. Opinions on abortion are influenced by religion (and many feminists see in the Roman Catholic Church's denial of contraceptives a desire to condemn women to passivity), complicated by the historical experience of racist genocide, or the experiences of black women who faced enforced sterilisation.

De Beauvoir approaches abortion in the context of the increasing control women are exercising over reproduction; legislation in favour of abortion therefore represents an enormous advance for women because its use is an exercise of freedom and agency. De Beauvoir, nevertheless, is torn by contradictory feelings; on the one hand, the refusal to permit abortion is a gauge of resistance to women's freedom and power, yet, on the other hand, having a foetus aborted is one of the cruellest experiences a woman is ever likely to have to undergo. Moreover, in many circumstances, perhaps the vast majority, the context of the abortion decision involves the cynical double-dealing of men.

> Men universally forbid abortion, but individually they accept it as a convenient solution of a problem; they are able to contradict themselves with careless cynicism. But woman feels these contradictions in her wounded flesh; she is as a rule too timid for open revolt against masculine bad faith; she regards herself as the victim of an injustice that makes her a criminal against her will, and at the same time she feels soiled and humiliated. She embodies in concrete and immediate form, in herself, man's fault; he commits the fault, but he gets rid of it by putting it off on her; he merely says some words in a suppliant, threatening, sensible, or furious tone: he soon forgets them; it is for her to interpret these words in pain and blood. Sometimes he says nothing, he just fades away ... [Women then] learn to believe no longer in what men say ... the one thing they are sure of is this rifled and bleeding womb, these shreds of crimson life, this child that is not there ... For many women the world will never be the same (1953: 474).

De Beauvoir is caught in the existentialist criteria of affirmation and taking control of one's existence; she adopts one of the key defining points of modernity, that of domination over nature as the hallmark of the modern person, and uses this as her key principle of worth. However, although personal agency need not be defined by control over events, the appeal of the technology of contraception and abortion lies in their giving substance to the liberal talk of rights. If the liberal, however, remains in a

---

28   The point may well be 'offers'. Feminists point out that the technology has been developed by commercial companies largely in the hands of men and the use of such technology may have the effect of making women more sexually available at a lesser social cost to men. Morgan (1970: xxv) is rhetorically compelling: 'We know that the so-called sexual revolution was only another new form of oppression for women. The invention of the pill made millions for the drug companies, made guinea pigs of us, and made us all the more 'available' as sexual objects; if a woman didn't want to go to bed with a man now, she must be hung up'.

discussion of the justice of rights, s/he may be hiding from the reality of women's potential freedom, from feminism itself. The distance from a philosophical discussion of the rights involved in abortion to feminism's concern with the power of women is both tiny and huge.

Liberal legalism against feminism: the case of Ronald Dworkin's Life's Dominion

The leading liberal jurisprudent Ronald Dworkin argues that the abortion debate has been wrongly described as conflicting opinions concerning whether the foetus is a person with rights and interests of its own from the moment of conception, including a right not to be killed. He proposes that the underlying point really concerns whether, and if so how and why, human life has 'intrinsic value' (that is, 'its value is independent of what people happen to enjoy or want or need or what is good for them' (1993: 71)), and whether abortion is wrong because it 'denies and offends the sanctity or inviolability of human life' (ibid: 24).

Dworkin builds his argument step by step with the constant theme that underlying the abortion issue is a core of 'detached' moral arguments 'about how and why human life has intrinsic value, and what that implies for personal and political decisions about abortion' (ibid: 24). As elsewhere, Dworkin's search is for a full constitutional theory which yields integrity and enables a principled decision to be made. He concludes that women have an abstract, privacy-based constitutional right to 'procreative autonomy', and that the state lacks a compelling interest in protecting the detached sacred value represented by the foetus when this would seriously curtail the mother's liberty interest and where the community is divided about what respect for this value requires. He offers a compromise: states must not ban abortion, but may force pregnant women to reflect responsibly on the abortion decision, so long as they do not coerce women into making a particular decision.

Dworkin's discussions are notable for their interpretative stance; he seeks to apply his liberal interpretative methodology to lay bare a rational structure behind current (confused) debate and the appropriate legal cases (Roe v Wade, 410 US 113, 1973; and Planned Parenthood v Casey, 112 S Ct 2791, 1993); but the same criticism levelled against the foundations of his interpretative community apply. The point is simple: in constructing his argument, Dworkin either 'simply misunderstands feminist critiques of privacy discourse' (McCaffrey and Novkov, 1994: 203), or displays a naivete towards the politics of the feminist enterprise. Regarding the first, Dworkin's transformation of debate into an aura of principles cannot acknowledge the extent that the positions of writers such as MacKinnon relate to existential features of a woman's life. As McCaffrey and Novkov summarise:

> MacKinnon is not making an argument about the intrinsic value of the foetus but rather about the material relationship between the woman and the foetus she carries. The relationship is deeply contextual and carries with it the history of its formation. It may thus be rendered problematic by the way it came into being: if a woman becomes pregnant through an act of coercive sexuality, her relationship with the foetus she bears will be different from her relationship with a foetus she has conceived willingly ...

MacKinnon seeks to focus upon the contextualised history of the foetus's origins and the effect that these origins have upon the woman who carries it (ibid: 205–6).

MacKinnon's solution to the abortion dilemma is to situate it within the changing forms of social structure and hopes for sexual equality. If sexual relationships can become less unequal and coercive (both personally and structurally) there not only will be less of an issue quantifiably (in that there would be fewer foetuses due to more free choice) and the relationship to the foetus in any individual case would be different. Dworkin's reading of Gilligan also picks up on the idea of responsibility but downplays the connected idea of relationship. In short there is a gulf between Dworkin's focus upon the sanctity of life (and his corresponding vague theory of the sacred) and the role of abortion in women's lives. From a feminist stance: 'state attempts to regulate abortion are really about adopting particular views of women's proper roles in society' (*ibid*: 224).

Abortion is a political issue in American and British New Right campaigns and takes on the appearance of a religious issue; to many women this is ideological mystification, the real issue is the economic and political marginalisation of women's interests. For feminists abortion is not a question of rights alone; it is a vitally important site overloaded with historical struggles concerning the family, motherhood, sexuality, self-sufficiency, and only by guaranteeing women's status as full and equal members of society can the problem of abortion be seen in greater existential depth.

Cultural feminism and difference theory

Philosophy, both ideal and material, has not found women's praxis in giving birth interesting; rather it has sustained a nagging death fetish, a preoccupation with finitude. Death without birth is not only abstract and unrealist, but signals an odd unwillingness to give meaning to species' persistence as the material substructure of temporality. I want to suggest that such an elision is possible only where thought is masculine (O'Brien, 1989: 84).

For cultural feminism, male domination is based on the grounding of the modern structure of thought (reason) on the male experience and the force of violence, but many things of value are lost to humanity by the downgrading of the experiences and perspectives of women. Even in the liberal irreducible core of jurisprudence – law as the barrier which holds back death, personal and collective – the fundamentality of woman's material bond with life-giving and nurture is downplayed.[29] Cultural feminism endeavours to repair this deficiency, to present the reasoning of the feminine 'other'.

Carol Gilligan

Gilligan is an American educational psychologist at Harvard who has developed a thesis on a 'woman's voice' and an ethic of care which has proved highly controversial.

---

29 To preserve the supremacy of the male the problem of birth and interrelationships must be removed from centre stage: men are of woman born, but must find their essence somewhere else than in relation to women; as Descartes asked 'from what do I derive my existence?' and gave his ultimate answer as God. The word of God is to be transcribed and translated by men.

In her *In a Different Voice: Psychological Theory and Women's Development* (1982) Gilligan responded to the work of Lawrence Kohlberg (1973, 1976, 1981, 1987), who had established a scale of cognitive moral development in which women were consistently outperformed by men. Gilligan's work argued that women's moral reasoning was not inferior, it was simply different, emphasising contrasting values. Under the six-stage model of human development (originally based on an empirical study of 84 boys over an period of 20 years) developed by Lawrence Kohlberg, women's judgments seemed to exemplify the third stage of development, where goodness was equated with pleasing and helping others. Kohlberg explained this as a result of the life experiences 'allowed' to women and implied that if women had a greater role in the public sphere they would move onto the higher stages that typify men's judgments. By contrast Gilligan asserts that her empirical research reveals what she calls a woman's voice, a different voice, not necessarily inferior to the (hu)man's voice which psychologists have traditionally described.

Kohlberg developed a notion of structurally categorised motives for engaging in moral action by tests such as the following 'moral dilemma' to which the student must respond:[30]

> In Europe, a woman was near death from cancer. One drug might save her, a form of radium that a druggist in the same town had recently discovered. The chemist was charging £2,000, 10 times what the drug cost him to make. The sick woman's husband, Heinz, went to everyone he knew to borrow the money, but he could only get together about half of what it cost. He told the chemist that his wife was dying and asked him to sell it cheaper or let him pay later. But the chemist said, 'no'. The husband got desperate and broke into the chemist's store to steal the drug for his wife. Should the husband have done that? Why?

There is a developmental list of answers which do not provide an absolute right or wrong response. Instead, disagreements are possible at each stage. Nevertheless, stages are defined by principles of reasoning, that is, by form, not content.

There are two stages of *preconventional morality*:

Stage 1: Action is motivated by avoidance of punishment and 'conscience' is irrational fear of punishment.

> Pro – If you let your wife die, you will get into trouble. You'll be blamed for not spending the money to save her and there'll be an investigation of you and the chemist for your wife's death.

> Con – You shouldn't steal the drug because you'll be caught and sent to jail if you do. If you do get away, your conscience would bother you thinking how the police would catch up with you at any minute.

Stage 2. Action is motivated by desire for reward or benefit. Possible guilt reactions are ignored and punishment viewed in a pragmatic manner (this differentiates own fear, pleasure, pain from punishment-consequences).

---

30 The following discussion of Kohlberg's dilemma is largely derived from William M Sullivan, *Reconstructing Public Philosophy*, 1982: 128–131.

Pro – If you do happen to get caught you could give the drug back and you wouldn't get much of a sentence. It wouldn't bother you much to serve a little jail term, if you have your wife when you get out.

Con – He may not get much of a jail term if he steals the drug, but his wife will probably die before he gets out so it won't do him much good. If his wife dies, he shouldn't blame himself: it wasn't his fault she has cancer.

Next comes *conventional morality*, which is reflex of group membership. 'The conventional individual subordinates the needs of the single individual to the viewpoint and needs of the group or the shared relationship' (Kohlberg).

Stage 3. Action is motivated by anticipation of disapproval of others, actual or imagined-hypothetical (eg guilt) (this differentiates disapproval from punishment, fear, and pain).

Pro – No one will think you are bad if you steal the drug but your family will think you're an inhuman husband if you don't. If you let your wife die, you'll never be able to look anybody in the face again.

Con – It isn't just the chemist who will think you're a criminal, everyone else will too. After you steal it, you'll feel bad thinking how you've brought dishonour on your family and yourself; you won't be able to face anyone again.

Stage 4. Action motivated by anticipation of dishonour, ie institutionalised blame for failure of duty, and by guilt over concrete harm done to others (this differentiates formal dishonour from informal disapproval; this differentiates guilt for bad consequences from disapproval).

Pro – If you have any sense of honour, you won't let your wife die because you're afraid to do the only thing that will save her. You'll always feel guilty that you caused her death if you don't do your duty to her.

Con – You're desperate and you may not know you're doing wrong when you steal the drug. But you'll know you did wrong after you're punished and sent to jail. You'll always feel guilty for your dishonesty and law-breaking.

In *postconventional morality* abstract principle rather than group affiliation is the criterion of moral judgment. Morally autonomous individuals criticise social rules in the light of rational principles.

Stage 5: Concern about maintaining the respect of equals and of the community (assuming their respect is based on reason rather than emotions). Concern about own self-respect, ie to avoid judging self as irrational, inconsistent, non-purposive (this differentiates between institutionalised blame and community disrespect or self-disrespect).

Pro – You'd lose other people's respect, not gain, if you don't steal. If you let your wife die, it would be out of fear, not out of reasoning it out. So you'd just lose self-respect and probably the respect of others too.

Con – You would lose your standing and respect in the community and violate the law. You'd lose respect for yourself if you're carried away by emotion and forget the long-range point of view.

Stage 6. Concern about self-condemnation for violating one's own principles (this differentiates between community respect and self-respect; this differentiates between self-respect for general achieving rationality and self-respect for maintaining moral principles).

Pro – If you don't steal the drug and let your wife die, you'd always condemn yourself for it afterwards. You wouldn't be blamed and you would have lived up to the outside rule of the law but you wouldn't have lived up to your own standards of conscience.

Con – If you stole the drug, you wouldn't be blamed by other people but you'd condemn yourself because you wouldn't have lived up to your own conscience and standards of honesty.

The stage theory judges the form of the reasoning, not the content. The higher stages are judged to be more advanced because they are more formally adequate in that the criteria governing the higher stages subsume the lower, each stage advancing closer to an ideal reciprocity of transaction and the universe of moral principles and individual rights.[31] The invariant sequence of stages, if empirically demonstrated, would set firm limits on the arbitrariness of genuine moral principles. At the same time, these valid principles would be universal and established independently of a substantive conception of human ends beyond maturation of natural, presumably genetic, potential. The moral principle of justice thus becomes a procedural norm of rational co-operation.[32]

By contrast Gilligan argues for a distinctive women's voice based on similar dilemmas and interviews with men and women.[33] In particular she conducted interviews with college students, and other studies on identity and moral development in their early adult years, carried out an abortion decision-making study on the relation

---

31 Kohlberg defines a moral principle as a mode of choosing which is universal, a rule of choosing which it is felt desirable for all people to adopt always in all situations.

32 Kohlberg's psychology is designed in part to complement empirically the moral claims of the social contract doctrine as elaborated by Kant and Rawls. According to that view, justice is an obligation to contract which requires impartiality in administering the law and the right of individuals to equal treatment. The theory is an elaborate contemporary re-statement of the liberal argument for the self-evidence of the moral scheme of the social contract. Kohlberg can then argue that moral education should proceed by focusing on the form, not the content, of moral beliefs and action. From the perspective of the social contract, that is, Stage 5 morality, all moral 'contents' or ends are fundamentally arbitrary. Obligation is defined in terms of contract, as respect for mutual rights, especially the right to be treated as an end in oneself and never as a means to another's end. The cognitive basis of moral reasoning is a developing ability to see the elements of that concrete thinking, the particular acts of persons, in abstraction from their experienced context so as to focus on the formal quality of reciprocity.

33 Gilligan (1982: 26-39) contrasts the responses of Jake, as typical of the young male, and Amy, as typical of the young female. Jake depicts the moral dilemma as a conflict between the right to life and the right to property; he posits that the right to life has greater importance than the latter and concludes that theft of the drug is morally justified. Amy seems more torn between stealing the drug and confronting the death of Heinz's wife; she looks for middle ways such as a loan to buy the drug, and depicts the principle moral issue as the chemist's refusal to compromise and find a way for Heinz to obtain the drug. Gilligan thus claims Amy's response would be placed on a lower level of moral development than Jake (since Amy did not see the issue in terms of a conflict of rights), but she interprets Amy's response as valuing accommodating continual relationships and understanding the interconnectedness of all those involved in the scenario.

between experience and thought and the role of conflict in development and rights and responsibilities, a study on conceptions of self morality, experiences of moral conflict and choice,[34] and judgments of hypothetical moral dilemmas. She concludes:

1   *Women conceive relationships in a different mode from men.* While men see relationships as a hierarchy, women conceive them as a web. For men the hierarchy is unstable, the desire is to reach the top and the fear is that someone else will come too close to that position at the top. For women the web is stable, the desire is to be at the centre and the fear is being too far out on the edge. Gilligan argues that these fears and desires 'give rise to different portrayals of achievement and affiliation, leading to different modes of action and different ways of assessing the consequences of choice' (1982: 62).

2   The abortion study had revealed *a distinct moral language* for women of 'selfishness and responsibility, which defines the moral problem as one of obligation to exercise care and avoid hurt. The inflicting of hurt is considered selfish and immoral in its reflection of unconcern, while the expression of care is seen as the fulfilment of moral responsibility' (1982: 73). Women reconstruct hypothetical dilemmas in terms of the real and often request further information. They tend to see abstraction in hypothetical discussion, as threatening to inflict harm through ignorance of the social consequences of a decision. Gilligan claims that women see the process of constructing hypothetical arguments as a process of abstracting out of and destroying real social life. Thus we can cause social harm by ignoring the real social locations and the social webs people are located within. Abstraction may be useful for the 'distillation and refinement of objective principles of justice and for measuring the formal logic of equality and reciprocity' but it is not conducive to 'the understanding of cause and consequence which engages the compassion and tolerance repeatedly noted to distinguish the moral judgments of women' (*ibid*: 100).

3   *Women give a distinctive construction to moral problems,* seeing moral dilemmas in terms of conflicting responsibilities. Care is the most important guide in the resolution of conflicts, while men see rights and justice as the key to resolution. *Thus women have an ethic of care or responsibility and men have an ethic of rights or justice.* Gilligan argues that her research demonstrates 'the centrality of the concepts of responsibility and care in women's constructions of the moral domain [and] the close tie in women's thinking between conceptions of the self and morality' (*ibid*: 105).

4   The conception of self and world is thus one of *relationship rather than domination* and separation. Self-description reveals women's identity and is defined in the context of relationships and judged by a standard of responsibility and care: 'masculinity is defined through separation while femininity is defined through attachment' (*ibid*: 7–

---

34 Such as studies of girls and boys at play which tended to show that in cases of cheating, the boys tended to remonstrate with the transgressor and ostracise him from the group, while if they realise that not all will play by the rules, girls will seek to change the game and maintain cohesion in the group. Gilligan (1982: 10–11) interprets this in terms of contrasting demands for strict enforcement of the rules and the maintenance of group cohesion.

8). One of her subjects describes being alone or unconnected as 'like the sound of one hand clapping ... there is something lacking' (*ibid*: 160). In contrast, the male self-descriptions, while speaking of attachments, were characterised by adjectives of separation.

Involvement with others [was] tied to a qualification of identity rather than to its realisation. Instead of attachment, individual achievement rivets male imagination, and great ideas or distinctive activity defines the standard or self-assessment and success (*ibid*: 163).

Are these poles total? What is the growth of a person and what is maturity? For Gilligan true maturity for both sexes would be to move away from the absolutes with which they are associated. That is, men must move away from the absolutes of rights, truth and fairness, to a realisation of differences between other and self and a recognition that multiple truths exist. Similarly, women must move away from the absolute of care and recognise a claim for equality and rights that transforms their understanding of relationships and their definition of care.

For Carol Smart:

Gilligan's work therefore constitutes the basis of a critique of any system of justice (criminal and civil) which celebrates the masculine voice of moral judgment as a form of universal justice. This can be developed in a number of ways. For example, it becomes possible to re-examine the criminal 'justice' system in terms of whether the application of a masculine mode of judgment is inherently and necessarily 'unjust' in its treatment of women. It raises the question of whether penal sanctions based on this masculine mode (eg institutional incarceration or economic penalties) are not unusually harsh when applied to women because they are derived from a mode of thought devised by men for male offenders. Equally, it is possible to develop an argument which criticises the system in terms of its treatment of both men and women. Gilligan looks forward to a 'more generative view of human life'. For her the ethic of justice (that everyone should be treated the same) should be added to the ethic of caring (that no one should be hurt) to produce a better outcome. Her conclusion is thus not to produce a separatist system of justice for women, not to replace the ethic of justice with the ethic of caring (1989: 74).

Smart states that in some ways this is a disappointing conclusion as it can be argued that some systems already claim to do this (for example, the appointment of women magistrates, the operation of the juvenile bench with juvenile justice). Thus Gilligan's work merely revives old concepts. Others have argued that Gilligan's work is essentialist[35] or reproduces the reductionist positions that male-led discourse gave women. Gilligan, however, never suggested that women's voices were biologically determined or even that they are only found in women. As she put it in her introduction:

... the different voice I describe is characterised not by gender but theme. Its association with women is an empirical observation and it is primarily through women's voices that I trace its development. But this association is not absolute, and the contrasts between male and female voices are presented here to highlight a distinction between two modes

---

35 In other words, the female developmental model in her work is a parallel universalism to the developmental model of Kohlberg.

of thought and to focus a problem of interpretation rather than to represent a generalisation about either sex.

Catherine MacKinnon reacts sharply, claiming Gilligan is actually reinforcing women's oppression; Gilligan's work only cerebrates the view women have been allowed to develop:

I am critical of affirming what we have been, which necessarily is what we have been permitted, as if it is women's, ours, possessive.

... the way women reason morally is [not] morality 'in a different voice'. I think that it is morality in a higher register, in the feminine voice. Women value care because men have valued us according to the care we give them ... Women think in relational terms because our existence is defined in relation to men. Further, when you are powerless, you don't speak differently. A lot, you don't speak. Your speech is not just differently articulated, it is silenced. Eliminated, gone. You aren't just deprived of a language with which to articulate your distinctiveness, although you are; you are deprived of a life out of which articulation might come ... All I am saying is that the damage of sexism is real, and reifying that into differences is an insult to our possibilities (1987: 39).

This is the opposite criticism to essentialism. For MacKinnon, Gilligan does not describe what women actually are, but what women have been socialised to be. Gilligan therefore describes and then reifies gender oppression. Viewed in this light Gilligan's work is regressive.[36] Nevertheless, in the United States, applying Gilligan's work to transform legal perspectives – at least academically – has been a fertile field of theorising.[37] Partly this is a critique of existing laws: because the whole paradigm of political and moral philosophy upon which they are legitimated is individualist, the legal theory of constitutionalism is individualist (Suzanna Sherry, 1986); the debates over progressive taxation or tax-cutting are dominated by ideas of separateness with little concept of social responsibility (Kornhauser, 1987); bankruptcy laws are revealed as a male-dominated field of activity with no concern for the poverty-inducing effects of its operation (Gross, 1990); tort laws would receive a different notion of responsibility and harm (Bender, 1990);[38] and applying the 'web of connection' to constitutional law would yield greater protection (Karst, 1984).

---

36 Joan Williams, in 'Deconstructing Gender' ((1989) 87 *Michigan Law Review* 797) illustrates how Gilligan has been used in litigation to women's detriment. In *EEOC v Sears* 628 F Supp 1264 (ND Ill 1986), Sears successfully argued that women were under-represented in higher paying commission sales jobs because women 'lacked' interest in sales, not because Sears was discriminating against them. Gilligan was cited in expert testimony to support Sears' argument that women have different career aspirations to men which make them less interested in high-powered jobs. The court accepted a very 'Gilliganesque' picture of women as nurturers and carers, adverse to capitalist virtues such as competition. Joan Williams claims that Gilligan and other cultural or relational feminists are simply rehashing Victorian domestic ideology that constructed women as more caring, less competitive and more moral then men. She argues that even in Victorian times this concept of women was cast in a positive light, but it ultimately led to their increased subordination.

37 Reviews of this work are in Katharine T Bartlett, *Gender and Law* (1993), and Leslie Bender, *From Gender Difference to Feminist Solidarity: Using Carol Gilligan and an Ethic of Care in Law* (1990).

38 Bender uses Gilligan's work both as a source of critique of existing tort law and a source of ideas for transformation. She argues that an ethic of 'rights' and the idea of separation dominates the field; in tort responsibility is largely seen in terms of fiscal responsibility, and not responsibility for taking care of others.

Robin West – separation and connection in legal and feminist theory

In a classic article, Robin West (1988) contrasted the different perspectives. West claimed that male legal theorists exhibit a specific form of reasoning because they experience the world firstly and fundamentally as separate, autonomous individuals; the foundation of both traditional and 'critical' masculine jurisprudence is a 'separation' thesis. Conversely, women:

> are not essentially, necessarily, inevitably, always, and forever separate from other human beings ... [but] are in some sense 'connected' to life and to other human beings during at least four recurrent and critical material experiences: the experience of pregnancy itself; the invasive and 'connecting' experience of heterosexual penetration, which may lead to pregnancy; the monthly experience of menstruation, which represents the potential for pregnancy; and the post-pregnancy experience of breast-feeding (1988: 2-3).

Women reason out of a 'connectedness' which men cannot experience. This counter-experience of women provides the basis of an alternative to legal theory which, through the presuppositions of the separation thesis, has become 'essentially and irrevocably masculine' *(ibid*: 2). West develops a set of contrasting hopes and fears through a stylistic presentation of the positions of legal liberalism, critical legal theory, cultural feminism and radical feminism.

Legal liberalism

Legal liberalism presupposes autonomous individualism and takes as its central value the notions of separation and freedom; freedom is defined as distance from the 'other' and the social space for the individual to pursue his/her own ends.[39] Freedom and autonomy is the 'official value' of liberalism, its hope; the fear lies in the vulnerability of the human condition and the danger that the discrete, separate 'other' may annihilate you.[40] To protect themselves from this 'other', human beings create and respect the state.[41] The foundational supposition of liberal legalism is that human beings experience the world as separate individuals, unconnected to others unless they so choose: as a result the value that is put forward above all else is the right to pursue our lives relatively free of outside control.

The critical legal theorists' view

For *critical legal theorists*, separation is not a 'perpetual celebration of autonomy, but rather, a perpetual longing for community, or attachment, or unification, or

---

39 For West, Ronald Dworkin expresses this perfectly: 'What does it mean for the government to treat its citizens as equals? That is ... the same question as the question of what it means for the government to treat all its citizens as free, or as independent, or with equal dignity' (Ronald Dworkin, 1985: 191, cited in West, 1988: 6).

40 This time West returns to the fear Hobbes expressed. 'If two men desire the same thing, which nevertheless they cannot both enjoy, they become enemies; and in the way to their end ... endeavour to destroy, or subdue one an other' (Thomas Hobbes, *Leviathan*, cited in West, 1988: 8).

41 The 'minimal state treats us as inviolate individuals ... [which] allows us, individually or with whom we choose, to choose our life and to realise our ends ...' (Robert Nozick, 1974: 333-4, cited in West, 1988: 9)

connection'. Human beings do not truly fear annihilation, as liberalism claims, but isolation and alienation.[42] Critical legal theory is the 'unofficial story' of masculine legal theory; in opposition to liberalism's focus on autonomy, it presents the individual as really desiring the opposite of what the dominant culture tells him he desires. Whereas the dominant culture in America (liberalism) says that autonomy is the key to happiness, inside himself the individual knows that connection and community are the key. The 'unofficial value' of masculine legal theory is connection and community and the 'unofficial harm' is alienation and isolation.[43] West claims that although women may fear intimacy as the destruction of their personhood (through their unique physical structure which makes them subject to the invasion of the penis) they do not fear it in the way that men do. Thus in criticising liberalism the Critical Legal Studies movement is trapped within the same separation thesis. Conversely:

> women are actually or potentially materially connected to other human life. Men aren't. This material fact has existential consequences. While it may be true for men that the individual is 'epistemologically and morally prior to collectivity', it is not true for women. The potential for material connection with the other defines women's subjective, phenomenological and existential state, just as surely as the inevitability of material separation from the other defines men's existential state. Our potential for material connection engenders pleasures and pains, values and dangers, and attractions and fears, which are entirely different from those which follow, for men, from necessity of separation (1988: 14).

Cultural vs radical feminism

In seeking a positive mode of thought and morality in the experiences that women endure,[44] cultural feminism develops the connection thesis, but closes off analysing the material conditions in which this development takes place. Its essential truth lies in connection, a truth which 'ought' to be universal:

---

42 As Roberto Unger puts it (1975: 201 cited in West, 1988: 10): 'Consciousness, then, is the sign of self's distance from the world. If one could imagine this separateness from nature in its pure form, before it was counterbalanced by the effects of human activity, its sign would be the experience of terror before the strangeness of the world. Because this terror is the mark of that very separation between self and nature upon which consciousness itself is based, it has never been driven completely out of conscious life.'

43 West's commentary upon the 'fundamental contradiction' which Duncan Kennedy finds at the basis of social life stresses its masculine structure: 'According to Kennedy, we value *both* autonomy and connection, and fear *both* annihilation by the other and alienation from him, and all for good reason. The other is both necessary to our continued existence and a threat to that continued existence. While it is true that the dominant liberal story of autonomy and annihilation serves to perpetuate the *status quo*, it does not follow from that fact that the subjective desires for freedom and security which those liberal values reify are entirely *false*. Rather, Kennedy argues, collectivity is both essential to our identity and an obstacle to it. We have contradictory desires and values because our essential human condition – physical separation from the collectivity which is necessary to our identity – is itself contradictory.'

44 West defines cultural feminism in relation to Carol Gilligan (*In a Different Voice*), Nancy Chodorow (*The Reproduction of Mothering* (1978)), and Suzanne Sherry ('Civic Virtue and the Feminine Voice in Constitutional Adjudication' (1986) 72 *Va LR* 543); Andrea Dworkin (*Intercourse* (1987)), Adrienne Rich (*On Lies, Secrets and Silence* (1979)), and Catherine MacKinnon (*Feminism Unmodified*).

Intimacy is not just something women do, it is something human beings ought to do. Intimacy is a source of value, not a private hobby. It is morality, not habit (*ibid*: 18).

While liberalism speaks of the fear of annihilation, women fear isolation and separation; women most often have trouble when a separate self must be asserted.[45]

Radical feminists, conversely, view the connection thesis as a starting point of women's experience, yet argue it is also a source of women's debasement, powerlessness, subjugation, and misery. In their search for intimacy, women actually experience invasion and intrusion; cultural feminists mistakenly characterise as connection and caring harmful invasions of women's bodies and minds.[46] West argues that each of the category presents radically different descriptions of humanity and womanhood. The significance of this is two-fold: (i) the perspectives of liberal legalism speak not of humanity but of men;[47] and (ii) there is a real contradiction in women's lives as a result of the conflicting experiences of intimacy and invasion.[48]

---

45 Note a contrast with liberal theory. Whereas Hobbes sees the 'other' as an equal who is potentially dangerous, the 'other' women most commonly encounter – the foetus or child – is anything but dangerous and equal. There is a natural inequality between a woman and her child – it is physically, emotionally and mentally weaker than her – but this does not prompt the woman to aggress against it (as Hobbes presumes men will do), rather it promotes in her feelings of responsibility, care and nurturing. As a result: 'Men respond to the natural state of equality with an ethic of autonomy and rights. Women respond to the natural state of inequality with an ethic of responsibility and care' (West, 1988: 28).

46 Thus while Unger claims that 'love helps man overcome the distinction between self and nature' (Unger, *Knowledge and Politics*: 205), cultural feminism does not accept that women have a distinction between the self and nature. For West women value love and intimacy because they express the unity of self and nature through our own selves. 'Intimacy is not something which women fight to become capable of. We just do it. It is ridiculously easy. It is also I suspect, qualitatively beyond the pale of male effort. The difference might be put pictorially: the intimacy women value is a sharing of intersubjective territory that pre-exists the effort made to identify it' (West: 1988: 40).

47 'When Hobbes, Ackerman, Dworkin, Rawls and the rest of the liberal tradition describe the natural human predicament as one of natural equality and mutual antagonism, and describe human beings as inevitably separate and mutually self-interested, thus definitionally excluding pregnant women and breast-feeding mothers from the species, they are ... mistaken in a particular way and for a particular reason. Gabel has confused his male experience of separation and alienation with 'human' experience, and liberals have confused their male experiences of natural equality, mutual separation, fear of annihilation, and pervasive, through-and-through selfishness with 'human' experience, and they have done so because women have not made it clear that our day-to-day, lived experience – of intimacy, bonding, separation, sexual invasion, nurturance and intrusion – is incommensurable with men's. We need to flood the market with our own stories until we get one simple point across: men's narrative story and phenomenological description of law is not women's story and phenomenology of law. We need to dislodge legal theorists' confidence that they speak for women, and we need to fill the gap that will develop when we succeed in doing so' (West, 1988: 65).

48 '... women 'officially' value intimacy (and fear separation) in spite of subjective desires to the contrary not (solely) because of the legitimating power of patriarchal ideology, not (solely) because of the power of denial, but rather, because women's existential and material circumstance is itself one of contradiction. The potentiality for physical connection with others that uniquely characterises women's lives has within it the seeds of both intimacy and invasion, and therefore women rightly value the former while we dread and fear the latter, just as the necessity of physical separation, for men, carries within it the seeds of both intimacy and alienation, and men rightly value the former and dread the latter. If this is right, then all four accounts of human experience – liberal legalism, critical legalism, cultural feminism and radical feminism – are saying something true about human experience. Legal liberalism and critical legalism both describe something true about male experience, and cultural feminism and radical feminism both describe something true about female experience (1988: 53).

FEMINIST FEARS AND UTOPIA

West's distinctions may be too sharply drawn; the contrasts in fears and hopes may be reflections of aspects of human fears, hopes and desires. Each perspective fixes upon one or other tendency in the human condition at the expense of others. Andrea Dworkin, for example, identifies cultural feminism's official value (intimacy) as a cover for harm. Most feminists would accept that unwanted intercourse, rape, is a harm and that to some women unwanted pregnancy is a harm, but radical feminists push their argument much further than this, often presenting the idea that pregnancy and motherhood constitute harms *per se*, because the foetus and the child are intrusive. For radical feminists, intercourse, including voluntary intercourse, is a harm since it 'divides a woman internally' – it 'pre-empts, challenges, negates, and renders impossible the maintenance of physical integrity and the formation of a unified self' (West, 1988: 35).

Radical feminists are torn between denying the inhumanity and alienation of individualism and claiming that because intimacy constitutes a harm, women long for individuation. Conversely, they wish to free women of the colonisation of their minds by the hegemony of patriarchy. The dominant culture tells women that they value intimacy and dependency to make them more easily governed by men; separation and independence are what they actually need, but this risks returning the liberalism.

Contrasting the interaction of the male–female body

Again the perceptions of the body are vital. In the 1980s various radical feminist critiques of intercourse depicted it in terms of a profound invasion of the self's physical integrity. Andrea Dworkin's book *Intercourse* is one of the prime proponents of this argument.

> ... There is the outline of a body, distinct, separate, its integrity an illusion, a tragic deception, because unseen there is a slit between the legs, and he has to push into it. There is never a real privacy of the body that can co-exist with intercourse: with being entered. The vagina itself is muscled and the muscles have to be pushed apart. The thrusting is persistent invasion. She is opened up, split down the centre. She is occupied – physically, internally, in her privacy ... her hole is synonymous with entry ... By definition she is intended to have a lesser privacy, a lesser integrity of the body, a lesser sense of self ... She is defined by how she is made, that hole, which is synonymous with entry; and intercourse, the act fundamental to existence, has consequences to her being that may be intrinsic, not socially imposed (1987: 122–3).

What then of love? The more mystic writings of Luce Irigaray call for an intermingling of experiences, a revelation of the divine in humanity by an 'amorous matrix' where human flesh is not to be regarded with suspicion and where 'the evanescence of the caress' talks to a celebration of life in an ethics of touching:

> The most subtly necessary guardian of my life being the other's flesh. Approaching and speaking to me with his hands. Bringing me back to life more intimately than any regenerative nourishment, the other's hands, these palms with which he approaches without going through me, give me back the borders of my body and call me back to the remembrance of the most profound intimacy. As he caresses me, he bids me neither to

disappear nor to forget but rather, to remember the place where, for me, the most intimate life holds itself in reserve. Searching for what has not yet come into being, for himself, he invites me to become what I have not yet become. To realise a birth still in the future. Plunging me back into the maternal womb and, beyond that, conception, awakening me to another – amorous – birth (Irigaray 1986: 232-3).

The identity of the female body has been lost in the demarcation of the mother role from the object of desire for the male lover. In Igarary's emancipation of the body it is the territory neither of the one who gave the woman her body (the mother), nor of the one who calls upon it to join his (the lover); instead the coming together denotes the search for a 'moment of ultimate sympathy', a return to 'the deepest level of elemental flux, where birth is not yet sealed up in identity' (ibid: 234).

Life dances with death, but one does not keep death at bay by (legitimate) domination of the other, nor by sealing off the other (boundary drawing), but by constant rebirth. The caress speaks to a 'future coming, which is not measured by the transcendence of death but by the call to birth of the self and the other ... Prior to any procreation, the lovers bestow on each other – life. Love fecundates each of them in turn ... reborn each for the other ... ' (ibid: 232, 235).

Beyond difference: feminism as humanism?

Drucilla Cornell's utopian methodology is of an 'ethical feminism' in which working for the feminine is also imagining a new structure for humanity beyond domination:

Ethical feminism 'envisions' not only a world in which the viewpoint of the feminine is appreciated; ethical feminism also 'sees' a world 'peopled' by individuals, 'sexed' differently, a world beyond castration. Through our 'visions' we affirm the 'should be' of a different way of being human. The 'goal' of ethical feminism, which 'sees' the 'should be' inherent in the feminine viewpoint, is not just power for women, but the redefinition of all of our fundamental concepts, including power. Feminine power should not, in other words, be separated from the different, ethical vision of human 'beings' sought after in the feminine, understood as a redemptive process (1991: 131).

INTO MULTIPLE SUBJECTIVITIES: THE IMPACT OF BLACK, OR CRITICAL RACE, FEMINISM[49]

That man over there says women need to be helped into carriages, and lifted over ditches, and to have the best place everywhere. Nobody ever helps me into carriages, or over mud-puddles, or gives me the best place! And ain't I a woman? Look at me! Look at my arm! I have ploughed, and planted, and gathered into barns, and no man could head

---

49 It is even controversial to speak of black feminism. Although women such as Maria Stewart, Sojourner Truth and Anna J Cooper (who discussed the viewpoint of the black women in her 1892 book *A Voice from the South by a Black Woman of the South*) presented a black women's perspective, they usually presented their argument as an argument for the whole race (since 'a stream cannot rise higher than its source'); a self-conscious black feminism is relatively recent. Frances Beale (1970) coined the term 'double jeopardy' to characterise the condition of being both female and black. Alice Walker prefers the terminology of womanism, defined as a commitment 'to the survival and wholeness of entire people, male and female ...'

me! And ain't I a woman? I could work as much and eat as much as a man – when I could get it – and bear the lash as well! And ain't I a woman? I have born 13 children, and seen most of them sold off to slavery, and when I cried out with my mother's grief, none but Jesus heard me! And ain't I a woman? (Address by Sojourner Truth, 1851, quoted in Bartlett and Kennedy, 1991:256)[50]

A black feminist ideology ... declares the visibility of black women ... Second, black feminism asserts self-determination is essential. Black women are empowered with the right to interpret our reality and define our objectives. Third, a black feminist ideology fundamentally challenges the interstructure of the oppressions of racism, sexism, and classism both in the dominant society and within movements of liberation. Finally, a black feminist ideology presumes an image of black women as powerful, independent subjects (Deborah K King, quoted Jewell, 1993).

The discourse of (particularly American) black women was originally an oral tradition and latterly usually has been that of the literary, the poetic and (blues, jazz) song. Today black feminists consciously take up the narrative tradition while demarcating themselves from 'feminism, in general'.[51] While one tendency of black consciousness may be a retreat to purity – an attempt to find a stable identity that is untouched by the legacy of colonisation, domination and the discourses of inferiority, other, perhaps post-modern, black scholarship denies universalisms (eg, Harris, Angela P, 1990), speaks to specificality and uniqueness, while stressing the commonality of interest in the differences of humanity.[52]

There are many themes but one is a movement to reclaim a self from the structures of slavery and multiple oppression. As bell hooks (1990, 1991) put it: ' ... no black woman can become an intellectual without decolonising her mind'. How does decolonising work? Take Judy Scales-Trent:

Another empowering act has been to take charge of defining my group, of naming myself. Naming oneself, defining oneself and thereby taking the power to define out of the hands of those who wield the power over you, is an important act of empowerment ... The act of self-definition thus makes clear our worth and entitlement, and sets forth our view of ourselves as one which will have to be reckoned with (quoted, Jewell, 1993: 103).

Or, in the famous words of the black American poet Audre Lorde, the African-American woman, heir to a tradition where her forebears were slaves, must not only

---

50 Sojourner Truth's appearance at the Akron Convention on Woman's Suffrage in 1851 was fought against by several of the organiser's – Frances Gage – colleagues. As Gage relates the advice was simple: 'don't let her speak, Mrs Gage, it will ruin us. Every newspaper in the land will have our cause mixed up with abolition and niggers, and we shall be utterly denounced' (quoted in Linda Ammons, 1995: 1041).

51 *Note*: with feminist scholarship the pattern has been that its analyses tended to reflect the experiences of white, middle-class women in America and some western European countries. While they were arguing that traditional scholarship universalised from limited perspectives their own was similarly limited. However, feminism has become aware that the voices left out from the main discourses of modernity have not only been women's but those of the many social groups which appeared as 'other' to the mainstream. However, feminism is still largely the pursuit of white middle-class women.

52 As Audre Lorde expresses it, the differences between white and black American feminists may relate to real differences in life position: 'Some problems we share as women, some we do not. You fear your children will grow up to join the patriarchy and testify against you, we fear our children will be dragged from a car and shot down in the street, and you will turn your backs upon the reasons they are dying' (1984: 119).

create positive messages and modes of articulating the situation black women find themselves in, but develop other forms of support which enable a degree of self-sufficiency and independence: *for the master's tools will never dismantle the master's house.*[53] Much of the traditional language and imagery of black female writers has concerned pain and suffering – understandably, since their historical reality (even when recounted by white males[54]) has often been a living hell – does this doom their tradition to one of recounting victimisation?[55] A poetry of the oppressed? Audre Lorde (1984) draws parallels with the traditional fear of the elites of the rich associative and musical language of poetry and its fear of the black skin, of the female, of darkness, of the dark 'other'. Lorde argues that black scholarship can only work as meaningful analysis if it sees in the experiences of black women sources of wisdom and not just examples of victimisation.[56]

Patricia J Williams constructs in *The Alchemy of Race and Rights: a Diary of a Law Professor*, a vigorous series of essays intermixing insights gained through personal experience, legal scholarship and flights of allegory and metaphor. Williams locates her message(s) by narrative recall. Positioning (her) subjectivity as a site of multiple forces and cultural messages, her self almost dissolves; battles over identity are not just for academic seminars and the struggle for recognition is social, racial and personal.[57] While

53 '*For the master's tools will never dismantle the master's house.* They may allow us temporarily to beat him at his own game, but they will never enable us to bring about a genuine change. And this fact is only threatening to those women who still define the master's house as their only source of support' (Audre Lorde, 1981: 99).

54 As the slave trader, John Newton (1962) recalled in his *The Journal of a Slave Trader* 1750-1754: 'when the women and girls were taken on board a ship, naked, trembling, terrified, perhaps almost exhausted with cold, fatigue, and hunger, they are often exposed to the wanton rudeness of white savages. The poor creatures cannot understand the language they hear, but the looks and manner of the speakers are sufficiently intelligible. In imagination, the prey is divided, upon the spot, and only reserved till opportunity offers. Where resistance or refusal would be utterly in vain, even the solicitation of consent is seldom thought of.'

55 'The sale began – young girls were there,
   Defenceless in their wretchedness,
Whose stifled sobs of deep despair
   Revealed their anguish and distress.
And mothers stood with streaming eyes,
   And saw their dearest children sold;
Unheeded rose their bitter cries,
   While tyrants bartered them for gold ...' (Ellen Watkins Harper, extract from *The Slave Auction*, 1857)

56 For a detailed and extensive review of imagery and social position of black women and how this impacts upon a particular field of living law see Linda Ammos, 'Mules, Madonnas, Babies, Bathwater, Racial Imagery and Stereotypes: The African-American Woman and the Battered Woman Syndrome', *Wisconsin Law Review*, 1995, 5.

57 One of the main tactics of feminist writing has been to breathe new life into narrative as a form of scholarly work. In the hands of Patricia J Williams, narrative is used to give her a sense of self which forms the basis of the 'character' who will do the jurisprudential writings. Her themes are of the difficulty of gaining a coherent sense of self in a dislocating post-modern world, particularly for blacks who have the legacy of white discourse to construct their identities with. 'There are moments in my life when I feel as though a part of me is missing. There are days when I feel so invisible that I can't remember what day of the week it is, when I feel so manipulated that I can't remember my own name, when I feel so lost and angry that I can't speak a civil word to the people who love me best. Those are the times when I catch sight of my reflection in store windows and am surprised to see a ...'

Williams demands that the reader question all the abstractions of reifications of the law, her work is also an essay of joy at the promise of law. In particular, she chronicles the hope blacks have expressed in rights.

> In the law, rights are islands of empowerment. To be unrighted is to be disempowered, and the line between rights and no-rights is most often the line between dominators and oppressors. Rights contain images of power, and manipulating those images, either visually or linguistically, is central in the making and maintenance of those rights.

Black perceptions of the capacity of rights demonstrate an almost religious belief and hope in the potential of real rights, to help their position:

> It must be remembered that from the experiential perspective of blacks, there was no such thing as slave law. The legal system did not provide blacks, even freed blacks, with structured expectations, promises, or reasonable reliances of any sort. If one views rights as emanating from either slave 'legal' history or from that of modern bourgeois legal structures, then of course rights would mean nothing because blacks have had virtually nothing under either ... When one's experience is rooted not just in a sense of being illegitimate but in being illegitimate, in being raped, and in the fear of being murdered, then the black adherence to a scheme of both positive and negative rights – to the self, to the sanctity of one's own personal boundaries – makes sense (1991: 154).

What does reading Williams achieve? Perhaps, a sensitivity to pain, to difference – a hope in a more open world – a kind of magical feeling; an awareness of the complexity of meaning in social relations; an appreciation of the reality of hegemony and reification. Along with Lourdes Teodoro (*Agua-Marinha Ou Tempo Sem Palavra*, extract from *The Generation of Fear*, trans Iain Bruce, 1978), black writers speak of:

> how difficult it's become to be
> but it was always difficult to be in vain.

POST-MODERN FEMINISM

In part post-modernism is the difficulty of accepting any settled position, any statement of essence, and identity as the single answer. Women are not an homogenous group, as the conflicting arguments of radical and cultural feminism make clear. Feminism is a loose range of discourses and practices – there can be no meta-theory. In each different feminist argument we may find different illuminations of the human condition.

The feminism movement(s) have not given rise to a dominant perspective and there are many diverse interpretations. Some aspects have not escaped from some of the faults that it criticises traditional theorising as displaying. In part feminists have reproduced the universalising tendencies they abhor in the traditional. Also they have been too quick with their treatment of the traditional – while it may be that particular assumptions and rhetorical positions have become dominant there have been many perspectives and

---

57...whole person looking back. Those are the times when my skin becomes gummy as clay and my nose slides around on my face and my eyes drip down to my chin. I have to close my eyes at such times and remember myself, draw an internal picture that is smooth and whole; when all else fails, I reach for a mirror and stare myself down until the features reassemble themselves like lost sheep.'

positions created by men, only some of which are worthy targets for feminists. Feminists have to recognise their own embeddedness; their contextuality. While demanding that traditional perspectives have not faced up to their specific historical context, feminists have often neglected to turn this demand upon themselves. The post-modern concern with reflexivity causes constant self-assessment and complicates all attempts to define an essential identity – the subject is not a rational transparent entity able to organise and confer a set of homogeneous meaning to the field of her endeavour. Many feminists believe that if they do not see women as a coherent entity then a coherent feminist movement is impossible. But post-modernity encourages one to think in terms of varied social relations and of a multiplicity of social spheres where there are many obstacles and opportunities for advancing liberty and the treatment of self and others as equals. The post-modern condition demands that women abandon any supposed unity and homogeneity in answering the 'woman question' and look to analyse and intervene in a multiplicity of relations of subordination, transforming oppression into an affirmation of life's possibilities and opportunities.

If in recent years feminist jurisprudence has seemed to lose direction – as has feminism in general – this is a reflection of the process whereby once the multiplicity of subjectivities are recognised then it becomes very difficult to tell a master story. What will the future course entail? Part of the dilemma involves rejecting or regenerating the processes of modernity. Those who wish to reject the process of modernity say that it has been a sham, it has allowed domination over real freedom, it has destroyed and not built the free, the just, the good. Those who wish modernity reinvigorated say this is partly correct – there has only been an incomplete modernity. But they ask us to seize the moment and attempt, in our various ways, to play a part in the building of a truly human civilisation from which women have traditionally been excluded in the name of irreason and the ethnic minorities excluded in the name of non-civilisation. In its best forms feminism talks to the politics of the 'other', or that which the law has often served to constrain and render silent. The struggle for that humanity which lies beyond the past that we have been, and lies undeveloped in the future that might be, is the issue. In this sense whatever one thinks of any one feminist writer, feminism serves as the demand to consider who we are, and who a truly social 'we' would be; it asks us to consider again and again, what is there to unify and give foundations to our real differences.

CHAPTER 18

CONCLUDING REMARKS: or reflections on the temptations for jurisprudence in post-modernity

I stand on the end platform of the tram and am completely unsure of my footing in this world, in this town, in my family. Not even casually could I indicate any claims that I might rightly advance in any direction. I have not even any defence to offer for standing on this platform, holding on to this strap, letting myself be carried along by this tram, nor for the people who give way to the tram or walk quietly along or stand gazing into the shopwindows. Nobody asks me to put up a defence, indeed, but that is irrelevant. (Franz Kafka, 'On The Tram', in *The Collected Short Stories of Franz Kafka*, 1988: 388)

As for law, it too partakes of the radical uncertainty of the rest of life, the want of firm external standards. But it is also a special kind of living on these conditions, a way of making standards internally, out of our experience, as we make ourselves in our talk. The law is in fact a method of cultural criticism and cultural transformation, as well as cultural preservation ... law is in structure multivocal, always inviting new and contrasting accounts and languages. (James Boyd White, 1986: 1386)

ENDGAME: THE AMBIGUITY OF THE POST-MODERN?

This text started with reflections upon the complexity of asking general questions about the nature of law. It has subsequently conducted a narrative from existential origins through readings of jurisprudential writers from Classical Greece to the present. There is no easy ending; the journey's consummation is simply the context of our times – a period many commentators have come to call post-modernity. There is no easy description or definition of this concept; we are, perhaps, too involved in the complexity and confusion of the present to be able to define with certainty its major processes and structures.[1] What is clear is that our considerations of law reflect the ambiguities, hopes, confusions and fears of the post-modern condition. The dialectic, for example, between the fear of the alienating effects of law embedded in the CLS

---

1   What is post-modernity? It is clear to most commentators that radical changes have occurred in social order over the last 30 years. To describe these changes social theorists have coined various labels including the Media Society, the Society of the Spectacle, the Consumer Society, the Bureaucratic Society of Controlled Consumption, the Post-industrial Society, the globalised society, the society of advanced world capitalism, the post-capitalist information order, and lately, and most fashionably, the description of post-modernism. Certain key writers are responsible for this term, among them Jean François Lyotard (1984), who, in a well known book *The Post-modern Condition*, coined the term post-modern to reflect changes in the level of science and technology, in particular the development of computers, mass communication and increasing emphasis upon language in social and cultural studies. For other writers, post-modernity is characterised by a feeling of extreme ambivalence to the hopes and social structures of the last 200 years; a mood of nostalgia; cultural relativism; moral conventionalism; scepticism and pragmatism; a dialectic of localism amidst globalism; ambivalence towards organised, principled political activity; and a distrust of all strong forms of ethical or anthropological foundations. Above all, certain commentators suggest (for example Eagleton, 1996), it is the feeling of failure and deep confusion where next to go, either personally, or in terms of striving to create social projects aiming at a just society.

movement, and the pride in law demonstrated by Ronald Dworkin, is daily reproduced between those who see the effect of globalisation as entrapping the underdeveloped world in webs of western (legal) domination and those who see in globalisation the spread of a legal culture of human rights, equality of opportunity, and the opening up of individual life projects for new subjects. Others, however, point to the rise of the 'Asian Tiger Economies', which combine capitalism with social traditions of patriarchy and relative authoritarianism, and fear that in the new world economic order the benefits of western legal liberalism will increasingly come under fire and a new fascism emerge. Commentators cannot agree either upon the health of the world order – is it an enormous mess, or is today the best time to be alive in world history – or as to the prospects for social order – is the nation state now redundant and do we need a new international world order and law? While realist commentators point to record absolute amounts of poverty,[2] others (for example, Richard Rorty, 1989) note that never before have so many people appeared to care about the lives of others, or, for that matter, had the technology to know about other's lives. Certainly, jurisprudence cannot ever be again – at least with good conscience – an abstract study of philosophical models. Its aim is wisdom as to law's being and law's effects. One is reminded, however, of Hegel's hopes, and of his statement that wisdom will only arrive when human activity has ceased; must this be so? It appears, perhaps at this time more than ever before, that this is the case. The diversity of modes of approaching law – modes which also serve to constitute their domain of study – render impossible a settled definition of law. Law, for instance, has become an vital cultural manifestation – its language mediates the very forms of social construction it buttresses – and its instrumentality cannot be reduced to merely facilitating political or economic interests, or the enabling of desires to be satisfied, for its expressive function is not mere ideology. Law enables forms of life – from the self-regulating zones of privacy prescribed in the classic liberalism of John Stuart Mill – to that of the structured world of the fundamentalist Islamic society. Stanley Fish (1991) once said that 'the law wishes to have a formal existence', by which he meant that the law wishes to be distinct, not something else, and it wishes its autonomous existence to be self-declaring, in case its autonomy – perhaps its 'integrity' – would be compromised. The enterprise of legal positivism sought to protect the formal self-sufficiency of law from morality, but, in so doing, rendered empirical law the amoral servant of social forces. In the post-modern context, law's uniqueness flows more from its versatility and the openendedness of the social forms it structures, than from its purity. As James Boyd White, a proponent of an emerging 'law and humanities movement', states, in the second of the opening quotations, law cannot help but partake of the radical uncertainty of (post-modern) life, and its multivocal structure renders it implicated in many contrasting accounts and languages. Law's flexibility ensnares it in

---

2   As Jacques Derrida (1994: 85) put it in his argument for the continual need for a tradition of critical rationality: 'Instead of singing the idea of the advent of liberal democracy and the capitalist market in the euphoria of the end of history, instead of celebrating the "end of ideologies" and the end of the great emancipatory discourses, let us never neglect this obvious macroscopic fact, made up of innumerable sites of suffering: no degree of progress allows one to ignore that never before, in absolute terms, never have so many men, women and children been subjugated, starved or exterminated on the earth.'

the post-modern dialectic of multi-directionality against directionless preformivity. The writer Franz Kafka may provide an appropriate witness to elements of post-modernity with which to conclude.

Franz Kafka as a narrator of the post-modern

... No one, no one at all, can blaze a trail to India. Even in his day the gates to India were beyond reach, yet the King's sword pointed the way to them. Today the gates have receded to remoter and loftier places; no one points the way; many carry swords, but only to brandish them, and the eye that tries to follow them is confused. (Kafka, The New Advocate, 1988: 415)

In the foundational text of modernity, Hobbes' *Leviathan*, law is the sword of the Sovereign who is to watch over us and within whose dominion we can pursue our legitimate desires. In time, the idea of social progress was joined with law so that law was seen as an instrument to guide us to that land and time of our happiness. Law was to be the guarantor of modernity, sure in its purpose, the instrument of rational power. Writing, however, during a time which should have been infused with the hopes of organised modernity, the 'central-european jewish' writer Franz Kafka, conveyed an existential condition of extreme ambivalence.[3] Many carried swords, but 'only to brandish them'; law seemed to have lost its rationality, how could a pattern of coherence or a common social goal be believed in? The dominant discourses told of the creation, through historical struggles and the granting of legal rights, of a modern subject which was being incorporated – by a process of assimilation – into the practices of organised, structured modernity. Instead, however, of contentment and reasoned satisfaction, Kafka relates feelings of personal suspension and ambiguity.[4] In Kafka's stories the subject is forced to live a situation of contingency and choice; longing for a life of relative peace and contentment within a socially just and acceptable social order, the subject finds only a rapidly moving terrain where little makes sense, where there are few places to rest and insufficient time to attain certainty. Kafka's characters become increasingly confused and bewildered as they attempt to ascertain the truth of their social context and the essence of the institutions which surround and position them. In this uncertain world, neither the law nor their cultural heritage offer certainty.[5] We students of the various horrors of

---

3   I use the phrase 'central-european jewish' in acknowledgement of the condition Kafka reproduces of a subject who is asked to be at home everywhere and anywhere and can not feel safe anywhere. Kafka's writings reflect his own beingness, specifically that of an extra-historical homeless condition, a condition of location not within the traditional constraints of time and space – a particular socio-cultural identity, as Zimmermann defines it: 'He was no Czech, he was no German. This fact, through substraction and the merciless syllogism of Prague politics, made him a jew' (quoted, Bauman, 1991: 180, upon whom I draw for my understanding of Kafka's personal situation).

4   In part, Kafka was relating aspects of being jewish (many have claimed that the essence of being jewish is that of a permanent stranger or being everywhere out of place), but the story of the jewish identity in organised central european modernity looks increasingly like the harbinger of the identity of the subject of the post-modern condition.

5   Take the sense of language. Kafka wrote and spoke German. His participation in that linguistic community did not give him any sense of settled identity; rather it was a technology.

our century know this only too well. In the lead-up to the holocaust, the legal subjectivity of the German jews – their citizenship – was by law taken from them. What was given by law could be taken away by law. Was there, then, in the light of modernity's excesses, any legitimate foundation, any truth, to our acceptance of modernity's creations?[6] And if not, what ought we to do? Various answers, or, perhaps, more appropriately, temptations, arise.

Temptation one: to accept radical relativism and the denial of any meaningful answers to questions of essence

One of the themes which concerned Kafka was the search for the truth of law. In *The Problem of Our Laws,* Kafka (1979) depicts a community which is governed by a very secretive and traditionally legitimate nobility which claims exclusive access to the knowledge of the law and its obligations. The nobility also ensures that all the other social groups remain ignorant of the truth of the law. The nobility achieve domination over 'the common people' on the grounds that tradition has established that the nobility know the secret of the law and wield it fairly and without self-interest: 'the nobles stand above the law, and that seems to be the very reason why the law has been given over exclusively to their hands' (1979: 128). The nobility, with its claim to integrity, stands in contrast with the apparent subjectivity of all other social groups, which have their specific projects to pursue. Only the detachment of the nobility can guarantee that they will not abuse 'truth'. Paradoxically, however, this claim is circular: the nobility are accepted as self-evidently neutral precisely because they control the law.

Kafka places the subjects of this story in the grip of a subtle bind: the rule of law is taken for granted, but in practical terms this means that the rule of the nobility is placed beyond question. Since the secret of the law is known only by the nobility, only they can claim to know what is to be done, and indeed, what has to be done; the populace – as Hart (1961) admitted – ultimately need only trust that the officials are doing their task with appropriate integrity. (It is tempting to replace Kafka's nobility with 'experts' and we have the picture of domination in a supposedly rational modernity founded on the

---

6   The experience of the German jews (and other European jews who came under Nazi control) points to the ever-present possibility of the collapse of the 'freedoms' which modernity has created. In *Long I Have Looked For The Truth* (contained in Bretolt Brecht, 1980) the German jewish poet Bertolt Brecht recounts that he had long looked for the truth of man's social life, a life that is crisscrossed, tangled and difficult to understand. But he strove to tell it as he found it. However, the Nazi's came and shot at the poor and those who strove to tell of complex truths. As Brecht relates, the Nazi's took both 'truth' and material comforts:

> 'From me they took my little house and my car
> Which I had earned by hard work.
> (I was able to save the furniture)
> When I crossed the frontier I thought:
> More than my house I need the truth.
> But I need my house too. And since then
> Truth for me has been like a house and a car
> And they took them.'

deepest irrationality.) But an ironical doubt creeps in to this otherwise watertight situation. If the law is only known by the nobility, and if everyone else is necessarily ignorant of its essential form, then perhaps it is actually the case that law does not have a core of meaning. The essence of law, the answer to the question 'what is law?' and 'what ought law to be guided by?' may not exist. Perhaps the only secret is the secret that there is no answer? In other words, the domination of modernity is actually founded upon an abyss of meaning, and a subtle fascism. There is no secure grounding from which to issue injunctions as to the quality of law, the only thing that legitimates the rule of the rulers, is the very success of their domination. But our knowledge of this outcome is deeply ambiguous, for whilst it may deprive the rulers of the master principle of their domination, it also removes the instrument by which the people were meant to control them; since, to hold the rulers accountable, we need strong ethical and political arguments.[7]

In Kafka's stories, structures of complex bureaucracy and reification hide the abyss created by the deconstruction of natural artifice. A formal belief in the existence of law's secret restrains the abyss of meaning from breaking into social consciousness: 'There is a tradition that [the meanings of law] exist and are entrusted as a secret to the nobility, but this is not and cannot be more than an ancient tradition to which age lends authority' (Kafka 1979: 128). Could modernity survive the knowledge that there was no great destiny? Kafka reads the story of the destiny of the human condition as the same as the study of law's imagination. Both share a 'belief that one day the time will come when both the tradition and our study of it will arrive ... at their conclusion. All will have become clear ... the law will at last belong to the people, and the nobility will vanish' (Kafka 1979: 129). Through its role as the goal of the relentless pursuit of knowledge, the idea of coming to know the truth of being becomes the transcendental signifier in relation to the obscurity and utterly reified relationships of the present. We join with Plato's transcendence of the cave, not by actually having achieved it, but by our belief that we will achieve it in the future. But Kafka declares this is a self-delusion. The future time and place in which the secret of law will be known by all and in which the nobility has quite disappeared can never arrive. There is only the void – thus we must face, forever, the need to assert power without extra-human guarantees. We cannot escape

---

7   Modernity was an attempt to create a just society of organised and transparent structure – a world of coherent practices organised around rules, where the rules themselves took their legitimation from a belief in some underlying structure or their inherent functionality, or in terms of their purity. The post-modern condition is ushered in with the growing realisation of the lack of deep structure. The mainstream of politics in the post-modern condition sees the desperate attempt to avoid ideas and return political speech to common sense. On opposing flanks are, on the one hand, those who argue for the benefits of radical pluralism and diversity; whilst on the other hand, we witness the most grotesque ethnic cleansing and search for secure identities – the rise of new tribalisms. But post-modernity is no return to the pre-modern. Unlike the pre-modern world of the ancients, it respects no absolute boundaries except those which are themselves the creation of law (for example, human rights, international law). As Nietzsche recognised, this implies that law is a guarantor of social structure, since within this world there might well be nothing natural which can never be transgressed. Consequently, this world might actually be meaningless without the simple assumption and tradition that it is meaningful. Additionally, however, as Foucault (1977; 1979) alerted us, the power of the sword of law, is in partnership with the processes which render contingent social practices 'normal', and encourage us to accept socialisation into the 'norm'.

from the need for the nobility: 'The one visible and indubitable law that is imposed upon us is the nobility, and could it really be our wish to deprive ourselves of this solitary law?' (Kafka 1979: 130). Ought we, then, to make ourselves into a new nobility?

Kafka's story points also to dialectic involved in the very idea of progress and modernity. Our belief in the continuance of progress depends on a fully modern society – the society of perfect justice – never actually being achieved, but we cannot tell ourselves this fact, in case such a realisation would mean that we gave up upon the enterprise: 'rather are we inclined to hate ourselves because we cannot yet be judged worthy of the law' (Kafka 1979: 129). The modern person has to assume, or has to be told, that perfection – truth – is a realistic, albeit futurist, possibility. In that way the struggle for justice, the political commitment to justice, the march into the future and out of the past, is provided with some sort of meaning and purpose. By contrast, post-modernity is the growing awareness that that linkage is absurd. Put another way, post-modernism is the realisation that there can be no utopia of the just society – the voyage is doomed – and, by implication, we are at the destination, the problem is that the destination is no conclusion. There is no end(ing).

Temptation two: abandoning the search for the wisdom of law in favour of preformivity

Can jurisprudence, as a search for the big picture – for the wisdom of law – survive, or is it doomed to descend into a babble of competing discourses with no common threads and little relevance? How do we account for the proliferation of jurisprudential discourse, and yet, the feeling of powerlessness? In part it is a question of the compatibility of discourse with power. For Lyotard (1984) the social meaning of knowledge has changed; the miniaturisation and commercialisation of information machines has changed the way in which learning is acquired, classified, made available and exploited. The new technologies rank knowledges in terms of their compatibility to the technology and its applications. Forms of knowledge not capable of being articulated in quantitative form suitable for translation into computer language are down graded and have difficulty surviving. The old principal where the acquisition of knowledge was associated with the training of minds or even of individuals is becoming obsolete; knowledge becomes a commodity produced in order to be sold.

The question of knowledge is closely linked to the question of government. Lyotard suggests the functions of regulation and therefore reproduction at being further and further withdrawn from human administrators and intrusted to machines – politics becomes the battle for imagery and public opinion polls. Knowledge is what makes someone capable of forming not only good speech but also good prescriptive and good evaluative utterances. But how are these to be assessed? In Lyotard's reading they are to be judged to be good by how they conform the relevant criteria of justice, beauty, truth and efficiency excepted in the social circle of the knowers, interlocutors or peer group. For Lyotard each field constructs its own language games and each utterance is as a move in a game; in his image of the language game, conflict is essential. Lyotard's persuasive metaphor is war, some positions are indefensible, some attack, demolish, shoot down, undercut other's arguments: 'In a discussion between two friends, the interlocutors use any available ammunition; questions, requests, assertions and narratives are launched pall mall into battle. The war is not without rules, the rules allow and encourage the greatest possible flexibility of utterance' (1984: 17).

It is little wonder then that CLS-influenced discourse plays off with the Law and Economics Movement. The central theme of the CLS movement was to return social organisation to human concerns, to less alienated forms of social life and human interaction. Conversely, proponents of law and economics tend to ask jurisprudence to speak only in the language understood by economic power - money.[8] Economics is the language most computer-friendly, most minimalist in its claims concerning human nature. The discourse of the law and economics movement speaks a post-modern language.

Scientific knowledge is not however self-sustainable. It exists in competition and conflict with other forms of knowledge which Lyotard labels as narrative and which dominated in traditional societies.[9] While modernity waged war on narratives, narrative survived bestowing legitimacy upon the social institutions and providing positive and negative forms of integration into the established institutions.[10] Thus we witness the growing law and humanities movements and the narrative style of feminism – but their power base is ambiguous.

---

8   As Richard Posner (1981) a leading exponent argues: 'The most important thing to bear in mind about the concept of value is that it is based on what people are willing to pay for something rather than on the happiness they would derive from having it ... Equivalently, the wealth of society is the aggregate satisfaction of those preferences (the only ones that have weight in a system of wealth maximization) that are backed up by money, that is, that are registered in a market.'

9   In Lyotard's reading, two great myths or narratives that have served as justification of institutional scientific research are that of the liberation of humanity and of the speculative unity of all knowledge. The first of those narratives is a political militant activist one, the second is based around the concept of totality under the idea of a system. The first of these narratives, humanity, is the hero of social progress. The state uses narratives of freedom, every time it assumes direct control over the training of the people under the name of the nation in order to point the people towards progress. But these master narratives no longer function to the same degree in contemporary society. The grand narrative for Lyotard has lost its credibility regardless of whether it is speculative narrative, or a narrative of emancipation; in this space post-modernism arrives. The declining grip of narrative progress, shifts the emphasis from the ends of action to its means, while we see an explosion and different kinds of technics and technologies. The criteria for legitimation changes. Lyotard argues the goal in science is no longer truth but preformivity. The ethos of the modern scientists, technicians and the design of instruments are orientated not to find truth but to argument preforming power. Educational policy changes to become more functional, the emphasis is on skills, rather than ideals. Knowledge is no longer transmitted once and for all to young people, rather it becomes an *a lá carte* menu available to adults as part of their job retraining in continuing education. Knowledge, along with the capability to doubt, becomes something translatable into computer language and the traditional teacher is replaced by memory banks and teaching intrusted to machines linking memory banks, libraries etc and computer data banks to terminals which are placed at the students use and practitioner is disposed of. The driving force, however, behind change is no longer 'is it true?' but 'what use is it?'. Or, 'is it saleable?'. Consumerism, it appears, becomes a dominate motive of the post-modern writer.

10 Science is supposed to rely upon objective criteria, however, Lyotard argues, scientific knowledge cannot know, and make it known that it is the true knowledge without resorting to other narrative kinds of knowledge, which from its own point of view is actually no knowledge at all; in short, the truth of the scientific depends upon the known truth, the narrative. Science must pass itself off as the largest story in town and the states own credibility is based on that epic story.

Temptation three: to abandon modernity for a dialectic of tribalism and rampant subjectivity

Throughout the developed Western world, social and cultural modernism has come under attack from many diverse quarters. From the right, conservatives argue that modernism has undercut the values of every day life and common sense. Principal and unlimited self-realisation, the demands for authentic self-experiences, the replacement of objectivism by subjectivism have placed a huge onus on the self. The self is meant to see the world as the site of projects and to use the objects of the world as the means to obtain the self's ends. To the conservative right, this has unleased hedonistic desires irreconcilable with the discipline modern life requires (Gottfredson, M and Hirschi, Travis, *A General Theory of Crime*, 1990; contrast Morrison, 1995). Hedonism, lack of social identification, lack of obedience, self-love, the withdrawal of deference from authority, are seen not as features of successful modernisation, but of a social and cultural modernity which has lost its way. Conversely, for those on the left, the post-modern problem, is that of the incomplete modernisation of the world (for example, Habermas). When Lyotard claims that in post-modern condition the grand narratives have lost their credibility at the same time as we keep on playing the games that were formerly legitimated by those grand narratives, and do so at a greater level of proformivity, he repeats Nietzsche's warning that nihilism is the condition engendered when we have killed God but continue to act as if he exists. The narratives of mastery and conquest of nature leave us with a technological emphasis upon control and domination, without, however, a purpose in mind. In this reading, an individualistic, fragmented society, in which law and rights are weapons of small scale conflict, seems our fate. No wonder in these conditions the nostalgia for a pre-modern traditional society surfaces and a multiplicity of little narratives develops. The lack of meta-narrative or meta-language to tie together late modernism is to be remedied by a resurgence in localised narratives or story telling. As narratives bind together the teller and audience, so, for Lyotard, post-modernity is to retain the flexibility of the narrative form yet, somehow, avoid the imposition of total belief systems. We are to escape from domination by the splitting up of different stories; society is depicted as working much better through an unstructured variety of micro events, and a society of a multiplicity of centres is better than a consciously planned society. Whilst big stories are bad, little stories are good. All we can expect of law is its involvement in a multiplicity of small battles, moves in a social order comprised of a vast diversity of competing language games.

The downside of this imagery is that social life may instead become a civilized Hobbesian war of all on all – mediated by the weapons of law. Instead of enabling justice, giving law to the people encourages litigation upon litigation. Without a belief in the grand narratives life becomes a mass of little games; yet Lyotard appears oblivious to the soulessness of this post-modern gaming. In his analysis, the grand narratives stand accused of legitimating the vast political programmes of the communist party or programmes of domination (the Cold War), whilst little narratives are associated with localised creativity. But from another point of view, such as that of the American critic Fredick Jamerson, the games of post-modernity are simply pastiche and doom us to schizophrenia.[11] Jamerson defines post-modernism as a nostalgia for the past where, at the same time, we seem to lose our ability to locate ourselves historically. We become incapable of embedding ourselves in a time-space contingent that makes sense. How then can we commit ourselves to social projects, since to commit to a social project means to commit oneself to a certain continuum of commitment and hope?

In similar terms, references to totality and fragmentation, to the dialectic of globalism and localism, run through post-modernist jargon. In a sense, post-modernity denotes a feeling of loss, in that we can no longer grasp what is going on in society, or indeed the globe as a whole, yet at the same time we need to know what is going on at this level of totality in order that we can say that it is no longer possible to say what is going on. Thus, whilst it is fashionable to say that there is no single theoretical discourse which is going to offer us explanations of all forms of social relations and make possible legitimate modes of political practice and legal intervention, this itself is, reflexively, a theoretical understanding of totality.[12]

Temptation four: to misunderstand the nature of deconstruction

Along with the realisation of contingency and the dreams of dynamic flexibility, the post-modern cultural consciousness is obsessed with the process of deconstruction (heavily influenced by the projects of Jacques Derrida). Deconstruction enters jurisprudence first through the law's textual nature, and, secondly, through the modernist (functional) linkage of law with social structure. By asking a continual series of questions, deconstruction seeks to sap the strength of a social structure whose substance lies in the prohibition of asking. There are two forms of deconstruction:

(i) The deconstruction of the text. It is a commonplace that the study of law and the transmission of the law involves texts. To search for the truth of the law is to engage in the interpretation of texts. Do the texts of law contain the meaning of (the) law?[13] Deconstruction is the technique of showing that any settled law of the text is open to destabilisation. Every interpretation which tries to replace the openendedness of the basic text with a final – authoritarian – interpretation usurps the life of the text with an early death. Instead of finality, deconstruction reads every interpretation as either enriching or lessening the potential of the original text, adding or subtracting

---

11 Jamerson uses the term schizophrenia to denote a feeling of a more intense experience of the-very-given-present which presents, however disorientatingly, a fragmentation or set of perpetual pressures of temporal and discontinuous experiences. Instead of the various events which impinge upon us being mere problems on a coherent life course, events are dislocated intrusions which threaten to arouse reactions which will split our very being.

12 The rejection of totality by Lyotard is itself a rather large narrative, although it, of course, stresses a fragmentation of language games, time, the human subject and society itself. But what do we find, what is the mood by which we cope with this dissolving of unity, what can give coherence and yet autonomy to individuals work?

13 Note that the search for the meaning of being through the study of the texts of that being stems from the study of 'the word of God'. In the Judaic, Christian, Muslin traditions, the gift of god lies in his provision of texts for mankind; texts which appear to change, develop and reveal a multiplicity of meaning(s) every time they are interpreted. Only by stabilising the tradition of interpretation – by creating a sect – can the canons of interpretation and the resultant meaning(s) be stabilised.

from a reservoir of meaning, but deconstruction requires that any reading be the subject of further and further study. Deconstruction announces that the goal of reducing the meaning(s) interpreted in a text to any one single latent referent is not only intellectually bankrupt but dangerous.

(ii) The deconstruction of the social order. To repeat a claim advanced against the legal positivism of HLA Hart, much of mainstream jurisprudence treats the contingency of late modernity as the normal and downplays the role of power behind the law. In his deconstructive reading of law, Derrida (1992) returns the foundations of modern anglo-american jurisprudence to the realist constructionism of Hobbes. Derrida returns to law the concept of force,[14] thus reversing the story of Hart – namely to avoid Austin's centrality of power to law – to tells us of a fatal mystery beneath law's presence. All forms of legitimation can be deconstructed – as with the final 'as-if' nature of Kelsen's basic norm, or the rule of recognition of Hart – at some stage there is, quite literally, no grounding for law. Justice is only the search for justice – it cannot ever be securely ascertained (except by our contingent agreement upon some procedure of recognition – which might always have been some other). As a result:

Since the origin of authority, the foundation or ground, the position of the law can't by definition rest on anything but themselves, they are themselves a violence without ground. Which is to say that they are in themselves unjust, in the sense of 'illegal'. They are neither legal nor illegal in their founding moment. They exceed the opposition between founded and unfounded, or between any foundationalism or antifoundationalism. Even if the success of performatives that found law or right ... presupposes earlier conditions and conventions ... the same 'mystical' limit will reappear at the supposed origin of said conditions, rules, or conventions, and at the origin of their dominant interpretations. (1992: 14)

For Derrida deconstruction is a form of humanism,[15] deconstruction's uncovering of the infinite regress of truth's being is not a denial of the task of enlightenment, but a call to remember that the task of philosophy is not to capture truth but to enable us to live in the spirit of truth. To live amidst the process of deconstruction is the fate of the modern person who retains both a critical distance from acquiescing in the power of the sword,[16] and who seeks to unpack the normalising process of everyday discipline.[17]

---

14 Derrida's text is dense but replays close analysis. He begins by noting an english expression 'to enforce the law': 'The word "enforceability" reminds us that there is no such thing as law (droit) that doesn't imply, in itself, *a priori*, in the analytical structure of its concept, the possibility of being enforced, applied by force. There are, to be sure, laws that are not enforced, but there is no law without enforceability, and no applicability or enforceability of the law without force, whether this force be direct or indirect, physical or symbolic, exterior or interior, brutal or subtly discursive and hermeneutic, coercive or regulative, and so forth' (1992: 5).

15 Seminar, Queen Mary and Westfield College, London, 1995.

16 One might say that, in this respect, deconstruction is to take HLA Hart's critical citizenship test to the extreme, and in contrast to those who assert that it is usually a good thing to obey the law.

17 Another form of inquiry related to deconstruction lies with the critical analysis of what Foucault called, in the section concluding the first volume of the *History of Sexuality*, the 'Right of Death and Power over Life'; the exercise of 'bio-power' or the disciplines of the body and the various extra-legal forms of regulating 'normal' life in the population (the disciplines of physical health, beauty, sexuality, mental health, in short normalcy as opposed to the deviancy which can only be understood by contrast to the 'normal').

Temptation five: to refuse the burden of deconstruction by retreating into gamesmanship

Beyond deconstruction lies the mystery of the jurisprudential quest. In a world where everything can be doubted, where justice is authenticity – rather than guarantee – the burden of existence moves, inescapably upon our shoulders.

Through everyday academic and professional practice the lawyer plays the game of rational reconstruction – doctrine is developed, sometimes new kinds of law are won – such as 'Restitution Law' – out of the battles of legal language games. Law's effects are either raised in our concern or forgotten. In this process of playing the games of the text(s) and creating the text(s) of the game(s) the words of Marx – that the law book was the people's bible book of freedom – become both a hope and a mirage. Instead Wittgenstein's injunction that henceforth the only place where philosophical problems could be tackled and resolved would be the railway station looks more apt. Post-modern life is a life on the run in conditions of great preformability.

Do the games have any stability? Other than the temporal satisfaction or frustration of the players desires? It is ironical to see in Hart's amoral theory of rules and games the prophet of post-modernity. Out of the structure of rules, the game is given order and the game develops its order. The order may hang over the heads of the players as if they were natural laws, but their structure is born ever anew informed by the 'authorities' willingness to develop the game and the players' willingness to obey the rules. If the desire to play the game by the rules were to dissipate, then the structure and foundation of the game would evaporate. Herein lies the attraction of Hart's liberalism: all of social order ought to be like a game (although, of course, it is what few, if any, real orders are in reality). In the context of the game, and no matter how meticulously the rule-bound order is observed, discipline is never considered or experienced as oppression, rather it is the context of judging worth and skill, and the penalties applied are judged mistaken or apt, but never seen as enslaving. The ideal liberal order is that which enables, empowers, and which comes with knowledge of how to continue and develop the palyer's projects. The order conjured up by the play of games appears so attractive that no late-modern order can avoid stealing some of its seductive power and speak of carrying out its obligations as normative, of moving as the rules command, as role-playing, of hiding the coercion if the law as being merely the effects of the rules of the game.

One cannot, of course, play the game and subvert the rules; this is the paradox of the law of the game. To play a game is to play by the rules; there is no way of playing other than by the rules. To fail is to cheat, and that is not to play. One cannot be sceptical concerning the rules of the game; one can only constructively interpret them (Dworkin). One cannot move in such a way as to transgress the game's rules without leaving oneself open to the (justified) penalty; one can only leave the game, refuse to play, or develop another game.

The games of life, the games of law respond to the need for recognition. Jurisprudence as the search for the truth of law, is the desire for wisdom. That humanities follow desire, rather than instinct, is the source both of our power and our existential problems. Through speech, desires one articulated, through the traditions of reason we seek to encode those most ambivalent of all human artifacts; the ideas of dignity and the sacred. The language-games of contemporary jurisprudence speak to the multi-focused nature and sources of these desires. Desire becomes mobile, transitory, unfocussed or, put more correctly, moves in a continual state of (re)focusing.

But we should remember that the games of the post-modern, like the games of the pre-modern, are not self-sustaining or ahistorical. In the games of post-modernity, as with the Chariot races of Classical Rome portrayed on the cover of this text (from the etching of the painting by the Spanish artist Ulpiano Checa, 1891), it matters whether one is a slave or a freeman, a winner or loser. It matters who gains from the performance and what the stake of the rulers is; it matters what the position of the game in the social order is. The games of the post-modern may again be games of paganism (Lyotard and Thebaud, 1985) – for who in good conscience would wish to reinvent God – but having looked at the abyss in the heart of modernism – there is no need to flee from the challenge of deconstruction – to face the irreducible mystery of the sacredness of being. To humanise the claims of reason – which post-modernity dislocates and lessens – we can use in everyday life the claims of Humean empathy and sympathy, but we also need a transcendental signifier. Perhaps in the post-modern condition, we must acknowledge the impossibility of escaping from our existential inadequacy; we need to recognise the mystery of a depth we can do little other than to call the realm of the sacred. That we will always be defeated by our attempts to know it, is no reason not to live by its spirit. Thus the challenge of the post-modern is to continually ask the meaning of being human, in full consciousness of the fact that any answer offered, and any social order thereby constructed, is only a temporary respite, an embodiment of some of our desires, solace to our fears.

BIBLIOGRAPHY

Acton, HB (1970) *Kant's Moral Philosophy*, New Studies in Ethics, London: Macmillan Education Ltd

Adorno, Theodor W and Horkheimer, Max (1972) *Dialectic of Enlightenment*, trans John Cumming, New York

Anschutz, RP (1953) *The Philosophy of JS Mill*, Oxford

Ammos, Linda (1995) 'Mules, Madonnas, Babies, Bathwater, Racial Imagery and Stereotypes: The African-American Woman and the Battered Woman Syndrome', *Wisconsin Law Review*

Aquinas, St Thomas (1945) *Introduction to St Thomas Aquinas (The Summa Theologica, The Summa Contra Gentiles)*, Anton C Pegis, ed, New York: The Modern Library

Arendt, H (1964) *Eichmann in Jerusalem: A report on the banality of evil*, New York: Viking Press

Arblaster, A (1984) *The Rise and Decline of Western Liberalism*, Blackwell: Oxford

Aristotle (1956–64) *Opera*, Oxford: Clarendon Press

(1962) *The Politics*, Trans TA Sinclair, Harmondsworth: Penguin Books

Auden, WH (1976) *Collected Poems*, London: Faber & Faber

Augustine (1972) *City of God*, David Knowles, ed, Harmondsworth: Penguin Books

(1907) *The Confessions of St Augustine*, Trans EB Pusey Everyman's Library, London: Dent and Sons Also (1969) *St Augustine's Confessions: The Odyssey of Soul*, Cambridge Mass

Austin, John (1954 [1832]), *The Province of Jurisprudence Determined*, Weidenfeld & Nicolson, London

(1873) *Lectures on Jurisprudence or The Philosophy of Positive Law*, 4th edn, revised by Robert Campbell, London: John Murray

(1859) 'A Plea for the Constitution', Fraser's Magazine (April)

Bailyn, Bernard (1967) *The Ideological Origins of the American Revolution*, Cambridge, Mass Harvard University Press

(1969) *The Origins of American Politics*, New York

Balkin, JM, (1987) 'Deconstructive Practice and Legal Theory', *96 Yale Law Journal* 743

Barnett, H (1995) *Constitutional Law*, London: Cavendish Publishing Ltd

Bartlett, Katherine (1990) 'Feminist Legal Methods', *103 Harvard Law Review*

(1993) *Gender and Law*,

and Kennedy, Rosanne (1991) *Feminist legal Theory: Readings in Law and Gender*, Bolder: Westview Press

Baudrillard, Jean (1983) *In the Shadow of the Silent Majorities*, Trans P Foss, P Patton and J Johnston, New York: Semiotext(e)

Bauman, Zygmunt (1987) *Legislators and Interpreters: On modernity, post-modernity and intellectuals*, Oxford: Basil Blackwell

(1989) *Modernity and the Holocaust*, Cambridge: Polity Press

(1991) *Modernity and Ambivalence*, Cambridge: Polity Press

(1993) *Postmodern Ethics*, Oxford: Blackwell

Baxter, James K (1980) *Collected Poems*, Wellington/Oxford: Oxford University Press

Beauvoir, Simone de (1953) *The Second Sex*, trans HM Parchley, London: Jonathan Cape

Beck, Lewis White Beck, (1960) *A Commentary on Kant's Critique of Practical Reason*, Chicago: University of Chicago Press

Bender, Leslie (1990) 'Changing the Values in Tort Law', *25 Tulsa LJ*

(1990) 'Feminist (Re)torts: Thoughts on the Liability Crisis, Mass Torts, Power and Responsibilities, *Duke LJ*

(1990) 'From Gender Difference to Feminist Solidarity: Using Carol Gilligan and an Ethic of Care in Law', *15 Vermont L Rev*

Benditt, TM (1974), 'Legal Theory and Rules of Law', *University of Western Ontario Law Review*, 13

Benjamin, Jessica (1980) 'The bounds of love: rational violence and erotic domination', *Feminist Studies, vol 6, no 1*

Bentham, Jeremy (1787) 'Panopticon', in *The Works of Jeremy Bentham*, New York: Russell & Russell, 1971

(1970), *Of Laws in General*, HLA Hart, ed, London: Athlone

(1987 [1789]) *An Introduction to the Principles of Morals and Legislation*, Harmondsworth: Penguin Classics

Berger, Peter (1967) *The Sacred Canopy*, Garden City

Berlin, Isaiah (1969) 'Two Concepts of Liberty', in *Four Essays on Liberty*, Oxford

Beyleveld, D and R Brownsword (1982), 'Critical Legal Studies', *Modern Law Review*, 47
(1986) *Law as a Moral Judgement*, London: Sweet & Maxwell

Blackstone, William ([1765–9] 1973) *Commentaries on the Laws of England*, G Jones, ed, London

Bloch, Ernst (1985) *Natural Law and Human Dignity*, trans Dennis J Schmidt, Cambridge, Mass: The MIT Press

Bloor, D (1983) *Wittgenstein: A Social Theory of Knowledge,* London: Macmillan

Bodin, J (1962) *The Six Books of a Commonwealth*, Cambridge, Mass: Harvard University Press

Bottomely, A (1995) *Feminist Perspectives on the Foundational Subjects of Law*, London: Cavendish Publishing Ltd

Boyle, James (1985) 'The Politics of Reason: Critical Legal Theory and local Social Thought', *University of Pennsylvania Law Review*, 133

Brecht, Bertolt, (1980) *Bertolt Brecht Poems 1913–56*, John Willett and Ralph Manheim, eds, London: Eyre Methuen

Brown, P *et al* (1981), 'A daughter: a thing to be given away', in *Women in Society,* Cambridge Women's Studies Group, ed, London: Virago

Bruno, Giuliana (1987) 'Ramble City: Postmodernism and Blade Runner', *October*, 41 Summer

Bryson, Valerie (1992) *Feminist Political Theory: an introduction*, Basingstoke: MacMillan

Buchheim, Hans (1968) 'Command and Compliance', in Krausnick, Helmut Buchheim, Hans Broszat, Martin and Hans-Adolf Jacobsen (1968) *Anatomy of the SS State*, London: Collins

Cain, M and A Hunt (eds) (1979), *Marx and Engels on Law,* Academic Press, London

Calhoun, George C (1944) *Introduction to Greek Legal Science*, Oxford: Clarendon Press

Callinicos, Alex (1989) *Against Postmodernism: a Marxist Critique*, Polity Press

Cardozo, Benjamin (1921) *The Nature of the Judicial Process*, New Haven, Conn

Cavafy (1984) *Collected Poems*, Edmund Keeley & Philip Sherrand Trans, George Savidis, ed, London: The Hogarth Press

Chambliss, WJ and H Siedman (1971), *Law, Order and Power*, Reading, Mass: Addison-Wesley

(1983), *Law, Order and Power* (2nd edn), Reading, Mass: Addison-Wesley,

Codrington, RH (1891) *The Melanesians: Studies in Their Anthropology and Folk-Lore*, Oxford

Cohen, GA (1982) *Karl Marx's Theory of History: A Defense*, Oxford: Oxford University Press

Collins, H (1982) *Marxism and Law*, Oxford University Press, Oxford

Comte, Auguste (1973) *System of Positive Polity*, Trans R Congreve and H Hutton 4 Vols New York: Burt Franklin

(1974) *The Positive Philosophy*, New York: AMS Press Inc

Coole, D (1988) *Women in Political Theory*, Brighton: Wheatsheaf

Cornell, Drucilla (1988) 'Institutionalisation of naming, Recollective Imagination and the potential for transformative legal interpretation', *University of Pennsylvania Law Review 136*

(1991) *Beyond Accommodation: ethical feminism, deconstruction, and the law*, London: Routledge

Cott, N (1987) *The Grounding of Modern Feminism*, New Haven and London: Yale University Press

Cotterrell, R (1984) *The Sociology of Law: An Introduction*, London: Butterworths, (2nd edn 1992)

(1989) *The Politics of Jurisprudence: A Critical Introduction to Legal Philosophy*, London: Butterworths

(1995) *Law's Community: Legal Theory in Sociological Perspective*, Oxford: Clarendon Press

Crozier, M (1964) *The Bureaucratic Phenomenon,* London: Tavistock

Davies, Howard and Holdcroft, David (1991) *Jurisprudence: Texts and Commentary*, London: Butterworths

Davies, Margaret (1994) *Asking the Law Question*, Sydney: The Law Book Company

Derrida, Jacques (1992) 'Force of Law: The "Mystical Foundation of Authority"', in Cornell, Rosenfeld and Carlson, eds, *Deconstruction and the Possibility of Justice*, New York: Routledge

(1994) *Specters of Marx*, London: Routledge

Descartes R (1984) *The Philosophical Works of Descartes*, trans J Cottingham, R Stoothoff and D Murdoch, Cambridge: Cambridge University Press

De Souza Santos, B (1991) 'The postmodern tradition: Law and Politics', in *The Fate of Law*, Austin Sarat and Thomas Kearns, eds, Ann Arbour: The University of Michigan Press

Devlin, Lord (1965) *The Enforcement of Morals*, Oxford: Oxford University Press

Douzinas, Costas, McVeigh and Warrington, Ronnie (1992) 'Is Hermes Hercules' Twin? Hermeneutics and Legal Theory', in A Hunt, ed, *Reading Dworkin Critically*, Oxford: Berg Publishers

Douzinas, Costas and Warrington, Ronnie (1994) *Justice Miscarried: Ethics, Aesthetics and the Law*, London: Harvester Wheatsheaf

Drucker, Peter F (1993) *Post-Capitalist Society*, Oxford: Butterworth-Heinemann

Dworkin, A (1981) *Pornography: Men Possessing Women*, London: Women's Press

(1987) *Intercourse*, New York: Free Press

Dworkin, Ronald (1967) 'The Model of Rules', *University of Chicago Law Review*, 35

(1975) 'Hard Cases', *Harvard Law Review*, 88

(1977) *Taking Rights Seriously*, New Impression with Reply to Critics, Duckworth, London

(1978) 'No Right Answer', *New York University Law Review*, 53

(1978) 'Liberalism' in Stuart Hampshire, ed, *Public and Private Morality*, Cambridge

(1980) 'Law as Interpretation', *Texas Law Review*, 60

(1983) 'A Reply by Ronald Dworkin', in M Cohen ed (1983) *Ronald Dworkin and Contemporary Jurisprudence*, London: Duckworth

(1986) *Law's Empire*, Cambridge, Mass: Harvard University Press

(1993) *Life's Dominion: An Argument About Abortion, Euthanasia, and Individual Freedom*, New York: Alfred A Knopf

(1996) *Freedom's Law: The Moral Reading of the American Constitution*, Cambridge, Mass: Harvard University Press

Elias, Norbert ([1939] 1978) *The Civilizing Process: The history of Manners*, New York: Urizen Books

(1982) *Power and Civility*, trans Edmund Jephcott, New York: Pantheon

Engels, Frederick ([1884] 1973) *The Origin of the Family, Private Property, and the State: In the Light of the researches of Lewis H Morgan*, New York: International Publishers

Estrich, Susan (1987) *Real Rape*, Cambridge, Mass: Harvard University Press

Fienburg, Joel (1984) *Harm to Others*, Princton: Princton University Press

Finley, MI (1954) *The World of Odysseus*, New York: Viking Press

Finnis, JM (1980) *Natural Law and Natural Rights*, Oxford University Press, Oxford

Firestone, Shulamith (1970) *The Dialectic of Sex*, New York: Bantam Books

Fish, S (1980) *Is There a Text in This Class? The Authority of Interpretative Communities*, Cambridge Mass: Harvard University Press

(1982) 'Working on the Chain Gang: Interpretation in Law and Literature', *Texas Law Review*, 60

(1991) 'The Law Wishes to Have a Formal Existence', in Austin Sarat and Thomas R Kearns eds *The Fate of Law*, Ann Arbor: The University of Michigan Press

Fitzpatrick, Peter (1992) *The Mythology of Modern Law*, London: Routledge

Flew, A (1971) 'Theology and Falsification', in Mitchell, B, ed, *The Philosophy of Religion*, Oxford: Oxford University Press

Forbes, Duncan (1975) *Hume's Philosophical Politics*, CambridgeYork: Cambridge University Press

(1979) 'Hume and The Scottish Enlightenment' in *Philosophers of the Enlightenment*, SC Brown ed Sussex: Harvester Press

Foucault, M (1977) *Discipline and Punish: The Birth of the Prison*, trans A Sheridan, Harmondsworth: Penguin

(1980) *The History of Sexuality*, vol 1, An Introduction, trans New York: Robert Hurley

Franklin, JH (1963) *Jean Bodin and the Sixteenth-Century Revolution in The Methodology of Law and History*

(1973) *Jean Bodin and the Rise of Absolute Theory*, Cambridge: Cambridge University Press

Freud, S (1961) *Civilization and its Discontents*, J Strachey, trans, New York: Norton,

Fukayama, Francis (1989) 'The End of History', *The National Interest*, Summer

Fuller Lon (1940) *The Law in Quest of Itself*, Chicago: Foundation Press

(1954) 'American Legal Philosophy at Mid-Century', 6 *Journal of Legal Education*

(1958) 'Positivism and Fidelity to Law - A Reply to Professor Hart', 71 *Harvard Law Review* 630

(1969) *The Morality of Law*, rev ed, New Haven, Conn: Yale University Press

Gabel, Peter (1980) 'Reification in Legal reasoning', in 'Research in Law and Sociology', Vol 3 25–46 *Critical Legal Studies*

(1984) 'The Phenomenology of Rights-Consciousness and the Pact of the Withdrawn Selves', 62 *Texas Law Review*

and Kennedy, D (1984) 'Roll Over Beethoven', 36 *Stanford Law Review*

Gadamer, Hans-Georg (1982) *Truth and Method*, G Barden and J Cumming Trans, New York: Crossroad

Galbraith, John Kenneth (1992) *The Culture of Contentment*, London: Penguin

Gandhi, Mohandas K (1957) *An Autobiography: The Story of My Experiences With Truth*, trans, Mahadev Dessai, Boston

Garner, Richard (1987) *Law and Society in Classical Athens*, Beckenham, Kent: Croom Helm

Geertz, Clifford (1973) *The Interpretation of Cultures*, New York

Gellner, Ernest (1987) *Culture, Identity, and Politics*, Cambridge: Cambridge University Press

(1994) *Conditions of Liberty: Civil Society and Its Rivals*, London: Hamish Hamilton

Gewirth, Alan (1985) 'Rights and Virtues', *Review of Metaphysics, 38*

Giddens, A (1990) *The Consequences of Modernity*, Cambridge: Polity Press

(1992) *The Transformation of Intimacy: Sexuality, Love and Eroticism in Modern Societies*, Cambridge: Polity Press

Gilligan, Carol (1982) *In A Different Voice: Psychological Theory and Women's Development*, Cambridge Mass: Harvard University Press

Gilmore, Grant (1977) *The Ages of American Law*, New Haven: Yale University Press

Goodrich, Peter (1992) 'Critical Legal Studies in England: Prospective Histories' *12 Oxford Journal of Legal Studies*

Gordon, R (1982) 'New developments in Legal Theory', in David Kairys, ed, *The Politics of Law: A Progressive Critique*

(1987) 'Unfreezing Legal Reality: Critical Approaches to law', *Florida State University Law Review* 15

Gottfredson, Micheal and Hirschi, Travis (1990) *A General Theory of Crime*, Stanford, CA: Stanford University Press

Gluek, Sheldon (1946) 'The Nuremberg trials and Aggressive War', 59 *Harv LR*

Gramsci, A (1971) *Selections from the Prison Notebooks*, London: Lawrence and Wishant

Grigg-Spall, I and Ireland, P (1992) *The Critical Lawyers' Handbook*, London: Pluto Press

Gross, Karen (1990) 'Re-Vision of the Bankruptcy System: New Images of Individual Debtors', *88 Mich L Rev*

Guest, Stephen (1992) *Ronald Dworkin*, Edinburgh: Edinburgh University Press

Habermas, J (1981) 'Modernity versus Postmodernity', 22 *New German Critique*

Hall, Jerome (1960) *General Principles of Criminal Law*, 2nd edn, New York: Bobbs-Merrill

Hamburger, Lotte and Joseph (1985) *Troubled Lives: John and Sarah Austin*, Toronto: University of Toronto Press

Harris, Angela P (1990) 'Race and Essentialism in Feminist Legal Theory', *42 Stan L Rev*

Harris, J (1980) *Legal Philosophies*, London: Butterworth

Harris, W (1988) 'Justice Jackson at Nuremberg' IL V 20 No 3

Hart, Henry (1958) 'The Aims of the Criminal Law', *Law and Contemporary Problems*, 23

Hart, HLA (1954) 'Definition and Theory of Jurisprudence', 70 *Law Quarterly Review*

(1958) 'Positivism and the Separation of law and Morals', *Harvard Law Review*, 71

(1961) *The Concept of Law*, Oxford: Clarendon

(1963) *Law, Liberty and Morality*, Oxford: Oxford University Press

(1965) 'Book Review' 78 *Harvard law Review*

(1977) 'American Jurisprudence Through English Eyes: The Nightmare and the Noble Dream', *Georgia Law Review*, 11

Harvey, David (1992) *The Condition of Postmodernity*, New York: Blackwell

Hay D (1975) 'Property, Authority and the Criminal Law', in D Hay et al, *Albion's Fatal Tree*, Harmondsworth

Hegel, F ([1895] 1963) *Lectures on the Philosophy of Religion*, EB Speirs and J Burden, eds, London: Routledge and Kegan Paul

(1896) *Lectures on the Philosophy of History*, Elizabeth S Haldane and Frances H Simson, trans, London: Kehan Paul, Trench, Trübner

Hegel, GWF (1952) *Philosophy of Right*, trans TM Knox, London: Encyclopaedia Britannica, Inc

(1969) *Science of Logic*, AV Miller, trans, London: George Allen & Unwin

(1971) *Faith and Knowledge*, Walter Cerf, trans, Albany: State University of New York Press

(1977) *Phenomenology of Spirit*, AV Miller, trans, New York: Oxford University Press

Heller, Agnes (1987) *Beyond Justice*, Oxford: Basil Blackwell

Heller, Agnes and Feher, Ferenc (1988) *The Postmodern Political Condition*, Cambridge: Polity

Heidegger, M (1962) *Being and Time*, J Macquarrie and E Robson, trans, New York: Harper & Row

Hobbes, Thomas ([c1642] 1991) *Man and Citizen: De Homine and De Cive*, ed Bernard Gert, Indianapoilis: Hackett Publishing [reprint of 1972, Garden City: Doubleday and Co (A collection of both The Man and The Citizen)]

([1651] 1991) *Leviathan*, Richard Tuck, ed, Cambridge: Cambridge University Press

Hobsbawm, EJ (1969) *Industry and Empire*, Pelican, Harmondsworth

Holmes, OW (1897) 'The Path of Law', 10 *Harvard Law Review*

Holland, RF (1980) *Against Empiricism: On Education, Epistemology and Value*, Oxford: Basil Blackwell

Hooks, B (1981) *Ain't I a Woman: black women and feminism*, Boston: South End Press

(1984) *Feminist Theory: from margin to centre*, Boston, Mass: South End Press

Horwitz, Morton J (1992) *The Transformation of American Law 1870–1960: the crisis of legal orthodoxy*, Oxford: Oxford University Press

Hitler, Adolf, (1943) *Mein Kampf*, trans Ralph Manheim, Boston

Hume, David (1957) *Dialogues Concerning Natural Religion*, ed Henery D Aiken, New York: Hafner Publishing

(1978 [1739-40]) *A Treatise of Human Nature* LA Selby Bigge, ed, 2nd edn, text revised by PH Nidditch, Oxford: The Clarendon Press

(1975 [1777]) *Enquiries concerning Human Understanding and concerning the Principles of Morals*, Introduction and Index by LASelby-Bigge, 3rd edn, text revised and notes by PH Nidditch, Oxford: The Clarendon Press

(1966) 'On Refinement in The Arts', in *Essays, Moral, Political, and Literary*, Oxford: Clarendon Press

Hunt, A (1985) 'The Ideology of Law', *Law and Society Review*, 19

(1987) 'The Critique of Law: What is "critical" about Critical Legal Theory?', in Fitzpatrick and Hunt (1987), ed, (1992) *Reading Dworkin Critically*, Oxford: Berg

Irigaray, Luce (1984) *Ethique de la difference sexuelle* [The Ethics of sexual Difference] Paris: Les Editions de Minuit

(1985) *This Sex Which Is Not One*, Ithaca, New York: Cornell University Press

(1986) 'The Fedundity of the Caress: A Reading of Levinas, "Totality and Infinity, Section IV, B, 'The Phenomenology of Eros'"', in Richard A Cohen, ed, *Face to Face with Levinas*, New York: State University of New York Press

Jewell, Terri, ed (1993) *The Black Woman's Gumbo Ya-Ya: Quotations by Black Women*, Freedom, CA: The Crossing Press

Kafka, Franz (1979) *Description of a Struggle and Other Stories*, Harmondsworth: Penguin

Kairys, D (1982 [revised edn 1990]) *The Politics of Law*, Pantheon, New York

(1984) 'Law and Politics', *George Washington Law Review*, 52

Kamm, J (1977) *John Stuart Mill in Love*, London: Gordon and Cremonesi

Kantorowicz, Ernst H (1957) *The King's Two Bodies: A study in medieval political theology*, Princeton: Princeton University Press

Kant, Immanuel (1902) *Prolegomena: to any metaphysics that can qualify as a science*, Paul Carus, trans, Illinois: Open Court

(1930) *Lectures on Ethics*, Louis Infield, trans, rpt (1979), Indianapolis: Hackett

(1949) *Critique Of Practical Reason and Other Writings in Moral Philosophy*, Lewis White Beck Trans, Chicago: University of Chicago Press

(1959 [1785]) *Foundations of The Metaphysics of Morals*, Lewis W Beck, trans, Library of Liberal Arts, Indianapolis: Bobbs-Merrill

(1960) *Religion Within The Limits of Reason Alone*, Theodore Green and Hoyt Hudson Trans and notes, London: Harper Torchbooks, Harper & Row

(1965) *Critique of Pure Reason*, Norman Kemp-Smith Translator, New York: St Martins

([1797] 1965) *The Metaphysical Elements of Justice*, John Ladd, trans, (Being part 1 of *The Metaphysics of Morals*), The Library of Liberal Arts, Indianapolis: Bobbs-Merrill

(1974) *Anthropology From A Pragmatic Point of View*, MJ Gregor, trans, The Hague: Martinus Nijhoff

(1983) 'Idea for a Universal History from a Cosmopolitan Point of View', in *Kant on History*, Lewis White Beck, ed, Indianapolis: Merrill Publishing Co

(1991) 'On the Common Saying: "This may be true in Theory, but it does not apply in Practice"', in Hans Reiss, ed, *Kant, Political Writings*, Cambridge: Cambridge University Press

Kaufmann, Walter (1974) *Nietzsche: Philosopher, Psychologist, Antichrist*, Princeton, NJ: Princeton University Press

Kelly, JM (1992) *A Short History of Western Legal Theory*, Oxford: Clarendon Press

Kelman, M (1984) 'Trashing' 36 *Stanf L Rev* 293

(1987) *A Guide to Critical Legal Studies*, Cambridge, Mass: Harvard University Press

Kelsen, Hans (1934) 'The Pure Theory of Law: Its Method and Fundamental Concepts: Part 1', *Law Quarterly Review*

(1935) 'The Pure Theory of Law: Its Method and Fundamental Concepts: Part II', *Law Quarterly Review*

(1941) 'Law as a Specific Social Technique', *University of Chicago Law Review*, Vol 75

(1945) *General Theory of Law and State*, New York: Russell & Russell

(1965) 'Professor Stone and the Pure Theory of Law', 17 Stanford Law Review

(1970) *Pure Theory of Law*, trans of 2nd edn by Max Knight, Berkeley: University of California Press

(1973 [1922]) 'God and the State', trans, P Heath, in O Weinberger, ed, *Hans Kelsen – Essays in Legal and Moral Philosophy*, Dordrecht, Holland: D Reidel

(1957, rev edn 1971) *What is Justice?: Justice, Law, and Politics in the Mirror of Science*, Berkeley: University of California Press

(1973) *Hans Kelsen – essays in Legal and Moral Philosophy*, O Weinberger, ed, Dordrecht, Holland: D Reidel

Kennedy, D (1976) 'Form and Substance in Private Law Adjudication', *Harvard Law Review* 89

(1979) 'The Structure of Blackstone's Commentaries', *Buffalo Law Review 28*

(1982) 'Legal Education as Training for Hierarchy', in Kairys (1982)

and P Gabel (1984) 'Rollover Beethoven', *Stanford Law Review*, 36

Keynes, JM (1919) *The Economic Consequences of the Peace*, London: Macmillan

(1949) *Two Memoirs*, London: Rupert-Davis

Kinsley, David (1975) *The Sword and the Flute: Kali and Krisha, Dark Visions of the Terrible and the Sublime in Hindu Mythology*, Berkely

Koedt, A (1970) 'The Myth of the Vaginal Orgasm', in L Tanner, ed,

Kohlberg, Lawrence (1971) 'Stage and Sequence: The Cognitive-Development Approach to Socialisation', in David A Goslin, ed, *Handbook of Socialisation Theory and Research*

(1976) 'Moral Stages and moralisation: The Cognitive-Development an Approach', in Thomas Lickona, ed, *Moral Development and Behaviour: Theory Research and Social Issues*

(1981) *The Philosophy of Moral Development*, San Francisco: Harper & Row

Kolb, David (1986) *The Critique of Pure Modernity: Hegel, Heidegger, and After*, Chicago, Chicago University Press

Kornhauser, Marjorie (1987) 'The Rhetoric of the Anti-Progressive Tax Movement: A Typical Male Reaction', *86 Mich L Rev*

Kramer, Mathew (1991) *Legal Theory, Political Theory, and Deconstruction: Against Rhadamanthus*, Bloomington: Indiana University Press

Krausnick, Helmut Buchheim, Hans Broszat, Martin and Hans-Adolf Jacobsen (1968) *Anatomy of the SS State*, London: Collins

Kronman, A (1983) *Max Weber*, London: Edward Arnold

Kymlicka, Will (1990) *Contemporary Political Philosophy: an Introduction*, Oxford: Clarendon

Lacey, Nicola (1995) 'Feminist Legal Theory: Beyond Neutrality', *Current Legal Problems*, London

Latour, Bruno (1993) *We Have never Been Modern*, London: Harvester Wheatsheaf

Lee, Desmond (1974) 'Translator's Introduction' in Plato *The Republic*, 2nd rev edn, trans, Desmond Lee, Harmondsworth: Penguin Classics

Lee, Keekok (1990) *The Legal-Rational State*, Aldershot: Avebury

Lee, Simon (1988) *Judging Judges*, London: Faber and Faber

Lenin, VI (1966) *Imperialism: The Highest Stage of Capitalism*, Moscow: Progress Publishers

(1970) *On the Foreign Policy of the Soviet State*, Moscow: Progress Publishers

Levinas, Emmanuel (1988) *The Provocation of Levinas Rethinking the Other*, ed, R Bernasconi and D Wood, London: Routledge

Levy, Peter (1975) *The Downfall of the Antisemitic Political Parties in Imperial Germany*, New Haven

Llewelyn, K (1961) *The Common Law Tradition*, Little Brown, Boston

(1962) *Jurisprudence,* University of Chicago Press

and EA Hoebel (1941) *The Cheyenne Way*, University of Oklohoma Press

Locke, Lock (1960) *Second Treatise on Government*, Peter Laslett, ed, Cambridge: Cambridge University Press

Lorde, Audre (1981) 'The Master's Tools Will Never Dismantle the Master's House', in C Morgan and G Anzaldua, eds, *This Bridge called My Back: Writings by Radical Women of Colour*, New York: Kitchen Table Press

(1984) *Sister Outsider: Essays and Speeches by Audre Lorde*, Trumansburg, NY: The Crossing Press

(1984a) 'Uses of the erotic', in *Sister Outsider*, Crossing Press: Trumansburg, NY

(1984b) 'An open letter to Mary Daly', in *Sister Outsider*, Crossing Press: Trumansburg, NY

Lloyd, G (1984) *The Man of Reason 'Male' and 'Female' in Western Philosophy*, London: Methuen

Luxemburg, Rosa ([1913] 1951) *The Accumulation of Capital,* trans Agnes Schwarzschild, London: Routledge

Lyotard, Jean-Francois (1984) *The Postmodern Condition: A Report on Knowledge*, Manchester: Manchester University Press

    and Thebaud, Jean-Loup (1985) *Just Gaming*, Minneapolis: University of Minnesota Press

Machiavelli, Niccolo (1977 [1513]) *The Prince*, New York: WW Norton

MacCormick, N (1977) 'Challenging Sociological Definitions', *British Journal of Law and Sociology,* 4

    (1978) 'Dworkin as PreBenthamite', *Philosophical Review* 87

    (1981) *HLA Hart*, Edward Arnold, London

MacIntyre, A (1966) *A Short History of Ethics*, New York: Macmillan

    (1981) *After Virtue A Study in Moral Theory* (2nd edn, 1985) London: Duckworth

    (1988) *Whose Justice? Which Rationality?*, London: Duckworth

MacKinnon, C (1982) 'Feminism, Marxism, Method and the State: an agenda for theory', in *Feminist Theory,* Keohane, NO *et al*, eds, Harvester: Brighton

    (1987) *Feminism Unmodified: Discourses on Life and Law*, Harvard University Press: Cambridge, MA

    (1989) *Toward a Feminist Theory of the State*, Harvard University Press: Cambridge, MA

MacPherson, CB (1962) *The Political Theory of Possessive Individualism: From Hobbes to Locke*, Oxford: Oxford University Press

Maine, Henery Summer (1893) *Lectures on The Early History of Institutions*, London: John Murray

Marcel, Gabriel (1964) *Creative Fidelity*, Robert Rostel, trans, New York

Marrus, Michael R (1989) *The Holocaust in History*, London: Penguin

Marx, Karl (1971) 'Preface to the Contribution to the Critique of Political Economy', in *A Contribution to the Critique of Political Economy* (ed and Intro Maurice Dobb) London: Lawrence & Wishart

    (1856) 'Speech at the Anniversary of the Peoples Paper', in *Collected Works*, The Free Press

    ([1867] 1967) *Capital, vol 1*, London: Lawrence and Wishard

    (1964) *The economic and political manuscripts of 1844*, trans, M Milligan, ed, DJ Struik, New York: International Publishers

    (1975) 'Preface to A Contribution to a Critique of Political Economy', in *Earl Writings*, Q Hoare, R Livingstone, ed, and G Brown, trans, New York: Random House

Marx, Karl and Engles, F (1978) *The Marx-Engels Reader*, Robert C Tucker, ed, 2nd edn New York: Norton

Marx, Karl and Engels, Friedrich (1980) *Collected Works*, New York: International Publishers

Matsuda Mari (1986) 'Liberal Jurisprudence and Abstracted Visions of Human Nature: A Feminist Critique of Rawl's Theory of Justice', *16 New Mex LJ*

McCaffrey, John C and Novkov, Julie (1993–94) 'The Emperor Wears No Clothes: Life's Dominion and Dworkin's Integrity (Book Review)', *Review of Law & Social Change XXI*

Menkel-Meadow, Carrie (1987) 'Excluded Voices: New Voices in the Legal Profession Making New Voices in the Law', *42 U Miami L Rev*

Milgram, S (1963) 'Behavioral Study of Obedience', 67 *Journal of Abnormal and Social Psychology*

(1974) *Obedience to Authority*, New York: Harper & Row

Mill, John Stuart (1869) *The Subjection of Women*, rept 1974, Oxford University Press: Oxford

(1868) *Dissertations and Discussions*, Boston

(1965) *On the Logic of the Moral Sciences*, ed Henery M Magid, Indianapolis

(1966) 'Autobiography', in *John Stuart Mill, A Selection of His Works*, ed, John Robson, New York

(1974 [1859]) *On Liberty*, Harmondsworth: Penguin Classics

Mill, John Stuart and Bentham, Jeremy (1987) *Utilitarianism and Other Essays*, Alan Ryan, ed, Harmondsworth: Penguin Books

Mill, JS and Mill, HT (1970) *Essays on Sex Equality*, Rossi, AS, ed, University of Chicago Press: Chicago

Millet, K (1985) *Sexual Politics*, London: Virago

Mitchell, J and Oakley, A, eds, (1976) *The Rights and Wrongs of Women*, Penguin: Harmondsworth

Mixon, Don (1989) *Obedience and Civilization*, London: Pluto Press

Moles, R (1987) *Definition and Rule in Legal Theory – A Reassessment of HLA Hart and the Positivist Tradition*, Oxford: Basil Blackwell

(1992) 'The Decline and Fall of Law's Empire', in A Hunt, ed (1992) *Reading Dworkin Critically*, Oxford: Berg Publishers

Monod, Jacques (1972) *Chance and Necessity: an essay on the natural philosophy of modern biology*, A Wainhouse, trans, London: Collins

Morgan, Robin, ed, (1970) *Sisterhood is Powerful*, New York: Random House

(1989) *The Demon Lover: On the Sexuality of Terrorism*, New York: WW Norton

Morison, WL (1982) *John Austin*, London: Edward Arnold

Morrison, Wayne (1995) *Theoretical Criminology: from modernity to post-modernism*, London: Cavendish

(1996) 'Modernity, imprisonment and social solidarity: notes on a bad relationship', in Roger Mathews, ed, *Prisons 2000*, London: Routledge

Mulhall, S and Swift, A (1992) *Liberals and Communitarians*, 2nd edn 1995, Oxford: Blackwell

Nehamas, Alexander (1985) *Nietzsche: Life as Literature*, Cambridge, Mass: Harvard University Press

Newman, Stephen (1984) *Liberalism at Wits' End: the Libertarian Revolt against the Modern State*, Ithaca: Cornell University Press

Newton, John (1962) *The Journal of a Slave Trader 1750–1754*, eds, Bernard Martin and Mark Spurrell, London: Epworth

Nietzsche, Friedrich (1888) *The AntiChrist*, in (1968) *The Portable Nietsche*, Walter Kaufmann, trans and ed, New York: Viking Press

(1966) *Basic Writings of Nietzsche*, Walter Kaufmann, trans, New York: Random House

(1886) *Beyond Good and Evil*, in Basic Writings of Nietzsche

([1888] 1969) *Ecce Homo*, Walther Kaufman, trans and ed, New York: Vintage

(1882) *The Gay Science*, Walter Kaufmann, trans, New York: Random House

([1887] 1969) *The Genealogy of Morals*, Walther Kaufmann and RJ Hollingdale, trans, New York: Vintage Books

(1878) *Human All Too Human*, in Basic Writings of Nietzsche

([1886–88] 1968) *The Will to Power*, Walter Kaufmann and RJ Hollingdale (trans and eds), New York: Random House

Norton, David Faith (1982) *David Hume: a common-sense moralist, sceptical metaphysician*, Princeton: Princeton University Press

Nozick, R (1974) *Anarchy, State and Utopia*, Blackwell: Oxford

Nye, A (1990) *Feminist Theory and the Philosophies of Man*, London: Routledge

Oakeshott, Michael (1975) *On Human Conduct*, Oxford: Clarendon Press

O'Brien, Mary (1981) *The Politics of Reproduction*, Boston: Routledge & Kegan Paul

(1989) Reproducing the World, *Essays in Feminist Theory*, Boulder, CO: Westview Press

O'Donovan, K (1981) 'Before and after: the impact of feminism on the academic discipline of law', in *Men's Studies Modified*, Spender, D, ed, Pergamon: Oxford

Offe, Claus (1987) 'The Utopia of the Zero-Option: Modernity and Modernization as Normative Political Criteria', *Praxis International* 7

Okin, SM (1980) *Women in Western Political Thought*, London: Virgo

(1989) 'Reason and Feeling about Justice', *Ethics*, vol 99, no 2

(1990) *Justice, Gender and the Family*, New York: Basic Books

Olsen, Frances (1984) 'Statutory Rape: A Feminist Critique of Rights Analysis', *Texas Law Review 63*

Pagels, E (1979) *The Gnostic Gospels*, New York: Random House

Pappe, HO (1960) 'On the Validity of Judicial Decisions in the Nazi Era', 23 MLR

Parekh, B (1973) *Bentham's Political Thought*, London: Croom Helm

Parsons, Talcott (1951) *The Social System*, New York: The Free Press

(1970) 'On building social system theory: a personal history', In T Parsons, *Social Systems and the Evolution of Action Theory*, New York: Free Press (1977)

Pashukanis, EB (1978) *Law and Marxism*, London: Ink Links

Pateman, C (1988) *The Sexual Contract*, Cambridge: Polity Press

(1989) *The Disorder of Women*, Cambridge: Polity

Paul, J (1981) *Reading Nozick: essays on Anarchy, State and Utopia*, Oxford: Basil Blackwell

Pearce and Tombs (1989) 'Realism and Corporate Crime', in *Issues in Realist Criminology*, London: Sage

Peller, Gary (1985) '*The Metaphysics of American Law*', *California Law Review* 73

Plato (1900–15) *Opera*, J Burnet, ed, Oxford: Clarendon Press

(1961) The Collected Dialogues of Plato, eds, E Hamilton and H Cairns, Princeton: Princeton University Press

(1970) *The Laws*, Trevor J Saunders, trans, Harmondsworth: Penguin Books

(1974) *The Republic*, 2nd rev edn, trans Desmond Lee, Harmondsworth: Penguin Books

Pock, Max A (1962) 'Gustav Radbruch's Legal Philosophy' 7 *St Louis University Law Journal*

Pocock, JGA (1973) *Politics, Language and Time*, New York

(1975) *The Machiavellian Moment: Florentine Political Thought and the Alantic Republican Tradition*, Princeton

(1985) *Virtue, Commerce and History*, Cambridge

Popper, Karl (1945) *The Open Society and Its Enemies* (in two volumes, Vol I *Plato*; Vol II *Hegel & Marx*), London: Routledge

(1959) *The Logic of Scientific Discovery*, London: Hutchinson

(1969) *Conjectures and Refutations*, London: Routledge and Kegan Paul

(1976) 'The Logic of the Social Sciences', Adorno, TW et al, eds, The Positivist Dispute in German Sociology, London: Heinemann

Posner, Richard (1981) *The Economics of Justice*, Cambridge, Mass: Harvard University Press

Pound, Rosco (1907) 'Spurious Interpretation', *Columbia Law Review* 7

(1921) 'A Theory of Social Interests', 15 *Papers and Proceedings of the American Sociological Society*

(1943) 'A Survey of Social Interests', 57 *Harvard Law Review*

(1954) *Introduction to the Philosophy of Law*, rev edn, New Haven: Yale University Press

Radbruch, Gustav (1947) *Vorschule der Rechtsphilosophie*, Heidelberg

(1950) 'Legal Philosophy', *The Legal Philosopies of Lask, Radbruch and Dabin*, Wilk, K, trans, Cambridge, Mass: Harvard University Press

(1950) *Rechtsphilosophie*, Wolf, E, ed, 4th edn, Stuttgart, extracts Fuller, Lon, trans, 69 *Leg Ed* 484

Ramakrishna Sri (1974) *The Gospel of Sri Ramakrishna*, Swami Nikhilananda, trans, Abridged ed, New York

Rawls, J (1971) *A Theory of Justice*, Cambridge: Mass: Harvard University Press

(1985) 'Justice as Fairness: Political not Metaphysical', *Philosophy and Public Affairs*, 14, 3

(1985) 'Kantian Constructivism in Moral Theory', *Journal of Philosophy*, 77

(1993) Politician Liberalism, New York: Columbia University Press

Raz, J (1970) *Concept of a Legal System*, Oxford: Oxford University Press

(1975) *Practical Reason and Norms*, London: Hutchinson

(1979) *The Authority of Law*, Oxford: Clarendon Press

Redner, Harry (1982) *In the Beginning was the Deed: Reflections on the Passage of Faust*, Berkeley: University of California Press

Redpath, T (1990) *Ludwig Wittgenstein: A Student's Memoir*, London: Duckworth

Rees, John (1977) 'The Thesis of the Two Mills', 25 *Political Studies*

Richards, JR (1982) *The Sceptical Feminist*, Harmondsworth: Penguin

Rifkin, Jeremy (1995) *The End of Work: the decline of the Global Labour Force and the Dawn of the Post-Market Era*, New York: Putnam Book

Robinson, Daniel N (1989) 'Moral and Social Science and Justice', in *Issues in Criminal Justice*, Fred Bauman and Kenneth Jensen, eds, Charlottesville: University Press of Virginia

Rorty, Richard (1979) *Philosophy and the Mirror of Nature*, Princeton: Princeton University Press

(1983) 'Method and Morality, in N Haan et al, eds, *Social Science as a Moral Enquiry*

(1989) *Contingency, Irony, and Solidarity*, Cambridge: Cambridge University Press

Rose, Nikolas (1990) *Governing the Soul: the shaping of the private self*, London: Routledge

Rosen, Stanley (1969) *Nihilism: a philosophical essay*, New Haven: Yale University Press

(1985) *The Limits of Analysis*, New Haven: Yale University Press

Rothbard, Murray (1982) *The Ethics of Liberty*, New Jersey: Humanities Press

Rousseau, J-J (1973) *The Social Contract and Discourses*, trans, GDH Cole, revised JH Brumfitt and John C Hall) London: Dent and Sons, Everyman's Library

Rumble, Wilfrid E (1985) *The Thought of John Austin: Jurisprudence, Colonial Reform, and the British Constitution*, London: The Athlone Press

Rundell, John A (1987) *Origins of Modernity; The Origins of Modern Social Theory from Kant to Hegel to Marx*, Cambridge: Polity Press

Russell, B (1929) *Mysticism and Logic*, London: Allen and Unwin

Sabine, George H and Thorson, Thomas (1973) *A History of Political Theory*, 4th edn Hinsdale, Illinois: Dryden Press

Saint-Simon, Henri Comte (1952) *Selected Writings*, FMH Markham, ed, Oxford: Basil Blackwell

Sampford, Charles (1989) *The Disorder of Law: A Critique of Legal Theory*, Oxford: Basil Blackwell

Sandel, M (1982) *Liberalism and the Limits of Justice*, Cambridge: Cambridge University Press

Savigny, FCV (1975) *On the Vocation of our Age for Legislation and Jurisprudence* (1831), trans, A Hayward, Arno Press, New York

Seidman, Steven (1983) *Liberalism and the Origins of European Social Theory*, Oxford: Basil Blackwell

Schauer, Frederick (1991) *Playing By the Rules: A Philosophical Examination of Rule-Based Decision-Making in Law and in Life*, Oxford: Clarendon Press

Scheppele, Kim Lane (1991) 'Facing Facts in Legal Interpretation', in Robert Post, ed, *Law and the Order of Culture*, Berkeley: University of California Press

Schmitt, Carl ([1922] 1985) *Political Theology*, George Schwab, trans, Cambridge, Mass: MIT Press

(1976) *The Concept of the Political*, George Schwab, trans, New Brunswick: Rutgers

(1985) *The Crisis of Parliamentary Democracy*, E Kennedy, trans, Cambridge, Mass: MIT Press

Semple, Janet (1993) *Bentham's Prison: a study of the Panopticon Penitentiary*, Oxford: Clarendon Press

Shange, N (1987) 'Interview', *Spare Rib*, May, pp 14–18

Sherry, Suzanna (1986) 'Civic Virtue and the Feminine Voice in Constitutional Adjudication', 72 Va L Rev

Shklar, Judith (1964) *Legalism*, Cambridge, Mass: Harvard University Press

Simmonds, Neil (1986) *Central Issues in Jurisprudence: Justice, Laws and Rights*, London: Sweet and Maxwell

Skinner, Q (1978) *The Foundations of Modern Political Thought*, 2 vols, Cambridge: Cambridge University Press

Smart, Carol (1989) *Feminism and the Power of Law*, London: Routledge

(1990) 'Law's Truth/Women's Experience' in Regina Graycar ed *Dissenting Opinions: Feminist Explorations in Law and Society*, Sydney: Allen & Unwin

Smith, Adam (1976 [1759]) *The Theory of Moral Sentiments*, D Raphael and A Macfie, eds, Oxford: The Clarendon Press

(1970 [1776]) *The Wealth of Nations*, Harmondsworth: Penguin Books

Smith, B and Smith, B (1981) 'Across the kitchen table' in *This Bridge Called My Back*, C Moraga and G Anzaldua, eds, New York: Kitchen Table

(1984) 'Between a rock and a hard place', in *Yours in Struggle*, Bulkin, E, MB Pratt and B Smith, eds, New York: Long Haul

Smith, Norman Kemp (1941) *The Philosophy of David Hume: a critical study of its origins and central doctrines*, London/New York: MacMillan

Soltan, Karol (1987) *The Causal Theory of Justice*, Berkeley/London: University of California Press

Sophocles (1947) *The Theban Plays* [includes 'Antigone'], Harmondsworth: Penguin

Stephen, James Fitzjames (1861) *Liberty, Equality, Fraternity,*

Stewart, Iain (1980) 'The Basic Norm as Fiction', *Juridical Review*

    (1986) 'Kelsen and the Exegetical Tradition' *Essays on Kelsen*, Tur, Richard and Twining, William, eds, Oxford: Clarendon Press

Strauss, Leo (1953) *Natural Right and History*, Chicago: University of Chicago Press

    (1958) *Thoughts on Machiavelli*, Chicago: University of Chicago Press

Strawson, PF (1966) *The Bounds of Sense*, London: Methuen

Stroud, Barry (1978) *Hume*, London: Routledge & Kegan Paul

Summers, Robert (1971) 'The Technique Element in Law', *California Law Review*, Vol 59

Tanner, L, ed, (1970) *Voices from Women's Liberation*, New York: Mentor

Taylor, Charles (1975) *Hegel*, Cambridge: Cambridge University Press

    (1979) *Hegel and Modern Society*, Cambridge: Cambridge University Press

    (1985) *Philosophical Papers* Vol 1 and Vol 2, Cambridge: Cambridge University Press

    (1990) *Sources of the Self*, Cambridge: Cambridge University Press

Taylor, H (1983) *The Enfranchisement of Women*, London: Virago

Teubner, G (1987) 'Juridification – Concepts, Aspects, Limits, Solutions' in G Teubner, ed, *Juridification of Social Spheres*, Berlin: Walter de Gruyter

Thompson, EP (1975) *Whigs and Hunters: The Origin of the Black Act,* London: Allen Lane

Thompson, W (1983) *Appeal of one half of the Human Race, Women, against the pretensions of the Other Half, Men, to retain them in Political, and Thence in Civil and Domestic Slavery,* London: Virago

Trotsky, Leon (1994 [1939]) *Their Morals and Ours: The Moralists and Sycophants against Marxism*, Union Books

Trubek, DH (1977) 'Complexity and Contradiction in the Legal Order', *Law and Society Review*, 11

Tuck, Richard (1991) 'Introduction' in Hobbes, *Leviathan*, Cambridge Texts: the History of Political Thought, Cambridge: Cambridge University Press

Tur, Richard (1986) 'The Kelsenian Enterprise' *Essays on Kelsen*, Tur, Richard and Twining, William, eds, Oxford: Clarendon Press

Tushnet, M (1984) 'Perspectives on Critical Legal Studies', *George Washington Law Review* 52

    (1986) 'Critical Legal Studies: An Introduction to its Origins and Underpinnings', *Journal of Legal Education*, 36

Unger, RM (1975, 2nd rev edn 1984) *Knowledge and Politics*, New York

(1976) *Law in Modern Society*, Free Press, New York

(1982) 'Critical Legal Studies', *Harvard Law Review* 96

(1984) *Passion: An Essay on Personality*, New York: Free Press

(1986) *The Critical Legal Studies Movement*, Cambridge, Mass: Harvard University Press

(1987) *Social Theory: Its Situation and its task A Critical introduction to Politics, a Work in Constructive Social Theory*, Cambridge: Cambridge University Press

(1987b) *Politics, a Work in Constructive Social Theory, vol 2, False Necessity Anti-Necessitarian Social Theory in the Service of Radical Democracy*, Cambridge: Cambridge University Press

Vaihinger, Hans (1965) *The Philosophy of 'As-If': A System of the Theoretical, Practical and Religious Fictions of Mankind*, London: Routledge Kegan Paul

Vattimo, Gianni (1992) *The Transparent Society*, Cambridge: Polity Press

Vernant, Jean-Pierre (1982) *The Origins of Greek Thought*, London: Methuen

Vico, G (1968) *The New Science*, trans, TG Bergin and MH Fisch, New York

Voegelin, Eric (1975) *From Enlightenment to Revolution*, John Hallowell edn, Durham: Duke University Press

Wagner, Peter (1994) *A Sociology of Modernity: Liberty and Discipline* , London: Routledge

Waltzer, M (1983) *Spheres of Justice A Defense of Pluralism and Equality*, New York: Basic Books

Wardle, M (1951) *Mary Wollstonecraft: a Critical Study*, London: Richards Press

Weber, Max (1947) *The Theory of Social and Economic Organisations*, trans, by Talcot Parsons and A Henderson, New York: Free Press

([1917] 1949) 'The meaning of Value Freedom in Sociology and Economics', reprinted in *The Methodology of Social Sciences*, AE Shils and HA Finch, trans, AE Shils, Glencoe, Ill: Free Press

(1966) *General Economic History,* [compiled by S Hellman and M Palyi from his students' notes of the 1919–20 lectures 'Outlines of Universal Social and Economic History'] New York: Collier

(1970) *From Max Weber*, H Gerth and C Wright Mills, eds, London: Routledge

(1974) *The Protestant ethic and the spirit of capitalism*, London: Allen and Unwin

(1978) *Economy and Society*, 2 vols Berkeley: University of California Press

(1984) 'Legitimacy, Politics and the State', in W Connolly ed *Legitimacy and The State*, Oxford: Basil Blackwell

Wellershoff, Dieter (1985) 'Germany - a state of flux', in *Observations on 'The Spiritual Situation of the Age'*, Jurgen Habermas, ed, Cambridge, Mass: MIT Press

West, Robin (1988) 'Jurisprudence and Gender' 55 *University of Chicago Law Review*

Whelan, Frederick G (1985) *Order and Artifice in Hume's Political Philosophy*, Princeton: Princeton University Press

White, James Boyd (1986) 'Is Cultural Criticism Possible?', *Michigan Law Review* 84

    (1987) 'Thinking about Our Language', *Yale Law Journal* 96

Williams, Bernard (1978) 'A Critique of Utilitarianism', in *Utilitarianism: For and Against*, JJ Smart and B Williams, Cambridge: Cambridge University Press

Williams Joan (1989) '*Deconstructing Gender*', 87 *Michigan Law Review*

Williams, Patricia J (1991) *The Alchemy of Race and Rights: diary of a law professor*, Cambridge Mass: Harvard University Press

Wittgenstein, L ([1921] 1961) *Tractatus Logico-Philosophicus*, London: Routledge & Kegan Paul

    (1958) *Philosophical Investigations*, Oxford: Blackwell

    (1969) *On Certainty*, Oxford: Blackwell

Wolfenden Report (1957) *Report of the Committee on Homosexual Offences and Prostitution*, Cmnd 247, London: HMSO

Wollstonecraft, M (1787) *Thoughts on the Education of Daughters: With Reflections on Female Duties, in the more Important Duties of Life*, Joseph Johnson: London

    (1789) *A Vindication of the Rights of Woman*, repr 1967, Norton: New York

Wood, Gordon S (1969) *The Creation of the American Republic 1776–1787*, Chapel Hill

Lord Wright, (1946) 'War Crimes Under international Law', 62 LQR

INDEX